D0855357

HISTORY OF THE CHURCH

VII

HISTORY OF THE CHURCH

Edited by
HUBERT JEDIN
and
JOHN DOLAN

Volume VII

THE CHURCH BETWEEN REVOLUTION AND RESTORATION

by

Roger Aubert

Johannes Beckmann

Patrick J. Corish

Rudolf Lill

Translated by

Peter Becker

CROSSROAD · NEW YORK

1981

The Crossroad Publishing Company

18 East 41st Street, New York, N.Y. 10017

Translated from the *Handbuch der Kirchengeschichte*

Vol. VI/1: *Die Kirche in der Gegenwart: Die Kirche zwischen Revolution und Restauration,* chapters 1 through 21, 2d edition

Printed in the United States of America

Library of Congress Cataloging in Publication Data

Main entry under title:

The Church between revolution and restoration.

(History of the church; 7)

Translation of Die Kirche in der Gegenwart,

pt. 1: Die Kirche zwischen Revolution und

Restauration, chapters 1–21.

"A Crossroad book."

Bibliography: p.

Includes index.

1. Catholic Church—History—Modern period,

1500– I. Aubert, Roger. II. Series:

Jedin, Hubert, 1900– ed. Handbuch der

Kirchengeschichte. English; v. 7.

BR145.2.J413 1980, vol. 7 [BX1386] 270s

[282'.09'034] 80-16017

ISBN: 0-8245-0004-0 Previously ISBN: 0-8164-0446-1

CONTENTS

PREFACE

During the nineteenth and twentieth centuries the Church became in fact what it always had claimed to be: a World Church. While Europe retained its spiritual leadership, the old and new churches on the other continents assumed greater importance, promoted by a world economy and world-wide communications. The speed and the extent of their growth become evident when one compares the composition of the participants at the First and Second Vatican Councils. But these councils also demonstrated that in matters of theology and spirituality Europe held on to its leading role. In order to do justice to both aspects, it became necessary to allow more space in this series to the nineteenth and twentieth centuries. Thus we have several volumes dealing with this period in an attempt to trace the roots of ecclesiastical developments during the past century. Needless to say, the small temporal distance separating us from the nineteenth century and the availability of sources do not permit us to make final judgments.

While volume VI was able to continue the subsequent developments which had started with the Reformation in volume V, the nineteenth and twentieth centuries present such a differentiated picture of the Churches of the Reformation that it is no longer possible in this series to give them the attention due to them. They are therefore mentioned in this and the subsequent volumes only to the extent necessary for the understanding of the history of the Catholic Church. We want this limitation to be understood as an ecumenical expression which was also the basis for the *Atlas zur Kirchengeschichte* with whose help the external development of the Christian Churches can be followed.

Hubert Jedin

PREFACE TO THE ENGLISH EDITION

The decision to divide the original German *Die Kirche in der Gegenwart* into three volumes was, at least in part, dictated by the revisionism that has characterized so much of historical writing in recent times. As the reader will find, this is reflected in the content of this work as well. It is now generally agreed that the two salient features of the early nineteenth century, revolution and romanticism, demonstrate how expectations far outrun the realities of objective change. As the Jewish historian J. L. Talmon remarks, the vast discordant forces released in 1789 reached a tragic denouement in 1848. All the problems, ideas, and conflicts of the modern age are there in *statu nascendi.*

In this volume the authors are concerned to a great extent with the Restoration and how the Church attempted to come to grips with a world drastically changed by a generation of war and revolution. In the twilight zone between revolutionary rationalism and romanticism, some ecclesiastics attempted a synthesis of the two. Few personalities of this period better epitomize the traumatic effects of the revolution on an entire generation than Lamennais, the counterrevolutionary apologist who turned to the social salvation of religious authority to counter the effects of extreme rationalism. Called by Dupanloup "the idol of the young priests, but a thorn in the side of the older clergy and the pious faithful," he fought a losing battle in his efforts to reconcile the Church and democracy. Many will find parallels between his call for reform and the avant-garde of postconciliarism in our own time, the impetuosity, the lack of sound theological training, and a superficial understanding of religion.

Of special interest in this volume are the fresh treatment of the origins of neo-scholasticism, the Church in Congress Poland, the role of Consalvi in reestablishing the Papal States, and the revived interest in the Eastern Churches and the missions. In the former one finds the Latinization and centralization so much a part of the ecumenical effort of the nineteenth century. Much of the adulation given the missionary efforts of Gregory XVI, "le grand pape missionnaire du XIXe siècle," has been toned down. It is now clear that the new direction in missionary activity during his pontificate harbored serious shortcomings. Active missionary work became almost exclusively the concern of religious orders and congregations, while the administration of the reorganized Congregation for the Propagation of the Faith was in the hands of secular priests completely lacking in missionary experience. Association with the colonial powers, especially England and France, formed the basis of a political reorientation of the missions which have repercussions in the Third World to this day.

Like other institutions of this time, the Church was often ill prepared to deal with the new problems because it failed to distinguish between the surviving framework of an earlier society and the tremendous change of self-awareness in the people it served.

John P. Dolan

LIST OF ABBREVIATIONS

ADRomana *Archivio della Deputazione Romana di Storia Patria,* Rome 1935seqq. (1878–1934: *ASRomana*).

AFP *Archivum Fratrum Praedicatorum,* Rome 1931seqq.

AGKKN *Archief voor de Geschiedenis van de Katholieke Kerk in Nederland,* Utrecht 1959seqq.

AHPont *Archivum historiae pontificiae,* Rome 1963seqq.

AHR *The American Historical Review,* New York 1895seqq.

AHRF *Annales historiques de la Révolution française,* Paris 1924seqq.

AHSI *Archivum historicum Societatis Iesu,* Rome 1932seqq.

AHVNrh *Annalen des Historischen Vereins für den Niederrhein, insbesondere das alte Erzbistum Köln,* Cologne 1855seqq.

AIA *Archivo Ibero-Americano,* Madrid 1914seqq.

AkathKR *Archiv für Katholisches Kirchenrecht,* (Innsbruck) Mainz 1857seqq.

Albers, *Herstel* P. Albers, *Geschiedenis van het herstel der hiërarchie in de Nederlanden,* 2 vols., Nijmegen–The Hague 1903–04.

Albers, *Lib. saec.* (P. Albers) *Liber saecularis historiae Societatis Iesu ab anno 1814 ad annum 1914,* Rome 1914.

Ammann A. M. Ammann, *Abriß der ostslawischen Kirchengeschichte,* Vienna 1950.

AMrhKG *Archiv für mittelrheinische Kirchengeschichte,* Speyer 1949seqq.

Anthropos *Anthroposophische Internationale Zeitschrift für Völker- und Sprachenkunde,* Mödling 1906seqq.

Antonianum *Antonianum,* Rome 1926 seqq.

AÖG *Archiv für österreichische Geschichte,* Vienna 1865seqq.

AOP *Analecta Sacri Ordinis Praedicatorum,* Rome 1892seqq.

ArchSR *Archives de Sociologie des religions,* Paris 1956seqq.

ArSKG *Archiv für schlesische Kirchengeschichte,* K. Engelbert, ed., I–VI Breslau 1936–41, VIIseqq. Hildesheim 1949seqq.

ASRomana *Archivio della Reale Società Romana di Storia Patria,* Rome 1878–1934 (*ADRomana* after 1935).

ASS *Acta Sanctae Sedis,* Rome 1865–1908.

AstIt *Archivio storico Italiano,* Florence 1842seqq.

Aubert, *Pie IX* R. Aubert, *Le pontificat de Pie IX* (ed. by A. Fliche and V. Martin, *Histoire de l'Église depuis les origines jusqu'à nos jours,* 21) Paris 1962.

Aubert, *Vat* R. Aubert, *Vaticanum I,* Mainz 1965.

Aubert-Martina R. Aubert, *Il pontificato di Pio IX,* translated by G. Martina with notes and supplement, Turin 1969.

Backmund N. Backmund, *Monasticon Praemonstratense* I–III, Straubing 1949seqq.
Bastgen F. Bastgen, *Die römische Frage,* 3 vols., Freiburg im Breisgau 1917–19.
Baunard L. Baunard, *Un siècle de l'Église de France 1800–1900,* Paris 1902.
Becqué M. Becqué, *Le cardinal Dechamps,* 2 vols., Louvain 1956.
Bellesheim, *Irland* A. Bellesheim, *Geschichte der Katholischen Kirche in Irland,* 3 volumes, Mainz 1890–91.
Bellesheim, *Schottland* A. Bellesheim, *Geschichte der Katholischen Kirche in Schottland,* Mainz 1883.
Belvederi R. Belvederi, *Il'papato di fronte alla Rivoluzione ed alle conseguenze del Congresso di Vienna* (1775–1846): P. Paschini and P. Brezzi, eds.,.*I Papi nella storia* II, Rome 1951, 767–930.
Bernasconi A. M. Bernasconi, *Acta Gregorii Papae XVI, auspice cardinal Vanutelli recensita,* 4 vols., Rome 1901–04.
BIHBR *Bulletin de l'Institut historique belge de Rome,* Brussels–Rome 1919seqq.
Bihlmeyer-Tüchle K. Bihlmeyer and H. Tüchle, *Kirchengeschichte,* I: *Das christliche Altertum,* Paderborn 1955; II: *Das Mittelalter,* Paderborn 1955; III: *Die Neuzeit und die neueste Zeit,* Paderborn 1968.
BLE *Bulletin de littérature ecclésiastique,* Toulouse 1899seqq.
BnatBelg *Biographie nationale. Publiée par l'Académie de Belgique,* 35 vols., Brussels 1866–1970.
Boudou A. Boudou, *Le Saint-Siège et la Russie. Leurs relations diplomatiques au XIX*[e] *siècle,* 2 vols., Paris 1922–25.
Brugerette J. Brugerette, *Le prêtre français et la société contemporaine,* 3 vols., Paris 1933–38.
BStBiS *Bolletino storico-bibliografico subalpino,* Turin 1896seqq.
BullRomCont *Bullarii Romani Continuatio,* A. Berberi and A. Spetia, eds., 19 vols., Rome 1835–58.
Burnichon J. Burnichon, *La Compagnie de Jésus en France. Histoire d'un siècle,* 4 vols., Paris 1914–22.

Cath *Catholica. Jahrbuch (Vierteljahresschrift) für Kontroverstheologie,* (Paderborn) Münster 1932seqq.
CathEnc *The Catholic Encyclopedia,* C. Herbermann, ed., 15 vols., New York 1907–12.
Catholicisme *Catholicisme. Hier-Aujourd'hui-Demain,* G. Jacquemet, ed., Paris 1948seqq.
CH *Church History,* New York–Chicago 1932seqq.
CHR *The Catholic Historical Review,* Washington 1915seqq.
ChStato *Chiesa e Stato nell' Ottocento. Miscellanea in onore di P. Pirri,* ed. by R. Aubert, A. M. Ghisalberti, E. Passerin d'Entrèves, 2 vols., Padua 1962.
Cîteaux *Cîteaux. Commentarii cistercienses,* Westmalle (Belg.) 1950seqq.
CivCatt *La Civiltà Catthōlica,* Rome 1850seqq. (1871–87 Florence).
CodCanOrFonti *S. Congregazione per la Chiesa Orientale. Codificazione Canonica Orientale. Fonti,* 3rd ser., Rome 1931seqq.
Colapietra R. Colapietra, *La Chiesa tra Lamennais e Metternich,* Brescia 1963.
ColLac *Collectio Lacensis: Acta et Decreta sacrorum conciliorum recentiorum,* ed. by Jesuits from Maria Laach, 7 vols., Freiburg im Breisgau 1870–90.
CollFr *Collectanea Franciscana,* Rome 1931seqq.
CPF *Collectanea Sancta Congregationis de Propaganda Fide* I (1622–1866), II (1867–1906) Rome 1907.

D H. Denzinger, *Enchiridion Symbolorum, Definitionum et Declarationum de rebus fidei et morum,* Freiburg im Breisgau 1967.

DACL *Dictionnaire d'archéologie chrétienne et de liturgie,* F. Cabrol and H. Leclercq, eds., 15 vols., Paris 1903–53.

Daniel-Rops Daniel-Rops, *L'Église des Révolutions,* 2 vols., Paris 1960–63.

Dansette A. Dansette, *Histoire religieuse de la France contemporaine,* 2 vols., Paris 1948–51.

DBI *Dizionario biografico degli Italiani,* A. M. Ghisalberti, ed., Rome 1960seqq.

DDC *Dictionnaire de droit canonique,* R. Naz, ed., 7 vols., Paris 1935–65.

Debidour, *Histoire* A. Debidour, *Histoire des rapports de l'Église et de l'État en France de 1789 à 1870,* 2 vols., Paris 1891.

Debidour, *IIIe République* A. Debidour, *L'Église catholique et l'État sous la Troisième République, 1870–1906,* 2 vols., Paris 1906.

de Clercq C. de Clercq, *Conciles des Orientaux catholiques* (*Histoire des conciles* XI), 2 vols., Paris 1949–52.

Delacroix *Histoire universelle des missions catholiques,* S. Delacroix, ed., 4 vols., Paris–Monaco 1957–59.

de Montclos X. de Montclos, *Lavigerie, le Saint-Siège et l'Église, 1846–1878,* Paris 1965.

DHGE *Dictionnaire d'histoire et de géographie ecclésiastiques,* A. Baudrillart, ed., Paris 1912seqq.

DictEngCath *A Literary and Biographical History or Bibliographical Dictionary of the English Catholics from 1534 to the Present Time,* by J. Gillow, 5 vols., London–New York, 1885seqq.

DSAM *Dictionnaire de Spiritualité ascétique et mystique. Doctrine et Histoire,* M. Viller, ed., Paris 1932seqq.

DThC *Dictionnaire de théologie catholique,* A. Vacant, E. Mangenot and É. Amann, eds., 15 vols., Paris 1930.

Dupeux G. Dupeux, *La société française 1789–1969* (*Collection U, série Histoire contemporaine*) Paris 1964.

Duroselle J.-B. Duroselle, *Les débuts du catholicisme social en France 1822–1870,* Paris 1951.

DVfLG *Deutsche Vierteljahresschrift für Literaturwissenschaft und Geistesgeschichte,* Halle 1923seqq.

ECatt *Enciclopedia Cattolica,* 12 vols., Rome 1949–54.

ED *Euntes docete* (*Commentaria urbana*), Rome 1948seqq.

EEAm *Enciclopedia Universal Ilustrada Europeo-Americana,* 70 vols., Barcelona 1908–30.

Éfranc *Études franciscaines,* Paris 1909–40; n.s. 1950seqq.

Ellis, *AmCath* J. T. Ellis, *American Catholicism* (*The Chicago History of American Civilization*), Chicago 1956.

Ellis, *Documents* *Documents of American Catholic History,* J. T. Ellis, ed., Milwaukee 1956.

Engel-Janosi F. Engel-Janosi, *Österreich und der Vatikan,* 2 vols., Graz 1958–60.

EnI *Enciclopedia Italiana di scienze, lettere ed arti,* 35 vols., Rome 1929–37, Supplement 1938, Index volume 1939, 2 Supplements (1938–48), Rome 1948–49.

ÉO *Échos d'Orient,* Paris 1897seqq.

EThL — *Ephemerides Theologicae Lovanienses* (Bruges), Gembloux 1924seqq.
Études — *Études,* Paris 1856seqq. (until 1896: *Études religieuses*).

Feine *RG* — H. E. Feine, *Kirchliche Rechtsgeschichte* I: *Die katholische Kirche,* Graz 1964.
Fliche-Martin — *Histoire de l'Église depuis les origines jusqu'à nos jours,* published under the direction of A. Fliche and V. Martin, Paris 1935seqq.
FreibDiözArch — *Freiburger Diözesan-Archiv,* Freiburg im Breisgau 1865seqq.
Friedrich — J. Friedrich, *Geschichte des Vaticanischen Conzils,* 3 vols., Nördlingen 1877–87.
FZThPh — *Freiburger Zeitschrift für Theologie und Philosophie* (before 1914: *Jahrbuch für Philosophie und spekulative Theologie;* 1914–54: *DTh*), Fribourg.

Goyau — G. Goyau, *L'Allemagne religieuse au XIX*[e] *siècle,* 4 vols., Paris 1905–09.
Gr — *Gregorianum,* Rome 1920seqq.
Grabmann *G* — M. Grabmann, *Die Geschichte der katholischen Theologie seit dem Ausgang der Väterzeit,* Freiburg im Breisgau 1933.
GregMC — *Gregorio XVI. Miscellanea commemorativa* (*Miscellanea historiae pontificiae* XIII/XIV), 2 vols., Rome 1958.
Grimaud — L. Grimaud, *Histoire de la liberté d'enseignement en France,* 6 vols., Grenoble–Paris 1944–54.
GRM — *Germanisch-Romanische Monatsschrift,* Heidelberg 1909–42 and 1951seqq.
Gurian — W. Gurian, *Die politischen und sozialen Ideen des französischen Katholizismus 1789–1914,* Freiburg im Breisgau 1929.

Hagen *R* — A. Hagen, *Geschichte der Diözese Rottenburg,* 3 vols., I, Stuttgart 1957.
HAHR — *Hispanic American Historical Review,* Durham (N.C.) 1918seqq.
Hajjar — J. Hajjar, *Les chrétiennes uniates du Proche-Orient,* Paris 1962.
Hales — *Pio Nono, A Study in European Politics and Religion in the 19th Century,* London 1954.
Heimbucher — M. Heimbucher, *Die Orden und Kongregationen der katholischen Kirche,* 3 vols., Paderborn 1907–08.
Hermelink — H. Hermelink, *Das Christentum in der Menschheitsgeschichte von der Französischen Revolution bis zur Gegenwart* I–III, Stuttgart–Tübingen 1951–55.
HistCathFr — A. Latreille, J. R. Palanque, É. Delaruelle, and R. Rémond, *Histoire du catholicisme en France* III: *La période contemporaine,* Paris 1962.
HJ — *Historisches Jahrbuch der Görres-Gesellschaft* (Cologne 1880seqq.), Munich 1950seqq.
Hocedez — E. Hocedez, *Histoire de la Théologie au XIX*[e] *siècle,* Brussels–Paris, I, 1948, II, 1952, III 1947.
Hochland — *Hochland,* Munich 1903seqq.
Holzapfel — H. Holzapfel, *Handbuch der Geschichte des Franziskanerordens,* Freiburg im Breisgau 1909.
HPBl — *Historisch-politische Blätter für das katholische Deutschland,* F. Binder and G. Jochner, eds., 171 vols., Munich 1838–1923.
HRSt — *Historical Records and Studies of the United States Catholic Historical Society,* Philadelphia 1884seqq.
HS — *Hispania Sacra,* Madrid 1948seqq.
Hurter — H. Hurter, *Nomenclator literarius theologiae catholicae,* 6 vols., Innsbruck 1903–13; I, 1926, F. Pangerl, ed.

IER — *The Irish Ecclesiastical Record,* Dublin 1864seqq.
Irénikon — *Irénikon,* Amay-Chevetogne 1926seqq.

JEH — *The Journal of Ecclesiastical History,* London 1950seqq.
Jemolo — A. C. Jemolo, *Chiesa e Stato in Italia negli ultimi cento anni,* Turin 1963.
JLW — *Jahrbuch für Liturgiewissenschaft,* Münster 1921–41 (now: *ALW*).
JP — *Jus pontificium de Propaganda fide, Pars I complectens Bullas, Brevia, Acta Sancta Sedis,* R. De Martinis, ed., 7 vols., Rome 1888–97.
Jürgensen — K. Jürgensen, *Lamennais und die Gestaltung des belgischen Staates. Der liberale Katholizismus in der Verfassungsbewegung des 19. Jahrhunderts,* Wiesbaden 1963.

Katholik — *Der Katholik,* Mainz 1821seqq.
KuD — *Kerygma und Dogma,* Göttingen 1955seqq.

Latourette, *Christianity* — K. S. Latourette, *Christianity in a Revolutionary Age. A History of Christianity in the Nineteenth and Twentieth Centuries,* 5 vols., New York 1958–62.
Latourette, *Expansion* — K. S. Latourette, *A History of the Expansion of Christianity,* 7 vols., New York–London 1937–45.
Le Bras S — G. Le Bras, *Études de sociologie religieuse,* 2 vols., Paris 1955–56.
Lecanuet — E. Lecanuet, *L'Église et l'État en France sous la Troisième République,* 4 vols., Paris 1907–30.
Leflon — J. Leflon, *La crise révolutionnaire 1789–1846* (*Histoire de l'Église depuis les origines jusqu'à nos jours* 20, A. Fliche and V. Martin, eds.) Paris 1949.
LJ — *Liturgisches Jahrbuch,* Münster 1951seqq.
Lösch — S. Lösch, *Döllinger und Frankreich. Eine geistige Allianz, 1823–1871,* Munich 1955.
LThK — *Lexikon für Theologie und Kirche,* Freiburg 1957–68.

Maass — F. Maass, *Der Josephinismus. Quellen zu seiner Geschichte in Österreich* I–V, Vienna 1951seqq. (*Fontes rerum Austriacarum* II/71–74).
MAH — *Mélanges d'archéologie et d'histoire,* Paris 1880seqq.
Mansi — J. D. Mansi, *Sacrorum conciliorum nova et amplissima collectio,* 31 vols., Florence–Venice 1757–98; reprinted and continued by L. Petit and J. B. Martin, eds., in 60 vols., Paris 1899–1927.
Mathew — D. Mathew, *Catholicism in England,* London 1936.
McAvoy — T. McAvoy, *A History of the Catholic Church in the United States,* Notre Dame 1969.
MCom — *Miscelánea Comillas,* Comillas/Santander 1943seqq.
MD — *Maison-Dieu,* Paris 1945seqq.
Mellor — A. Mellor, *Histoire de l'anticléricalisme français,* Paris 1966.
Mercati — A. Mercati, *Raccolta di Concordati su materie ecclesiastiche tra la Santa Sede e le autorità civili,* 2 vols., Rome 1919–54.
Meulemeester — M. de Meulemeester, *Bibliographie générale des écrivains rédemptoristes* I–III, Louvain 1933–39.
MF — *Miscellanea francescana,* Rome 1886seqq.
MH — *Missionalia Hispanica*
MIÖG — *Mitteilungen des Instituts für österreichische Geschichtsforschung,* (Innsbruck) Graz–Cologne 1880 seqq.

MiscMercati *Miscellanea Giovanni Mercati,* 6 vols., Rome 1946.
Mollat G. Mollat, *La Question romaine de Pie VI à Pie XI,* Paris 1932.
Moroni G. Moroni, *Dizionario di erudizione storico-ecclesiastica,* 103 vols., Venice 1840–61.
Mortier A. Mortier, *Histoire des maîtres généraux de l'ordre des frères prêcheurs,* Paris 1903seqq.
MÖSTA *Mitteilungen des Österreichischen Staatsarchivs,* Vienna 1948seqq.
MThZ *Münchener Theologische Zeitschrift,* Munich 1950seqq.

NAG *Nachrichten von der Akademie der Wissenschaften in Göttingen* (until 1940: *NGG*), Göttingen 1941seqq.
NDB *Neue Deutsche Biographie,* Berlin 1953seqq.
NRTh *Nouvelle Revue Théologique,* Tournai–Louvain–Paris 1849seqq.
NZM *Neue Zeitschrift für Missionswissenschaft,* Beckenried 1945seqq.

ÖAKR *Österreichisches Archiv für Kirchenrecht,* Vienna 1950seqq.
ÖBL *Österreichisches Biographisches Lexikon,* Graz–Cologne 1954seqq.
OrChrP *Orientalia Christiana periodica,* Rome 1935seqq.

Pastor L. von Pastor, *Geschichte der Päpste seit dem Ausgang des Mittelalters,* 16 vols., Freiburg i. Br. 1885seqq.
Pouthas C. Pouthas, *L'Église catholique de l'avènement de Pie VII à l'avènement de Pie IX* (*Les Cours de Sorbonne*), Paris 1945.
PrJ *Preußische Jahrbücher,* Berlin 1858seqq.
PrOrChr *Le Proche-Orient chrétien,* Jerusalem 1951seqq.

QLP *Questions liturgiques et paroissiales,* Louvain 1921seqq.

RACHS *Records of the American Catholic Historical Society,* Philadelphia 1884 seqq.
RAM *Revue d'ascétique et de mystique,* Toulouse 1920seqq.
Rémond R. Rémond, *La Droite en France, de la Première Restauration à la Ve République,* Paris 1963.
RevSR *Revue des Sciences Religieuses,* Strasbourg 1921seqq.
RF *Rázon y Fe,* Madrid 1901seqq.
RGB *Revue générale belge,* Brussels 1945seqq.
RH *Revue historique,* Paris 1876seqq.
RHE *Revue d'histoire ecclésiastique,* Louvain 1900seqq.
RHEF *Revue d'histoire de l'Église de France,* Paris 1910seqq.
RHLR *Revue d'histoire et de littérature religieuse,* Paris 1896–1907.
RHM *Revue d'histoire des missions,* Paris 1924seqq.
RHPhR *Revue d'histoire et de philosophie religieuses,* Strasbourg 1921seqq.
RhVJBll *Rheinische Vierteljahresblätter,* Bonn 1941seqq.
Rigault G. Rigault, *Histoire générale de l'Institut des Frères des Écoles chrétiennes,* 9 vols., Paris 1936–53.
Ris *Risorgimento,* Brussels 1958seqq.
ROC *Revue de l'Orient chrétien,* Paris 1896seqq.
Rogier *KG* *Geschichte der Kirche,* ed. by L. Rogier, R. Aubert, and D. Knowles, IV, Einsiedeln 1966.
Rogier, *KathHerleving* L. Rogier, *Katholieke Herleving. Geschiedenis van Katholiek Nederland sinds 1851,* The Hague, 1956.

RömHM *Römische Historische Mitteilungen,* Graz–Cologne 1958seqq.

Roskovany A. de Roskovany, *Romanus Pontifex tamquam Primas Ecclesiae et Princeps civilis e monumentis omnium saeculorum demonstratus,* 20 vols., Nitra 1867–90.

RPol *Review of Politics,* Notre Dame 1939seqq.

RQ *Römische Quartalschrift für christliche Altertumskunde und für Kirchengeschichte,* Freiburg im Breisgau 1887seqq.

RQH *Revue des question historiques,* Paris 1866seqq.

RRosm *Rivista Rosminiana,* Stresa 1906seqq.

RSIt *Rivista storica Italiana,* Naples 1884seqq.

RSoc *Recherches sociographiques,* Quebec 1960seqq.

RSPhTh *Revue des sciences philosophiques et théologiques,* Paris 1907seqq.

RSR *Recherches de science religieuse,* Paris 1910seqq.

RSTI *Rivista di storia della Chiesa in Italia,* Rome 1947seqq.

RStRis *Rassegna storica del Risorgimento,* Rome 1913seqq.

RStT *Rassegna storica toscana,* Florence 1955seqq.

Saeculum *Saeculum. Jahrbuch für Universalgeschichte,* Freiburg im Breisgau 1950seqq.

Salvatorelli L. Salvatorelli, *Chiesa e Stato dalla Rivoluzione francese ad oggi,* Florence 1955.

SC *Scuola Cattolica,* Milan 1873seqq.

Scheffczyk *Theologie in Aufbruch und Widerstreit. Die deutsche katholische Theologie im 19. Jahrhundert,* ed. by L. Scheffczyk, Bremen 1965.

Schmidlin *PG* J. Schmidlin, *Papstgeschichte der neuesten Zeit* I–IV, Munich 1933–39.

Schmitz *GB* P. Schmitz, *Histoire de l'ordre de Saint Benoît* IV and VII, Maredsous 1948/56.

Schnabel *G* F. Schnabel, *Deutsche Geschichte im 19. Jahrhundert,* Freiburg im Breisgau, I, 1948, II, 1949, III, 1954, IV, 1955.

Scholastik *Scholastik,* Freiburg im Breisgau 1926seqq.

Schrörs, *Braun* H. Schrörs, *Ein vergessener Führer aus der rheinischen Geistesgeschichte des 19. Jahrhunderts, Johann Wilhelm Joseph Braun,* Bonn 1925.

Schulte J. F. von Schulte, *Geschichte der Quellen und der Literatur des kanonischen Rechts,* 3 vols., Stuttgart 1875–80.

SE *Sacris Erudiri. Jaarboek voor Godsdienstwetenschapen,* Bruges 1948seqq.

Seppelt-Schwaiger F. X. Seppelt, *Geschichte der Päpste von den Anfängen bis zur Mitte des 20. Jahrhunderts,* I, II, IV, V, Leipzig 1931–41; I, Munich 1954, II, Munich 1955, III, Munich 1956, IV, Munich 1959.

Simon, *Rencontres* A. Simon, *Rencontres mennaisiennes en Belgique* (*Académie royale de Belgique, Mémoires de la Classe des Lettres* LVI/3), Brussels 1963.

Simon, *Sterckx* A. Simon, *Le cardinal Sterckx et son temps,* 2 vols., Wetteren 1950–51.

SM *Studien und Mitteilungen aus dem Benediktiner- und Zisterzienserorden bzw. zur Geschichte des Benediktiner-ordens und seiner Zweige,* Munich 1880seqq.

Sommervogel C. Sommervogel, *Bibliothèque de la Compagnie de Jésus* I–IX, Brussels–Paris 1890–1900; X (Supplements by E. M. Rivière), Toulouse 1911seqq.; XI (*Histoire* by P. Bliard), Paris 1932.

SourcesHist.rel.Belg. *Sources de l'histoire religieuse de la Belgique. Époque contemporaine. Colloque Bruxelles 1967* (*Centre interuniversitaire d'histoire contemporaine, Cahiers* 54), Louvain–Paris 1968.

SpAzLCIt *Spiritualità e Azione del laicato cattolico italiano,* 2 vols. (*Italia sacra* 11/12), Padua 1969.

Spini — G. Spini, *Risorgimento e protestanti,* Naples 1956.
SPM — *Sacrum Poloniae Millenium,* Rome 1954.
StdZ — *Stimmen der Zeit* (before 1914: *Stimmen aus Maria-Laach*), Freiburg im Breisgau 1871seqq.
StL — *Staatslexikon,* ed. by H. Sacher, Freiburg im Breisgau 1926–32.
StMis — *Studia Missionalia,* Rome 1943seqq.
Streit — *Bibliotheca Missionum,* started by R. Streit, continued by J. Dindinger, (Münster-Aachen) Freiburg im Breisgau 1916seqq.
StudFr — *Studi francescani,* Arezzo–Florence 1903seqq.
SZG — *Schweizerische Zeitschrift für Geschichte,* Zürich 1951seqq.

ThGl — *Theologie und Glaube,* Paderborn 1909seqq.
ThJ — *Theologische Jahrbücher,* Leipzig 1842seqq.
ThQ — *Theologische Quartalschrift,* Tübingen 1819seqq.; Stuttgart 1946seqq.
TThZ — *Trierer Theologische Zeitschrift* (until 1944: *Pastor Bonus*), Trier 1888seqq.

Villoslada — R. G. Villoslada, *Manual de historia de la Compañia de Jesús,* Madrid 1954.

Walz — A. Walz, *Compendium historiae Ordinis Praedicatorum,* Rome 1948.
Weill, *Cath. lib.* — G. Weill, *Histoire du catholicisme libéral en France 1828–1908,* Paris 1909.
Weill, *Idée laïque* — G. Weill, *Histoire de l'idée laïque en France au XIX*[e] *siècle,* Paris 1929.
Winter, *Byzanz* — E. Winter, *Byzanz und Rome im Kampf um die Ukraine,* Leipzig 1942.
Winter, *Russland* — E. Winter, *Russland und das Papsttum II: Von der Aufklärung bis zur Oktoberrevolution,* Berlin 1961.
WiWei — *Wissenschaft und Weisheit,* Düsseldorf 1934seqq.
WZ — *Westfälische Zeitschrift. Zeitschrift für vaterländische Geschichte,* Münster 1838seqq.

ZAGV — *Zeitschrift des Aachener Geschichtsvereins,* Aachen 1879seqq.
ZBLG — *Zeitschrift für Bayerische Landesgeschichte,* Munich 1928seqq.
ZGObrh — *Zeitschrift für die Geschichte des Oberrheins,* Karlsruhe 1851seqq.
ZKG — *Zeitschrift für Kirchengeschichte,* (Gotha) Stuttgart 1876seqq.
ZKTh — *Zeitschrift für Katholische Theologie,* (Innsbruck) Vienna 1877seqq.
ZMR — *Zeitschrift für Missionswissenschaft und Religionswissenschaft* 34seqq., Münster 1950seqq. (*Zeitschrift für Missionswissenschaft* 1–17, Münster 1911–27; *Zeitschrift für Missionswissenschaft und Religionswissenschaft* 18–25, Münster 1928–35; *Zeitschrift für Missionswissenschaft* 26–27, Münster 1935–37; *Missionswissenschaft und Religionswissenschaft* 28–33, Münster 1938–41, 1947–49).
ZRGG — *Zeitschrift für Religions- und Geistesgeschichte,* Marburg 1948seqq.
ZSKG — *Zeitschrift für schweizerische Kirchengeschichte,* (Stans) Fribourg 1907seqq.

PART ONE

The Catholic Church and the Revolution

Introduction

The Catholic Church at the End of the Eighteenth Century

The Crisis of the Church during the Old Regime

Today it is increasingly recognized that the "crisis of the European spirit, between 1680 and 1715," of which the French literary historian Paul Hazard wrote in 1935, was in reality a crisis of growth during which many positive elements which were important for the future attempted to find cautious expression and form on the level of thought and institutions. On the other hand, it can not be ignored that the eighteenth century was an exceedingly difficult period for all Christian Churches and that the Roman Church especially displayed the appearance more of decadence than of renewal. While on the surface the Church still possessed the power of immeasurable riches, countless privileges, and state support, its authority was shaken. Each year there were further discords. Finally, the disparity between a world which was in the process of full economic, social, and cultural development and that of a clerical hierarchy which was simply incapable of differentiating between the real requirements of faith and the nonessential accessories with which the Church and religion had surrounded themselves in the course of centuries became evident. The Church clung tenaciously to completely obsolete positions.

This was especially evident in the case of the Holy See. Gallicanism and Febronianism were not limited to the theses of a certain school of thought. Both were more accurately the doctrinaire expression of a sentiment hostile to Rome which became more widely accepted throughout Catholic Europe. Many members of the clergy, of the higher civil service, and of the judiciary came to accept the notion that the spiritual supremacy of the Pope was nothing more than an honorary privilege. The devaluation of the authority of the Pope was strengthened by the ambiguity of his position as a small Italian territorial ruler. Under Europe's enlightened despotism, governments attempted to improve the economic conditions of their states, and to reform governmental institutions so as to provide a more rational direction, and to promote general education. In light of such circumstances, the backward administration of the Papal States generated widespread sarcastic and critical commentary. This vulnerable state was also in a rather difficult position internationally. It was the object of rivalry between Vienna, Paris, and Madrid, and thus forced its ruler constantly into accommodations and compromises. It was impossible for the Father of all the faithful to rise above party factions and to exercise his really supranational authority. Temporal power, which was demanded from the world as an irreducible prerequisite for the independence of the papacy, had in reality become an additional cause of the weakness of this institution. Other matters were becoming of even graver consequence.

With the exception of the pontificate of Benedict XIV, one must agree with Professor Rogier's assessment of the papacy in the eighteenth century. "In general, the actual influence of Rome on international happenings was extremely small; its contributions to the development of thought exhausted themselves in stereotype and sterile protest. Surveying the cultural history of the eighteenth century, one repeatedly misses the participation of the Church and its supreme leadership in the discussions of the burning issues of the period. If Rome contributed at all, it did so only negatively: with an admonition, an anathema, or an exhortation to silence. Regrettably, Rome not only failed to join in dialogue with a generation as strongly affected by the currents of the age as that of the eighteenth century, it systematically avoided it."[1] On the eve of the upheavals of 1789, the 1740 formulation of President Charles de Brosses was still valid: "If in Europe the credit of the Holy See is shrinking daily, this loss stems from an unawareness by the papacy of its antiquated modes of expression."

The broad masses of the population continued to perform their religious duties. The performance of these duties, however, was frequently more an accommodation to the structure of social tradition than a matter of conviction. In particular, the nobility and the educated bourgeoisie, under the influence of the Enlightenment, adopted an increasingly emancipated stance. Philosophy, influenced positively by the progress of the empirical sciences, and negatively by the endless and fruitless Jansenist controversies, gradually came to provide the intellectual constructs which formerly had their origins in theology. This shift was promoted by the insistence of the official Church that it was the champion of a global concept of the world, science, society, and education which was immutably fixed. Consequently, in the area of thought or of practical implementation, there was no room left for progress. The reaction against these increasingly anachronistic pretensions was unavoidable in a world obsessed by modernity. The tendency grew stronger to reorder social life on a secular basis, to glorify the autonomy of the individual against all political and clerical authorities, and to demand a "natural religion" corresponding to what man had determined. Religion was to tolerate all opinions and to replace not only

[1] Rogier, *KG* 29.

ridiculous exercises of piety, regarded as revelations of superstition, but also dogmas, sacraments and the entire clerical organization.

The movement began in England and rapidly spread first to France and then to Germany. In Germany, the Protestant north quickly caught up with the Catholic south, whose urban areas after the Thirty Years War were the cultural centers of the country. After the middle of the century, the Protestant north actually became the carrier of future values, in contrast to the stagnation of the important Catholic centers of learning, for which the old Jesuitic *ratio studiorum* was in the process of becoming an antiquated iron collar. The "Catholic Enlightenment" attempted to marshal all its vital forces to defeat the Protestant challenge, to prevent the spread of religious indifference and unbelief, to fight the sclerosis of the Church of the Counter Reformation, and to bring about the victory of the mysticism of salvation parallel to the development of the profane sciences and the striving of mankind for an improvement of its earthly condition.[2] The number of its followers, however, was relatively small. In addition, the Catholic Enlightenment was frequently compromised in France and Italy because of its relationship to the Jansenists. Above all, its searching attempts, although intuitively auguring well for the future, were for the time being a rather shy groping, which among many—similar to the fermentation following the Second Vatican Council—awakened an impression of doctrinal confusion and disintegration of traditional Catholicism. All of this could only strengthen the impression among contemporaries that Catholicism was dealing with a double crisis, because to the attacks from the outside had been added a profound internal discontent.

The responsible leaders of the Catholic Church lacked the acuity necessary to develop a new religious anthropology to respond to the message of revelation as well as the spiritual reorientation of the age. They were equally incapable of clearing away the confusion which stemmed from the Middle Ages with respect to the difference between real clerical structures based on the gospel and the aristocratic structure of the Church of the Old Regime. One of the chief sources of dissatisfaction was the system of benefices. Since the Council of Trent it had been impossible to improve or to abolish the system of benefices, because sovereign princes, who used it to satisfy the nobility by assigning them to younger sons, resisted any change. The intolerable nature of the system, which had been aggravated by numerous abuses, became increasingly evident on the pastoral as well as the social level. It was not

[2] See the illuminating discourse of B. Plongeron in his article "L'Aufklärung catholique en Europe occidentale, 1770–1830" in *Revue d'histoire moderne et contemporaine* 16 (1969) 557–605.

inconceivable that if the opportunity were provided, it would be swept away in a large part of Europe by the spirit of the age. Even though reform of the structure might be basically healthy, there was danger that it might be regarded by many as a prelude to the disappearance of the Church as a whole.

Toward the end of the Old Regime many ecclesiastical institutions were failing to function well. Noteworthy were the problems within the monastic systems. It would be an inaccurate generalization to say there were not large numbers of zealous monks. But in the eyes of the world the monastery had for some time ceased to be a place to exercise the virtues of the Gospel. To be sure, monasteries were not the dens of iniquity painted in certain types of literature, but it must be admitted that the religious atmosphere within their walls was in general rather mediocre. Aside from some particularly strict orders such as the Carthusians, the Trappists, and the Carmelites, the world often regarded monasticism as an easy life which provided good incomes to the monks who administered extensive pieces of real estate and undertook expensive construction projects. It was also complained that many of the monasteries which had been founded in the Middle Ages were now half empty. The mendicant orders provoked less criticism with their lack of riches, but their members suffered from a crisis of belief to which was added, especially in the southern countries, a crisis of discipline. One found among the mendicant orders many an eager preacher and apostle of charity, but a substantial number of their members formed a rather less impressive ecclesiastical lower class which was an easy target for the scorners of monastic vows. The opponents of monastic life criticized not only the frequent enervation of these institutions, but also asserted that the orders were totally useless to society. In their eyes only those orders were acceptable which devoted themselves exclusively to education and the care of the sick. Consequently, in the second half of the eighteenth century, it was not surprising to see governments, encouraged by public opinion, secularize a part of the monasteries. The proceeds from secularization were used to found parsonages for the growing population and to subsidize public education and welfare, areas which many people would have preferred to be made into public agencies. In this sense, the radical measures ultimately taken during the French Revolution were only the culmination of a policy which had been developing for a quarter of a century in all Catholic countries and against which the ecclesiastical authorities, although fully aware of the unhealthy conditions, had protested only feebly. An example of government secularization may be found in the Republic of Venice where, between 1748 and 1797, 127 monasteries were closed down. Similar measures were taken in Tuscany, the Duchy of Parma, Lombardy,

Spain, and, in an especially systematic way between 1780 and 1790, in the various provinces of the Austrian monarchy. In France, such an action had been suggested and organized by the clergy itself despite the protests of the Pope. A Commission of Regulars[3] was formed under the driving force of Lomenie de Brienne, the archbishop of Toulouse. The archbishop, an expert administrator and a man worried about the good standing of the Church in society, but "closer to the philosophes than to Christianity," in 1768 suggested a number of steps to the King. The proposed changes would raise the age for taking monastic vows, in order to better guarantee the voluntariness of the action; reform the structure of the old orders in order to take into account their spiritual progress since their founding; strengthen the control of the bishops over the monasteries not under their jurisdiction; and prescribe a minimum number of monks for each house. The result of the proposal by the commission was the dissolution of 426 monasteries, whose lands were turned over to the dioceses, and the disappearance of a number of smaller congregations which, admittedly, as Chevallier said "constituted the truly ruinous part of the monasteries." The Commission of Regulars doubtless had in mind more a reform of orders than their abolition, but nevertheless it appealed to the power of the state, ignored systematically all protests of the Holy See, and assumed a far more utilitarian than religious position. Precisely this kind of procedure created a "precedent which the Constituent Assembly was to remember twenty years later" (Latreille).

While the crisis was particularly painful for the monasteries, it was also felt among the secular clergy with major differences from country to country. In the Belgian provinces and in the Rhineland, for example, the situation was relatively satisfactory, but lamentable in the kingdom of Naples and in some areas of Spain. The fact that a very large number of priests lived from the income of benefices or other murky sources without performing any pastoral work illuminates one of the most evident defects of the Church toward the end of the Old Regime. One could in fact notice during the course of the eighteenth century an attempt in many areas to upgrade the intellectual and spiritual education of the lower clergy, and, by the end of the century, educated priests and self-sacrificing pastors were more numerous than a century earlier. This did not alter, however, the existence of many abuses which an enlightened public opinion was no longer willing to countenance. In this context, as in so many others, factual determinations must not allow the historian to forget that psychological reactions also played a consider-

[3] Cf. P. Chevallier, *Lomenie de Brienne et l'ordre monastique, 1776–1789,* 2 vols. (Paris 1959).

able role. A striving for an improved education did indeed exist among the lower clergy, but a large number of the clergy, not only in France but in Italy and western Germany as well, became interested in Richeristic doctrines whose goal it was to reduce the authority of the Pope and the bishops and which prepared the way for the democratic notions which found a reflection in the Civil Constitution of the Clergy. The acceptance of Richeristic doctrine was facilitated by the desire of many pastors to reduce episcopal "despotism" and an unjust distribution of the income from the estates of the Church. To this must be added that in the rural areas of such countries as France the dissatisfaction created by unpopular tithing was aggravated by a feudal reaction of the landlords. Further friction arose from the attitude, taken by many civil servants, that the clergy was merely a depository of immense land wealth and that its prerogatives were dependent upon the decisions of the sovereign. This view won increasing acceptance among the circles concerned with the modernization of religious and secular institutions.

The various foundations of the power of the Church in the Old Regime, its wealth, its prestige, and its moral authority were questioned systematically. In spite of sporadic and embryonic attempts to reach a highly necessary adjustment, the Catholic Church on the eve of the revolution made a weakened impression, and the still remaining spiritual forces, whose strength became evident in the course of affliction and which were to explain why the Church was able to regenerate itself so quickly, proved ineffective. Catholic resistance was made more difficult because not only did it lack a cohesive leadership but also because of the prevailing confusion of concept and opinion regarding the role of the Church. The situation was aggravated by the fact that the upper clergy and the secular leadership were accustomed to intervention by the government in ecclesiastic affairs. Missing at the head of the Church was a highly gifted man with extraordinary energy. When the storm of revolution broke loose in France, the greater part of Catholic Europe eventually became involved. At that moment, there sat on Peter's chair a Pope who was conscientious but who lacked precisely those characteristics which were needed under such trying circumstances.

Pius VI

After the death of Clement XIV, the more than four-month-long conclave between October 1774 and February 1775 faced the nightmare question to what extent the Society of Jesus was to be dissolved. The cardinals representing the chief powers could not agree among themselves. Representatives from Austria and France desired a moderate interpretation, while those from Spain and Portugal were in favor of a radical implementation. Although both factions faced opposition from the group of so-called "zealots" who regretted Clement XIV's capitulation to the great powers, they were undecided among the several candidates. After numerous vain attempts, Zelada, who functioned as mediator, succeeded in getting all zealots to unite behind Braschi, who, although he was regarded as a partisan of the Jesuits, had kept away from political and religious controversies under the two previous pontificates. The candidacy of Braschi was supported emphatically by Cardinal de Bernis, the French legate, who skillfully managed to remove the remaining doubts of the Austrians and Spaniards. The result was Braschi's unanimous election.

Gianangelo Braschi, who adopted the name of Pius VI because of his high esteem for Pius V, was born on 25 December 1717 at Cesena in the northern region of the Papal States. He studied law and only became a priest in 1758. The protection of Cardinal Ruffo, legate at Ferrara, and his personal characteristics assured him of a quick rise in the Curia. In 1766, Clement XIII appointed him treasurer of the apostolic chamber, i.e., as secretary of the treasury, and he succeeded in improving somewhat the strongly shaken economic and financial position of the Papal States. Misfortune which pursued Pius VI in his later years has given rise to his idealization and has marked him as a martyr Pope. There was a great difference, however, between the myth and the reality. The new Pope was indeed pious and honest, and he demonstrated irreproachable and genuine courage in the face of adversity. But Pius VI was not a prepossessing personality. He was vain, worldly, and proud of his handsome appearance. Moreover, he was determined to imitate Leo X as promotor of art and architecture. Pius VI spent large amounts of money for the beautification of the Eternal City, encouraged archeological digs, and surrounded himself with such scholars as Cardinal Garampi and Cardinal Gerdil. He also revived nepotism once more and practiced it to a greater degree than any other Pope during the eighteenth century. For his sister's son, Luigi, he built a splendid palace in Rome. During the course of his quarter of a century pontificate he repeatedly showed that he lacked both energy and acuity. Pius VI was reluctant to make decisions and was totally absorbed by secondary problems of prestige. For example, he became absorbed in a ridiculous dispute with the King of Naples over the white horse which the King owed in annual tribute to the Pope as his liege lord. Yet Pius VI was also able to act independently. In the conclave he had been the candidate of the zealots, but he immediately disassociated himself from their position and pursued a flexible and moderate policy which did not offend the European courts. In pursuing this policy, however, he ignored his secretary of state, Cardinal Pallavicini, who had been pressed on him by the powers, and allowed the Cardinal little initiative. Concerned with both the welfare of his subjects and the defense of the rights of the Church, Pius VI conscientiously pursued the double task of secular ruler and Pontiff.

Still relatively young at the time of his election, Pius VI nurtured a number of major plans. With regard to the administration of the Papal States, he introduced reforms which were in part inspired by mercantilistic theories. These undertakings were frequently badly planned or badly implemented, but some of them are of interest. For example, the introduction with the help of Cardinal Boncompagni Ludovisi[4] of a land register, even though this reform foundered on the opposition of the large landlords. The Pope also improved roads, modernized the ports of Anzio and Terracina, and drained a large part of the Pontine Swamp. These public works projects required financial means which Pius VI did not have at his disposal and, in combination with the huge expenditures which he committed toward immortalizing his memory in Rome, led to a tremendous rise in the public debt. Pius constantly wavered between a policy of improving conditions in the Roman Campagna and a protectionist policy in the area of manufacture and trade. Moreover, he was unfortunate in the selection of his staff and suffered from the indifference of influential Roman factions, even though their leaders were infected by the spirit of reform.

From the beginning, Pius VI met with difficulty in maintaining the traditional position of the Pope. The Holy See encountered increasingly hostile public opinion toward the Curia, and governments became more determined to exact from the Pope one concession after another, with the goal of strengthening their influence over the national clergy. The situation was not altered by the fact that in France and Portugal a certain improvement of the general situation was recorded. The new French King, Louis XIV, showed himself to be favorably inclined toward the position of the Pope, and in Portugal Pombal fell into disgrace and was dismissed after the coronation of the pious queen, Mary I, in 1777. Examples of the weakening papal position were the futile defense which Pius VI mounted against the religious policy of the Austrian Emperor, Joseph II; the conflict between the Pope and the German prince-bishops in the Munich nunciature controversy and the Ems draft treaty; the problems arising from the reforms of the Grand Duke Pietro Leopoldo and the adjacent position of the Duchy of Tuscany to the Papal States; and the recurring tension with Russia over the integration of Polish Catholics as a result of the annexations of 1772, 1793, and 1795. Aware of his weakness, Pius VI tried within reason to gain time. The Pope was

[4] See U. Coldagelli in *DBI* XI, 713–19.

more forceful in counteracting attempts at Jansenist reform in Rome, and he succeeded in the resignation of Bishop Scipione de Ricci. After hesitating for eight years, Pius VI, with the Bull *Auctorem fidei* of 28 August 1794, finally condemned the main decrees of the Synod of Pistoia. With regard to the Jesuits, he maneuvered exceedingly carefully so as not to offend the Bourbon courts, and finally tacitly allowed the Jesuits to secretly regroup themselves around the nucleus which continued to exist in the western part of the Russian Empire.

The outbreak and the subsequent effects of the French Revolution in 1789 introduced a much more threatening period for the Catholic Church in general and for the Holy See in particular. But during his last years Pius VI increasingly failed to supply a much needed decisive stance and became torn by the opposing factions of his entourage. He displayed, as Godechot stated, "more courageous obstinacy than real political sensitivity."

CHAPTER 1

The French Revolution and Pius VI

For a number of years following the French Revolution, the concept grew not only in France but also in the United States that the revolution and the period beginning around 1770 was not merely a remarkable national event, but one which comprised a part of a larger "Atlantic Revolution," which had transformed the entire western world.[1] This interpretation is certainly justified from a social and political point of view; yet it does not change the fact that from the point of view of the Catholic Church the events which occurred specifically in France between 1789 and 1801 were totally predominant. France was not only the country with the largest Catholic population, it also was the country in which the monastic orders had their largest number of houses; the country whose theological and spiritual influence was particularly strong both for all of Europe and America. It was incontestably the epicenter of the earthquake which within a few years caused the fall of the antiquated structures of the Catholic Church in a large part of Europe and profoundly transformed the position of the Catholic Church, especially in Germany and the Netherlands, relative to the Protestant Churches. Beyond this, the policy of revolutionary France in Italy considerably

[1] See R. Palmer, *The Age of the Democratic Revolution* (Princeton 1959); J. Godechot, *Les Révolutions, 1770–99* (Paris 1963).

affected the situation of the papacy. After a decade of conflict, the new solutions worked out by Napoleon and Pius VII influenced and lastingly determined the relationship between Church and state in the course of the nineteenth century. For this reason the first two chapters of this volume are devoted exclusively to the development of the religious crisis in France.

The Gallican Church on the Eve of the Revolution

A first view of the Church in France in 1789 gives a solid impression of strength and power. In reality, though, its standing among the educated had been weakened. Debilitated by internal wrangles and new ideas which had found fertile soil, the level of institutions showed indications of arteriosclerosis that became ever more noticeable.

The Catholic Church in France, as in other Catholic European countries, was an official institution linked to the state and one which enjoyed significant political, juridical, and financial privileges. Roman Catholicism was the established religion in France, and as such it was supported by the secular power. The concept of religious tolerance, which increasingly had gained ground during the past several decades in the Anglo-Saxon and German states, found hardly an echo among the bourgeois institutions of France. Public divine services for non-Catholic denominations remained outlawed. Although the Protestants had succeeded by the edict of 1787 in gaining recognition for marriages performed without the services of a Catholic priest, this regulation was opposed by clergy and laymen alike. The principle of unity of faith in the kingdom thrived and toleration continued to be equated with atheism. In spite of the concessions of 1784, which were limited to Alsace, the position of Jews also remained a delicate one.

The relationship between the Church in France and the Holy See continued to be governed by the concordat of 1516, whose implementation gave rise to no major complaints. The concordat conceded important rights to the King. Among these were the right to distribute benefices. Even though in the case of bishoprics and abbeys the King was required to seek the consent of the Pope, his selection always was the decisive one. Thereby the King assured himself the loyalty of the clergy. To these rights were added the traditional esteem in which the monarch always had been held. Coexistent was the equally traditional distrust toward all ultramontane demands and the frequent differences of opinion between Rome and Versailles in the arena of international politics. The combination of these factors explains the widespread popularity of the Gallican doctrines. During this time a balance had been reached between the rights of the Holy See and the rights of the crown, and both the clergy and the faithful felt more commitment to the Pope than might be gathered at first sight.

The clergy enjoyed a predominant position in every respect. It constituted an estate equal to those of the nobility and the commoners and was in fact the only estate with an organization which acted increasingly like a pressure group of nobles. The delegates of this estate met every five years in general convention. In Paris, its representative was the *Agence Générale.* Talleyrand had succeeded between 1780 and 1785 in changing this agency into a type of permanent ministry of the clergy.[2] The clergy retained the right to its own system of justice, although interventions by the fiscal solicitor as representative of the state became more frequent and occasionally extended even to religious matters. The French Church was divided into 135 remarkably unequal dioceses with antiquated and inexpedient districts.[3] The clergy consisted of approximately fifty thousand priests laboring in the parishes and between fifteen thousand and eighteen thousand canons who served virtually no function. There were also twenty thousand to twenty-five thousand monks and thirty thousand to forty thousand nuns. The French clergy thus comprised approximately one hundred twenty thousand persons. Additionally, there were a large number of sacristans and chorists, as well as businessmen and staff who took care of worldly concerns. This secular and regular clergy possessed impressive economic power. It owned numerous urban buildings and, more importantly, ecclesiastical real estate in the countryside in amounts which fluctuated from region to region. In the south, the Church owned between 4 and 6 percent of the land. The actual amount in the Auvergne was only 3.5 percent, but rose as high as 20 percent in Brie and in Picardie and constituted as much as two-thirds of the land in Cambresis. In the whole country, the

[2] See L. S. Greenbaum, *Talleyrand, Statesman Priest. The Agent-General of the Clergy and the Church of France at the End of the Old Regime* (Washington 1970). Also M. Peronnet in *AHRF* 34 (1962), 8–35.

[3] In Provence and also in Languedoc there were numerous tiny dioceses, stemming from the time of Gallico-Roman settlements. Several dioceses ranged on both sides of a border, for example the diocese Glandève which numbered thirty-four parishes in France and twenty-five in the Kingdom of Sardinia. Seven dioceses even had their capitals in foreign countries, for example Tournai and Basel. The diocese of Strasbourg belonged to the church province of Mainz, while the dioceses of Metz, Toul, and Verdun belonged to that of Trier. With respect to income there was a tremendous disparity between the poor bishoprics in the south (incomes between seven thousand and fourteen thousand Livres) and some large dioceses in the north or the east (diocese of Strasbourg forty thousand Livres, diocese of Cambrai two hundred thousand Livres, and the diocese of Beauvais ninety-six thousand Livres).

Church owned about 10 percent of the land and received an annual income of more than 100 million Livres. The tithe, which also fluctuated from region to region and which, after 1770, led to actual peasant uprisings, produced an equal amount. Wherever the Church owned little land, it contributed as much as 80 percent of the income of the parish priests. The income was almost tax-free. The Church was obliged to pay no more than a voluntary contribution to the state, and toward the end of the Old Regime this amounted to no more than 4 million Livres, or less than 2 percent. On the other hand, this tax privilege was compensated for by heavy expenditures, especially the costs of education and welfare. In spite of their high cost, however, these activities guaranteed the Church a considerable influence in French society and one which it was to long for during the subsequent century.

The influence of the Church was especially strong in the countryside. While the monks and cathedral canons were often regarded as burdensome landlords, the parish clergy was held in esteem, because it provided education, maintained the register, and supported the poor. In some areas, however, the peasants gradually dissociated themselves from the Church. This was especially true in Bordelais, Santogne, and Aunis, where the forced conversion of Protestants in the preceeding century had led to religious indifference. Among many segments of society, above all among the landed bourgeoisie, local civil servants, innkeepers, and retired soldiers, free spirits abounded. The distancing process was acute in the cities, where in such places as Auxerre, Rouen, and Bordeaux a considerable number of people no longer performed their Easter rites.[4] The concepts of the philosophes touched not only the educated circles, but other population groups as well. This condition should not be generalized too much, however, as foreign travelers in France in 1780 reported that the people continued to cling to their traditional religion in more than a merely surface fashion. Foreign travelers were particularly impressed by the seriousness and the piety which people displayed during services, even in such urban centers as Paris. Even the civil service was not lacking in pious families, and among the nobility, according to D. Mornet, the "philosophical" landlords were hardly in the majority. The success of the Freemasons should not lead to erroneous conclusions about a general lack of piety. While it is true that Freemasonry created a suitable climate for the idea of a "natural religion," one which frees man from submission to a Church, no respectable historian will defend the assertion that in the lodges of the eighteenth century there existed a systematic conspiracy against the

[4] Y. Hilaire in *L' information historique* 25 (1963), 57–58.

Church.[5] This reservation must be made, because it makes comprehensible the resilience of the old religion during the storms of the revolution. On the other hand, it must be admitted that, aside from the older anticlericalism of the trade guilds, the influence of the philosophes increasingly constituted the major competition to the influence of the Church among the rising bourgeoisie.[6] The impact of this development was enhanced by the fact that the refutations of enlightened thought by Catholic apologists were overwhelmingly of rather mediocre quality, and that responsible officials generally preferred to hide behind the skirts of secular power and censorship instead of acknowledging that in many areas a serious attempt at accommodation was urgently needed.

The situation was especially apparent among the orders in France as well as elsewhere. The contemporary literature illustrates a fashionable trend toward denouncing the sloth, greed, and immorality of the monks. Indeed, many of the monks had been urged into monastic life by their families and consequently led frivolous and occasionally scandalous lives, read the most daring works of the philosophes, and a few years later constituted a significant portion of the revolutionary nucleus. Many a monastery had abandoned completely its vows of poverty and had squandered its best efforts in controversies with debtors. Such orders no longer were concerned with works of charity and serving God. The case was especially so in the many monasteries whose abbots were nominated by the King. These monasteries had become ecclesiastical sinecures, distributed among courtly favorites, most of whom did not take up residence. In 1789, of a total of 740 abbeys no fewer than 625 had been awarded as prebends. Their tenants enjoyed the income of their benefices while being exempted from clerical duties. Countless abuses and grievances, therefore, called urgently for reforms; reforms which needed to go deeper than the rather inept efforts which had been considered by the Commission of Regulars between 1766 and 1768. It

[5] On Freemasonry in France on the eve of the revolution see *AHRF* 197 (1969) and as an example of monographic treatment see A. Le Bihay, *Francs-Maçons, parisiens du Grand Orient de France à la fin du XVIIIe siècle,* 3 vols. (Paris 1966–72). See also the bibliographic entries in the *Handbuch der europäischen Geschichte* IV, ed. by F. Wagner, 297–98, notes 29–33. On the thesis of the alleged plot against the Church which was promoted by the Eudist Lefranc in 1791 and spread in popular form by the Jesuit Barruel in his *Mémoires pour servir à l'histoire du jacobinisme,* 3 vols. (Hamburg 1797–99), see A. Gérard, *La Révolution française, mythes et interprétations* (Paris 1970), 22–24; M. Defourneaux in *AHRF* 37 (1965), 170–86; J. Droz in *RH* 226 (1961), 313–38.

[6] In connection with R. R. Palmer, *Catholics and Unbelievers in XVIIIth-Century France* (Princeton 1940) it is advisable to read the analyses of L. Trenard and Y. Hilaire, "Idées, croyances et sensibilité religieuse du XVIIIe au XIXe siècle," *Bulletin de la section d'histoire moderne du Comité des travaux historiques* 5 (1964), 7–27.

would be too simplistic to assert that on the eve of 1789 a general decadence prevailed. Spiritual laxity was the exception rather than the rule in the convents. The contemplative female orders recorded a constant stream of admissions in spite of the spirit of the time. Public opinion, formed in the light of Diderot's novel *La religieuse,* viewed the solemn vows of the old orders with hostility, but valued the services of the numerous new congregations with their simple or total lack of vows. Such congregations as the Sisters of Mercy, who performed services in the areas of education and charity, met with approval. With respect to the monasteries, historians note the reduction in the number of monks between 1768 and 1789.[7] The depopulation differed among orders and between regions. It is remarkable that in the case of such different orders as the Benedictines, Dominicans, and the regular canons of Saint Geneviève, the curve of admissions began to rise again after 1780. This development, coming after a long decline, caused a problematical relationship between the younger members, who were more open to the new ideas, and the older monks, who did not understand the desire for reform. Although there were many poorly qualified monks who were pleased to regain their freedom as a result of the decisions of the Constituent Assembly, B. Plongeron has noted some cases of genuine fervor and the "continuation of truly religious and priestly attitudes." This is a confirmation of the fact that one cannot characterize the entire spiritual history of the eighteenth century, as Bremond did, as a "retreat of the mystics." The hasty generalizations of earlier historians are explained also by Plongeron, who pointed out that one could find "firm religious convictions under totally irreligious behavior." The palpable existence of abuses and grievances all too easily permitted the assumption of a general decay, and one cannot overemphasize the fact of crisis within the monasteries. This condition, however, should not be equated with general decadence. It can be interpreted as a crisis of adaptation which in actuality was a sign of vitality. Such an interpretation cannot be expected to have been reached by the upper clergy prior to the events of 1789 nor could they be expected to assign a proper perspective to the strivings of numerous orders for a trenchant reform of monastic life.

Even the upper clergy, who occupied a position of major responsibility, cannot be condemned out of hand. Neither scandal, scepticism, or unbelief associated with some of the bishops, nor the worldly conduct of others, who preferred to live at court and left the administration of their dioceses to subordinates, should make one forget that the overwhelm-

[7] Between 1768 and 1789 the number of monks at Cluny sank from 671 to 301. The Franciscans went from 2385 to 1544, the Capuchins from 4937 to 2674, and the Dominicans from 1432 to 1006.

ing majority of the French bishops in the second half of the eighteenth century led a life of dignity and conscientiously attempted to fulfill the duties of office. There was no lack of such genuinely pious and virtuous pastors as Lefranc de Pompignan. Others, as Gurian points out, acted more "as provincial administrators than as administrators of sacraments," and concerned themselves primarily with economic and social reforms. Their conduct was determined by their conviction, growing out of the spirit of the time, that faithful adherence to the Gospel required them to labor for the improvement of the lot of the common man. These members of the episcopate for some years had been recruited from the nobility and the aristocracy and therefore demonstrated the bad as well as the good characteristics of this social class. Their social background provided them with a broad education, magnanimity, and a sense of honor; but these aristocratic bishops, who owed their appointments more to their birth and their connections than to their personal qualifications, had only a superficial theological knowledge; a deficiency which was particularly alarming at the moment when the French Church required an extraordinarily strong and firm spiritual leadership. Privileges were jealousy defended and benefices were regarded as the quite natural accumulation necessary for the kind of life which these aristocratic bishops expected to be accorded their position. Moreover, bishops of this type moved almost exclusively within circles of clerics and laity from their own background. They appeared as nothing more than part of a caste system to the middle clergy of canons, seminary professors, and scholarly priests who came from the upper middle class and whose spiritual role and influence at the local level was considerable. The parish clergy, which was drawn also from the middle class, resented the arrogance of the aristocratic bishops and angrily compared the ostentatious life style of these bishops with their own often meager incomes.

Monographs concerning individual dioceses, however, require a correction of the popular conception regarding the small incomes of the country clergy.[8] They demonstrate that parish priests in many dioceses enjoyed genuine comfort. This was particularly true wherever the official incomes were augmented by generous contributions of the parishioners. It is true that this was not the case everywhere, and in some areas the withholding of the tithe by the landlords made the salaries of country clergy inadequate; an inadequacy which these parsons, who mostly stemmed from the middle urban bourgeoisie, felt

[8] See for example the articles by D. Julia on the diocese of Reims in *Revue d'histoire moderne et contemporaine* 13 (1966), 195–216 and by Ch. Girault on the Department of Sarthe in *La Province du Maine* 33 (1953), 69–88.

acutely, as they were desirous of maintaining the life style of their class. There were some isolated cases, as in the Dauphiné and in Provence in 1779, where, in defiance of the law, parish priests formed a kind of labor union to effect an improvement of their situation. However, on the eve of the events of 1789, the complaints of the lower clergy were primarily concerned with the social, pastoral, and theological situation, rather than with their economic status. These sons of the middle class utilized their strength to defend an elitist position which they saw as threatened and were angered by the aristocratic pretensions displayed toward them by the bishops. Agreeing with Richer, who saw in the parsons the successors of the seventy-two disciples, they assumed the point of view that "the real ecclesiastical body is the body of the officiating pastors which is merely presided over by the bishop and that everything else, such as cathedral benefices, abbeys, other property, and colleges with the right to tithe, is the result of a history of centuries." They demanded from the bishops, who never bothered to consult them, the reintroduction of diocesan synods in order to discuss with them the means for a reform of the Church to achieve greater equality and spiritualization. The indifference with which the Church hierarchy responded to a movement which was agitating the lower clergy from one end of France to the other contributed to the deepening division between the bishops and the priests. Even if it did not result in actual class warfare, as it did in Nancy, there is no doubt that many priests were prepared to accept radical changes in the position of the oligarchy; an oligarchy which had established a leadership monopoly within the Gallican Church.[9] One has to agree with A. Latreille when he writes: "The resentment of a bourgeoisie, which was aware of its economic and social importance, and enraged that the privileged classes continued to oppress them, has often been mentioned among the causes of the revolution; analogously, one must realize that a sizable portion of the clergy was convinced of the injustice of its established order and was driven spontaneously to rise against it."[10] The meeting of the Estates General left no doubt that the Church in France constituted its own estate within the state, but one which was severely lacking in homogeneous social unity.

The Constituent Assembly and the Church

Nothing in the summer of 1789 signaled that the incipient revolution was to develop into the most dramatic period in the history of the

[9] See M. G. Hutt, "The Curés and the Third Estate. The ideas of reform in the pamphlets of the French lower clergy in the period 1787–89" in *JEH* 8 (1957), 74–92.
[10] *HistCathFr* III, 51.

French Church. In the grievances prepared for the Estates General, there were rather frequent complaints about the privileges and the abuses of the Church, and about the tithe and the degeneration of monasticism, but only rarely was a dissolution of the orders mentioned and even less often was the official position of the Church and its leading role in the fields of education and charity called into question. Generally, there was a desire that necessary reforms be effected with the advice and cooperation of concerned circles. Under pressure from the priests, those groups concerned with reform made a number of suggestions and supported various political, legal, and fiscal demands of the Third Estate.[11] During the period in which the Estates General transformed themselves into the Constituent Assembly, it became clear that the clergy, after an initial hesitation, was again willing to be cooperative. However, at first, a rather considerable number of the lower clergy as well as the upper clergy did not show itself in agreement with the reform proposed by the Third Estate to vote by heads instead of by Estates; a reform which would grant it a predominating position with respect to the other two privileged Estates. Finally, the small group of priests who were in favor of this change were able to convince two-thirds of their brethren to vote for it. On 23 June the King attempted to save the situation by closing the meeting hall. About eighty priests joined with the members of the Third Estate in refusing to disperse and, by remaining, contributed to the success of the revolution.

A few weeks later, on the famous night of 4 August, the clergy accepted almost unanimously the abolition of feudalism, the discarding of the tithe, and all of the consequences for the Church resulting from this action. In the following week the Assembly declared that it bore no ill will toward the Church and would take care that expenses for services, for the support of acolytes, and for the support of the poor would be covered in other ways. On 12 August an ecclesiastical committee was constituted to find solutions to these problems.

A much more radical measure was to be considered on 2 November. The increasing gravity of the financial situation made it obligatory to discuss once again a problem which for years had concerned both lawyers and economists. This was the confiscation by the state of Church lands. This time, many members of the Church, even priests like Henri Grégoire, who normally were favorably inclined toward reforms, resisted such a proposal. They considered it dangerous to change the

[11] In addition to the outdated work of L. Chassin, *Les cahiers des curés de 1789* (Paris 1882), see B. Hyslop, *A Guide to the General Cahiers of 1789* (New York 1936); J. Richard, *L'élaboration d'un cahier de doléances. P. Cl. Perrot, curé de Brazey* (Dijon 1961); A. Dupront, "Cahiers de doléances et mentalités collectives" in *Acts du 89e Congrès des Sociétés savantes* (Paris 1969), 375 ff.

clergy into salaried officials of the state. Many of the secular delegates also hesitated to break with the tradition of centuries. The bishop of Autun, Charles-Maurice de Talleyrand, who was disappointed by the incoherence of royal policy and wanted to confirm the new order, delivered a skillful address and helped to change the prevailing sentiment. In all, the debate lasted three weeks. In its course, Abbé Maury forcefully defended the legal thesis of the inviolability of the rights of the Church, while a few moderate groups, following the respected Bishop Boisgelin of Aix, in vain suggested a compromise solution. The Assembly's final decision was influenced more by the specter of bankruptcy than by the ideal of secularization. By a vote of 510 to 346, the Church lands were nationalized under the conditions that priests were to be paid a minimum salary of 1,200 Livres, more than double the amount which many had received, and that the state would assume the care of the poor. The sale of Church lands began in the following month.[12] Initially, the bishops exerted little pressure upon the faithful to abstain from the purchase of Church lands. Soon, however, such pressure began to be exerted on the local level, and as early as 1790 in many areas of France good Catholics hesitated to bid during sales. In subsequent years, the clergy, especially the emigrated clergy, increasingly opposed such sales and characterized them as sacrilegious. This attitude resulted in a marked anticlericalism among many of those who bought such properties.

At the same time in which the Constituent Assembly dealt with the problem of Church property, it also took up the question of the monasteries, as the nationalization of Church lands implied their secularization. Many of the regular clergy were convinced in any event that monastic vows were incompatible with the Rights of Man. A decree of 13 February 1790 forbade such vows for the future and, simultaneously, dissolved all orders and congregations with solemn vows which were not active in education or the care of the sick. Monks and nuns had two alternatives: they could return to public life and draw a pension from the state or they could gather in a number of houses which would remain at their disposal until they died. Even though in the past civil law had regulated the legal consequences of monastic vows, the matter was carried much further this time, and many bishops protested that this

[12] Numerous regional monographs concern themselves with these countless transfers of title and their social consequences. For ten years they constituted a substantial portion of the income of the republic, regardless of corruption in some instances. The bourgeoisie benefitted most and so did the wealthy peasants; in contrast the condition of the poor peasants was often aggravated by the sale, because the old collective rights had been changed in favor of the property rights of the new owners. See a tentative conclusion by G. Lefebvre in *Revue d'histoire moderne* 3 (1958), 189–219.

decree constituted secular intervention into an area where it had no jurisdiction. The new regulation, which, for the time being, allowed the "useful" orders to continue their work, caused hardly a ripple in the country, where, initially, it was interpreted fairly benevolently. Whereas the male orders recorded many departures, most of the nuns declared their intention to remain faithful to their houses. The nuns were permitted to remain in their houses, which were then merely sequestered. Only in August 1792 did the Legislative Assembly dissolve all congregations, including those in the service of the poor, and complete the dispersal of the monastic orders.

Many members of the Church noted with concern the progressive destruction of the traditional structures of the Gallican Church. In Paris, several anticlerical demonstrations by the excited masses had been staged. A number of bishops and aristocratic priests expressly dissociated themselves from the measures taken, but, initially, most of the clergy, some with resignation and some with enthusiasm, accepted the religious policy of the National Assembly. The Assembly, far from having decreed the separation of Church and state, attempted to connect the Church intimately with the revolution. This was shown by the decree of 23 February 1790, which ordered all decisions of the Assembly to be read and commented upon from the pulpit in all parishes. Subsequent developments demonstrated, however, that the general acceptance of the alliance between the Church and Third Estate had come about on the basis of mutual misconceptions. The problem of the legal status of non-Catholics caused the first major rift in April 1790. In August of the previous year, a small group of Protestant delegates, supported by liberal nobles, had demanded complete equality of religion during the vote on the Declaration of Rights of Man and the Citizen, a vote against which no objection had been raised from the Catholic side. The Assembly failed to grant the equality to Protestants, and instead limited itself to a negative formulation which provided that no one could be molested because of his convictions, including his religious beliefs. In the south, however, the fanaticism of the priests and of the population directed itself against the wealthy Huguenots. This situation subsequently was to be exploited by the forces of counterrevolution. The Catholics of the south demanded recognition of Catholicism as the established religion in the constitution. When a motion to this effect was introduced on 12 April by the Carthusian monk Gerle and voted down, many Catholics saw in this rejection a national apostasy. Although this rejection had in truth a political rationale, many priests overreacted and dissociated themselves from the progressive wing of the revolution. A more serious result, illustrated by contemporary newspapers, was that the unrest among many Catholics was capitalized upon by several bishops in organizing resistance in the provinces against the whole religious policy of the National Assembly. Consequently, the Left became convinced of an aristocratic and clerical conspiracy. It was in this aggravated political and religious atmosphere that the debates on the new status of the French Church took place; debates which were to lead to an open break between Church and state.

The reform of the ecclesiastical organization appeared to the Constituent Assembly as a natural consequence of the general transformation of all institutions and of the radical change of the economic foundations of the French Church. The bishops would have preferred to leave the implementation of reform to a national council. There was the fear, however, that such a council, which would be composed almost exclusively of aristocrats, might become a tool of the reactionaries. Therefore the legal experts adopted the eighteenth-century principle that the Church stood within the state, and joined with numerous priests in accepting the difference in canon law between dogma and discipline. They, therefore, asserted that the Constituent Assembly had the right, as long as it did not touch doctrine, to reform ecclesiastical institutions along with all others. This was held to be doubly true as the state had agreed to pay the salaries of clergymen and thus needed to be able to control their number and recruitment. The idea of a Civil Constitution of the Clergy was born.

The formulation of this constitution was placed in the hands of the church committee of the National Assembly, whose composition had been changed in favor of the Gallican Jansenists in order to assure a majority. One accepted position was that a substantial reduction of the personnel of the Church was absolutely necessary, for reasons of economics as well as with respect to the principle of social utility which did not justify a preservation of cathedral or collegiate chapters and monasteries. In conflict with this aim was the desire to return as much as possible to the customs of the early Church. Antiquity was fashionable and all proponents of such a course were seduced by different principles. The philosophes dreamed of a return to a golden age of equality and brotherhood; the Gallicans were inveigled by the prospect of a Church independent from Rome; the Jansenists were motivated by the prospect of a life which adhered more closely to the Gospel; and the Richerists hoped to restore presbyterial collegiality.

After two months of sometimes heated debate,[13] the Constituent

[13] Parallel to the debates within the Constituent Assembly (see *Archives parlementaires* 1st Series, vols. XV–XVII) there were also heated polemical exchanges in the press, analyzed by J. Haak.

Assembly, on 12 July 1790, passed the Civil Constitution of the Clergy. It produced three substantive changes. First, dioceses were to be redivided and reduced to eighty-three and their boundaries were to be made the same as those of the Departments. This meant the disappearance of fifty-two dioceses and a strong reduction in the number of parishes. Secondly, bishops, priests, and vicars were to be paid salaries by the state with the condition of performing all religious services free of charge. Thirdly, there was to be election of bishops and priests by electoral colleges on the level of Department and districts, and the canonical investment of the bishops by the metropolitan without prior confirmation by the Pope. Bishops only were to be entitled to inform the Pope of their election. Allied with this regulation was to be a severe reduction of episcopal authority through a council of priests, which was to participate in the administration of the diocese.

In spite of their appearance, these decrees had no specifically revolutionary content. They were simply an inheritance of the past and belonged more to the Old Regime than to the new.[14] They owed very little to a philosophy of laicistic inspiration and instead were designed to underline the intimate connection of Church and state. In their essential part, the decrees were the expression of the Gallicanism of the eighteenth century; a Gallicanism which demanded not only the autonomy of the priests toward the bishops and the autonomy of the bishops toward the Pontiff; but also, primarily, the political Gallicanism of the jurists and parliamentarians, who, aside from dogma, regarded the state as having the responsibility for the whole field of ecclesiastical life. This last position was the cardinal error of the Constitution. Many ordinances of the decree were acceptable in themselves, especially if one looks at them from the perspective of Gallican ecclesiology rather than from the viewpoint of later concepts which gained validity after Vatican I. Some of the ordinances were excellent, regardless of such small details as the inclusion of a few non-Catholics among the electors for priests and bishops. But the Constitution raised the claim to have the right to make changes in the area of religion without the participation of the Church, and the error of this position was stated firmly by thirty dissenting bishops (not including Talleyrand and Gobel) who were still members of the Constituent Assembly.[15]

Even if one concedes that quite special circumstances justified the unilateral cancellation of the concordat of 1516, with respect to ecclesiastical legal considerations so closely concerning the life and the

[14] Leflon, 59

[15] *Exposition des principes de la constitution civile,* published on 30 October 1790.

fundamental structures of the Church, spiritual authority should have been consulted. This point was made throughout the debate by almost all of the bishops, even those with the most opportunistic and conciliatory views.[16] Inasmuch as the Constituent Assembly rejected the idea of a national council, only the Pope would have been competent to play this role. The Assembly, however, refused to consult him and tacitly allowed the King and the bishops to act for it. On 1 August, Louis XVI ordered Cardinal de Bernis, the French ambassador in Rome, to obtain the agreement of Pius VI.

In Rome, even before the arrival of the first emigrants, who formed themselves into a powerful group and exerted strong antirevolutionary pressure, the reaction to the events of the summer of 1789 in France had been negative. Without focusing upon the depressing turn of events at Avignon, one discovers objections being raised to the abolition of the annates, the confiscation of Church property, and the destruction of the monasteries, as well as to the declaration of political and religious freedom which was seen as incompatible with the God-given social order. Although the enemies of the revolution tried to drive the Pope to a firm statement of objection, Pius VI, determined not to aggravate the position of Louis XVI, whom he trusted, decided to adopt a reserved attitude and to limit himself secretly to condemning the Rights of Man in an address to the consistory. He stuck to this cautious conduct even when he was asked to comment on the Civil Constitution of the Clergy. The Pope charged a special congregation of cardinals with an examination of the problem.[17] These cardinals, confused by the rapid changes which had taken place in France and concerned not to engage the Holy See carelessly, examined the truly complex issues in detail and came to decisions only with great caution. There were also very real problems of both a political and religious nature.

On the political level, a confrontation with the French Assembly was to be avoided so as not to cause the sudden annexation of the county of Avignon, whose inhabitants were demanding union with France. On the religious level, irritation of the sensitive Gallicans was to be avoided, as well as the temptation to dictate the conduct of the French episcopate which jealously guarded its prerogatives. The danger was exaggerated

[16] With respect to the central problem the episcopate was indeed of divided opinion: while many bishops, and not only those who had emigrated toward the end of 1789, but also a portion of those who had remained in France, more or less clearly opposed the draft of the civil constitution, others thought it a suitable vehicle to improve the situation of the Church.

[17] For the appointment of this *Congrégation pour les affaires ecclésiastiques de France* see L. Pásztor in *AHPont* 6 (1968), 193.

that a strong statement could drive the most powerful established Church into schism. Finally, the view prevailed everywhere that the revolution was a fever attack which would pass quickly, and that it was better to leave things alone and not compromise oneself. The result was an eight-month irreparable delay, during the course of which in an unforeseen way a concatenation of circumstances caused the very schism which it had been hoped would be avoided.

The French bishops demanded to await the papal agreement and to put the constitution into effect only after its arrival. The death on 30 September of the bishop of Quimper forced the Constituent Assembly to a decision. It ordered the election of a successor according to the procedures laid down in the Constitution. Expilly, priest, delegate, and chairman of the religious committee, was designated by the electoral college of Finistere[18] to fill the vacancy. This action signaled the intention systematically to ignore the Pope and to introduce without delay innovations which would make clergymen who were in no way allied with the aristocratic opposition into enemies. Such action reinforced the fermentation which had begun to spread throughout the countryside and which aimed against other directives of the National Assembly. In such areas as Alsace and the south of France, agitation against the sale of Church lands intensified. Notified by the local authorities, the National Assembly determined to have its way and, with the decrees of 27 November and 26 December 1790, demanded from all clergymen in a public function, i.e., from all bishops, priests, and vicars, the same oath as from all other civil servants. Clergymen were to swear to be loyal to state, to the laws, and to the King and to protect the constitution with all of their power. The oath included agreement to the new regulations of ecclesiastical affairs which were embodied in the constitution. Refusal to swear the oath was tantamount to resignation from office, and agitators were to be tried in court.

The Two Churches: Constituent and Refractory Priests

Much to the surprise of everyone, two thirds of the clerical representatives and all but seven bishops, four of whom were already discredited because of their unbelief or their scandalous lives, refused to take the oath. Almost half of the parish clergy refused as well. In some areas in the north and in Alsace, between 80 to 90 percent of the lower clergy refused to swear the oath. In other areas between 60 and 70 percent also refused. Even though in Paris and its environs and in the southeast

[18] See *DHGE* XVI, 257–61.

of France a large, and sometimes very large, majority took the oath,[19] it frequently was with reservations which the local authorities silently accepted. Moreover, recantations followed soon afterward. The National Assembly refused to rescind its decisions in spite of the disappointing vote. Although it was driven by its old longing for political unity based on religion and by an increasing desire to extirpate any and all opposition, it removed the refractory priests from their offices and substituted for them priests who had taken the oath. In the beginning this was fairly easy to do in many dioceses with respect to the parish clergy, as the government was able to employ former monks, many of whom, at least for the time being, were willing to take the oath.[20]

The situation was different wherever massive refusals occurred. In spite of the reduction of the number of parishes, an action which was highly resented by the rural population, hundreds of positions needed to be filled and the number of applicants was small in spite of the decree of 7 January 1791 which eased the conditions for taking over a parish. Consequently, some refractory priests had to be left in office for a time. The reconstruction of the dioceses posed other problems as well, because there were virtually no metropolitans who could ordain new bishops. The Constituent Assembly, on 15 November 1790, ordered that the newly elected clergy were to address themselves to the departmental authorities, who would nominate French bishops who would ordain them. But six of the seven prelates who had taken the oath refused to perform this function. Finally Talleyrand, who according to Pioro's findings[21] played a much more significant role in the reordering of the dioceses than had been known, agreed to ordain two bishops. During the subsequent two months, Gobel, who had meanwhile ad-

[19] These are rather approximate numbers, for the statistical examination by Ph. Sagnacs in *Revue d'histoire moderne et contemporaine* 8 (1906–07), 97–115, as well as other monographs which later attempted to add to it, was rendered questionable by the neglect of methodological prerequisites to which B. Plongeron drew attention in a basic article in *AHRF* 39 (1967), 145–98, continued in *Conscience religieuse en Révolution,* 17–100.

[20] Here also, with respect to motivation, the too simplistic judgments of earlier historians must be differentiated. See above all B. Plongeron, *Les réguliers de Paris devant le serment constitutionnel. Sens et conséquences d'une option* (Paris 1964), to be augmented by his articles in *Notre vie eudiste* 9 (1962), 68–80 and *Oratoriana* 4 (1964), 34–65. Because of the representative situation of Paris toward the rest of the country, Plongeron comes to the conclusion that the number of members of orders taking the oath was, contrary to widespread opinion, rather small and that in many cases they were men whose religious values and whose honesty could not be doubted.

[21] "Institution canonique et consécration des premiers évêques constitutionnels" in *AHRF* 28 (1956), 346–80.

vanced to the position of archbishop of Paris, ordained another twenty-six bishops.

The Pope was compelled to react. On 10 March 1791, in his Brief *Quot aliquantum,*[22] he condemned the Civil Constitution of the Clergy because it had mortally wounded the divine constitution of the Church with its canonical investment of bishops, the election of priests, and the creation of episcopal councils. In the following Brief *Caritas,* he declared the ordinations of the new bishops sacrilegious, prohibited them from performing their offices, and threatened with suspension all priests who refused to recant their oaths. On the same occasion, the Pope strongly condemned the declaration of the Rights of Man as contradictory to Catholic doctrine regarding the origin of the authority of the state, freedom of religion, and social inequality.

The Constituent Assembly was disappointed and fought back by expanding the required oath to still other groups of clergymen. While on the one hand the Constituent bishops denied the authenticity of the papal briefs and relied on the Gallican liberties to assert that the Pope had no authority to punish the French Church, during the summer other priests, who had honestly believed that they were permitted to take the oath, began to recant in substantial numbers. The Church, which eighteen months earlier had been so united, was now deeply cleft, and the rift increased for religious, social, cultural, and political reasons. The controversy between the two ecclesiologies, which disagreed about the rights of the Pope and of the state to intervene in the affairs of the Church, was complicated further by a far-reaching difference of opinion that the rights of man could be deduced from the Christian principle that Christianity is a religion of freedom and fraternity, and that the revolution would bring about a Christian renewal. One of the most representative defenders of this group was Henri Grégoire, priest and representative in the Constituent Assembly, who at the beginning of 1791 was elected as Constituent bishop of Blois.[23] Another part of the Church was convinced that the principle of equality necessarily had to lead to the republicanization of the Church and that the principle of liberty left the common man no opportunity to defend himself against

[22] A. Theiner, *Documents inédits relatifs aux affaires religieuses de la France 1790–1800* I (1857), 32–71. On the papal brief of 13 April 1791, ibid. I, 75–88.

[23] On Henri Grégoire, whose actions and concepts for a long time were portrayed in a rather partisan light, and who has not yet received the exhaustive treatment he deserves, see J. Tild, *L'abbé Grégoire* (Paris 1946); L. Pouget, *Les idées religieuses et réformatrices de Grégoire* (Paris 1905); N. Ravitch in *CH* 36 (1967), 419–39; chiefly "L'abbé Grégoire" in *Europe* 34 (Paris 1956) no. 128–129.

religious error. For these clerics, the political and social principles of the Old Regime constituted the necessary prerequisites for the defense of Catholicism. For this reason, any other social philosophy which might have been able to reconcile the Catholic faith with the democratic movement was ruled out. Opposition to the Assembly grew more fierce also because the dissatisfaction of many of the faithful, who were encouraged by the priests loyal to Rome to reject the priests not recognized by Rome, was exploited by the royalist forces for the benefit of their counterrevolutionary plans. This situation led quickly to the simplistic identification of the clergy loyal to Rome with the reactionary aristocrats and salved the consciences of all those who were newly congregated to the Constituent church.

For a long time, traditional Catholic historiography harshly condemned the Constituent clergy. Today it has become clearer that it was not merely a ragbag of renegades and apostates, but that there belonged to it many respectable priests and important personages. Without a doubt, the vacancies in many dioceses were filled with hasty ordinations and through the employment of questionable people. But many Constituent bishops and priests were irreproachable and hard-working clergymen who proved themselves in the hour of danger. Also it should not be overlooked that the reasons which made them take the oath were complex and occasionally very honorable. Many of these clerics wished to underscore their break with an ecclesiastical organization from which the revolution had freed them or, if they were aged, to avoid having to lead a life of difficulty. Others took the oath because an educated and pious adviser had assured them that it was all right to do so; because their ecclesiastical principles allowed them to judge the civil constitution less harshly; or because they were convinced that the oath was a necessary evil if they were to be able to serve the Church better and not abandon their flocks. Many also did not view their election by political corporations as evil. They regarded election as totally and doctrinally justified in the name of an ecclesiology and a political theory which was condemned wholesale by the ultramontanes and counterrevolutionaries of the nineteenth century, but whose significance and validity are again acknowledged today.[24]

Both hostile parties were convinced of the rightness of their positions and fought one another with the passion commonly associated with religious controversies. If, for religious reasons, most of the former bishops preferred to vacate their sees in favor of their Constituent competitors and to join the emigrants outside of France, the same was

[24] See the chapter on the two contrasting ecclesiologies in B. Plongeron, *Conscience religieuse*, 179–290.

not true of all parish clergy. Frequently the non-juring priests stayed, celebrated the Mass, and contested the church-building with the new priest. This created confusion for the faithful, many of whom, especially in the rural areas, did not comprehend the jurisdictional struggles. In many areas the only important matter was that somehow the parish be administered, and it did not matter whether the priest had taken the loyalty oath or not, as the parishioners could not understand why an oath of a political nature should make a priest a schismatic. However, the liberality of the Constituent priests, some of whom even demanded the right to marry, together with the accusations of the non-juring priests, led many of the faithful to doubt the validity of the sacraments dispensed to them. Conflict broke out between priest and parishioners, with the faithful demanding to have "good" priests again. In the cities, where the issues were better understood, the competition between the two Churches was particularly sharp. The Constituents attempted at first to end the controversies through radical measures. Soon they were forced into the realization that it was impossible to impose the Constituent Church on the whole country. A limited legalization of the nonconformist religion was attempted, according to which the non-juring priests would be entitled to celebrate the Mass in a parish church, but could not preach, baptize, or perform weddings. This attempt satisfied neither the Constituent nor the refractory priests, as both parties were intent on seeing their Church recognized as the established one. Under pressure from the political clubs, which fell prey to the error of marking the non-jurors as enemies of the revolution, the authorities were finally forced into administrative persecutions.

Persecutions and Dechristianization

The Legislative Assembly which followed the Constituent Assembly on 1 October 1791 was composed of people who were farther to the left both politically and religiously. Their major faction and driving force, the Girondists, were members of the bourgeoisie who, completely absorbed by the contemporary philosophy, had dissociated themselves from the Church and were occasionally irreligious. The Girondists considered the pangs of conscience of the refractory priests as irrelevant. The Constituent Assembly had recognized that the religious unrest which spread in many areas of France, chiefly in the West, was a warning sign which threatened national unity. Shortly before the end of its mandate, the Constituent Assembly had attempted a defusion of the issues by ordering a general amnesty. The Legislative Assembly, however, under pressure from the press and the political clubs in the larger cities which continued to characterize the non-jurors as bad citizens and agents of the counterrevolution, made a complete turnabout. In spite of protests from many representatives, who on the basis of the Rights of Man demanded freedom of conscience, it began to persecute its opponents. A decree of 29 November 1791 ordered that clergymen, regardless of whether they ministered to parishes or not, who did not take the oath within eight days would be regarded as rebelling against the law and as having evil intentions against the country. These clergymen would lose their pensions and would be removed from their residences. The veto which Louis XVI cast against the measure, as well as against the measures taken against the emigrants, compromised the priests loyal to Rome by lumping together their religious cause with the political reaction of the aristocrats. Under pressure from a campaign directed by the Jacobin Club and implemented on the local level, the civil authorities immediately began to jail clergy who refused to comply with the November decree.

In May 1792, France went to war with Austria and Prussia. When the Pope subsequently appointed Abbé Maury, who was known for his antirevolutionary stance, as legate to the Emperor in Germany, his action was seen as a direct challenge to the Legislative Assembly. The result was that clergymen who had refused to swear the oath because of their loyalty to the Pope now began to be regarded not merely as accomplices of the reactionaries but also as a "fifth column" prepared to assist the invaders. The "second revolution" on 10 August 1792, and the seizure of power by the radicals hastened the process. The congregations in the service of education and charity, which in the decree of 1790 had been spared for being "useful," were dissolved; the remaining monasteries were closed; the property of church administrations was sold; the wearing of clerical garb was prohibited; processions in Paris were forbidden; and, after the deposition of the King, when all earlier oaths had become invalid, a new oath, the so-called Liberty-Equality Oath, was instituted. The oath was visibly without religious significance, and as such explains why Jacques-André Émery, a highly respected theologian and general superior of the Congregation of Saint-Sulpice, declared it as permissible. However, the oath posed a problem of conscience for those who asked themselves whether it was possible to preserve liberty and equality after the Pope had condemned the Rights of Man.[25] On 26 August the deportation of all priests loyal to Rome was ordered. This action was followed a few days later by the September

[25] Bibliography on this oath, about which Pius VI in spite of contrary claims by the Roman college of cardinals and most of the migrated bishops made no official statement, see Leflon 86 and 99, note 3.

Massacres of 300 clergymen and three bishops who had been jailed in Paris prisons.[26]

In the following months, more than thirty thousand clergymen fled the country. During the first few months of the revolution the upper clergy had emigrated voluntarily. Now, the lower clergy were being exiled by legal means.[27] On 7 July 1793 two additional decrees of the National Assembly further aggravated the situation. These decrees provided for the death penalty within twenty-four hours for all priests who had not obeyed the decree of 26 August and left France, and the deportation to Guyana of all non-officiating priests who had refused to take the Liberty-Equality Oath. In spite of this, several thousand priests endangered their lives by remaining in France and going into hiding in order to continue to dispense the sacraments to their flocks.

By the end of 1792, the situation was desperate for the clerics who had remained loyal to Rome. In spite of their courage and inventiveness. the support which they enjoyed from many of their flocks, and even the tacit help of authorities in some areas,[28] they were under persecution and bereft of all structural support. The Constituent Church, which had succeeded in taking hold in most of France and which occasionally had gloated over the measures taken against its rivals, soon found itself in the same unenviable situation. At first, Constituent clergy had to suffer the step-by-step deprivation of their official status. On 20 September 1792 the Assembly removed the keeping of civil registries from the Church and transferred it to the civil authorities. Thus began the process of separating Church and state. Then legal permission for divorces and priests to marry was decreed, and the

[26] The works of P. Caron, *Les massacres de septembre* (Paris 1935) and J. Hérissay, *Les journées de septembre* (Paris 1946) receive required differentiation by B. Plongeron, *Conscience religieuse*, 36–74, who shows that the motives for this massacre, which was occasioned by the excitement of the mob upon hearing of the approach of Prussian troops, were essentially political in nature.

[27] With respect to the emigrated or deported clergymen, consult the copious bibliographies in G. Bourgin, *La France et Rome* XIII, note 6 and Leflon, 88. They can be augmented by T. de Raemy, *L'émigration française dans le canton de Fribourg* (Fribourg 1935); R. Picheloup, *Les ecclésiastiques français émigrés dans l'État pontifical* (Diss. Tulouse 1968); L. Sierra, "La inmigración del clero francés en España" in *Hispania* 28 (1968), 393–422. These works are confined almost exclusively to statistics and methodology and concern themselves very little with the mentality and activities of the immigrants.

[28] The reasons for this support were complex. Sometimes the motive was a superficial but genuine Catholic conviction; occasionally also the devotion to tradition, or the pleasure of outwitting the bureaucrats, or the social antagonism which pitted the peasants against the revolutionary bourgeoisie who was buying up property.

Constituent Church found itself undermined and confronting the same stricture of conscience as the non-jurors of 1791. Torn between compliance with the law and adherence to its theological principles, the Constituent Church split into two camps. Much to the great consternation of their confreres for whom the intervention of the state in ecclesiastical matters had gone much too far, a number of priests and a few bishops pushed revolutionary logic so far as to marry. The second camp of the Constituent Church sincerely deplored the political development which had led from a limited monarchy to a republic. In numerous locations, the Constituent clergy supported the federalist movement which by July 1793 agitated about sixty Departments and thereby made the Constituent Church as suspect to the revolutionaries as the non-jurors. Now the Constituent Church also began to be called an enemy of the people. The enormous wave of dechristianization which swept over the country between the summer of 1793 and the summer of 1794 completed the ruin of the Constituent Church and drove it underground.

Of course, the role of dechristianization[29] in the history of the Church during the revolution should not be exaggerated. It must be noted that the impulse for the dechristianization came from the Departments and not from Paris, and also that its extent differed markedly from region to region.[30] The area between the Saône and Loire was most affected, and more so within the villages than the cities. Above all, it must be understood that the concept of dechristianization was totally alien to the eighteenth century and would more correctly be interpreted as anticlericalism or secularization. Except in those areas where this phenomenon had developed since the middle of the century, there was actually little genuine effect. Often, what was seen in the course of the revolutionary changes was a more or less vehement reaction against the excessive interference of the Church in the everyday life of the population. This effect was aggravated by the fact that the entire Church, Constitu-

[29] A good summary of the theories about dechristianization from Aulard on can be found in Leflon, 104–06. The problem has been raised anew by B. Plongeron in *AHRF* 40 (1968), 145–205 and his *Conscience religieuse en Révolution,* 101–77. He provides more room for sociological aspects and an analysis of the various attitudes.

[30] A. Soboul, *Les sans-culottes parisiens de l'an II* (Paris 1958), 290–91; R. Cobb, *Les armées révolutionaires, instument de la Terreur dans les départements*, 2 vols. (Paris 1961–63). This work provides numerous precise details about the antireligious action of these political police organizations that were used to fight domestic opposition and a very useful calendar, but several interpretations have been questioned. See among others J. Godechot in *RH* 232 (1964), 502 and chiefly B. Plongeron in *AHRF* 40 (1968), 145–205. Concerning the special case of the southeast, see M. Vovelle in *Annales du Midi* 76 (1964), 529–42.

ent as well as Roman, was regarded as a social class politically hostile to the Jacobin ideology.

Although it is known now that the National Convention and the majority of the Committee of Public Safety were opposed to exaggerated hostility toward religion, extremists such as Hébert succeeded in pushing through a number of radical measures designed to extirpate any and all of the country's memories of the Christian legacy. The old calendar was replaced by a republican calendar; Sundays were eliminated in favor of the tenth day of the three decades into which each month was divided; purely secular feast days were organized; and a revolutionary cult of the Goddess of Reason was introduced, although its ridiculousness was soon recognized and countered by Robespierre's own spiritualistic cult of the Supreme Being. For several months, however, the observance of Catholic ritual and even that of the Protestants and Jews as well was radically disturbed. The persecution of suspected clergymen was stepped up and pressure was exerted to effect the apostasy of priests, although the extent of this phenomenon has more nuances than has been acknowledged so far in traditional historiography.[31] Most of the churches were closed or torn down, and their liturgical equipment was looted.[32] When the faithful attempted to organize services away from the churches, these also were forbidden under the pretext that they were only a cover for counterrevolutionary intrigues. Even the lodges of the Freemasons were not spared, an act which confirms the predominant political motivation of the measures. It should be noted, however, that radicalism was implemented with little overall planning and frequently was of temporary duration. Its effect was minimized wherever the faith was still strong, ecclesiastics could organize effective resistance,[33] and in areas where religious conformism was shaken by the excesses of the reign of terror and genuine revivals

[31] On 17 November 1793, the Sansculottes forced the Parisian archbishop Gobel and his vicars general to do so. Such renunciations were particularly frequent among the Constituent clergy, but it must be remembered that by this time the refractory priests in the great majority had left France. The topic was reexamined in a regional context under the direction of M. Reinhard and collected under the title *Les prêtres abdicataires pendant la Révolution française* (Paris 1965). They confirm the regional differences of the phenomenon and underscore its complexity. The resignations were sometimes the manifestation of militant apostasy, sometimes the result of a collective panic, occasionally also a meaningless formality which did not prevent the continued celebration of the Mass.

[32] See S. J. Idzerda, "Iconoclasm during the French Revolution" in *AHR* 60 (1954), 13–26. On the attempts to save the artistic and literary heritage of the ecclesiastical institutions see P. Riberette, *Les bibliothèques françaises pendant la révolution* (Paris 1970).

[33] There is no dearth of stories about the vitality of religion during these dark years. But information is not nearly so rich about the clandestine administration of dioceses during this period. For example, see J. -B. Lechat in *Annales de Normandie* 17 (1957), 263–79.

were taking place.[34] However, enormous dislocations, whose traces were visible for a long time, occurred in those areas which had been undermined by skepticism or, as was the case around Paris and Vendée, had experienced the systematic extremism of nearby large urban areas.

The Separation of Church and State

Confronted by the growing dissatisfaction of the population, the National Convention was forced to reverse its course. At first it attempted to stop the attempts to finish off Catholicism. When this met with qualified success, the Convention moved in the direction of separation of Church and state, a move more motivated by the pressure of events than by philosophical preference. In April 1794, the payment of salaries to the Constituent priests was stopped, and on 18 September the budget item for public religious exercises was officially removed. At the same time, the spirit of toleration made progress in spite of the hostility toward the Church of the Thermidoreans. In the course of negotiations with Spain and Tuscany, the French government agreed to treat Catholicism considerately, and in France itself freedom of religion was demanded both by Grégoire, who called for it in the name of the Constituent Church, and by the rebels in the Vendée, who made permission for religious freedom a nonnegotiable issue for the restoration of order. Religious freedom was granted by the decree of 21 February 1795, although with some important reservations. Catholics, for example, were prohibited from using churches. However, the fall of Robespierre was erroneously interpreted in many of the provinces as the end of the system of oppression, and many churches reopened spontaneously and many priests, Constituent as well as Roman, resumed their priestly functions.[35] The Convention had no choice but to accept these changes as accomplished facts, and a new decree of 30 May 1795 liberalized the previous one. The Convention demanded from the priests in return for this concession a declaration that they would submit to the laws of the republic and be obedient to it. In theory, the Roman priests as well as the Constituent ones were entitled to make this declaration.

[34] For an example see B. Plongeron, "Autopsie d'une Église constitutionelle, l'Indre-et-Loire de 1793 à 1802" in *Actes du 93ᵉ Congrès des Sociétés savantes* II (Paris 1971), 134–90.

[35] Numerous examples are listed by E. Soreau, "La résurrection religieuse après la Terreur" in *Revue des études historiques* 100 (1933), 557–74 and by L. Mirot, ibid. 101 (1934), 193–206.

The Church, however, was split over the permissibility of the oath. Some, such as Jacques-André Émery, were of the opinion that this oath had a purely political meaning, while others regarded it as a global submission to legislation, totally in opposition to the principles of the Church. Dissension increased with regard to the reconciliation of Constituent priests, priests who had resigned from their offices, and repentant married priests. Some churchmen, led by Émery and the eleven bishops who had remained in France, were in favor of leniency, which they felt was justified by the extraordinary circumstances; while others, on the advice of the emigrated bishops, demanded humiliating recantations and long atonements.[36] An additional confrontation arose between the followers of the Jesuits and the Jansenists over the question of what attitude should be taken toward the faithful. Here it was a conflict between the active priests, who were of the opinion that the salvation of souls could compensate for many arrangements with regard to doctrinal strictness, and the purists, who placed purity even above evangelization.[37]

These controversies made the restoration of the Catholic religion immensely more difficult. In many cases extraordinarily confused situations arose because most of the legitimate bishops remained outside of France. However, until 1797, the reorganization of the Church was largely successful, and many emigrated priests returned, even though it was difficult for them to adapt to radically altered conditions.

Paralleling these attempts, the Constituent Church, which now presented itself as the Gallican Church, also tried to attain a renewal. The driving force behind this rejuvenation was Grégoire, who cooperated with such deeply religious and intelligent men as Le Cox and joined in the Committee of Reunited Bishops which expressed episcopal collegiality and was totally opposed to religious democracy. In August 1797, they succeeded in bringing about a National Council, the ground for which had been prepared by consulting the diocesan presbyteries.[38] More interested in giving preference to quality than quantity and in

[36] On the "Parisian method" see P. Pisani, *L'Église de Paris et la Révolution IV,* ch. 3; on the "Lyon method", Ch. Ledré, *Le culte caché sous la Révolution. Les missions de l'abbé Linsolas* (Paris 1949). It is to be noted that under the influence of Jansenistic rigorism the Constituent Church often acted even more harshly against the abdicators and the married priests.

[37] J. R. Suratteau, *Le département du Mont-Terrible sous le régime du Directoire* (Paris 1965), 250.

[38] J. Leflon, "La reconstitution de l'épiscopat constitutionnel après Thermidor" in *Actes du 81e Congrès National des Sociétés savantes* (Paris 1956), 475–81. On the council of 1797 see also the correspondence between Grégoire, Dufraisse, and Ricci, published by M. Vaussard.

planting in France a Church true to Catholic tradition, these men jointly worked out a rechristianization program which was directed less exclusively toward a return to the past than the program which eventually received Rome's concurrence. The program had the merit of making allowances for the psychological and structural shifts and for the universal longing and changes in mentality which were the constant preoccupation of the priests who had remained in France.[39] This attempted reform met with many obstacles. Foremost was a shortage of qualified people, because both episcopate and Church had been decimated by resignations, marriages, deaths, and still increasing recantations. Added to these problems were the internal struggles between episcopalists and presbyterians, and between adherents and opponents of the use of the native language in worship.[40]

At the beginning of the Directory, Catholics of both persuasions enjoyed relative freedom. They were permitted to distribute their own publications; the *Annales de la religion* by the Constituents, and the *Annales religieuses, politiques et littéraires* by the Romans. At the end of the summer of 1797, however, the political crisis which led to the coup d'état of 18 Fructidor again endangered the precarious improvement of the preceding two years. Not without reason, the Directory accused the Catholic clergy of continuing to support the royalist opposition and decided to return to a sharply anticlerical policy. One of the Directors, La Révellière, wanted to fashion a new revolutionary religion out of the "Theophilanthropy" which was being promoted by the end of 1796. La Révellière attempted to make it into an official religion, an attempt which was countered by Merlin de Douai. The supporters of this government-protected sect occupied many of the churches, especially in the cities; yet at no time were they a realistic danger to the old religion.

Much more important were the measures taken against the priests. The decrees of 1792 and 1793, which had exiled the Roman priests from France, were activated again. All priests were required to swear a new oath of "royal hatred." A number of bishops and casuists considered it acceptable, while all of the emigrated bishops and many theologians declared publicly that it was insupportable, especially for a priest, to make God witness to a vow of hatred. The Roman congregation for French affairs reached the same conclusion, but Pius VI again declined to publicize this decision officially. A strong minority of the priests

[39] B. Plongeron, *Dom Grappin correspondant de l'abbé Grégoire* (Paris 1969), 4.
[40] See M. D. Forstier in *MD* 1 (1945), 74–93.

swore the oath in the conviction that its formulation made it the lesser of two evils and that to take it would be better than to leave their flocks again without worship or religious instruction. Many priests refused to take this oath, however, and became subject to legal punishments which, while no longer as bloody as during the reign of terror, were of a more calculated cruelty. These priests were either incarcerated in prison ships or deported to Guyana. The number of victims of this renewed persecution was smaller than during 1792 and 1793, however, because there were fewer priests and the execution of the decrees fluctuated widely from Department to Department. In some areas the law remained a dead letter due to the cooperation of the population and occasionally even that of the local authorities. The other extreme could be found in the Department of Yonne where not a single church remained open and in Sarthe where a quarter of the Roman priests were arrested even though the population remained loyal to the old religion.[41]

Certain positive facets of this situation must not be overlooked, regardless of how grim the final period of the Directory may have been. Many of the faithful, who earlier had practiced a largely passive conformism, now became aware of their responsibility to the Church. In areas where there were no longer any priests, prayer meetings were organized, children were given religious instruction, and Mass was celebrated. Former nuns took advantage of the article of the Constitution of the Year III which permitted private instruction and formed new groups,[42] thus preparing during this chaotic time for the resumption of monastic life. In the rural areas, especially in the north and the west, many priests, disturbed by the growing religious ignorance of children and the neglect of the sick, encouraged pious young girls to devote themselves to these duties, thereby planting the seed for the future congregations so typical of the nineteenth century. Another indication of the surviving vitality of the French Church during these harsh times were the Daughters of the Heart of Mary, whose congregation was founded in 1791 in the search for a modern form of life devoted to God and adjusted to the new conditions.[43] By 1799 there were 267

[41] V. Pierre, *La déportation ecclésiastique sous le Directoire* (Paris 1895). An insufficient number of monographs have been written on the regions of France under the Directory, but see R. Daniel in *Bulletin de la société archéologique du Finistère* 92 (1966), 212–53.

[42] A number of examples for Paris are recounted by J. Boussoulade, *Moniales et hospitalières dans la tourmente révolutionnaire* (Paris 1962), 179–216. Characteristic is the subtitle "Épreuves et renouveau"—"Visitation and renewal."

[43] See A. Rayez, *Ad. de Cicé et P. de Clorivière* (Paris 1966).

Daughters of the Heart of Mary in ten dioceses from Brittany to the Jura. The members of this new congregation wore no external sign, retained their occupations, and continued to live with their families.[44]

Effects in Neighboring Countries

By the end of 1792, the French Republic was bent on conquest. In November 1792, it annexed Savoy and shortly afterwards Nice, both belonging to the Kingdom of Sardinia, and in March 1793, the region of Pruntrut in the Jura, from which the Department of Mont-Terrible was formed. Belgium, at that time comprised of the Austrian Netherlands and the Ecclesiastical Principality of Liège, was first occupied in the winter of 1792–93, reoccupied after the victory of Fleurus in June 1794, and annexed on 1 October 1795. The left bank of the Rhine, which had been occupied temporarily in the fall of 1792, was again occupied in the summer of 1794. French institutions were introduced, but the Rhine territory was not officially incorporated into France until the time of Napoleon. The Greek islands won from Venice were annexed in October 1797, and French authorities were brought in contact with the Orthodox Church.[45] Geneva became a French Department in April 1798, and Piedmont was annexed in February 1799. With the aid of the army of the Directory six satellite republics were created on the borders of France, whose institutions corresponded to those of the *Grande Nation.* These were the Batavian Republic (1795), the Cisalpine Republic and the Ligurian Republic (1797), the Roman Republic and the Helvetic Republic (1798), and the Parthenopean Republic (1799). Together with the principles of 1789 and the institutions which embodied them, France also exported its religious policy to these countries, aided by the French army. The army was not interested in providing those populations which clung firmly to their belief[46] with additional

[44] Religious freedom was in effect not only for the two rival Catholic Churches, but also for Protestants and Jews who, especially after 1796, were able to reorganize their communities without in any way having to suffer from the revival of anticlericalism after Fructidor.

[45] E. Rodocanachi, *Bonaparte et les Îles Ioniennes* (Paris 1899). The commissioner of the Directory attempted to introduce equality for the Orthodox, the Jewish, and the Roman religion. This irritated the majority of the population which, consequently, warmly received the Russian troops in 1799.

[46] Indeed, the difficulties which the French conqueror encountered were only secondarily the result of religious factors. At least this is one of the conclusions of the colloquium *Occupants, occupés, 1792–1815* (Brussels 1969) which J. R. Suratteau summarizes as follows: "It was known already that the importance of this factor was of lesser weight in Belgium. The religious motivations in Switzerland as well as in Spain were smaller than has often been said, and weak in the Rhineland and in Switzerland. In any case they evidently belong into a socio-religious context," *RH* 240 (1968), 257.

reasons for resistance. It was eager to prevent brutal conduct and local traditions survived best in the religious sphere.

Belgium was a country strongly rooted in the Catholic religion. Its reaction to the reform attempts of Joseph II had proven clearly how ultramontane it was. Therefore, the occupation troops at first were considerate of the "prejudices" of the population. The Convention ordered the confiscation of Church property, but delayed its sale for months. Only in the summer of 1796 did the Directory dare to transfer civil registers to the authorities of the state and to close the monasteries. Even then, the orders devoted to education and the care of the sick were not touched. But the openly demonstrated anticlericalism of officers and officials, especially that of the Belgian Jacobins, led to the arrest of priests and monks on the local level, about thirty of whom were executed. The Cult of Reason destroyed monasteries and profaned churches. Aside from the short and bloody persecution of the summer of 1794, however, the exercise of religion was little affected until 1797. This enabled the vicars general, who remained in communication with the bishops who had left the country, to administer the dioceses in a more or less regular fashion. Interestingly, the officials of the Departments and communities showed no hurry to force the priests to take the oath of submission to the laws of the republic.

The Belgian Church rejected the oath much more completely than in France, even though several vicars general considered it permissible. Conditions worsened with the arrival of Fructidor. The congregations which had been spared so far were dispersed, the University of Louvain and the seminaries were closed, the wearing of clerical garb was prohibited, and each priest was obligated to take the oath of hate against royalty as a precondition for conducting religious ceremonies. Led by Cardinal von Franckenberg, who was jailed and then deported to Germany, the majority of the clergy, except in the Department of Ourthe, refused to take the oath. Shortly thereafter the priests were unjustly made responsible for the peasant revolts in Kempenland and the Ardennes,[47] and the government ordered all non-jurors to be deported. Of more than eight thousand priests thus affected, only about 10 percent actually were arrested, however, because the almost unanimous help of the population enabled them to hide themselves and to exercise their pastoral tasks in secrecy. These three years of secret religious exercises indeed did give the coup de grâce to such old forms of piety as confraternities, but, at the same time, they were the foundation for the new

[47] See T. Vandebeeck-J. Grauwels, *De boerenkrijg in het departement van de Nedermaas* (Hasselt 1961) and G. Trausch, *La répression des soulèvements paysans dans le département des Forêts* (Hasselt-Luxembourg 1967).

more individualistic forms of piety which later were to become characteristic of the piety of the nineteenth century.[48]

In the Rhineland, the French occupation brought about the disappearance of the ecclesiastical principalities, but did not affect the structure of the Church. Initially the troops, who did not molest the Protestants, adopted a hostile stance toward the Catholic clergy because of its resistance to the propaganda for unification with France. But Hoche, who at the beginning of 1797 became commander of the Army of the Rhine, introduced a much more moderate religious policy. He saw a great similarity between the conditions in the Vendée, where he had recently restored order, and those of the Rhineland, where the population strongly clung to its traditional religion. Hoche granted favorable treatment to the lower clergy and allowed the orders to continue, and his successor continued Hoche's policy after his death. No restrictions were placed on the continued exercise of religion within the churches, and clergymen continued to receive their salaries from the sequestered Church lands. But the bishops who had emigrated to the right bank of the Rhine incited the priests and monks against the French, which resulted in a stiffer attitude toward the monasteries in particular, even though they were not closed. As in Belgium, the Rhineland population also helped those priests to go underground who had run into difficulties with the occupation forces. The local authorities also frequently sabotaged the measures against the Church.

In the former United Netherlands, in contrast to Belgium and the Rhineland, Protestantism was the privileged religion, and Catholics, who constituted approximately 40 percent of the population, were oppressed by the ruling oligarchy. Therefore, they generally acclaimed the French revolutionaries as liberators, much to the dismay of Nuncio Brancadoro, who headed the Dutch mission. Only the southern provinces, which initially had witnessed the hostility of the French troops toward the Belgian Church, remained rather reserved. The majority of the Catholic clergy, on the other hand, under the leadership of a group of Amsterdam priests supported the Patriot Party, which early in 1795 overthrew the Old Regime with the aid of the French. The constitution of the new Batavian Republic granted Catholics full civil rights and complete freedom of religion, and most of the priests at once took the oath of "eternal hate" against the Old Regime.

The time of the Batavian Republic was for the Catholics in the United Netherlands a period of emancipation and progress, without dissonances and persecutions. Within a few years, scores of new churches were

[48] See L. Preneel in *Sources Hist. rel. Belg.,* 7–36 and J. Grauwels, *Het Oude land van Loon* 13 (1958), 177–246.

opened and were staffed without difficulty due to the number of Flemish and Rhenish priests who had gone into exile. Inasmuch as the University of Louvain had been closed by the French, three seminaries were opened in the Batavian Republic in 1799. Beyond this, a few Catholic notables and a number of priests drew the logical consequence from the new liberal regime which resulted from the separation of Church and state. Because they no longer wished to have Italians, who were unfamiliar with the country, at the head of the Church, they raised the question of the restoration of the episcopal hierarchy.[49] But the Holy See, for which the period of the Directory was a period of increasing hardship, was not in any condition to deal with this problem.

In Switzerland, as well, the Catholics were less numerous than the Protestants. Until the end of the eighteenth century they had been grouped in homogeneous masses in the nearly sovereign cantons. On the basis of the constitution of the Helvetic Republic created in 1798,[50] they suddenly found themselves as a minority in a Protestant state, a circumstance which led to great discontent and to armed revolts in Wallis and the small original cantons.[51] While the constitution granted freedom of religion and conscience, it contained some limitations directed at the Catholics and their relationship to the papacy. With respect to the practical implementation of these ordinances, the Roman Church suffered additional limitations. The Helvetic government prohibited those bishops who resided outside of Switzerland, and this was true in most cases, from exercising their jurisdiction in Switzerland. The right to assign benefices, the tithe, and the separate judicial system of canon law were abolished. Although not all orders were dissolved, they were forbidden to recruit novices, their lands were sequestered, and some monasteries were closed immediately. In contrast to Holland, Jews were not granted legal equality. Thus the religious policy of the Helvetic Republic differed fundamentally from the truly liberal religious policy of the Batavian Republic.

In Italy, the religious policy had a much more conservative character.

[49] Rogier, *KathHerleving* 10–11.

[50] It should be remembered that at the same time the old republic of Geneva was incorporated into France in the same way in which this had been done in March 1793 with the ephemeral Rauracic Republic, which in the preceeding year had been formed with the old bishopric of Basel. In this area the revolutionary laws against the Catholic clergy were applied as in the rest of France and most of the priests fled to the Catholic cantons which remained independent until 1798; guided by a vicar from Solothurn they could easily return and exercise their offices. Some of them preferred, however, to await the end of visitation in safety. See J. R. Suratteau in *Mémoires pour l'histoire du droit et des institutions des anciens pays bourguignons, comtois et romands* 24 (1963), 167–88.

[51] See J. R. Suratteau, *Occupants, occupés 1792–1815* (Brussels 1969), 165–220.

The understanding with the French occupation forces was facilitated by the fact that numerous Italian priests and officials, who earlier had been won to Josephinist policies, were inclined to regard positively any reform measures directed against ultramontane practices. At the same time, the leaders of the French military and many Italian patriots who wanted to introduce a republican form of government strove not to alienate the broad mass of the people, which was strongly Catholic. Bonaparte, the commander of the Army of Italy, because he was both a realist and of Mediterranean background, understood the situation much better than the Directory. He made a few concessions to the hardline Italian Jacobins, and depended chiefly on moderate Catholics. He agreed to the preferential position granted the Catholic Church by the Italian Republics between 1796 and 1799, even though the French constitution of the year III with its radical separation of Church and state had been their model. This direction had also been taken in 1796 by the authors of the first constitution written after the arrival of the French. This Constitution of Bologna made no reference to religion, but an advisory of the senate stated that with respect to faith and dogmas no innovations would be introduced. Although this led most of the clergy, despite the protest of a few Catholics, to accept this constitution, it never became effective, because Bologna shortly afterwards was incorporated in the new Zispadanic Republic.

The Zispadanic Republic was comprised of the Duchy of Modena and the provinces of Romagna and Emilia which had been taken from the Pope. During the sessions devoted to the writing of the constitution for the new republic, the problem of the position of the Church in the state had led to passionate discussion. The thesis defended by democrats and enlightened people that religion is a private matter was supported by the Jansenists, who expected a renewal of religious fervor with the separation of Church and state. Victory was carried by the contrary thesis. Catholicism became the established religion of the republic (the Jewish religion was tolerated but did not receive equality) because religion "constrains the masses." After brief hesitation, Bonaparte concurred with this article even though it completely deviated from the principles of the Directory, because he realized that this would win him the sympathy of the people and the clergy. But a few months later, in 1797, when he himself wrote the constitution of the Cisalpine Republic, he returned to the principle of complete equality of religions and the religious neutrality of the state. The Cisalpine constitution contained a limitation, later removed from the second constitution of 1798, which empowered the executive to deny the right to officiate to those ministers who had lost the confidence of the government. Consequently, many clergymen, although they favored the republican system, felt that their consciences did not permit them to take the oath under these circumstances.[52] In the process of the practical application of the constitution local influences became noticeable. The new republic accepted a nuncio in Milan and in turn sent an ambassador to Rome. In fact, a number of ordinances which had been in effect since the time of Joseph II simply were applied again. Concrete reality resulted in the following: while separation of Church and state had been nearly accomplished in France, the Catholic Church in the Cisalpine Republic depended strongly upon the state and was subjected to a renewed Josephinism. The only really new aspect was religious equality, although civil equality of Jews was not implemented without resistance by the population. The influence of the Jansenists led to the introduction in 1797 of difficult-to-enforce compulsory civil marriages. The influence of the Jacobins, in turn, spawned a number of increasingly petty measures, irritating the people severely.[53] It was Jacobin agitation which resulted in the dissolution of the ecclesiastical orders. But their plan to nationalize the lands of the parish clergy failed just as did their intention to abolish the tithe.

The constitution of Rome in 1798 and that of the Parthenopean Republic in 1799 adopted the principle of separation of Church and state from the constitution of the year III and the constitution of the Cisalpine Republic. In contrast, the constitution of the Ligurian Republic appears as the most Catholic of all of the constitutions adopted on the Italian peninsula. The Jansenists, who were especially influential in Liguria, refused to agree to the principle of separation, but, on the other hand, wanted to specify that the awarding of all ecclesiastical benefices and the granting of marriage and other dispensations should occur independently from the Roman Curia. The majority of the clergy protested against this intention, and Bonaparte, eager to avoid conflict, urged a change in the draft in order to accommodate the priests and monks. The Jansenists immediately availed themselves of freedom of the press, revived Degola's[54] *Annali politico-ecclesiastici,* and continued to plead their

[52] There is no work and no statistics available on the problem of taking the oath in the Cisalpine Republic.It is known, however, that in the diocese of Brescia alone not fewer than 484 priests were suspended *a divinis* upon the return of the Austrians in 1799, because they had applied Cisalpine religious laws. Cf. A. de Gubernatis, *E. Degola* (Florence 1882), 246.

[53] See Leflon, *Pie VII,* 380: "Bonaparte, whose clear plans the Italian Jacobins far exceeded, was not to forget in 1800 the lessons of such an irritating experience."

[54] Eustachio Degola (1761–1826) was the "most original and strongest personality of Italian Jansenism" at the end of the eighteenth century (Codignola). He was a deeply religious man of great and inflexible moral strength who was in close touch with Sc. de'Ricci and then with Abbé Grégoire. See *DHGE* XIV, 160–62; E. Codignola, *Carteggi di giansenisti liguri* I (Florence 1941) CIII–CCLIX and III 105–563; S. Banacchi, *La vita e la teologia di Eustachio Degola* (Pistoia 1949).

case after the ratification of the constitution. Their harsh criticism of the wealth of the monasteries, together with the criticism of the writers of the Enlightenment, who also were interested in a thorough ecclesiastical reform, led to the law of 4 October 1798, which permitted the dissolution of certain monasteries if this was deemed of value to the state.

Although the revolutionary period in Italy from 1796 to 1799 changed the institutional situation of the Catholic Church in Italy much less than elsewhere, one cannot conclude that this brief period was without significance. For the past thirty years Italian historians have focused their attention upon the influence which the controversies and the hopes kindled during these years exercised upon the development of the mental attitude of the Italian Catholics with respect to liberal and patriotic ideas as well as to the striving for reform of the Church; ideas which ultimately converged in the movement of the *Risorgimento* in the second half of the nineteenth century.

While in Belgium and the Rhineland the antichristian policy of the French national convention had driven an already conservative clergy completely into the camp of the antirevolutionaries, the attitude of the Italian clergymen was more differentiated. Many priests, chiefly from the upper clergy, faced the new regime with distrust, but only a few resisted from the beginning. Most of them considered it wise in view of the conciliatory stance of the French to go along with them and to attempt to save as many rights of the Church as possible. They promoted reconciliation with the new governments by pointing to the indifference of the Church toward matters of civil authority. Many of the clergy, including some bishops,[55] emphasized the Christian character of the principles of equality and fraternity. Others went further and openly welcomed the French republicans. While constituting only a small minority,[56] they had a large influence because they included monks who had been absolved of their vows, as well as many intellectuals and honorable priests. Can these persons be characterized simply as Jacobins? Stamped with this brand[57] were such diverse groups as cardinals who had adapted their religion to the Enlightenment, vague Deists

[55] Best known is the case of Cardinal Chiaramonti, bishop of Imola (the future Pope Pius VII); but there were other bishops of like mind, for example Bishop Dolfini of Bergamo. On the Romagna see J. Leflon, *Pie VII*, 439–43. The *Raccolta di tutte le lettere pastorale*, published by G. Zatta, contains several forgeries.

[56] In Piedmont during the reaction of 1799 a total of 448 clergymen were persecuted as "Jacobins". They were not quite 3 percent of the secular clergy and 4.36 percent of the regular clergy. Cf. G. Vaccarino, *RSIt* 77 (1965), 27–77. After the lawyers, however, these clergymen were the largest faction (14 percent) of the Jacobins.

[57] See D. Cantimori, *Giacobini italiani* I, 407–13; P. Villani, *La storiografia italiana nei ultimi vent'anni* I (Milan 1970), 612–18.

hostile to the Christian religion, and followers of a *Vicaire savoyard.* It is better to speak with V. Giuntella of "Catholic democrats" if one wishes to characterize priests and laymen who endeavored to return to the sources of Holy Scripture and patristics and to separate the essence of the Christian faith from the contingent aspects which it had assumed in the course of centuries. The Catholic democrats thought they could demonstrate the complete harmony of genuine Catholicism with democracy by separating the spiritual area from the secular.

Often these democratic Catholics have been identified with the Jansenists, and they in turn with the Jacobins. Today the profound differences between these groups are more easily recognizable. Most of the Jansenists cooperated with the Jacobins in order to obtain a new religious policy, but this was only a tactical alliance. After the Jansenists failed to obtain backing for their program from the princes, they saw in the structural reforms which the Jacobins urged out of hostility toward the Church the prerequisite for a return to the Church in its original purity. To the Jansenists such prerequisites included renunciation of all Church treasure not essential for worship, abolition of ecclesiastical titles, abolition of benefices, colleges, monasteries and confraternities, and the reduction of the number of ecclesiastical feast days. This was the intention of Degola, who devised a plan for the civil organization of the Ligurian Church. The aim of the plan was to free this Church from the authority of Rome and to rejuvenate it according to the example which the French Constituent Church had provided in keeping with the guidelines worked out by Grégoire at the national council of 1797.[58] Such sympathies with the Civil Constitution of the Clergy should not be misunderstood, however. There were, after all, fundamental differences between the Jacobins who wanted to destroy the Church and the Jansenists who wanted to reform it. Most of the Jacobins were Deists and put their trust in human nature; the Jansenists, disciples of Augustine, regarded the principles of 1789 with distrust and interpreted the enthusiasm of the Jacobins for liberty and progress as Pelagianism. Thus the Jansenists and the democratic Catholics, regardless of their frequent cooperation in the area of practical implementation, adopted fundamentally different points of view on an ideological level.

The common efforts of the Catholics and Jansenists favorably inclined toward the French Revolution formed a significant connection between the writers of the Enlightenment of the 1770s and the reformers at the Synod of Pistoia on the one hand, and liberal Catholics and reformers of

[58] On the echo which this council and that of 1801, in which several Italian Jansenists participated, found in Italy, see M. Vaussard, *Jansénistes et gallicans aux origines religieuses du Risorgimento*, 55–59.

the 1830s such as Raffaele Lambruschini and Rosmini on the other, a connection which deserves the special attention of the historian. At that time, however, their expectations were quickly disappointed. The resumption of persecutions in France after Fructidor, the looting of Church treasures and monasteries, and finally the expulsion of the Pope from Rome awakened in many the fear of a return to the antireligious excesses of the years 1793–94. Such apprehensions together with other social and political stresses resulted in 1799 in several popular revolts. These revolts, frequently led by priests or monks, appeared as a defense of the faith against those who cooperated with the occupation forces.[59] The democratic Catholics, never more than a minority, lost all credibility among the broad masses, and the political developments after 18 Brumaire completed their total defeat. The concordat concluded between Bonaparte and Pius VII destroyed the plans of the Jansenists to establish in Italy a rejuvenated Church according to the example set by the French Constituent Church.

The Destruction of the Holy See

The revolutionary wave which swept over Italy did not spare the Papal States. The central administration of the Church was damaged to such a degree that many came to the conclusion that they were witnessing the end of the papacy as an institution.

The events in France left Pius VI in a particularly difficult position. He felt lonely after the departure of his secretary of state, Boncompagni, and was informed rather tendentiously. The émigrés who flooded Rome during the first two years saw the events through the distorted lens of their own political prejudices. After the termination of diplomatic relations between Paris and Rome in May 1791 there remained only one official envoy in France, who combined much naivety and vacillation with exaggerated obstinacy.[60]

At the beginning of 1791, Pius VI had missed the opportunity to clearly define the true significance of his condemnations of the revolution. In spite of suggestions by several French bishops and representatives of the Constituent Assembly, he refused to deal with the difference between the necessarily immutable principles of religious order and

[59] See also the chapter "Paura e religiosità popolare nello Stato della Chiesa" in R. De Felice, *Italia giacobina* (Naples 1965), as well as G. Cingari, *Giacobini e sanfedisti in Calabria nel 1799* (Messina 1957).

[60] Cf. Ch. Ledré, *L'abbé de Salamon, correspondant et agent du Saint-Siège pendant la Révolution* (Paris 1965).

acceptable transactions in the civil sphere. He totally compromised himself a year later when he sent Abbé Maury to Germany with the charge to win the sovereigns for armed support of the counterrevolution in France.[61] In spite of the warm reception of many French émigrés in the Papal States;[62] in spite of the harsh measures which were taken against Romans suspected of sympathy for the French ideas; and even in spite of the assassination of the French legate Bassville by the mob in January 1793, the French Republic after the annexation of Avignon was not in the position to intervene against the papacy directly. The peninsula was cordoned off by Austria's military forces in conjunction with those of Piedmont and was additionally protected by the British and Neapolitan fleets.

This situation changed drastically, however, in the spring of 1796 after the lightning strikes of General Bonaparte and the occupation of Milan. In the preceeding year, Pius VI had contemptuously rejected an offer of the Spanish ambassador, Azara, to mediate between France and Rome with a view toward resuming full relations. Confronted with the new dangers, the Pope was now prepared to avail himself of such mediation services, but initial talks foundered on the French conditions. The French demanded heavy reparations, and above all the renunciation of all condemnations which the Pope had uttered against the Civil Constitution of the Clergy and the revolutionary principles since 1790. After the French conditions were rejected by Rome, Bonaparte occupied the northern portion of the Papal States. A march on Rome was threatened when negotiations continued to stall. Now the Pope, who feared a revolt of his subjects if the French advanced, decided to submit in order to save the essentials. On 20 June an armistice was signed which contained only territorial and financial clauses; the problem of his renunciation of his condemnations was postponed until a treaty of peace.

The question of who first had the idea to use military pressure on the Papal States in order to obtain from the Pope a pacifying intervention in the religious affairs of France has been much discussed. Was it Bonaparte who regarded as both unrealistic and politically unwise the express directives of the Directory to shake the foundations of the universal Church?[63] This view has been maintained by A. Sorel, L.

[61] Consult also L. Madelin, "Pie VII et la première coalition" in *RH* 81 (1903), 292–306.

[62] See Surrel de Saint-Julien, *L'œuvre pontificale des émigrés français et son organisation.* Mgr. L Caleppi in *Annales de St-Louis des Français* 1 (1897).

[63] *Actes du Directoire*, ed. by A. Debidour IV, 787.

Madelin, and, more recently, by G. Filippone. Or was it, as R. Guyot maintains, the Directory itself which was less obstinate and less simplistic than has been thought? As in so many things, the truth of the matter is probably to be found in the middle between these two extremes. Within the Directory there were two opposing factions. Some of its members did not close their minds to the view of those like F. Cacault who stated that contrary to appearances the papacy still constituted a considerable spiritual and diplomatic strength and one which it would be better to spare and to dominate and use in order to erect the banner of liberty in Rome. But while the Directory wallowed in conflicting intentions which were not followed by actions, Bonaparte immediately recognized the advantage of their suggestions and managed to translate them into a coherent policy.

The negotiations for a peace treaty began in Paris during the summer. Following Azara's advice, the Curia composed a memorandum which reminded French Catholics that the true faith was not created to overturn civil laws and which recommended their submission to the government. This action implicitly recognized the legality of the government's existence. The Directory, however, was not satisfied with the concession of the Brief *Pastoralis sollicitudo,* although it was so significant that Royalists and Romans alike thought it incredible. Upon the urgings of Grégoire, who at all costs wanted to prove that the Constituent Church had never ceased its ties to Rome, the Directory continued to demand from the Pope the renunciation of the condemnations of the Constituent Church. Pius VI refused, of course. In September there were further negotiations in Florence, but they also produced no results. In the meantime, the military situation in Italy appeared to develop favorably for Austria, and Secretary of State Zelada, who favored a conciliatory approach, was replaced by Cardinal Busca. Busca called off the armistice and attempted in vain to persuade the kings of Spain and Naples as well as the Emperor to resume armed resistance. As soon as Bonaparte had solved his problems in northern Italy, he began preparations to march on Rome and forced the Pope, on 16 February 1797, to accept the treaty of Tolentino. By agreeing to additional heavy reparations and ceding to France the wealthiest part of his states, the Pope saved his secular position which, in view of the current conditions, he regarded as the indispensable foundation for the functioning of the government of the Church. Bonaparte, who now felt strong enough to ignore the orders of the Directory, also no longer spoke of a renunciation of earlier papal documents, and thereby laid the groundwork for the future religious pacification of France.

After the bellicose Cardinal Busca had been replaced by the moderate francophile Cardinal Doria, and after France had appointed as its emissary in Rome[64] Joseph Bonaparte, the brother of the general who had refused to destroy the Holy See, the Pope could rest in the conviction that the essence of his power had been saved. However, the situation deteriorated again. In France the coup d'état of Fructidor restored the old virulence of Jacobin anticlericalism. The zealots in Rome interpreted the popular revolts which occurred in several places as the harbingers of a general rising against the French occupation and poured oil upon the flames. In this tense atmosphere, General Duphot was assassinated on 27 December 1797. The Directory, dominated by La Révellière-Lépeaux, a sworn enemy of Catholicism and apostle of the new religious movement of Theophilanthropy, ordered the immediate occupation of the Papal States. On 15 February 1798 Roman Jacobins, covertly led by French agents, proclaimed the Roman Republic.[65] For the first time, the secular sovereignty of the territory, which for a thousand years had constituted the Papal States, was placed in question. An indication of the rapid maturing of opinions in the matter was the advice of the ultramontane theologian Bolgeni who urged, much to the irritation of the zealots, the acceptance of the new political regime in order to preserve the spiritual authority of the Pontiff.[66]

The Pope, now eighty-one years old, pleaded to be allowed to die in peace in Rome. Instead, he was forced to flee to the still-independent Duchy of Tuscany. Separated from almost all of his advisers and in very frail health, the Pope found it difficult to act effectively as supreme head of the Church. He did publish a few briefs; among them on 13 November 1798 an addendum to the constitution of 11 February 1797, regarding how to conduct the conclave under these emergency conditions. With the aid of the nuncio in Florence, who acted as secretary of state, he directed appeals to all sovereigns of Europe, including Paul I of Russia, in which he asked for their help against the occupation of the Papal States. Thus, to some degree the Pope promoted the formation of the second coalition against France. Its successes induced the French, who had occupied Tuscany, to deport Pius VI to France. The dying Pope was transported first to Grenoble, and then to Valence, where he died on 29 August.

[64] For the first time the Vatican was in this case willing to receive a diplomat who represented a not officially Catholic state. Cf. R. Graham, *Vatican Diplomacy* (Princeton 1959), 40–41.

[65] This Roman Republic found it difficult to exercise its authority outside the city limits of Rome. During the entire year of 1798 there were domestic rebellions and even where the new regime asserted itself without friction it was frequently a case of "Holy-water-Jacobinism." For an example see R. Lefèvre, "La rivoluzione giacobina all'Ariccia" in *RStRis* 47 (1960) 467–520.

[66] *DBI* XI, 276.

At this point little remained of the former machinery of the Holy See. The work of the Curia was totally disorganized, the Sacred College was dispersed, and several cardinals had been imprisoned. It was not surprising that many people thought, some with joy and others with apprehension, that with the death of Pius VI, the papacy as the coping stone of the Catholic Church was disappearing under the hammer blows of the French Jacobins.

Chapter 2

Napoleon and Pius VII

The Election of Pius VII and the First Restoration of the Papal States

Pius VI realized that the next conclave would take place under quite extraordinary circumstances. For this reason he decreed even before his death that it should be convoked by the most senior cardinal at a place in the territory of any Catholic sovereign. Actually, Rome was meanwhile liberated by Neapolitan troops who drove out Frenchmen and Jacobins; about ten cardinals were residing in Rome. But King Ferdinand was suspected of wishing to increase his territory at the expense of the Holy See and to attempt to obtain a new Pope who would be favorably inclined toward his territorial ambitions. Spain was far away and in any case had been an ally of the French for five years and was thus suspected of being dependent. For this reason Cardinal Albani, the senior cardinal of the Sacred College who, with many other cardinals had fled to Venice (Austrian territory since 1797), preferred to place the conclave under the protection of Emperor Francis II. The Emperor had the monastery on the Island of San Giorgio refurbished for the purpose and assumed the expenses of the conclave which began its work on 1 December 1799. Of the forty-six living cardinals thirty-five participated. Of the latter, thirty were Italians. Two parties quickly opposed one another. The first was composed of the "politicians," whose concern was to adapt themselves to the new European situation and to maintain the bridges with France; they were discreetly supported by Spain. The other consisted of the "zealots," whose primary interest was to retain the heritage of the past undiminished and to maintain good relations with Austria. Good relations with this state seemed important to them because of Austria's hostility toward France and because they considered it the best means to regain from the Emperor the largest portion of the Papal States, which he had meanwhile conquered. The "politicians" were led by Cardinal Braschi and agreed on Cardinal Bellisomi, who quickly was able to obtain two-thirds of the votes. The "zealots" were led by the authoritarian Cardinal Antonelli, who was not moved by egotistical considerations, of which he was later accused by Consalvi, but by the consequences resulting from an objective analysis of the situation.[1] They were supported by Maury, the only French cardinal present who acted under power of attorney from Louis XVIII (whom the Sacred College had officially recognized as King of France, after Pius VI had steadfastly refused to do so) and by the Austrian cardinal Herzan, who was ordered to express the imperial veto against any candidate suspected of not being fully behind Vienna. The candidate of this party was Mattei, moderately opposed to the French. The bumbling manner with which the Emperor's plenipotentiary opposed the almost certain election of Bellisomi and pushed that of Mattei irritated the majority, and Mattei's last chances were gone when the cardinals learned that Spain would in no way recognize him. Spain was being directed by Bonaparte, who meanwhile had become France's virtual master. For three months a stalemate existed. By 12 March there was the outline of a solution: Antonelli was to get the support of the zealots—who would thus have the honor of having cast the decisive votes—for Cardinal Chiaramonti. A moderate and intelligent man, he had consistently voted with the "politicians," but had not made enemies of the opposition. The action was started by Cardinal Ruffo of condottieri fame who, with his Sanfedisti, had liberated Calabria. As we know from the recently discovered diary of Consalvi, the tactic "was skillfully suggested to him by someone who was not a cardinal but had a great part in the success without anyone being aware of it." Was it, as L. Pásztor thought, Consalvi himself, inasmuch as he was responsible for the material organization of the meeting? Or was it, as Monsignor Leflon wrote, the secret Spanish legate Despuig, who from the beginning had favored the candidacy of Chiaramonti? Both men knew one another well from business with the Rota, probably acted in agreement with one another, and with accomplished patience created the conditions for their successful candidate, whom they preferred much more for diplomatic and political than religious reasons. Be that as it may, Antonelli agreed to this compromise solution and so did Herzan after a discussion with the new candidate. Within forty-eight hours everything was settled and on 4 March 1800, Chiaramonti, in spite of the unconcealed displeasure of Maury and the reluctance of some colleagues who considered this fifty-eight-year-old cardinal rather young, was elected with only one negative

[1] On his apprehensions immediately before the conclave, see L. Briguglio in *RStRis* 45 (1958), 449–57.

vote. For reasons of devotion to his predecessor, who had also been his protector, he assumed the name of Pius VII.

Barnaba Chiaramonti came from a noble family closely related to the Braschi family. Like Pius VI he was born in Cesena, a small town of the Papal States, on 14 August 1742. The vivacious, vigorous, independent man from the Romagna, always open to new ideas, came to control the biting, arrogant aspects of his temperament. In mature age he displayed energy tempered by friendliness, an untiring patience, and realism fed by acuity and a sense of proportion. In contrast to his predecessors in the eighteenth century, who chiefly had been administrators or politicians, he turned out to be a man of doctrine and a shepherd of souls, always interested in distinguishing between the spiritual and the secular concerns of the Church and always giving pronounced preference to the religious goals. He had the courage of his convictions, but always had great tolerance for opinions which differed from his own. His earlier experiences prepared him well for the serious problems which a world in full transition posed for the Holy See. J. Leflon has illuminated for us the early segment of his life. During the conflict which in the eighteenth century confronted the supporters of the Jesuits with those who were vaguely called "Jansenists," the young Chiaramonti did not fight on the side of the Jesuits. Later, during the three years of revolution, he did not regard the undifferentiated condemnation of the principles of 1789 as the best method for defending religious interests.

In view of this conduct it is understandable that earlier biographers at the time of the reawakening of ultramontanism preferred to leave the formative years of Pius VII in a cautious and imprecise twilight. At the age of fourteen, Chiaramonti joined the Benedictines, studied in Padua and Rome, and from 1766 to 1775 was professor of theology in Parma. It was a period when in the circle around du Tillot and his French supporters plans for a reform of society, Church, and state were being discussed. The catalogue of his library at that time reveals that his mind was open to the modern ferment of thought; his library held few works of scholastic theology, but many critical editions of the Church Fathers, works by Muratori, Mabillon, Martène, and Tillemont, and the *Encyclopedia* of d'Alembert and Diderot. After he became professor at Saint Anselm in Rome, many colleagues accused him of too much sympathy for the reform attempts of young monks, and Pius VI, in order to remove him from such hostility, appointed him Bishop of Tivoli in 1783. In 1785 he was created a cardinal and transferred to Imola in the Romagna where he had an opportunity to learn of the shortcomings of the papal government. For a period of fifteen years he demonstrated that he possessed considerable pastoral ability and that he knew how to preserve his independence from the papal legate in Ferrara as much as from Jacobin officials and the occupation forces. In a situation which was particularly difficult because three different regimes—the papal, the Cisalpine Republican, and the Austrian regime—followed one another, he proved to be a courageous, skillful and imaginative leader during the difficult times of reaction and white terror. As a diplomatic mediator he had an outstanding ability to hold without breaking and to reconcile without bending. Shortly after the French invasion took place, he preached a sensational homily on Church and democracy[2] at Christmas 1797. He declared that the democratic form of government was not in opposition to the Gospel, and that religion was even more important in a democracy than in any other form of government. During the three-year existence of the republic he constantly attempted to separate the political and religious aspects of problems, tried not to identify the clergy with the opposition to the democratic regime, and demonstrated his ability to compromise in trivial matters in order to preserve the essentials.

Immediately after his election, the new Pope demonstrated that he had insight, was independent, and decisive. He refused Herzan's recommendation to appoint as his secretary of state a cardinal who was obligated to Austria. Instead his choice was Consalvi,[3] the young prelate to whom he owed his tiara. Consalvi was a conservative reformer, in keeping with the enlightened spirit of the eighteenth century, possessing both energy and flexibility. Consalvi had no experience in diplomacy but assisted the Pope, who concentrated on the religious aspects of problems, with his strong talent for an intelligent and cautious policy. He remained his right-hand man until the end of his pontificate. Emperor Francis II tried to hold the new Pope in his state, but Pius VII was firmly determined to free himself from Austrian tutelage and returned to Rome as soon as the opportunity presented itself (3 July 1800).

Consalvi began his diplomatic and administrative tasks without delay. One was the restitution of the papal territories occupied by Austrians, Neapolitans, and Frenchmen. Although the French maintained their position, the others eventually gave in and gradually the powers restored their representations at the Holy See.[4] Another problem was a papal administration completely disorganized by more than thirty

[2] Imola 1797. Subsequently this homily found wide distribution.

[3] Ercole Consalvi (1757–1824) was the perfect type of a non-ordained prelate (he became a priest only in 1822), passionately devoted to the Roman Church. He advanced quickly in the papal administration, in 1799 became secretary in the conclave of Pius VII, then pro-secretary of state, and on 11 August 1800, cardinal and secretary of state.

[4] For the first time in history a Protestant came to Rome as a diplomat, the Prussian Minister Humboldt. Cf. R. A. Graham, *Vatican Diplomacy* (Princeton 1959), 42–53.

months of foreign occupations; it needed to be made functional again. In addition, institutions whose obsolete character had been underscored by the introduction of the French system needed to be rejuvenated. Consalvi was fully aware of these matters, which were aggravated by numerous abuses, and was prepared to introduce a number of innovations, but encountered the reactionary opposition of the majority of the Curia. For this reason the papal Bull *Post diuturnas* of 30 October 1800,[5] prepared by a commission of cardinals, prelates, and expert laymen, provided only for a rather modest reform of institutions. It removed a number of evident abuses and added a few noble laymen to an administration which heretofore was completely reserved for clergymen. Economically, a number of useful steps was taken. These were chiefly freedom of trade (11 March 1801); a limited land reform (15 September 1802); a compromise solution with respect to the secularized estates of the Church; a partial solution for the catastrophic financial condition; and a simplification of the fiscal system. Such initiatives, in practical terms continuing the reforms envisioned by some popes of the eighteenth century, were no doubt commendable in a state in which there was a tendency to regard as sacrosanct every condition once it had reached a certain age. Professor Demarco, for example, described some of the measures as revolutionary. But on the whole the realization remained far behind the plans, the more so as Pius VII, who was so clear and decisive when important decisions for the Church were at stake, liked to leave details of administration to subordinates, who by a long shot were not all men like Consalvi.[6] Thus the Papal States, undermined by passive resistance of opponents from right to left, in spite of some incontestable improvements remained in an extraordinarily precarious administrative and economic situation until its annexation by Napoleon.

The Concordat of 1801

Shortly after the return of Pius VII to Rome, at the very time when the renewed arrival of French troops for the purpose of restoring the republic was feared, the Bishop of Vercelli arrived with a suggestion by the First Consul to begin negotiations with the aim of settling the religious affairs of France.

[5] *BullRomCont* XI, 48–71.

[6] L. Pásztor points out that the creation of cardinals during the first years of Pius VII's pontificate were not made with the intention to gain fresh forces for the reorganization of the life of the Church and the Papal States, but to reward the closest collaborators of his predecessor and some nuncios; see *RHE* 65 (1970), 479.

Immediately after the elimination of the Directory by the coup d'état of 18 Brumaire (9 November 1799), a reduction of tension on the religious level had set in. The persecution of the non-oath takers was suspended, many churches reopened again, and adherence to the "decades" was no longer obligatory. All of this indicated that the policy of systematic dechristianization was being abandoned. This development, regretted by many republicans in leading positions, was the direct result of a decision by the First Consul. It was not made for religious reasons—although it seems that he was less areligious than has been asserted[7]—but for political ones. He had become convinced that France, especially rural France, wished to remain Catholic, and his experiences in Italy had taught him that in a Catholic country the influence of priests constitutes a power which it is better to use than to fight. Some people advised him to depend for support on the Constituent Church as a republican and Gallican Church, then involved with its reorganization and about to convene its second national council for 29 June 1801. But Bonaparte realized that if he took the side of the Constituent Church he would force the numerically strongest and most influential clergy back into dependence on the hostile emigrant bishops, not to mention the strongly ultramontane Belgian and Rhenish Departments. He also sensed that an agreement with the papacy would redound to his prestige among Italians, Spaniards, and the great powers of the Old Regime. The victory of Marengo (14 June 1800) enabled him to negotiate with Rome from a position of strength. He hurried to exploit his opportunity without worrying too much about the discontent of the numerous opponents of the Church among political and administrative officials, in the army and among the buyers of Church lands. Pius VII on his part knew well that a better understanding with revolutionary France would be protested strongly by a large segment of the Curia and the majority of the émigrés. He was irritated when he realized that Napoleon wanted to bargain for an agreement, but also immediately recognized the tremendous advantage which he could gain. He understood completely what the restoration of peace and religious unity in the most important Catholic country of Europe would mean for the Holy See and for a French Church shaken to its foundations. Besides, a ceremonious act of international law would also acknowledge the superior position of the *pontifex maximus* at the head of the Catholic hierarchy.

Negotiations were begun, proved to be extraordinarily protracted, and were concluded successfully only after a year. The first session took place in Paris between November and February. The Church negotiators were Monsignor Spina, a prelate of the Curia who had

[7] See M. Guerrini, *Napoléon devant Dieu* (Paris 1960).

accompanied Pius VI to France, and Father Caselli, a theologian. France was represented by Abbé Bernier. He had played a large role in the pacification of the Vendée and now placed the tools of a subtle theology and an occasionally ambiguous diplomacy in the service of a reconciliation between France and Rome. He also succeeded in neutralizing the opposition of the French secretary of state, Talleyrand, without bringing the fight into the open. After four drafts a fifth one was finally sent to Rome, where the second phase of negotiations took place between March and May. The Curia, under the leadership of Cardinal Antonelli, declared the text which had been suggested by Bonaparte as unacceptable. The Curia drafted a counterproposal, which in turn occasioned numerous objections by the French legate Cacault. Angered by the Roman delays, Bonaparte transmitted an ultimatum and Pius VII decided to send Consalvi with power of attorney to Paris. In the time from 20 June to 15 July frequently stormy discussions took place at the highest level. Until the last minute there was the danger of a termination of the negotiations, for Bonaparte absolutely refused to yield in several points, as he had to reckon with the stiff-necked opposition of a large part of his entourage, among whom Jacobin anticlericalism remained virulent. But Consalvi used all of the abilities of his flexible genius in order to achieve the acceptance of conciliatory formulations, and an agreement was finally reached at midnight on 15 July.

The relatively brief text,[8] including the recognition by the Pope of the republic as the rightful government of France, was preceded by a preamble in which the Catholic religion was acknowledged as "the religion of a large majority of Frenchmen." This was a compromise wording, for the Curia had insisted that the Catholic religion be acknowledged as the dominant religion among all religions whose equality before the law was tacitly affirmed by Rome. Article 1 declared the Catholic religion to be public and free, but with the limitation that "it must agree with police regulations which the government might pass in the interest of maintaining public peace." Consalvi had vainly tried to exclude this clause, as it seemed to open the door to all kinds of chicanery, but had to be satisfied with the addition of the last part of the sentence which at least put a limit on capricious acts. After this basic declaration, which carried with it the renunciation of all earlier laws of restrictive character, the subsequent articles had a double objective.

The difficulties which had arisen between Church and state since 1790 were to be removed and the French Church was to be reorganized on new foundations. Two problems created difficulties. One was the sale of nationalized Church lands, with which the Holy See agreed after

[8] Mercati I, 561–65.

it had vainly attempted to achieve at least the restitution of those lands which had not yet been sold. The second was the existence of a dual episcopate. Bonaparte quietly left the Constituent Church to its own devices, and the Pope agreed in embarrassed language (Article 3) to ask all surviving bishops of the Old Regime for their resignation in order to clear the way for the creation of a totally new episcopate. With respect to the future organization of the Church of France, only general principles were stated. These included the right of the Holy See to a reorganization of the dioceses, and the right of bishops to a reorganization of the parishes, but in both cases only with the prior agreement of the government; the appointment of bishops as under the Old Regime by the head of state, their canonical investment by the Pope; appointment of parish priests by the bishops after agreement by the government; the right of bishops to a cathedral chapter and a seminary, but without any obligation of the government to pay for their maintenance; the obligation of the government to pay appropriate salaries to bishops and parish priests as compensation for the nationalization of Church lands; and finally, in spite of initially brusk rejection, the right of the faithful to make gifts to the Church. Nothing was said in the concordat about religious congregations.

Now the compromise had to be ratified. Without a doubt it was of considerable benefit for both sides. It strengthened Bonaparte's prestige, confirmed several important accomplishments of the revolution, and conceded to the French government the right to control the Church in several significant areas. On the other hand it was the Holy See which had granted these privileges to the state on the basis of its own authority and not on the basis of a right of the state. This afforded the Church a good deal of satisfaction, as it was a matter of principle. Furthermore, the schism which had split the Church for more than ten years was healed and the foundation had been laid for a modernized restoration of the old ideal of a Christian Church based on the state. Finally, last but not least, the right of the Pope to intervene in the affairs of national Churches was strengthened. To be sure, every or almost every article contained as many intended or inadvertent ambiguities as it resolved. The commission of cardinals in Rome began to demand changes. Consalvi, in any case convinced that the achieved political advantages outweighed the theological and pastoral worries of the zealots, judged the situation with greater realism and assured the cardinals that no further improvement could be attained. Cardinal Antonelli noted with deep regret that only the shadow of a religion was being restored in France, but in spite of everything also considered it necessary to accept the document which, paradoxically, underlined the supreme spiritual jurisdiction of the Pope in the former stronghold of Gallicanism. Yet only fourteen of twenty-eight cardinals voted for unconditional acceptance. Pius, however, ignored the vote, publicly declared the Holy See's acceptance on 15 August 1801, and asked the legitimate bishops to submit their resignations. In Paris, strangely enough, Bonaparte hesitated to confront the hostility of the deliberative assemblies. In order at least partially to counter their objections, which were supported by the determined resistance of Talleyrand and Fouché, he resorted to a subterfuge: the text of the "Convention de Messidor," as the concordat was officially called in France, was submitted for approval with two other bills. One regulated the Protestant religion, attesting the willingness to be totally nonpartisan in religious questions, and the other placed Catholics under a comprehensive church regulation, consisting of seventy-seven "Organic Articles."[9]

They in part retracted what had been conceded, as the Church was now being subordinated to the state in the old royal fashion. The clergy required the permission of the government before it could publish papal documents, convoke a provincial or national council, create new parishes, and even establish private chapels. Seminarians had to be taught about the Declaration of 1682; the old diocesan catechisms had to be replaced by a uniform catechism; priests were forbidden to perform church weddings before the civil ceremony; the confirmation of nuncios and other papal legates was strongly limited; each infraction of rules by priests or even bishops was to be treated like a felony and to be dealt with by the Council of State.

Other articles defined the rights and obligations of bishops with the harshness and precision of military regulations, and imposed upon the Church an organization corresponding to that of other state agencies. From now on there was no longer a French episcopate, but only bishops strictly controlled by the Ministry of Religion, permitting the bishops no organic connection and prohibiting any collective action. In their turn, the bishops were virtually given the rights of prefects in their dioceses, with a discretionary power over their parish priests, which exceeded what had been known under the Old Regime. The formerly so powerful and growing cathedral chapters were relegated to a purely decorative function, while the priests, whose desire for a synodal and democratic rejuvenation of diocesan life had been fulfilled by the Civil Constitution of the Clergy, saw themselves reduced to the role of merely carrying out orders. They were obligated to strict obedience, having lost the protection which their benefices once afforded them. The vast majority of them could be removed upon the slightest suspicion. Napoleon granted the bishops this virtually unlimited power because he wanted to

[9] See *DDC* I, 1064–72.

utilize the concordat to assure the cohesion of a nation rent by the existence of two Churches, and because he realized that this extremely difficult fusion could only be accomplished by imperial means. This strengthening of episcopal authority, dictated by the moment, was to have lasting consequences. Assured of an obedient civil-service-like clergy, the bishops lost their taste for criticism within the Church. Among the priests, likewise, the parallel between the ecclesiastical organization and the civil service and the fact that they received their salaries from the state also augmented their view of themselves as regular officials. They increasingly adopted the mentality of officials, with increased respectability and punctuality and decreased initiative and sense of responsibility. The institution thereby won cohesion and functioned better, but lost freedom and innovative spirit.[10] These changes strongly influenced the image of bishops and priests not only in France, but in all of western Europe. Aside from all this, Napoleon, by authoritatively substituting his ideal of administrative centralism for the old Gallican and presbyterian traditions of the old Church of France, unwittingly helped to prepare the triumph of ultramontanism. It would raise its head again as soon as the government was no longer sufficiently despotic to pose a counterweight to papal power.

But these future consequences could not be foreseen at that time. More immediately, Rome was worried about the unilateral changes, and therefore falsification, of the concordat by means of a strong state control over the life of the Church. Pius VII protested vigorously.[11] In Paris, where Bonaparte's maneuver had succeeded in disarming the opposition so that the new laws on religion were passed on 8 April 1802,[12] the government pretended amazement and replied that the Organic Articles did not introduce new law, but were merely a renewed sanction of old principles of the Gallican Church.[13] This was only partially correct, of course, inasmuch as the articles intensified earlier directives through the introduction of new ones which could be reconciled with the letter of the concordat (only with difficulty).[14] Pius VII and Consalvi once again proved their realism. They knew that the reconciliation of the Church with the new society created by the revolution was possible only by paying this price. They did not pursue the matter further, inspired by the hope that the future would permit them

[10] Observe the appropriate notes of J. Godel in *Revue d'histoire moderne et contemporaine* 17 (1970), 837–45.

[11] Consistorial address of 24 May 1802, in A. Boulay, *Documents* V, 584 ff.

[12] Still, there were twenty-one nays and fifty-one abstentions.

[13] J. Portalis, *Discours* 113.

[14] See the concise criticism of Pouthas, 112–14.

to improve a situation which they were helpless to change unless they wished to jeopardize what had been gained.

The Reorganization of the Church of France

The concordat and the Organic Articles established the principles for the reorganization of the Church of France. They needed to be implemented on both national and local levels. On the national level the work was done jointly by three men. One was Cardinal Caprara,[15] whose age, physical constitution and character disposed to a willingness to compromise bordering on weakness. He had already demonstrated this as nuncio in Vienna. In spite of reluctance by Pius VII and Consalvi, Bonaparte had succeeded in having him appointed as papal legate. Another man was Jean Portalis,[16] in charge of religious affairs, one of the few Catholics among the leading politicians, and a conscientious lawyer. He was a dedicated proponent of the principles of parliamentary Gallicanism, but within the framework of the possible also willing to advance the cause of the Church. Finally and foremost there was the inconstant Bernier. He provided undeniable services in sometimes questionable fashion, especially by lending his skillful and subtle pen to both sides in an attempt to formulate the questions as well as the answers, which to him seemed the best means to reconcile both.

On the whole, Bonaparte succeeded in gaining most of his objectives with the concordat. He saw in it an essential element of his policy of pacification and wanted to fashion the Church into one of his most useful tools.

The first problem was the adjustment of the dioceses to the administrative organization of France. The simplest solution would have been a return to the civil constitution, i.e., one bishopric for each Department. But Pius VII was reluctant to favor what had been rejected by Pius VI. Chiefly, however, it was the French government which deemed this solution as too expensive. Its proposal envisioned ten archbishoprics, to correspond to the area of jurisdiction of the appellate courts, and forty bishoprics for the 102 Departments of which France was then composed. At the last minute Bonaparte raised the figure to sixty. He did this not for pastoral reasons, but with the intention to strengthen the ecclesiastical organization of the conquered areas.[17] The papal bull of 13 De-

[15] See *DHGE* XI, 944–57 and S. Delacroix, 60–64, on Giovanni Battista Caprara (1733–1810).

[16] See L. Adolphe, *Portalis et son temps* (Paris 1936) and S. Delacroix, 77–97.

[17] Half of the additional bishoprics were established in the following areas: Liège and Ghent in Belgium, Mainz on the left bank of the Rhine, and Chambéry and Nice in Savoy.

cember 1801 and Caprara's executive order of 9 April 1802 confirmed the reorganization legally. There were now twenty-four dioceses consisting of two, and 6 consisting of three departments each. About ten dioceses were larger than 5750 square miles and thirty-seven had more than five hundred thousand inhabitants. Some memorable episcopal sees such as Reims, Arles, and Sens disappeared, while many of the new dioceses formed an artificial mosaic composed of fragments of sometimes up to eight of the old dioceses, all with their own traditions and mentality. Naturally this mixture caused the bishops great difficulties during the first generation.

Before appointments could be made to the new sees, the resignation of the old office holders had to be effected. Reluctantly, fifty-nine Constituent bishops went along with the wishes of the government. After some disputes with respect to the eventual formulation, they directed a common letter to the Pope in which they accepted the condordat and the principles which the French government and His Holiness confirmed in it. Of the ninety-two surviving bishops of the Old Regime, all those who had returned to France and those who had fled to Italy submitted their resignations without creating any difficulties. Not so with some others. Monsignor Dillon was the leader of an opposition group in England and his ideas spread to a considerable number of the prelates who had fled to Germany and Spain. Among this group loyalty to the King assumed precedence over loyalty to the Pope, the more so as their Gallican theology[18] convinced them that the Pope had exceeded his constitutional authority. Finally only fifty-five bishops, including nine from the annexed territories, resigned. Most of the others were at least prudent enough no longer to intervene in their old dioceses and to go so far as to advise their clergy and their laity to subordinate themselves to their new bishops. Two of them, however, Thémines and Coucy, organized an open resistance to the concordat and thus created a new schism. It was numerically insignificant, but in some areas persisted until Vatican II.[19] Generally, though, the old refractory clergy, after a

[18] It found its reflection in their *Mémoire* of 23 December 1801, and in their *Réclamations canoniques* of 6 April 1803 and 15 April 1804.

[19] Behind the *Petite Église* with which we are here dealing, there is in actuality concealed a complex movement which commingles to varying degrees Gallican traditions, royalist sentiments, religious fanaticism, peasant resistance against innovations, and the actions of some leaders with a peculiar psychology. See C. Latreille, *L'opposition religieuse au concordat* II (Paris 1910), augmented by the revealing article by M. Rebouillat, "Étude comparée des schismes anti-concordataires en France" in *Revue du Bas-Poitou* 73 (1962), 27–38, 212–19, 458–83. Depending on the area, the movement had different effects. Three main centers can be differentiated: a) the west, to which can be added the area of Blois. Here the schism, centering on Bishops Coucy and Thémines, was chiefly regally inspired and initially numbered thirty thousand dissidents. The at first episcopal

brief period of being upset, acted like the future bishop Eugène de Mazenod: "Loyal to the monarchy, he considered Bonaparte as a usurper, but as a son of the Church he placed the interest of his religion and his obedience toward the Holy See ahead of everything else."[20]

The designation of the new bishops raised a sticky problem. Bonaparte insisted that as with his appointments to prefectures, so also with the appointment of bishops, his principle of integration be applied. The new episcopate was to consist simultaneously of bishops of the Old Regime, of Constituent bishops, and of new men. The Holy See, which regarded the Constituent bishops as schismatics, demanded from them an official recantation. Most of the government nominees from this group refused, however, to declare themselves as schismatics. Caprara, on whom Bernier worked skillfully, eventually had to be satisfied with a compromise, even though it was inadequate in the eyes of Rome.

Delicate negotiations took place in which Bernier and Émery played an eminent role; they went on from October 1801 to October 1802. Eventually the new episcopate consisted of sixteen, in some cases rather aged, bishops of the Old Regime; twelve former Constituent bishops, among them many vicars general, most of them relatively young. To this group also belonged an uncle of Bonaparte, Fesch, who was named Archbishop of Lyon. Although political considerations played a role, the nominations generally turned out to be good. While there were few strong personalities, the episcopate on the whole consisted of fair, level-headed, and conciliatory men—at that time of utmost importance—who performed their tasks conscientiously and proved to be excellent administrators under extremely difficult conditions.

---

and then presbyterian schism quickly became a popular issue, which explains why it persisted even after the demise of its originators. See A. Billaud, *La Petite Église dans la Vendée et les Deux-Sèvres, 1800–30* (Paris 1962); R. de Chauvigny, *La résistance au concordat de 1801* (Paris 1921); L. Chesneau, *Les dissidents vendômois de la Petite Église* (Vendôme 1924); J. Leflon, *Bernier* II, 252–58. b) the area of Lyon, in which the schism was not so vociferous, but cooler and more persistent, and colored by Jansenism; see C. Latreille, *Histoire de la Petite Église de Lyon* (Paris 1910); E. Dermenghem: *Bulletin de la Société d'Études historiques des Hautes-Alpes* (1957), 115–47. c) the south; see P. Mouly, *Concordataires, constitutionnels et enfarinés en Quercy et Rouergue* (Sarlat 1945); Gabent, *Les illuminés ou anticoncordataires de l'ancien diocèse de Lombez* (Auch 1906). In England there was a clerical schism without believers. Almost nine hundred priests followed Abbé Blanchard who distributed numerous pamphlets; see A. Dechène, *Contre Pie VII et Bonaparte. Le blanchardisme* (Paris 1932). The case was different with the Belgian Stevenists; they protested not against the concordat, but against the acceptance of the Organic Articles by the new bishops. See J. Soille, *C. Stevens* (Gembloux 1957); id., *Notes pour servir à l'histoire du stévenisme,* 2 vols. (Gembloux 1958/63); E. Torfs: *Annales du Cercle archéologique d'Enghien* 10 (1955), 9–154, 11 (1956), 2–56; Th. Van Biervliet, *Het stevenisme in Vlaanderen* (Louvain 1956).

[20] J. Leflon, *E. de Mazenod* I (Paris 1957), 248–49, 317.

Everything had to be reconstructed and newly created. The new diocesan administrations not only needed to be put in place, but also had to adjust to the meager means available. The parish boundaries had to be arranged according to the directives of the government, and in them economic considerations also had to be taken into account. Church buildings which during the revolution were alienated from worship and employed for profane purposes[21] had to be reconsecrated for divine services. A new parish clergy had to be created and this point raised complex problems. At first sight there seemed to be no lack of qualified personnel. To be sure, there had been few ordinations during the past few years and many priests had resigned from their offices; but now, after the signing of the concordat,[22] many of these and married priests attempted to reconcile themselves with the Church. The former prebendiaries and monks also constituted a formidable reserve.[23] But aside from those who for political or theological reasons declined to enter the concordat Church, many were actually unsuited for a parish position. Some were too old or too discouraged by the new material or psychological conditions; the members of former chapters generally belonged to a university and had no pastoral training, while among the former monks many hesitated to become so engaged, as they momentarily expected a restoration of their orders or simply preferred the life of an itinerant preacher, sheltered by pious old ladies, to the sedentary existence of a poorly paid vicar.[24] Consequently quite a number of posts could not immediately be filled and this situation did not change for years. As late as 1808, 10,477 places, i.e., 21.2 percent, were vacant.

Another problem was that this numerically inadequate clergy was also quite disparate in other respects. It consisted of persons who came from different dioceses with different traditions; of monks alien to their new areas who brought with them new aspects of spirituality; of émigrés who for ten years had virtually lived a life of idleness; and of former Constituents, who were regarded suspiciously by their confreres and their parishioners, and whose reconciliation posed a number of delicate

[21] On 14 October 1801, Napoleon had banned the adherents of Theophilanthropy from the churches.

[22] A precise census of the priests in 1801 is virtually impossible. See J. Leflon, *Bernier* II, 283, 356–91, and S. Delacroix, 134–44.

[23] A brief of 15 August 1801 had given Caprara far-reaching authority. A total of 3,224 priests, 2,313 of them secular priests and 911 priests of orders, sought absolution. Cf. S. Delacroix, 443–56.

[24] In 1808 in all of France 25 percent of the priests were still without office, in some dioceses such as Mecheln the percentage rose to 46. Many of them, especially those in the cities, raised formidable difficulties for the concordat bishops because of their latent opposition.

problems.[25] According to Bonaparte's plans one-third of the clergy was to come from the former Constituents. In reality this proportion was not reached, unless a bishop happened to be a former Constituent himself. State officials closed their eyes to this fact, knowing fully well that the rural population did not care for priests who had sworn the oath.

The absolutely essential personnel were placed quickly, sometimes too quickly. No serious repercussions occurred, unless a bishop or a prefect, as in Namur, lacked the necessary tact. Thought also had to be given to replacements, for in contrast to the bishops, the clergy had reached advanced middle age. In 1809 more than 33 percent of the priests were older than sixty years of age, and this ratio increased from year to year.

The reopening of the seminaries was a troublesome and protracted project. Money was lacking, as the government initially had not budgeted any sums for this purpose. Many bishops had to wait five or ten years for the return of the former seminary buildings. There was also a lack of competent teachers. It was necessary to fall back on prerevolutionary teachers, who in no way were able to cope with the temper of the times.[26] Finally, there was also an initial lack of students for the seminaries, because the small parochial schools in which they received their first training had disappeared ten years earlier, and the high officials of the public education system were eager to preserve their monopoly and reluctant to see them reintroduced. Ordinations increased from year to year, especially after seminarians had been exempted from military service and the government provided stipends for

[25] See S. Delacroix, 315–35 on the conflict of May–June 1802 between Caprara and the government over the phrasing of recantation. On the local level, the attitude differed among the various dioceses. Some bishops, like Fesch or d'Aviau were very strict, others, like Bernier, generous; the Constituent bishops were understandably even more generous, going so far in some cases, such as that of Saurine, bishop of Strasbourg, to question the principle of recantation. Other difficulties resulted especially in the Belgian dioceses in connection with the renunciation of the oath of hate against the monarchy. See, for example, J. Plumet, op. cit. 211–35 and C. de Clercq, *Bulletin de la Société d'art et d'histoire du diocèse de Liège* 38 (1953), 71–107. There were even disputes among the former refractory clergy, some of them, the "Purists," accusing the others of having taken the oath to the constitution of the year VIII even before the regulation of the religious question. The faithful sided in part with one, in part with the other group, giving rise to suspicion and arguments.

[26] In order to obtain higher standards of education, Portalis would have preferred to create in each Church province a metropolitan seminary reserved for the most talented. But the bishops opposed his plan, fearing that they would not be able to control his activity. On the reorganization of the seminaries, see J. Leflon, *M. Émery* II, 202–64.

them. Still, there were only six thousand ordinations between 1801 and 1815, a figure which corresponded to ordinations in 1789 alone. Besides, the material condition of the rural clergy during the first few years was anything but attractive; only district pastors were paid by the state, the other nine-tenths received room and board from their communities which were not always generous.[27] Under such conditions, the reorganization of ecclesiastical administrations could be completed only after 1809.[28] Gradually the general situation improved, for the government was eager to retain the good will of the clergy. The budget rose from 1,200,000 francs in 1802 to 17,000,000 francs in 1807, making it possible to pay all parish administrators an annual salary of 500 francs (Decree of 31 May 1804).

Cooperation between state and Church took place not only in the financial sphere. Several measures strengthened the prestige of the Catholic Church. A law of 1 April 1803 decreed that children had to be given names of saints; a decree of 13 July 1804 ordered military honors for altar sacraments carried in processions and granted ecclesiastic dignitaries a place of honor in the official sequence of precedence (cardinals before state ministers, archbishops before prefects). On the local level, the bishops generally could count on the cooperation of officials, even if some prefects did not display their best side. Of course, the Church in turn had the obligation to cooperate with the state in maintaining order and the strict control to which all of its activities were subjected by the ministry of religion. After all, it was created by Bonaparte for the purpose of supervising the Church in the same way in which other ministries supervised other state agencies.[29] The rigidity and strictness of this centralization should not be overestimated, however. The men who had to implement on the local level decisions which had been reached at the national one, acted less servile, especially in important matters, than had long been thought. Occasionally they interpreted their directives in a rather personal way, such as was done in the diocese of Grenoble or the diocese of Ghent. All told, the situation differed from region to region, sometimes from one diocese to a neighboring one, depending on local circumstances as well as on the personality of the bishop or the prefect.

[27] E. Dupont, *La part des communes dans les frais du culte paroissial* (Paris 1906). See also A. Sicard, "Quinze années de budget des cultes à la charge des fidèles 1792–1807" in *Le Correspondant* 220 (1905), 209–38.

[28] See J. Gennart in *Annales de droit et de sciences politiques* 21 (Brussels 1961), 3–42.

[29] Portalis died in 1807. His successor was Bigot de Préameneu, a devoted Catholic, who felt he had to comply with every wish of the master of France. See J. Savant, *Les préfets de Napoléon* (Paris 1959), 69–72.

Although the concordat was silent on them, a limited official restoration of religious congregations took place. Napoleon and most of his advisers were quite hostile toward male orders; not only did they consider them useless, but even dangerous, as they were not under the control of the bishops. When it was noted that the Fathers of the Faith, who correctly were suspected of preparing the way for the resurrection of the Society of Jesus, had opened a number of schools thanks to the protection of Cardinal Fesch, a decree on 22 June 1804 ordered the immediate dissolution of all not officially sanctioned congregations. Government permission was granted only to mission congregations (priests of foreign missions, Fathers of the Holy Spirit, and the Lazarists) who were considered useful for the dissemination of the French spirit abroad, to the friars in the parochial schools on the basis of the irreplaceable and practically free services which they rendered for the education of the people,[30] and to some monasteries which were used as way stations at Alpine passes. The "useful" female congregations, on the other hand, i.e., congregations which devoted themselves to education and the care of the sick, not only were not molested in any way, but were in fact often encouraged officially. A breach in the revolutionary laws was made in December 1800, with the permission for the Daughters of Charity of Saint Vincent de Paul. They also received permission to train pupils for service in hospitals and eight years later there were 1653 Daughters of Charity in 274 houses. In the course of the first decade of the new century a thoroughgoing revival took place. The restoration of dissolved monasteries which had begun under the Directory continued. The contemplatives often emphasized education and explained that their novices were to take care of the aged Sisters. There were several new creations, some of which were to have a great future. Following the example of the Fathers of the Faith, Madeleine Barat in 1800 founded the Sacred Heart Society in Paris for women who devoted themselves to the education of girls. In 1803, the Belgian Pierre-Joseph Triest founded in Ghent the Sisters of Charity of Jesus and Mary, who in 1806 were officially acknowledged as the first new congregation. In 1804, Marie-Rose-Julie Billiart founded the Sisters of Notre Dame in Amiens for the education and training of girls; in 1809 the order was transferred to Namur. In 1807, Jeanne-Elisabeth Bichier des Ages founded the Daughters of the Holy Cross of Saint Andrew in

[30] Napoleon was much concerned with control over higher education which trained the future leadership, and the decree of 15 November 1811 strengthened his supervision of the private high schools and the boys' schools, but he was not interested in elementary education. See L. Grimaud, *Histoire de la liberté d'enseignement en France III/IV* (Paris 1946).

Poitiers for the purpose of educating children, nursing the sick, and taking care of the poor.[31]

A decree of the Emperor of 23 March 1805 made his mother the protector of the Sisters of Mercy in the entire Empire. In 1807, Napoleon convoked in Paris a meeting of all congregations devoted to the care of the sick. His penchant for organization was disturbed by the great number of small congregations and he wished to see them unite in one large organization. When he realized that it was not possible to effect this plan, he limited himself to decreeing on 18 February 1809 common guidelines defining the age of novices, the duration of their vows and similar matters, and ordered the congregations to have their statutes approved by the government before the end of the year. By this time there were 2057 convents with 16,447 nuns devoted to the care of the sick and the poor.

Religious Revival

"It was not Napoleon's intention to rechristianize France, but to exploit for his own benefit the religious feeling which still existed," stated G. Lefebvre correctly. The work by S. Delacroix illustrates in detail this utilitarian and often cynical attitude toward religion. Yet the aim of rechristianizing France, not shared by Napoleon, was pursued by a considerable number of the concordat clergy, assisted by the reviving religious congregations and an elite of laymen. They were able to record a limited but undeniable success. These forces were aided by the ministry of religion, at least in the first few years after the signing of the concordat, a support which was due to the circle of clergymen from Provence who gathered around Portalis and Cardinal Fesch.

There were, of course, many priests among the randomly collected clergy who were totally lacking in apostolic spirit and who had no difficulty performing their office of "pious administration" to which the government wished to limit them. But many others and numerous bishops, among them many former Constituents who stood out by their special zeal (regardless of what may have been said about them before), were firmly convinced that reintroduction of religion and worship was not enough. They undertook a gigantic effort to clean up a situation whose roots went back to prerevolutionary times, but which had been aggravated by the revolution. It must be noted, though, that the reopen-

[31] See L. Baunard, *Histoire de Madame Barat,* 2 vols. (Paris 1876, 1925); L. Cnockaert, *Le chanoine Triest et ses fondations* (Diss. Louvain 1971); Th. Réjalot, *La bienheureuse Julie Billiart* (Namur 1922); E. Domec, *Vie de Ste. Jeanne-Élisabeth Bichier des Ages* (Paris 1950).

ing of the churches almost everywhere was greeted joyfully, that the faithful set about putting up the torn-down crosses, and that the jubilee pronounced at the end of 1803 was a great success. But despite all external devotion to old customs, festivities, and forms, religious indifference prevailed quite frequently in the cities. It was encountered even in the rural regions, where for a decade the population had not observed religious customs, where many abnormal conditions, especially in the area of marriages, had to be cleared up, and where most of the young people had had no exposure to a catechism and lived in deep religious ignorance.

The number of confirmations attests the seriousness with which the bishops undertook the systematic visitation of their dioceses. Some of them, like Monsignor d'Aviau, the pious Archbishop of Bordeaux, did not hesitate to preach all day long and hear confessions;[32] others organized catechismal instruction on the model of Saint Sulpice and were inspired by the advice of the respected Émery. After 1800, he transformed his revived society into one of the most active centers of religious revival and secretly remained the conscience of the Church of France until his death in 1811.[33]

The lower clergy was not idle either. Many priests organized retreats in order to encourage the zeal of their brethren. As early as 1799, still under the Directory, Abbé Allemand founded the first youth center in Marseille, an institution which was to have a great future in the nineteenth century. Others wanted to lead the intellectuals back to the Church and concentrated on a renewal of apologetic sermons, represented chiefly by Frayssinous in Paris. One must also look at the more modest parallel attempts which were undertaken in the provinces, with different rates of success and in different directions. Some, rejecting the compromise of the eighteenth century, preached an open return to the great religious century of Malebranche and Bossuet, while others tried to see the future of the Church in light of the undeniable facts of the revolution. Others again, more concerned with the salvation of the masses, organized missions in the parishes,[34] which assumed large proportions after the jubilee of 1803, owing to the assistance provided by de

[32] See Dom du Bourg, *Mgr du Bourg, évêque de Limoges* (Paris 1907), 391–408; J.-P. Lyonnet, *Histoire de Mgr d'Aviau* IV (Paris 1847), 528–31.

[33] See J. Leflon, *M. Émery* II, 177–99. On the Compagnie de St-Sulpice under Napoleon see J. Leflon, *E. de Mazenod* I, 309–409; C. Maréchal, *La jeunesse de Lamennais* (Paris 1913), 125–48; de Montclos, 5–17; J. Audinet, *L'Ecclésiologie au XIXe siècle* (Paris 1960), 115–39.

[34] See E. Sevrin, *Les missions religieuses en France sous la Restauration* I (Paris 1948), 11–21.

Clorivière's Priests of the Sacred Heart of Jesus and chiefly to Father Varin's Fathers of the Faith. While these missions were sharply watched by the police, they also frequently were aided and occasionally subsidized by the civil authorities. Cardinal Fesch planned a national mission society which was to be made part of the Grand Almonry under the direction of Abbé Rauzan, a famous missionary. But after his disagreement with Pius VII, Napoleon, on 26 September 1809, forbade the continuation of these missions, as he feared that these "itinerant and vagabond" priests could become propaganda agents in the papal cause. Through measures of this nature, which during the last years of the Empire followed one another in rapid succession and which impeded the traditional priestly apostolate, several initiatives of a more modest scope were of great value. Among others there were the Marian Congregations for students, founded in 1801 in Paris by the former Jesuit P. Delpuits. After their elimination in 1809, they played an active role in the religious resistance;[35] the congregations of young men and young women from all walks of life which after 1806 were founded in Bordeaux by Abbé J. Chaminade, secular institutions with the aim of forming religious nuclei on the level of different social classes;[36] and the Congregation of Lyon with an even more pronounced lay character. Its origins fell in the time before the concordat and contributed to placing the church of Lyon in the vanguard of the religious restoration of the nineteenth century.[37] On the other hand it must be noted that the disappearance of most of the confraternities during the revolution allowed the parish priest in all of France an exclusive leadership role. This, in turn, was all too often a reason for the faithful to ignore the religious life in the parish.

The various evangelization attempts bore fruit only slowly. There were indeed baptisms and first communions of adults, and the prominent people in communities once again attended Mass, but until the end of the Empire there was little call, especially among men, for the Sacraments. One characteristic detail serves to illuminate the picture. Only a few of the thousands of wounded in the Moscow military hospitals in 1812 demanded to see a priest. Such facts justify Grégoire's disappointed statement that while there was religious exercise in France,

[35] See G. de Grandmaison, *La Congrégation* (Paris 1890), 14–137. Not much is known about the activity in the provinces.

[36] P. Broutin, *NRTh* 65 (1938), 413–36; A. Windisch, *The Marianist Social System* (Fribourg 1964).

[37] Cl. Embruyen, *La vie a jailli des ruines. Le P. Roger* (Lyon 1947) and especially A. Lestra, *Histoire secrète de la congrègation de Lyon* (Paris 1967).

there was little religious feeling.[38] But in one area an encouraging development had begun: in the world of the intellectuals.

Revolutionary excesses and the failure of an ethical philosophy without God had caused many heads to turn away from the rationalistic philosophy of the eighteenth century. They began to see again in a religion of revelation the irrevocable basis for all of social life, and inextricably tied together the ideas of truth, tradition, and authority, applying the concept of authority to the authority of the monarch in a state as well as to the authority of God and the Church. If the works of Joseph de Maistre and Vicomte de Bonald, published in 1796 during the emigration and sketching the outlines of their traditionalist systems, found only a limited echo in France before 1815, they were nevertheless symptomatic of the mentality which grew from year to year. At the very moment when Napoleon reopened the churches, the great writer Chateaubriand contributed much to making Catholicism acceptable again in the eyes of the intellectuals. On 4 April 1802, he published *Le Génie du christianisme,* a radical "No" to Voltairean enlightenment. The book was a tremendous and lasting success, proving that it appeared at just the right time. In admirable language and with original force he orchestrated themes touched upon by many apologetic writers of the eighteenth century and directed the religious yearning of his contempories no longer to the vague Christianity of a Rousseau but directly to the Catholic Church, its dogmas, its Sacraments, its rites.[39] It savaged the prejudices of the eighteenth century, which had portrayed Catholicism as barbaric and mediocre, and described it instead as a wholesome haven for all whose bodies and souls suffer. To Chateaubriand it was the source of poetic inspiration, equally as fruitful as heathen antiquity.

Chateaubriand continued the success of *Le Génie du christianisme* in 1809 with his novel *Les martyrs ou le triomphe de la religion,* a Christian epic. In the meantime other writers, mostly émigrés, had also taken up the battle against the philosophy of the eighteenth century as the source of atheism, among them Ballanche, Michaud, and Royer-Collard with his *Journal de l'Empire.* These men found support in the drawing rooms of Paris, such as those of Madame de Rémusat, Madame de la Briche, and Élisa Bonaparte. After 1803 they were also supported by Fontanes, the chancellor of the university, a personally rather skeptical epicurean, who was convinced of the social utility of religion. He appointed Émery and Bonald to his General Council, and sent many members of the old

[38] *Mémoires* II, 423. On the situation in Paris see especially L. de Lanzac de Laborie, *Paris sous Napoléon* IV (Paris 1907), chapter 3.
[39] See V. Giraud, *Le christianisme de Chateaubriand,* 2 vols. (Paris 1925/28).

congregations with teaching experience into the high schools so that they could attack the dangerous philosophy of the eighteenth century.

To be sure, as Fontanes shows exemplarily, many of these Neo-Christians, as they were then called, were only sympathizers on the surface. They also constituted only a minority, for the ideologues, the heirs of the atheistic encyclopedists, still occupied strong positions in the important areas of the press, the literary salons, the scientific societies, and the humanities at universities.

In summary it can be said that by 1810 the concordat Church had justified reasons to be proud of the regained territory, but that in spite of everything its strength was weak and its successes mere seeds, to bear fruit only during the time of restoration. Before it, another storm had to be weathered.

The Pope and the Emperor

In May 1804, Bonaparte was proclaimed as Emperor of the French. To a high degree the leaders of the Church of France had fostered this development with the extravagant praises in their pastoral letters of the "modern Cyrus," the "new Constantine," and the "restorer of altars." Against the advice of the Curia, Pius VII decided to travel to Paris in order to anoint the new Emperor (2 December 1804), even though in the entire history of the Holy Roman Empire a Pope had never journeyed to Vienna for the coronation of an Emperor. Fesch, appointed ambassador to Rome in April 1803, convinced the Pope that direct contact with Napoleon could effect a change in the Organic Articles and the legislation on marriage and at the same time regulate the worrisome problems which the development of the situation in Germany and Italy posed for the Church. With respect to these issues, the Pope's stay in Paris produced only meager results. But it had useful effects for the Holy See insofar as the former Constituent bishops were finally forced to clear up their situation, a result which in France and Italy was seen as a victory of papal authority. It also gave numerous priests and the faithful, for whom the papacy in the past had been nothing more than an abstract concept, an opportunity to laud a man whose spiritual aura made such a deep impression that this journey saw the beginning of that devotion to the Pope which was to play such a large role in the church history of France during the nineteenth century. The anointment of the Emperor officially confirmed the rejection of the revolutionary ideology; it proclaimed the new alliance between throne and altar, which at that time appeared to most observers as the essential prerequisite for a religious restoration. For this reason the episcopate, followed by a large portion of the clergy, during the next three years increasingly lent the government a hand. Eventually this went so far as to include in the uniform catechism in use in all churches of the French Empire a passage which, under threat of eternal perdition, required from all the faithful "love, respect, obedience, loyalty toward Napoleon, our Emperor, service in the army, and payment of the taxes necessary for the maintenance and defense of the fatherland and its throne."[40]

The loyalty of the French clergy toward the Emperor, which only too frequently degenerated into servility, was shaken after 1808 by the conflict between Napoleon and Pius VII. Gradually such a change occurred in Napoleon's attitude toward the Church that during the last years of his reign one could believe to be back in the sad years of the Directory.

The conflict broke out when war with Europe was renewed. Napoleon, expanding his religious policy to continental dimensions, wanted to use the Pope in western Europe as he used his bishops in France, and wanted to force Pius VII to join him politically and morally. This pretension met categorical rejection because the Pope, as head of the universal Church, wished to maintain a strict neutrality. Convinced that Consalvi was behind the Pope's resistance, Napoleon demanded his dismissal. But Consalvi's resignation (17 June 1806) only strengthened the influence of the reactionaries. In 1807 a number of peremptory demands reached the Pope: Napoleon insisted not only on the Pope's joining an Italian league against "heretical England," but also made unacceptable demands with respect to church policy in Italy, and demanded the inclusion of additional French cardinals into the Sacred College until their number had reached a third of the total. Pius VII, accusing himself of having been too weak in the question of the Organic Articles, the equality of religions,[41] and the imperial catechism, this time did not give in and rejected Napoleon's demands.

[40] The catechism was edited independently from the bishops in the office of the *Direction des Cultes* by Abbé d'Astros and Bernier and personally corrected by Napoleon. To the great dismay of Rome it was accepted by the old legate Caprara, who once again had allowed himself to be outmaneuvered, as well as (with certain reservations) by the entire episcopate. In actuality it was hardly taught and many bishops avoided prescribing it in areas where there was strong resistance. See A. Latreille, *Le catéchisme impérial de 1806* (Paris 1935). In the Belgian departments resistance was almost universal, as their ultramontane sentiments were hurt by a procedure which reminded people of the interventions of Joseph II in ecclesiastical matters. See C. de Clercq: *Annales de la Féderation historique et archéologique de Belgique* 35 (1953), 319–78; id., *SE* 8 (1956), 378–420. On the resistance in Italy see R. Paschini in *RSTI* 17 (1963), 406–12.

[41] A last step in this direction was taken in 1806 when Napoleon decreed the equality of the Jewish with the Catholic and Protestant religions and permitted the reestablishment of the Great Sanhedrin. It is to be noted that Napoleonic policy was not favorable in all

The Emperor now ordered general Miollis to occupy Rome (2 February 1808), but left the Pontiff a faint degree of sovereignty in the hope that he would give in. Pius VII was not intimidated by this massive pressure. Quite the contrary: When fifteen papal officials were deported from Rome, he publicly accused the emperor of enchaining the government of the Church, and replied with the recall of ambassador Caprara from Paris and the refusal to perform the investment of bishops according to the concordat, i.e., by mentioning their nomination by the Emperor. After his secretary of state had also been exiled, he appointed Cardinal Pacca, the best head among the zealots, as his successor. Napoleon did not react immediately. But after his decisive victory over Austria he was firmly convinced that the collapse of Europe's sole remaining large Catholic monarchy had removed the Pope's last support. On 17 May 1809, he annexed the Papal States to France in order to put an end to the "improper combination of secular and spiritual power." On 10 June, as the papal flag was taken down and replaced by the French tricolor, Pius VII answered with the excommunication of all "robbers of Peter's patrimony," without mentioning Napoleon by name. Several weeks of indecisiveness followed. When the occupation forces feared a rebellion of the Roman population, they exceeded the directives of the Emperor[42] and placed the Pope and Cardinal Pacca in a carriage going north. After a hard journey of longer than a month, the Pope was given Savona on the Italian Riviera as residence. There he remained until the beginning of 1812, separated from all advisers and—in spite of the official respect which he was shown—increasingly cut off from contact with the outside world. It was impossible for him to act as Pope, i.e., to concern himself with the affairs of the universal Church.

The French administration concerned itself with the modernization of the Papal States, dividing it into three departments, and closed the foreign colleges, such as the German, the Spanish, and the Irish college. A number of the papal offices were transferred to Paris, where Napoleon intended to move the seat of the papacy as well. In the meantime, the Curia cardinals and the head of orders had to move to the French capital. They were treated at first with respect, but this changed rapidly when, upon the advice of Consalvi, thirteen of them refused to attend the wedding of Napoleon and Marie-Louise, the daughter of the Emperor of Austria. They refused to recognize the nullification of his first

---

points to the Protestants. Those of the Organic Articles applying to them robbed them of an essential element of Calvinistic church organization, the synods. Thus the restoration of the Protestant churches proceeded even slower than that of the Catholic churches. See D. Robert, *Les Églises reformées en France, 1800–30* (Paris 1961), 47–259; R. Anchel, *Napoléon et les Juifs* (Paris 1928).

[42] See H. Aureas, *Un général de Napoléon, Miollis* (Paris 1961), 151–54.

marriage, issued by the Paris office.[43] Napoleon at first prohibited them from wearing their insignias (resulting in the nickname "black cardinals"), then sequestered their possessions, and finally exiled them to the provinces.[44]

As a result of the vigilance of the office of censorship, the mass of the clergy and the faithful in France at first took no notice of the conflict, as it seemed to be a political struggle concerning merely the secular position of the Pope. Thus a vicar general could state to the pastors of Lyon: "The clergy of France lost its possessions, now the Pope lost his. But that did not change religion or his spiritual powers." But after the autumn of 1809, as a result of the activity of clandestine groups of laymen and clergymen,[45] a number of documents found their way into circulation, among them the papal bull of excommunication. Additionally, reports spoke of the inability of the imprisoned Pope to exercise his duties as the head of the Church. The people hostile to the Emperor, especially the members of the royalist opposition, were only too pleased to exploit his break with the papacy, a break which the sanctions against the "black cardinals" made completely evident.

The bishops were afraid that the French Church, so recently recovered, would be drawn into a new conflict with the state, a state which now was much more powerful than at the time of the Directory. At first there was therefore the attempt to still the increasing discontent with the expectation that soon a satisfactory solution would be achieved. Additionally, Gallican traditions and the memory of a similar conflict between Louis XIV and Innocent XI encouraged them not to take the whole matter too seriously. But the tactic of Pius VII to deny the canonical investiture to the bishops nominated by the Emperor eventually forced them to assume a less complacent attitude. By the summer of 1810 there were twenty-seven vacant dioceses and the flocks began to get worried. Some of the new imperially appointed bishops tried to assume their duties without papal investment, but met the opposition of the clergy, which was being seized by ultramontane ideas. When the

[43] The officialate made its decision according to Gallican law and no French bishop criticized it, not even Émery, whom no one could suspect of subservience toward the power of the state. But the Roman teachers of canon law judged differently. See L. Grégoire, *Le "divorce" de Napoléon. Étude du dossier canonique* (Paris 1957).

[44] See U. Beseghi, *I tredici cardinali neri* (Florence 1944). Also G. de Grandmaison, *Napoléon et les cardinaux noirs* (Paris 1895) and V. Bindel, *Le Vatican à Paris 1809–14* (Paris, no date).

[45] Mainly the "Congrégation de Lyon" and the "Aa" of the Sulpician seminaries. J. Verrier in *RHE* 54 (1959), 71–121, 453–91 shows the great role played by the Lyon layman F. D. Aynès in the spreading of these documents, and C. Bona, *Le "Amicizie"* (Turin 1962), describes the activity of the Turin group of Pio Lanteri.

Chapter of Paris under the influence of Vicar General d'Astros refused to reassign the administration of the diocese to Cardinal Maury, popular opinion was strongly impressed.[46] When several probes elicited no response from the Pope, Napoleon had no choice but to follow the advice of the committee of theologians, which he consulted in the matter. Their advice was to convoke a national council, which in view of the special circumstances was to decide to return to the "earlier custom" of investment of bishops by the metropolitan bishop. One hundred forty French, Italian, and German bishops participated in this council, which opened on 17 June 1811, in Paris.[47] Although a good number of the participants regarded the tactics of Pius VII as exaggerated, the council proved itself much more recalcitrant than had been expected. It stated that a council decree would not be possible without the agreement of the Pope. Napoleon was angry and imprisoned the three bishops leading the opposition.[48] But in actuality all of the bishops, even the most Gallican among them, after the experience with the revolution, refused to take the path toward a schism again. They understood full well that this time they would encounter the resistance of a large part of the lower clergy and of militant laymen, who were increasingly worried about the course of events.

After this attempt had failed, Napoleon tried to master the situation through political chicanery against the priests and against the Sulpicians, who were made responsible for the ultramontane behavior of the young clergy. After his return from Russia, he tried to force the Pope to give in. The Pope meanwhile had been brought to Fontainebleau and, after several days of angry negotiations, completely weakened by illness, agreed on 25 January 1813 to sign the draft of a convention which in essential points corresponded to the demands of the Emperor. Although the agreement was to remain secret and to serve merely as the basis for a final settlement, the Emperor published it immediately under the name of Concordat of Fontainebleau. But three days later the Pope decided to recant his act of weakness[49] and on 25 March wrote a long

[46] See G. de Bertier in *RHEF* 35 (1949), 49–58.

[47] The inadequate work by A. Ricard, *Le concile de 1811* (Paris 1894), has not yet been supplanted. See in addition to A. Latreille, op. cit. 214–25 and *RH* 194 (1944), 1–22, J.-B. Vanell, "Le concile de 1811 d'après les papiers du cardinal Fesch" in *Bulletin d'histoire du diocèse de Lyon* (1912/13) and V. Bindel, *Le Vatican à Paris* (Paris, no date).

[48] These were Mgr. de Boulogne, bishop of Troyes, Mgr. de Broglie, bishop of Ghent, and Mgr. Hirn, bishop of Tournai. The last two had allowed themselves to be influenced by the very ultramontane views of their clergy.

[49] This was proved by L. Pásztor: *ChStato* II, 597–606. See the text of the draft of Fontainebleau in Mercati I, 579–81 and the letter of Pius VII of 23 March 1813, id. 581–85.

letter to the Emperor. Napoleon pretended that he was unaware of the letter and celebrated the reconciliation between Church and state with religious services of praise and thanksgiving.

There was no doubt that the time of the concordat was over. Napoleon's conduct toward the spiritual power deeply angered the Catholic conscience. Catholics became increasingly excited and agitated, especially by an extraordinarily active secret society, the "Chevaliers de la foi," recruited from the ranks of congregations. This secret society was founded in May 1810 by a royalist nobleman, F. de Bertier, with the double objective of returning to the Pope his freedom and secular power and restoring the monarchy.[50] These "Knights of the Faith" accepted the views of Abbé Barruel on the freemasonic origins of the revolution,[51] and were largely responsible for convincing French Catholics that their faith was severely endangered as long as they had a government inspired by the principles of the Revolution. This secret propaganda actively prepared the Catholics to connect the cause of religion with the restoration of the Bourbons. The quickly flaring fire of anticlericalism accompanying Napoleon's Hundred Days completely stiffened the attitude of those who, after the disappointments of the final years of Napoleon's domination, saw the salvation of the Church solely in the triumph of counterrevolution. This was the negative aspect of this collision between wordly and spiritual power, and for several generations was to be a heavy burden for French Catholics. For the papacy it had a double advantage. For one, the problem of the freedom of the Church and the neutrality of the Holy See was posed for the whole world as a problem of international policy. For another, the fact that the papacy had had the courage to defy the tyrant when all other governments bowed before him, lent the papacy a moral prestige of which the governments of the subsequent generation had to take account.

Southern Europe

A large part of Italy did not belong to the French state, even though it was under the control of French armies. In this part the concordat of 1801 was, of course, not applied.

In the north, the former Cisalpine Republic was reorganized as the Italian Republic. Napoleon, aware that its population was even fonder

[50] See G. de Bertier, *Le comte F. de Bertier* (Paris 1948); Also A. Saitta in *RSIt* 62 (1950), 124–33.

[51] On the origin and the success of this thesis see chapter 1, footnote 5.

of its religion than the French,[52] in Article 1 of the new constitution recognized Catholicism as the established religion, much to the dismay of the local Jacobins. Allowing for the influence which the clergy had retained for itself, he appointed a committee of clerics—and not lay jurists as in France—under the leadership of Cardinal Bellisomi for the purpose of preparing the "Organic Law for the Clergy of the Italian Republic" (27 January 1802). In part, this law was modeled on the French concordat, but, in a whole series of points, was more favorable to the Church. It maintained the jurisdiction of the clergy in marriages, cathedral chapters and seminaries received subsidies, and Church lands not yet employed for other purposes were restored. Napoleon desired the confirmation of this law through a concordat with the Holy See. The negotiations in Paris between Cardinal Caprara and the Italian Republic's emissary dragged on for longer than a year, because in the meantime Vice-President Melzi d'Eril had passed a decree of pure Josephine inspiration (23 June 1802), subordinating almost every ecclesiastical activity to the power of the state. Pius VII expressly demanded the cancellation of the decree in the text of the concordat. A compromise formulation was eventually adopted, and the concordat was signed on 16 September 1803.[53] It was even more favorable for the Church than the Organic Law of 1802.

A severe disappointment was in store, though. On 24 January 1804, Melzi published an implementation order, which put in question several important gains. Not only did it enact a portion of the republican church regulations preceding the concordat—thus violating it—but also declared the government of the republic to be the successor to the rights of the former duke of Milan. In practical terms this amounted to the reintroduction of the Josephine laws in effect before the revolution. Strong protests of the Holy See had no immediate effect. But when in 1805 the republic, through the inclusion of Venetia, was changed into the Kingdom of Italy, Napoleon with his decree of 22 May 1805 lifted the Melzi order of 1804. In the following month several steps were taken, which on a disciplinary and financial level regulated the clergy, dissolved a number of monasteries, and reduced the number of parishes in order to increase the subsidies for the remaining ones. These steps on the whole were sensible and were received well by the clergy. But their unilateral character caused new Roman protests. The extension of the

[52] Which was not to say that everything was satisfactory. In June 1809 the bishop of Vercelli wrote: "A good third of the faithful no longer performs its Easterly obligations, especially since the revolution."
[53] Mercati I, 565–72.

concordat of 1803 and the laws resulting from it to Venetia without prior consultation also were protested, because these laws introduced the secularization of institutions to another area of the Italian peninsula. The introduction of the French civil code, and therefore of divorce, also raised objections from the Holy See. In the following years tensions between Rome and Milan increased. In October 1806 Pius VII began to deny investment to the bishops nominated by Napoleon for Italy, justifying it with the violation of the concordat. The introduction of the imperial catechism in Italy during 1807 occasioned additional polemics, just as did the inclusion of the Papal States in the Kingdom.[54] But the heightening tensions between Pope and Emperor soon moved the focus of conflict to France.

The situation in the other Italian states was hardly more satisfying for the Roman Curia. The only exception was Tuscany which had become the Kingdom of Etruria. Bishop Scipione de' Ricci completely subordinated himself to the Pope and the new King, Louis of Parma, in a way which was particularly favorable to Rome, thereby restoring almost total freedom to the Church. In 1802 the first Catholic journal in the nineteenth century was founded[55] in Florence as the organ of the militant Catholic group of the "Amicizie." Yet the objections of the French embassy and the incorporation of the Etrurian Kingdom in the French Empire after the battle of Austerlitz put a quick stop to the hopes of the Holy See, which after 1808 also had to suffer the dissolution of all monasteries.

In the Duchy of Parma and the Republic of Lucca the interference of the civil authorities with ecclesiastical matters caused Pius VII to protest repeatedly. But it was in vain, especially as the clergy, even before annexation, showed itself very subservient.

In the Kingdom of Naples, the negotiations toward a concordat foundered, in part because of Acton's refusal to give up the old Josephinistic laws, and in part because of the refusal of Pius VII to reduce the number of dioceses from 131 (in a population of five million!) to 50. When Napoleon's brother Joseph succeeded King Ferdinand in 1805, he at once began a radical reform of the Church, which until then had

[54] Bishops at first and then hundreds of priests refused to take the oath. See G. Cornaggia-Medici, "Una pagina di politica del Regno italico. Il giuramento di fedeltà dei vescovi dei dipartimenti del Metauro, Musone et Tronto (1808)," *Archivio storico lombardo* 41 (1934), 169–222; L. Madelin, *La Rome de Napoléon* (Paris 1906), 330–45, 435–53; A. Mercati in *RSTI* 7 (1953), 51–96. Other problems were raised by the dissolution of the monasteries. See C. A. Naselli, *La soppressione napoleonica delle corporazioni religiose. Il caso dei passionisti* (Rome 1970).

[55] "Ape" under active collaboration of Cesare d'Azeglio. Cf. C. Bona, *Le "Amicizie"* (Turin 1962), 248–52.

retained its Old Regime character. For ideological and primarily financial reasons, all abbeys and priories as well as a large portion of the houses of the mendicant orders[56] were dissolved between August 1806 and August 1809, beginning with the wealthiest. The secular clergy also was the objective of several steps designed to reduce the excessively high number of clergymen (there was one priest for every eight hundred inhabitants, and many priests lived in degrading circumstances). A considerable reduction of the number of dioceses was also planned, but diplomatic and military events as well as internal disturbances kept Joseph's successor, King Murat, so busy that he had no time left to pursue the plan. Additionally, Napoleon's violent conduct toward the Pope and other reform measures so alienated the clergy that now its secret opposition, just as effective as hard to defeat, stirred up the latent hostility of the population against the French.

Revolutionary ideas had not nearly the same success in Spain as in Italy. The reason was in part the strength of the political unity of the country at this time, in part the still strong influence of the Church and the power of the Inquisition.[57] Yet Spain was the only Catholic state which throughout the storms maintained cordial relations with revolutionary France. Godoy, King Charles IV's favorite, even based his foreign policy on the alliance with France. This also explains why Monsignor Despuig, the official representative of Spain, worked together with France during the conclave of Venice leading to the election of Pius VII.

Thus the last years of the eighteenth century did not mean for Spain, as they did for France, Italy, and Germany, the end of the Church of the Old Regime. Nevertheless, the church policy of the Spanish government created some concern for the Holy See. On one hand Madrid had the not unjustified impression that secular interests, especially Avignon and the Papal States, occupied the Pope and his advisers more than religious problems. It did not hide the opinion that the Church would gain enormously if the Pope were to renounce his secular power in order to become a purely spiritual force. On the other hand, the old claims of the government to deal with ecclesiastical matters independently from Rome, and the episcopal leanings of a part of the clergy,

[56] See P. Villani in *RStRis* 44 (1957), 508–13. Ultimately more than eleven hundred monasteries were sold and the proportion of real property owned by the clergy sank from 26 percent at the end of the eighteenth century to 13 percent in 1815. See also U. Caldora, *Calabria napoleonica* (Naples 1960).

[57] See R. Herr, *The Eighteenth-Century Revolution in Spain* (Princeton 1958). The bishops tried everything to prevent the incursion of revolutionary ideas. Even the emigrated French priests were looked upon with suspicion and carefully kept separate under surveillance. On the Spanish Inquisition at the end of the eighteenth century, see F. Marti Gilabert, op. cit., 155–90.

freshly fueled by the recent influence of Italian Jansenism, were strengthened by the political developments after 1797 in Italy. After all, it was not at all clear how the centralized system was to continue to function in the area of ecclesiastical appointments to benefices and the granting of dispensations, once Rome had come under French control and the Roman Curia was completely disorganized. For this reason—and not because of freemasonic and Jacobin influence as Menendez Pelayo asserted—M. L. de Urquijo with the support of the Jansenists started campaigning for a return to the old church discipline. He utilized the vacancy of Saint Peter's after the death of Pius VI to publish a decree by J. Espiga, a member of the Spanish Rota, on 5 September 1799, which transferred the right of dispensation of marriages from the Roman congregation to the Spanish bishops.

This decree was declared void immediately after the elevation of Pius VII because of the resistance of the majority of the Spanish clergy and the pangs of conscience of the King, and Urquijo was pushed aside. But in the following years Godoy wrested from the King a number of measures which limited the influence of the nuncio and the Inquisition and obtained from Rome the authorization to dispose of certain Church lands and to subordinate the orders more to the King. The orders were in fact a serious problem for the Church, for in 1797 there were no fewer than 53,098 monks and 24,471 nuns, approximately 1 percent of the population, with signs of decadence visible everywhere. Godoy succeeded in having the young Cardinal Luis de Borbon, who was sympathetic to his plans, put in charge of visiting all of the more than two thousand Spanish monasteries. After a rather superficial inquiry he had the King submit plans to the Pope on 30 May 1803, with the purpose of strengthening the supervision of the monasteries by the bishops and of obtaining for the mendicant orders, which constituted 84 percent of all monasteries, virtual independence from their superiors in Rome. After more than one year of negotiations the Spanish government was ready to reduce some of its demands, but the papal Bull *Inter graviores* of 15 May 1804 was still a satisfactory arrangement.[58]

After Napoleon had substituted his brother Joseph as King of Spain[59] for the dynasty of the Bourbons in 1808, the French administration backed the interests of the old Spanish royal prerogatives. They were represented at court by the expert in canon law, J. A. Llorente,[60] and by

[58] See chapter 12, footnote 8.

[59] Catalonia was incorporated into France. In 1811 the bishops retreated to Mallorca under the protection of the British fleet.

[60] See *EEAm* XXXI, 1063–65 and Schulte III, 766–67.

Urquijo, who again had become Minister. Consequently the interventions of the government in the ecclesiastical sphere multiplied. The court of the Inquisition was immediately dissolved and the estates of the confraternities were put up for sale. The decree of 1799 on the granting of dispensations from marriages was immediately reinstituted on 16 November 1809, even though this measure could be implemented only partially, owing to the revolt which, depending on the region, lasted until the return of King Ferdinand VII in December 1813. Napoleon contemptuously called it a monkish rebellion, but in actuality it was the consequence of the tremendous dissatisfaction which the French occupation caused in the economic, social, and political areas. Undeniably it was the religious factor which gave the resistance its special flavor. Only a few prelates such as Cardinal de Borbon, archbishop of Toledo, and the archbishop of Saragossa initially supported Joseph Bonaparte in the hope that the French administration would at long last modernize the worm-eaten structures of Church and state. The majority of the episcopate, which since 1790 had castigated the revolution as the work of Satan, played a significant role in the rebellious juntas, which called upon the very religious people to rise simultaneously for the liberation of the country and the preservation of the orthodoxy and purity of their religion. The papal bull of excommunication of July 1809 strengthened the campaign against "atheistic France." Many monasteries became centers of resistance, and numerous priests and monks, not satisfied with stoking the religious fanaticism of their flocks, frequently fought together with the guerrillas.

In liberated Spain the central junta, residing at first in Seville, cancelled the measures for the confiscation of Church lands and reintroduced the Inquisition on 28 December 1808. Even the old Jesuits were permitted to return. But during the work on the constitution by the Cortes of Cádiz in March 1812, the enlightened minority, which in no way should be identified with the adherents of French revolutionary ideas, carried the day over the traditionalist majority. They were supported by Jansenist clergymen like Joaquín Villanueva,[61] who desired a thorough overhaul of church law. They did not dare go so far as a civil constitution of the clergy, but fell back on a strengthened version of Godoy's policy. In the face of financial difficulties, the bishops did not dare protest against the economic measures, such as the collection of certain taxes and confiscation of certain church lands by the state, or the decision to close about one thousand monasteries with too few members. Although the occupation of a part of the area made collective action impossible,

[61] See J. S. Boa, *Doctrina canónica del doctor Villanueva* (Vitoria 1957).

the bishops, especially those of the north,[62] reacted sharply against the introduction of freedom of the press and against the declaration of the incompatibility of the court of the Inquisition with the liberal principles of the constitution. It must also be noted, however, that a portion of the episcopate reacted less hostilely to the demands of the civil power for independence from the Holy See, and that about one-half of the bishops sided with Cardinal de Borbon in the jurisdictional struggles which he carried on with Nuncio Gravina after 1809. The opposition reached its peak when the Primate and the government demanded the right to fill seats made vacant by death[63] as long as the Pope was Napoleon's prisoner. Ultimately, the nuncio was expelled in April 1813 and resided in Portugal until the restoration of Ferdinand VII.

[62] It must be remembered that in view of the chaotic conditions of the country many decisions of the Cortes of Cádiz remained dead letters outside of Andalusia and a few large cities.

[63] In 1813, sixteen sees, a quarter of the total, were vacant.

PART TWO

The Catholic Church and the Restoration

To a much more marked degree than at the election of Pius VII, the Church, now faced with a new Europe erected by the counterrevolutionary movement upon the ruins of the Napoleonic Empire and still deeply marked by the modern ideas which contemporaries termed "liberalism," had to begin a reconstruction. Pius VII concerned himself with this task immediately after his return to Rome in May 1814. With the increasing assistance of the brilliant Consalvi,[1] whom he reappointed as secretary of state, and supported by a religious renascence which had grown spontaneously in various countries, the Pope devoted the final nine years of his pontificate to laying a solid foundation for the rapid rise of the Church. His activity, on the spiritual level more than in the political sphere, determined the history of the Church in the first half of the nineteenth century.

The effort of Pius VII and his successor Leo XII toward the reorganization of the Church was the prerequisite for the revival of Catholic vitality.

Only Austria, Spain, and Portugal had not been affected by the French Revolution and therefore experienced no essential alterations of their ecclesiastical structures. In all other countries it was necessary to adjust dioceses to the new political boundaries, to rebuild ecclesiastical institutions, and to restore the almost extinct orders and patrimony of the Church. The conditions for this restoration differed in the individual countries. In France, the basic structure of the Church was already in line with the new conditions, even though religious policy had a changed orientation after the return of the Bourbons. In Germany, the Netherlands, and Italy, the spread of French ideas and secularizations had resulted in a profound shock, and for the Church there were also important territorial changes to which it had to adjust. In Great Britain, the growth of liberal ideas was used for the liberation of the Irish Catholics from their oppressed condition. In Russia, the new situation, created at the end of the eighteenth century by the inclusion of several

[1] See chapter 2, footnote 3.

million Polish Catholics into an Orthodox state, had to be negotiated with an autocratic ruler. Overseas there were serious problems as well. The declarations of independence in Spanish America required a new approach to the status of the Church, which heretofore had been dependent on Spanish patronage. With respect to the Near East, which had come much closer to the Occident psychologically in the course of the Napoleonic wars, the Holy See desired to establish closer ties with the Uniate patriarchs. Even the missionary apostolate had been compelled to acknowledge the result of the changes in Europe and was in need of a reconstruction.

Consalvi deplored the fact that an overwhelming number of cardinals in Rome were engaged in the restoration of the Papal States and the German ecclesiastical states and, therefore, must neglect the regulation of religious problems. During the Congress of Vienna[2] he negotiated future concordats with the representatives of Austria, Bavaria, Prussia, Württemberg, Switzerland, Russia, and France, and had discussions with Lord Castlereagh about the situation of the English Catholics. These were among the first achievements of an ecclesiastical restoration for which he labored untiringly until his death. It was a huge and difficult task, aggravated by the previous isolation in captivity of Pope and Curia. Thus, the major task was to regain firm control of the administration of the Church and to reconfirm papal authority.

[2] On the Holy See and the Congress of Vienna, consult I. Rinieri, *Il Congresso di Vienna e la Santa Sede* (Rome 1904); id., *Corrispondenza inedita dei cardinali Consalvi e Pacca nel tempo del Congresso di Vienna* (Turin 1903); A. Omodeo, *Aspetti del cattolicesimo della Restaurazione* (Turin 1946), 81–180; E. Ruch, *Die römische Kurie und die deutsche Kirchenfrage auf dem Wiener Kongress* (Basel 1917); Mollat, 102–27; *La missione Consalvi e il Congresso di Vienna*, ed. by A. Roveri, I (Rome 1970).

SECTION ONE

The Reorganization of the Churches

CHAPTER 3

The Catholic Church after the Congress of Vienna

The *orbis catholicus* in 1815

Until the end of the Napoleonic era, the Catholic Church, in spite of earlier missionary successes, remained in essence a European church, defined by the urban areas of Vienna-Naples-Cádiz-Brussels.

In Africa only a few missionary settlements were left in Senegal and Angola, and the number of Uniate Copts in the Nile valley had sunk to a few thousand. The number of believers in other Uniate patriarchates in the Near East was hardly higher, the only exception being the approximately two hundred thousand Maronites in Lebanon.[3] India numbered about one hundred thousand Catholics of the Eastern rite and fifty thousand of the Latin rite. In East Asia there were, aside from the Philippines, where a majority of the 1.5 million inhabitants were Catholic, and Annam with four hundred thousand Christians and 180 priests, only a few tens of thousands of Christians in China and Japan, who were virtually cut off from contact with Rome because of persecution.

Even the American churches constituted only a relatively small contingent in numerical terms. In North America there were barely two hundred thousand Catholics among the French-Canadians and in the United States only one hundred fifty thousand. Among the 15 to 18 million inhabitants of Latin America, most of whom were concentrated around the Antilles, many Indians and Mestizos had become Christian in name only.

In Europe in 1815 there were about 100 million Catholics, compared to 40 million Orthodox, 30 million Protestants, 9 million Anglicans, and a few million Mohammedans and Jews. Of the 100 million Catholics, more than 60 percent lived in three countries relatively untouched by the Industrial Revolution and in which the clergy, in spite of the increas-

[3] Precise statistics for this period do not exist, hence only magnitudes can be indicated.

ing importance of urbanization, continued to reflect mainly the values of their agrarian congregations. France numbered 28.5 million Catholics and seven hundred thousand Protestants; Spain had 10 million, and in the Habsburg Empire there were 24 million Catholics (about 80 percent of the population). The distribution of influence among these three Catholic states had changed since 1789. For a time, defeated France was forced to lay aside its claim to hegemony in Europe. Austria became the leading power and, of particular importance for Roman policy, gained a strong influence over Italy. In addition to Lombardy, Austria had also acquired Venetia and Liguria and exercised undisguised hegemony over the duchies of central Italy. After the treaty of Laibach (1821), this was also true with respect to the Kingdom of Naples. Spain, weakened by Napoleonic wars, dynastic quarrels, and the secession of its American colonies, lost much of its ecclesiastical importance. In fact, for the immediate future, only Austria and France remained great Catholic powers, engaged primarily in rivalries with one another.

Of the remaining 40 million Catholics, 14 million lived in the seven independent Italian states, 3 million in Portugal (which lost Brazil in 1822), nearly 3 million in Bavaria, and 4 million (out of a total of 6 million inhabitants) in the Kingdom of the Netherlands. The remaining 16 million Catholics constituted minorities in the non-Catholic states: among these were 4 million in Prussia, 1.5 million in the other German states, 4.5 million in Ireland, which was part of the United Kingdom of Great Britain, 3 million in Russian Poland, seven hundred fifty thousand in Switzerland, and five hundred thousand in Turkey.

The new distribution of Catholics which resulted from the changes in borders after the Congress of Vienna was not a satisfactory situation for the Holy See. The papacy noted with great sadness the dissolution of the ecclesiastical principalities in Germany, a dissolution which it had not been able to prevent. The shift in Catholic population centers resulted in the subordination of several million Catholics to Protestant princes and, compared with the Old Regime, resulted in a marked increase in the number of states with mixed religions. The Holy See also regretted the incorporation of Belgian Catholics into a state with Protestant leadership and the continuing subjugation of Polish Catholics by an Orthodox autocracy. Rome was further disturbed that a papal diplomatic inquiry concerning the sad lot of Christians in the Ottoman Empire remained unanswered. Finally, the influence of the powerful Habsburg Empire, whose church policy was still marked by Josephinism, over the old republics of Genoa and Venice, could hardly find approval in Rome, where Italian problems were always regarded with special concern.

Problems and Alternatives for the Catholic Church

The problems of adjusting the ecclesiastical geography following the shifts in state boundaries were neither the only nor the most difficult ones facing the Church. At the conclusion of a crisis which had lasted a quarter of a century, a new beginning had to be made in almost every area. For a certain group, called "ultras" in France, but with adherents to be found everywhere, the solution to the problem of reconstruction consisted simply of the destruction of the revolution and its results and the restoration of the order of yesterday. These groups wanted to reintroduce the Old Regime out of a double justification of legitimacy and counterrevolution. But was such a program possible or even desirable?

It is surprising to see that the so-called new institutions of administration, justice, finances, economics, and the military, encompassing more nominal than real changes, retained those forms which the French had given them. Where this form was destroyed, it was often restored a few years later as a result of revolutionary risings. In many instances, these new institutions were copied by countries which had not experienced a French occupation. These institutions were the juridical realization of an economic and social development which was unavoidable and irreversible. The development occurred in the individual countries rather quickly, and brought with it the destruction of the Old Regime and the creation of a new society of the bourgeoisie, which embodied the new tendencies and which was to play the predominant role for the next century.

Parallel to the social changes, there also took place a transformation of ideas, a development of far greater significance from the religious viewpoint. Was it not senseless to use police powers to attempt to turn back the clock for those who had absorbed the concepts of liberty and equality? Was the revolution really only an event brought about by violence or did one not have to recognize in it the result of a development reaching back to the Renaissance? Was it intelligent to try to reverse the wheel of history? Were these new tendencies wrong, or were there not beyond all the errors and excesses some basic values to be fostered? Pius VII had discussed this concept in his Christmas homily of 1797 on Christianity and democracy while he was still bishop of Imola. But only few of the men of 1815, having been victims of the painful experiences of the past, were prepared to pursue such a path. Totally misinterpreting the social and economic roots of the revolution, most believed to have found the explanation for it in the liberation of satanic forces. They preferred to long for what they called the golden days of Christianity in the past; an attitude which for decades was to support the reactionary stance of a majority of the Catholic clergy. Many a time it was acknowledged that the Old Regime had not been only good for the Church. In the Catholic countries it meant Gallicanism and Josephinism, among other evils, and such principles remained vital even in the Austria of Metternich, the France of the Bourbons, in Spain, and in the Kingdom of Naples in which the reaction triumphed.

Thus it became clear very quickly that the religious counterrevolution, in spite of the theses proclaimed by such lay theoreticians as Haller and Bonald, was, in fact, not identical with the political counterrevolution. This discrepancy became visible when Pius VII restored the Society of Jesus despite the disapproving attitude of most of the governments and rejected a proposal to join the Holy Alliance. Even if the Holy Alliance was undoubtedly inspired by a greater religiosity than historians have been willing to admit,[4] it nevertheless stemmed from an understanding of Christianity which was too little oriented toward the institutional not to cause the Roman authorities grave concern. The Holy See could not conceive of states in which the Church did not occupy a central position, and it was afraid to become involved in political plans whose originators believed in regalism.

The most fervent propagandists for revolutionary ideas were and remained the adherents of the philosophers of the eighteenth century, and as such declared enemies of the Church. Wherever the revolution had been successful, the Church had had to suffer. Was not, therefore, the expectation of advantages from a compromise with the revolution a game of self-deception? The dilemma which was to come into focus more dramatically during the nineteenth century was sketched only in vague outlines in 1815, and even circles advocating concessions limited to secondary aspects of the liberal demands saw in them merely a policy of the lesser evil. The rancor of the many victims of revolutionary unrest combined with the conviction that there existed a fundamental contradiction between the two dominant ideologies. Intitially this led Catholic laymen and clergy almost without exception to the side of counterrevolution. Their only uncertainty was whether the counterrevolution was to be conducted implacably or with a limited tactical flexibility.

Aside from this fundamental ideological decision, there also remained problems of a practical nature. In numerous countries the Church had lost the majority of its property. While the impoverishment was advantageous as a kind of purification, it created the problem of

[4] See also E. Susini, *L'Allemagne religieuse au XIXe siècle* (Cours de Sorbonne 1959/60) I, 97–107.

how to finance seminaries, schools, charitable institutions, and apostolic organizations. In Rome as almost everywhere, the ecclesiastical administration was in shambles, archives dispersed, and communications disrupted. Furthermore, the clergy in many countries had not only lost its privileged position, but in many areas had suffered also from a diminished interest among young people. The problem of successors became acute. The religious orders, always a valuable apostolic tool, also suffered acutely.

Far-reaching regeneration was imperative. But, as has been stated, the Revolution had disturbed minds even more than administrations. Spread by officials of the French Empire and its military throughout Europe, the new ideas had shaken the foundations of the traditional social and political order and had intensified a crisis of European conscience which had been developing for a century. The Church through its clergy still had a firm grip on the rural populations, as had been demonstrated by the revolts in the Vendée, the peasants' war in Belgium, the rising of the Neapolitan Sanfedists, the Spanish resistance, and the Tirolean rebellion. However, the young intellectuals had been awakened. Liberated suddenly from the strict control which the Inquisition and the censorship of books had exercised over them, many intellectuals had gone to the opposite extreme. Many crises of conscience were helped along also by the general laxity of morals. The task, therefore, consisted not merely of reopening monasteries and churches, but of healing souls.

Fortunately, the Church possessed several means with which to accomplish its enormous task. In addition to the spiritual advantage which the Church had gained through the secularization of its property, Catholicism could now count on the active support of the public purse. In addition, sovereigns as well as governments were one in believing that the altar provided the best protection for a throne and that the Church ought to have a place of priority among the institutions to be restored. Inasmuch as the institutions which served to maintain religion for the masses were of the utmost importance, the Church, at least for the moment, experienced enormous gain from the benevolent attitude of the state. A dangerous aspect for the Church of this common cause with the reactionary elements was that the young and dynamic elements among Catholics might be irretrievably driven to the ideas of the revolution. In the atmosphere of the moment, however, when upper and lower classes were still under the impact of the terrors of the revolutionary time, it was not easy to take account of the influence which these young elements would have in the future. The clergy's ability to look into the future was dimmed by the deceptive expectation of creating a new Christian society with the aid of counterrevolutionary governments and by the immediate advantage which this help constituted in the area of pastoral care and the rapid restoration of ecclesiastical foundations.

The signs of religious revival, evident in France after the end of Napoleon's reign, now became visible in all countries. This was a universal phenomenon; reversions to the faith on the Catholic side were mirrored in the Protestant world by revival movements. From both directions voices were raised calling for an alliance of all Christians against the propagators of the Enlightenment. The disorder of the past twenty years had made many people look toward religion for consolation and to doubt the validity of the rationalistic ideology which they held responsible for past catastrophes. Everywhere people turned away from the modern ideas of progress and back toward a tradition rooted in the Catholic Middle Ages. The influence of this return to tradition was felt even in Protestant circles, where a series of spectacular conversions to Roman Catholicism took place.

The shift in the intellectual climate, caused by the French counterrevolutionary thinkers, was intensified by the spreading of romanticism. The most deadly weapon against the Church had been its derogation by the aesthetes, who presented religion and especially Catholicism as marks of intellectual mediocrity and of obscurantism. But now, artists and writers, led by Chateaubriand in France, Stolberg in Germany, Schlegel in Austria, and Manzoni in Italy, praised Christianity as guarantor of high culture and Catholic rites as the fertile source of artistic inspiration. The romantic movement was not free of religious imperfections. It fostered immorality and uncritical raptures and thus was distrusted by many clergymen. Furthermore, even in the guise of Catholic romanticism, it frequently exchanged the Christian faith for pseudomysticism and a vague religiosity determined more by feeling than intellect. Romanticism was also ill-suited to deal with the problems of positivism which soon were to characterize the nineteenth century. But for the moment the Church had found powerful support in the change of mentality which led spirits from the progressive rationalism of the Enlightenment to mysticism and the heritage of medieval traditions.

These problems faced the entire Church, but especially Rome where the principles had to be determined which would govern not only the conduct of the Church in general, but the restoration of secular conditions in the Papal States in particular. In 1825 the Roman Curia was of divided mind in this matter.

One group, led by Consalvi, who were called "liberals" in a denigrating fashion by their opponents, wished to use chiefly political means to achieve the desired Catholic restoration. Its members possessed that awareness of realities which is needed for effective political action. The group considered it advantageous to keep an open mind toward some of the modern tendencies or at least not to oppose them too openly as long as the faith was not affected. Aware of the benefits which the Church could derive from the benevolent attitude of officials, these politically oriented men also exercised moderation in their relations with governments, preferring a cautious stance or even partial concession in the questions of juridical claims, if this price would assure good relations.

They encountered the determined opposition of the large majority of cardinals and prelates who were absolutely hostile to modern philosophy and all modern institutions. These churchmen favored political absolutism and return to an established religion. Simultaneously, they also wanted to see a Church free from any influence of the government and without any interference in the exercise of its doctrine and its apostolic mission.

This group of zealots, led by the aged Cardinal Pacca, consisted of conservatives who psychologically and sociologically were tied to the old customs and privileges and who placed their trust more in power and force than in admonitions and the peaceful power of clemency and tolerance. Many historians have made the mistake of seeing them only in this light. In actuality, they were driven much more by religious considerations than by reactionary attitudes; unpretentious men whose piety sometimes turned into bigotry, their chief interest was pastoral care, and they were uncompromising in moral matters and unshakeable in questions of faith. The group believed that the modern spirit of the liberals was basically nothing more than a continuation of the principles of the Protestant Reformation and that any, even the smallest, concession would invite heresy. In their attempt to shape society according to the dictates of religion, they were convinced that ecclesiastical power which represented God on earth stood above that of the princes, the servants of God and his Church. They also firmly believed that the victory of the true religion, if it was to be brought about by men of weak faith using diplomacy, would require the aid of providence. Therefore they preferred to look to the religious orders for assistance rather than to those clerics who had too much contact with the world. Finally, they saw no benefits arising from the compromises which the Church had made with the new ideas of the eighteenth century and thought an uncompromising attitude more appropriate. With the superior assurance of those who tend to see in human affairs merely the supernatural in action, they assumed an unyielding stance to all who did not think as they did. These zealots regarded the modernists as traitors to their religion and some went so far as to call them Freemasons.[5]

With the passing of the years, two subgroups formed within the camp of these uncompromising opponents to liberalism and religious Gallicanism; a split which was similar to a gap between generations. The proponents of one position remained essentially persons of the eighteenth century. Fixed in their fearful rejection of Jansenism and democratic Jacobinism and defenders of a total return to an idealized past, they saw a solution in a closer cooperation between princes and ecclesiastical authorities, with the princes absolutely subordinate to the Church. The adherents of the second position, involved as they were with the beginnings of the new ultramontane movement, did not hesitate to recommend the employment of some modern methods for the realization of their ideal. Disappointed by the insistent jurisdictionalism of the courts, and out of their knowledge of the support the masses had given the Church in its struggle against Napoleon, they favored an active Christian policy for regaining lost ground. Their plan would include a popular base and would make more use of the press and of lay organizations than of the powers of the police in addressing consciences directly and inculcating true principles as a foundation for the restoration of a society in the Christian spirit.[6]

The Three Restoration Popes

Pius VII was a religious person with a spiritual power which reached far beyond the limits of the Church. In the performance of his apostolic duties he was extremely conscientious. He showed an understanding for the concerns of the zealots and did not hesitate to hurl new condemnations against the Freemasons, who[7] in his eyes personified the incarnation of antichristian philosophy. The Pope also warned of the Bible societies,[8] whose Protestant origins made them suspect of spreading indifferentism. Cleverly and tactfully he tried to reestablish close relations between Rome and the clergy of the different countries. He was also concerned with reviving expressions of religious life. Where he could, Pius VII fostered the organization of parish missions and looked into the devotions of the clergy. Through the granting of indulgences,

[5] See V. Giuntella, "Profilo di uno zelante, Mgr. B. Gazzola" in *RstRis* (1956), 413–18.

[6] See R. Colapietra, op. cit. 36–55, 240–41, 247, 255–56.

[7] Bull of 21 September 1821 (*BullRomCont* XV, 446–48).

[8] Briefs of 29 June and 3 September 1816 (*ASS* IX, 580–87).The first Catholic Bible society was founded in 1805 in Regensburg by seminary regent Wittmann. On the influence of the conditions in Poland and Russia on the condemnation, see Boudou I, 110–123.

he encouraged the formation of confraternities and called for processions and pilgrimages. He increased the number of Marian feasts and began new sanctification processes in the conviction that the heroic virtues of the saints would inspire the simple believer to imitation. The Pope's abilities were evident from the beginning of his pontificate. Among his many strengths were his comprehensive education and alert intelligence, combined with a conciliatory spirit; his mistrust of systematicians; his sense for appropriate judgments, which enabled him to recognize essential points and to champion them while neglecting inconsequential details; and his realism which enabled him in spite of his respect for tradition to accept the good aspects of modern institutions. With respect to the administration of the Papal States and the orientation of religious policy in different countries, Pius VII agreed with the direction favored by Consalvi, and after Pius had reached the age of seventy he left these matters frequently to this cardinal. The strength of the Pope's personality was far greater, though, than has often been asserted, and his mind was also open to other currents of the times. When he thought it required by the interests of religion, he was capable of intervening in a way which often made the work of Consalvi much more difficult.

Supported by the confidence of his sovereign and enjoying the high reputation which his wide and moderate opinions had won him even among non-Catholic politicians, between 1815 and 1823 Consalvi guided the fortunes of the Papal States virtually by himself and with remarkable skill. Faithful to his training in the tradition of the great Roman canonists of the preceding century, he held to his belief in the irreducibility of papal sovereignty on earth and in the connection of throne and altar in individual countries. At the same time he was free of any prejudice, open to the currents of the time, and convinced that the majority of the changes during the past quarter century in Europe were irreversible. Consalvi was prepared to accept the loss of many concrete forms of the Old Regime and to acknowledge the utility of a clear separation of the ecclesiastical and secular spheres of interest. With this perspective, and almost alone in the Roman world of that period, he worked out a new method, better adapted to the circumstances of the nineteenth century, which would assure the Church a maximum of freedom of action in the political Europe of the restoration.

While Consalvi supported the work of the counterrevolution in countries such as France, Spain, and Portugal, where he hoped to gain advantages, in the interest of the Church he did not hesitate to emphasize the new ideals of liberty in the face of various forms of regalism or to improve the legal condition of Catholics in those countries in which they constituted a minority. Consalvi also recognized that the policy of the Popes of the seventeenth and eighteenth centuries to seek the support of Catholic monarchs was no longer appropriate for the new Europe. He attempted, with success, an improvement of the relations between the Holy See and the two great victorious powers of the Napoleonic wars, England and Russia. In particular, he sought the support of Russia in order to diminish Austria's influence in Italy, because he was aware of the negative effect of this influence on the patriotic tendencies of the younger generation. In spite of his basically antiliberal attitude, Consalvi recognized the danger of an uncritical acceptance of Metternich's system.[9] Ever since the Congress of Vienna, it was clear to Consalvi that, regardless of all attempts to stifle it, the spirit of revolution was alive. It seemed to him the better course to guide this new spirit and to channel it in order to avoid being swamped by it again.

But Consalvi was becoming increasingly more isolated within the Sacred College. The authoritarian and untiring secretary of state was accused of having concentrated all matters in his own hands. Some of the politically oriented regarded his attempts to loosen Austrian influence as unrealistic. But it was the zealots in particular who raised fundamental objections to his policy. They criticized his orientation toward reform of the administration of the Papal States and the continuation of some measures which had been introduced by French revolutionaries. They found fault in his weakness toward those governments who refused to countenance fully the demands of the Church. They disapproved of the signing of concordats, which served only to confirm government usurpations and which, under cover of an apparent peaceful agreement restoring some rights to the Holy See, actually encouraged new demands. But the fundamental objection, hitherto overlooked by many historians, was to the apparent preference which the secretary of state accorded to diplomacy over the religious concerns. Indeed, Consalvi wished to improve relations with the non-Catholic powers, especially England and Russia, in order to strengthen the position of the papacy within the European context,[10] and to assure institutionally the effective representation of the Holy See to these governments; more so, in fact, to maintain strict orthodoxy in doctrinal questions and to exercise a direct apostolate among the Christian masses.

[9] Typical is his attitude during the revolution in Naples, where he acted very cautiously in spite of pressure applied by Austria, which wanted to see Rome participate in a forceful repression. See J. H. Brady, *Rome and the Neapolitan Revolution of 1820–21* (New York 1937); S. Furlani in *Nuova Rivista storica* 39 (1955), 465–91, 40 (1956), 14–47; A. Tamborra in *AstIt* 118 (1960), 190–211.

[10] The interest of the great powers in the conclave of 1823 is proof of the success of his work.

When Pius VII died on 20 August 1823, the zealots, constituting a majority in the conclave, were determined to bar anyone's way who was not willing to remove Consalvi and to accord preference to a religious restoration which would take full account of the rights of ecclesiastical power. In vain, the "Party of the Crowns," led by Cardinal Albani but weakened by the division between Austria and France, promoted the candidacy of Castiglione, a moderate "zealot." The majority of the zealots feared that his election would not result in the necessary break with Consalvi. A bitter battle was waged over a period of three weeks, and the chances of the inflexible Severoli increased. But when Austria cast its veto against him because of his attitude toward Vienna's policies, Severoli threw his support to Cardinal della Genga. Della Genga was elected on 28 September 1823, and as Leo XII governed the Church until the beginning of 1829.[11]

Leo XII, relatively young but mature in outlook, was a strict and pious, simple and good man, who possessed extraordinary moral strength. He devoted a great deal of time to his pastoral tasks in the diocese of Rome. Motivated by a rigorous and active spirit of reform, he wanted to give Church and Curia a less political and more religious orientation, and soon aroused the ire of all those whose habits he disturbed. In addition, the Pope planned a necessary raising of standards in religious studies. Unfortunately, there existed a tremendous discrepancy between the leadership and administrative qualities of this former diplomat, who hardly had been successful in his various offices, and the degree of his personal ardor and virtue. Without the necessary skill, and always hesitant and too easily influenced by advisers who did not deserve his trust, Leo XII was not the man to master the delicate situation within the Church at that time. In spite of a few clearsighted judgments, he left the impression of a somewhat pale figure who was not in control of events.

Because the "zealots" had elected the Pope in order to put an end to the Consalvic system, many historians have regarded Leo XII as nothing more than a reactionary; but this opinion is too one-sided and takes into consideration only the last years of Leo's pontificate during which he

[11] Annibale della Genga was born on 22 August 1760 near Spoleto as the son of an aristocratic family. Pius VI had noticed him and appointed him as nuncio in Cologne in 1794, and subsequently as nuncio in Bavaria, and sent him on missions to Vienna and Rastatt. Pius VII had also entrusted him with several diplomatic missions and placed concordat negotiations with the courts of Bavaria, Baden, and Württemberg in his hands. Consalvi reproached him in 1814 for the failure of his negotiations concerning Avignon, whereupon Genga withdrew to his abbacy of Monticelli. In 1820 he became vicar general. See R. Colapietra, *La formazione diplomatica di Leone XII* (Rome 1966) and A. F. Artaud de Montor, op. cit.

relied on obsolete paternalism and police methods to administer the Papal States. The reality was much more diverse and, above all, much more complex.

The first actions of the new Pope indeed seem to indicate a clear break with the policy of the preceding administration. Merciless disfavor was shown to Consalvi, and a Congregation of State was created which, according to the wishes of the Pope's electors, consisted of declared enemies of Consalvi. The Congregation was to advise the Pope in all political and religious questions. Yet the appointment of the aged Cardinal della Somaglia (1744–1830) as secretary of state indicated an attempt by Leo not to be beholden to the group of intransigents who severely disapproved of his choice. Della Somaglia was a man without vision and his opinions placed him on the far left fringes of the zealots. After less than three months the Pope caused raised eyebrows by calling on Consalvi for advice.[12] After the meeting he appointed him prefect of the Congregation for the Propagation of the Faith, a position to which the Pope attributed special importance in light of his apostolic zeal and his concern over the maintenance of communications with the non-Catholic countries. The sensational rehabilitation of Consalvi occurred at almost the same time that the newly created Congregation of State diminished in influence. To be sure, measures such as the Pope's first encyclical in which indifferentism and tolerance received his condemnation, his strengthening of vigilance by the Index and the Holy Officiate, his favors granted to the Jesuits, his more religiously motivated selection of new cardinals, and his decision to celebrate the Holy Year of 1825 despite the general resistance of the state chancellory, all indicated that the Pope had not changed sides to the "politicals." The Pope's attitude became even clearer with his decision once again to levy a small tribute on commuters as a symbol of the vassal status of the King of Naples to the Holy See. In an astonishing letter to King Louis XVIII of France, on 4 June 1824, Leo accused him of failing to support the clergy sufficiently and of having failed to change laws inspired by revolutionary maxims.[13] At the same time, however, and particularly after the death of Severoli on 8 September 1824, Leo XII tended to become more independent and to exercise a moderate policy. Matters were arranged with the aid of his former secretary Consalvi and without the knowledge of

[12] Consalvi's advice concerned the following subjects: the increasingly close relationship with France because of its influence in the Levant; discretion in the hospitality toward the Bonaparte family; the usefulness of the Holy Year 1825; the attitude to be taken toward the new Spanish-American republics; distrust of the projects of the archbishop of Mogilev and the feasibility of an approach to the Russian church; and the emancipation of English Catholics.

[13] Printed in A. F. Artaud de Montor, op. cit., 234–39.

his secretary of state. Of his own accord, Leo resumed Consalvi's concordat policy and, after only a momentary yielding to the demands of the very reactionary Spanish ambassador, the Pope adopted an understanding policy toward Latin America.

Was Leo XII, then, a genuine zealot? The answer is yes. Among the zealots there were many gradations from the strict severity of Severoli to the eighteenth-century empiricism of della Somaglia.[14] Della Genga, like Pacca, stood in the center between these two extremes. He combined rigorism in religious matters with moderation in his relations to governments. His religious achievements consisted of strengthening the clerical influence in the administration of the Papal States, a closer alignment of the monasteries with the apostolic efforts of the Church; the introduction of a stricter way of life and an improved education for the clergy; the promotion of all initiatives designed to awaken the religious spirit of the masses and to facilitate Christian knowledge in society; resistance in work and deed against liberal indifferentism; and the attempt to remind Catholic sovereigns of their calling with respect to God and Church. At the time he was mindful of the fact that the religious division of Europe and its post-revolutionary conditions no longer permitted the traditional solutions which might have been appropriate for medieval Christianity. He was aware of the dangers inherent in antagonizing the possessors of power, and he had enough experience to realize that in his relationships with them moderation generally was more rewarding than inflexibility.[15]

Yet to understand the policy of Leo XII in all of its variations, another aspect needs to be considered. While the Pope as Cardinal della Genga had shared the restrained views of Pacca, during the first years of his pontificate he came under the strong influence of the young ultramontane generation and especially that of Father Ventura. This new type of zealot was convinced that after the irrevocable decay of the political and social structures of the Old Regime, the great chance for the Church consisted in using its intellectual and spiritual prestige to influence the new leading classes instead of putting all its hopes in the support of Catholic princes. They were also convinced that the papacy and not, as Metternich believed, the governments had to bring about the religious and social restoration of Europe by presenting itself as the spiritual

[14] See the analysis by R. Colapietra in *AstIt* 120 (1962), 82–84.

[15] Symptomatic is his declaration of 1828 with respect to a moderate attitude toward Martignac's decrees against boys seminaries in France: "This is perhaps not the language of a Pope of the zealots, but all decisions which I have made in my political career and the desire to apply them without hesitation to the situation in which God has placed me, have proven to me that the peace of the Church can only be preserved by this system of moderation" (cited by Leflon 395).

leader of humanity and by no longer relying on political action but on what later was called "Catholic Action." For a short time, Leo XII was swayed by these ideas, and they explain his first Encyclicals *Ubi primum* and *Quo graviora*,[16] and the declaration of 1825 as a Holy Year in order to afford an opportunity for restored contact between the Pope and the Christian people. It was during the time of this persuasion as well that Leo convoked a council of the Italian bishops in Rome in order to lend more weight to the apostolic initiatives of the Pope[17] and gave such a cordial reception to Lamennais when he visited Rome. Leo XII even seriously considered inviting Lamennais to be an expert to the council.[18]

But Leo XII did not wish to commit himself fully to this direction which, although it held possibilities for the future, was also fraught with danger. Would it not promote the growth of revolution if one placed his confidence in peoples rather than in kings? There was also the danger that the Holy See might become too isolated during such a process, the more so as the European episcopates were very reserved toward the ultramontane movements. After 1826, the removal of Ventura from his chair;[19] the rise of Cappellari; the appointment of Lambruschini as nuncio in Paris; and Bernetti's mission to the Tsar, who was regarded as the real foundation of the established order, demonstrated that the Pope had given up the course charted by Lamennais and his admirers and returned to the policy of collaboration by the Holy See with the conservative powers to fashion a common front against the rise of liberalism, a policy desired by Metternich, Villèle, and Nesselrode. This increasingly defensive and political orientation of Leo's pontificate, a pontificate which had begun under the sign of religious renewal and apostolic reconquest, intensified when della Somaglia was replaced by Bernetti, whom Consalvi had once regarded highly. But little time was left for Leo XII to profit from the new appointment. Continually ill, the Pope died on 10 February 1829, at a peak of unpopularity, despised by the Roman people, who did not think highly of his attempts at moral reform, looked down upon by the liberals who called him a tyrant beholden to the Holy Alliance, and unforgiven by the disappointed zealots for his turning away from their party.

In the conclave of 1829, lasting from 13 February to 31 March, politicians and zealots opposed one another as they had in 1823. Even though they were in the majority, the zealots were weakened in their

[16] *BullRomCont* XVI, 45–49 (5 May 1824) and Roskovany II, 24Off (13 March 1825).

[17] See P. Perali, ed., *Memoriale del Card. Pacca a Leone XII dell' 11.4.1825 sul projetto di convocare un concilio romano* (Rome 1928).

[18] About a possible elevation of Lamennais to a cardinalate, see chapter 14, footnote 16.

[19] R. Colapietra, "L'insegnamento del P. Ventura alla Sapiena" in *Regnum Dei* 17 (1961), 230–59.

prestige by the unpopularity of Leo XII. The zealots also lacked the unity of purpose which their common enmity to Consalvi had given them during the last conclave. The politicians, under the clever direction of Cardinal Albani, now had the support of the ambassadors of the Catholic powers and managed to form a sufficiently large block to eliminate de Gregorio, the candidate of the zealots, and to force them to accept the election of Francesco Saverio Castiglioni,[20] a candidate who had been rejected in 1823.

Choosing the name Pius VIII, Castiglioni indicated his intention to resume the tradition of Pius VII, who had wished to see him as his successor. But he was not given time to prove himself. Upon his election at the age of sixty-seven, he was seriously ill and died on 30 November 1830, after only twenty months in office. As an individual primarily interested in pastorate and orthodoxy, he was more concerned with the aftershocks of Jansenism than with the new problems which occupied the attention of the younger generation. He was little interested in political questions, and his training placed Castiglioni near the zealots, but he tended more toward the smooth policy which Consalvi had conducted within the Papal States as well as in his relations to foreign governments. Yet Pius XIII remained faithful to his office as Pope. He stood unflinchingly by his principles and the defense of the rights of the Church. He knew how to deal with contingencies and was prepared to make concessions in subordinate matters and to be conciliatory in exclusively political areas. He demonstrated the latter ability in his position toward mixed marriages and "ecclesiastical pragmatism," problems which had arisen in Germany, as well as in his decision, made without hesitation and against the advice of the majority of his Curia, to recognize Louis-Philippe as King of the French after the revolution of 1830.

But in other areas Pius VIII proved to be less open. In the matter of the former dioceses of Spanish America he remained closer to the legitimist view than either Leo XII or Cappellari. He also did not disguise his hostile attitude to the national emancipation movements which broke out in Belgium, Poland, and Ireland during the last months of 1830. Toward these movements, the influence of his most important elector, Cardinal Albani, who was totally in agreement with the Austria

[20] Born on 20 November 1761, as son of a noble family of the Papal States, he had received a chiefly canonistic education. He gained his first experiences in the diocesan administrations of zealous bishops, and in 1800 he himself became bishop of Montalto. Exiled by Napoleon between 1808 and 1814, he was transferred to Cesena and appointed cardinal in 1816. In 1821 he became Grand Penitentiary and Prefect of the Index congregation; in the conduct of his office he was always interested in balanced arrangements.

of the Holy Alliance, was noticeable. Pius VIII named Albani as his secretary of state and left the larger part of political matters to him, while the Pope devoted himself to religious problems. It is also partly as a result of Albani's influence that the policy which Pius VIII pursued during his pontificate was no longer the policy of the Church which Consalvi, the model of so many churchmen of the nineteenth century, had perfected. Instead it was the same policy as that of the dynasties in Vienna, Paris, and Madrid. This places Pius VIII politically as well as theologically among the stragglers of the eighteenth century, who were still so numerous in the period of restoration. These were certainly outstanding minds and men who by no means deserve to be cast simply as reactionaries, but none the less they failed to understand the problems of the new world forged by the Revolution.

The Restoration of the Papal States

The Papal States were the only ones of the former ecclesiastical states which were restored by the Congress of Vienna and were placed under the international protection of Europe. At the time of Napoleon's fall, the allied sovereigns, who from their recent experiences had gained the conviction that a totality of spiritual power in the person of a sovereign Pope would be a valuable guarantee for them, were most willing to acknowledge him. But the state chancellories at first understood this restoration to be limited in area. They stated that the papal provinces, which the Pope had renounced in the treaty of Tolentino, were French areas of conquest of which they could dispose freely. It required all of Consalvi's skill and months of negotiations to obtain the almost total restoration of the old territories.[21]

Even this success was to be the source of a number of problems for the Popes. The most developed areas of the states, with about 2.5 million inhabitants, particularly in the districts of the Romagna, which for more than fifteen years had been separate from Rome, had enjoyed modern methods of administration and feared even a partial return to the archaic prerevolutionary system. It would be easier, it was said, to transform the goddesses, whom Napoleon had painted in the papal palaces, into madonnas than to change the minds of the young, who had known only the French regime. The difficulties which continued to

[21] Agreement of 12 June 1815. The Austrian and Napoleonic officials showed reluctance to implement the conditions of the treaty, and negotiations over the enclave of Benevento and the evacuation of the northern provinces dragged on for several more years. See the unpublished dissertation of H. Breitenstein, *Metternich und Consalvi* (Vienna 1959) and for Benevento see A. Zazo in *Samnium* 26 (1953), 1–32.

surface during the course of the subsequent half century were to become an increasing source of worries to the Popes and one which would divert them from important religious problems.

While Consalvi was still negotiating in Vienna, the reorganization of the nucleus of the state, in which the Pope already exercised his rule, was begun immediately. In May 1814 Pius VII turned the reorganization over to a kind of provisional government under the chairmanship of Cardinal Rivarola. Rivarola was not satisfied to proceed against the collaborators of the destroyed Empire, as had been the case in all other countries which had belonged to the French Empire, but, with the unfortunate edict of 13 May 1814, managed to do away with all French governmental offices. In their place he restored the old terribly complicated administration together with the feudal law of the barons, a unique occurrence in western Europe.

Consalvi possessed an acute sense of historical development and, as early as 1801 on the occasion of the first restoration of pontifical power, emphasized the impossibility of a total elimination of the Jacobin-introduced French institutions. He protested sharply to Pacca against this inept and reactionary policy. This policy, which caused protests even in fairly backward areas, which had experienced the French only briefly, was totally inapplicable in the Marches and the Romagna, which had been regained as a result of the difficult negotiations in Vienna and which had attained a much higher stage of development. An edict of 5 July 1815 guaranteed them, for the immediate future, the continuance of the French administrative system, except in those matters which were in disagreement with canon law, as well as the continuation in office of all officials.

A year later, on 6 July 1816, a rescript gave final shape to the Papal States and thereby ended the governmental dualism.[22] It introduced a number of desirable administrative and judicial reforms, inspired by the Napoleonic system, which were designed to centralize and simplify institutions and which involved a more equitable tax system. The serious attempt to reform the archaic structure of the Papal States could not but produce a longing for Consalvi after the departure of the secretary of state. It was the source of the neo-guelfism of the following generation. But the significance of the reform should not be overestimated. For example, the part dealing with judicial reform was actually a regression when measured against the experiences of the Napoleonic times, and even the publication of a civil code modeled on the French civil code on 22 November 1817 was not able to improve matters. While Consalvi

[22] *BullRomCont* XIV, 47–196. See Schmidlin *PG* I, 149–54 and R. Colapietra, op. cit., 21–22.

was a moderate with an open mind, he was not a liberal reformer. He was a representative of enlightened despotism and convinced that the independence of a Holy See which had to be assured by temporal power was incompatible with a constitutional government in which the Pope had to share responsibility with his subjects. Thus not only did the political leadership remain unchanged in spite of the suggestions made by Austria and Russia at the congress of Laibach, but even in the sphere of administration Consalvi, in spite of his serious concern with an improvement of administrative methods, was unable to disregard a number of aspects which were incompatible with the spirit of modern institutions. In particular, the laicization of personnel remained strictly limited to subordinate functions.

The reform of 1816, limited as it was, nonetheless could have been the starting point for further improvements. But many felt it already had gone too far. For example, the conservatives who were damaged by the suppression of local particularisms or feudal privileges, the cardinals whose role was reduced as the reorganization transferred more decision-making to the secretary of state,[23] and, finally, the zealots who regarded Consalvi's work as a sign of philosophical Jacobinism, all opposed reform. This opposition from the right, under the leadership of cardinals Severoli, Rivarola, della Genga, and Somaglia, attempted to sabotage the implementation of the rescript, to prevent the promulgation of new and more modern civil and penal codes, and to reintroduce the old privileges and exemptions.

In resisting this systematic reaction, Consalvi remained isolated and often had to do with mediocre subordinates. Not only in the Sacred College and among the higher prelates did he encounter men who did not share his views and therefore whom he could not place at the head of provinces, but even among the Roman laity there was no segment which afforded him support. He could not count on the developing bourgeoisie, which, in spite of welcoming some of his measures, accused him of limiting himself to secondary reforms in economic affairs and of ignoring the awakening of Italian national feelings. The masses in turn were dissatisfied because the crisis following the French occupation had brought in its train a reduction of income, and they were unable to generate any enthusiasm for a government which in principle remained aristocratic. Thus, especially in the more developed Marches and the

[23] Cf. L. Pásztor, "Per la storia della Segreteria di Stato, la riforma del 1816" in *Mélanges Tisserant* V (Vatican City 1964), 209–72. Following Consalvi's order a filing system was introduced, inspired by the one employed in the Kingdom of Italy during the French regime. On the transformation and reduction of the Sacred College and the attempts of the cardinals to react to the situation, see L. Pásztor in *RHE* 65 (1970), 479–84.

Romagna, the opposition developed in the climate of general discontent. This opposition found expression in the revolutionary secret societies, harking back to the French era, and of which the "Carbonari" and the "Gulfi" were the most important. Pressured by Metternich, the Pope vainly renewed his condemnations of them because of their revolutionary character and their connections to the Freemasons.[24] Because of their more political than religious nature, these condemnations hardly made a dent in minds agitated by the liberal mystique, and contributed to making the Church appear in the eyes of all of Europe as an enemy of modern institutions and national movements alike.

In short, the restoration in the Papal States brought about less of a synthesis of traditions and new tendencies than in the neighboring states, and the deficiencies of the Consalvic reforms were magnified by the unwise opposition of conservatives and zealots.

After the death of Pius VII, the zealots took over the management of internal affairs and began to oppose previous policies directly. In retrospect it is clear that, just as the modern nature of Consalvi's work has often been exaggerated, the regressive character of Leo's XII government has been overemphasized. One should not overlook the administrative and judicial reforms of Pius VII. The new structure which he had given the state was left essentially untouched, regardless of a number of changes which found their organic expression in the rescripts of 5 October 1824 and 21 December 1827,[25] and this structure led in part to a strengthening of authoritarian centralization. The edict of 27 February 1826, reforming the charitable institutions, contained a number of positive aspects and was progressive in comparison to other Italian states. Useful but unpopular saving measures made it possible to lower taxes and to make financial policy more liberal, but they were not able to prevent a downturn in the economic situation. In some other areas, however, a clear regressive movement was evident: Jews were again confined to their ghettos; the feudal aristocracy regained its commanding position; the ecclesiastical courts returned to the position preceding the year 1800; the cautious laicization of the administration was slowed down; and university education was reformed according to regressive concepts with the aim of hindering the development of criticism.[26] But the most important change which also took place in the neighboring states, with the exception of Tuscany, was not a legal one,

[24] Bulls of 13 September 1821 and 13 March 1825.

[25] *BullRomCont* XVI, 128–255, XVII, 113–291.

[26] Constitution *Quod divina sapientia* of 28 August 1824 (*BullRomCont* XVI, 85–112). About their preparation see A. Gemelli and S. Vimara, *La riforma degli studi universitari negli Stati pontifici, 1816–24* (Milan 1932).

but one of attitude. It was manifested as a narrow-minded puritanism which had the aim of governing daily life; in systematic attempts to extinguish all memories of the atmosphere of the "Italian rule" in clerical circles; in having only bishops appointed who were either very old or too young to have occupied important positions during the Napoleonic time; in arrogant indifference toward the constantly increasing stagnation of the political, economic, and social life; and finally in replacement of the spirit of self-possessed moderation prevailing under Consalvi by a police state.

This change in attitude engendered a spy system which embittered moderates, and the brutal methods of repression—symbolized by the edict of Palotta in Campagna in May 1824, and Rivarola's judgment of 31 August 1825 in Bologna,[27] which were enforced only intermittently—could not stop the increasing activity of the Carbonari. The policy of the zealots, embodied in the Congregation of Vigilance, became increasingly illiberal in the hope of gaining the confidence of the conservative courts, and only led to the strengthening of the revolutionary movement which Consalvi had hoped to dampen. Even when Pius VIII softened the police state with his return to the policies of Consalvi and effected some sensible changes in the economic and social sphere, the gap between the papal government and the rising classes, especially in the Romagna, was too wide to hope for a peaceful development within the heated atmosphere of 1830.

[27] D. Berardi, ed., *Sentenza del Card. A. Rivarola legato a latere* (Ravenna 1970); R. Colapietra, op. cit., 189–214, 261–69.

CHAPTER 4

The Rejuvenated Position of the Holy See within the Church

Rome, the Center of the Universal Church

At the beginning of the nineteenth century, the position of a sovereign Pope in the Church seemed to be endangered by the confluence of two streams of thought: the Febronianist canonists and theoreticians of Josephinism and the Gallican jurists of the French Revolution and the Empire. However, the brutal conduct of Napoleon, who intended to limit the role of the Pope to that of a high ecclesiastical functionary in the Empire, had two results. First, it earned his intended victim the respectful adoration of the faithful, especially those north of the Alps, who in the past centuries had been rather indifferent toward a Pope who never left Rome, and secondly, it called the Pope to the attention of European state governments. The restoration of the Pope's earlier prestige received another support through the recognition by the governments and leading elements that it would be useful to anchor the work of counterrevolutionary restoration on the moral authority of the Pope, who suddenly appeared in the eyes of all of Europe as the symbol of the principle of order and authority. A twofold sign of this recognition were the decisions of the Congress of Vienna to acknowledge the nuncios as doyens of the diplomatic corps[1] and to increase the number of accredited diplomats in Rome. Between 1816 and 1823 the number of diplomats rose from eight to sixteen, among them eight representatives of Protestant sovereigns and the ambassador of Orthodox Russia.

Rome managed to exploit the new situation not only to the advantage of the secular interests of the Holy See, but also with respect to purely ecclesiastical concerns. Pouthas could justifiably say: "The papacy under Pius VII approached with determination the monarchization of the Church, reaching its peak with the victory of ultramontanism under Pius IX." At the very time that the principle of nationalism had come to the fore, a restoration of Roman authority in a supranational sense occurred; one which seemed to usher in a return to traditional Christianity.

The policy of concordats jointly carried out by Pius VII and Consalvi was one of the most important means toward this end. At the same time, as his predecessors after the great schism had done, Pius VII attempted to make Rome once again into a center of art and culture. He invited to Rome scientists such as Mai and artists such as Canova and Thorwaldsen, heaped gifts on the academies, the Vatican Library and the papal museums, promoted the construction or restoration of monuments, and continued the excavations in the center of Rome begun by the French. This policy had the disadvantage that monies were diverted for purposes which lacked economic usefulness; monies which could have been employed to finance the public works of which the Papal States were in such need. This was only one example of the antinomy which existed within the two-fold tasks of the Pope as both head of the universal Church and sovereign of an Italian state.

Leo XII not only continued this patronage, which contributed to directing the eyes of the Christian world to Rome, but also, in keeping with his personal predilections, directed activities of a more religious

[1] S. Schröcker, *Der Nuntius als Doyen des Diplomatischen Korps: Reich und Reichsfeinde IV* (1943), 214ff.

nature. Contrary to the advice of the political party of the Curia and in the face of the disapproval of most of the European Catholic and non-Catholic governments, the Pope decided to celebrate 1825 as a Holy Year. It was the first one in fifty years and attracted hordes of Italians, including a few sovereigns, and a small but remarkable number of foreign pilgrims, who once again discovered the path to Rome.[2]

In his effort to portray the papacy as the spiritual leader of the Christian world, Leo XII renewed the tradition of the great magisterial messages. On 3 May 1824, the Pope addressed the programmatic Encyclical *Ubi primum*[3] to the world. The encyclical condemned Gallicanism and Josephinism together with indifferentism and its two consequences: tolerance and liberalism. Pius VIII continued this tradition by beginning his pontificate with the Encyclical *Traditi humilitati nostrae,*[4] a renewed affirmation of Rome's supreme magisterial office. While in the preceding century it had met stiff resistance, the claim to the spiritual leadership of mankind was now well received among the younger clergymen. These clergymen were not familiar with the conditions of the Old Regime and were convinced, in these hard times for the Church, of the necessity to emphasize Roman unity more than Catholic pluralism.

Concordat Policy

Pius VII had begun his pontificate with the signing of a concordat with Napoleon which enabled the Pope to demonstrate the full extent of his powers through the recognition of the right to remove bishops on his authority alone. This was a particularly heavy blow to Gallican traditions. The mere fact that a concordat had been concluded which reorganized completely all aspects of the Church in a country was, by itself, a moral victory for the papacy. Now the Pope no longer was regarded as he had been during the preceding centuries, as a force to be ignored or, far worse, as a foreign power against which the governments might mobilize the national episcopate. On the contrary, he was viewed as an ally, whose supreme authority over the local clergy was acknowledged and whose cooperation was sought as a desirable alternative to regulating religious questions unilaterally.

That Pius VII once again had the opportunity actually to guide the fortunes of the Church makes understandable the path which he fol-

[2] See G. de Grandmaison, *Le Jubilé de 1825* (Paris 1910) and Colapietra, 143–44, 226–27, 237–38, 252–54, 291.
[3] *BullRomCont* XVI, 45–49.
[4] Ibid. XVIII, 17–20.

lowed.[5] In a situation which was more diplomatically favorable than in 1801, the Pope could make higher demands and protect the interests of the Church more effectively. The result was an even more pronounced and fundamental recognition of the rights of the Holy See. The zealots, on the contrary, argued that the concordats embodied some exaggerated limits to the right of the Pope to intervene. Actually, though, Consalvi, the intelligent negotiator of the concordats, had a clear understanding of reality and the possible. In addition to the creation of solid foundations for the rebuilding of the Church shaken by revolution (even at the price of concessions in some secondary matters), he recognized how important it was to induce numerous governments,[6] among them Protestant and Orthodox ones, through these diplomatic instruments to agree to a recognition of the Church as an independent and perfect society and to an acknowledgment of the leading position of Rome within the structure of the Catholic Church. Retrospect makes it easy for the historian of today to see that in large part it is owing to Pius VII's secretary of state that during the nineteenth century the universal Church assumed the place which the national Churches had occupied in the Old Regime.

In order to guide the reconstruction of Churches from Rome, Pius VII created a new Congregation for Extraordinary Ecclesiastical Affairs.[7] Because Consalvi was in Vienna at the time of its founding in 1814, Pacca implemented the new Congregation. Thus its membership, drawn from cardinals and theologians, consisted almost exclusively of

[5] Treaty with Tuscany in 1815; with Bavaria, France, and Piedmont in 1817; with Kingdom of the Two Sicilies and Russia in 1818; with Prussia and the Upper Rhenish states in 1821. Other agreements, sta[illegible] by Consalvi, were concluded during the following pontificate: with Hanover in 1824, with Duchy of Lucca in 1826; with Netherlands in 1827, and with Swiss Cantons in 1828.

[6] Two large Catholic states remained outside of this movement: Austria, because there the agreements entered into by the Emperor and also by Metternich encountered the opposition of the Viennese bureaucracy, and Spain, where anticurial prejudices were equally alive among the absolutist Godoy and the liberals.

[7] In contrast to what has often been said, there was no connection between this congregation, founded by decree on 19 July 1814, and that of the ecclesiastical affairs of France, created by Pius VI in 1790, nor with that of the same name established by Pius VII at the time of the preparations for the concordat with Bonaparte. Since the beginning, its organization was clear and unmistakable, but its nomenclature changed, and especially its tasks underwent strong changes during the first fifteen years. Its role during the preparations for the concordats at the time of Consalvi (and even under Leo XII) was much more limited than has been thought. During the short pontificate of Pius VIII the significant role of the new congregation was confirmed and simultaneously its function became more precise. On the first years of its efforts see the very rare collection *Raccolta dei rapporti delle sessioni tenute nell'anno (1814–1819) della S. Congregazione deputata sugli affari ecclesiastici del mondo cattolico*, 8 vols.

zealots, a condition which was to complicate life for the secretary of state upon more than one occasion. Consalvi was also severely handicapped by the presence of cardinals who were heads of several other important congregations and who did not agree with him with respect to the general policy line of the Church. Consalvi's intention to improve the mobility of the Curia caused him to concentrate in the secretariat of the state not only the leadership of the Papal States, but also of the universal Church. In order to put life into his plans, he created organizations outside of the institutional framework of the Curia. He appointed special ad hoc commissions and staffed them with prelates such as Capaccini, Sala, and Mazio rather than with cardinals. In addition to Consalvi, these prelates were the real authors of the policy of restoration. Hence in the history of the Roman Curia, the pontificate of Pius VII occupies a remarkable place in that it attempted to improve the functioning of the Curia not through a reform of already existing institutions, but by creating new ones.

The Ultramontane Offensive in France

At the same time that Rome attempted to gain firm control of the central leadership of the Church, the countries in which Gallicanism and Febronianism had grown underwent a similar and parallel development in their own awareness.

Robbed of its privileges and the support of the monarchy during the years of the revolution and the French Empire, the French clergy had come to acknowledge that its best policy would consist of closer relations with the head of the Church. The attempt to subdue the clergy through the civil constitution and Napoleon's efforts at the time of the council of 1811 to erect an established church had opened the eyes of many to the dangers of the principles of Gallicanism.

A remarkable proof for this spiritual development was provided on 8 November 1816 when five prelates of the Old Regime, who had been opponents of the concordat of 1801, following a request by the government, renounced their opposition and in the name of the entire Gallican Church promised their unconditional obedience to all measures which Pius VII might have to take for the welfare of religion in France. This step, which gave the *Petite Église*[8] a blow from which it did not recover, was an important moment in the decline of Gallicanism. With this decision, the French clergy, long before the recognition of this

[8] Where the opposition to the concordat gathered, now finding only the support of five of the old bishops, among them Thémines of Blois.

principle by Vatican I, acknowledged de facto the right of the Pope to intervene and unilaterally to decide matters for a national Church.

Even though the development did not stop, at first it seemed to slow down with the restoration of the Bourbons. The apparatus of this government remained wedded to the parliamentary Gallicanism of Pithou, which represented not only the independence of the state from the Church, but also the dependence of the Church upon the state in all matters which were not purely spiritual. The Bourbons emphasized and strengthened Gallicanism by continuing Napoleon's authoritarian methods of state socialism. They tended to regard relations between bishops and the Holy See as requiring royal permission, to maintain the grievance appeals embodied in the Organic Articles, and to appoint bishops without reference to Rome. The subjection of the Church to the government was designed to strengthen absolutism and to disarm the liberal opposition, whose aggressive tendencies were then to be diverted to the Holy See. The theoretical writings of André Dupin and Count de Montlosier in the defense of this system found an echo in public opinion, which regarded some of the clauses of the concordat of 1817 as humiliating to the state.

While the opposition of the clergy to the Organic Articles and to the submission of the Church to royal power was unanimous, a clear shift took place in favor of the articles of 1682, which now were interpreted very moderately. The prelates of the Old Regime who had returned with the King to France ordered the teaching of these Gallican articles. The Congregation of Saint Sulpice, which was in charge of many seminaries, remained faithful to Bossuet's tradition, and many clerics, who out of opposition to the Napoleonic despotism were open to ultramontanism and who, like Monsignor d'Astros, had defended the rights of the Pope even while they were in jail, now tended to give another chance to a traditionally moderate Gallicanism. It is also possible that they did so in order not to offend a government which so openly favored the Church.

Many individuals, especially the young, did not follow this line of thought, and soon ultramontanism became increasingly strong. Following the distribution of a Jesuit translation in French of the works of Italian ultramontanes, the first manifestation of the reawakening occurred in 1819 with the publication of the book *Du Pape* by Joseph de Maistre,[9] a Savoyard layman. In a simplified manner, Maistre defends the most extreme positions of the papalists by relying less on biblical or

[9] On de Maistre see bibliography, chapter 14. Critical edition of *Du Pape* with introduction by J. Levie and J. Chetail (Geneva 1966).

patristic witnesses than on analogies with political society as seen from the perspective of an absolute monarchy. Too theocratic to influence the politicians for whom it was chiefly intended and insufficiently theological for the clergy, the book nonetheless found readers among the broad public, whom it began to convert to the thesis of the infallibility of the Pope.

It was to be Abbé de Lamennais[10] who was to achieve the conversion of the French clergy to ultramontanism. Lamennais had become a follower of a moderate ultramontane position after 1810 and upon reading Maistre's book he was confirmed in his views. On the occasion of a press campaign for unrestricted education, he seized on ultramontane justifications. This was done in part to underscore the rights of the Church against the state and in part to discredit in the eyes of Rome and of Catholic public opinion the Gallican-oriented bishops who refused to oppose a school monopoly which endangered the faith of the young. Without advocating a return to theocracy (on the contrary, he depicted the Holy See as an arbiter who protects right against might), he now accused Gallicanism at every opportunity of introducing democratic principles into the Church. Lamennais accused Gallicanism of making attacks upon the divine constitution of the Church, which if successful would lead to the dependence of the spiritual power upon the political power and, in this case, upon a government corrupted by liberal ideas.

The author of the *Essai sur l'indifférence* had already gained a reputation as an apologist, and his ultramontane partisanship, or opposition to Gallicanism, to be more precise, quickly drew the attention of several young priests. With their help Lamennais was able within a few years to spread "Roman views" among the young clergy, in spite of the resistance of the hierarchy and the reserve of many older priests, who were alienated by the impetuous nature of these innovators and their lack of the sense of proportion so dear to their Sulpician teachers.

The bishops were not only angry at the disrespect with which the young clerics treated them; they also were concerned with justification about the development of a movement in which they saw the expression of a clerical anarchy; an anarchy which elevated a distantly residing sovereign in order to ignore an immediate superior. Yet many of them, especially the younger ones, realized that the Gallican system was obsolete. This became evident in 1826, when Monsignor Frayssinous, the minister for ecclesiastical affairs and the author of a classical and very modern work on *Les vrai principes de l'Église gallicane* wanted to see the episcopate take a stand against the slogans of Lamennais. The results of the consultation demonstrated the degree to which even at this time the

[10] On Lamennais, see bibliography, chapter 14.

principles of Gallicanism within the French episcopate had begun to waver, including the moderate wing.

Because Rome was aware of the inner logic of this development, it preferred to let it mature without hasty intervention which might lead to a more rigid attitude on the part of the bishops. The Holy See maintained a diplomatic silence because it did not wish to offend the pious King Charles X, and refused to lend open support to those who defended the ultramontane cause in France. This lack of support was a bitter disappointment to Lamennais. There was an additional reason for the Roman reticence.[11] Just as Rome had received de Maistre's *Du Pape* with reserve, in this case its theologians were dissatisfied with a depiction of ultramontane doctrine which gave insufficient importance to divine institutions and furthermore lacked clear definitions of the area of canon law and of the relationship of papacy and episcopate. Therefore, Rome avoided open approbation and confined itself to receiving with satisfaction the reports of success from the nuncio in Paris;[12] reports which recounted the steady progress of the ultramontane movement among the clergy and the pious laity.[13]

The Beginnings of the Development in Germany

The rebirth of ultramontanism in the German areas proceeded more modestly and at a slower pace. That it occurred, however, was an undeniable fact and the more remarkable because the way there was a more difficult one. The generally very moderate views of the school of Saint Sulpice had to be overcome as well as the much more radical and clearly episcopal outlook of Febronius and of the Josephinist canonists. Furthermore, the German bishops had for a long time shown themselves much more independent toward the Curia than was the case in France.

Secularization had reduced the power of the Rhenish archbishops. Once so proud in their relations to the Holy See, after twenty years of war and the numerous and long-lasting vacancies of episcopal sees which resulted from the many territorial redistributions, they now were forced to ask Rome for dispensations which heretofore they had reserved to themselves. This development led to a rediscovery of the thesis of the universal episcopate of the Pope. At the same time, several

[11] Cf. Colapietra, 443–47 and, with respect to de Maistre, J. Levie and J. Chetail, XXX–XXXIV.

[12] Who on his part acted very intelligently; see L. Lambruschini, *La mia nunziatura di Francia* (Bologna 1934), 50–55.

[13] The nuncio in Spain transmitted similar reports. At the University of Sevilla, for example, the works of the Roman canonist Devoti replaced those of Van Espen and Tamburini after the restoration of 1823 by Ferdinand VII.

of the governments wished to avoid the creation of an adversary in the form of a strong and unified Church. After the Congress of Vienna, they thought it better not to foster the reorganization of the German established Church which was promoted by all those who longed to return to the Old Regime. The governments merely wanted to regulate the condition of their Catholic subjects through an agreement with the Holy See, which at this time still appeared weak and distant.

Conditions, therefore, became more favorable for the awakening of ultramontanism in Germany. We see the first signs in the numerous influential circles which characterized the German Catholic restoration after the turn of the century. Among these were the Vienna circle of Clemens Maria Hofbauer and the convert Friedrich Schlegel; those of Münster and Munich in which the friends of Princess Gallitzin and of Görres placed the accent on unity with Rome as a factor of Catholic regeneration in Germany; and finally and chiefly the Mainz circle formed around a group from Alsace: the bishop of Colmar, the seminary director Liebermann, and Professor Räss, all of whom had received their training from Strasbourg Jesuits outside of the Gallican and Febronian tradition. All of them wanted to train the clergy in a Roman and very anti-Protestant spirit and for this purpose spread the ultramontane views of Bellarmine through their seminaries and their journal *Der Katholik.*

Gradually, ultramontane views entered theological education. Even Möhler, who had little interest in the hierarchical aspects of the Church, depicted the Pope as the vital center of the unity of the Church. Ultramontanism also became visible in the teaching of many canonists who broke with the Josephinist tradition and polemicized against the idea of a German established Church which had been propagated by Dalberg and Wessenberg. This was true with respect to Frey and Schenkle; Scheill, who belonged to the younger generation, continued the work of the other two, and was able to win a portion of the young clergy to their ideas. The movement was encouraged by the bold gesture of Pius VII, who, after long hesitation in 1820, finally dared to place the textbooks of canon law and church history by G. Reichsberger and R. Dannenmayer, which had been in use for the past thirty years in all Austrian universities, on the Index of Forbidden Books.

In contrast to the French radical ultramontanism of Joseph de Maistre and the followers of de Lamennais, during the first decades of the nineteenth century this German ultramontanism was a very moderate one. It was much more a reaction against the extreme positions of Febronius and of Josephinism than a general reconciliation with Roman theologians and canonists on the question of the privileges of the Pope. Although many bishops spurned the doctrine of the superiority of a general council over the Pope, they thought themselves entitled to guide their dioceses without recourse to the Curia and, especially in the case of mixed marriages, to do so without heed to Rome's specific directives. Similarly, the majority of theologians rejected the interpretation of papal primacy which would have concentrated virtually all ecclesiastical authority in the offices of the Roman Curia. Gradually, however, the thesis of the personal infallibility of the Pope gained ground. The German translation of de Maistre's *Du Pape* in 1822 influenced a few laymen who sympathized with the new movement from France, as in their romantic enthusiasm they held an idealized image of the medieval theocratic state. Terrified by the spiritual anarchy which had sprung from the rationalism of the eighteenth century, they now willingly emphasized the necessity for a magisterial office which expressed itself with absolute authority. From a base within the laity, these ideas gradually reached the clergy, and, after 1830, they were introduced into some of the universities by men such as Klee and Phillips.

Roman Catholics and Separated Christians

As a consequence of ultramontane enthusiasm, which brought with it a denominational hardening and a virtual expulsion of the Christians separated from Rome, the nineteenth century was to produce the peak of ghetto mentality within Catholic Church history. In spite of this, the Catholic Church, as well as other Christian denominations, experienced a revival of unifying tendencies during the first quarter of the nineteenth century; a revival generated by a variety of motives. In some cases, as in Germany and in Holland, unification was a manifestation of a dogmatic interconfessionalism which had developed in the course of the preceeding century within circles which had been in contact with the Enlightenment or pietism. It was fed by a romantic tendency to prefer religious subjectiveness to precisely defined aspects of dogma and church discipline. In other cases, there was no other aim than to gather all of the disciples of Christ in order better to counter the dangers of secularism and rationalism. Still others propagated the religious unity of Europe[14] as the best means against the progress of revolutionary ideologies. Many thought of this unity as following the precepts of the Holy Alliance and as a gathering in of all Christians regardless of frontiers and denominational boundaries. Finally, for such as Bonald, de Maistre, and Lamennais in France, it was a question of speeding up the "return" of the separated "sects" into an all-embracing Catholic unity.

[14] This is the title of an 1806 article by Bonald. See *Oeuvres* VII (Brussels 1845), 164–202.

In the view of these men the Roman Church, based on the principles of authority, was the only useful bulwark against atheism in religion and individualism in politics.

Considerations of this nature were in fact the cause for a number of conversions to the Roman Church; especially among the Russian aristocracy and in Germany, where enthusiasm for the Middle Ages was a contributing factor. Some people believed that these were the first signs of a movement which would spread in coming years. Some, encouraged in their utopian hopes by the rumors of the unity projects ascribed to the Tsars Paul I and Alexander I,[15] even thought possible an incorporation of the Russian Orthodox Church into the Roman Catholic Church.[16]

With respect to the Protestants in France, where even during the Empire rumors of a fusion or absorption abounded, it was hardly possible to escape triumphalistic apologetics. One example was the assertion, spread by the Catalan J. Balmes in 1841–1844 in the four volumes of his *El protestantismo comparado con al catolicismo*, that Protestantism corrupted all social virtues, while Catholicism fostered them. In Ireland in 1826, Bishop Doyle urged the government to begin theological talks between Anglicans and Catholics; talks which he wished to conduct in a spirit of irenicism and spiritual competition. In Germany, ultramontane circles fostered certain controversial apologetics, because they were concerned about tendencies toward syncretism and doctrinal indifferentism. Occasionally, however, as in Frankfurt, such individuals as Schlegel and the historian Boehmer began dialogues, which in some cases lasted until the middle of the century and demonstrated a serious effort to overcome divergences and a spirit approaching that of modern ecumenism.[17] Sailer also wrote in a spirit which exceeded the Catholic world,[18] and he counted many Protestants among his friends. Without a doubt the work of J. A. Möhler[19] at the beginning of the nineteenth century was the most fruitful contribution of Catholic Germany toward Christian unity, even though the majority of his ideas were to mature

[15] On Paul I see M. J. Rouët de Journel in *RHE* 55 (1960), 838–63. On Alexander I see Boudou I, 131–39; Winter, *Russland* II, 205–07; and "Lettres du Général Michaud à Nicolas Ier" in *L'Unité de l'Église* (1937), 129–33.

[16] So also the Bavarian priest H. J. Schmitt, who in 1824 published *Harmonie der morgenländischen und abendländischen Kirche. Ein Entwurf zur Vereinigung beider Kirchen.* Some time later the French priest L. Bautain entered into a very irenical correspondence with two Russians. See E. Baudin in *RevSR* 2 (1922), 393–410, 3 (1923), 1–23.

[17] A few examples in A. Mouchoux, *L'Allemagne devant les lettres françaises de 1814 à 1835* (Toulouse 1953), 315–16.

[18] See below, p. 221.

[19] See below, p. 246.

only at a later time. Study of the Church Fathers had enabled Möhler to regain a concept of the Church which had been lost to theology for a long time. He presented the Church as a dynamic unit encompassing all differences and possessing an inner affinity for all of them.

Rome, on the other hand, was receptive primarily to the conversion movement which characterized the first decades of the century and to the fact that a growing number of non-Catholic visitors were converging on Rome. These two occurrences were seen as an indication of diminishing antipapal prejudices. Although the Apostolic See would have liked to see itself again as the center of Christian unity, it hesitated to take steps which might cause consternation in London or Saint Petersburg. When the Greeks, after their first rising against the Turks in 1822, appealed for support from Rome, Pius VII did not dare to discuss their cause.[20] When in 1829 Chateaubriand invited Leo XII to place himself at the head of a comprehensive movement for Christian unity at the expense of a few concessions in the area of discipline, the Pope replied: "Matters must first mature and God himself must complete his work. Popes can only wait."[21] On the other hand, the Popes of this period did not hesitate to obstruct everything that might promote panchristian mixing, and this, above all else, was the reason for the negative attitude of the Holy See toward the Bible societies. It was quite evident that the papacy of this time did not wish to bring about the restoration of the Catholic Church by way of a genuine ecumenism.

[20] E. Duhaut-Lhéritier, *Histoire diplomatique de la Grèce* I (Paris 1925), 208–13.
[21] *Mémoires d'Outre-Tombe*, Edition Garnier, V, 110–12.

CHAPTER 5

The Alliance of Throne and Altar in France

The church history of the restoration period in France, long viewed only through the distorting prism of ideological passions, gradually has become the object of genuine scientific attention. It illuminates the naivety of a clergy believing it possible to regain the preeminent position it had occupied before 1789 through the support of the reigning nobility and compromising itself in the eyes of the rising classes by its agreement with the political and social forces of reaction. It also depicts the ecclesiastical and spiritual rebuilding of these fifteen years and its lasting effect.

The Restoration of the Catholic State

"The throne of Saint Louis without the religion of Saint Louis is an absurd concept." Chateaubriand's statement, which breaks with the ideal of those in the eighteenth century who wanted to revive the old monarchical institution by transforming it according to the precepts of the encyclopedists, corresponds to an attitude which reached far beyond the group of émigrés. During the trials of the revolution many people returned to religion; some of them came to believe that it was the first duty of a ruler to lead his subjects to God; others, more concerned with political reality, concluded that the best protection for the throne lay in the social power which Catholicism represented. Integrating their social and political philosophies of counterrevolution into a religious perspective, they united in the common task of restoring the traditional church system and a powerful and respected Church in a Christian state. This goal was pursued by the ultras to its extreme, but they had to take into consideration liberal opinion which, while only weakly represented in parliament, held strong positions in society. Hence, the individualistic and liberal civil code remained untouched. For a century it governed the religious and moral life of the country, in part through an increase in birth control, which had been introduced in the preceding century. In many areas a policy of compromise was mandatory. For this reason numerous prelates and especially Catholic journalists complained bitterly about the "weakness" of the government with respect to the support which the government afforded the Church. The majority of the episcopate exercised moderation, as factually and legally there was no doubt that the Church profited considerably from the favorable attitude of the government.

Immediately after his return in 1814, Louis XVIII established Catholicism as the official religion of the state and required the honoring of the sabbath. There were also movements for the abolition of freedom of religion and the restitution of Church lands. In the following year the Chamber outlawed divorce and attempted to return to the clergy all functions of the civil registry and education. At the same time, secret negotiations were undertaken at the behest of the representatives of the *Petite Église* who were behind the religious policy of the first restoration. This aim was to annul the concordat of 1801, return to the concordat of 1516, restore the old dissolved dioceses, and replace the Napoleonic episcopate. Pius VII and the zealots around him were indeed interested in negotiating a new treaty which would cancel the Organic Articles and be more favorable for the Church. But the Holy See did not wish to create the impression that it had erred and now disapproved of its negotiations with the "usurper," nor did it desire to return to the traditional status of the Church in France with its old Gallicanism. Besides, Consalvi was very skeptical about such a far-reaching counterrevolution. After three years of difficult negotiations a compromise was finally reached on 11 June 1817. In spite of the intentional vagueness of many of its clauses, it was a success for Rome and restored forty-two of the old dioceses.[1] But the reaction of Gallican jurists and of liberal opinion was such that the government did not dare submit the treaty to the ratification of both Chambers. This placed it in a quandary, but the skillful mediation of Portalis's son and the King's promise gradually to increase the number of dioceses from fifty to eighty (effected by October 1822), persuaded Pius VII to discard the idea of a new concordat. The concordat of 1801 remained in effect, paradoxically saved by the extreme demands of the ultras.

The failure of the concordat of 1817 is explained by the fact that upon the advice of Decazes Louis XVIII was seeking a reconciliation with liberal opinion. Basically prepared to improve the material and legal position of the Catholic Church, Louis above all tried to keep the state independent from the clergy, thus preventing the complete realization of the program of the ultras. But the assassination of the heir to the throne on 13 February 1820 fueled the resistance of clergy and nobility anew. It expressed itself in chicanery against the Protestants, a newspaper law of March 1822 which placed blasphemy of religion under penalty, and in increasing influence of the Church on education. The reaction deepened with the accession of Charles X in September 1824. He was the prototype of an émigré who, converted to piety, "atoned for the thoughtless sins of his youth through equally thoughtless exercises of devotion in his old age" (Dansette). His coronation at Reims appeared to be both symbol and program.

This clerical policy was supported by the even more extremist religious press, as well as by the secret ultra royalist and religious society known as Knights of the Faith,[2] a kind of Catholic counterfreemasonry. Its supreme goal was to serve religion and the monarchy; but soon it was infiltrated by a number of ambitious people. During the first years of the restoration it formed a regular secret government and until 1826, the year of its dissolution, not satisfied with bringing about the complete Christianization of institutions through legal reforms, it tried to gain control over the administration, systematically filled all influential positions with its members, and let it be known that religious zeal was the most important prerequisite for gaining high office.

[1] Text *MiscMercati* I, 597–601.

[2] See below, p. 229.

Strengthening of the Ecclesiastical Hierarchy

Parallel to this questionable public action, which soon turned against the very Church it professed to serve, the work of ecclesiastical reconstruction begun in 1801 proceeded in a less spectacular but much more useful way.

The rebuilding was done by an episcopate which on the basis of vacancies, of attrition, and the creation of thirty new sees was quickly "purified" (of ninety bishops appointed between 1815 and 1830, seventy were noblemen). But on the whole, the bishops of the restoration, selected by the Grand Almonry chiefly from émigrés and priests who had resisted Napoleon, were noticeably different from those of the Old Regime. Similar to the Napoleonic bishops, they were conscientious administrators, were too old, and had too little contact with the faithful and their priests. Yet they fulfilled their obligations eagerly if not always intelligently, and were irreproachable in their personal conduct. Dupanloup applauded their eagerness, but Foisset regretted the absence of new pastoral initiatives called for by the new situation ("Nothing was done to prevent the nineteenth century from being a continuation of the eighteenth century.") In the face of a society incapable of admitting that the past quarter century was not merely an episode, this episcopate certainly was the wrong one for the times.

One of the most important tasks was to recruit enough priests, and the results were good. With the aid of the government, which provided considerable sums[3] for stipends, seminarists, and higher salaries for the clergy, the bishops succeeded in overcoming the critical situation within a few years. Seen superficially, the number of thirty-six thousand priests in France in 1814 seemed to be adequate, even if it was only half the number of 1789, but many of the priests were rather old; only 4 percent were under forty. The steps taken to ameliorate the situation resulted in an improvement. The number of ordinations increased from year to year (918 in 1815, 1400 in 1820, 1620 in 1825, and 2337 in 1830; the last figure constituted an absolute high-point, as it was never reached again). The average age of the clergy decreased, and after 1825 a small increase in the absolute number of priests took place.

The young clergy, often from an agrarian background, was occasionally attracted by the glitter of a career newly provided with respect by the government, but Jean-Marie Vianney,[4] who in 1818 became pastor

[3] The church budget gradually increased from 12 to 33 million Francs per year. Simultaneously the contributions of the faithful increased considerably (42 million compared to 2.5 million during the Empire); they were favored by the law of 2 January 1817, which made possible the purchase of real estate and the receipt of legacies.

[4] R. Fourrey, *Le curé d'Ars authentique* (Paris 1964).

of Ars, was certainly not the only one who took his pastoral obligations seriously. Many priests came from families with strong religious traditions, had gone through the trials of the revolution, and received their calling in contact with uncompromising and strict priests of the "resistance." In newly organized seminaries in which the influence of Saint Sulpice predominated, they received a solid ascetic training which, compared to the neighboring states, gave the French clergy a relatively high standard. Some bishops attempted to uphold these standards with the help of retreats and priests' conferences. But with respect to humanistic and even theological knowledge, this clergy, even in the cities, was only half educated. The reason for this was the low standard of education in the seminaries and the total destruction of higher ecclesiastical education during the revolution.[5] Bautain, Lamennais, and a few others were rare autodidacts with the usual shortcomings.[6] Bishops like Monsignor Trévern of Strasbourg were exceptions and tried to deal with the unfavorable situation during a period of extraordinary spiritual ferment.

The regular clergy was not able to make up for the failure of the secular clergy in this respect, for of the old "intellectual" orders only the Jesuits played a role in the France of the restoration. Still small in numbers, they were absorbed with the reintroduction of their colleges and the missions to the people. Congregations engaged in ministering to the sick or teaching elementary school, however, were in full bloom, especially in the east, the southeast, and the west of France. As early as 1815 there were 14,226 sisters, divided among forty-three congregations in 1,829 houses; by 1830 there were 24,995 sisters in sixty-five congregations and 2,875 houses. The rapid increase of local congregations,[7] resulting from the isolation of some of the provinces, the attempts of some bishops to remain masters of their territory, and the narrowness of some founders, unfortunately were a waste of strength. Among the school brothers, there were local groups as well, but with much greater unity. Three congregations were particularly active: the institute of the Brothers of Christian Instruction at Ploërmel in Brittany,[8] founded in 1820 by Jean-Marie de Lamennais; the Marist Brothers of Marcellin Champagnat, founded at the same time in Lyon; and the Christian Brothers, who had never disappeared and whose

[5] See below, pp. 248ff.

[6] On Bautain, see below, pp. 249f.; on Lamennais see bibliography chapter 14. See also pp. 251–54 and 273–76 on the Mennaisian movement.

[7] List, incomplete in *NRTh* 82 (1960), 609–10; on the congregations of brethren see id., 612.

[8] H. C. Rulon and Ph. Friot, *Histoire des méthodes et des manuels scolaires utilisés dans l'Institut des Frères de Ploërmel* (Paris 1962).

strength quadrupled in fifteen years. In addition to these congregations, officially recognized because of their public usefulness, some old congregations reappeared in spite of the disapproval of some Gallican bishops opposed to any exceptions.[9] Others were new and ignored the regalistic laws which the government inherited from Napoleon. The government eventually weakened these laws by superceding them in 1825 with a new law. Because of its moderate nature it remained in effect until the end of the century.

The Attempt to Regain Society and Anticlerical Reactions

Administrative and legal advantages for the clergy, one-sided selection of civil servants, and reordering of ecclesiastical structures, all were in part designed to strengthen the monarchy; but for the Church the supreme goal was the rechristianization of society. The actual degree of dechristianization in the France of 1815 is difficult to ascertain. But in general the following can be said: The constant wars, the mutual recriminations after Napoleon's rupture with the Pope, and the discontent growing out of the tactlessness of the first restoration and its unrestrained exploitation during the Hundred Days, placed the Church in a very difficult situation, in spite of the religious renewal associated with the concordat of 1801. Of course, the conditions were different in different parts of the country. While, for example, not a single male inhabitant was religiously active in Périgueux, the population of Marseille was still very religious, and while some rural departments like Yonne and Charente contained a considerable number of unbaptized children, other areas were hardly touched by such phenomena. This was especially true for the areas on the periphery of France, like the north, the Vendée and Anjou, Aquitaine, the Provence, Franche-Comté, Lorraine, and Alsace. Generally it can be said that the old aristocracy as well as a few intellectuals returned to the old faith, professionals and notables of the provinces continued to be openly hostile to the clergy, and religious indifference was widespread in the world of commerce and industry. The mass of the people, on the other hand, in the rural areas as well as in some provincial towns, continued to adhere to Christian practices. But religious ignorance was profound, morals clearly had sunk lower, and the reception of Sacraments, especially among the men,

[9] The actual attitude of the local authorities differs with time and place. See for example F. Tavernier, "L'affaire des capucins à Aix et à Marseille" in *Provence historique* 8 (1958), 235–64.

had virtually disappeared.[10] The masses were influenced by the freethinking press, which was read aloud in drinking halls, and by the dime novels sold by street vendors. In short, even though not quite as catastrophic as depicted in some pastoral letters, the situation was worrisome. In addition to the comprehensive movements, to be treated in detail later,[11] the Church of France could look toward two significant means to regain its hold on the society which seemed to be slipping from its grip: the Christian education of the young and people's missions for adults.

The awareness that the rechristianization of the people would have to begin in elementary school explains both the hostility of the clergy to an education which was not single-minded[12] and the flourishing of the teaching congregations. Their work was facilitated by several legislative measures assigning the clergy an important role in the elementary schools, especially the ordinance of 2 April 1824, which placed all elementary education under the control of the Church. The Church was chiefly interested in secondary schools which were educating the future leaders. It would have liked the restoration to return to it the monopoly of education which, after it had been lost to the revolution, was turned over by Napoleon to the *"Université."* But the change could not occur from one day to the next. Therefore an attempt was made to establish a secondary ecclesiastical school system on the fringes of the state system,[13] and with the tacit permission of the government. At the same time, the state schools were given a more religious character. In addition to the catechism, daily Mass and weekly confession became obligatory. The almoners were given great authority; some pressure was exerted on young Protestants, although only rarely. Then Monsignor Frayssinous, after 1822 in charge of education, purged the universities and replaced important professors, whose religious or monarchical sentiments were suspect, by clerics (in 1818, 139 of 309 deans and 66 of 80 professors of philosophy were clerics). The purge seems to have had some positive results in a few small towns, but in many places, espe-

[10] The situation was particularly bad in Paris. In 1825 Nuncio Macchi wrote: "In Paris hardly an eighth of the population practices its religion and it is questionable whether there are ten thousand practicing Christians."

[11] See chapter 14. pp. 227–30.

[12] See R. Limouzin-Lamothe in *BLE* 57 (1956), 71–83.

[13] Seminaries for boys to which, in addition to future priests, young people were accepted who wanted to enter a professional career; private schools organized by pastors; even secondary schools established by orders which were entitled by the ordinance of 27 February 1821 to grade the same way as the royal secondary schools. One actually feared the bad influence which the children from liberal or enlightened circles might exert on children from Christian families.

cially Paris, it was a dismal failure. It merely resulted in hypocrisy on the part of the professors and animosity on the part of students, who were more hostile to religion when they left the royal secondary schools than when they had entered. This partial failure of the protectionist system also explains the success of Lamennais's work toward a liberal education,[14] in spite of the mistrust of most of the bishops, who suspected anything that had any connection with liberalism.

With respect to the missions to the people, the method employed reached back to the seventeenth century and was employed under Napoleon until he abolished it. In 1816 it was resumed with a hitherto unknown intensity. Several societies of diocesan missionaries were founded (in the south, in Lyon, in Besançon, in Tours) the most successful of which was the congregation of the Priests of Mercy of Abbé Jean-Baptiste Rauzan of Bordeaux. Some religious orders, Jesuits, Lazarists and Monfortians participated in this apostolate. Supported by the majority of the bishops and the parish clergy as well as occasionally by the civil and military authorities, these inspired apostles seized every opportunity for spectacular appearances in order to instill and revive the faith. At the same time, they urged them to be loyal to the Bourbons, as they were convinced of the solidarity between monarchy and religion. The frequent mixing of politics and religion was a severe mistake in an ideologically divided country, and the missionaries often emphasized the existing divergencies instead of bringing people closer together. Their provocative attitude toward the nonbelievers, their sermons on the restitution of Church lands, their diatribes against dancing, and the burning of books, reminding people in unpleasant fashion of the Inquisition, angered an influential minority. They were ultimately the reason for the rejection of these missions as well as for the stormy reaction directed toward the "mission crosses," whose theatrical erection usually concluded ceremonies. An objective examination of the missionary activity must admit, though, that it was relatively successful. Even if it had hardly any influence on the educated, it temporarily succeeded in stopping the process of secularization among the simple people, even if the emphasis all too frequently was more on public adherence to Catholicism than on the regular exercise of faith. In some cases the missionaries organized a "work of persistence," whose activity was felt for a long time. The general aim of the rechristianization of France certainly was not achieved; but one has to consider that, contrary to appearances, the number of these missions was rather small: perhaps fifteen hundred in fifteen years, perhaps one hundred per year, in a total of thirty-six thousand parishes.

[14] See below, pp. 233ff.

The outbreak of hate and violence against the Church accompanying the fall of the Bourbons in 1830 was the result of a steadily growing opposition. The provocative and tactless policy of the ultras, who identified religion with the counterrevolution and wanted to subordinate the state to the Church, produced hostility in a France which had not known the Old Regime and in the survivors of the old Gallican parliamentarism. The liberals constituted only a small but very dynamic minority; out of an enlightened hostility against religion and with the intention of taking a slap at the throne, which was in solidarity with the clerical reaction, they used all possible means to undermine the activity of the clergy. Inexpensive editions of the encyclopedists were distributed among the lower middle class and in most villages: 2,740,000 copies between 1817 and 1824, i.e., more than in the entire eighteenth century.[15] The liberal papers daily informed their readers of cases of intolerance or scandals among the clergy. The pamphletist Paul-Louis Courrier and the songwriter Béranger assisted the bitter struggle with their talents. A widespread concern with maintaining the predominating position of the state over the Church gained them the support of the moderate wing of the constitutional monarchists, who were very influential in the Chamber of Peers, in the academy, in the courts, and in the university. The uneasiness of the heirs to the Jansenist tradition, in the face of the increasing activity of the ultramontane congregations, also moved a number of Gallicans to join the anticlerical opposition. In 1826 an old Catholic nobleman, the Count of Montlosier, who also was a fanatic Gallicanist, placed himself at the head of a campaign against the Jesuits, who for many had become the symbol of the subordination of the state under the papacy.

The disappearance of the ultraroyalist majority after the elections of 1827 and the replacement of Martignac's ministry by Villèle assured the ordinance of 21 April 1828, withdrawing from the bishops a portion of their authority with respect to elementary schools, and the ordinance of 16 June, which removed members of nonauthorized orders from the educational system and which regulated the small seminaries in such a way that they could not be transformed into secondary schools. These were limited measures, but the Left was jubilant: "The scepter of the Inquisition has been broken." While the Jesuits dispersed without commotion, the episcopate, stirred up by the right-wing press, began to react with firmness. Leo XII, however, skillfully influenced by the emissaries of Charles X, did not wish to add to the problems of such a devout ruler and, happy to be able to exercise his pontifical authority over the French upper clergy, advised the bishops to give in. The gov-

[15] Precise figures in *Mémorial catholique* of May 1825 (III, 261–99).

ernment also showed itself tolerant in the application of the laws.[16] This first defeat of the priestly party far from pacified the liberal opposition, however; on the contrary it incited it more.

Balance Sheet of the Restoration

At the level of institutions, the zeal of the ultras and of the pious, ill-advised by the nunciature, brought the Church no gains. "Everytime it was thought that the lines drawn by coercion at the time of Louis XVIII could be erased with the hope of a social and religious counter-revolution, it was necessary to return wholly or in part to the Napoleonic solution of a differentiation between the spheres of jurisdiction of Church and state, as this solution corresponded best to the situation of a country changed by the revolution."[17] The intensity of the anticlerical reaction which became stronger in the fifteen years of the restoration, and the deplorable attitude of the students, educated in the royal secondary schools under strong ecclesiastical influence, sufficed to make evident the futility of a policy designed to change the religious thinking of Frenchmen by placing at the disposal of the Church the centralized administrative machinery created by Napoleon. To the thoughtless demands of a clergy incapable of analyzing the sociological causes of the religious indifference of the people or the true motives for the irreligiosity of the intellectuals was added the stupid resort to the secular power. It compromised the clergy with the reactionary party and damaged the Church permanently.

But, as we have seen, the balance sheet of the restoration with respect to religion is not entirely negative. A tremendous spiritual rebuilding was effected, to which the rapid increase in ordinations, the continuing renewal of the traditional life in the parishes, the flourishing of charities, an apostolate served by an elite of laymen, and the numerous cases of a return to the faith and to religious practice were eloquent testimony. Not all of these results were superficial and the intensity of the reaction of the enemies of the Church seems to confirm that France was more Christian in 1830 than in 1815. But it must not be forgotten that it was the aid and protection of the government which made possible the rebuilding of the Church in France and, at least in the provinces, a genuine and permanent change of the spiritual climate. One can there-

[16] In Marseilles, for example, everything remained unchanged (J. Leflon, *Mazenod* II, 332–33). Similarly in Lyon, where the authorities insisted on the implementation of the ordinances only under the July monarchy (C. Latreille: *Revue d'Histoire de Lyon* 11 [1912], 5–25).

[17] *HistCathFr*, 250.

fore justifiably ask with G. de Bertier: "Would the Church of France have been able, without these fifteen years of reconstruction and reconquest, to maintain and develop its enthusiasm for charity and the apostolate to the degree to which this was the case in the nineteenth century?"[18] It was an enthusiasm whose emanation to Europe and the world was significant, and it justifies the place which historians assign to the diverse manifestations of the Catholic life of this country.

[18] *La Restauration,* 324.

Chapter 6

The Continuation of the Old Regime in Southern Europe

The Italian States

After the end of the Napoleonic interlude, Italy had once again become a "geographic expression." It consisted of eight individual states: the Kingdom of Piedmont-Sardinia, enlarged by the former Republic of Genoa; the "Kingdom" of Lombardy-Venetia, which was a part of the Habsburg possessions; the Duchies of Parma, Modena, and Lucca, and the Grand Duchy of Tuscany, which were nominally independent but in reality were Austrian protectorates; the Papal States; and the Kingdom of the Two Sicilies.

The shortage of priests which France experienced did not exist in Italy, where the superabundance of clergy continued. But its quality often left much to be desired. In the southern part of the country, many priests had chosen the clerical vocation only because this was the customary prerequisite to becoming an educator or being able to devote oneself to studies. In central Italy, the landed nobility often used priests with a small living as administrators of their estates. In the Papal States, Monsignor Sala complained about the idleness of many priests who served no real function. In the northern part of the country, though, where the bishops were interested in an improvement of the seminaries and, like Monsignor Lambruschini in Genoa, began to organize exercises and retreats for the priests, the clergy definitely had higher standards. In Piedmont a number of lesser known imitators joined people like Giuseppe Cottolengo and Pio Lanteri.

But there were other urgent problems: determination of the relations between the Holy See and the new governments; adjustment of the diocesan borders (which received the form they have retained to this day) in keeping with the territorial changes; regulation of the problems caused by the nationalization of Church lands and the suppression of the monasteries during the French period; and regaining of the minds influenced by the anti-Roman Jansenism of the eighteenth century and the liberal ideas spread by the French.

The institutional reorganization was completed within a few years through a series of agreements, not all of which were easily reached. While the government counted on the assistance of the clergy in its counterrevolutionary undertakings, it was not at all prepared to give up old regalistic laws. In fact, the caesaro-papism of the eighteenth century developed into a kind of modern secular jurisdictionalism of Napoleonic character. Despite objections by the zealots, Consalvi ultimately accepted a number of concessions to this mentality. He acknowledged that, in spite of its unavoidably reactionary character, society refused to revert to the spirit of the Middle Ages. Besides, seen as a whole, this agreeable policy resulted in genuine benefits.

Immediately after his return to Naples, King Ferdinand I requested negotiations for a concordat. They proved particularly difficult, because the Roman zealots in their anachronistic pretensions wanted to see the feudal dependence of Naples on the Holy See confirmed and made demands on a state in which the jurisdictional tradition of Giannone had been strengthened by Murat's bureaucracy. But under the pressure exerted on the court by the pro-Jesuit party and by the flexible position of Consalvi, the negotiations were successfully concluded on 13 February 1818.[1] Like the concordat of 1801 with France, this one made concessions to modern ideas (ending the privileged position of the estates of the Church; limitation of ecclesiastical courts; reform of the dioceses which were too small;[2] and reduction of feast days) as well as to regalistic concepts (the right of the King to appoint bishops; the right of the government to intervene in the administration of estates of the Church). These concessions were compensated, however, by far greater advantages than the French concordat had permitted. Catholicism was recognized as the only religion, with all of the rights in the field of education and censorship of publications resulting from the privileged position; royal permission for administrative acts of the Church was abolished, and the right to appeal to Rome was authorized; the bishops received the exclusive right of jurisdiction over clerics; and the state granted far-reaching guarantees for the material support of the Church

[1] Text in Mercati I, 620–37.

[2] Fifty bishoprics were dissolved or consolidated by the bull of 3 April 1818 (*BullRomCont* XV 31f.). In Sicily, on the other hand, their number was slightly increased for pastoral reasons (Bulls of 28 June 1818 and 23 March 1822, id., 36–40, 487ff.).

by providing the clergy with fixed incomes, restoring unsold Church estates, and providing the monasteries with land. A bilateral commission was entrusted with the implementation, and in 1819 it began to reintroduce religious orders.

The agreement appeared to the inflexible as too advantageous for the state, and it caused the strong opposition of the upper classes because of the economic clauses. The government, counting on the customary docility of the southern episcopate, tried to expand the rights left to it and to maintain as much as possible the old privileges of the monarchy. Disagreements over several points endured until the time of Leo XII, especially the question of returning the jurisdiction over the convents to the nunciature. The zealots, on the other hand, had a certain satisfaction in a policy which was decidedly opposed to any softening toward the liberals; after the unrest of 1820–21 they were led by the Prince of Canosa,[3] who for some years was regarded as the head of the intransigent Catholics of Italy.

But the intransigents were not very numerous in the Kingdom of the Two Sicilies. They found no support among the educated classes, which lived under the influence of the enlightened reformism of the eighteenth century, and among whom the Freemasons of the Scottish Rite had numerous followers, nor among the people whose superstitious religiosity had nothing clerical about it. They found no echo even among the clergy itself, for in the south the clergy more often than not was liberally oriented.

In the states to the north of the Papal States, the Jansenist clergy, which frequently had concluded compromises with the French government, lost part of its influence. While this did away with one cause of opposition to the Roman Curia, Josephinist tendencies remained alive.

In Tuscany, Grand Duke Ferdinand III demonstrated a certain degree of flexibility after the brief interlude of Prince Rospigliosi, who had annulled all French ordinances which seemed to conflict with the Catholic religion. Although Ferdinand III refused the recision of the laws of mortmain desired by Pius VII as compensation for yielding a portion of the church lands, and equally was not prepared to readmit the Jesuits to his territories, a convention was relatively easily reached on 4 December 1815.[4] It permitted the continuation of the orders which still existed at the time of the conquest, but reduced the monasteries numerically, in view of the diminished patrimony of the Church. A compromise was also found with respect to the jurisdiction of canon

[3] See W. Maturi, *Il principe di Canosa* (Florence 1944).

[4] Mercati I, 585–90.

law. But the jurisdictionalistic tradition which had come down from Grand Duke Leopold soon proved so strong that a regression took place, and as early as 1819 the situation at the close of the eighteenth century had been reached again, namely a privileged but strictly controlled established religion. The accession of Leopold II in 1824 led to a reduction in the tensions with the Roman Curia, finding its expression in 1828 in the reestablishment of the nunciature at Florence, which had ceased to exist in 1788.

The situation was very similar in the duchies.[5] The authorities counted on the favorable cooperation of the clergy in their consolidation of absolutist governments and were therefore willing to restore the external power of the Church, which in turn was agreeable with respect to the secularized Church lands. But the governments were not prepared to renounce the Josephinist habits of the eighteenth century.

The same was especially true for the Kingdom of Lombardy-Venetia, which was under the direct influence of Vienna. It enjoyed a Josephinist administration and enlightened bishops like Archbishop Gaysruck of Milan, a conscientious pastor who objected to the gradually spreading religious congregations.

In the Kingdom of Sardinia, where the French concordat remained in force, King Victor Emmanuel I and his ministers, considering the Church as the best support for the throne, were well-disposed toward the Holy See. One of the first actions of the restoration rescinded the Napoleonic laws which had emancipated the Waldensians. The bishop of Pinerolo started a conversion campaign, supported by means of coercion, heralding a return to the persecutions of the preceding centuries. In 1817 a number of dioceses which Napoleon had abolished were reestablished and their boundaries were drawn in keeping with pastoral requirements.[6] The Jesuits, who in the eighteenth century had not experienced the same hostility as in the Bourbon states, quickly regained their dominant position, especially in the field of education. To be sure, the lay members, former Napoleonic civil servants, of the commission charged with the restitution of the unsold Church lands and the reestablishment of monasteries, dragged their feet so that a definitive agreement was reached only in 1828. But it must be admitted that the conduct of many monks and nuns gave rise to complaints and after 1825 Rome had to send out apostolic visitors in order to restore discipline and to eliminate sometimes scandalous abuses. On the other hand, the secular clergy was of higher quality than in the rest of the peninsula and

[5] Where dioceses were newly established in order to adjust them to the changes in borders (Bull of 11 December 1821, *BullRomCont* XV, 462–65).
[6] Mercati I, 601–19.

succeeded in forming small militant groups which, in a very reactionary spirit, became the forerunners of the future Catholic Action.[7]

But it proved to be more difficult to shape minds than to change institutions. Tridentine Catholicism without a doubt governed the conduct of the people. Its faith generally was viable, but lacked enlightenment. Even the elite uncritically accepted the slanderous pamphlets of the Jesuits and Redemptorists against modern ideas, which were represented as derived from Protestantism. For this reason the counterrevolution in Italy more than in other countries occurred in the spirit of the Counter-Reformation. But simultaneously there were, even in the patriarchal monarchy of Savoy, enough enlightened Catholics who, as heirs to the Jansenist tradition in Italy or to the encyclopedists, desired a reform of the Church as well as of the state. Especially among the middle-class youth in large parts of Italy a development could be noted which was analogous to that of France during the same period. In defiance of official coercion the students of Turin, Padua, Pavia, Pisa, and even of Bologna and the Papal States, evinced an anticlericalism which rarely went so far as unbelief, but which differentiated between Church and state. They complained loudly about the growing influence of the Jesuits and, particularly after the intensification of Roman antiliberalism occasioned by the election of Leo XII, turned more and more away from the papacy. Limited as the movement was to the intellectuals, it made visible, in spite of officially shown optimism, the growing rift between the Church and the "young Italy" of the Risorgimento.

The Iberian Peninsula

In Spain as well as in Portugal the French occupation had been too short and too violent to cause a profound change in thinking. Thus the restoration of the Old Regime was total. It was undertaken by an altogether too eager political party, which more than elsewhere equated religious with political restoration.

This was no real advantage for the Church. The governments continued to adhere to the regalistic ways of the eighteenth century and were not forced, as in other countries, to seek a just balance between tradition and new ideas. The clergy thus increasingly identified itself with a past which the intellectual elite and the bourgeoisie had outgrown. After having been under the influence of the encyclopedists,[8] they looked with envy toward England.

[7] See below, pp. 235ff.

[8] Without going as far as they did toward an absence of piety or even anticlericalism, for they spoke of adaptation, and not of discarding national traditions.

Yet the organization of the Spanish Church demanded far-reaching reforms. It suffered from unsuitable diocesan and parish boundaries and excessive wealth;[9] ignorance and sometimes lack of morality among the lower clergy; an unusually high number of people in orders (forty thousand monks and twenty-two thousand nuns in a population of 10 million) and forty-six thousand diocesan priests (proportionately twice as many as the considerable number of priests in Italy). The otherwise qualified episcopate lacked clearsighted men.

Consequently the interference of the Cortes of Cádiz in purely ecclesiastical affairs,[10] together with certain forms of conduct engendering a revolutionary demagogy according to the French model, brought into discredit any type of liberalism, even the most moderate kind derived from Suarez and Thomas Aquinas. For this reason the clergy passionately supported the violent absolutist reaction accompanying the return of King Ferdinand VII to Madrid in 1814, and during the suppression confused the "afrancesados" with the patriotic liberals. During the following years "Black Spain," supported by the masses of the people loyal to the Church, triumphed over an "enlightened" minority. The Inquisition was immediately restored and turned against all who between 1808 and 1814 had toyed with the "revolution," closed monasteries were reopened, and the Jesuits were permitted to settle again, but only on condition that they respect the rights of the crown. The crown determinedly held on to some aspects of the Old Regime, leading to occasional tensions with Rome, especially in the question of the appointment of bishops, not to mention American affairs.[11] Pius VII, with his acute sense for reality, gave in to several royal demands. In 1817 he agreed to charging nuns with the education of boys and girls wherever schools were inadequate. In 1818 he turned over a respectable portion of the income of the Church for cultural and social purposes.

Between 1820 and 1823 the liberals succeeded in gaining power and exacted heavy punishment from the Church for its concession to the reaction. Clerics who resisted the immediately restored constitution of 1812 were incarcerated or deported;[12] half of all monasteries were closed; the Jesuits were expelled; many Church lands were expropriated; and the Inquisition and episcopal censorship were outlawed.

[9] See some remarks in E. A. Peers, *Spain. The Church and the Orders* (London 1939), 18–20. See also the remarks of the author on the development of Spanish anticlericalism during the eighteenth and nineteenth centuries: "What had originally been in the main a struggle for power between Church and King became a struggle for property" (p. 63).

[10] See above, pp. 81f.

[11] See below, pp. 163–70.

[12] The episcopal resistance was led by P. Inguanzo y Rivero, bishop of Zamora, who became archbishop of Toledo in 1824.

Finally, the appointment of Canon Villanueva, a highly anti-Curial Jansenist, who had been the soul of all ecclesiastical reform projects, as ambassador to the Holy See led to a break with Rome and the expulsion of the nuncio.

Under these circumstances it was not surprising that bishops, priests, and members of orders fervently assisted the counterrevolution, and that numerous monasteries became bulwarks in the service of the traditionalist party and the so-called *Junta apostólica.* With the restoration of the absolutist government for another ten years (1823–33) by the "one hundred thousand sons of Saint Louis," the Church was again placed in its former position. Buyers of Church property were not compensated. But the few concessions which the King made to the liberals, such as his refusal to restore the Inquisition,[13] irritated the intransigents or "apostólicos," led by the Franciscan general and supported by Nuncio Giustiniani. Giustiniani was a representative of the Roman zealots and wanted to make of Spain an object lesson for a Catholic reconstruction of Europe on an antiliberal basis. Keeping this objective in mind, the clergy, and especially the regular clergy, placed its hopes in the impending accession to the throne of the brother of the King, Don Carlos. In spite of the firm trust of the people in the traditional religious customs, the clergy was incapable of understanding that the anachronistic attitude of the Church of the Old Regime could not but jeopardize it.

The restoration of the Church in Portugal was hardly more satisfying. Even more than in Spain, the entire Church needed to be cleansed, for the decadence of the orders and the low morals of the clergy[14] were even more pronounced. In its relationship to the Holy See the episcopate was much more emancipated, and the ideas of the French philosophes and of Freemasonry had developed deeper roots. Continuing along the guidelines of Pombal, the government wanted to reform the religious orders without Rome's involvement and experienced constant difficulties with the Pope over the appointment of bishops and their jurisdiction. But this did not protect the Church from the hostility of the liberals. Consequently, the seizure of power by the Freemasons after the revolution of 1821 was accompanied not only by the abolition of a series of ecclesiastical privileges and the closing of several monasteries, but also by violence against the clergy, including bishops. In

[13] This restoration was of symbolic value for the *Apostólicos.* They saw in it a challenge to liberal Europe. But the Holy See thought it more prudent not to add fuel to the fire (and also was not sad at the disappearance of this national tribunal which had not allowed appeals to Rome).

[14] There were very many of them, for in 1822 there were eighteen thousand priests in a population of fewer than 3.5 million (i.e., one priest per two hundred inhabitants).

order to find protection, they were compelled to seek it from Rome. The accession of Don Miguel in 1829 reintroduced absolutism as well as the privileged position of the Church.[15] But the removal of the fetters from the anticlerical press during the liberal administration had made evident the deep rift between the clergy and the intellectuals. The few clergymen open to modern ideas, like the Benedictine Father Saraiva, author of a constitutional draft in 1821 along the lines of the Cortes of Cádiz, were helpless to change the situation, the more so as they were chastised by both Rome and the Portuguese episcopate.

[15] Including, fourteen years later than Spain, the reinstatement of the Jesuits, although between 1834 and 1857 they were to be suppressed again. See L. Frías, *Historia de la Compañía de Jesús en su asistencia moderna de España* II/1 (Madrid 1944), 536–73.

CHAPTER 7

Ecclesiastical Reorganization and Established Church in the German Confederation and Switzerland

As a consequence of secularization the Catholic Church of Germany was bereft of its material foundations, its political backing, and its educational institutions, and was dependent on the states. It also needed to be adjusted to the new conditions and reorganized from the bottom up.

The Imperial Delegates Final Recess had promised an adjustment in imperial law, which, however, had not been effected during the agony of Germany's secularization, in spite of the efforts of Prince-Bishop Dalberg and the Court of Vienna. Dalberg's plans for a concordat for the Rhenish Confederation also had foundered.[1] The Curia, having just succeeded with the French concordat in setting up the prerequisites for a centralized reconstruction, was not interested in seeing an autonomous ecclesiastical organization reestablished in Germany. Even more determinedly, several medium-sized states, especially Bavaria and Württemberg, opposed any national or federal solution. They insisted on preserving their recently gained sovereignty, and for the first time in German history ecclesiastical particularism prevailed. It was combined with a blunt application of absolutist ecclesiastical sovereignty; in the medium-sized states whose borders had just been redefined, the estab-

[1] Concerning Dalberg's religious policy, see also R. Reinhardt, "Fürstprimas Carl Theodor von Dalberg im Lichte der neuen Forschung," *ThQ* 144 (1964); G. Schwaiger, "Carl Theodor von Dalberg," *Beiträge zur Geschichte des Bistums Regensburg* I (1967); *MThZ* 18 (1967).

lished Church, bereft of its independence, was intended to be an instrument of the states' integration policies.

Only the collapse of the insecure and unstable Napoleonic system and the political reorganization by the Congress of Vienna (September 1814 to June 1815) created the prerequisites for an ecclesiastical reorganization. An all-German solution was in the realm of the possible at Vienna and was promoted by the wise and tireless Coadjutor Ignaz Heinrich von Wessenberg, Dalberg's representative at the congress.[2] Adhering to a Febronian concept, Wessenberg strove for the creation of a national Church under the prince-bishop, virtually independent from Rome and secured by a federal concordat, and the inclusion in the constitution of the new German Confederation of the right to a state Church. While Wessenberg gained the support of Austria and Prussia, he met opposition by Rome and the medium-sized states. Cardinal Consalvi, successful in Vienna with the restoration of the Papal States and of the Pope as a European sovereign, had to fight on two fronts with respect to the problems of the German Church. He opposed Wessenberg's episcopalism as well as the demands of the individual states. Supported by the Hofbauer circle (see chapter 13 below) and the representatives of the ultramontane wing of the German Church, F. von Wambold, J. A. Helfferich, and J. Schiess, the cardinal favored a federal solution, allowing the Curia direct administrative powers over the Church in Germany. Wessenberg's as well as Consalvi's plans were defeated in Vienna primarily by Bavaria and Württemberg, which rejected any infringement of their ecclesiastical sovereignty. A single religious reference (Art. 16) was ultimately included in the Federal Act. It stated that the differences among the Christian denominations in the states of the confederation were not to be the basis for civil and political discrimination. Thus the denominations were not granted any corporative privileges but only equality of civil rights for their adherents.

This left the regulation of ecclesiastical problems to the individual states. While still in Vienna, Consalvi started negotiations with several state governments and continued them from Rome. The cardinal succeeded in including in his system of concordats the German states with large Catholic populations, even though a formal concordat was signed only with Bavaria. For the Protestant states, there were bulls of cir-

[2] See Wessenberg's autobiographical notes, especially 155–67, as well as his 1815 work *Die deutsche Kirche* (concerning it, see Becher, op. cit., 98f., 131ff.) More recent works on Wessenberg are W. Müller, "Die liturgischen Bestrebungen des Konstanzer Generalvikars Wessenberg," *LJ* 10 (1960); id., "Wessenberg in heutiger Sicht," *ZSKG* 58 (1964); E. Keller, "Die Konstanzer Liturgiereformen unter Ignaz Heinrich von Wessenberg," *FreibDiözArch* 85 (1965); F. Popp, "Studien zu liturgischen Reformbemühungen im Zeitalter der Aufklärung," ibid., 87 (1967).

cumscription and annotated briefs, i.e., papal decrees in form but genuine treaties with respect to their content.[3] They fixed the results of bilateral negotiations, and the participating states gave them the force of law without establishing precedents for the sovereign powers.

After the mediation of the bishops had removed the chief obstacle to the achievement of old Febronian demands, Bavaria between 1806 and 1809 had negotiated a concordat, but then decreed parity, toleration, and extensive state supervision of the Church with the religious decree of 24 March 1809. The negotiations, resumed again in 1815 and conducted on the Bavarian side by titular bishop (after 1818 cardinal) von Haeffelin, led to the concordat of 5 June 1817, giving in to the demand of the Church for independence from the state.[4] The Catholic Church was guaranteed the undiminished preservation of its privileges based on the "divine order and on canon law" (Art. 1). The bishops were assured of the right to administer their dioceses according to canon law, to communicate unhindered with Rome, and the unrestricted right to train their clergy (Art. 12). They were permitted to inform the state of books in conflict with faith and Church regulations, and the state promised their suppression (Art. 13). Insults to the Catholic religion were forbidden (Art. 14), and the reestablishment of monasteries was permitted (Art. 7). Conflicting state laws were to be repealed (Art. 16), and ecclesiastical matters not specifically mentioned in the concordat were to be settled only according to the doctrines and regulations of the Church (Art. 17). The state was divided into two Church provinces; Munich-Freising encompassed Augsburg, Passau, and Regensburg, and Bamberg consisted of Würzburg, Eichstätt, and Speyer (Art. 2); the Curia had objected to only one Church province, as its metropolitan might become too powerful and grow into the role of a Primate. The state promised adequate landed property for the bishoprics, cathedral chapters, and seminaries (Art. 4 and 5), amounting to a partial reversal of secularization.

In turn, the King and his Catholic successor were granted the right to appoint bishops, who had to swear an oath of loyalty and obedience (Art. 9, 15). The state also gained significant influence on the composition of cathedral chapters (priors, deacons, ten or eight canons). The appointment of priors was left to the Pope, but shortly afterwards he agreed to the right of the King to submit nominations; the King appointed the deacons and also the canons during the six "papal" (uneven) months (Art. 10). The patronage of the sovereign was confirmed and

[3] Concerning the legal aspects of the bulls of circumscription, see Huber, *Verfassungsgeschichte* I, 418f.

[4] Text: Walter, *Fontes,* 204–12; Mercati, *Raccolta,* 591–96.

extended to all parishes which previously had belonged to secularized monasteries and cathedrals (Art. 11).

Appointments, patronage, and the bishop's oath involved a degree of participation in the filling of Church offices that no other German state outside of Austria enjoyed in the nineteenth century. Yet the concordat encountered lasting resistance among the enlightened civil servants, the Protestants, and the liberal Catholics. The monopoly granted the Catholic Church was incompatible with the modern concept of state, the edict of 1809, and the existence of a substantial Protestant minority in Franconia, Swabia, and the Palatinate. In order to remove the self-inflicted difficulties, the Bavarian government employed a legally questionable procedure. The concordat was published in conjunction with the new constitution and as a supplement to the religious edict of 26 May 1818,[5] which imitated Napoleon's Organic Articles. The edict guaranteed religious freedom and equality of the three main Christian denominations, and the state's supervision of the Church was reinstated (such as royal consent and appeal of abuses). A good number of clergymen thereupon refused the oath to the constitution with the religious edict, and the representative of the Curia, Nuncio Serra di Cassano,[6] insisted on adherence to the treaty. The state ultimately agreed nominally: In the Tegernsee Declaration[7] of 15 September 1821, King Max I Joseph declared that the oath referred only to civil matters. He also promised strict compliance with the concordat, but the absence of any real-estate transfers denied it. The contradictions between edict and concordat were papered over but not removed, and during the subsequent century numerous misunderstandings resulted from them.

Prussia's population, traditionally intimately connected with Protestantism, had become two-fifths Catholic as a consequence of the Polish partitions, secularization, and the territorial shifts after the Congress of Vienna. About half of Prussia's Catholics were Poles. The result was a blending of denominational and national contrasts, as well as a fusion of German and Polish Catholics. Prussian law (1793) had granted freedom of religion and conscience to all subjects, but simultaneously it had strengthened the state's supervision of the Churches. Its application to the territories gained in the West complicated their already difficult integration. The Rhineland and Westphalia socially and politically had developed quite differently from Prussia, and the inclusion of the left

[5] Text: Walter, *Fontes,* 213–26.

[6] The Munich nunciature, vacant since 1800, was filled immediately following the signing of the concordat. Until 1925 it remained the only diplomatic representation of the Holy See in Germany. Prussia (and temporarily Hanover and the southwest German states) only maintained missions in Rome.

[7] Text: Walter, *Fontes,* 212f.

bank of the Rhine in Napoleon's progressive legal system had amplified the differences. Both government and papacy were interested in at least a formal regulation of the situation of the Catholic Church. Thanks to Prussian generosity in financial questions and to the skill of Niebuhr, after 1816 Prussian envoy to the Holy See, a partial agreement was reached relatively quickly; the Bull *De salute animarum*[8] and the Brief *Quod de fidelium*[9] (both of 16 July 1821) summarized the content.

The bull founded the Church provinces of Cologne (with Münster, Paderborn, and Trier) and Gnesen-Posen (with Kulm); the bishoprics of Breslau[10] and Ermland remained separate. The bishopric of Aachen, established by Napoleon, was dissolved.[11] In the cathedral chapters (priors, deacons, ten or eight canons, and four voting honorific canons), the appointment of priors was always based on royal nominations and that of canons only during the "papal" months. This, for a Protestant sovereign, unusual concession was the more important for the state, as the bull confirmed the right of cathedral chapters to elect bishops. The Brief *Quod de fidelium* exhorted the chapters to select only candidates acceptable to the King. It did not establish the positive right of nomination demanded by Prussia and always denied to non-Catholic sovereigns, but only a negative right of exclusion. An ambiguous formulation in the bull also enabled the government to continue the right of nominations employed in the chapters of Gnesen-Posen, Ermland, and Kulm.

The agreed-upon financial settlement after 1833 was to be based on real estate and property taxes, but, as in Bavaria, the implementation of this promise, which would have given the Church more independence, did not take place. Annual payments from the state were the rule.

The Bull *De salute animarum* was essentially implemented in the decade after 1821 by its executor, Bishop Joseph von Hohenzollern of Ermland, and the first bishops for the largely vacant dioceses were appointed by the Pope upon suggestions of the government. The bull regulated primarily organizational problems; in all other areas the dominant sovereignty of state law and the Organic Articles (in the Rhineland) prevailed. *Placet* and appeal of abuses were maintained, the state

[8] Text: Walter, *Fontes*, 239–62; Mercati, *Raccolta*, 648–65.

[9] Text: Walter, *Fontes*, 262f.; Mercati, *Raccolta*, 665f.

[10] Berlin, the province of Brandenburg and the province of Pomerania were subordinated to the bishopric of Breslau. See L. Jablonski, *Geschichte der fürstbischöflichen Delegatur Brandenburg-Pommern*, 2 vols. (Breslau 1929). Breslau retained its portions of Austrian Silesia, but the autonomous administrative district of County Glatz remained with the archbishopric of Prague.

[11] J. Torsy, *Geschichte des Bistums Aachen während der Französischen Zeit 1802–1814* (Bonn 1940).

controlled the administration of ecclesiastical property and educational institutions, and correspondence between bishops and Curia had to go through state agencies. Additionally, during the administration of Friedrich Wilhelm III (until 1840), the state in practice exercised the right of nomination in the filling of bishoprics, contrary to Rome's reservations, by indicating a *persona grata* to the voting chapter.

Negotiations were also started with the Kingdom of Hanover which since the secularization also comprised appreciable numbers of Catholics. Begun in 1817, they continued until 1824 because of the large demands of the state, especially in the right of nominating bishops. The Bull *Impensa Romanorum Pontificum,*[12] on 26 March 1824, confirmed the continued existence of the bishoprics of Hildesheim and Osnabrück which were adjusted to the state's borders. The cathedral chapters received the right to elect bishops based on the so-called Irish election system. Before the election the chapters had to submit to the government a list of candidates from which it could strike the less acceptable ones, although it was expected to leave an adequate number. The real-estate transfers agreed to by the state in Hanover also were replaced by monetary payments, and even these were made to the full extent initially only for the bishopric of Hildesheim. Osnabrück consequently remained under the provisional direction of a suffragan bishop; only in 1857 did it receive the endowment which made possible the establishment of a regular diocesan administration.

The Catholics of the other north and central German states were subordinated to neighboring bishops or vicars apostolic. For the Grand Duchy of Oldenburg, an officialate was founded in Vechta in 1830 and joined with the bishopric of Münster. The vicariate apostolic established in 1743 for the Kingdom of Saxony, whose Catholic dynasty governed a largely Protestant state, after 1816 was under the direction of a titular bishop. The vicar was nominated by the King, and after 1831 he also functioned in personal union as deacon of the cathedral of Bautzen. The seventeenth century vicariate of the northern missions remained responsible for Denmark, together with Schleswig-Holstein, the two Mecklenburgs, the Hanseatic cities, and the Duchy of Braunschweig. After 1841 the suffragan (after 1857 bishop) of Osnabrück acted as a provicar. In many small Protestant states, the Catholic religion long remained subject to restrictions contradicting the modern concept of state.

The reorganization was protracted and problematical in southwestern Germany, where established Church and Enlightenment were not deeply rooted. The problems were aggravated by the dispute over Wes-

[12] Text: Walter, *Fontes,* 265–75; Mercati, *Raccolta,* 689–96.

senberg; because of his reforms in Constance (revival of social structures, introduction of the native language into the liturgy) as well as because of his religious policy after 1815, when he favored a common religious policy of at least the southwest German states, he was in full disgrace in Rome. After the Pope had rejected his election as chapter vicar (after Dalberg's death in 1817), he could remain in office, in spite of his following, only as long as the government of Baden supported him. He thus suffered the fate which many reformers experienced in the nineteenth century: in order to realize at least a part of their anti-Curial plans, they were compelled to ally themselves with established church governments and therefore were doubly suspect to the Church.

But the Febronian concept won a partial victory, in that the governments of Baden, Württemberg, Hesse-Darmstadt, Electoral Hesse, and Nassau banded together for common action against Rome. At the Frankfurt Conferences, under the leadership of the Württemberg representative to the Federal Diet, K. A. von Wangenheim, they agreed in 1818 on a declaration designed for Rome based on Josephinistic principles. It was to be kept secret for the moment and later to be decreed as the law for an established Church. In the form of an ultimatum, the declaration demanded the establishment of state bishoprics and state governmental appointment of bishops from a list of three submitted by the chapters and the deacons.

When Consalvi rejected such a right of appointment, the governments at first pretended to act as defenders of the freedom of the Church; they knew they had the support of their own clergymen. But under the impact of the restoration after 1820 they became more conciliatory, as an understanding with the ecclesiastical authority appeared more important to them than the realization of the liberalizing ideas of Wessenberg and his friends. On 16 August 1821, Pius VII published the Bull of Circumscription *Provida sollersque.*[13] It provided for the establishment of the archbishopric of Freiburg (for Baden, instead of Constance) and the bishoprics of Rottenburg (for Württemberg), Mainz (for Hesse-Darmstadt), Fulda (for Electoral Hesse), and Limburg (for Nassau and Frankfurt), and determined the composition of the cathedral chapters (deacons, and between four and six canons) and their endowment. Only Mainz and Fulda had been bishoprics before.

The governments made the implementation of the bull dependent on a compromise in the question of filling episcopal sees, and in tough negotiations achieved an effective combination of the Prussian and Hanoverian veto rights. Leo's XII's Bull *Ad Dominici gregis custodiam,*[14]

[13] Text: Walter, *Fontes,* 322–35; Mercati, *Raccolta,* 667–78.

[14] Text: Walter, *Fontes,* 335–39; Mercati, *Raccolta,* 700–03.

of 11 April 1827, decreed the right to election by the cathedral chapters according to the listing procedure and equal participation by the states in the appointment of cathedral canons; the Brief *Re sacra,*[15] of 28 May 1827, obliged the chapters to confine themselves to nominating only candidates who were acceptable to the sovereigns. Both bulls were implemented and the first bishops appointed. The governments insisted on Febronian-oriented clergymen, but Wessenberg, the exposed head of the movement, had to retire from his offices as a consequence of the dissolution of the bishopric of Constance.

The reservation of sovereign privileges had particularly grave consequences in southwestern Germany. On 30 January 1830, the five governments published identical ordinances,[16] imposing on the Church a uniform system of state control as secretly agreed to in 1818. These involved assent, *recursus ab abusu* with simultaneous exclusion of Roman tribunals, loyalty oath of bishops and clergymen, participation of the state in ecclesiastical education and administration of property, adaptation of the ecclesiastical administrative structure to that of the state, state service instructions for deans, and sovereign patronage for most parishes. Synods also had to have governmental permission. In addition to pushing back Rome's participation, the ordinances also agreed with some of the other demands of Wessenberg. Education of clergymen was to take place in the theological departments of state universities, and an excellent theological knowledge and pastoral experience, an academic position, or a public office were to be prerequisites for the appointment as bishop or cathedral canon. The ordinances by the sovereigns were accepted by the bishops and firmly applied by state agencies in which clergymen also were active (in Baden the High Consistory, in Württemberg the Catholic Consistory). Papal protests were successful only in Electoral Hesse, where the regulations were applied less stringently.

The ecclesiastical reorganization of Germany, which in its basic forms has continued into the present, largely followed the example of the French concordat. It also corresponded far more to the schema of a universal Church than the arrangement ending in 1803, whose complex legal titles and traditions had fostered autonomy and self-assurance. In contrast, the new arrangement rested solely on legal actions of the papacy and on its agreements with the governments; it practiced visibly and efficiently a combination of Roman jurisdictional primacy and ecclesiastical sovereignty of the state. In the process, the Curia had been

[15] Text: Mercati, *Raccolta,* 703.

[16] Text: Walter, *Fontes,* 340–45. The papal protest (Brief by Pius VIII of 30 June 1830) ibid., 345–48.

compelled to make more concessions than the ultramontane doctrine wished to acknowledge, viewing the Pope as the only guarantee of ecclesiastical freedom. Especially in the question of filling episcopal sees and other high Church offices, the governments had achieved an extensive participation not justified by the subject matter.

The division of the Church of Germany into small, weak, and isolated territorial Churches corresponded exactly to the wishes of the states and of the Curia. Intermediate layers had not been reinstated. From now on, no priors and archdeacons stood between pastors and bishops, no powerful metropolitans between bishops and Pope, and for political reasons the rights of archbishops were reduced and several bishoprics were exempt. The new, more "Roman," church organization afforded the Curia numerous opportunities for intervention. The system of established Churches served to stimulate this movement, for the time being inhibited but in the long run increasingly centralized, and fostered the development of an alliance between papacy and people's Church. As dependent minorities, the German Catholics had no recourse but to affiliate more with the Roman central office. Initiatives for the expansion of ecclesiastical freedom generally could not be expected by the cathedral chapters and diocesan curias staffed with people trusted by the state, but only from the secular clergy and laity. Appeals against abusive extensions of governmental privileges could only be made to the Pope, who alone was entitled to negotiate with the governments on the level of international law and diplomacy.

Austria was relatively little affected by the secularization. The bishoprics, whose incumbents had to renounce their sovereign rights (Salzburg, Brixen, Trent), continued to exist with adequate financial means, just as much as the monasteries permitted by Joseph II. But the government utilized the secularization in order to implement in Salzburg, Tirol, and Vorarlberg[17] the new alignment of diocesan borders, which in the other Habsburg possessions had been undertaken between 1782 and 1788. Since then, the dioceses of the monarchy were almost exclusively limited to Austrian territory,[18] approximately equally large, and corresponded to the political and administrative or-

[17] The definitive reorganization took place in 1818. Salzburg lost its episcopal territory and its metropolitan privileges in Bavaria. The portions of Chur in South Tyrol were divided among Brixen and Trent; Brixen received Vorarlberg (until then largely with Constance) and as compensation ceded South Tyrolean deanships to Trent, which after 1825 became part of the Salzburg church province.

[18] The Josephinist principle of church organization was not implemented only in Silesia. Concerning the problem of adapting ecclesiastical to state boundaries, see R. Kottje, "Diözesan- und Landesgrenzen" in *Reformata Reformanda, Festgabe für Hubert Jedin* II (Münster 1965), 304–16.

ganization of the state. The emperor nominated almost all bishops. Only in Olmütz and Salzburg was the election privilege of the cathedral chapters unchanged, and the archbishop of Salzburg retained the singular privilege of appointing bishops in three of his suffragan bishoprics.[19]

In general, Austrian religious policy during the long reign (1792–1835) of Emperor Francis II (I), was conducted under the precepts of moderate Josephinism, and not without difficulties it was extended to the newly won and regained territories after 1815. Its principles also initially guided Metternich, who after 1809 was in charge of foreign policy. Between 1814 and 1816 he promoted Wessenberg's plans for a federal concordat, with whose help he hoped to extend Josephinism to the other German territories, to give the new confederation a greater uniformity, and to enlarge Austria's influence. Peace between Church and state occupied an eminent position in Metternich's conservative concept of society. Earlier than others he recognized the utility of close cooperation between a restored papacy and a restored Empire, and he did not ignore suggestions from Hofbauer's circle with respect to ecclesiastical policy.[20] After the foundering of the plans for a federal concordat, he weighed the possibility of mitigating Josephinist laws and concluding a concordat between Austria and the Holy See. But the Emperor and the highest officials, led by Count Wallis, insisted on preserving the state's sovereignty over the Church, achieved under Maria Theresia and Joseph II, which, of course, also meant protection for the Church and its activities within the limits drawn by the state. Only in the last years of his reign did Emperor Francis adopt Metternich's suggestions and start the alliance of throne and altar.

The French occupation of Switzerland (Helvetic Republic 1798–1803) had resulted in the dissolution of the monasteries and the expulsion of the nuncio, but the mediation constitution written in 1803 under Napoleon's influence improved the situation. A new nuncio, Testaferrata, was sent to Lucerne; fought against the reforms being introduced from Constance, which found many followers in Switzerland, and passed on to Rome the complaints and suspicions about Wessenberg. In order to prevent a further spreading of his ideas, Swiss territory was separated from Constance and placed under the provisional direction of

[19] In Lavant and Seckau the archbishop had the right of appointment every time, in Gurk every third time. See H. Bastgen, "Die Prärogativen der Salzburger Metropole," in *HJ* 33 (1912).

[20] Metternich's turning away from Josephinism: H. von Srbik, *Metternich. Der Staatsmann und der Mensch* (Munich 1925, reprint Munich 1957) I, 308ff., II, 40–45, 455, and elsewhere; A. Posch, "Die Vorgeschichte des österreichischen Konkordats von 1855," in *Religion, Wissenschaft, Kultur,* 7/1 (1956); Weinzierl-Fischer, *Konkordate,* 15ff. See also chapter 13, pp. 219ff. and especially chapter 20, pp. 340ff.

the strictly Catholic-minded prior of Beromünster, Goldin von Tiefenau.

The federal treaty of 1815, reconstituting Switzerland as a federal state with twenty-two cantons under guarantee of the Congress of Vienna, essentially reintroduced an established Church and contained a guarantee for monasteries. Similar to the constitution of 1803, the federal treaty adjusted several borders, creating religiously heterogeneous cantons and sowing the seed for many future discords. The reorganization also made evident the main cause for the conflicts beginning in the 1830s, namely the radicalism of many liberals and the continuing contrast between Febronian and ultramontane Catholics.

The Church in Switzerland also needed to be reorganized. After the idea of one national bishopric which the Swiss had favored was rejected by Rome, the difficulty was how to reconcile the rival demands of the cantons. The creation of a new structure for the entire country required the constant efforts of ten years, mediated by the nunciature in Lucerne. Only the bishopric of Sitten remained unchanged. The area of Constance and the Swiss portion of the prince-bishopric of Basel in 1828 were combined in the bishopric of Basel, with its seat in Solothurn. It comprised seven cantons, whose governments had the right to influence the composition of the cathedral chapters electing the bishop. Only candidates could be chosen who were acceptable to the governments.[21] Chur, reduced by the loss of its Austrian territory, was united in 1823 with Sankt Gallen (until 1836). In western Switzerland, enlarged by a few Catholic strips of land, the old bishopric of Geneva was reconstituted in 1821 and combined with Lausanne. The four bishoprics remained exempt, allowing the Holy See a direct influence. Tessin remained a part of the Italian dioceses of Milan and Como until 1859.

[21] The treaties on the founding of the bishopric of Basel together with circumscription bull: Mercati, *Raccolta,* 711–24.

CHAPTER 8

The Other European Churches

The Catholics in the Kingdom of the Netherlands

As an artificial creation of the Congress of Vienna, comprising the former, mainly Calvinistic, United Provinces and the nine Catholic Belgian departments and ruled by a Protestant monarch, William I of Orange, the new Kingdom of the Netherlands ecclesiastically presented a most disparate view. In the north, the "Dutch mission," dependent on the Congregation for the Propagation of the Faith, numbered about three hundred twenty-five thousand Catholics, i.e., one fifth of the population of the area. Since the closing of the nunciature in Brussels it was administered by a Vice Superior, Monsignor Ciamberlani, who resided in Münster in Westphalia. In reality, however, the archpriests and members of orders who supervised numerous city parishes possessed a large degree of autonomy, naturally leading to inadequate religious discipline. The centralized training of the clergy in the seminary at Warmond was strongly influenced by the German Catholic Enlightenment with all of its positive and negative aspects. In north Brabant and the other areas conquered by the Dutch in the seventeenth century, Catholics were in the majority (about four hundred thousand) and, except for the remainder of the old diocese of Roermond, whose bishop was still alive, divided into two vicariates apostolic: 's-Hertogenbosch and Breda (where in 1811 Napoleon intended to create a bishopric by decree). The cultural standards of the clergy, accustomed to being on the fringe of national life, left much to be desired. In the southern provinces lived 3.5 million Belgians with a long tradition of post-Tridentine Catholicism, divided into five dioceses which were established by the concordat of 1801.[1] Their reorganization, after the troubles of the revolutionary period a dire necessity, was not yet completed. This was the more necessary as during Napoleon's final years the administration by prelates, installed without permission of the Pope, encountered the growing resistance of a strongly ultramontane clergy, which was encouraged by its successful resistance against Joseph II. The difficulties which almost from the beginning placed the Church in opposition to the Dutch government delayed reorganization even longer. But at least the number of ordinations rose appreciably and, at least until the closing of the seminaries as a consequence of the decisions of 1825, permitted a gradual filling of the vacancies caused by the revolution.

In this denominationally divided state the only sensible solution was the principle of religious freedom, which was in fact imposed by the powers in July 1814 and anchored in the constitution. But while the Dutch Catholics, long treated like second-class citizens, regarded the new system as progressive in spite of the limitations imposed by the Organic Articles, the Belgian and above all the Flemish clergy, whose

[1] Rome and The Hague at first hesitated, but after 1816 there was indeed a partial provisional renewal. See H. Wagnon, "La reconductions du Concordat de 1801 dans les provinces belges du Royaume Uni des Pays-Bas" in *Scrinium Lovaniense* (Louvain 1961), 514–42.

reactionary position had been strengthened by Napoleon's religious policy, would have preferred a restoration of the Church in the southern provinces to the privileged position it had occupied before the French occupation. This was especially true for the field of education. Consequently, the diocesan authorities under the leadership of the energetic bishop of Ghent, Monsignor de Broglie, the heroic opponent of Napoleon, by their doctrinal judgment of September 1815 condemned the indifferentism of the new constitution and forbade Catholics to take the oath on it. Incited by the *Spectateur catholique* of Abbé De Foere, founded in 1815 in the service of counterrevolutionary traditionalism, many bowed to this exhortation. On the other hand, the former prince-bishop of Liège, Francois-Antoine de Méan, a member of the Estates General and raised in a less strict theological tradition than the clergy of the former Austrian Netherlands, was prepared to swear the oath. Shortly afterwards he was appointed by the King as archbishop of Mechelen. In Rome, where a commission of cardinals had approved the doctrinal judgment, there was initial reluctance to confirm the appointment. But under pressure from Metternich and thanks to the flexibility of Consalvi, ultimately a compromise formula was adopted, which stated that the oath applied only to civil matters and had no dogmatic significance. In 1817 the archbishop received his bull of appointment, and in 1821 after months of protracted negotiations the King finally agreed that Catholics could take the oath "with the understanding of de Méan." This calmed the emotions for the time being.

In the meantime new difficulties had arisen. The government, brooking no interference in its sphere of competence, in 1815 had prohibited Monsignor Ciamberlani from concerning himself with the affairs of the Belgian dioceses and had ordered his deportation. Additionally, in order to counter the resistance of a portion of the clergy, it reinstated in 1816 the Napoleonic Organic Articles, which became a source of many administrative and police chicaneries. Likewise in 1818, Napoleonic laws concerning orders were reinstated in order to limit the reestablishment of orders to those which were devoted to works of charity.[2] Even if the laws were applied only very cautiously in the beginning, obstacles increased noticeably after 1822. At the same time, these steps led to the laicization of education, an area in which the Belgian clergy was particularly sensitive. Between 1822 and 1824 numerous Catholic schools were closed, especially those of the Christian Brothers, who were accused of being French agents. In June 1825, two royal ordinances dis-

[2] A list of the monasteries with the number of their members can be found in Stockmann, op. cit., 404–50. Additional facts can be gleaned from the numerous descriptions concerning themselves with local conditions.

solved all free secondary schools, including the boys' seminaries. Simultaneously, there was established at Louvain a College of Philosophy, attendance at which was to be obligatory for all young men interested in becoming clergymen. Its entire faculty was to be appointed by the King independently from the bishops.

These measures, hardly touching the Catholics in the north, were joyously greeted by the Catholic middle class of the south, which had absorbed the ideas of the eighteenth century and viewed as an anachronism the intention of the clergy to resume control over public life. They were also accorded a friendly reception by some priests, influenced by the Enlightenment and German Febronianism, especially in the north and in the province of Luxemburg, which before the revolution had belonged to the diocese of Trier. The diocesan officials were worried, but protested only mildly; the majority of the bishoprics were vacant or occupied by prelates weakened by old age and illness. Archbishop Méan was chiefly interested in maintaining cordial relations with the government. But the majority of the clergy as well as some militant Catholics reacted vociferously. Following the ordinances of 1825, two Dutchmen, the lawyer Van der Horst and the priest Van Bommel, soon joined by the vicar general of Mechelen, E. Sterckx, opened a vehement campaign against the educational policy of the government.

Belgians especially were convinced that the King secretly aimed at Protestantizing the country, but actually the King was only interested in raising the cultural standards of the southern provinces, which were far inferior to the United Provinces. In the tradition of enlightened despotism[3] and based on his *ius circa sacra,* the King wished to exercise strict control over the Church, which was regarded as the chief educational institution (interestingly enough, he behaved even more dictatorially toward the Reformed Church when he imposed a regulation on it in 1816).

Under the influence of his minister Van Maanen, a good legal mind but bare of all psychological sensitivity, and surrounded by advisers, who for the most part were Catholic but motivated by Febronianism, Josephinism, and Napoleonic Gallicanism and prepared to smash clerical power, William I, after the foundering of the concordat negotiations in 1822 and 1824 and in order to settle the problem of nominating bishops, adopted the idea of a national Church guided by the state and only tenuously connected with the Holy See.

But the objections to the College of Philosophy touched on the

[3] Concerning his earlier attitude to the Catholics, see J. A. Bornewasser, *Kirche und Staat in Fulda unter Wilhelm Friedrich von Oranien, 1802–06* (Fulda 1956).

training of the clergy, and the diocesan curias considered this as the limit of possible concessions. The resumption of negotiations with Rome for a new concordat became unavoidable. These led to an agreement[4] for the entire country on 18 June 1827. It extended the conditions of the 1801 concordat to the northern provinces, where two new bishoprics were to be created (Amsterdam and 's-Hertogenbosch), and compromised on the nomination of bishops: the Protestant monarch was not to nominate the bishops who would be elected by cathedral chapters, but he had the right of veto.

Calm returned for only a few months, however. Giving in to the complaints of the Dutch Calvinists and Belgian liberals, the government let it be known that it intended to defer the application of the concordat, viewing it as too favorable to the Catholics. Indeed, the efforts of Monsignor Capaccini, sent by Leo XII, failed in spite of some partial successes because of the visibly lacking desire of the commission charged with the affairs of the Catholic religion. As before, the commission was Josephinistic and anticlerical. While de facto religious instruction in the schools was continued, the government persevered in its intentions to laicize education and thereby drove Catholics to increasingly bitter resistance. Van Bommel, elected bishop of Liège in 1829, continued to hope for an agreement with the King, who in fact was ready to make concessions. But the Belgian clergy, more ultramontane than the Pope himself, had definitely lost confidence in a solution by the government. Under the leadership of Sterckx it now demanded the complete independence of the Church from the state, and was willing to conclude an alliance with the opponents of the government in order to obtain "freedom in everything and for everything."[5]

In this situation, the Belgian clergy was almost exclusively occupied with institutional problems and the rebuilding of a Catholic society which was supposed to resemble the prerevolutionary one. Severely handicapped by the rudimentary training which the clergy received in the seminaries, staffed by professors who were self-taught themselves, and paralyzed by the largely unfounded fears of a Protestantization of the country, the clergy was little concerned with adapting the Gospel to the antireligious ideas imported from France and Germany. The only positive note was that the clergy, supported by some active laymen, as for example L. de Robiano and P. Kersten, was quick to recognize the importance of the press.

It was also a layman, J. G. Le Sage ten Broek, who in 1818 in Holland founded the first Catholic monthly, *De Godsdienstvriend.* This successful

[4] Mercati I, 704–10.

[5] Concerning the stages of this development, see below, pp. 271ff.

publicist, a man of action, eccentric, and full of initiative, was more responsible than anyone else for shaking the Dutch Catholics out of their lethargy, forcing them to emerge from the virtual underground in which they had lived since the seventeenth century, and publicly defending their rights. Son of a Protestant minister and convert, inspired by the great movement of the "Awakening," he was tirelessly working to win his peaceloving countrymen for a militant ultramontanism and did not limit himself to confronting medieval Catholic tradition with Protestant innovations. With equal passion he attacked the infiltration of rationalistic ideas among some of his fellow believers, such as the priest Schrant, who preferred to seek their inspiration from the Germany of the Enlightenment rather than from the France of de Maistre and the early Lamennais. In this fashion he warned the Dutch Catholics of the temptation of a dogmatic Christianity based on natural morality. He equally participated in shaping a strictly denominational mentality, viewed all manifestations of tolerance and irenicism with suspicion, and categorically rejected Sailer's heritage as well as the Catholicism of those clergymen who had accepted Hegelianism and Josephinism.

Briefly, the developments after 1815 were disappointing from the institutional point of view. But they served to strengthen Catholicism in the north, and allowed to grow a new attitude in the south, which soon would seize Europe under the name of Catholic liberalism.

The Political Emancipation of Catholics in the British Isles

After the Act of Union by which Ireland in 1800 became a part of the United Kingdom, Catholics constituted a quarter of the population. Except for the community of faith and the common loss of many civil and political rights, there hardly existed anywhere else larger differences than those between the handful of English Catholics, with their status of a missionary society, and the Church of Ireland. Through all persecutions it had preserved its episcopal hierarchy and its hold on 4 million faithful, and since the middle of the eighteenth century had seen increasing normalization.

Unaffected by any establishment tradition,[6] the Irish Church drew its strength from the people. They had the status of semi-serfs, as the English conquerors had taken approximately 95 percent of all land, but for centuries they had been accustomed to defend with equal passion their religious faith and their national traditions. French revolutionary ideas encouraged them in vigorously demanding their religious, social,

[6] The suggestion spread in 1801 and 1824 that the state should take over the remuneration of the clergy was rejected by the great majority of bishops and priests.

and political independence, three aspects closely intertwined in their eyes. In this atmosphere, a new generation of priests, not trained abroad but in the national seminary of Maynooth and unfamiliar with the punitive laws directed against Catholics, turned uninhibitedly to a reorganization of pastoral life and promoted the development of expressions of faith. The clergy, which maintained close contact with the people in spite of an improved material condition, continued to be assisted by the religious congregations, which after a downturn in the eighteenth century[7] experienced a rapid growth in the first decades of the nineteenth century. The old orders, again able to function more freely, were joined by native foundings such as the Christian Brothers, who were an Irish imitation of the French Christian Brothers. Founded in 1804, the Christian Brothers received their ultimate form in 1817 from Monsignor D. Murray, archbishop coadjutor in Dublin.

In England, on the other hand, the members of the Roman Church constituted only 2 percent of the total population. Their preference for a Catholicism of stark sobriety resulted in part from their desire not to attract undue attention from the public, in part from the British temperament, and in part from their reaction against the emotionalism of the Protestant sects. The Roman Church was divided into four vicariates apostolic, whose geographical extension made an effective guidance of pastoral care difficult. Even in 1815, most of the Catholics lived isolated lives in the rural areas in the vicinity of manor houses, whose owners maintained an almoner more because of tradition than because of religious convictions. With the beginning of the nineteenth century and Irish immigration to London and the industrial cities of the north, the Catholic community began to orient itself to them. The number of the faithful doubled within one generation, and in 1814 surpassed the two hundred thousand mark, requiring the construction of nine hundred new chapels. Catholicism began to develop an urban character, while the landed gentry gradually lost its monopoly on the Church to the enterprising middle class.

Simultaneously, there occurred in the leading segments of England a transformation in the attitude toward Catholicism. The decadence of the Anglican Church and the growth of indifferentism among the upper class favored a tolerant attitude. Contact with French émigrés, together with the romantic rediscovery of the Middle Ages by Walter Scott, removed some deep prejudices against "papism." They even effected

[7] As a consequence of the closing of the noviciates, imposed by Rome in 1751 upon the suggestion of some bishops, the number of regular clergy, consisting in 1742 of between seven hundred and fourteen hundred priests, by 1802 had sunk to two hundred fifty compared to nineteen hundred secular clergy.

some conversions such as those of Kenelm Henry Digby in 1823 and of Ambrose Phillipp de Lisle in 1829. The attitudinal change was fostered by the firm position assumed by Pius VII toward Napoleon and promoted the resumption of official contacts between the Holy See and the British government after two hundred years of nearly complete interruption.[8]

The confluence of these diverse elements contributed to an easier resolution of the problem of the emancipation of Catholics, i.e., the lifting of the legal restrictions under which they had been forced to live since the Reformation, a problem which for decades had presented itself with increasing intensity. In 1813 a solution was close, even at the price of numerous concessions which the Catholic nobles as well as the Congregation for the Propagation of the Faith were willing to make. But the Irish were supported in their opinion by John Milner (1752–1826), the fervent vicar apostolic of the Midlands. He was an Englishman, but a decided opponent of the exclusive Anglo-Gallicanism of the Cisalpine Club, and regarded such a solution as an attempt to subordinate the Church to a Protestant state. The efforts for a resumption of negotiations by Consalvi, who had no objections to a limited control of the clergy by the government and by Castlereagh, who viewed the British arrangement as anachronistic, foundered on the uncompromising stance of the Irish, who under no circumstances were willing to diverge from their demand for the freedom of the Church. They also failed because the Irish did not believe they had to take account of the Roman viewpoint or of the Tories in the House of Lords. The latter's demand to have veto power over the appointment of bishops was not merely a sign of antipapism, but also, in view of the situation in Canada, a security measure.

In spite of growing sympathy by the Liberals, negotiations for years remained at dead center. Regularly introduced petitions in Parliament produced virtually no result, the only exception being a bill in 1817 facilitating the appointment of Catholic officers to the army. The English Catholics were willing to wait patiently for better times, but not the Irish Catholics, whose national concerns fueled their religious demands. The press campaign started in *The Chronicle* by John England, the director of the seminary of Cork, and the thirty-two letters published by Hierophilus between 1820 and 1823 against the preferential rights of

[8] These contacts were made at the Congress of Vienna and were increasingly necessary as a result of the growing importance of the Catholics in Ireland and Canada, and the establishment of England in Malta and the Ionian Islands. The deaths of Castlereagh and Consalvi and the accession of the very antipapal George IV after 1823 resulted in a cooling of relations, without, however, leading to a rupture. See N. Miko in *ZKTh* 78 (1956), 206–14.

the Anglican Church in Ireland, were the first signs of a new tactic. Hierophilus was the pseudonym of John McHale,[9] a professor of dogmatics at Maynooth who, like John England, was typical of the new generation of the clergy. Their efforts supplanted diplomatic negotiations and cautious initiatives, most of which had been undertaken by the English. A mass action was started in Ireland with the intention to ease up on the pressure only after victory had been achieved. A first decisive step was taken by Daniel O'Connell, a popular speaker and eminent organizer, who for twenty years had headed the struggle for national and religious freedom. In 1823 he transformed the old Catholic Association, heretofore confined to bourgeois circles, into a mass movement by decreasing the annual contribution of twenty shillings to one penny a month. With the aid of voluntary propagandists, who undertook the political indoctrination of the uneducated peasants even in the smallest of villages, the association organized peaceful agitation within the law.

Many priests at first hesitated to join a movement which clearly had political objectives, but following the example of some bishops like Monsignor Doyle of Kildare and under the influence of the seminary of Maynooth, the clergy gradually joined and supported the Catholic rent by making their churches available for election meetings. Soon the entire firmly united Catholic population of the island joined the man who was called the uncrowned King of Ireland in the spirit of a crusade. The British government, vainly having attempted to stop O'Connell's campaign, felt overwhelmed. The triumphant election of the Irishman in 1828 as the Member of Parliament for Clare, even though legally he did not qualify, made the more clearsighted Tories understand that concessions had to be made if a civil war was to be avoided. In the face of resistance by the royal family, the Anglican bishops, numerous peers, and the majority of the population, Wellington, who by no means was the blind enemy of Catholics as he was often depicted, threw his reputation as the victor of Waterloo behind the Catholics. Supported by Robert Peel, he managed to curtail drastically the political activities in Ireland; in return, he received the King's approval in April 1829 for a bill which with few exceptions granted Catholics equality in civil and personal rights[10] without compelling them to concede to the government the right to veto in the election of bishops. This victory, gained

[9] See *The Letters of M. Rev. J. MacHale* (Dublin 1847), 9–155.

[10] Catholics could fill all offices except those of the Lord Chancellor, the Lord Keeper, and the Lord Lieutenant for Ireland; they could be elected to Parliament, but had to take a special oath "not to disturb or weaken the Protestant religion" and affirm that the Pope had no political rights over England. Additionally, the recruitment of regular clergy was forbidden, but not that of nuns. Their presence, especially that of the Jesuits, was subject to strict control.

through Irish agitation, was beneficial for all Catholics under the British crown, in England and Scotland as well as in Canada and the other colonies.

The undeniable significance of the legal restructuring for the future of Catholicism in the British Empire does not alone account for the changes which the Catholic community underwent. In Ireland, Protestant propaganda during the 1820's grew more intensive and was able to record some successes. On the other hand, the work of ecclesiastical renewal begun since the end of the eighteenth century began to quicken, especially under the favorable leadership of a number of capable prelates such as P. Curtis in Armagh (1819–32); J. Doyle in Kildare (1819–34); and chiefly D. Murray in Dublin (1823–52; coadjutor after 1809), one of the principal promoters of Catholic renewal on the island during the first half of the century. The development in England was slower, but no less effective. To be sure, the weight of the few hundreds of landed gentry around whom the Catholic population had centered for two hundred years remained noticeable until the 1820s; their social and economic influence and the Gallican and Jansenist education given to the French-educated clergy was the explanation for the continuing existence of the "Cisalpine" spirit. It insisted strongly not only on independence from Rome but also from the hierarchical authorities in England, and was hostile to any Catholic initiative which might offend the Protestants. But the vicars apostolic who in 1818 had reopened the English College in Rome distanced themselves from the lay nobility and strove to regain firm control over a clergy accustomed by long tradition to being independent. In 1826, William Poynter prescribed annual priestly exercises for the first time. But the new mentality was best represented by John Milner, from 1803 until 1826 the pugnacious vicar apostolic of the Midlands. He was the dominating figure during the first quarter of the century not only because of his uncompromising support of emancipation for the Irish, but equally because of the strength of his ultramontanism[11] and his innovative pastoral methods, which made him the forerunner of Manning. He was vehemently polemical and narrow-minded in his view of Protestants, but he was one of the first to grasp the significance of Irish immigration to England and to recognize that the future of English Catholicism was in the cities. He also opposed the formality of exercises of piety and introduced continental forms of devotion, such as the Sacred Heart of Jesus devotion. Finally he was one of the first to take advantage of the influence of the press. He supported the efforts of William Eusebius Andrews, who in 1813 had founded the

[11] The eagerness with which he defended the rights of the Holy See against his Gallican-infected confreres earned him the nickname "Athanasius of England."

Orthodox Journal, the first English Catholic monthly, whose polemic harshness gradually disturbed Rome's clever tactics.

Intellectual life also showed some tentative signs of renewal. Without a doubt, seminary training generally remained highly superficial and was limited to morals and practice, but progress could be noted in Ushaw College.[12] Even if the works of Poynter and Milner betrayed a very one-sided anti-Protestantism, they nevertheless pointed to the desire of Catholics to be heard again. But above all it was John Lingard's[13] *History of England,* appearing between 1819 and 1830, which impressed everyone by its scholarly character and objectivity and persuaded many Englishmen to throw their antipapal and outdated prejudices overboard. Unfortunately, the effectiveness of the Bible Society, founded in 1803 by laymen, was soon hampered by ecclesiastical censorship.

The Difficult Situation of Catholics in the Russian Empire

While the condition of the Catholics dependent on the British crown appreciably improved between 1815 and 1830, a worsening of the situation occurred in the Russian Empire, which with the annexation of a large part of Poland numbered several million Catholics of both rites. After the 1830 Polish revolution, the situation grew worse yet.

But immediately after 1815 hope did not appear unfounded. At the Congress of Vienna, Tsar Alexander I in the name of conservative principles actively contributed to the restoration of the Papal States, and Consalvi after an interruption of ten years succeeded in reestablishing diplomatic relations. The Tsar desired direct contacts with the Holy See in order better to counter Austrian influence in the Balkan states and, in spite of Pius VII's disappointing refusal to join the Holy Alliance, to gain the support of the Roman Church in the political restoration of Europe. Perhaps he also was interested in a unification of the Russian Orthodox and Roman Catholic Churches and harbored certain personal sympathies for Catholicism.[14] General Tuyll's mission from 1815 to 1816 was a failure, but that of Italinski, Alexander's emissary to Rome from 1817 to 1823, brought some positive results, which were enhanced by Alexander's visit to Pius VII in 1822. Yet while the Tsar and his advisers were willing to regard the Pope as an ally in their common resistance to the rise of revolutionary forces, they wanted the Catholic Church in the Empire to remain under the strict control of the govern-

[12] See D. Milburn, *A History of Ushaw College* (Durham 1964), 26–145. The seminary was not controlled by the bishop, but by the clergy of the district.

[13] See M. Haile and E. Bonney, *Life and Letters of J. Lingard* (London 1911); G. Culkin in *The Month* 192 (1951), 7–18.

[14] See the description of the situation in Winter, *Russland,* 205–07.

ment and contacts with Rome were to be held to a minimum. The Russian state, since Peter the Great directly involved in its own national Church, could not but regard as unacceptable the demands of the papacy in favor of an alien, barely tolerated, Church. This was true all the more so as the Catholic Church was seen as the soul of the resistance in Poland and as a Trojan horse in the service of Austrian aims in Eastern Europe. Besides, the Church could hardly be called independent from the state in the neighboring Habsburg Empire in which Josephinist laws were still in effect. To this initial material for conflict between the two great powers, which started from two incompatible totalitarian principles, another one was added. After being open to western influences during the Enlightenment, explaining the success of the Jesuits and the forming of a group of "papalists" around the ambassador from Savoy, Joseph de Maistre, the campaign of 1812 had awakened the patriotic spirit in Russia and caused a movement of national reaction. Considering revolutionary Europe on the way to dechristianization, it insisted on bringing back the virtues of Slavism as embodied by the Orthodox Church. A few spectacular conversions to Catholicism in the aristocracy[15] spurred in the circles of the reaction, fostered by Prince Golitsin, minister for education and religion, a strong desire to fight back. In 1816 the Jesuits were expelled from Moscow and Saint Petersburg, and in 1820 from all of Russia. Fed by romanticism and the success of idealist philosophy, the slavophile movement came into its own with the ascendancy of Nicholas I in 1825. He was determined to proceed even more determinedly than his brother and without paying any attention to Roman complaints. Until the eventual realization of his ideal, a Russia united by the single faith of Orthodoxy, the Catholic clergy of the Empire was to be increasingly isolated from Rome and subjected to the sole jurisdiction of the Russian state. He systematically avoided all discussions with the Holy See on the grounds of religious freedom of his subjects and denied the justification of the concerns presented to him. The implementation of this policy of tacit and continuing infringements was initially facilitated by the hesitation of the Pope and his advisers to oppose tsarist Russia, which, having emerged strengthened from the Napoleonic wars, appeared to them as a model of order.

In this continuingly worsening atmosphere there were repeated discussions between Rome and Petersburg which hoped to find a mode for coexistence, even though the fundamental differences made this vir-

[15] See Winter, *Russland,* 165–66, 178; J. Gagarine, *Le salon de la comtesse Golovine* (Paris 1879); M. J. Rouët de Journel, *Une russe catholique, Mme Swetchine* (Paris 1929). In 1817 Joseph de Maistre departed, having been one of the promoters of the group of "papalists" and whose *Du Pape* was intended as the answer to A. Sturdza, *Considérations sur la doctrine et l'esprit de l'Église orthodoxe.*

tually impossible. Three problems were in the center of these negotiations: the condition of the Catholic Church in the autonomous Kingdom of Poland, the condition of Roman Catholicism in Russia proper, and finally the condition of the Uniates.

The blows of fate which the last ones had been forced to endure in 1839 led to a forced incorporation into the Orthodox Church. Until his death in 1826 the very controversial Monsignor Siestrzencewicz, archbishop of Mogilev, was the leading figure of Latin Catholicism in Russia.[16] Ultramontane historiography of the nineteenth century, influenced by the Jesuits, who often were unhappy with him, depicts him as an ambitious courtier, more concerned with winning the favor of the Russian sovereign than with representing the rights of the Holy See, and as a man hostile to the orders, especially the Society of Jesus. From a more precise examination by A. Brumanis, however, he emerges as a zealous defender of the Church, even though he liked worldly honors and power. Like many other bishops, he did not appreciate the exemption of regular clergy, but his skillful and sometimes unpredictable actions on the whole produced positive results. Through his persistent efforts to remain *persona grata* at the court, a matter of outstanding importance in an autocratic regime, he left at his death a blossoming diocese with dozens of new parishes, an almost adequate secular and regular clergy, and active charitable works. At the price of some manipulations of canon law, he also succeeded in gaining respect for the Catholic Church from the authorities, who regarded it as an alien body, and in securing for it the prerequisites for its viability without loss of its fundamental principles.

Between 1815 and 1820 he was severely reproached by the Jesuit-influenced Catholic circles of Russia and by Rome for his membership in the Russian Bible Association, which was of Protestant origin and counted several Orthodox bishops among the members of its general council.[17] In part his position was doubtless determined by an enlightened interdenominationalism, but he also took care that the translation for the Catholics was done according to the Vulgata. After the Congress of Vienna, the archbishop was also accused of supporting, possibly of provoking, the demands by the tsarist government to make him a primate. In most matters, including the canonical investment of

[16] In addition to the Catholics in the annexed Polish provinces after 1795 and the Baltic states, there were also German colonies in the area of the Volga and around Odessa; Catholics of French and Flemish origin lived on the shores of the Black Sea in the Caucasus. The former largely inhabited the dioceses of Vilna, Samogitia, Minsk, Luck, and Kamenez, while the latter formed the huge archdiocese Mogilev.

[17] Concerning the Russian Bible Society, see Boudou I, 105–23 and A. Brumanis, op. cit., 282–91.

bishops appointed by the Tsar, such a position would have freed him from consulting Rome. But in the light of the most recent developments in ecclesiology we have a better understanding of the resistance which Monsignor Siestrzencewicz put up against the centralizing tendencies of the Curia[18] by appealing to the autonomy that the Churches enjoyed during the first centuries. Our understanding also rests on the knowledge that he was there at the time and probably knew better the limits of the possible; he also knew that by open confrontation instead of skillful tactics nothing would have been gained, and probably a lot would have been lost.

This is not to say that the situation was ideal. While the diocese of Mogilev was in a relatively good position, this was not the case in the other dioceses in which most of the Catholics lived. The material and moral condition of the priests was often inadequate, inasmuch as the authorities disagreed with the bishops over the training of the clergy. Several dioceses were without leadership for long years (Vilna from 1815 to 1830, Minsk from 1816 to 1831), or the Tsar assigned them unqualified and unsuitable bishops. Siestrzencewicz's successor as archbishop of Mogilev, Monsignor G. Cieciszewski, also appointed without prior consultation with Rome, was an energetic and learned prelate, but he was a frail old man of eighty years of age no longer able to oppose the Russification policies of the authorities in Petersburg and Moscow. When he died in April 1831, the government, planning a reorganization of the dioceses in Russia, delayed the appointment of a successor until 1839. In 1832 Catholic institutions were hard hit by a series of ukases. Of the total of 291 monasteries and convents 202 were dissolved[19] with the claim, only justified in a few cases, that they had decayed morally, and parish schools in Podolia and Volhynia were taken away from Catholic priests and assigned to Orthodox priests.

In Congress Poland the situation was hardly better, in spite of its relative autonomy and the fact that by the constitution of 1815 Catholicism had been declared the established religion. The rationalistic tendencies of the eighteenth century had resulted in decreasing religious interest among the upper class. The Latin clergy, especially in the rural areas, were accused, often with reason, of ignorance and immorality, and the orders, although they still possessed many houses, suffered heavily from the various partitions of the country. Only in the second

[18] Who justifiably could fear that in this period of the prevailing regalistic and Josephinistic atmosphere a concession of quasi-patriarchal rights, which Austria and other countries would have demanded immediately, would have endangered not only the Roman primacy but all of ecclesiastical life.

[19] See documents X and XI in *Allocuzione . . . del 22 luglio seguita de una Esposizione corredata di documenti* (Rome 1842), 16–25.

third of the century did Poland experience the religious revival which the other European Churches had seen since the beginning of the nineteenth century.

Without consulting the Holy See, Tsar Alexander I in 1817 had changed the Organic Fundamental Law of the Church in the direction of larger royal influence. A commission for religion and education was established for the purpose of supervising the clergy, acting as obligatory arbiter between the clergy and the authorities, nominating bishops according to the suggestions of the chapters, and authorizing the publication of papal bulls. Pius VII, in need of the Tsar's support, thought it better to ignore the new regulations and to accept the establishment of the archbishopric of Warsaw[20] in order to cooperate with the Russian government in freeing the Polish dioceses from the influence of the Primate of Gnesen, whose seat was on Prussian territory. A brief of 3 October 1816 granted the University of Warsaw the privilege to award doctoral degrees in theology and canon law, thereby substantially facilitating the control of the government over the education of the upper clergy. The Pope, always eager to prove his willingness to accommodate, empowered the archbishop of Warsaw to dissolve some monasteries. But this permission was far exeeded, and the decree of 17 April 1819, forced from the mortally ill archbishop, dissolved more than forty abbeys and monasteries in spite of Roman objections.[21] A further step on the path toward regalism was taken in 1825 when the Diet, ignoring objections from the episcopate, placed marriage under the jurisdiction of the civil courts and thereby made divorce possible even for Catholics. At the same time, the orderly administration of the dioceses became increasingly difficult through the suppression of synods and canonical visitors, the appointment of questionable ambitious creatures to important positions, and arbitrary sanctions against clergymen who refused to violate canon laws and to follow the dictates of the government. These conditions were aggravated by the lengthy vacancies of the episcopal sees.

A further worsening of the situation occurred after the failed Polish revolution of 1830, in which the clergy and several bishops had actively participated. After the constitution of 1817 was repealed and Poland became an integral part of the Russian Empire, the Catholic Church was subjected to increasing control by the authorities and Russification of its

[20] Bull *Militantis Ecclesiae* of 12 March 1818 (*JP* IV, 552; see 568–69). It was complemented by the Bull *Ex imposita Nobis* of 30 June 1818 (Mercati I, 638–48), which adjusted the borders of the eight dioceses of the Kingdom to the border changes caused by the Congress of Vienna.

[21] Concerning the dissolution see Z. Olszamowska: *Ochrona Zabytków* (Warsaw 1952).

leading personnel. The mobility of the clergy was limited in 1834, and the faithful were pressured to convert to Eastern Orthodoxy. Gregory XVI, very disconcerted by the wave of revolutions shaking Europe, regarded the Polish uprising not as a crusade against a schismatic oppressor, but as a subversive movement instigated by radicals and Freemasons. Following the suggestions of Metternich and some reactionary cardinals, he twice, on 19 February 1831 and 9 June 1832, condemned[22] the rising against the "legitimate power of the sovereigns," which he ascribed to "a few cunning and treacherous agitators." To the utter horror of western Europe's liberal Catholics, he advised the bishops to heed Saint Paul and preach submission and recommended to the Polish Catholics loyalty "to their powerful sovereign, who would show himself gracious to them." The position of the Pope originated from a feeling of mutual interest of the conservative powers. In return for his intervention, which gravely offended many Polish Catholics and led to their apostasy, he also expected the Tsar to alter his religious policy. For this reason he followed up his encyclical of 9 June 1832 with a confidential memorandum to Prince Gagarin, in which, citing precise cases, he denounced "the malice and chicanery of the government in Poland which had caused the decline of the Church."[23] The document remained unanswered, as did a complementary note by Secretary of State Bernetti. When Gregory XVI a while later was about to protest even more vehemently against the closing of two-thirds of Russia's monasteries, Metternich persuaded him not to do so. He promised a personal intervention of the Austrian monarch with the Tsar, but it produced no results. Equally unproductive were protest notes between 1836 and 1840 against the coercive measures to which Monsignor Gutkowski, O.P., bishop of Podlachia, was subjected. He was one of the few prelates who dared to protest the measures of the government and had

[22] *Acta Gregorii* XVI, I, 143–44 and *BullRomCont* XIX, 571–72. Erroneously the second document has been called *Cum primum,* occasionally with the words *Superiori anno,* which, however, introduced a harsher document, which was never sent (Lamennais received word of it). Concerning the drafting of this encyclical and the possible role of the Russian ambassador, see Boudou I, 178–87 (against F. Lamennais, *Les affaires de Rome* [Brussels 1836], 122–28), M. Żywczyński, op. cit., 168ff. and K. Piwarski, op. cit., 42ff. Did Gregory XVI regret the sending of this document when he learned of the large degree of the Russian suppression? The question cannot be answered unequivocally (see P. Lescœur, *L'Église catholique en Pologne* I, 201–16 and A. Simon, *Rencontres mennaisiennes en Belgique,* 259; on the other hand, Boudou I, 187–88). On the reactions in Poland see G. Bozzolato in *RStRis* 51 (1964), 328–38 and L. Le Guillou, *Les Discussions critiques. Journal de la crise mennaisienne* (Paris 1967), 23–25.

[23] Text in *Allocuzione . . . del 22 luglio seguita da una Esposizione corredata di documenti,* 11–14 (see ibid., 26–27).

to pay for his courage with expulsion.[24] Only after the affray of 1842 was there finally hope for alleviation.[25]

The Latin Catholics in the Ottoman Empire

For the first three decades of the nineteenth century all Balkan and Danube states, with the exception of the Ionian Islands,[26] which passed from the Venetian sphere of influence under British protection, remained with the Ottoman Empire. In spite of the Muslim preponderance in this enormous Empire, about one-third of the population was Christian and almost 10 percent were Roman Catholics.

Since their conquest, the Christians enjoyed a limited freedom in the exercise of their religion and the organization of their communities. Nevertheless, their situation was not an easy one. Quite to the contrary, despite the right of protection officially accorded the French consuls but also exercised by the Austrian and Russian representatives, Christians were exposed to constant injustices at the hand of the local authorities. Occasionally the Christians were affected by measures which were caused less by religious antagonism than by political agitation or racial hate. The first interventions of the Christian powers—France, Austria, Russia, and England—in the Ottoman Empire produced political spoils which they hungrily wished to divide among themselves. Similarly, the successful Greek revolt of 1829 produced only greater Turkish suspicions of the Christians, who were thought to be receiving their orders from foreign countries and awaiting an opportunity to revolt also.

The Catholic group, imbedded in the mass of the Orthodox Christians among whom the Greek element attempted to gain dominance over the Slavs and Arabs, did not constitute a homogeneous bloc. More than half of them, especially in Syria and Egypt, belonged to other rites and had their own hierarchy. But there was also an appreciable number of Latin Catholics spread over the entire Empire. They numbered about two hundred thousand in 1815 and steadily increased in the course of the century. The growth was caused in part by conversions which the prestige of the West, then at its height, occasioned, in part by high birth rates in the rural and mountainous areas, and in part by Italian, French, and Austrian immigration to the centers of commerce.

The majority of the Latin communities were in a very bad position. The interruption of normal communications with Rome and the chaos following the Austrian-Turkish and Napoleonic wars had produced fre-

[24] See Boudou I, 246–96.

[25] See vol. VIII in this series, chap. 11.

[26] Where at this time there were about four thousand Catholics, who were chiefly concentrated on the island of Corfu and had a native secular and regular clergy.

quent vacancies in the episcopal sees, a reduction of missionaries, and a lack of discipline among the lower clergy. The delegates of the Congregation for the Propagation of the Faith systematically devoted themselves to an alleviation of these conditions as soon as they had reorganized themselves after the return of Pius VII to Rome, but often lacked the necessary desirable tact.

The densest Latin center, even then accounting for only 20 percent of the population, was Albania (seventy-five thousand Catholics), where six bishoprics existed from the time of the Middle Ages, and Bosnia-Herzegovina (one hundred thousand Catholics), where in contrast to Albania virtually no secular clergy were left and where the parishes were administered by Franciscans, whose three authorized monasteries were the centers of Catholic education.

Another relatively important center was the Rumanian principality of Moldavia, which during the first half of the century experienced a particularly rapid growth of Catholics (from sixteen thousand to sixty thousand). But the apostolate in this area, entrusted to Italian and Hungarian conventuals, encountered great difficulties because of the wide dispersion of the believers and the ethnic hatreds between Rumanians and Magyars. Attempts undertaken between 1808 and 1818 by Rome with the aid of Vienna, which had assumed the place of the former protector Poland, to restore the old bishopric of Bakau met determined resistance from the Orthodox hierarchy which received support from the Rumanian boyars. Catholicism was the religion of Hungary, which was even more hated than the Turks.

An analogous reaction developed at the same time in Wallachia, whose prince tolerated the unobtrusive existence of some rather insignificant Catholic centers but who rejected proselytism. Inasmuch as the missions in Bulgaria had been totally dissolved on account of the wars between Turkey and Austria, the bishop of Nikopolis, an Italian Passionist, at the beginning of the nineteenth century had withdrawn with the paltry survivors of his flock to the area of Bucharest, an area with relative autonomy. At first this fact remained unnoticed, but when in 1815 the Congregation for the Propagation of the Faith selected Monsignor Ercolani as new bishop, there quickly came protests from the Orthodox bishops when Ercolani, an antischismatic zealot, ignored the advice of the Austrian resident to act cautiously. Monsignor Ercolani, who with his reforming inflexibility also aroused the enmity of the few Franciscans who long had been residents of the area, was forced to resign in 1822 and the see remained vacant for several years. Through skillful behavior his successor gradually succeeded in reducing mistrust, and in 1833 he was able to settle in Bucharest and with Austrian aid establish a few Catholic schools.

In the south of Bulgaria, where the few surviving Catholics lived without resident clergy, Austrian Redemptorists settled in 1830 in Philippopel, and from there began to spread over the country. The situation in Serbia was hardly better, although the Orthodox clergy there was more tolerant than in other areas.

Before 1830, Roman Catholicism was hardly represented on the Greek peninsula, and on the islands, where for a long time Latin groups of Venetian and Genoan origin had resided, the Catholic presence had been reduced to scant remains by the exodus of Italian settlers as well as by mixed marriages. The center of Catholicism was on the island of Syros. Between 1815 and 1822, the group was severely disturbed by the justified grievances of the clergy and their flocks against Bishop Rossini, who finally was forced to resign. The arrival of numerous Orthodox refugees during the course of the wars of independence caused this "Island of the Pope" to lose its long preserved exclusively Latin character. On the other hand, the recognition of independence by the London Protocol of 1830, which guaranteed complete freedom to the Catholic religion, and the subsequent installation of a Catholic sovereign, Otto von Wittelsbach, in Athens,[27] allowed Catholicism to take hold in continental Greece. Monsignor Blancis, the new bishop of Syros (1830–51), was appointed as apostolic delegate in 1834. Concurrently he was charged with the reorganization of the Latin Church in the entire Kingdom, in the course of which he had to remove abuses in the diocese of Naxos. He was also to maintain contact with the government, which in 1838 accredited him as the official representative. But Gregory XVI was looking farther into the future. As former prefect of the Congregation for the Propagation of the Faith he was fully informed of the problems of the Christian East. He knew that the Latin rite had no future among the Greek population, and in 1836 offered to send young Greeks to the reopened Greek College in Rome, there to train them in the Eastern rite. But this was a false hope; for in spite of the successes which the schools established by French and Italian orders had with the Orthodox Christians, the articles of the constitution of 1844 forbade proselytism and decreed that the successor to the throne had to belong to the Orthodox religion. There was no doubt that the new Greece wished to remain faithful to its national Church.

In Constantinople and even more in the other port cities of the Levant, the Catholic missions were in full decay after the suppression of the Society of Jesus. In 1800, they had fewer than six thousand mem-

[27] The selection was a relief for the Vatican, which feared the influence of Russia. Earlier, Leo XII had made representations to the king of France for the same reason (see L. Manzini, *Il cardinale Lambruschini* [Vatican City 1960], 121–23.

bers. They were mainly foreigners and barely held together by a few Italian Lazarists and Capuchins. After French diplomats, not entirely altruistically, had succeeded in achieving a limited improvement, the Congregation for the Propagation of the Faith in 1817 began the reorganization of this area. It reestablished the Archbishopric of Smyrna, which for two centuries had been reduced to the rank of a vicariate apostolic, and the vicariate apostolic of Aleppo, vacant since 1774, and conferred on it the jurisdiction over all missions in Syria, Palestine,[28] and Egypt.

Around 1830, new prospects developed for the Christians in the wake of the growing interest of the European chancellories in the eastern problems and the shift in the balance of power occasioned by the temporary occupation of Syria and Palestine by Egyptian pascha Mohammed Ali. The suggestion by the historian-diplomat Bunsen to declare Palestine an open area, in which Christianity could freely develop under a Christian government, was ignored. But the denominational map quickly changed with the acceleration of Anglo-Saxon missionary penetration,[29] begun in 1825. The establishment of an Anglo-Prussian episcopal see in Jerusalem in 1841 was symbolic of the new interplay of political and ecclesiastical forces at work in the Middle East.[30]

The Roman authorities observed with concern this growing influence of Protestant England and Orthodox Russia[31] in areas in which heretofore Rome had enjoyed the nearly total support of French and Austrian diplomats. Nevertheless, they tried to gain the greatest possible benefit from the settlement of a growing number of Europeans in the Levant, which the crisis of the Ottoman Empire opened to the political and economic competition of Europe. The growth of the Catholic population, largely of European origin, justified the establishment of new Latin missionary stations. They were expected, more than the still insignificant numbers of the Uniates, to become centers of attraction for schismatic easterners, thanks to the prestige of western schools and in recognition of the services performed by hospitals and dispensaries for the

[28] In Jerusalem the custody of the Holy Land entrusted to the Franciscans continued its traditional policy of a slow infiltration of the Eastern communities. In 1818 the Greek patriarch asked the Sultan for a decree which would force the converts to return to the Orthodox Church, but at the request of Pius VII the Catholic powers intervened in Constantinople in order to avert the threat (*JP* IV, 566, and note 1. F. Engel-Janosi, *Die politische Korrespondenz der Päpste mit den österreichischen Kaisern,* 137–40).

[29] Latourette, *Expansion* VI, 20–26, 38–55; Rogier *KG,* 374–79; J. Hajjar, *L'Europe et les destinées du Proche-Orient,* 5–16, 33–62, 230–60.

[30] See J. Hajjar, op. cit., 373–458.

[31] Concerning the Russian action in Palestine, see J. Hajjar, op. cit., 17–26, 460–82.

poor. The revival of the orders in the European countries, especially France, favored this policy. The numbers of Franciscans, Capuchins, and Lazarists, pitifully small at the beginning of the nineteenth century, underwent a steady growth. The Jesuits reappeared in Syria at the beginning of the 1830s, and in 1839 settled in Beirut, the new Lebanese capital. The Sisters of Charity in 1838 settled in Constantinople and in 1839 in Smyrna; they were followed in 1841 by the Christian Brothers, and the entire movement grew until the end of the nineteenth century.

The vast majority of the members of these orders, whose cultural and spiritual influence was without a doubt beneficial for the moment, unfortunately had received no introduction to the specific problems of the Christian East. Therefore only a systematic Latinization appeared to them as an effective guarantee of Catholic unity. They refused to consider the objections which their blind zeal caused among the Uniate hierarchy already established in the area. They also ignored exhortations to be prudent by the Congregation for the Propagation of the Faith, which with its historical experience had a deeper insight. They were only interested in increasing the conversions of Uniates to the Latin rite and gradually were able to win to their view the responsible people in Rome. It was in this connection that the thought of a reestablishment of the Latin Patriarchate in Jerusalem arose. But it was effected only ten years later, during the first months of the pontificate of Pius IX,[32] as Rome feared offending the Uniate hierarchy. It constituted a landmark in the Latinization process of the Christian East, and was to have its effects in the second half of the century.

[32] Bull *Nulla celebrior* of 23 July 1847 (*JP* VI/1, 42ff.). See J. Hajjar, op. cit., 482–514.

Chapter 9

The Churches of America

Schmidlin described well the paradoxical situation of Catholicism in America at the beginning of the nineteenth century in this fashion: "In Latin, Central and South America, the Church, although overtly both Christian and Catholic, was internally deteriorating and close to dissolution; in Anglo-Saxon and French North America, Catholicism was only in its infancy and still partially in the phase of persecution, but everywhere nascent and spreading its wings."[1]

[1] *PG* I, 314.

Spanish America

When the Napoleonic interlude came to an end in 1814, and the Roman Curia was again free to make contact with the Churches of the world, there were forty bishoprics in Spanish America[2] serving a population of about 15 million, which was centered largely in the Caribbean area. In spite of the continuing attachment of the population to the Catholic faith, an attachment which was especially concerned with external manifestations and a clear tendency toward religious syncretism among the American Indians in Mexico, Peru, and Bolivia, the Church was confronted with some extraordinarily difficult problems after the revolt of the old colonies against Spain. The revolutions, which had begun toward the end of the eighteenth century, by 1810 had led to the actual independence of most of the colonies.

Among these were financial problems. The substantial ecclesiastical property had been used by the two contending parties to cover their expenditures, and the Church, although formerly too wealthy, now was compelled to cancel some of its charities and even to close seminaries due to a lack of funds.

There were also problems of internal discipline. To the quantitative as well as qualitative regression and the turmoil produced by years of civil and military unrest for both the secular and the regular clergy[3] there often was added a kind of ecclesiastical anarchy. A majority of the Spanish upper clergy, many of whom were closely allied with the legitimist party, left the country voluntarily or by force and it was nearly impossible for the members of the orders (who also were angry over the confiscation of the majority of their lands) to remain in contact with the commissioners general of their orders, who resided in Spain and for centuries had been the normal link to the central authority.

Finally, the relationship between Church and state and the consequences of this relationship carried with them extremely delicate problems. The King of Spain resorted to his patronage, which his lawyers did

[2] Eight dioceses for Mexico, four for the Antilles, four in Central America, three constitute the province of Caracas, four that of Bogotá, ten that of Lima, and seven that of Charcas or Chuquisaca in Bolivia.

[3] Concerning the frequently very active role of the young clergymen (especially the secular clergy, in which Creoles played a larger role than among the regular clergy) in the movement for independence, see principally M. André, *La fin de l'empire espagnol d'Amérique* (Paris 1922). One must not look upon all patriotic priests as bad priests, however. Cf. the biography of the Colombian Dominican *Fray I. Mariño OP, Capellán general del Ejercito libertador* (who always behaved exemplarily) (Bogotá 1963) by R. M. Tisnes. And even if the examples of priests and friars living in concubinage or being more devoted to politics than to the apostolate were very numerous in all areas, Monsignor Muzi during his stay in Buenos Aires in 1824 was nevertheless highly impressed by the exemplary conduct of secular and regular clergy alike.

not regard as a papal privilege but as an irrevocable right of the civil power. Without his permission, he did not allow the Pope to install new bishops in the area in which revolts had broken out but which he still considered as part of his Empire. The new republican governments, however, considered themselves heirs to that same patronage, and wanted to have direct influence not merely upon the administration of Church lands but also upon such internal affairs of the Church as the election of the chapter vicars in vacant dioceses and the decisions of the provincial chapters of the orders. This made the jurisdiction of those who had been placed in positions of authority through violations of canon law questionable, if not invalid. In many places situations were created which, strictly speaking, were "schismatic." But concretely and psychologically the situation was much more fluid, and the only formal schism occurred much later in 1829 in the diocese of San Salvador.[4]

With the exception of some politicians, whose regalism exceeded even that of the radical Gallicanists of Europe, the majority of the leading laymen as well as the entire clergy were soon convinced that the only possible solution was contact with the Holy See, which, because of its universal significance, alone could correct this fundamentally irregular situation. The first efforts in this direction were made in 1813 and 1814 when the Spanish King Ferdinand VII was a prisoner at Bayonne and it was hoped that Napoleon, whose sympathies for American independence were well known, could exert pressure on the Pope to be as conciliatory as possible. However, the developments in both America and Europe delayed the continuation of such efforts by several years. Between 1814 and 1817, the significant military successes of Spain made possible the provisional restoration of its authority over the area except for the provinces of La Plata, and Rome, under the influence of the spirit of restoration, saw in the nationalistic American movements only a delayed effect of the French Revolution, which it hoped could be assigned to the past. In these circumstances, Pius VII, who until 1819 received inadequate information about America solely by way of Madrid, tacitly accepted the measures of the Spanish King against the patriotic bishops. Without the slightest pressure from the Spanish King, on 13 January 1816, the Pope, in his Encyclical *Etsi longissimo,* exhorted the bishops of the New World to aid the reinstallation of the legitimate authorities.[5] Vehement polemics by the republican press[6] against Rome

[4] P. de Leturia, *Relaciones* II, 296–97, 317–19.

[5] Text ibid., 110–12. With respect to all documents concerning this problem, consult P. de Leturia, ibid. II, 95–116, III, 385–437. Father de Leturia was the first to point to the role played in this matter by F. Badan, a Genovese in the service of Spain.

[6] Especially in the independent United Provinces of La Plata where he contributed for many years to amplify the anti-Roman sentiments of the government.

and the loyalist bishops followed, and the Church in America became the victim of the same principle of legitimacy which was beneficial for the Church in Europe.

Soon the encyclical itself was to be overtaken by events, and Consalvi was astute enough to recognize this fact quickly. Between 1818 and 1820, as a result of Bolivar's victories, Latin America regained its independence. Then, when between 1820 and 1823 a liberal regime came to power in Spain and followed a pronounced anticlerical policy, the pro-Spanish sympathies still harbored by many South American clergymen disappeared quickly. The Holy See also, turning more to the pastoral aspects of the matter, disregarded the Spanish viewpoint in the solution of the problem. Under the changed conditions, many of the bishops appointed since 1814 with the approval of Ferdinand now fled or were handicapped in the exercise of their authority. The condition of the Church constantly worsened, and Rome began to eye a new, more realistic stance. A first public echo of this was a letter of 7 September 1822, from Pius VII to Bishop Lasso, who, after having been a glowing defender of legitimism until 1820, had taken Bolivar's side. In the letter, which was widely publicized by the South American press, the Pope affirmed the neutrality of the Holy See with respect to the political changes in America, an affirmation which was tantamount to an actual desertion of the Spanish cause, and was an implicit renunciation of the unfortunate "legitimist encyclical" of 1816.

The new papal position coincided with the arrival in Rome of the first official emissary from a South American republic, Canon Cienfuegos. Cienfuegos had been delegated by the Chilean government[7] to ask the Pope to fill the vacant dioceses, if only with titular bishops, and to transfer the right of patronage, once held by the King of Spain, to the new government. In the spring of 1823, Pius VII sent Monsignor Muzi as vicar apostolic to Chile. The vicar apostolic arrived with extensive authorization to deal with the ecclesiastical situation in Chile. Before his departure, Monsignor Muzi was given jurisdiction over all areas of America no longer administered by Spain and whose further development Consalvi observed with growing concern. Unfortunately, Muzi's mission ended in failure. In Buenos Aires, where the vicar apostolic in keeping with his secret instructions was to attempt the settlement of a number of very delicate ecclesiastical problems, he encountered the firm regalism of Rivadavia and of the administrator of the diocese of Zavaleta, in addition to a hostile climate, which had been in existence since the encyclical of 1816. While Muzi received a friendlier reception in the

[7] In 1821 Greater Colombia and Mexico also considered sending agents to Rome to settle ecclesiastical problems, but such plans did not mature.

provinces of La Plata, his lack of tact and political sensibility poisoned the situation in Chile. Dictator O'Higgins,[8] who had occasioned the Roman mission, had just been replaced by a government which was much more hostile toward the intervention of the Holy See in national ecclesiastical concerns.

The new head of government, General Freire, and his foreign minister, Pinto, posed unacceptable conditions for the consecration of two new titular bishops, whose appointment was one of the most important objectives of the mission, and were equally unwilling to negotiate with respect to the orders. Muzi also encountered the intrigues of chapter dean Cienfuegos. Cienfuegos wanted to become bishop and did not hesitate to accept his appointment from the government as administrator of the diocese of Santiago, the legitimate bishop being accused of having sided with the Roman emissary and driven out. Thus Muzi, who had come to Chile to stabilize the hierarchy, through his ineptitude deprived the country of its only remaining bishop and thus the source of priests for years to come. Furthermore, blinded by his reactionary attitude, which equated striving for independence with revolution, he made the mistake of rejecting Bolívar's official invitation to visit Greater Colombia. In doing so, he failed to employ his stay to begin the reorganization of these areas which were much more densely settled than those south of the equator.

In the meantime, Leo XII had become Pius VII's successor, and with the end of the liberal regime in Madrid, the Spanish ambassador Vargas Laguna, then at the height of his prestige, reappeared in Rome. Laguna was a bitter defender of the principle of legitimacy and for this reason was hostile to any contacts between the Holy See and the insurgents even for the settlement of purely spiritual problems. Supported by the ambassadors of Austria and Russia, Laguna succeeded on 24 September 1824 in wringing from the new Pope the legitimist Encyclical *Etsi iam diu.*[9] This document was to constitute no more than an interlude. In America it did not lead to the feared reaction against Rome, because many regarded it as apocryphal. Its effect was further weakened by knowledge of the true feelings of the Pope and his advisers. Leo XII was extremely sensitive in pastoral matters, and Monsignor Muzi's first-hand information had confirmed the leaders of the secretariat of state and of the Congregation for the Propagation of the Faith in their conviction

[8] See J. Eyzguirre, "La actitud religiosa de don Bernardo O'Higgins" in *Historia* 1 (Santiago de Chile 1962), 7–46.

[9] Text in P. de Leturia, *Relaciones* II, 165–271. Concerning the origin of this document and the reactions it caused, see ibid., 241–81 and G. Mönkeberg Barros, *Anales de la Universidad católica de Valparaiso* 3 (1956), 239–58. Several historians have questioned its authenticity (for a critical discussion, see P. de Leturia, *Relaciones* II, 243–59).

that there was much to be lost if Rome adopted an extreme position. After Varga's sudden death, this opinion gained ground, and the Holy See was convinced that it should not become involved in the political struggle between Spain and its former colonies, but should confine itself to safeguarding the spiritual interests of America's dioceses. A first important step in this direction was taken in the summer of 1825. In agreement with Fra Mauro Cappellari, the future Pope Gregory XVI, who soon was to grow into an expert on Latin American affairs, Leo XII decided to follow the advice of the cardinals of the Congregation for the Propagation of the Faith to comply with the request of the episcopate of Greater Colombia. He appointed a bishop *in partibus* without informing the government in Madrid.

This was only a provisional step. In order not to provoke the radical elements and to have to face the equivalent of a Civil Constitution of the Clergy, direct negotiations with the government with respect to the entire situation of the Church were imperative. In March 1826, due to the intercession of the French cabinet, the Spanish King agreed to have J. Sánchez de Tejada, one of Bolívar's delegates, who had been recalled from Rome in 1824 at Madrid's request, approved as a simple emissary of the bishops and the chapter of Greater Colombia. Negotiations were now finally begun and facilitated by Rome's growing fear that South America's new governments would join the schism. Tejada, who as a good Catholic desired a positive conclusion, exercised great diplomacy and managed to reduce the demands of his superiors without losing patience in the face of Rome's hesitation. Additionally, Bolívar himself, regardless of his own religious attitude, realized that a policy favorable to Catholic interests, symbolized by an agreement with Rome, would make it easier to tie the clergy, which still exercised a considerable influence on the masses, to the new government.[10] Such circumstances and Cappellari's bold vision introduced a new phase in 1827. Without regard to the prerogatives once accorded the Spanish King, the Pope appointed resident bishops rather than titular ones to the vacant sees of Greater Colombia. In order to avoid the appearance of a political arrangement, the appointments were made *motu proprio* and not officially in response to the suggestions of the government (even though in every case the appointed bishops corresponded to Bolívar's nominations).

Hardly had Leo XII made this gesture, which raised great hopes in all of Spanish America, than he appeared to reverse his position. Having always had legitimist tendencies, the Pope bowed to Ferdinand's furious objections and, in spite of the advice of Cappellari, who meanwhile had

[10] On Bolívar's church policy, see P. de Leturia, *Relaciones* III, Supplement 1, 4, 12, 13, and 15, and C. Mendoza, ibid. I, XXI–XXXV.

become prefect of the Congregation for the Propagation of the Faith, promised to appoint only vicars apostolic in the future,[11] except in the evidently very rare case in which the King had approved the particular person. In line with this decision, the Pope on 15 December 1828 suggested to the Consistory the appointment of two vicars apostolic for Chile, where the prejudices against Rome had diminished since Muzi's visit and where the constitution of 1833 soon was to concede numerous privileges to the Church. The Argentine crisis, particularly serious because the provinces of La Plata had not had a single bishop for years and because the government with its unilateral interference in ecclesiastical matters had gone very far, was handled by Pius VIII in similar manner in the following year when political forces propelled men into power who were less hostile to Rome.

A parallel development in Mexico, where almost half of the Catholics of Spanish America resided, also raised hopes for an arrangement before too long. But the government's emissary, canon Vázquez, was uncompromising in one point. He considered it humiliating for his country to have to be satisfied with vicars apostolic, while Greater Colombia had been assigned resident bishops. Cappellari advised the Pope to fulfill this reasonable request, but Pius VIII remained true to the views enunciated eight years earlier by Consalvi as more in agreement with his own legitimist principles. The election of Cappellari, who in 1831 became Gregory XVI, put an end to the problem. Within three weeks, the new Pope appointed six resident bishops in Mexico and published his reasons in the Bull *Sollicitudo Ecclesiarum.*[12] In the following year, the vicars apostolic of Argentina and Chile received the status of resident bishops and shortly afterwards (1834–35) moved to reorganize the Peruvian hierarchy, to end the schism in San Salvador (1839–42), and to settle the ambiguous situation of Paraguay (1844).

After the official recognition of New Granada (Colombia) by the Holy See in 1836, an internuncio was sent to Bogotá. His jurisdiction was to encompass all of Spanish America,[13] and his appointment signal-

[11] This compromise solution was naturally of a kind which irritated the sensibilities of the republics; beyond that, they also had the disadvantage of having no connection with the ecclesiastical traditions of Spanish America, soon creating legal conflicts between the new apostolic vicars and the governments.

[12] See below, p. 266.

[13] The nunciature in Rio de Janeiro established in 1829 had the secret mission to concern itself with all of Latin America, but the communications with Colombia, Central America, and Mexico were extremely bad (see W. J. Coleman, op. cit., 59). Yet the apostolic delegation for Latin America soon had to be entrusted to the nuncio of Rio de Janeiro, as the internuncio of Bogotá was not able to fulfill his responsibilities. An attempt in 1837 to establish a third nunciature was not successful (P. de Leturia, *Relaciones* II, 4–5).

led a new phase in the normalization of the relations between Holy See and the new South American republics.[14]

The length of time required for this normalization was owing in part to grave legitimistic scruples and antirevolutionary reflexes on the part of the Roman Curia and in part to the all too frequent compromises by the native clergy with the colonial governments. But the influence of these compromises should not be overestimated. The frictions between Church and state in the La Plata states were particularly vehement, and the episcopate soon took the side of the national revolution. Moreover, after 1820, agreement between Church and Spanish monarchy became rare. Difficulties from other basic causes did continue, however. These problems were primarily of a social nature, because the Church was often allied with the large land owners, while the new government officials came from the intellectuals of the cities. There were also ideological causes. The majority of the clergy wished to retain as much as possible the former control of the Church over the press, education, and society in general. The class now in power, which had been strongly affected by Freemasonry, was not yet ready for a rationalistic laicism—most of the constitutions still embodied Catholicism as the state religion[15]—but was in favor of the main principles of the Enlightenment, the independence of the civil power, and a control of the Church by the government. The orders became the first victims of this attitude. In a way similar to Europe in the eighteenth century, the state did not confine itself to the partial confiscation of property, but also limited recruitment, designated a minimum age for taking vows, forbade the recruitment of foreigners, and occasionally suppressed such institutions as the Franciscan missions to the Indians in Mexico. The secular clergy, not immediately affected, was concerned nevertheless when its traditional privileges were limited by an appeal to the principles of 1789. This concern was indeed justified, as the politically liberal governments still laden with the regalistic heritage of the Bourbon era rarely were able to reconcile themselves to liberty for the Church. The result was

[14] The recognition of New Granada in October 1835 was followed in 1836 with Mexico, 1838 with Ecuador, and 1840 with Chile. In the case of the other republics, Rome waited until their political situation was clarified.

[15] Even in Argentina, where non-Catholic religions were treated with great toleration in deference to the English, whose support had been decisive in the liberation of the country. In other countries the opinion of the Chilean jurist J. de Egaña generally prevailed. In his repeatedly printed work *Memoria política sobre si conviene en Chile la libertad de cultos* he defended the thesis that allowing several religions would lead to unbelief and, in the civil sphere, to discords. See M. Gongora, "El pensamiento de J. de Egaña sobre la reforma eclesiástica" in *Boletín de la Academia chilena de la historia* 30 (1963), 30–53.

that the lower clergy, which at the beginning of the independence movements often had sympathized with the liberal constitutions, after 1830 tended to become more conservative. This tendency was reinforced by the influence of the priests and regular clergy arriving from Europe.

Brazil

The political development of Brazil was far less problematical for the Holy See than that of the former Spanish colonies; in spite of some republican riots in which a number of clergy also participated, it did not lead to the same clear break with the Old Regime. In 1808, the Portuguese King João VI had settled in Rio de Janeiro after fleeing Napoleon's invasion. He was followed by the nuncio of Lisbon, Caleppi, who handled the sale of Church lands well and was able to prevent the appointment of bishops by the archbishops without the participation of Rome. In 1822, after João VI's return to his capital, the large Brazilian landowners persuaded Don Pedro, the hereditary prince, to declare himself as the ruler of an independent Empire which was officially recognized by Portugal. Leo XII received the ambassador of the new state in 1826.

With the continuation of the monarchial organization and the common dynasty assured, Rome did not hesitate to transfer to the Emperor the rights of patronage which heretofore the King of Portugal[16] had exercised over the Church and to arrange a reorganization of the diocesan hierarchy in line with this change. In view of the extremely regalistic pretensions of the government, Rome quickly dropped plans for a concordat and decided to solve problems on an ad hoc basis. After some initial difficulties, it was possible to establish in Rio de Janeiro the first nunciature on the American continent; a symbol of the cooperation between Church and state.

But the cooperation was not entirely untroubled; it also produced difficult moments for the Holy See. These problems were occasioned principally by the Gallican and Febronianist attitudes of the clergy, attitudes strongly influenced by the writings of the Oratorian Pereira de Figueiredo and by Freemasonry. Monsignor Azevedo Coutinho (1743–1821), who had reorganized the seminary of Olinda, and the learned Monsignor da Silva Coutinho, bishop of Rio de Janeiro (1767–1833), both of whom had been trained at Coimbra, were typical rep-

[16] Bull of 15 May 1827 (*JP* IV, 685). On the relations between Church and state as determined by the constitution of 1824 and the amendment of 12 August 1824, see K. Rothenbücher, *Die Trennung von Staat und Kirche* (Munich 1908), 362ff.

resentatives of an "enlightened" clergy. They regarded it as normal that the government subjected all acts of the Holy See to its approval, viewed the Church as a kind of state service controlled by the government, and took increasingly restrictive steps at the expense of the orders. This latter act quickly brought about the deterioration of the once flourishing Benedictine abbeys. Even if Brazil did not experience the same tensions that were created in Portugal by liberal anticlericalism, the spirit of Pombal was more alive there than ever.

The United States

At the time of the Declaration of Independence of the thirteen American states, the Catholic population was very small: only twenty-five thousand in a population of 4 million in 1785. Catholics were chiefly concentrated in the two states with more tolerant legislation: sixteen thousand in Maryland, and seven thousand in Pennsylvania. There were nineteen priests in Maryland and five in Pennsylvania, principally members of the Jesuit Order. The remainder of the faithful was spread among the other states and had no native priests. In the course of the last twenty years of the eighteenth century, however, a rapid change came about. Under the influence of democratic ideals, the principle of religious freedom and the equality of all faiths was recognized.[17] At the same time, a native Catholic hierarchy developed. After the vicar apostolic of London was no longer able to exercise his authority in the former colonies, the Holy See decided, after contemplating placing the territories under the jurisdiction of the bishop of Quebec, to succumb to the insistence of the Jesuits and to appoint one of them as head of the missions, although directly subordinated to the Congregation for the Propagation of the Faith. The choice was John Carroll (1735–1815), brother of one of the authors of the Declaration of Independence of 1776. Carroll, an experienced priest, although a man of the world, was both deeply Roman Catholic and fully American and completely convinced of the principles of separation of Church and state and of tolerance toward other religions. In the course of the years, he came to believe that only someone with episcopal authority could lead the diverse flock which posed so many problems for him. The Holy See concurred with his assessment and on 6 November 1789 established the diocese of Baltimore.[18] After Carroll's consecration in England on 15

[17] Article 6 of the constitution of 1789 and the first amendment, adopted in 1791 ("Congress shall make no law respecting an establishment of religion or prohibiting the free exercise thereof").

[18] Letters *Ex hac apostolicae*, whose text is in D. C. Shearer, *Pontificia Americana*, 81–84.

August 1790, he successfully continued the difficult work of organizing the new diocese. He made use of a few French priests whom the revolution had driven from France, and, with the help of four Sulpicians, in 1792 opened the first seminary in the United States in Baltimore. In the preceding year he had founded a boys college at Georgetown, under the direction of the Jesuits, who again were given regular status as an order in 1806. A good number of settlers moved to the Middle West, and a few Irish Dominicans followed them. It was much more difficult, however, to find nuns in Europe willing to take care of parish schools. In 1809, a young widow, the convert Elizabeth Bayley Seton (1774–1821), founded the first native congregation, the Sisters of Charity. It developed rapidly and acted as model for other similar congregations.

The growth of the young Church soon required the division of the huge diocese of Baltimore, which comprised the entire United States with the exception of Louisiana, which, as a French colony, had its own bishops residing in New Orleans since 1793 and was annexed in 1803. On 8 April 1808, Pius VII established four new dioceses: Boston, Philadelphia, and New York (vacant until 1814) on the East coast and Bardstown (renamed Louisville in 1841) in Kentucky. When Archbishop Carroll died in 1815, the number of Catholics had grown to one hundred fifty thousand, ministered to by one hundred priests. This figure corresponded to only a small diocese in western Europe, but the progress was to continue unabated. A quarter of a century later, shortly before the huge wave of immigrants began in the 1840s, the number of Catholics had quadrupled. This was a consequence both of the general increase in population as well as the steady immigration, particularly from Catholic Ireland. Success occurred in spite of the problems posed by the Protestant environment and the vast geographical distances. To be sure, the six hundred sixty-three thousand Catholics in the United States in 1840 were less than the Catholic population of Cuba and only 4 percent of the total population of the United States, but the percentage had doubled since 1815. The fact that the Holy See founded twenty new dioceses between 1820 and 1837 demonstrated its prompt efforts to provide this new, growing Church with ecclesiastical administration. In Rome, the United States was still viewed as a missionary area, but in spite of many obstacles the North American Church quickly developed its own character and orientation.

The first of these difficulties was the shortage of priests. In spite of the gradual growth of the Sulpician seminary in Baltimore and the efforts of the bishops to establish boys' schools, native priests remained few for a long time. In order to provide the huge areas coming under settlement with a minimum of service, it was necessary to use European priests even at the risk that Catholicism might be viewed as an alien religion. A record of 1838 shows that of 430 priests and vicars in America only 20 percent were native born; and 132 were Irish, 95 French, and 41 Belgian. Among the priests who had come from Europe there were a substantial number of adventurers and vagabond members of orders, who were gladly released for emigration by their superiors and who created quite a few worries for their new bishops.

The national rivalries of this heterogeneous clergy further complicated the situation. The priests who had left France in order not to expose themselves to the iniquities of the revolution were without a doubt the best educated and almost always irreproachable in their conduct. Many of the new bishops and their assistants were selected from their ranks and from the persons recommended by them. Unfortunately this was sometimes a course of action fraught with disadvantages. These pastors had mastered the English language only imperfectly. The increasing number of Irish priests, full of enterprise and often boisterous, suffered under the moderation of the French prelates educated in the Sulpician spirit, a moderation which appeared to the Irish as lack of ability. Indeed, the impression could not be avoided that the Frenchmen were too rigid in their views for a country which was developing quickly and in a spirit alien to the European mentality. Repeated representations of American Irishmen at the Holy See, supported by the Irish bishops and by Irishmen residing in Rome, gradually resulted in a change. In the 1840s, the American episcopate began to take on the Irish character which was to remain for almost a century. The Irish characteristics were not without disadvantages, but at least they had the advantage that they provided American Catholicism with pastors who did not expect state subsidies or who were able to exercise their apostolate in a society dominated by Protestant leaders.

To the problems of an impetuous clergy was added the independent spirit of the laity in some parishes, an independence which led to the crisis of trusteeship with effects throughout the century. Religious denominations were not permitted to own property, and therefore an administrative corporation was created in each parish. Its members, the trustees, were laymen chosen by the community through election. In some areas, particularly in New England and the Middle West, this system generally functioned without many problems. However, some trustees, influenced by their Protestant environment, imbued with a radical democratic spirit, and often backed by rebellious priests, thought they had a right of patronage, which extended even to the selection of the communal clergy. The matter had already been a grave problem as early as the time of Monsignor Carroll.

After Carroll's death, a number of particularly grave incidents occurred in Charleston, Philadelphia, New Orleans, and Norfolk. The trustees in Norfolk went so far as to encourage a disgruntled Irish Franciscan to have himself consecrated bishop by the Jansenist prelate of the Netherlands in order to found an independent Church. Between 1817 and 1826, the Pope was forced to intervene several times.[19] Monsignor England, an Irishman who had been appointed as the first bishop of Charleston in order to deal with the crisis there, devised a system which associated the clergy and the lay delegates of the parishes with the bishop in administering the diocese. But this solution appeared as too democratic to his colleagues. The problem of the trustees gradually was normalized during the second third of the century with the legal rulings of the provincial councils of Baltimore, which decided that new churches could be constructed only if the contracts were drawn up in the name of the bishop.

After 1825, the Catholic Church was confronted with another problem, this time coming from outside the Church. A wave of hostility toward aliens, which gave the name of nativism to the movement, caused an aggressive revival of anti-Catholic sentiments. An objection by the Catholic hierarchy to the obligation of Catholic students in the public schools to attend Protestant Bible classes was presented at the very moment when there was a general renewed interest in the Bible. The objection was interpreted as proof of Catholic disregard of Holy Scripture, and a ferocious campaign began in the press, and meetings, backed by the Protestant Association, were held against the "godlessness and the corruption of papism." The growing number of Catholic immigrants from Ireland and Germany buoyed the agitation. A part of the population saw its standard of living threatened by cheap immigrant labor, and others saw in it a plot by the Holy See and the Holy Alliance to smother political and religious freedom in the United States with a flood of Catholic immigrants who would blindly obey a reactionary clergy. The result was a number of assaults on churches and monasteries between 1834 and 1836 which, after a brief phase of quietude, erupted again with renewed virulence after 1840.

The "nativist" campaign had at least the one positive result that it impelled Catholics to leave their ghettos and to defend their cause in word and print. Thus it brought about the rise of the Catholic press. Following the *United States Catholic Miscellany,* the first Catholic weekly in the United States, published in 1822 by the former journalist Monsignor England, scarcely a year passed during the subsequent quarter of a century in which a Catholic paper was not founded somewhere in the country.

[19] Letters *Litteras tuas* of 9 July 1817 (*JP* IV, 557f.), *Non sine magno* of 24 August 1822 (ibid., 619f.), and *Quo longius* of 16 August 1828 (ibid., 705ff.).

Publication was not the only area in which the influence of John England (1786–1842), Charleston's dynamic bishop, became known. A contemporary said of him that he was the first person to gain respect for the Catholic religion in the eyes of the American public. It was because of his persistence that the first council of the Church province of Baltimore, which had been scheduled to convene in 1812, was finally convoked in October 1829. The immediate results were a series of decrees regarding the rights of the bishops as opposed to the clergy and the trustees, the construction and maintenance of churches; catechisms and schools; clothing of the clergy; sports; the Catholic press; and the living conditions of orders. At the conclusion of the session the archbishop and his six suffragans composed two pastoral letters. One was directed to the clergy with the admonition to study the Scriptures and not to become too involved in earthly matters, and the other exhorted the laity to contribute to education and the press and to beware of religious indifferentism under the guise of liberalism. The second council, meeting in 1833, urged Rome to consider the advice of the bishops when appointing new ones. Reserving the principle of freedom of action to the Holy See, the Congregation for the Propagation of the Faith accepted an arrangement according to which the names of candidates should be suggested by the American episcopate in the future. This system was retained until 1866. A third provincial council took place in 1837, and subsequently the bishops met regularly every three years.

As already mentioned, one of the problems dealt with by the first provincial council of Baltimore concerned the orders. To alleviate the shortage of secular clergy, the bishops had sent a plea for help to the European orders and congregations. The Jesuits, Sulpicians, Augustinians, and Dominicans already present at the time of Monsignor Carroll were joined by the Lazarists (1816); the Redemptorists (1832), chiefly active in the Middle West among the people of German descent; the Holy Cross Fathers (1841); and the Franciscans (1844). Among the convents of such European congregations as the Sisters of the Sacred Heart (1818), the Sisters of Saint Joseph of Cluny (1831), and the Sisters of Our Lady of Namur (1840), there very soon were native congregations to testify to the vitality of the young American Church. To the first native congregation of Elizabeth Seton's Sisters of Charity were added, in 1812, the Sisters of Charity of Nazareth and the Sisters of Loreto in Kentucky, and shortly afterward the black congregations of the Sisters of Providence (1829) and the Sisters of the Holy Family (1842).

The sisters were engaged chiefly in the parish schools and charitable efforts. The Church hierarchy was also involved with the creation of reception stations for Catholic immigrants through the generous help of

European mission organizations such as the French Society for the Spreading of the Faith, Austria's Leopoldine Foundation, and the Bavarian Mission Society. The Church administration in the United States had no experience in the area of Catholic education, but the necessity to acquire such experience very quickly became evident. The arrival of the Irish had a positive effect, and the start provided by Monsignor Carroll produced a gradual growth. In 1840, there were two hundred parish schools, half of them west of the Alleghenies. With respect to charitable works, the first Catholic orphan home was opened in Philadelphia in 1814 by the Sisters of Charity, who because of the generosity of a layman from St. Louis also were able to open the first Catholic hospital there. Thus the tight network of institutions independent from the government, which is so characteristic of present-day Catholicism in the United States, had its roots in the first decades of the nineteenth century. They were generated by the immediate needs of a Church which constituted a minority in a Protestant country, but which because of a constitutionally guaranteed separation of Church and state could develop unhindered and in complete freedom.

The young American Church was firmly determined to turn away from French and Spanish traditions which might have expanded from the mission stations of the Great Lakes or the eighteenth century Churches of Louisiana and Florida. The atmosphere of Catholic romanticism and the longing for medieval Christianity was alien to this new Church, and it developed its strength by concentrating increasingly upon the urban centers of the East Coast, charting a new hitherto unknown path toward the future of its visionary prelates. As early as 1784, John Carroll had written: "America may give proof to the world that general and equal toleration, by providing a free climate for fair argument, is the most effectual method of bringing all denominations of Christians into a unity of faith."[20]

Forty years later, the most important Church leader of the next generation, John England, sounded the same note with increased optimism in a letter to O'Connell: "I am convinced that a total separation from the temporal government is the most natural and safest state for the Church in any place where it is not, as in papal territory, a complete government of churchmen."[21] These and similar concepts appeared in the Roman Curia as dangerous paradoxes, and Rome was frequently concerned about the happenings in a Church about which it knew so little. Yet the American example soon impressed European observers, and, from

[20] Quoted by Ellis, *Documents,* 151.

[21] Quoted by J. T. Ellis in *Harper's Magazine* 207 (1953), 64.

Lamennais to the "Americanists" of the closing nineteenth century, it continued to encourage the defenders of Catholic liberalism.

Canada

While only a few tens of thousands of Catholics lived in the United States at the beginning of the nineteenth century, there were one hundred fifty thousand of them in Canada, and this number grew to four hundred sixty-five thousand by 1931. Under the aegis of Bishop John Octave Plessis (1806–25) the Canadian Church, which since the conquest by England had to suffer under administrative chicaneries, experienced a period of prosperity. In 1763, the clauses of the Treaty of Paris, detailed in the Quebec Act of 22 June 1774, guaranteed the Canadian Catholics "the free exercise of the faith of the Church of Rome" and the retention of its traditional institutions, among them the right of the clergy to tithe. After some hesitation, the British government also granted permission for the establishment of a bishopric in Quebec. The head of the bishopric was only to employ the title of "Superintendent of the Romish Church," but was to have the privilege of appointing parish priests without the approval of the governor.[22] The rebellion in the colonies of the United States had a positive effect upon the Canadian Church, because the Catholics constituted a rather significant element in the portion of the British colonies which survived the War of Independence. The government in turn was prepared to augment the loyalty of the Catholics with new concessions. It permitted the Catholics to hold political meetings with a simple oath of loyalty to the King instead of the anti-Catholic formulation demanded in England. Furthermore, in 1791, the Sulpician seminaries of Quebec and Montreal were allowed to reopen and regained the use of their property. Finally, several dozens of French priests, victims of the revolution, were permitted to settle in Canada in spite of the ban decreed after the British conquest.

New vexations began, however, with the new Anglican Bishop Mountain, whom George III in 1794 appointed as "Lord Bishop of Quebec." Mountain had the backing of Governor Craig and especially of the secretary for South Canada, Ryland, both of whom held that the best means of Anglicizing the new colony was the promotion of the development of the Anglican Church. The Catholics, among others, were compelled to accept the control of the government over ecclesiastical appointments and the income of the Church.

It was under these conditions that Monsignor Plessis, coadjutor since

[22] See A. Gosselin, *L'Église du Canada après la conquête, 1760–75* (Quebec 1916).

1800, became bishop of Quebec in 1806. This prelate, combining strength of character with an enterprising spirit, became the backbone of resistance to the anti-Catholic attacks of British local governments. At the same time, he was clever enough to remain loyal to London and gained the appreciation of the British during the War of 1812 with the United States. Bishop Plessis was rewarded with membership in the Legislative Council, where he became rather influential, as well as with the official recognition of his title as bishop of Quebec (1817); a title which initially had been rejected. Now thought could be given to dividing the Quebec diocese, which hitherto had stretched from the Atlantic to the Pacific. In spite of some obstacles posed by London, five vicariates apostolic were established between 1817 and 1820. Two of these were in the maritime provinces, where many Irish and Scottish immigrants had joined the descendants of the original Nova Scotians. One of the new vicariates, that in Montreal, even began to overtake Quebec in importance, and in the one in Kingston on Lake Ontario after 1817 an English-speaking Catholic community grew up around A. Macdonnell, a former army chaplain. In a fifth vicariate in Manitoba, Lord Selkirk called for priests for the settlers of the new community of Rivière Rouge, whose German population explains the name Saint Boniface for the new church. After Kingston (1826) and Charlottetown (1829), Montreal received in 1836 the rank of an independent diocese, following a lengthy quarrel with the Sulpicians.

The Catholic schools were severely threatened by the founding, at the urging of the Anglican bishop, of the *Institution royale,* but were saved by the *Société d'éducation* of Quebec. With the backing of Protestant dissenters, who also fought against Anglican confiscation, a pluralistic school regulation was ultimately agreed upon, which allowed the parochial schools to develop without hindrance. There was a long fight over the property of the seminary of Quebec which was finally settled satisfactorily in 1839.

Monsignor Plessis always took a legal approach in his actions and thus incurred the displeasure of some fanatics who envisioned a rapid increase in the number of French Canadians. After Plessis's death, against the will of the bishops, an autonomist agitation developed under the pretext of religious demands, which between 1837 and 1838 led to armed riots that could have created an uncomfortable situation for the Church. But the government was understanding, and the act of union between Quebec and Ontario in 1840, which initially was viewed with suspicion by the Catholics, eventually proved to be very advantageous because it extended to the entire country the religious guarantees which in 1791 had only been granted to Lower Canada.

Yet while the legal position of Catholicism improved, its religious condition seemed to be rather mediocre, at least in Quebec, where the majority of the Catholics were located. The faithful demonstrated an undeniable religious indifference fed by Enlightened thoughts, a reaction against the English loyalism among the high clergy, and also by the excessive rigorism of many priests who during the eighteenth century stopped being missionaries in order to become officials.[23] The number of priests was far too small, and the ban on recruiting priests in France led to a Canadianization of the clergy.[24] In spite of the founding of seminary colleges in several small towns such as Nicolet in 1807 and Saint Hyacinthe in 1811, the first part of the nineteenth century was a poor time for recruiting priests. The number of the faithful per priest rose from three hundred fifty at the time of conquest to eighteen hundred in 1830. The shortage of priests, the vast distances, the long winters, and the open way of settling made already difficult working conditions even more difficult. Under such conditions it was not surprising that some priests, influenced by Richer's thought, were little concerned with the authority of the bishop, even though they led irreproachable lives. On the other hand, the clergy of this time were not concerned with politics.

[23] M. Trudel, *Situation de la recherche sur le Canada français* (Quebec 1963), 25.

[24] Forty-five priests, fleeing before the revolution, did indeed enter the country between 1794 and 1802, but as welcome as their addition was, it was inadequate in the face of the rapid growth of the population.

CHAPTER 10

The Churches of the Eastern Rite

The Uniates of the Near East

In the West, ecclesiastical reorganization began as early as 1815, but the efforts to regain the Christian communities in the Ottoman Empire met great obstacles. This is particularly true for the religious minorities which, with the exception of the Maronite Patiarchate, had just begun to mature by the beginning of the nineteenth century. In order to bring the work of renewal to fruition it was necessary, even more than in the European provinces of Turkey, to effect those structural changes which after 1830 were to change the civil and religious physiognomy of the Near East. But this change also had its dark side. The liberal attitude of the Ottoman government favored the Uniates, but at the same time facilitated missionary penetration from the West, exposing the still-weak Uniate communities to Protestant, Anglican, and Russian-Orthodox competition. It also promoted the Latinizing infiltration and the Roman process of centralization, which was to become characteristic for the history of the unity movement of the entire nineteenth century.

The Maronite Patriarchate was by far the most important group of Uniate Christians in the Near East. The crisis of authority which it underwent in the second half of the eighteenth century was resolved under the leadership of the patriarchs Yohanna Al-Halu (1809–23) and Yussef Hobeich (1823–45). Hobeich was a man of energy and vision, who based his work of ecclesiastical reconstruction on full cooperation with the apostolic delegates and a political and religious France.

After his reconciliation with Monsignor Gandolfi, the representative of the Holy See, Yohanna Al-Halu in 1818 convoked a council at Lowaizeh.[1] It decided at last to implement the decisions of the council of Lebanon, made a century earlier in 1736. But the most important objectives were implemented only under Hobeich. In 1826 he dissolved the double or mixed monastic institutions and established an episcopal residence in each diocese, so that after 1835 the bishops at long last had a firm place of residence. He also founded several new seminaries and thereby assured the training of a relatively well educated clergy and of many school principals. But the support of his work by the French resulted in a strengthening of Latinizing tendencies, to which the publication of the ritual (1839–40) attests. With its close to two hundred thousand faithful,[2] the Maronite Church numerically far surpassed all other Eastern Uniate communities, many of which were still at a very low stage of development in 1815.

This was especially true for the Copts, who were still dependent on the Franciscan mission in Egypt and received an autonomous ecclesiastical organization only under the pontificate of Leo XIII. The letter with which in 1822 Pius VII asked the Monophysite patriarch of Alexandria to profess the Catholic faith and to send young Copts to Rome for study[3] remained unanswered, and until 1831 the number of the Uniates was only 2,624 with fourteen priests, dispersed over the entire country. Nevertheless, trusting in forged letters from Mohammed Ali, Leo XII in 1824 decided to reestablish a Coptic patriarchate. The consequences of the forgery, originated by a Sicilian Franciscan, were avoided through

[1] Decrees in de Clercq I, 479–83; cf. 308–13.

[2] According to a report of 1844 they were ministered to by 1205 priests, with an additional 1420 monks and 330 nuns in eighty-two monasteries and convents.

[3] *JP* IV, 529–30.

the quick action of the French consul at Alexandria,[4] but for a long time burdened the fate of the Coptic movement of union.

The Uniate Chaldean Church, developed as a consequence of the Roman adherence by several Nestorian prelates in the seventeenth and eighteenth centuries,[5] was buffeted by a number of vicissitudes at the beginning of the nineteenth century. Its hierarchy was firmly established by this time, though, and the Church numbered twenty thousand faithful. In addition to being isolated in Upper Mesopotamia under extremely poor living conditions, the Uniate Chaldeans were also split by the rivalry of the two candidates for the patriarchal position, the metropolitan of Mosul, John Hormez, and the metropolitan of Diarbekr, Augustine Hindi. After the death of the latter in 1828, a decision by the Congregation for the Propagation of the Faith put a stop to the crisis which had reached its peak in 1826. The Congregation decided to unify the patriarchal jurisdiction and to appoint as "Patriarch of Babylonia" John Hormez, who until this time had been viewed by Rome with mistrust. Under the new designation, which replaced the traditional title *Katholikos,* Hormez became the first of the patriarchs of the contemporary Uniate Chaldean Church. A further step in the process of reorganization was taken by the Congregation in 1838. Breaking with a 300-year tradition, according to which a patriarch was always succeeded by a nephew, it attached Nicholas Zeya as coadjutor with the right of succession to Patriarch Hormez. It could not be foreseen that his selection was so unfortunate as to compel Gregory XVI in 1846 to withdraw him from office. More important than these institutional changes was the adherence to Rome in 1828 of the influential monastery Rabban Hurmuz. With this monastic center as focal point, the Chaldean union movement was immensely strengthened spiritually. In 1845, Gregory XVI recognized the rules of the monastery, which were based on the ideas of Saint Anthony.

The small Syrian community, newly organized in 1782, underwent a fairly parallel development during the first half of the nineteenth century. Here also the fights of rivaling parties delayed a reorganization until 1830, a delay which was complicated by the clumsy interference of the Congregation for the Propagation of the Faith. Following the ten-

[4] For details of this embarrassing affair, typical for the improvisational character of the policy of the Holy See during those years concerning the Christian East as the Congregation for the Propagation of the Faith was then only just being formed, see G. B. Brocchi, *Giornale IV* (Bassano 1841), 210–14.

[5] In Malabar also, in southern India, there lived a number of Catholics of Nestorian origin who, however, had no bishops and were subordinate to the jurisdiction of a Latin vicar apostolic. Only after 1850 did they make contact with the patriarchate of Mesopotamia.

dentious information submitted by Monsignor Gandolfi, the Congregation wanted to remove Pierre Jarweh (1820–51) from the patriarchal see. He had been duly elected, but was suspected of being willing to make compromises with English Protestants. But after the circumstances of Gandolfi's inadequate information had been cleared up, the Congregation recognized Jarweh in 1828. It gave this dynamic man the chance to devote himself to a restructuring of his Church more in keeping with the demands of modern times. He changed the monastery of Scharfeh, in which he lived, into a seminary and replaced the monastic vows by the simple acceptance of celibacy, a vow of obedience, and some testamentary obligations of the former students. The Congregation in 1828 at first rejected the proposal, but accepted it in 1841. Between 1827 and 1836 the Syrian community became known as the Syrian Church in order to distinguish it from the Jacobite-Monophysites and so that it would profit from the traditional reputation of the Christian community of Antioch. The Church experienced a very fortunate development in that several Jacobite bishops declared their loyalty to Rome and thereby added about twenty thousand believers to the Church. But the resulting predominance of the formerly "heretical" bishops worried Rome, and Jarweh was encouraged to exploit the liberalizing steps of the Ottoman Empire for the transfer of his patriarchal see to Aleppo so as to provide him with a better center of operations.

The return of Jacobite prelates to Roman Catholicism was due to the new Melkite Patriarch Maximos III Mazlum (1833–55). Through his diverse and persistent activities he transformed his languishing community[6] into a flourishing Church, yet was determined to defend the autonomy of the Byzantine tradition within the framework of the Roman Church. Until 1830, the Melkite Church suffered from the consequences of the council of Karkafeh (1806)[7] to which some bishops, headed by Germanos Adam, had given a definitely Gallican orientation because they were tired of the interference of Latin missionaries and were disadvantaged by their theological inferiority. The joint reaction of the Maronite patriarch and all of the missionaries placed the Melkite Church in dependence on the apostolic delegate, Monsignor Gandolfi, who intended to master the situation by "breaking the back of the eminent personalities, weakening the hierarchy, and forcing upon it the awareness of defeat" (Hajjar). Fearing Gallican indoctrination, he de-

[6] Whose numbers he was able to increase from thirty-thousand to seventy-five thousand through individual and collective memberships. Around the middle of the century there were about two hundred clergymen, chiefly members of orders.

[7] Concerning the council of Karkafeh, given life by the Gallican bishop of Aleppo, Germanos Adam, and his condemnation by Rome (1835), see de Clercq I, 337–60.

manded that the seminary of Ain-Traz, founded in 1811, remain closed. As the Melkite clergy had no other educational institutions available, and since the best educated among the laity demanded a schooled clergy, they preferred to confess to the Latin missionaries and listen to their sermons. A first step toward the reopening of Ain-Traz in 1831 was taken when Mazlum, who since 1814 had lived in exile in Rome where he had earned the respect of the future Gregory XVI, returned and brought with him a few Jesuits for the seminary. Two years later he was elected patriarch and with determination devoted himself to a general reform of the ecclesiastical institutions. He raised the religious standards of his flock, encouraged the training of an educated and pious clergy, and adjusted the legislation and the structure of the diocesan organization, which stretched across the entire Near East, to the new political and social realities of his country.[8] As defender of patriarchal privileges against the missionaries, the apostolic delegates, and the Roman congregations, this "indefatigable fighter," very suspect in ultramontane circles, but ultimately and justifiably rehabilitated by P. Hajjar, succeeded in freeing his Church from the oppressive monopoly of official orthodoxy. He did so with great persistence by emancipating his national Church, a process which was started in 1831 by an ordinance of the Sultan in favor of Catholic Armenians.

As trading people, the Armenians were spread across the entire Near East and some of them had entered a union with the Roman Catholic Church. A few thousand lived dispersed in the Russian Empire, and after 1635 a Uniate Armenian archbishop resided in Lemberg in Poland, while in Venice, and after 1811 also in Vienna,[9] two communities of learned monks, the Mechitharists, contributed to acquainting the West with some traditions of the Christian East. Within the Ottoman Empire they were found especially in Cilicia and Syria—headed by a *Katholikos*, who after 1750 resided in Bzommar in Lebanon—and in Constantinople, where in spite of the impressive number of fifteen thousand members they did not have their own prelate but were dependent on the Latin vicar apostolic. In 1830 they received an archbishop of their rite, who was independent of the patriarch. In keeping with the secular legislation of the Ottoman Empire, the Uniate Armenians were dependent on the schismatic Armenian patriarch for all civil needs, just as the other Uniate Churches were subordinated to the Orthodox patriarch. The Turkish government did not distinguish be-

[8] See de Clercq I, 379–414 on the two councils of Ain-Traz (1835) and Jerusalem (1849).

[9] About the origins of this founding see V. Inglisian, *150 Jahre Mechitaristen in Wien* (Vienna 1961).

tween Catholic and non-Catholic Christians as long as they belonged to the Eastern rite. In connection with the Greek rebellion in 1827, the Gregorian (i.e., non-Uniate Armenian) patriarch denounced Constantinople's Catholics as accomplices of the rebels and caused them to be persecuted. Leo XII, deeply shocked by such conduct, intervened together with France and Austria and in 1830 obtained from the Sultan, in addition to a limit to the expulsions, the emancipation of the Catholic Armenian communities. From now on they were free to build new churches and received their own civil *patrik.* As a consequence of the liberal development after Mohammed Ali's victories, the jurisdiction of this priest by the decree of 3 June 1834 was expanded to all Uniates, Maronites, Melkites, Syrians, and Chaldeans. The government at Constantinople thereby acknowledged their legal existence for the first time.

The next step was the recognition of the autonomy of each of these communities. The Melkite Patriarch Mazlum played an eminent role in the process. At the same time that he vehemently fought and won the "Battle of Kallous" (a cylindrical cap which only Orthodox priests were permitted to wear), he also suceeded in 1837, with the backing of French diplomacy and despite Russian objections, in obtaining from the Sultan recognition as the civil head of the Catholic Melkites. He remained subordinate to the Armenian *patrik* only formally. A further step was taken in 1844 when, again under the protection of the French ambassador, the Uniate patriarchs of the Syrians and Chaldeans were given an analogous position. But they lived rather reclusive lives and thought it advisable to reach an agreement with the Armenian *patrik.* Mazlum, however, continued his fight and finally on 7 January 1848 obtained a decree which freed his Church community even from any nominal tutelage.

The emancipation of the Uniate groups from the corresponding Eastern Churches, resulting from the political developments in the Near East, constituted an important turning point in the history of the unification movement. The Uniate Churches from now on were able to develop and organize freely and unhindered. But the consolidation at the same time led to a deepening of the rift which separated the Uniate Churches from those from which they had sprung. Thus they could no longer function as bridges between them and Rome. Their growth and the cultural and apostolic rejuvenation of which they had urgent need could only be effected with aid from the West; by the same token, the West's juridical, theological, and spiritual impact could be nothing but disastrous for communities which tended to have feelings of inferiority. The spontaneous and often unintentional development which increasingly estranged the Uniate Churches from the unadulterated Eastern tradition was amplified by the policy of the apostolic delegates. Sometimes with good intentions and often with tactless intransigence, which in some cases exceeded their instruction, they attempted to subordinate the Uniate patriarchates to Rome's central control. To be sure, the efforts of the Holy See to establish closer bonds between these Churches and Rome were understandable. But the almost total ignorance of the Eastern institutions and the general opinion that true unity could only be achieved through uniformity had the consequence of removing, even though done in good faith, the substance of the institution of the patriarchate and the synodal organization of the Church. This Roman policy, which aimed at a redefinition of the authority of the patriarchs in keeping with the purely nominal prerogatives of the Latin archbishops, was pursued with utmost determination only by Pius IX, but its beginnings could be noted during the pontificate of Gregory XVI. An important way station was the decision of the Congregation for the Propagation of the Faith of 23 May 1837, based on the initiative of Monsignor R. Fornari.[10] It decreed that the Uniate patriarchs had to ask the Roman Pope for a confirmation of their election and the investiture with the pallium, and were entitled to assume the other aspects of their jurisdiction only after receiving it. Furthermore, it demanded the approval of the Holy See for decisions of councils before they were published, and forbade the patriarch and his synod to publish decrees which deviated, even if only implicitly, from the discipline approved by the Roman authority. This decree, hardly noticed at the time, introduced a veritable revolution in Eastern law, signifying the distance which within a few decades had been traversed concerning the restoration of papal prerogatives.

The Romanian and Slavic Groups

While the Uniate Churches of the Near East were the focus of attention because of initially appearing difficulties and their pronounced efforts in the defense of the autonomy of the Eastern patriarchical system against Latin attacks, they were not alone among the Uniate Christian communities of the Eastern rite tied to the Apostolic See. In Eastern Europe there were several millions of Uniates, mostly belonging to the Austro-Hungarian Dual Monarchy, who even in the eyes of Rome were a natural bridge for the encounter with Slavic Orthodoxy.

Transylvania was the home of half a million Romanians,[11] grouped in

[10] *CodCanOrFonti,* 1st ser., II (Rome 1931), 439. Cf. Hajjar, 270.

[11] In 1840 there were 571,400 Greek Uniates in Transylvania compared to 686,300 Orthodox, 601,100 Protestants, and 207,400 Roman Catholics.

two dioceses of the Hungarian Church province of Gran; Blaj was their ecclesiastical and cultural center and also served as the residence of the bishop of Făgăras. Between 1782 and 1830 the position was held by John Bob, educated in the Josephine spirit, who put an end to Uniate Monachism which counted among its followers such eminent men as Peter Maior, one of the pillars of the Romanian cultural renaissance. He and his colleague Vulcan, bishop of Oradea Mare (Grosswardein) (1806–39), continued the reintegration into the Catholic Church of the schismatic parishes from the time of Maria Theresia and awakened in the secular clergy a new awareness of its pastoral obligations. In spite of receiving little help from Latin Catholics, they developed a network of educational institutions,[12] which assured the flock of their Church an intellectual level far above that of the other Uniate Churches, as the synods of Blaj (1821 and 1833) attest.[13] John Bob's successor, I. Lomeni (1833–50), continued his work by promoting the religious impact of his clergy and gathered able professors in Blaj to serve both religious and national aims. In the revolution of 1848 he, together with the Orthodox bishop, presided over the National Assembly; his role caused the Hungarian government to call for his dismissal during the reaction following the revolution.

Much more important was the group of the Ruthenians or Ukrainians who after the Union of Brest (1595) had fallen away from the Russian Church. After two centuries of uninterrupted Polish oppression, the Ruthenians had succumbed to the attraction of the powerful and rich Latin Church to a larger degree than the other Uniates and adopted a number of western customs in the area of devotional exercises and discipline. These were acknowledged and strengthened by the Council of Zamosc in 1720 and ultimately led to their clear differentiation from the Orthodox Church.

The Polish partitions at the end of the eighteenth century split the Ruthenians into Austrian and Russian groups. The Russian government understandably was hostile to the Latin and Polish strains of the Uniate Church of the Ukraine and immediately began efforts to lead them back to the fold of Orthodoxy through the use of force, attempts at conversion, and elimination of the clergy. Alexander I's (1801–25) desire to effect a union of the two Churches made possible a lessening of the tension, leading to a partial restoration of the hierarchy which had been suppressed almost totally under Catherine II. But the deterioration could no longer be stopped. The relation of the Holy See to the Uniate

[12] Details in *DThC* XIV, 31–51.

[13] Text in J. Moldovanu, *Acte sinodali* II (Blaj 1872), 68–74, 63–68. On the synod of 1821, see L. Pásztor in *AHPont* 6 (1968), 251–52, 300.

Church continued to be difficult, and the representative of the Catholic Church in Russia, Monsignor Siestrzencewicz, who viewed the end of the Uniates as inevitable, attempted to lead as many Uniates as possible to the Latin rite, mindless of the protests of the Ruthenian clergy and the prohibitions of Rome. At the time of the accession of Nicholas I in 1825, the Uniate Church in the Russian Empire was still represented by 1.5 million believers, two thousand priests, and six hundred monks, but it was in the process of decay. The deterioration was enhanced by the fighting between some secular clerical dignitaries, trained in the Josephine spirit at the general seminary of Vilna, with the pro-Roman Basilian monks, whose wealth was the envy of the others. Catherine II's plan of a radical Russification was disinterred with the help of some ambitious subjects like that of the intriguer J. Siemaszko. Under the pretext of strengthening the Uniate Church, its structure was refashioned in the likeness of the Orthodox Church by the ukase of 22 April 1828. The liturgy was adapted; the clergy systematically indoctrinated; and the episcopal sees were staffed, without paying any attention to Rome, with men who agreed with the government. After they had circulated among the clergy a petition with 1305 signatures, Siemaszko together with two other bishops in February 1829 at the Synod of Polozk drafted a bill of union with the Orthodox Church. Opposition from the population was ignored, and a number of the opponents thereupon fled to Galicia, while others secretly maintained their loyalty to Rome. Only the diocese of Chelm escaped immediate integration, as it was located in the Kingdom of Poland and thus belonged to another governmental jurisdiction. Its agony was delayed for about forty years because of the resistance of its bishop, Monsignor Szumborski.

The fate of the Ruthenians of Galicia, subordinated to Austria, was a happier one. In order to make them immune to Russian influence, Pius VII in 1807 created a new Church province[14] and revived the old title of the Metropolitan of Halicz which he awarded to the bishop of Lvov, with Přzemysl and Chelm as suffragan sees.[15] Within this new framework, the Uniate Ruthenian Church of the Habsburg Empire, numbering 2 million believers in 1840, was able to reorganize itself under the leadership of the able prelates Monsignor M. Lewicki in Lvov (1816–58) and Monsignor J. Suigurski in Přzemysl (1818–47). Pursuing the directives of the synod of Přzemysl of 1818,[16] they increased the number

[14] *JP* IV, 493ff.

[15] From 1795 until 1815 the diocese of Chelm actually was part of the areas belonging to the Habsburgs. After it had come under Russian domination, Leo XII in 1828 separated it from the Lemberg metropole.

[16] Documents in G. Lakota, *Tri sinodi peremiski* (Přzemysl 1939), 153–65.

of parishes and schools and worked at a quantitative and qualitative improvement of the spirit of the Enlightenment. But the results of these efforts were limited, as the Ruthenians no longer had a leading class ever since the majority of the aristocracy had turned away from the Eastern rite in order to enjoy the privileges reserved to the Poles. People ultimately became accustomed to have the "peasant faith" of the Ruthenian serfs on one side and the "landlord faith" of the Latin rite on the other. The feeling of inferiority growing out of this situation was the reason for a greater inclination to adopt western rites. Yet the development did not prevent frequent tensions with the Latin clergy inasmuch as it, especially on the urging of Primate Archbishop A. A. Ankwicz (1815–33), favored the change of rite. The Latin clergy thus followed its own nationalistic Polish feelings and the conviction that in this fashion the Ruthenians could best be strengthened in their Catholic faith. The attitude of the Holy See, however, was more differentiated. It encouraged Latinization, but did not wish to see the suppression of the Ruthenian rite. On the contrary, Gregory XVI in 1843 considered the appointment of a patriarch for the Uniates in the Habsburg Dual Monarchy,[17] because he wanted to encourage the return to the Roman faith of many of the Orthodox still there (nearly 3 million, principally in Hungary) and to protect the Uniates better against the attraction of the Russian Church.

In the Habsburg Empire of the seventeenth century, there lived in Podcarpathia another group of several hundred thousand Uniate Ruthenians who had never belonged to Poland and whose customs therefore in some points deviated from those of the Galician Ruthenians. After 1781 they had their own diocese of Mukačevo. The growing number of converts moved Pius VII in 1818 to establish a second diocese in Presov. Zealous and expert bishops, who towered above the intended mediocrity of the prelates of the Russian Ukraine, lent a new buoyancy to the religious life with the help of the Catholic revival of the Habsburg Empire. The rivalry between Austria, to which Galicia belonged, and Hungary, to which Podcarpathia was subordinated, prevented the connection of the two dioceses with the metropolitan see of Lvov. Thus, just as the Romanian Uniate dioceses of Transylvania, they remained part of the Latin province of Gran, with the result that regulations concerning the Hungarian clergy were also accepted by these Uniates.

Immediately after 1815, the Austrian government for a brief time nourished the hope that the Serbs of Dalmatia, who after the dissolution of the Venetian republic in 1799 had hurriedly returned to Orthodoxy,

[17] A. Baran in *Analecta Ordinis S. Basilii* 3 (1958/60), 454–88.

could be induced to return to Rome and thus form another group of "Uniate Greeks." But all of its efforts were to no avail;[18] in this area there survived only the small diocese of Križevci, founded in 1777 in Bosnia, which in 1847 was attached to the metropolitan see of Zagreb.

The unsuccessful efforts of the Vienna government in Dalmatia, as well as the more effective support which it granted to the more or less Latinized reorganization of the Uniate dioceses in Transylvania, Galicia, and Podcarpathia, were part of a comprehensive larger plan aiming at the largest possible absorption of the remaining Orthodox groups in the Empire. It did not do so, as was the case with Rome,[19] for confessional reasons, but rather for the political reason of preventing the formation of beachheads of Russian influence in the area of the Balkans and Danube. Such ulterior motives behind the Uniate policy of the Habsburg states for a long time to come poisoned the relationship between the Vatican and the Russian Orthodox Church.

[18] See G. Markovič, *Gli Slavi e i Papi* II (Zagreb 1897), 431–34.

[19] And also for some Eastern clergymen in the Dual Monarchy such as the priest A. Horvath, the bishop of Székesfehérvár, J. Horvath, and chiefly the Benedictine abbot I. Guzmics, who wrote extensively on Christian unity (see *DSAM* VII, 697–98).

CHAPTER 11

The Resumption of Missionary Work

The Beginnings of Restoration prior to Gregory XVI

The French Revolution had no direct catastrophic effect upon missionary work. Only a few French possessions in the Antilles and in India were affected by it. At home, however, the destructive consequences of the activity of the encyclopedists and the deists were more than evident. Until the turn of the century, the situation in the missionary countries was approximately as described by the secretary of the Congregation for the Propagation of the Faith, Stefano Borgia, in his comprehensive treatment of 1773.[1]

This far-seeing secretary and future prefect of the Congregation also attempted to help the Chinese Church, threatened by continuing persecutions and a growing shortage of missionaries, by ordaining Chinese bishops. Although his memoranda of 1785 were dealt with negatively

[1] N. Kowalsky OMI, *Stand der katholischen Missionen um das Jahr 1765 an Hand der Übersicht des Propagandasekretärs Stefano Borgia aus dem Jahre 1773* (Part of the series of *NZM* 16) (Beckenried 1957).

by the cardinals of the Congregation in 1787,[2] they were taken up again in 1817 after his death in response to the deteriorating situation. Ultimately they were rejected in 1819,[3] and only one hundred years later were his suggestions implemented.

At the turn of the century, the problems of the missions required particular attention because it was a time of growing turbulence. The uninterrupted wars following the French Revolution and especially those under Napoleon made normal communications between the central office of the missions and the non-European areas almost impossible, and even the work of the central office itself was seriously disrupted. This disruption occurred first in 1798, when General Berthier occupied Rome and the offices of the Congregation. Hardly reorganized after 1800, the Congregation was almost totally destroyed after 1808 when Pius VII was taken into French captivity. The estates of the Congregation became the property of the French state; the printing house was closed down and its valuable type was handed over to the French state printing house; and finally, the entire archives of the Congregation were transferred to Paris.[4] Only after the fall of Napoleon and the return of Pius VII was the Congregation gradually able to resume its orderly function and, after 1817, to improve its financial situation slightly.[5]

Although Napoleon's plans to transfer the Pope and the Congregation as well to Paris failed, they indicate that the Emperor appreciated the great importance of missionary work, at least as a political activity. In a letter to Pius VII of 28 August 1802, Napoleon offered the Pope

[2] Published by V. Bartocetti in *Pensiero Missionario* VI (1934), 231–47.

[3] J. Beckmann, "Beratungen der Propagandakongregation über die Weihe chinesischer Bischöfe von 1787–1819" in *ZMR* 30 (1940), 199–217.—The great concern of Rome to help the threatened missions was embodied in the plans of the secretary of the Congregation for the Propagation of the Faith, Monsignor Coppola, in 1805 and subsequent years to found a seminary for secular priests who were to function as professors for the training of a native clergy in the various countries. J. Metzler OMI, "Missionsseminarien und Missionskollegien. Ein Plan zur Förderung des einheimischen Klerus um 1805" in *ZMR* 44 (1960), 257–71.

[4] J. Schmidlin, "Die Propaganda während der napoleonischen Invasion" in *ZMR* 12 (1922), 112–15.

[5] The archives were returned in 1817, but many volumes were lost. Only in 1925 were seventy-four volumes returned from the Vienna State Archives to the Propaganda archives in consequence of the efforts of the Austrian legate and historian Baron von Pastor. These volumes constituted the *"Fondo di Vienna."* N. Kowalsky, *Inventario dell'Archivio storico della Santa Congregazione "de Propaganda Fide"* (Publication of the *NZM* 17) (Beckenried 1961); id., "L'Archivio della Santa Congregazione "de Propaganda Fide" ed i suoi Archivisti" in *Annales Pont. Univ. Urbaniana* (Rome 1964), 33–53.

the protection of France for all missions in the Near East and China.[6] In a memorandum in the same year Minister Portalis spoke of the political value of French missionary work, citing concrete examples of English efforts to establish such a protectorate in China.[7]

The leading circles in France soon added to this political interpretation by an understanding of the religious concern for the propagation of the faith. The savior of the mission seminary in Paris and future general of the Congregation, Denis Chaumont (1752–1819) was a quiet but successful spokesman for missionary work. From his exile in London he tried to revive the missionary spirit through strong exhortations and the publication of mission reports.[8] In 1805, an imperial decree restored the Paris mission seminary together with the seminary of the Fathers of the Holy Spirit, who were chiefly active in the French Antilles.[9]

This success was prepared by René de Chateaubriand's (1768–1848) *Le Génie du Christianisme* (1802). The work principally served to revive the Catholic religion in France and the missions, especially in America, with which Chateaubriand was personally acquainted.[10]

The book by this romantic was proof of the intimate connection between a revived Catholicism and the activity of spreading the faith. This connection explains why the Church in France, although for a long time affected by rationalistic and anti-Christian forces, was gradually able to hold a position of supremacy in Catholic missions. The focus of spreading the faith increasingly shifted from the Iberian countries to

[6] Streit XII, 17.

[7] F. Combaluzier CM, "Les missions au temps de Napoléon" in *RHM* 14 (1937), 258–66, 395–402, 521–24 (Portalis's memorandum, 261f.). A summary of the efforts of England to gain the favor of Catholic missionaries and a missionary protectorate can be found in L. Wei Tsing-sing, *La politique missionnaire de la France en Chine 1842–1856* (Paris 1960), 70–76.

[8] In China since 1776, he went to Paris in 1874 as the representative of the China mission, was forced to flee in 1792, and returned in 1814. His financial contribution made possible the purchase of the confiscated seminary buildings. After 1814 he was general-superior. A. Launay, *Mémorial de la Société des Missions Étrangères* II (Paris 1916), 126f.

[9] Text of the decree in A. Launay, *Histoire Générale* II (Paris 1894), 377–78. The mother house of the Lazarists was returned to Paris only in 1817 in response to a rather optimistic memorandum of the former China missionary J. Fr. Richenet (1759–1836): "Note de M. Richenet CM sur la Mission des Lazaristes en Chine" in *T'oung Pao* XX (1920/21), 117–29. The government paid for the newly acquired generalate in the Rue de Sèvres.

[10] He described them in the fourth book and parts of the fifth and sixth books. J. Schmidlin, "Chateaubriand und Maistre über die Mission" in *ZMR* 21 (1931), 295–97; J. Beckmann, "Chateaubriand et les Bethléemites," *NZM* 19 (1963), 130f.

France. Here new missionary orders and congregations sprang up. In 1805, the Congregation of the Sacred Hearts of Jesus and Mary (Picpus Fathers) was founded, a congregation which provided the first complete group of Catholic missionaries in Oceania,[11] and in 1807 the Sisters of Joseph of Cluny began continuous work in Africa and Asia.[12] In 1816, the Oblates of the Immaculate Virgin Mary became the modern apostles to Canada,[13] and in 1836 the Marian Society (Marists) was given responsibility for a huge area in the South Seas.[14]

While French orders and societies trained and sent out new missionaries, Marie-Pauline Jaricot as well (1799–1862) sought to help the missionaries by founding in Lyon in 1822 the Association for the Spreading of the Faith. The Association offered its help through regular prayers by the members and through collection of a weekly "penny for the missions."[15] Although the initial efforts of Marie-Pauline Jaricot were made in close contact with the Paris mission seminary, as early as the founding meeting plans were made to encompass all Catholic missions, a plan heartily supported and inspired by the two French bishops in America, Flaget (1763–1850) and Dubourg (1766–1833). The fact of such "Catholicity" was probably the reason for the fast growth of the association beyond the French borders at first to the neighboring countries of Savoy and Piedmont,[16] then to Switzerland (1827)[17] and the Netherlands (1830),[18] and ultimately to America, Portugal, and Spain.[19] Due to the exclusively French direction and administration, indepen-

[11] St. Perron, *Vie du T.R.P. M.-J. Coudrin, fondateur et premier supérieur de la Congrégation des Sacrés-Cœurs de Jésus et Marie* (Paris 1940).

[12] Founded by Anne-Marie Javouhey (1779–1851). G. Goyau, *Un grand Homme: Mère Javouhey, apôtre des Noirs* (Paris 1929).

[13] Founded by Ch. J. E. de Mazenod (1782–1861). J. Leflon, *Eugêne de Mazenod. Évêque de Marseilles, Fondateur des Missionnaires Oblats de Marie* I-III (Paris 1957/65).

[14] Founded by J. Cl. Colin (1790–1875). G. Goyau, *Le Vénérable Jean Colin* (Paris 1913). See also the summary description of these orders in L. Deries, *Les congrégations religieuses au temps de Napoléon* (Paris 1928). (*Les missions et les missionnaires au temps de Napoléon*, 107–19).

[15] De Lathoud, *Marie-Pauline Jaricot*, 2 vols. (Paris 1937).—On the precursors of the association, especially within the framework of the Paris mission seminary, see H. Sy, "Précurseurs de L'Œuvre de la Propagation de la Foi" in *NZM* 5 (1949), 170–88.

[16] On the quick expansion of the association see A. Schmidlin, "Zur Zentenarfeier des Vereins der Glaubensverbreitung" in *ZMR* 12 (1922), 65–76; M.-A. Sadrain, "Les premières années de la Propagation de la Foi" in *RHM* 16 (1939), 321–48, 554–79. In Piedmont the establishment of the association was intimately connected with the religious renewal. See C. Bona IMC, *La rinascita Missionaria in Italia* (Turin 1964).

[17] J. Beckmann, "Die katholischen Schweizermissionen in Vergangenheit und Gegenwart" in *StMis* 9 (Rome 1956), 135–36.

[18] A. J. J. M. van den Eerenbeent, *Die Missie-actie in Nederland (1600–1940)* (Nijmegen 1945), 81–84.

[19] A. Schmidlin, op. cit., (Note 16), 88.

dent associations sprang up in Austria and Germany, where several missionary circles had been formed. People in Vienna founded the Leopoldine Foundation[20] in 1828; people in the Rhineland organized themselves as the Xaverius Society[21] in 1834, and in Bavaria the Ludwig Society[22] was founded in 1838. In 1824, the journal *Annales de la Propagation de la Foi* began to appear regularly, at first in French and then in translation throughout most of Europe.[23] After the Congregation for the Propagation of the Faith had been looted twice, first by revolutionary troops and then by Napoleon, the Association for the Spreading of the Faith became the most important source of money for the missions in modern times.[24]

The Bull *Sollicitudo omnium,* published by Pius VII on 17 August 1814, restored the Society of Jesus. This was an act of the greatest consequence for the missions. Shortly after assuming office, the Pope had affirmed the existence of the order in Russia. The Society had continued to exist there under the protection of Catherine II, but only papal recognition brought about an increase in its membership in Russia.[25] The restoration of the Society was intended to rejuvenate the old Jesuit mission to China as well. The Russian government expected that by placing this mission under its protection, an improvement of its relations with China could be effected. Several attempts to do this were fruitless.[26] But they illustrated symbolically the great esteem which the China mission still enjoyed in leading circles. Together with that in

[20] J. Thauren, *Ein Gnadenstrom zur Neuen Welt und seine Quelle. Die Leopoldinenstiftung zur Unterstützung der amerikanischen Missionen* (Mödling 1940); G. Kummer, *Die Leopoldinen-Stiftung (1829–1914)* (Vienna 1966).

[21] The Rhenish Circle was active for the Association for the Spreading of the Faith in Lyon as early as 1827, but the founding of the Xavier Association was possible under a new name and independent direction only in 1834. The Aachen physician Heinrich Hahn (1800–82) was the life and soul of the efforts. Biography by C. Bäumker (Aachen 1930); G. Schückler, *Brücken zur Welt. 125 Jahre Aachener Missionszentrale* (Aachen 1967).

[22] W. Mathäser OSB, *Der Ludwig-Missionsverein in der Zeit König Ludwigs I. von Bayern* (Munich 1939). In Bavaria also support for the central office in Lyon went back to the year 1827.

[23] Streit, I 571–73, lists editions in nineteen languages. Inasmuch as especially in the first decades the missionary bishops themselves or their representatives composed the reports, the volumes covering the nineteenth century are one of the most important sources for missionary history in our time.

[24] According to the accounting of the association, it contributed 500 million francs to the missions during the first hundred years of its existence (A. Schmidlin, op. cit., [Note 16], 69).

[25] J. A. Otto, *P. Roothaan,* 9ff.—When the order was dissolved in Russia in 1820, 350 Jesuits, who were active in thirty-two settlements, were forced to leave the country.

[26] J. A. Otto, op. cit., 64–81; G. Garraghan SJ, "John Anthony Grassi SJ (1775–1849)" in *CHR* 23 (1937), 273–92.

Indochina, the China mission was the only one which, in spite of all obstacles, had maintained a vibrant religious life.

Of fundamental importance for all of China was the first synod in Szechuan conducted by the martyr Bishop Gabriel Taurin Dufresse (1750–1815) together with fourteen Chinese and three European priests. The minutes of the synod were approved and published by the Congregation for the Propagation of the Faith in 1822, and a decree of 1832 made the decisions of the synod applicable to all of China.[27] Although this synod with its far-reaching decisions gave the impression of peaceful conditions in China, in fact, local chicaneries continued and in 1805 and 1811 grew into general persecutions. The mission in Peking became a victim of the persecution of 1805, and its missionaries were forced to leave the country. In consequence of the imperial decrees of 1811, Bishop Dufresse of Szechuan died a martyr's death in 1815, and the same fate befell the Italian Franciscan Giovanni da Triora of Shansi in 1816 and the French Lazarist Francois Clet (1748–1820) in 1820. In addition to persecutions, the Franciscan missions in the north suffered also from internal difficulties. The vicar apostolic G. B. de Mandello was removed from office because of differences with native priests.[28]

However, despite all of these persecutions, the external organization of the dioceses and vicariates apostolic in China not only remained intact, but the European and Chinese missionaries also managed to create new Christian centers. These centers were small and widely scattered, but, in the course of the nineteenth century, they expanded to regular communities.[29] By 1815, eighty-nine Chinese and eighty European priests devoted themselves to missionary work and ministered to two hundred ten thousand Christians.[30] The relatively high number of Chinese clergymen illustrates the active way in which the European missionaries had conducted their training and education. To the existing training centers in Macao and distant places in inner China was added in 1808 the newly opened general seminary of the Paris missionaries in Pulo-Penang.[31]

[27] Streit, XII, 22f., 89.

[28] K. S. Latourette, *A History of Christian Missions in China* (New York 1929), 175ff.

[29] Monsignor Dufresse in 1814 reported the following details for his area: in East Szechuan there were 123 centers, 73 in the west, 73 in the north, and 183 in the south, altogether 577. In addition, the provinces of Kweichow (10) and Yinnan (25) were under his jurisdiction. J. Beckmann, "Die Lage der katholischen Missionen in China um 1815" in *NZM* 2 (1946), 222.

[30] Ibid., 217–23.

[31] P. Destombes, *Le Collège Général de la Société des Missions Étrangères* (Hong Kong 1934). The seminary had existed since 1665 in Siam, had to flee a hundred years later after the invasion of the Burmese, but after several attempts was finally reestablished on British territory.

Efforts by Pius VII to provide support for beleaguered Catholics elsewhere, such as in South Africa, Australia, India and Oceania, had only short-lived results or were total failures. It was his missionary zeal, however, that reorganized the Congregation for the Propagation of the Faith, restored the Society of Jesus, confirmed new missionary societies, and aided the Association for the Spreading of the Faith. Pius VII prepared the way for the restoration period under the pontificates of Leo XII (1823–29) and Pius VIII (1829–30).[32]

The Restoration of Missionary Work under Gregory XVI (1831–46)

In 1831, the Camaldolensian Cardinal Mauro Cappellari was elected Pope. Since 1826 he had been prefect of the Congregation for the Propagation of the Faith,[33] and as such was well acquainted with the deficiencies, obstacles, needs, and tasks of missionary work. As Pope, he was eager to promote and to instill new life into the various missionary endeavors.[34]

Gregory XVI saw as his first task the acquainting of the Church of the western world with the duties and tasks of spreading the faith, a task which heretofore had been conducted primarily by the use of patronage powers. To do this, the Pope used his first papal mission Encyclical *Probe nostis* of 15 August 1840,[35] extensive support of the Association for the Spreading of the Faith,[36] and recognition and support of the Holy Childhood Association,[37] founded in 1843 by Bishop Charles de Forbin-Janson of Nancy. The national mission associations in Aachen,

[32] Schmidlin, *Papstgeschichte* I, 307–43, Leflon, 343–56, Delacroix, III, 45–51.

[33] J. Schmidlin, "Gregor XVI. als Missionspapst (1831–46)" in *ZMR* 21 (1931), 209–28; id., *Papstgeschichte* I, 662–75; C. Costantini, "Gregorio XVI e le Missioni" in *Gregorio XVI, Miscellanea Commemorativa* II (*Misc. Hist. Pont.* XIV/2) (Rome 1948), 1–23; R. S. Maloney SX, *Mission Directives of Pope Gregory XVI (1831–1846)*, Partial edition (Rome 1959).

[34] C. Costantini, op. cit., 6–8 with a list of all decrees issued by Gregory as prefect of the Congregation.

[35] *JP* V, 250–53.

[36] The partial edition of Maloney's dissertation mentioned in footnote 33 deals with this aid. It was the Pope's purpose to establish the international and missionary character of the association. With this objective in mind even the work of the Catholic apostolate of Vincent Pallotti, personally approved by the Pope earlier, was dissolved in 1838. On the other hand, he approved the expenditure of association funds for the construction of a new Jesuit college at Schwyz but withdrew his permission in 1835 after a protest by Cardinal Fransoni, prefect of the Congregation.

[37] P. Lesourd, *Un grand cœur missionnaire: Monsignor de Forbin-Janson (1785–1844), Fondateur de l'Œuvre de la Sainte-Enfance* (Paris 1944).

Vienna, and Munich also received support from Gregory XVI, who attempted to subordinate them to the direction of Lyon.[38]

One of the chief concerns of the Pope was to increase mission personnel. Spain and Portugal, which in the past had provided most of them, in the course of persecutions between 1834 and 1836 had dissolved almost all of the orders and religious associations and expelled or imprisoned their members.[39] These persecutions had detrimental consequences for the Spanish successor states in America and for the Portuguese missions. Although the Jesuits were the most persecuted group in the Iberian states, France and Switzerland, Gregory XVI sought help for their beleaguered missions. The Pope's position was also adopted by the Jesuit General Johann Philipp Roothaan (1785–1853), and found enthusiastic readiness among the Jesuits just as in the sixteenth and seventeenth centuries. Ever since the Dutch general had taken over direction of the order in 1829, it had become internally and externally strengthened; and at his death it again numbered 5209 members.[40] Even more important for the organic growth of the Church was the fundamentally positive attitude of General Roothaan toward the central mission office of the Congregation for the Propagation of the Faith. He engaged tirelessly in completely adjusting the work of the Jesuit missions to this highest organ of missionary activity. His struggle for cooperation by both parties was to be of benefit not only for all mission work, but also for the activity of other orders and congregations.[41] The end of this development saw a strategy in effect to this very day: the division of missionary areas and their transfer to the various orders and congregations.

The Paris mission seminary also followed the new trend. Until the nineteenth century it had provided the vicars apostolic for the Far Eastern mission areas, but had sent missionaries only in isolated cases. Now the bishops were joined by missionaries of specific societies, who took entire mission areas under their care. Bishop Luquet (1810–58) exercised lasting influence in the process. As seminarist, he wrote the guidelines for the establishment of a native hierarchy, including cardinals, and the training of a native clergy, thereby reviving the ideas which had

[38] Maloney, op. cit., 49–55.—These different associations became branches of the Association for the Spreading of the Faith, tied in more or less closely, depending on the circumstances.

[39] Schmidlin, *Papstgeschichte* I, 614–27.

[40] J. A. Otto, *P. Roothaan*, 106.

[41] Ibid., 504–20.—Concerning the historical development of the legal aspect, see S. Masarei, *De missionum institutione ac de relationibus inter Superiores Missionum et Superiores Religiosos* (Rome 1940), especially 59–84.

guided the seminary in the period of its beginnings.[42] In fact, the seminary became the principal mission society for the Far East in the nineteenth century.

One of Monsignor Luquet's associates was Franz Maria Libermann (1802–52),[43] the son of a rabbi and a converted Catholic. In 1841, Libermann founded the Association of the Missionaries of the Holy Heart of Mary, which, in 1848, united with the Society of the Holy Ghost[44] and adopted its name. This association operated entirely in the service of the blacks, who at his time were virtually without missionaries. In 1841, the association began its mission and pastoral work on the island of Mauritius and in 1842 on the island of Réunion. The first ten missionaries, seven priests and three friars, arrived in Senegal in West Africa in 1843, but within one year all but one of them had succumbed to the tropical climate. In spite of all losses the ranks were refilled again and again, and in West and East Africa[45] one mission area after the other was entrusted to the Congregation of the Holy Ghost. The fruitful development of missionary work was due not only to the heroic efforts of the missionaries, but also to the visionary instructions of Libermann, who, very much like Monsignor Luquet, never lost sight of a native Church.[46]

Before Libermann's spiritual sons reached Africa, a devout woman,

[42] *Lettres à Monseigneur l'évêque de Langres sur la Congrégation des Missions Étrangères* (Paris 1842).—In 1845 Luquet was appointed suffragan bishop of Pondichéry by Gregory XVI, but was not accepted by his co-workers. A. Launay, *Mémorial de la Société des Missions Étrangères* II (Paris 1916), 411–13; R. Roussel, *Un Précurseur: Monseigneur Luquet, 1810–1858* (Langres 1960); J. Millet, *La Pensée missionnaire de Monseigneur Luquet* (Unpublished dissertation, Paris 1962).

[43] Literature by and on Libermann in Streit XVII, 422–28; also P. Blanchard, *Le Vénérable Libermann 1802–52,* 2 vols. (Paris 1960).

[44] The society, founded by Father Poullart des Places (1679–1719), devoted itself principally to missionary and pastoral work in the French colonies. J. Michel CSSp, *Claude-François Poullart des Places. Fondateur de la Congrégation du St. Esprit, 1679–1719* (Paris 1962); J. Janin CSSp, *La Religion aux Colonies Françaises sous l'Ancien Régime* (Paris 1942); V. Lithard CSSp, *Spiritualité Spiritaine. Étude sur les Écrits Spirituels de Monseigneur Poullart des Places et du Vénérable Libermann* (Paris 1948); H. J. Koren and M. Carrignan, *Les Écrits de Monseigneur Claude-François Poullart des Places, fondateur de la Congrégation du Saint Esprit* (Pittsburgh-Louvain 1959).

[45] H. J. Koren, *The Spiritans. A History of the Congregation of the Holy Ghost* (Pittsburgh-Louvain 1958).

[46] For example, Libermann wrote to the first missionaries in Dakar: "Become Negroes with the Negroes in order to educate them the way they need to be educated. Do not educate them in the European fashion, but let them keep their characteristics! Act toward them like servants toward their master . . ." Cited in A. Engel CSSp, *Die Missionsmethode der Missionare vom Heiligen Geiste auf dem afrikanischen Festland* (Knechtsteden 1934), 41.

Anna Maria Javouhey (1779–1851) had begun the work of spreading the faith. In 1807, she founded the Congregation of the Sisters of Saint Joseph of Cluny with the purpose of reviving the languishing religious life in France. When she heard of the great misery in Africa, she sent her sisters to the island of Réunion in 1817 and to Senegal in 1819. Accompanied by six companions, she herself brought aid to the suffering sisters in West Africa, organized mission work in Senegal and neighboring Sierra Leone and, after 1827, devoted herself principally to the blacks in America and Guyana. Convinced of the urgent necessity of having missionary priests, she intended founding such an organization but deferred to Father Libermann when she heard of his efforts. Mother Anna's enterprise laid the foundation for the work of the sisters in Africa.[47] Moreover, not only did she act as the pathfinder for missions in Africa; the example of her sisters was also the signal for a general participation of women in the modern Catholic apostolate overseas.

Even before the dissolution of the orders in the Iberian countries, the shortage of missionaries had negative results in the vast reaches of Asia which were part of the Portuguese patronage. Gregory XVI, as former prefect of the Congregation for the Propagation of the Faith, was well acquainted with the local conditions and from the beginning of his pontificate sought to ameliorate the situation. In 1832 he gave Portugal the choice of either fulfilling its duties as patron or of resigning from the patronage. When Portugal failed to respond to the papal request, the Pope himself undertook the reorganization of ecclesiastical affairs in Asia, beginning first in India.

After solving a number of problems which had originated in part from the participating orders and in part from the governments of Portugal and England, Gregory XVI in 1834 reestablished the vicariate apostolic of Bengal (Calcutta),[48] where the British East India Company, which virtually ruled the area, had its headquarters ever since 1733. Here, in 1819, was created the first Anglo-Indian bishopric. But here also the Portuguese Augustinians tenaciously clung to their traditional patronage and acknowledged only the bishop of Meliapur or his representative as their ecclesiastical superior.[49]

A similar situation existed in Madras, where the British had built a

[47] Literature in Streit XVII, 383–86. The best biography is G. Goyau, *Un grand Homme: Mère Javouhey, apôtre des Noirs* (Paris 1929). Her letters appeared in 5 volumes (Paris 1909/17). Beatified in 1950.

[48] *JP* V, 95f.; The separation from Meliapur occurred in 1835, ibid., 135–36.

[49] N. Kowalski OMI, "Die Errichtung des Apostolischen Vikariats Kalkutta nach den Akten des Propagandaarchivs" in *ZMR* 36 (1952), 117–27, 187–201, 37 (1953), 209–28. For the history of the Jesuits in Calcutta at this time, see J. A. Otto, *P. Roothaan*, 257–83.

fort as early as 1641, and never had permitted admission to Portuguese missionaries. Pastoral care here was in the hands of French Capuchins.[50] As in Calcutta, the establishment of the vicariate apostolic of Madras in 1832 did not fully untangle the jurisdictional problems. The same was true for the vicariates of Pondichéry, Ceylon, and Madura, all of which were established in 1836.[51]

Rome's unusual and significant intervention in India's mission situation was not accepted well everywhere by the patronage clergy. Some priests and their communities refused to obey the new bishops, who in turn demanded from Rome an unequivocal decision which would put an end to the disastrous double jurisdiction. It was not until 28 April 1838 that Gregory XVI signed the Decree *Multa praeclare,*[52] and he failed to inform Portugal and the corresponding administrative levels in India of his decree in the correct form. His brief dissolved the patronage bishoprics of Kotschin, Kranganore, and Meliapur in India and the bishopric of Malacca in Indochina. The effect was disastrous, and the sporadic opposition to the vicar apostolic now hardened to a united front and in the subsequent period resulted in increased confusion.

Multa praeclare shook Portugal out of its lethargy. The Portuguese government nominated the Benedictine José Maria da Silva Torres (1800–54) for the archepiscopal see of Goa, vacant since 1831, and in 1843 Gregory XVI accepted him.[53] Unfortunately the Pope appointed Torres according to the example of earlier bulls and only a private letter *Nuntium ad te* obligated the new archbishop to acknowledge the Brief *Multa praeclare* and the subsequent reduction of the archbishop's jurisdiction.[54] As a Portuguese national, the new archbishop was compelled to act in accordance with *Multa praeclare,* while the vicars apostolic acted according to *Nuntium ad te.* Thus from the beginning the two points of view clashed irreconcilably and poisoned India's religious-ecclesiastical climate.[55]

[50] N. Kowalsky OMI, "Die Errichtung des Apostolischen Vikariats Madras nach den Akten des Propagandaarchivs" in *NZM* 8 (1952), 36–48, 119–26, 193–210.

[51] *JP* V, 97, 161, 168.—For Ceylon: J. Rommerskirchen OMI, "Die Errichtung des Apostolischen Vikariats Ceylon" in *ZMR* 28 (1938), 124–32. For Madura: J. A. Otto, *P. Roothaan,* 283–339.

[52] *JP* V, 195–98.—J. Metzler OMI, "Die Aufnahme des Apostolischen Breve *Multa praeclare* in Indien" in *ZMR* 38 (1954), 295–317.

[53] J. Metzler OMI, "Die Patronatswirren in Indien unter Erzbischof Silva Torres (1843–49)" in *ZMR* 42 (1958), 292–308.

[54] *JP* V, 316–17.

[55] It is no longer correct to describe the situation thus created as "Goan schism", as—aside from subjective opinion and ignorance—the position of the archbishop cannot be called schismatic. A. Lourenço, *Utrum fuerit Schisma Goanum post Breve "Multa praeclare" usque ad annum 1849* (Goa 1947) rejects the earlier interpretation with documents and fresh reasoning.

Gregory XVI in 1834 established the vicariate apostolic of Sardhana[56] and in 1845 the vicariate of Patna in the Capuchin mission of Hindustan. To the latter, he appointed the Swiss Capuchin Anastasius Hartmann.[57] Less troublesome than the reorganization of the dissolved Portuguese dioceses of India was that of Malacca which, first joined with Burma (vicariate apostolic of Ava and Pegu) and then after 1840 combined with Siam, was divided into two vicariates in 1841.[58]

The most vivid growth of Christianity in Indochina took place in the former empires of Tonking and Cochinchina. Under Emperor Gialong (died 1821), who had ascended the throne with the help of the French and notably that of the vicar apostolic Pierre Pigneau de Behaine (died 1799), the mission experienced a period of rest which enabled it to heal the damages of the persecutions of the eighteenth century. In 1830, under his successor, Ming Mang (died 1841), however, a bloody persecution began which claimed hundreds of Christians, twenty Vietnamese priests, nine European missionaries, and four bishops as its victims.[59] Gregory XVI in 1839 directed a letter of consolation and encouragement[60] to the persecuted Church and, in a public consistory of 27 April 1840, praised the Christian fortitude of the individual martyrs.[61] The Church was able to continue its existence only under the protection of the forests and rivers.

In spite of persecutions and a shortage of missionaries, the China mission survived relatively intact during the first half of the nineteenth century.[62] That this was so was owed principally to the uninterrupted maintenance of the office of the Congregation for the Propagation of the Faith in Macao.[63] Another factor was that Gregory XVI dealt more

[56] *JP* V, 108–10 in addition to other documents of Gregory (letter to the prince), S. Noti SJ, *Das Fürstentum Sardhana* (Freiburg 1906).

[57] *JP* V, 351, 352.—A. Jann a Stans OMCap, ed., *Monumenta Anastasiana* I/1 (Lucerne 1939), 1st appendix 970–1152, also documents for the antecedents of Patna, i.e., of the Capuchin mission of Hindustan; W. Bühlmann OFMCap, *Pionier der Einheit. Bischof Anastasius Hartmann* (Paderborn-Zürich 1966).

[58] Schmidlin, *Papstgeschichte* I, 670.

[59] F. Schwager SVD, "Aus der Vorgeschichte der hinterindischen Missionen" in *ZMR* 3 (1913), 146–56.

[60] *JP* V, 318–20.

[61] *JP* V, 229–31.

[62] J. Beckmann, "Die Lage der katholischen Kirche in China um 1815" in *NZM* 2 (1946), 217–22.

[63] Under Gregory as cardinal prefect of the Congregation for the Propagation of the Faith and as Pope, this office was held by Raffaele Umpierres (until 1834), then Theodore Joset, and by Antonio Feliciani after 1842. A history of this institution, so significant for the Asiatic missions, has not yet been written. For the years 1834–42, see J. Beckmann, "Monsignor Theodor Joset, Prokurator der Propaganda in China und erster Apostolischer Präfekt von Hongkong (1804–42)" in *ZSKG* (1942), 19–38, 121–39.

circumspectly with the bishoprics there than in India.[64] For example, in 1838, after the death of the last bishop of Nanking, Gaetano Pirés Pereira, who was never able to leave his residence and work in Peking, the Pope appointed only an apostolic administrator, the Italian secular priest L. de Besi. The establishment of the vicariate apostolic of Korea in 1831 and of the vicariates apostolic of Manchuria in 1838 and Mongolia in 1840 hardly touched upon Peking's interests. Only the vicariate apostolic of Shantung was separated from the bishopric in 1839. The establishment of other vicariates in 1838 in Hu-Kuang, Kiangsi, and Chekiang concerned only areas which were already under the jurisdiction of the Congregation. A real collision with Portuguese officials did occur, however, when the Congregation claimed jurisdiction over Hong Kong, which the Chinese had ceded to the British. In 1841, the Congregation elevated the area to a prefecture apostolic and appointed the procurator in Macao, Theodor Joset, as prefect apostolic. Joset was expelled from Macao and in 1842 died of deprivation in a straw hut in Hong Kong.[65]

It was also during Gregory XVI's pontificate that the first three missionaries of the recently reinstated Society of Jesus were sent out. In 1841 the missionaries arrived in Macao and soon became active in the diocese of Nanking.[66] According to the plans of General Roothaan, the China mission was to be a bridge for the reopening of the mission in Japan. Korea, the nearest and most natural connection with Japan, was difficult to reach. Only in 1837 was a missionary priest able to step upon Korean soil, to be followed in 1838 by the first bishop, Monsignor Imbert, who in the following year became the victim of bloody persecution. In 1836, the Ryukyu Islands were assigned to the Korea mission in the expectation that they would facilitate the entry into Japan. The Paris missionary Father Forcade was appointed in 1846 as vicar apostolic,[67] but all attempts to establish a mission in Japan proper failed.

A new epoch in Chinese mission history was introduced with the Chinese-French treaty of Whampoa in 1844, which had arisen out of the unfortunate Opium War and the subsequent treaty of Nanking. At Whampoa, the French plenipotentiary De Lagrené succeeded in obtaining not only the freedom of action which France wanted, but also, albeit

[64] The reason for such caution was probably the procurate of the Congregation in Macao. It exercised its function until 1842.

[65] J. Beckmann, "Monsignor Theodor Joset," 132–37; A. Choi, *L'érection du premier vicariat apostolique et les origines du Catholicisme en Corée* (Schöneck–Beckenried 1961).

[66] J. A. Otto, *P. Roothaan*, 350–83.—The administrator of Nanking, Count de Besi, had fallen out with the French Lazarists. A conflict with the new missionaries caused him to resign in 1848 and to leave China.

[67] *JP* V, 359.

to a limited degree, freedom of religion as well.[68] This treaty concluded the period of the old China mission. The new mission, especially in the second half of the nineteenth century and the twentieth century, stood in the shadow of the French protectorate.

In the Philippines, the spreading of the faith was continued during the nineteenth century within the framework of the established hierarchy, and in Indonesia, established in 1831 and designated as vicariate apostolic in 1842, was compelled to limit its activity to the European population. The missions in Oceania, however, found a vast new field.[69] The first Catholic representatives, the Picpus Fathers, arrived in Honolulu in 1827; Protestant missionaries had been active there since 1797. In 1833, Polynesia became a vicariate apostolic,[70] and in 1836 West Oceania was separated from Lyon for the benefit of the Marists, a portion of which was elevated to the vicariate of Central Oceania in 1842.[71]

The contrast between denominations, so evident in Oceania from the very beginning, was accentuated by political differences as well, with the Protestants siding with England and the Catholics with France. Both denominations, following the example of the old Paraguay mission, had established autonomous theocracies in their areas, headed by native chieftains. But these social creations were not impervious to the increasing European penetration of the South Seas, and the missionaries were forced to look for new supports. They found these in their home states, with the Protestants looking toward England and the Catholics toward

[68] A. Grosse-Aschhoff OFM, *The Negotiations between Ch'i-Ying and Lagrené 1844 to 1846* (St. Bonaventura/N.Y. 1950).—According to this examination, resting on Chinese documents, Lagrené had neither the order nor the personal inclination to demand religious freedom for the missionaries. The pertinent clauses were virtually pressed upon him by the Chinese, who probably had the hope of playing the French against the English. Aside from a few private letters, missionaries did not influence the negotiations. Older descriptions, as well as that by B. Wirth, *Imperialistische Übersee- und Missionspolitik, dargestellt am Beispiel Chinas* (Münster 1968), 20, are therefore incorrect. See also L. Wei Tsing-sing, *La Politique missionnaire de la France en Chine 1842–1856* (Paris 1960).

[69] Of the literature listed by Streit XXI, the following two surveys stand out: J. Braam MSC, "Die Gestaltung der ozeanischen Kirche" in *ZMR* 26 (1936), 241–55; J. Schmidlin, "Missionsmethode und Politik der ersten Südsee-Missionare" in *ZMR* 26 (1936), 255–63. It was against the latter article that A. Perbal OMI directed his defense *Les missionnaires français et le nationalisme* (Paris 1939).

[70] *JP* V, 78–80 and letter of appointment of the first apostolic vicar Monsignor Saint Rouchouz.

[71] *JP* V, 157–58, 295–98.—Bishop Pompallier SM arrived in his mission area in 1837, and transferred Wallis Island to the future Bishop Bataillon and Futuna Island to Saint Pierre Chanel, the first martyr of Oceania. See Streit XXI, 174–83, as well as *Écrits du P. Chanel 1803–41,* ed. by Claude Rozier (Paris 1960).

France, thus laying the base for the political attitudes of the future.[72] On the other hand, it was often the Catholic missionaries who tried to protect their Christian flocks from French exploitation. An example was Father Honoré Laval (1838–80), who after 1834 built up a Christian center at Mangareva in the Gambier islands. Because of his defense of the natives, the French exiled him to Tahiti.[73]

With colonial powers as well as missions expanding into the South Seas, the African continent, aside from a few areas on its rim, had not yet awakened any great colonial or missionary interest.[74] In North Africa, after the French occupation, the diocese of Algiers was established in 1838 and the vicariate apostolic of Tunis in 1843. In Abyssinia, the Lazarist Giustino de Jacobis (1800–60) resumed the long-interrupted missionary work,[75] and the Capuchin Guglielmo Massaia (1809–89) was appointed by Gregory as vicar apostolic to the heathen Gallas.[76] Missionary work in West Africa first began in Liberia, a new state formed with liberated slaves from America. Monsignor Edward Barron (1801–54) arrived in Liberia from the United States in 1841, as a result of the council of Baltimore in 1833, which had stipulated that Catholics in the United States should be involved in the establishment of black missions. In 1842, Barron also became vicar apostolic for Upper Guinea, but was unable to take care of this gigantic area. Almost all of the missionaries to Upper Guinea died within a short period of time.[77] Senegambia and Gabun were ceded to the Holy Ghost Fathers[78] in 1844, and Monsignor Barron returned to the United States a sick man. In South

[72] A. Koskinen, *Missionary Influence as a Political Factor in the Pacific Islands* (Helsinki 1953).—This work exceeds all earlier ones in thoroughness and depth, although it is limited to Polynesia. The author concludes that both denominations could not act differently in the interest of the missionary work they had started. A good survey of the French-Catholic point of view is offered by C. W. Newbury and P. O'Reilly in the introduction to P Honoré Laval, *Mémoires pour servir à l'histoire de Mangareva ère chrétienne 1834–1871* (Paris 1968), LXXXVIII–CVIII and 244–49.

[73] H. Laval, *Mémoires.* He concludes his remarks about his expulsion and his memoirs with the words: "Est-ce donc là ma récompense de trente-six ans de Mission!!" (p. 629). Gregory XVI already in 1840 had sent a congratulatory letter to the newly converted Prince of Mangareva (*JP* V, 256–57).

[74] Even the secular priest Henri de Solages, who in 1829 was appointed apostolic prefect of the island of Réunion, directed his gaze principally to Oceania and in 1830 became prefect of the South Sea Islands. But in 1832 he went to Madagascar, where he died the same year. G. Goyau *Les grands Desseins Missionnaires d'Henri de Solages (1786–1832),* (Paris 1933) and valuable additions in A. Boudou SJ, *Les Jésuits à Madagascar au XIXe siècle* I (Paris 1942).

[75] Streit XVII, 428–33.

[76] Ibid., 540–48.—Massaia was able to reach his field of activity only in 1852.

[77] M. Bane, *The Catholic Story of Liberia* (New York 1950).

[78] Streit XVII, 448–51.

Africa, the vicariate of Cape Town was established in 1837, and the first missionaries ministered principally to the white Catholics.[79] Although the Pope, who knew little about the still-unexplored continent, was able to take few positive actions on behalf of Africa, he nevertheless tried to help the blacks through his Apostolic Constitution of 3 December 1839, in which he condemned the slave trade.[80]

Georges Goyau has called Gregory XVI *"le grand pape missionnaire du 19e siècle,"*[81] and J. Schmidlin has called him *"Missionspapst."*[82] Other historians, however, have been more reluctant to give him such titles.[83] Certainly Gregory XVI was not the "great missionary Pope of the nineteenth century." He generated no deep or lastingly effective missionary efforts, either with respect to strategy or method. He did approve the directives of 1845 from the Congregation for the Propagation of the Faith regarding the formation of a native clergy in India,[84] but careful examination of the origins of these directives indicates that the instructions were inspired by the Synod of Pondichéry in 1844 and brought about by a detailed memorandum written by Monsignor Luquet.[85] Gregory did give all mission work a new imprint, but he did so less because of personal considerations than because he was prompted by contemporary events. In many instances, in fact, he was virtually forced to do so. The system of vicars apostolic, only tentatively begun by his predecessors, became regular procedure during his pontificate. "Under Gregory XVI the papacy finally assumed the leadership of the entire missionary movement through the efforts of the Congregation for the Propagation of the Faith, and during this pontificate forty-four new mission bishoprics were established."[86]

[79] *JP* V, 188–89 with the letter of appointment for Monsignor Raym. Griffith OP. W. Rörig OMI, "Die Entwicklung der katholischen Mission in Südafrika von 1836–1850" in *ED* 22 (1969), 129–75.

[80] *JP* V, 223–25; *CPF* I, 503–05; J. Margraf, *Kirche und Sklaverei seit der Entdeckung Amerikas* (Tübingen 1865), 227–30. Gregory's Constitution, more than the ordinances of his predecessors which he cited, was a futile gesture against the slave trade, for neither the Arab slave traders in the east nor the Portuguese in the west of Africa worried about the papal decree (Brazil outlawed slavery only in 1888). England, on the other hand, banned slavery in its territories as early as 1834.

[81] Chapter heading in his work *Missions et Missionnaires* (Paris 1931), 106–27, similarly Mulders, *Missionsgeschichte,* 364.

[82] "Gregor XVI. als Missionspapst" in *ZMR* 21 (1931), 209, similarly *Papstgeschichte* I, 662; also Cardinal C. Costantini headed a chapter of his assessment with "Il Papa Missionario" (Note 33), 8–10.

[83] Thus P. Lesourd in Delacroix III, 52–71; J. A. Otto, P. Roothaan, 102 ("The great restorer of world missions").

[84] *CPF* I, 541–45.

[85] C. Costantini, "Ricerche d'Archivio sull'istruzione 'De Clero Indigeno'" in *Miscellanea Pietro Fumasoni-Biondi* (Rome 1947), 1–78.

[86] J. A. Otto, *P. Roothaan*, 103.

The increased number of vicariates apostolic established during subsequent pontificates "renewed" all missions in the sense that they received a structure which they hitherto had not known. By assigning entire vicariates or mission areas to single orders or religious associations, a number of advantages ensued. Among these was that the earlier tensions between missionary orders and the hierarchy ended, because the new bishops were selected from the missionaries of the same order. Also, gradual separation of powers between superiors of Church and orders enabled the orders not merely to concern themselves with the religious-ethical life of their members but actually obligated them to do so. This practice involved the officials of the orders back home, to whom was left the task of appointing the superiors in the field, more closely than before in the missionary activity of their confreres. As a consequence, the home orders gave more material help to the missions and simultaneously enhanced their own spirituality. Finally, the logical consequence of this reorientation was that the entire academic and religious education of the missionaries was no longer a matter for the mission administration but instead for the individual orders themselves.[87]

However, the new direction of missionary activity also harbored grave disadvantages. The missions now felt more acutely the effects of centralization and bureaucracy. Active missionary work became almost exclusively the concern of orders and congregations. The administration of the Congregation, however, with few exceptions, remained in the hands of secular priests who often lacked the most fundamental knowledge of missionary work. To this was added a new political direction. The Spanish-Portuguese influence had diminished, but its place was now occupied by the modern colonial powers, in particular England and France. Although connection with them was not sought by the missionaries, it was actively sought by the congregations and the vicars apostolic of the various countries.[88] There can be no doubt that Gregory's close cooperation with the restoration and the conservative powers formed the basis for the political reorientation of the missions. The reason for any lack of missionary effort may be found in these political and spiritual ties.

[87] As a consequence of the anticlerical, rationalistic, and freemasonic tendencies of most state universities, the education of the orders and thereby also of missionaries increasingly went its own ways, i.e., separate from the education of the nation as it used to be in preceding centuries. See J. Beckmann, "Die Universitäten vom 16.—18. Jahrhundert im Dienste der Glaubensverkündigung" in *NZM* 17 (1961), 24–47.

[88] In this connection must also be mentioned the as yet unexamined position of the apostolic vicar in London for missionary concerns; also the incontestable preference given to the American missions, i.e., the strengthening of the Church in the United States. Into the twentieth century, the term "missionary" in German-speaking countries had the same meaning as pastor in America.

SECTION TWO

The Awakening of Catholic Vitality

CHAPTER 12

The Rebirth of the Old Orders and the Blossoming of New Congregations

Although by the end of the Napoleonic era all clerical institutions suffered from revolutionary unrest and its consequences, none of them were harder hit than the religious orders. Severely shaken in the second half of the eighteenth century by the spirit of the Enlightenment and Josephinism, the orders appeared to have received the coup de grâce through the secularization measures in all of western Europe during the final quarter of the century. Although Bonaparte had dissolved only a portion of the monasteries, such was the case in France in 1790, in Belgium in 1796, in Germany between 1803 and 1807, in Italy between 1807 and 1811, and in Spain in 1809. A few countries escaped the storm, but the decadence of many monasteries in these areas had progressed so far that a resurgence was highly improbable. Within less than a generation, however, a restoration movement was initiated which "in breadth and complexity has no equal in history" (H. Marc-Bonnet) and which became one of the focal points of Church history in the nineteenth century. With the exception of the disappearance of some twenty houses, the old orders began to be restored, and particularly in France and in northern Italy numerous new congregations were formed. These congregations were better adapted to the needs of the time and provided an undeniable sign of a revitalized Catholicism.

A spectacular decision by Pius VII, himself a former member of an order, brought about a sudden change in events. The Society of Jesus, which since 1773 had been officially suppressed, was reestablished. In reality the society had never totally disappeared; with the tacit consent of Pius VI, it continued to exist in Russia and served as a haven for many former members. Pius VI had encouraged the diplomatic José Pignatelli[1] to keep in contact with the Russian Jesuits, though without traveling to Russia. Until his death in 1811, Pignatelli was so active in

[1] J. M. March, *El restaurador de la Compañia de Jesús, Beato José Pignatelli y su tiempo,* 2 vols. (Barcelona 1935/36).

his attempts to keep alive the spirit of Saint Ignatius that today he is rightfully regarded as the connecting link between the old and the new Society of Jesus. It was Pignatelli who in 1795 established a noviciate in the Duchy of Parma and in 1804, with the official permission of Pius VII, once again established the Jesuits in the Kingdom of Naples. Other simultaneous initiatives also prepared the ground for the general restoration of the Society of Jesus. In England and in the United States shortly after 1800 groups of ex-Jesuits joined with the Russian Jesuits. In France, during the time of suppression Father de Clorivière founded the Institute of the Heart of Jesus, a secret organization modeled on the Society of Jesus. In Louvain, two emigrated Sulpicians, Tournely and de Broglie, in 1794 founded the Society of the Sacred Heart of Jesus, which in 1799 fused with a similar congregation founded two years earlier by N. Paccanari at Spoleto. This society was then known as the Society of the Faith of Jesus. Under the leadership of Father Varin and with the cooperation of the Knights of the Faith this society actively supported the resistance of Pius VII against Napoleon. Thus the restoration of the Society of Jesus spread throughout the entire Church. Upon his return to Rome in 1814, Pius VII accepted a petition from the Jesuits asking for formal restoration. Encouraged by Cardinals Pacca and Consalvi, who had abandoned their old prejudices, the Pope immediately granted the petition.[2] In doing so the Pope ignored all political caution, especially with respect to Spain and Austria, both of which could have been expected to advise postponement of the decision.

The Pope's action was greeted with strong reservations by such enlightened Catholics and romantics as Görres and his friends. Liberals also reacted with dismay to this act of "counterrevolution," and for several years the government in Vienna resisted the resumption of Jesuit activity in the Empire.[3] Many bishops and the majority of militant Catholics, however, greeted the readmission of the Society of Jesus with acclaim. After 1805 the general of the order was Thaddeus Brzozowski, who maintained the headquarters of the society in Russia in order to dispel the suspicions of the tsarist government toward an organization which was again beginning to assume an international character. Brzozowski received many inquiries regarding the reopening of old colleges and residences of the order, and the now somewhat

[2] Bull *Sollicitudo omnium Ecclesiarum,* 7 August 1814 (*BullRomCont* XIII, 325–27).

[3] In Spain, however, the pressure exerted by the bishops was successful in countering the footdragging of the administration. On 29 May 1815 a royal decree authorized the partial resumption of the activity of the Society of Jesus, and a new decree of 17 June 1816 lifted all restriction in the entire kingdom (see also L. Frias, op. cit. I, 69–97, 349–88).

more heterogeneous membership increased.[4] The increased membership brought about certain problems in subsequent years, because the temptation was great to be lax in selection in view of the need of new members. These difficulties were amplified by the conflicts between different trends within the order. Some, especially the older members, saw the preservation of the true spirit of the Society of Jesus in a full return to the order as it had been prior to 1773. Others, under the leadership of Father Angiolini, who was very influential with Pius VII, were deterred by the mistakes of the order at the time of its dissolution and were inclined toward an accommodation. This group was supported by a number of the younger members, who were led by Father Rezzi and Father Pietroboni, the assistant for Italy. These younger members did not cling to the old traditions and, conscious of the tremendous changes in the world in consequence of the French Revolution, attempted to adapt the spirit of the society and its institutions to the new times by using the dubious terminology of the bull of restoration. After the death of Brzozowski (5 February 1820) the younger faction succeeded in winning the vicar general of the order, Petrucci, and Cardinal della Genga to their ideas. Thanks to the perspicacity of Consalvi, however, the general congregation,[5] convened in Rome in September 1820, saw through the maneuver, and insisted on retaining the society as an effective instrument for the Holy See. The innovators were excluded, and Father Luigi Fortis was elected general (1820–29). The rules and constitutions of the old society were adopted and an end was put to all attempts to refashion the society. After Della Genga became Pope Leo XII, he returned the Collegium Romanum to the Jesuits and in 1826 confirmed their old privileges, including those in the area of exemptions.[6]

Just as the material condition of the society was restored, its activity in the areas of the colleges, preaching, and missions to the people were redeveloped. To be sure, growing opposition was encountered from the liberals in Spain, where the society was once again banished during the three years of constitutional government from 1820 to 1823, and in France, where the "Black Men" were treated as scapegoats for all sins committed by the ultras; but the society had the satisfaction of once again establishing itself in the Habsburg Empire. In 1820, the Habsburg government permitted the entry of some Jesuit Fathers who had been

[4] Immediately after the readmission of the Jesuits, there were about 800 Fathers (337 in Russia, 199 in Sicily, 84 in England, 86 in the United States, and 47 in France). As early as 1820 there were about 2,000 (436 of them in Spain, 400 in the Papal States, 198 in France).

[5] The Jesuits were banished from Russia in 1820.

[6] *BullRomCont* XXVIII, 449–52.

banished from Russia so that they might conduct the education of Polish youth in Galicia. Finally, after long negotiations and difficulties with some bishops and the civil government, a modus vivendi was reached on 18 November 1817. The first breach in the Josephinist legislation had been made.[7]

While the Society of Jesus experienced a rebirth which was as rapid as it was brilliant, the reorganization of the old orders proceeded rather slowly. The problem was a dual one. It was necessary to reopen a number of houses for the surviving members and to provide them with the material conditions for the resumption of their communal life. In addition, in those provinces not affected by secularization a number of abuses which had spread for two hundred years and had become aggravated owing to the unusual circumstances of the past few years needed to be abolished. These were laxness of discipline and communal life; violations of the vow of poverty; neglect of choir prayer; and, in some convents, disregard of seclusion. The abolition of abuses was a rather difficult task, because of the obstacles posed by some of the more regalistic governments and by bishops who were anxious over their jurisdictions. These groups resented the interventions of the generals of orders established in Rome or the visitors sent by the Holy See. As a result of such problems, a genuine revival in Austria was possible only after the middle of the century.

In Spanish America as well, the monasteries, which had lost a good portion of their estates as a result of the wars of independence, were no longer able to maintain contact with their superiors in Europe. This had fateful consequences for their discipline and religious life and offered a further justification for systematic attempts at suppression by the diverse liberal governments during the course of the century. In Spain, the papal Bull *Inter graviores* of 15 May 1804[8] posed a special problem. Under the pretext that after the dissolution of a number of houses of the mendicant orders in western Europe the monasteries dependent on the Spanish crown (including the Philippines) were now in the majority, King Charles IV managed to obtain from Pius VII a separation of the Spanish provinces. It was agreed that the two groups were to be governed in turn by a general and a virtually independent vicar general.

After his return to Rome in 1814, Pius VII was eager to provide a model for restoring the orders. In the Papal States he created a special reform congregation and charged it with conducting disciplinary reforms as well as the regrouping of a number of houses in an effort to

[7] Maass, V, 74–96, 271–72.

[8] *BullRomCont* XIII, 164ff. See also B. de Rubi, *Reforma de regulares en España a principio del siglo XIX. Estudio histórico-jurídico de la bula "Inter Graviores"* (Barcelona 1943).

increase their vitality. For a brief time Pius even considered dividing all the monasteries of his state into two congregations, one for the black monks and another one for the white ones. The project was reconsidered by Leo XII and ultimately was not implemented. Pius VII also watched with great interest the revival of the large mendicant orders and more than once intervened personally, with differing results, in order to promote necessary reforms.

The mendicant orders emerged from the revolutionary age weakened from two causes. All monasteries in France, Belgium, and Germany, and some of those in Italy, had been dissolved; and the monasteries in Spain, the only other country beside the Russian part of Poland in which they had continued to exist in large numbers, were removed from the jurisdiction of the central administration and finally dissolved during the secularizations of 1834–36. The Dominicans, eager to save what they could attempted a regrouping of their Fathers in Italy. In this way, eighty of the five hundred monasteries in existence at the end of the eighteenth century were reestablished. For forty years these monasteries provided the order with new blood for its central administration and enabled it to safeguard its traditions, although in a somewhat attenuated form. At the same time a new beginning, led by Father Hill, was evident in England as well as in Holland where, in 1824, a school was opened. In the United States, Father E. A. Fenwick laid the foundation for the Province of Saint Joseph.

Unlike the Dominicans, the Franciscans managed to recover only with great difficulty. The Capuchins were able to revive themselves under the leadership of their energetic general, the future Cardinal Micara (1824–30), who pushed reform at the risk of his own life, and the order was able to regain a foothold in France in 1824. The Conventuals, however, whose large monasteries had been especially desirable to civil officials looking for administrative buildings, never completely recovered from the crisis.[9] The Minor Friars were weakened by tension between their various orientations, especially between the two largest groups, the Spanish and the Italians. An inept attempt by General J. Tecca de Capestrano to impose a uniform statute on all Franciscans in 1827 failed. None of the non-Spanish provinces was willing to attend the general meeting called for 1830 at Alcalá de Henares. Only in 1844 was the Belgian province finally reconstituted, to be followed by France in 1850. The Clarissas, who except in Spain had almost totally disap-

[9] By the middle of the nineteenth century they had not yet reached a membership of fifteen hundred, while in 1773 there had been twenty-five thousand. By the same time the Minorites had already reached 20 percent and the Capuchins 40 percent of their memberships prior to the revolution.

peared, quickly rose again. Even before the fall of Napoleon the former sisters had begun to regroup, and the order quickly spread under the influx of new members. The same was true for the Carmelite Sisters, who reappeared in the first few years of the nineteenth century in France. The Carmelite Brothers, on the other hand, did not appear again until 1830, and were never able to regain the influence which they had exercised prior to the revolution. An apostolic visitation noted several abuses within the order, together with a general decline in education, and even the measures taken by Leo XII in 1830 had only limited success. This was also true for the Augustinian Eremites, who in the post-Napoleonic period managed to hold a few places in Ireland, Holland, and, in addition to the sporadically recreated Italian provinces, in the United States, where they grew into flourishing provinces.

The different branches of the Benedictine community as well as the monasteries of the regular canons were especially hard hit. The crisis of the resolution had come to them in an already attenuated condition. In most instances that vital force which the mendicant orders possessed in their tight organizations was also absent. Such organization among these orders either had never existed, as in the case of the Benedictines, or, as in the case of the Cistercians and the Premonstratensians, who had their seat in France, had been destroyed. However, a number of reopenings came about through personal initiatives. Dom de Lestrange, having newly constituted his Trappist community at La Valsainte in Switzerland, regained his former monastery in 1814. During subsequent months, the Trappist monasteries of Melleraye, Aiguebelle, and Gard were occupied again. Repossession of Westmalle in Belgium occurred in 1814, and of the two Roman abbeys of Santa Croce and San Bernardo in 1817. To be sure, the rather strict rules which de Lestrange wished to impose upon his monks had to be canceled after his death in 1827 but, nevertheless, with full justification he can be called the "Savior of the Trappist Order."

The Cistercians of the *observantia communis,* who had survived in part in Spain and Portugal, reorganized themselves in southern Germany. In 1821, Pius VII gathered the monasteries of Italy within one congregation. Inasmuch as Cîtaux had been dissolved, the Pope had appointed the abbot of one of the Roman monasteries as general superior in 1816. In 1816 also, the Grande Chartreuse was reopened. The Premonstratensians, who had regained their large abbeys in central Europe, revived slowly in Belgium after 1830 and in France after 1856. It was not until 1869, however that they were able to convene their first general chapter.

The experience of the Benedictines was similar to that of the Premonstratensians, even though the Benedictines enjoyed the personal sympathy of the Pope. In the course of the revolutionary disturbances they had lost more than a thousand houses, and the remaining monasteries were beset by uncertainty in the face of the enmity of the regalistic governments in the Habsburg and Russian Empires and the temporary closing of numerous houses in Spain in 1809 and in 1820–23. It was possible to reopen twelve abbeys in Italy, and in 1821 the congregation of Monte Cassino was reorganized. In France and Belgium, a number of Benedictine convents reappeared, in some instances before Napoleon's fall, but it was not possible to reopen the monasteries until the second third of the nineteenth century. In spite of the concordat with Bavaria in 1817, which had called for the restoration of a few monasteries, the Bavarian government procrastinated. Also lacking was a readiness on the part of former monks to return to the life of the order. Thus only in 1830, thanks to the enthusiasm of Ludwig I for all things medieval, was there a gradual restoration of the abbey of Metten, followed by the abbeys of Saint Stephen in Augsburg in 1834, of Saint Boniface in Munich in 1835, of Scheyern in 1838, and Weltenburg in 1842.

In contrast to the rapid revival of the Society of Jesus, therefore, the rebirth of the old orders of medieval origin proved to be much more difficult. Yet the foundations were laid at this time from which their renewal was to come during the two next generations. This happened in spite of the Spanish and Portuguese decrees between 1834 and 1836 which destroyed the still existing representative centers of the orders. A few modern institutions, however, which were better adapted to the times, as early as the first decades of the nineteenth century profited from a development which would have been unthinkable during the Old Regime. This was particularly true for some charitable women's congregations such as in France the Sisters of Saint Joseph, inspired by Mother Saint Jean Fontbonne; the Daughters of Wisdom, led by Father Gabriel Deshayes (1820–41); and, especially, the Sisters of Saint Vincent de Paul. The last-named, after their official recognition by the government in 1809, spread outward from France and developed their specific religious character during the course of the nineteenth century.

Several male congregations also flourished at the beginning of the restoration. Among these were the Brothers of Christian Schools, who had retained only a few of their houses in the Papal States. In 1803, they were reintroduced by Brother Frumence, whom Pius VI had appointed in 1795 as vicar general. As early as 1810, the order held a general chapter and by 1814 already numbered fifty-five houses. Such a revival was experienced by the Redemptorists whom Klemens Maria Hofbauer (1751–1820) had introduced in central Europe, chiefly in Austria. Emperor Francis I, after his trip to Rome in 1819, guaranteed their safety, in spite of the Josephinist legislation inimical to the orders. From Austria, the order, under the leadership of Hofbauer's successor J. Passerat (1772–1858), expanded to France (1820), Portugal (1826), Switzerland (1827), Belgium (1833), Bulgaria (1836), and the United States (1832). In spite of the rapid revival of the Italian mother congregation, the new houses of the order generated a far more impressive apostalic dynamic.

The most noteworthy development during the period was the growth of new congregations. Frequently the influence of these congregations, especially in the case of women's congregations, did not extend beyond a diocese, and in many cases not even beyond a few parishes, but some of them developed both extensively and quickly and within a few decades assumed a place of prominence next to the great old orders. The male congregations were oriented chiefly toward two models: The school brothers followed the system introduced by Jean-Baptiste de la Salle during the preceding century. The priestly congregations followed French models of the seventeenth century, which allowed them a supple formula for many apostolic activities. The de la Salle model was followed by the Marist Brothers of M. Champagnat in the area of Lyon (1817, 1839); the Brothers of Christian Instruction of Jean Marie Lamennais; the Brothers of Saint Gabriel, founded by Father G. Deshayes (1821); The Sacred Heart Brothers of Abbé A. Coindre (1821); the Christian Brothers (1802, 1820), created in Ireland through episcopal initiative: the Brothers of Saint Patrick (1808); and the Brothers of Charity of Peter Joseph Triest at Ghent (1807), who in addition to education also devoted themselves to caring for the sick and the insane.[10] Among those congregations adopting the French models were the Picpus Society (1800, 1817) founded in France in the midst of the revolution by J. P. Coudrin. This society devoted itself to both Eucharistic veneration and preaching and, after 1826, with missions to Oceania. Others established on the French model were the Fathers of Mercy of Jean-Baptiste Rauzan, (1808, 1834); the Oblates of Mary Immaculate (1816, 1826), founded by Eugène de Mazenod, who concentrated on the missions to Canada after 1841; the Fathers of Jean Claude Colin, who at first devoted themselves to preaching in the rural areas around Lyon and then were selected by Gregory XVI for missions to foreign countries (1816, 1822); the Priests of the School of Charity of the brothers Cavanis in Venetia (1802, 1828); the Oblates of the Virgin Mary of Bruno Lanteri in Piedmont (1815, 1826); the Institute of Charity of A. Rosmini in Lombardy (1828, 1838); and the Marianists of

[10] The dates in parentheses indicate the founding of each institute and, when listed, of the first papal approbation.

Guilleaume-Joseph Chaminade (1817, 1839), forerunner of the Catholic Action and of secular institutes. He was aware of the necessity to organize different social groups as a counterweight to the individualism of the time and, in contrast to most of his contemporaries, recognized the need for a close cooperation between priests and laymen.

Among the women's congregations, it is noteworthy that there was an increase in a type of small congregation which devoted itself equally to charity and education. These congregations were in the immediate service of the parish clergy and generally were created by them for specific purposes such as the education of novices. Such small groups had the disadvantages of creating local splintering. The precise number of such communities has never been determined; nor would it be easy to discover it, because of the numerous fusions and splits and great similarity of names. Father de Berthier described the history of the creation and development of these numerous small congregations of sisters in picturesque fashion: "The history of these foundings is the same in almost all cases. In order to grasp the confusing multiplicity in such identical tasks, one must always be aware of the isolation in which the various provinces lived. A pious girl spontaneously or upon the advice of a priest devotes herself to the care of the sick or the poor or to education; soon she is joined by likeminded companions; the lady of the local manor grants her moral and financial support and the priest either encourages her or raises obstacles in her path; a spiritual guide from the Jesuits or some other order then appears in the background; soon the foundation takes form; a house is bought and the bishop becomes involved; in order to receive the bishop's permission, rules for the group must be established, a habit be selected, and a responsible superior, name, patron saint, and noviciate be chosen. All of this crystallizes gradually and the day for applying for authorization by the Holy See and the government arrives. A new congregation has been born."[11]

This phenomenon was particularly evident in France[12] after the concordat, but could be seen everywhere in western Europe during the subsequent years.[13] To the ulterior designs of some parish priests to

[11] *La Restauration*, 312.

[12] Where legislation was petty for male congregations, but was much more liberal for women's institutes, especially after the law of 24 May 1825. The sisters raised their numbers from 12,400 in 1829 houses in 1815 to 25,000 in 2872 houses in 1830, not counting the many communities still in a tentative stage of development which had not yet asked for administrative authorization.

[13] With local variations, of course. While in France the majority of the foundings took place in the rural areas, they occurred in Italy primarily in the cities. Custom in Italy for a long time forbade that the sisters, unlike those north of the Alps, also devote themselves to the care of sick males. In the Germanic countries, on the other hand, there was much less demand than in France and Italy for teaching sisters.

remain masters in their own houses was frequently joined the impossibility of receiving assistance from the busy larger congregations. At the outset, the founding priests could often turn to former sisters who had been secularized during the French Revolution, but soon most of these sisters were motivated not only by the serious purpose of aiding Church and neighbors in daily life, but also by other considerations. The surplus of women and the late date of marriage made possible a longer time for choosing a spiritual life; and the respect that women in orders enjoyed in the religious community, together with the expectation of upward social mobility provided especially in the teaching orders, made such a choice attractive. In contrast to the conditions under the Old Regime, most of the aspirants came from the lower economic strata and occasionally from the aristocracy. Rarely did the middle class choose the vocation.

Among the founders were many simple souls who passively had allowed themselves to be guided by a clerical adviser. But there were also among them some strong, complex personalities, who combined great spiritual abilities with a developed sense of action and organization. To these belong St. Marie Madeleine Postel, the Norman founder of the Sisters of the Christian Schools of Mercy (1807), who later were widely accepted in the Germanic countries; the blessed Julie Billiart, founder of the Sisters of Notre Dame de Namur (1808); the Marchesa di Canossa, founder of the Daughters of Charity (1816) in Verona; and St. Emilie de Rodat, founder of the Sisters of the Holy Family (1817) in southern France. Many of these congregations grew quickly beyond regional boundaries and underwent a national or, in some cases, even international expansion. This was the case with the Society of the Sacred Heart begun by St. Madeleine Sophie Barat in 1800. Her congregation, inspired by Saint Ignatius, was of an apostolic character. Its nuns were to be a female elite of the Christian spirit. After receiving their constitution in 1815, houses were established in the United States in 1818, in Turin in 1823, in Rome in 1828, in Brussels in 1825, and in Austria and England a short time afterwards. Another important figure was Mother Javouhey, the founder of the Sisters of Saint Joseph of Cluny. After 1817, these sisters became active as nurses and teachers in African missions and by the middle of the century had settlements in all five continents. These types of orders were not begun only by French women, however. The Sisters of Mercy, founded in Münster in 1808, after the model of the French Sisters of Charity, gradually spread to the various states of Germany and Austria. The Poor Teaching Sisters of Our Lady, founded in 1833 by K. Gerhardinger, a pupil of G. M. Wittmann, settled in thirteen European countries and in the United States. The Sisters of Mercy, founded in Ireland in 1829 by

C. MacAuley, quickly spread to England, the Colonies, and the United States. This list could easily be expanded.

The rapid development of these numerous congregations, so different from the old orders and so often delayed in acquiring a definitive form, presented the Holy See with subtle problems of canon law. "The multiplicity of inquiries which frequently reach us from France," Leo XII explained to Mazenod in 1825, "persuaded the congregation to devise a special type of approval and to applaud and to encourage, without, however, granting formal approbation."[14] The *decretum laudis,* the first step of a papal approbation, originated in this time in answer to problems of these congregations. The Holy See, long hesitant about women's congregations with simple vows and whose members were not secluded, changed its attitude when it was realized that this new type of order was especially well suited to many of the new conditions. The Sisters of Love of Ghent were the first to receive the special approbation from the Congregation of Bishops and Religious in 1816.[15] Once again the circumstances of changing times provided the impulse to adapt canon law.

[14] Quoted by J. Leflon, *Mazenod* II, 281–82.

[15] Father Callahan, *The Centralization of Government in Pontifical Institutes of Women with Simple Vows* (Rome 1948) 34, 44–45. The author lists the following approbations: Filles du S. Cœur de Marie d'Angers (1821), Sœurs de la Miséricorde de Cahors (1824), Sœurs de l'Instruction chrétienne of Ghent (1827), Canossiane (1828), Sœurs de Ste. Thérèse de Bordeaux and Sœurs du Bon Pasteur d'Angers (1835).

CHAPTER 13

The Beginnings of the Catholic Movement in Germany and Switzerland

Historically speaking, the spiritual rebirth which the Catholic Church in Germany experienced during the first decades of the nineteenth century was more significant than the organizational reconstruction. This rebirth received its impulse from native forces, independent of the official Church. The common denominator was the determination to overcome the crisis caused by the radical Enlightenment. Redefinition of the essence and the tradition of the Church became a valid alternative to the rationalistic depletion of theology, tendencies toward secularization of society, and the far-reaching submission of the Church to the state. An important prerequisite was the existence of an unbroken tradition in all areas of the Church, especially outside of the courtly and urban elements of educated society. Some achievements of the moderate Enlightenment, such as the cultivation of positive theology, reforms of liturgy, preaching and pastoral care, as well as a basic ecumenical sentiment present in some localities also contributed their share. The experience of the French Revolution and its consequences shook the Church out of its lethargy and simultaneously heightened the defensive character of the incipient movement. Because of radical consequences of the Enlightenment and the modern theories of the state, both revolution and secularization made themselves suspect in the eyes of Catholics. From its beginnings, therefore, the Catholic defense had to aim at the two concrete goals of restoring ecclesiastical liberty and replacing destroyed centers of education.

Romanticism provided strongly differing impulses in keeping with the multiplicity of its essence. In its universal aspects, romanticism reached back to early Christian ideas and values in the areas of the arts, science, and societal order. It emphasized the irrational, historic, and organic roots of the present. In contrast to the focus of the Enlightenment upon the individual, reason, and progress, romanticism often went to the opposite extreme of awarding primary value to community, feeling, mysticism, tradition, and continuity. The Church was again viewed as a living and historical organism, and romantic inclusiveness strove for a synthesis of religious and profane cultures. Among the Protestants, romanticism promoted the concepts of revival and nation, but many of its representatives were attracted by the Catholic Church, whose structure and forms of piety corresponded more closely to their ideals. Eminent converts had a decisive influence on the beginnings of the Catholic movement in Germany. The new appreciation of the Catholic Church was often a consequence of the rediscovery of the essentially Catholic Middle Ages and its artistic and spiritual creations. In addition, romanticism fostered the German patriotism of Catholics. Its emphasis on continuity and organic structures led to a concept of restoration which idealized Emperor and Empire and, following the wars of liberation, the value placed upon people and nation allowed the growth among German Catholics of a feeling of affinity for religion and nationality.

Consonant with the customs of society at the time, the Catholic movement grew out of small circles, often in conjunction with attempts to revive religious studies.[1] Roman influence was totally absent and French philosophy of restoration only began to play a role in the 1820's,

[1] Thus the Tübingen School of Theology together with its publication *Theologische Quartalschrift* after 1819 provided educated Catholics with a new and profound self-assurance.

primarily through the people involved with the Mainz seminary and associated circles in the Rhineland.[2]

Even before the French Revolution, Princess Amalie Gallitzin (1748–1806), who had resided in Münster since 1779, gathered around her a number of people who were concerned with deepening their faith through imbuing it with emotion and who raised the reaction against the Enlightenment to the level of an antiintellectual belief. Among the advisers of the princess were the religious instructor and educator Bernard Overberg (1754–1826) and the canon Franz von Fürstenberg (1729–1810). Since 1762, Fürstenberg had administered the cathedral chapter of Münster in exemplary fashion, and, in contrast to his own bishop, who was also the Elector of Cologne and had freely opened his court at Bonn to modern ideas, had resolutely resisted the Enlightenment. After Fürstenberg in 1780 had been forced to give up his political offices, he concentrated on internal improvements and pedagogical reforms, aided by his close collaborator Overberg, whom he entrusted with the training of teachers. The Gallitzin circle, regarding itself as a *"familia sacra,"* also counted as members several professors of the academy founded by Fürstenberg. Among these were the Church historian Theodor Katerkamp and the exegete Bernard Georg Kellermann, as well as younger people who were deeply influenced by the circle, such as the brothers Droste-Vischering.

Close relations existed with the pietistic Lutherans, such as Matthias Claudius, Friedrich Perthes, Count Friedrich Leopold zu Stolberg, and Johann Georg Hamann. The Enlightenment had influenced the circle insofar as it had emphasized the common elements of the denominations, albeit the aims of the circle were of an anti-Enlightenment direction. The faithful were supposed to unite against rationalism as the common enemy. In 1800 Stolberg became a Catholic, and his conversion, the first of an impressive number, created a sensation. He settled in Münster and together with other members of the *"familia sacra"* wrote the *History of the Religion of Jesus Christ,* which interpreted Church history in a universal sense and as the passion and salvation of Christ. This interpretation reawakened in German Catholicism the historical consciousness buried by the Enlightenment.[3] In spite of his apologetic approach, Stolberg also incorporated such Lutheran elements as the belief in salvation exclusively through God's mercy, and his concept of the Church was comprehensive and included episcopal elements.

[2] E. Fleig, "Zur Geschichte des Einströmens französischen Restaurationsdenkens nach Deutschland" in *HJ* 55 (1935), 501–22.

[3] The work appeared in 15 volumes (Hamburg 1806/18). See L. Scheffczyk, *Friedrich Leopold Stolbergs "Geschichte der Religion Jesu Christi"* (Munich 1952).

The writings of Overberg, together with those of Sailer, founded a new Catholic pedagogy. Although Overberg favored educational discourse and growth of the students within the meaning of the Enlightenment, he saw the "higher assurance of the Christian faith" exclusively in revelation. For this reason he made revelation the focal point of religious instruction and acquainted a wide readership among teachers and families with this concept through his frequently reprinted *History of the Old and New Testaments.*

Under the impact of the rising against Napoleon (1809), Vienna developed into a radiating center of German romanticism. Through the circles around Clemens Maria Hofbauer (1751–1820) and Friedrich Schlegel (1772–1829) it also raised a new religious consciousness. Hofbauer, the first German Redemptorist from southern Moravia, addressed members of all classes as teacher, preacher, missionary, and organizer of ecclesiastical life. Schlegel, who had converted in Cologne, entered the Austrian civil service. He also taught religious history in Vienna and developed his comprehensive interpretation of European spirit and culture against the background of a Catholic Christianity[4] which was influencing all aspects of romanticism. Other North German converts with great influence joined him. Among these were the political scientist Adam Müller, the painter and educator Klinckowström, and the poet Zacharias Werner. For a time Franz von Baader, Brentano, Eichendorff, and Johann Friedrich Schlosser also joined the circle which, especially during the time of the Congress of Vienna, established continuing relations with like-minded people in all of the German states.

Schlegel, Müller,[5] and their friends attempted to prove monarchical authority and hierarchical social order as natural and divinely inspired. For this reason they propagated a corporative state, based on religion and national characteristics and modeled on medieval concepts. State and Church were to be connected and equal partners. They saw the most legitimate guarantee of the preservation of continuity within the hierarchical order of the Catholic Church. They agreed with the objectives of de Maistre and tried to provide them with the deeper religious and philosophical support which they found missing in his writings. The concept of society held by the Vienna circle contributed to that ideol-

[4] Especially in his lecture series of 1810 and 1812 *On Modern History* (Vienna 1811) and *History of Classical and Modern Literature* (Vienna 1815), also in the periodicals *Deutsches Museum* (Vienna 1812/13) and *Concordia* (Vienna 1820/22).

[5] Müller's chief works: *Die Elemente der Staatskunst,* 3 vol. (Berlin 1810, reissued by J. Baxa, Jena 1922); *Von der Notwendigkeit einer theologischen Grundlegung der gesamten Staatswissenschaft* (Leipzig 1820, reissue Vienna 1898); *Ausgewählte Schriften Müllers zur Staatsphilosophie,* ed. by R. Kohler (Munich 1923).

ogy of the restoration in whose formulation another convert, Karl Ludwig von Haller (1768–1854), political scientist from Bern, played a leading role.[6] Schlegel, Müller, and Baader also derived the first postulates of social Catholicism from the corporative principle. Their demands for a just wage and the integration of the lower classes, for subordinating the economy to social policy, and for a just balance between agriculture and industry had no direct effect, but did have lasting influence upon the development of Catholic social theory.

While the Emperor, the government, and the majority of Austrian clergy, especially the prelates, still adhered to Josephinism, the Hofbauer circle initiated its spiritual conquest.[7] Bishops Zengerle (1824–48 bishop of Seckau) and Ziegler (1827–52 bishop of Linz), who emerged from the Hofbauer circle, promoted the new spirit in their dioceses. As a young priest the future Cardinal Rauscher received his direction from the Hofbauer circle.

Hofbauer fought the Enlightenment with uncompromising and often abrasive vigor, and during the Congress of Vienna he was Wessenberg's most important spiritual opponent. The argumentative Redemptorist also favored the restoration of a church organization applicable to all of Germany. Moreover, his group was the first among the circles of Catholic revival to conduct this reconstruction in close collaboration with Rome. Hofbauer and his friends presented this position to the Vienna nuncio Severoli and also to Cardinal Consalvi during the Congress. After 1815, the Hofbauer circle attempted by way of Schlegel and Schlosser to influence the religious negotiations referred to the Frankfurt Diet. The circle was convinced that only the papacy, which was regaining its strength at that time, could provide the German dioceses with bishops who were free of the belief in an established Church and Febronianism. This position explains the group's strong defense of a centralistic and authoritarian church regulation. Secretly Hofbauer's circle informed on people who thought differently and thus started in Germany the denunciation of ecclesiastical opponents. It was an embarrassing accompaniment to ultramontanism. At the same time Hofbauer demanded a greater consideration of Germany from the Curia in the interest of the Roman-German alliance which he envisioned, and he joined many anti-Curialists in their criticism of Roman ignorance of German conditions.

[6] Especially through his *Handbuch der allgemeinen Staatskunde* (Winterthur 1808) and *Die Restauration der Staatswissenschaften,* 6 vol. (Winterthur 1816/26, [2] 1820/34), which coined the name of the period.

[7] Beginnings of an overcoming of Josephinism in A. Reinermann, "The Return of the Jesuits to the Austrian Empire and the Decline of Josephinism 1820–1822" in *CHR* 52 (1966/67).

The Hofbauer circle influenced similar groups in neighboring Bavaria, such as the confederates of the Würzburg Suffragan Bishop Zirkel and the Görres circle in Munich. Hofbauer also approached the Bavarian Crown Prince Ludwig who, however, preferred to follow the suggestions from Landshut and Munich.

Johann Michael Sailer (1751–1832), the leader of the Landshut circle, built upon the philosophical and literary heritage of the period and initiated the encounter of Catholicism with the modern intellectual culture of the nation. At the same time, his main concern was the intensification of traditional religion, and he early began to oppose deism. Adopting a position similar to that of the Münster group, Sailer maintained a friendly relationship with such Protestants as Lavater, Claudius, Savigny, and the princes of Stolberg-Wernigerode. Sailer, an eclectic, adopted the moral philosophy of Kant, the religious philosophy of Jacobi, and the pedagogy of Pestalozzi.

Accused of illuminatism and being a proponent of the Enlightenment, Sailer was forced to leave the University of Dillingen in 1794. Five years later Montgelas, the defender of a bureaucratic established Church, appointed Sailer professor of moral and pastoral theology at the University of Ingolstadt, which, in 1800, was transferred as a Bavarian state university to Landshut. Holding fast to his humanism and the rejection of scholasticism during the following two decades, Sailer became involved in activities which ran counter to the ideas of Montgelas and thus were stopped. Sailer pleaded for a rejuvenation of the Church arising from its internal strengths, and it was his very acquaintance with the Enlightenment which qualified him as a credible opponent. He developed a theology of revelation and spirituality which was new for his time and which had a biblical and patristic basis.[8] His concept of the Church, which was related to Stolberg's, attempted to mediate between Curialism and Febronianism. In his Bible-oriented pedagogy, Sailer, as had Overberg, transcended the Enlightment.

Sailer was not only an effective teacher and publicist, but also a charismatic pastor and counselor. He gathered around him an unusually large circle of students and friends from all walks of life and faculties. The zealotry of Hofbauer, who regarded him as suspect, was alien to him. It was due to the intrigues of Sailer's enemies that he failed to be appointed bishop of Augsburg in 1819. Only after difficult negotiations between the government and the Holy See did he become suffragan

[8] Sailer's chief works: *Vorlesungen aus der Pastoraltheologie,* 3 vol. (Munich 1788/89; *Neue Beiträge aus der Pastoraltheologie,* 2 vol. (Munich 1809/11); *Beleuchtung einiger Hauptideen der katholischen Theologie,* 3 brochures (Munich 1816/21); *Handbuch der christlichen Moral,* 3 vol. (Munich 1817).

bishop and coadjutor of Regensburg in 1822 and bishop in 1829. Other clerics from Sailer's circle continued to promote his religious and ecclesiastical concerns. Among them were Georg Michael Wittmann (1760–1833) and Franz Xaver Schwäbl (1778–1841), his successors as bishops of Regensburg; the educator Christoph von Schmid (1768–1854); the exegete and Bible translator Joseph Franz von Allioli (1793–1853); and Melchior von Diepenbrock (1798–1853).

Because Crown Prince Ludwig belonged to Sailer's admirers, the Landshut circle influenced Bavarian domestic policies. Two members of the circle, the physician Johann Nepomuk Ringseis (1785–1880) and the jurist Eduard von Schenk (1788–1841) became his advisers on cultural policy. Crown Prince Ludwig, having brought about the fall of Montgelas in 1817, ascended the throne in 1825 as Ludwig I. The King held fast to parity and established Church, but in all other respects he followed the path of romantic restoration. He also wanted to see Bavaria become the leading state of German Catholicism. Schenk headed the new section for religion and education in the ministry of justice. Benedictines, Franciscans, and several women's congregations were permitted to return; teacher training was largely turned over to the Church; royal seminaries for priests were established; the missions received financial support; and numerous church buildings were restored.

Ringseis became the first president of the Bavarian State University, which was moved from Landshut to Munich in 1826, and his consistent policy of appointments made it into the most important Catholic center of the period. In addition to Ringseis, important leaders were found in three of the new professors, Josef von Görres,[9] Franz von Baader, and Ignaz von Döllinger. These men prepared the ground for Catholic federations and fought rationalism and liberalism on the level of philosophy and history. To an increasing degree this group also fought an alliance between Protestantism, rationalism and liberalism. The anniversary of the Reformation in 1817 produced a first confrontation, and in general the revived Churches were developing a new denominational self-assurance.

The circle around Ringseis and Görres initiated the periodical *Eos,* but had to relinquish it only two years later in 1830. The antiliberal polemics of the publication had aroused the ire of the King, who did not wish to be totally identified with any party. Yet almost at the same time, his religious policy permitted the introduction of two Church newspap-

[9] Görres must be counted in the conversion movement of the time insofar as he, like Brentano, returned to his innate Catholic faith under the influence of romanticism.

ers,[10] which also treated non-Bavarian matters and became very influential in Church policy. These periodicals, together with *Katholik,* founded a few years earlier in Mainz, constituted the first development of a German Catholic press.

With greater efficiency than Hofbauer's friends, a number of people in Mainz began to promote a centralistic-authoritarian rejuvenation of the Church. Its first leaders were Johann Ludwig Colmar (1760–1818), who had been appointed by Napoleon as bishop of Mainz, and Franz Leopold Liebermann (1759–1844). Both men had been part of Alsatian Catholicism, which had kept out of internal French developments but which finally was forced to undergo the most radical consequences of the Enlightenment during the revolutionary disturbances. In 1805, Colmar founded a Tridentine seminary headed by Liebermann in place of the theological faculty of the university, which had been destroyed by secularization. In 1816, another Alsatian and student of Liebermann, Andreas Räss (1794–1887), was appointed to teach there. In contrast to the other circles of revival, the leaders of the Mainz group were all clerics. Like all defenders of purely ecclesiastical concentration, they were opposed to theological departments at state universities. Because of this, they contributed greatly to the training of priests at seminaries in Germany, a method which was also desired by Rome. Their justification was that at many state universities theologians were teaching who were rationalistic and in favor of an established Church. Colmar and Liebermann based theological instruction upon a return to scholasticism,[11] while Räss and his friend Nikolaus Weis (1796–1869) also included French restoration philosophy. The Mainz circle was convinced that strict spiritual and organizational concentration of the Church was of the essence in the face of the Enlightenment and its consequent concept of an established Church. They pleaded for a retreat to the seemingly secure bastion of the old doctrine, coupled with an innovative activation of the faithful, while remaining unaffected by romanticism. Their program coincided with that of the "zealots" in the Roman Curia, who had gained the upper hand after the election of Leo XII in

[10] With the active support of Räss (Mainz) and of members of the Munich Görres circle, Johann Baptist von Pfeilschifter in 1829 in Aschaffenburg founded the *Katholische Kirchenzeitung,* which during the following decade achieved great eminence; in Würzburg there appeared after 1828 the *Allgemeiner Religions- und Kirchenfreund* (ed. Franz Georg Benkert).

[11] Liebermann's textbook, the *Institutiones theologiae dogmaticae* (Mainz 1819/21) was read widely and long ([10] 1870), just as the speculative, sharply anti-Hermesian dogmatic of his student Heinrich Klee (Mainz 1834/35, [4] 1861), who shortly before his early death in 1840 received an appointment at Munich University.

1824.[12] Since that time, the Mainz group had been even more in favor of close collaboration with Rome. Their simplistic belief was that episcopalism would lead to the established Church of the Enlightenment, while papalism would bring with it freedom of the Church. They had been forced to suffer Napoleon's sovereignty over the Church, but they opposed the religious policy of the weaker German states. This brought them quickly into opposition to the Hessian government.

In order to influence the clergy and laity toward the Mainz program, in 1821 Räss and Weis founded the monthly publication *Der Katholik.* Under pressure from the government the editor's office had to be transferred to Strasbourg a year later, and in 1827 it was possible to move it to Speyer in Bavaria. Through *Der Katholik* and several popular pamphlets, the Mainz theologians fought against the Enlightenment, an established Church, and the forces of Protestantism. They also opposed Catholic lines of thought which were unacceptable to them, such as Hermesianism, which was spreading in the Prussian Rhineland.[13] The authoritarian defense upon which they relied throughout this process was well suited to the exigencies of the period, but their generalizations contributed toward excluding the Catholic Church from intellectual developments and toward placing it within the very ghetto in which its enemies wished it to be.

Three eminent bishops came from the Mainz circle; the first two were Räss (bishop of Strasbourg after 1842) and Weis (after 1841 bishop of Speyer); the third was Johannes von Geissel, who as archbishop of Cologne was the leader of the Prussian episcopate in the 1840s and 1850s.

The fighting spirit of the Mainz seminary also reached to Bavaria and influenced many another Catholic circle. At first such Catholic circles initiated internal revivals on the local level, but with increasing effectiveness they defended themselves against bureaucratic ecclesiastical regimens. Among such groups were one in Kassel led by Josef Maria von Radowitz; another in Frankfurt led by Johann Friedrich Schlosser, one in Koblenz led by Clemens Brentano and Hermann Josef Dietz, and finally one at Bonn led by the professor of canon law Ferdinand Walter[14] and the philosopher Karl Josef Windischmann. Circles also

[12] See above, pp. 95–99.

[13] See below, pp. 243ff.

[14] The textbook of canon law, published by Ferdinand Walter (1794–1879) as early as 1822 at Bonn ([14] 1871), contributed considerably to the defeat of Febronianism. As most of the other representatives of his movement, Walter, of course, did not hold the same concept of the Church as accepted under Gregory XVI and Pius IX. He taught papal infallibility as little as Liebermann; only from the eighth edition of his work

formed at Cologne, led by Haxthausen, in Aachen led by Martin Wilhelm Fonck and Leonhard Aloys Nellessen, and in Düsseldorf under the guidance of Josef Binterim. The Rhenish circles maintained close contact with one another. Common to all of them was the hostility to the Hermes School which was pursued so markedly at Bonn. In Koblenz the first steps toward a modern Caritas were developed, while at Cologne attention was primarily directed to the maintenance of medieval-Catholic traditions and buildings.

Persons and forces contributing to the ecclesiastical renewal were later opposed or pushed aside by the strengthening Catholic movement. Wessenberg initiated a biblical-liturgical reform movement which was in force for a long period.[15] Out of the Hermes School came a generation with an optimistic pastoral outlook; a generation which was convinced of the compatibility of the old faith with new ideas.[16] Many outstanding bishops such as Spiegel in Cologne, Gebsattel in Munich, and Hommer in Trier promoted internal reconstruction. By incorporating positive aspects of the Enlightenment and attempting to evade conflicts with the governments, they distinguished themselves from their pugnacious successors who stood under the influence of the revival movement.

The beginnings of the revival movement in Germany included the entire range of Catholic thought ranging from a universal interpretation resting on the spirit and the tradition of the Church to a defensive-hierarchical concentration. From this broad beginning, reaching into romanticism, it was possible for the last time in modern German history to have active cooperation in the shaping of the intellectual and artistic life of the nation.[17] But for the inner development of the Church, the narrower and stricter direction was decisive. The circles around Hofbauer and the Mainz seminary understood how to provide a clear and easily acceptable program to the majority of Catholics, who were confused by the intellectual shifts and oppressed by the established Church. Recognizing the fundamentally conservative state, these circles de-

---

onward (1839) did he begin to accept the spreading doctrine. See Vigener, op. cit., 62–70.—Under the influence of the Bonn circle, Carl Ernst Jarcke, then Instructor of Law, converted to Catholicism in 1825.

[15] See Th. Klauser, *Kleine abendländische Liturgiegeschichte* (Bonn 1965), 122.

[16] H. Schrörs, "Hermesianische Pfarrer" in *AHVNrh* 103 (1919), 76–183.

[17] Beyond the general influence on romanticism, the Catholic movement also participated in the forming of the Nazarene movement and New Gothic, as well as a revival of classical polyphony.—H. Beenken, *Das 19. Jahrhundert in der deutschen Kunst* (Munich 1944); Schnabel, *G* IV, 220–49; W. Nauss in *LThK* VII, 849ff.; H. Schade-H. Kirchmeyer in *LThK* VII, 9, 21ff. See also W. Weyres-H. Mann, *Handbuch zur rheinischen Baukunst des 19. Jahrhunderts* (Cologne 1968).

manded from it fulfillment of the promised parity. Within Catholicism they created the first modern mass consciousness in Germany; a consciousness which achieved political relevance after the unrest at Cologne.[18] The movement, initially varied, eventually joined the forces of the ultramontane restoration, which had come to the fore in Rome in the 1820s and were systematically supported by the papacy after the election of Gregory XVI.

The regrouping of the Swiss dioceses[19] was only a prerequisite for the revival of Catholic life in Switzerland, a revival which was as urgent there as it had been in neighboring countries. In Geneva the most active pastor was Vuarin, who was in close contact with the French Catholic movement. However, the indifferentism of the Enlightenment and the anti-Roman stance of Wessenberg deeply influenced the minds of laity and clergy in many cantons. Wessenberg's ideas were spread chiefly through the "Helvetic Society" and men such as pastor Müller and the teacher Dereser of Lucerne. The reaction against philosophes and Jacobins and against the Febronian reformers was led in an especially active fashion by a group of professors of the Lucerne seminary. These professors, headed by J. Gügler, one of the first representatives of romantic theology, and by F. Geiger, the founder of the *Swiss Church Newspaper,* were students of Sailer. At the same time, the great schools of Solothurn and Einsiedeln resumed their activity in a clearly clerical sense. In addition, the Jesuits became active again in Brig in 1814 and in Fribourg in 1818 and, as the Capuchins had done, missionized the people and founded confraternities and congregations. Although the efforts of the governments to control the work of the seminaries did not simplify matters, pious and hard-working prelates effectively contributed to a revival. Among them were the vicar apostolic B. Göldlin, who from 1815 to 1819 was administrator of the areas which were separated from the diocese of Constance; C. -R. Buol, bishop of Chur from 1793 to 1833; and, at a later date, A. Salzmann, the new bishop of Basel. These men also influenced the revival of Swiss Protestantism, even though their development was quite distinct with respect to their goals and manifestations.

Finally, the Catholic revival was accompanied, as in Germany, by a number of conversions.[20] Some of them, especially that of K. L. von Haller (1817), a jurist from Bern, aroused special attention. In spite of

[18] See chapter 20.

[19] For example, in 1826 the archbishop of Paris on a journey to the abbey Rheinau had to confirm six thousand persons (Henrion, *Vie de Mgr. de Quélen* [Paris 1840], 168–70).

[20] See D. A. Rosenthal, *Konvertitenbilder aus dem 19. Jahrhundert* (Regensburg 1868), 348ff.

his voluntary exile in Paris from 1820 to 1830, a number of Catholic ultras gathered around Haller, who, in violent opposition to Jean-Jacques Rousseau, the revolution, and liberalism, combined an irreconcilable ultramontanism with political concepts of a patriarchal and legitimistic inspiration. The majority of Haller's compatriots, however, turned toward a liberal progressivism.

Chapter 14

The Catholic Movement in France and Italy

The Catholic Action of the Laity in France

The French clergy counted on the strong support of the government, but saw no reason to remain inactive itself. Its efforts were effective especially within the framework of the parishes. These efforts consisted of extended instructions in the catechism;[1] services which were made more attractive by the addition of music which, corresponding to a tradition of the eighteenth century, was derived from popular songs; and membership for the faithful in pious organizations, chiefly in the confraternities of penance, which became attractive again during this period. Some enterprising priests set up youth organizations, analogous to those of Abbé Allemand at Marseille,[2] but more often with the atmosphere of a hothouse than in the style of training for the apostolate.

This priestly activity, however, could flourish only in the more backward rural areas; for the needs of urban populations it was inadequate. In order to appeal to them, a large number of organizations were created during the course of the restoration in which the laity assumed an eminent place. Of course, the clergy continued to hold a leading position in founding and direction of these works, but the laity played a great participatory role not only as executors but also as initiators and cofounders. This was a new phenomenon, and one must go back as far as the *Compagnie du Saint-Sacrament* in the seventeenth century in order to find an analogous event in France. The intrusion of the laity into a sphere long reserved to the clergy is in part explained by the lack of priests and orders, but it was also the result of an awareness of the new conditions of the apostolate: "I am convinced that priests can no longer be the most successful apostles," one of them wrote. We see here the

[1] Some later bishops such as Quélen, Borderies, Feutrier, and Gallard gained their reputation through their activity in the *catéchisme de persévérance.* See p. 434.

[2] P. Gaduel, *Le directeur de la jeunesse, J. J. Allemand* (Marseille 1885).

beginnings of the modern Catholic Action, an action directed toward a specific social environment.

At the beginning of many of these laymen's works stood the Congregation, whose description as the "Central Office of Catholic Action" may perhaps be overblown, but whose efforts on the national level resulted in a significant achievement. Founded in Paris in 1801 by an ex-Jesuit in imitation of the Marian Congregation, it was banned by Napoleon in 1809 and ultimately reestablished in 1814. The Jesuit Pierre Ronsin was its spiritual creator, but its prefects and assistants were laymen. Approximately sixty similar bodies, often founded in provincial towns in connection with missions to the people, were associated with it. It comprised only a limited number of members, almost all of whom came from socially prominent circles. In contrast to the former confraternities, for which religion was often no more than a pretext for merry get-togethers, the Congregation charged its members with performing all kinds of charitable and apostolic works designed to influence the masses and represented by branches throughout the country. To them belonged the Society of Good Works, founded in 1816, which engaged in three forms of charity—visits to hospitals, visits to prisons, and religious instruction for young chimney sweeps—performed by the members on an individual basis; the Society of Saint Joseph, founded in 1822, which comprised about one thousand small employers in order to assure the Christian welfare of young workers; the Society of Beneficial Studies, also founded in 1822, which was a forerunner of study groups of university students; and the Catholic Society of Good Books, founded in 1824, whose purpose in imitation of similar groups in Bordeaux, Grenoble, and Turin[3] was to counter the spread of antireligious tracts through the publication of books of monarchical and Catholic content. They were priced moderately in order to appeal to the middle class (1,600,000 were published within six years).

The Congregation was attacked severely by opponents of what they called the "Party of Priests." It was accused of being a secret club, dominated by the Jesuits, for the purpose of controlling state and society. Historians for a long time were uncertain about the justness of this allegation. But Father de Bertier succeeded in clearing up the matter conclusively through the use of hitherto unknown documents. He proved what Catholic authors, and especially G. de Grandmaison, had always asserted. The Congregation as such always avoided any direct political activity and neither it nor its branches ever acted as lobby groups for the filling of influential positions. But there was also no doubt that the majority of the leaders of this organization were con-

[3] See below, p. 236.

vinced that the religious future of France was closely tied to the Bourbon dynasty; this orientation gave Catholic Action an undeniable monarchical direction. A number of influential members of the Congregation were also, in conjunction with their official positions in the government or their prominent social standing, eager partisans of an ultramontane policy and active members of the secret monarchical Knights of the Faith. Thus the liberals were not wrong when they accused the people associated with the Congregation of being leaders of a secret club bent on acquiring control of the government. "Their understandable error consisted of ascribing to the Congregation the function of an organization responsible for all of these political and religious activities, while in reality it was only one of those clearly differentiated institutions whose undeniable simultaneous appearance found sufficient explanation in the fact that they were all headed by the same people with identical ideals and principles."[4]

It remains to be added that even on the purely religious level the Congregation possessed no monopoly of inspiration. It had no connections at all either with the Society of Good Literature or with the Catholic Library. It was independent from the congregation founded in Bordeaux by Father Chaminade for young people, adults, and women. The same is true for the Congregation of Lyon which was founded by laymen at the end of the Revolution and was connected to groups from Savoy and Piedmont as well as to the Knights of the Faith. In spite of the veil of secrecy with which it surrounded itself, this society was very active under the leadership of the merchant Coste. Because of his zeal he was called the "First Christian of the Diocese" and in 1818 founded several autonomous branches, which pursued varied activities in the area of charitable works. This group from Lyon played a signal role, especially in cooperation with Pauline Jaricot, a pious young girl, in the founding of the Society for the Propagation of the Faith.[5]

Nonetheless, many of these lay works, even if they were not creations of the Paris Congregation, lived under its strong influence, at least until the death in 1826 of Mathieu de Montmorency, the leading personality of the first generation of the Congregation. After his death, which coincided with the great offensive of Montlosier and the liberals against the Congregation, a new generation took over its leadership. Berryer, Bailly, and Gerbet and Salinis, followers of Lamennais, introduced a

[4] G. de Bertier, op. cit., 406.

[5] See A. Lestia, op. cit. and G. Gorrée, *Père Jaricot, une laïque engagé* (Paris 1962). Abbé Jaricot and his sister Pauline founded a society for the support of the missions in America. The principle of aid for missions in the entire world was agreed on in a convention of the congregation on 3 May 1822 at Lyon; the cooperation of the Knights of the Faith expanded the activity to Paris and all of France.

new spirit. They exercised little influence on the government—which, incidentally, explains the quick decline of all those organizations which existed because of official support—and instead turned more directly to fashioning public opinion. It was they above all who were involved in the beginning of the Association for the Defense of the Catholic Religion, the first of the societies for the defense of Catholicism against anticlerical currents. Founded in June 1828 following the formation of the Martignac ministry, it aimed at the establishment of branches in all of France, and for this purpose founded the paper *Le Correspondant.*[6]

Catholic Publications in France

Several of the societies listed above took it upon themselves to promote the distribution of good books, as the Catholics had clearly recognized the great importance of the press for winning public opinion on behalf of the Church. After being freed from Napoleonic censorship, Catholic publishing houses developed a remarkable activity. Reprints of apologetic works of the eighteenth century and publications of new apologies of the Catholic Church as well as of monarchical government became increasingly numerous, a process in which quality was often sacrificed to quantity. In addition to Lamennais, there were four figures who for a period of fifteen years radiated from Paris to the rest of Europe a political-religious ideology based on the combination of Catholicism and monarchical authority. It was an ideology which took the place of the earlier rationalistic and liberal ideology which likewise had emanated from France during the two preceding generations. It was characteristic for the intellectual condition of the Church in France toward the end of the revolutionary era that these four persons were laymen and that three of them were foreigners.

Count Louis de Bonald (1754–1840) throughout the restoration period continued his little-read but frequently quoted publications against the individualistic and critical philosophy of the eighteenth century. Tirelessly and with imperturbable logic he treated topics which for half a century became the focus and point of departure of political and social traditionalism on one hand and of philosophical and religious traditionalism on the other. The Savoyard Joseph de Maistre (1754–1821), a writer with a brilliant and sharp pen, who became for the Society of Jesus, under rather different conditions, what Pascal was for Port-Royal (Thibaudet); he paled much sooner, but was also much more appropriate for his time. From the excesses of the revolution he derived the necessity of monarchical absolutism and theocracy and became the

[6] See below, p. 276, footnote 8.

defender of the infallibility of the Pope. In his *Soirées de Saint-Pétersbourg* (1821) he became the "lay theologian of providence" (Brunetière). The Swiss Karl Ludwig von Haller (1768–1854), opponent of Rousseau and defender of the principle of authority, arrived at a rejection of Protestantism through the extension of his ideas to the field of religion. His *Letter to his Family, in Order to explain to it his Return to the Catholic Church* (1821) saw more than fifty editions. It was published in Paris, where he lived from 1824 to 1831, and through his writings and personal contacts exercised a remarkable influence on the Catholic restoration in the intellectual world. Finally there was the Dane Nikolaus von Eckstein (1790–1861), who in 1809 converted to Catholicism and after 1816 resided in Paris. He was a prolific, often confused, but also occasionally original author, thanks to his German professors Schlegel and Görres, for the spread of whose thoughts in France he was largely responsible. He intended to collect in a comprehensive synthesis everything that in contemporary research concerned the Christian dogma and seemed to support the Christian faith. He wanted to incorporate the findings of Brognart, Cuvier, and Humboldt in geology and ethnology, as well as those of philology, jurisprudence, orientalism, and prehistory. As a defender of tradition within the meaning of the German historical school, but more open-minded toward political freedom, Eckstein in a certain sense was also the precursor of Catholic liberalism. This unfortunately rather neglected publicist for a number of years, in addition to Lamennais, constituted "a focus for some young Christians who, like him, saw the essence of modern times in science and politics" (L. de Carné). In order better to propagate his ideas, he founded the monthly *Le Catholique* in 1826, following the example of the Mainz *Katholik.*

The Catholic champions intended to serve throne and altar not only through books and pamphlets. Lamennais as early as 1814 thought of founding a paper for the defense of Catholic interests, and on a regular basis he contributed articles to political newspapers which he regarded "not only as a tribune, but as a pulpit." Thus he contributed to Chateaubriand's *Conservateur,* to Genoude's and Bonald's *Défenseur,* and finally he published in *Drapeau blanc,* whose editor he was temporarily, eloquent indictments of the politics of concessions to the secular state as it had emerged from the revolution.[7] To be sure, many Catholics turned to journalism, but few possessed the talent of the Breton abbé. Most of the Catholic papers founded during the period of the restoration were

[7] His articles were printed in the *Premier mélanges* (Paris 1819) and *Nouveaux mélanges* (1826). Concerning Lamennais as journalist, consult C. Maréchal, *La dispute de l'Essai,* 81–195 and *Lamennais au "Drapeau blanc."*

rather colorless, first among them the most widely read *L'ami de la religion et du roi,* edited by Michel Picot, a man full of zeal but also of great limitation.

In addition to the support provided by writers and a few journalists, Catholicism during the restoration could also count on poets who continued to travel the path first taken by Chateaubriand twenty years earlier. In his *Méditations,* which turned out to be the literary event of 1820, Lamartine demonstrated that and how religion illuminated the problems of human destiny. Under the influence of Lamennais and as a result of his own experiences, Lamartine reverted to the faith of his youth. In spite of some vagueness in his thinking, his writings during the subsequent ten years created an atmosphere favorable to the Christian faith. In the circle around Nodier, the leaders of the new romantic school, especially the young Victor Hugo, celebrated the beauty of the Bible, of Gothic cathedrals, and of Catholic liturgy. But the situation was not as favorable as it might appear at first glance, and among the French romantics one could not speak of a Catholic culture to the same degree as with Görres and Manzoni. A few years sufficed to demonstrate the superficial character of an "elastic Christianity" (Viatte), in which the desire to merge with nature or the longing for a medieval past outweighed a rational agreement with a clearly defined faith. Besides, the romantics, after certain circumstances had connected them temporarily with the extreme right, began to distance themselves from this unnatural connection under Charles X and turned to the new liberal generation, the opponents of the established order, whose anticlericalism and even freethinking they frequently adopted.

The Appearance of Abbé de Lamennais

Several times the activity of Lamennais has been mentioned. In the course of the last years of the restoration he dominated to an increasing degree the Catholic movement in France and in other countries, chiefly in the Netherlands and Italy, and in some manner was connected with the beginning of the great intellectual development of Catholicism in the nineteenth century.

Félicité Robert de Lamennais (1782–1854) in 1804 found his way back to his faith and decided to work in the service of the Church in the future. He read extensively, especially the Bible, Bossuet, Malebranche, and Bonald. Interrupted by long periods of depression, together with his brother Jean-Marie he wrote a work against rationalism and another one against the religious policy of Napoleon. After long hesitation he finally allowed himself to be persuaded by his spiritual mentors to enter the priesthood in 1815.[8] In addition to his collaboration with ultraroyalist newspapers he then turned to the writing of comprehensive apologetic works designed to establish an effective protection of religion and the freedom of the Catholic Church. In the *Essai sur l'indifférence en matière de religion* he attacked less the unwillingness of individuals to concern themselves with religious questions as the attitude of the government, which refused openly to defend the only true religion.

The first volume, published in December 1817, reveals an intimate knowledge of the mentality of his time. It was written in a style of concentrated emotion which to us may appear high-flown, but it met the taste of the readers of the *Génie du Christianisme* and in the following years became a gigantic success in spite of the reticence of the left as well as the right press. "This book could bring the dead back to life," admitted Frayssinous. Overnight the young unknown priest had risen to the first rank of literary eminence, even though since the death of Massillon (1742) "no cleric in France had achieved the reputation of a writer or an outstanding person" (Lacordaire). It was his pleasure to witness that under his influence several of the young romantic writers again came closer to the Church. The volumes subsequently published between 1820 and 1823 were written in a more sober style, confused the public, and displeased the critics. But they inspired a number of young priests, who in consequence of an inadequate philosophical training in the seminaries were without protection exposed to the thought processes of an apparently relentless logic. They believed to have found in Lamennais the man of the future, able to breathe life into the religious restoration by adapting it to the spirit of the times.

To the same degree they applauded the passionate polemicist who in the press directed severe attacks against the weakness of a government whose policy, especially with respect to education, lacked sufficient Christian content. He also attacked the submissive spirit rooted in the Gallican influence with respect to the civil powers which prevented the bishops from taking effective action against this "treason." The famous *Lettre au grand-maître* of August 1823 was a high-point of his attacks in which he accused Monsignor Frayssinous of using his authority in covering up the "practical atheism" of the royal high schools.[9] It earned Lamennais the first episcopal reprimand and he was excluded from the *Drapeau blanc.* But two of his initial admirers, the Abbés Gerbet and

[8] See P. Dudon, *La vocation ecclésiastique de Lamennais: Le recrutement sacerdotal* (Reims 1912), no. 1.

[9] See C. Maréchal, *Lamennais au "Drapeau blanc"*, 160–285; M. R. Henrion, *Vie de Mgr. Frayssinous* II (Paris 1844), 425ff.; A. Garnier, *Frayssinous et la jeunesse* (Paris 1932).

Salinis, pastors to the students,[10] in January 1824 decided to take a page from models in Germany and Italy and founded an independent newspaper. With the cooperation of their master and with the intent to spread his ideas, it was designed to deal with religious, philosophical, and literary problems from a modern vantage point in place of political discussions. The resulting *Mémorial catholique* generated a vivid echo even in liberal minds, and was a surprise not only because of its "youthful verve and fervent proselytizing spirit" (Sainte-Beuve) but also because of the breadth and variety of the questions raised.[11] It went considerably beyond what the remaining contemporary press had to offer,[12] and strove to acquaint its readership with the most important foreign publications. But it had the disadvantage of introducing into ecclesiastical literature a belligerent, provocative, and frequently intolerant tone which characterized Lamennais and his adherents and a good deal of French publications in the nineteenth century.

It increasingly strengthened the opposition to Lamennais and the young reformers of the apostolate surrounding him. The bishops were enraged over the lack of constraint with which these "religious Jacobins" (Frayssinous) treated hierarchical authority in their attacks against Gallicanism. The sense of tradition and of the fitting of the Sulpicians was offended, and the Jesuits were not at all convinced that Lamennais was the greatest thinker whom the French Church had produced since Bossuet; they feared that his intemperance could cause a reaction among the liberals, whose first victims they would be. Finally the clerics had to fear for the advantages which the Church derived from the protection of the civil power, and therefore they condemned the virulent attacks of the new school against the state. The reproaches became even stronger when Lamennais published his sensational *De la religion considerée dans ses rapports avec l'ordre politique et civil* (1825/26). In it he attacked Gallicanism more strongly than ever before and recommended that the Church separate itself openly from the government of the Bourbons. The overdrawn formulations especially attracted the young, who, as so often is the case, were exposed to great danger in an apparently favorable situation. With the electric effect of his writings, the prophetic character of his ingenious intuitions, and the magical charm of

[10] As almoners of the College of Henry IV, they created a new type of study group called "conferences," which served to train a number of men for the Catholic movement of the middle of the century, such as E. d'Alzon, the brothers Boré, L. Dulac, E. de Casalès, and L. de Carné.

[11] C. de Ladoue, *Gerbet* II, 74–81 and chiefly J. R. Derré, op. cit., 169–225.

[12] The much more solid *Catholique* of Eckstein appeared only two years later.

his personality,[13] Lamennais succeeded in surrounding himself with an enthusiastic elite of young clerics and laymen. Among them were most of the leading minds of French Catholicism of the subsequent decades,[14] even though more than one of them, as for example Guéranger, later preferred to treat these youthful associations with silence.[15] Encouraged by the benevolent reception which Leo XII accorded the talented apologist and defender of ultramontane doctrine on the occasion of his journey to Italy in 1824,[16] the sickly little priest became the leader of a new generation, and his influence ultimately was so great that Duine could speak of his spiritual dictatorship over the French Church.

One of the reasons for this extraordinarily great influence was that Lamennais, however much importance he attached to his intellectual work, in equal measure was concerned with the "Catholic Action"—he coined the term—as the practical realization of his new Christian philosophy and the vital religious currents which inspired it. He wanted to encourage his followers in a complete reform of Catholic society[17] and the work of the Church in the world by asking them to solve all problems of social life not with a respectful neutrality toward all opinions but from the vantage point of revealed divine doctrine. His passionate interest, which he brought to bear especially on the question of a free Catholic education, must be seen from this perspective. It gained strength following the laws of 1828, as did the development of his political ideas. This former ultra eventually became the leader of Catholic liberalism, but still pursued the reconquest of society for Catholicism.[18]

The Beginnings of Catholic Action in Italy

In Italy also the Catholic restoration, as in other countries of western Europe, was not only a political movement, but to an equal degree a

[13] Especially evocative in this respect are the *Souvenirs de jeunesse by* Charles Sainte-Foi (=Elie Jourdain) (Paris 1911) and the *Journal* by Maurice de Guérin (Paris 1862).

[14] Not all of them, however. Lacordaire remained reserved for a long time and Dupanloup, closely affiliated with the Sulpician circle, always remained hostile to him.

[15] See E. Sevrin, *Dom Guéranger et Lamennais* (Paris 1933).

[16] Whether he actually wanted to make him a cardinal is dealt with by L. Le Guillou, *L'évolution de la pensée religieuse de Lamennais* (Paris 1966), 135–36 and Colapietra, 326–29.

[17] Already in 1822 he had written in *Drapeau blanc* of the unhappy conditions of the workers in the new liberal society, the first landmark of social Catholicism in France. See Duroselle, 36–40.

[18] See chapter 16.

manifestation of religious vitality in which laymen played a significant role. To be sure, there was nothing on the Italian peninsula which could rival the dynamic of the religious circles of the Rhineland or Bavaria or the initiative of the groups around Lamennais. But there also, especially in the north, were a number of priests and laymen who placed all of their strength in the service of religious restoration. Some of them, such as the future Monsignor J. M. Favre or Father Mermier, concentrated on preaching to the people according to the French example. Others, like B. Rubino, the founder of the Oblates of Saint Louis of Gonzaga, and Father Aporti devoted themselves to the apostolate among the young or tried to ameliorate the needs of the poor, as was done by the unique Giuseppe Cottolengo.[19] Others attempted to influence the opinion of the educated and to make a front against the prevailing mentality at the end of the eighteenth century. They attacked philosophies which were hardly compatible with Christian spiritualism, turned against the *Illuminismo* which sailed in the wake of the encyclopedists and followed rigoristic tendencies in morality, and were opposed to regalism and to those who disapproved of papal prerogatives. Among the latter, three names were dominant in 1820: Ventura in Naples, Rosmini in Lombardy, and Lanteri in Piedmont. Pio Brunone Lanteri (1759–1830), whom circumstances often forced to act secretly or anonymously, is least known. Historians have only recently recognized the significance of the role which he played for half a century after the deluge of the French Revolution. He was a witness to priestly work which all too often was neglected. As a teacher he used a portion of his wealth to distribute small pamphlets, often written by him, in order to dispel the errors of his time. But he was also an organizer who wanted to assure his activities of the greatest possible effectiveness through the creation of clubs[20] or the rejuvenation of already existing organizations.

It was primarily his efforts which brought back to life in completely new form in 1817 a society for the distribution of good books which had been founded forty years earlier by the ex-Jesuit Diesbach. This *Amicizia cattolica* was subsequently headed exclusively by laymen, without exception members of the nobility, and no longer placed the personal salvation of its members into the foreground but concentrated on mass action to be effected through publications. In its spiritual form, it adopted the organization of the Freemasons. Its chief supporter was the

[19] Concerning Cottolengo (1786–1842), see A. Scheiwiller, *G. Cottolengo* (Freiburg i. Br. 1937); *Il Cottolengo. L'uomo, l'opera, lo spirito* (Turin 1950).

[20] He was involved in the creation of the Oblati di Maria Vergine, for which in 1826 he received the approbation of Leo XII against the will of his archbishop, as well as of the Convitto ecclesiastico of Turin, which in 1817 was founded by his student Guala and from which later G. Cafasso and Don Bosco were to emerge.

Marchese Cesare d'Azeglio, who in 1824 introduced in Piedmont the French work of dissemination of the faith and thus established the first center of missionary lay work outside of France.[21] Several societies related to the *Amicizia* of Turin were created either under its direct influence (in Rome and Novara) or in imitation of its principles and methods.[22] Among the latter a special place was occupied by the *Società degli amici* and its branches in Venice and Lombardy, founded in 1819 by Rosmini in Rovereto. Its attitude was neither fearful nor conservative and it was oriented toward Italy. On the other hand, its aims were far-reaching; it wanted to devote itself both to charitable work and to an intensification of Catholic education. The *Amicizie* in general concentrated their efforts on the struggle against liberalism, and for this purpose distributed small pamphlets, easily accessible to the public, which were not limited to religious-political polemics or an emphasis of the social utility of religion. Simultaneously they promoted spiritual and theological aims awakened by the Society of Jesus, such as the veneration of the Sacred Heart of Jesus or the Virgin Mary, frequent communion, a less rigoristic morality, and the belief in the infallibility of the Pope.

After the unrest of 1820/21, Catholic publications received a new form through the founding of newspapers for the defense of Catholic and monarchical principles. The first, the *Enciclopedia ecclesiastica e morale,* was founded in Naples in 1821 as a result of collaboration between Father Ventura and the Prince of Canosa, a layman. It was their aim to confront liberal tendencies, against which the police were powerless, with an ideological bulwark based on religion. In the following year, Cesare d'Azeglio realized a long-planned project by founding in Turin the *Amico d'Italia.* Father Baraldi in Modena founded the *Memorie di religione, di morale e di letteratura,* and in 1825 similar papers appeared,[23] in Rome the *Giornale ecclesiastico,* strongly influenced by Ventura, and in Florence the *Giornale degli apologisti della religione cattolica.* But already by this time the mediocre results of these efforts brought about a weakening of the initial zeal; genuine journalistic talent was lacking and this also limited the power to influence. All of these papers, which unceasingly and in all areas countered social and intellectual anarchy with the principle of authority, were inspired, albeit with con-

[21] See C. Bona, *La rinascita missionaria in Italia. Dalle "Amicizie" all'Opera per la propagazione della fede* (Turin 1964).

[22] His influence reached to France and even to the Netherlands. See C. Bona, *Le "Amicizie,"* 357–61.

[23] Concerning the differentiating nuances of the *Memorie* (Modena) from the *Giornale ecclesiastico* which was designed to appeal chiefly to the common Christians, see Colapietra, 238–42.

siderable variations, by the counterrevolutionary ideology developed at this time in Paris and Vienna. In contrast to many conservatives, who above all desired a political and social restoration for whose implementation they wished to use the Church, the editors of these Italian Catholic papers were more or less firmly convinced that the Church was the only and indispensable guarantee for social order. They also believed that the political revolution of 1789 was nothing more than the logical consequence of the religious revolution of the sixteenth century and that for this reason an integrated religious restoration was necessary. With the aid of this restoration they wanted to return, aside from all deviations of the Gallicanism of the Old Regime, to a medieval Christianity in which the Church, represented by the Pope, formulated the duties of the state.

Such ideas, which even some members of the Roman Curia considered excessive or at least inopportune under the prevailing circumstances, could hardly be to the liking of the regalistic governments of the time, and in fact the papers were one by one suppressed. The enthusiasm, however, with which these circles greeted the campaign of Lamennais in favor of theocracy and ultramontanism is easily understandable. In this connection there was often talk of influence; rather, it was a confluence of several strains of thought. Frequently there were laudatory allusions to Lamennais in these papers. His works were translated several times, and contacts by letter with the main representatives of the Catholic movement, especially with the Piedmontese group, became more frequent and reached a peak on the occasion of his journey to Italy in 1824. Yet it was not Lamennais to whom they owed their convictions; they merely recognized in the French writer an excellent means to propagate their ideas. Thus it was not surprising that in contrast to Belgium his Italian readership dwindled at the very moment when, in 1825, he began to promote the separation of Church and state. After the publication of his *Progrès de la révolution* in 1829, outright hostility developed in many cases, one of whose exceptions was Father Ventura.

This development in the attitude toward Lamennais was characteristic for the Italian, and above all the Piedmontese, Catholic movement of the restoration period. It lacked a certain cultural open-mindedness—the unequivocal opposition to romanticism is typical—and that sensitivity for new religious and political problems which lent the French movement of Lamennais its conquering dynamic. Their efforts were limited to a rather superficial concept of the activity of the Church in the world, assigning more significance to the Christianization of institutions than to the development of conscience. We see here—and this consideration justifies the importance assigned to this movement in spite of its immediate lack of success—the beginnings of the intransigent current whose strength in Italian Catholic life grew more important in the second half of the century.

Not all Catholic forces, however, oriented themselves in this conservative direction. Rosmini separated himself from it in spite of his connections to the restoration movement and his sympathies for Haller and German traditionalism. On the cultural level he was concerned with a rejuvenation of traditional Christian philosophy and on the political level with the national problem. On the other hand there were also convinced Catholics in the romantic movement which, in contrast to France and especially to Germany, in Italy had a much stronger continuity with the *Illuminismo* of the eighteenth century. The most striking figure in this context is Alessandro Manzoni (1785–1873), much more so than Gioberti, who despite his influence on liberal Catholics remained on the fringes of Catholicism and wavered between deism and skepticism. Manzoni moved from revolutionary encyclopedism to Catholicism by way of the moral endeavors of Jansenism and Calvinism. His religious ideas were the cause for many controversies,[24] but there can be no doubt about the seriousness of his faith following his conversion in Paris in 1810. His frequently reprinted *Osservazioni sulla morale cattolica* (1819), in which he corrects the Protestant Sigismondi, who attributed the political decadence of the Italians to Catholicism, constituted the first remarkable manifesto of a cultural patriotism in Italy which openly was as one with the Catholic tradition. The ethical-religious topics here sketched were taken up again a few years later in the famous novel *I promessi sposi* (1826/27) which gave the Italy of the nineteenth century a literary masterpiece of a depth different from that of Chateaubriand's *Génie du Christianisme.* Even if Manzoni's thinking at this time cannot yet be called liberal, it implied liberal consequences which made Manzoni one of the most important originators of Catholic liberalism in Italy during the second third of the century. In an environment, then, which in essence remained reactionary, the seeds for a rejuvenation of Catholic mentality were planted which approached modern values with greater openness.

[24] See G. Busnelli, *La conversione di A. Manzoni* (Rome 1913); G. Salvadori, *Libertà e servitù nel pensiero-giansenista e in A. Manzoni* (Brescia 1932); F. Ruffini, *La vita religiosa di A. Manzoni* (Bari 1931); and P. Fossi, *La conversione di A. Manzoni* (Bari 1933).

CHAPTER 15

The Complex Revival of Religious Studies

The eighteenth century, although productive in the areas of exegesis, Church history, and pastoral care, was on the whole not a glorious time for theology. The following century began under even worse conditions. In spite of a rich apologetic literature, Catholic thought lacked force and determination. In Italy and Spain, theologians were absorbed by sterile polemics and religious thought languished in mediocrity. In France, the magical style of a Chateaubriand could not conceal the doctrinal poverty, and works which were tied to the classics were ill-suited to a modern mentality. In Germany, a majority of theologians, influenced by the rationalism of their environment, stood in danger of emptying Christianity of its supernatural content. In addition, the old centers of education were disorganized as a consequence of the French Revolution.

Between 1810 and 1820, the very depth of the crisis in Catholic thought, a crisis which could no longer be ignored, brought about a reaction. Within a few years, a number of initiatives were taken. Although inept, these actions were more impressive and positive than the neo-scholasticism at the turn of the century was willing to admit. They had as their aim the regaining for Catholicism of that esteem among the educated which it had lost almost completely. These attempts were strongly supported by the romantics, in spite of the inherent ambivalence of their philosophy. The literary and theological revival not only occurred simultaneously, but theology also received lasting influences from romantic thought and adopted such concepts as a sensibility to the coldness of reason, a mystical understanding of the universe, a reaction against individualism in favor of the values of the community, and a desire for the rehabilitation of tradition and history. This mentality was reflected in a somewhat exaggerated philosophy, which fostered a daring idealism in search of comprehensive harmonious syntheses and a history in which the organic development of the idea through the ages was accentuated. In theology, this attitude led to a revaluation of the confession of faith, occasionally even sliding into fideism; to a shift in emphasis in religion from the moralism of the eighteenth century to a mystical and supernatural position; to a view of the Church as a living organism which, although it had occasionally neglected the personality of the believer, was also the soil from which dogmas developed; to a rediscovery of the meaning of the past and especially of the Church Fathers; and even, in consequence of the admiration of the Middle Ages, to a renewed interest in scholasticism. It was also recognized that there were internal connections and an organic unity between the various theological sciences, such as between dogmatism and morality, and exegesis and Church history. This new view led in similar fashion to a rapprochement between theology and profane culture. In spite of the profound differences which separated the two, in this area the strivings of the Hermes School and the Tübingen theologians coincided with those of a Lamennais in France or a Rosmini in Italy.

Germany: Between Rationalism and Romantic Idealism

In contrast to Austria, where the structure of the theological university departments had hardly been touched by the disruptions at the end of the eighteenth century, in Germany the secularization of the ecclesiastical principalities and abbeys in the wake of the suppression of the Jesuits had led to the dissolution of most of the ecclesiastical centers of education. Thanks to the firm organization of the Catholic theological departments at a number of universities the interruption was mercifully brief. The new arrangement whereby theology was studied at state universities, an arrangement which has lasted to this day, offered the Catholic scholars the opportunity of close contact with non-Catholic sciences; an exchange which turned out to be fruitful. However, the new order noticeably limited the degree of control over educational content exercised by the ecclesiastical authorities. This academic freedom occasionally promoted an exaggerated sense of independence[1] and even actual deviations from correct doctrine. The danger was particularly great during the first years, when teaching appointments were made without adequate consideration of the orthodoxy of the candidates.

The Mainz seminary, which was reorganized by the French regime, under Liebermann became the center of the future neo-scholastic movement in Germany.[2] Two strong and equally dangerous tendencies dominated theology and apologetics at the beginning of the nineteenth century. The rationalism of the preceding century, strengthened by the success of the great post-Kantian philosophical systems, still exerted a strong attraction. Many efforts to defend Christianity were characterized by an unjustified accommodation to the positions of the opponents and thus incurred the risk of unseemly concessions. In some cases

[1] The declaration of the Bonn professors of 1820 was characteristic for this tendency. See H. Schrörs, op. cit., 134ff.

[2] Between 1819 and 1820 he published a four-volume textbook, *Institutiones theologiae dogmaticae,* frequently reprinted during the first half of the century. He intended to provide in it a precise description of the doctrines of the Church from an unequivocally anti-Protestant perspective. See L. Lenhart, op. cit., 25–53.

the tendencies to make a compromise were very strong. Professors like Fingerlos, Berg, and Gratz interpreted the miracles of the Gospel according to the method introduced by Heinrich Paulus and disregarded certain dogmas which they qualified as mere subtleties, even, upon occasion, questioning the Godhead of Christ. In addition to these extreme cases, the thinking of many pious theologians remained anchored in the Enlightenment or succumbed to Kantian criticism and idealistic pantheism. To this group belonged men such as Oberthür, who described theology in the language of Herder's humanism, and Zimmer, who interpreted dogma according to Schelling. In contrast to these tendencies, however, there was a reaction against the dry moralism and the cold rationalism of natural religion. The concepts adopted by such philosophers as Jacobi and Schleiermacher, the Protestant "Court Philosopher of Romanticism," in spite of the superiority of their emphasis on the nonreducible originality of the Christian experience and religious dynamism, led frequently to an antiintellectualism which endangered the rational foundations of the confession of faith. In some cases, they encompassed a concordism which regarded Catholicism and Protestantism merely as two different aspects of the same mystical Church. Even circles such as that of the Princess Gallitzin in Münster, whose orthodoxy was beyond question, believed to have found in fideism the true Christian answer to the excesses of rationalism.

As always in turbulent times and intensive intellectual fermentation, a few probing attempts were made to combine the different movements of the period. Two converts, Count Friedrich Leopold von Stolberg[3] and Friedrich von Schlegel,[4] whose intellect and character had been formed by the classicism of the eighteenth century, but who also had adopted the findings and values of romanticism, contributed substantially to the rehabilitation of Catholicism among the educated classes. Through their writings, the style of which was more impressive than their content, they treated history, literature, and the philosophy of religion in equal measure. Friedrich Leopold von Stolberg, from 1800 on a member of the Münster circle, placed all of the knowledge which his excellent classical education had provided him in the service of his passionate faith in order to demonstrate the superiority of the Catholic faith over that inspired by ancient philosophy. His fifteen-volume *History of the Religion of Jesus Christ* (1806/18), written with more spiritual zeal than scholarship and critical spirit, opened to the study of Church history, which hitherto had been influenced by a Febronian and Josephinist mentality, a new and more universal horizon and one which

[3] See above, p. 218.

[4] See above, p. 219.

did justice to the essentially religious and saving mission of the Church in the development of humankind. Another attempt at synthesis arose from the work of Schlegel, an admirer of Goethe and student of Fichte and Schelling, who, after 1810, taught at Vienna in close contact with the circle led by Clemens Maria Hofbauer. Schlegel's research in the history of religion led him to explore the concept of revelation. In his *Lectures on Modern History* (1811) he developed the basis for a Catholic philosophy of history,[5] and his *History of Ancient and Modern Literature* (1813), with its revelation of the literary and artistic significance of the Bible and the Middle Ages, played a role in Germany comparable to that of the *Génie du Christianisme.*

Johann Michael Sailer,[6] professor of pastoral theology at Landshut from 1800 to 1821, is characteristic of the theologians of the transition from the Enlightenment to Catholic romanticism. Sailer was an eclectic, but possessed a certain creativity, and was one of the first to again integrate theology with Christian spirituality. Starting from a position still firmly imbedded in the views of the eighteenth century, he gradually moved from vivacious religiosity to the life of the Church by first discovering the patristic concept of tradition and then that of the Church as a spiritual organism whose supernatural life is shared by its members.[7]

Between 1820 and 1830, Bonn, Tübingen, and Munich were the three centers of learning which most influenced religious thought in Germany.[8] At Bonn, after 1819, the influence of a school founded by Georg Hermes (1775–1831) was to last for a generation. Hermes, who earlier had been a professor of dogma at Münster and a member of the circle of the Princess Gallitzin, was a priest with great apostolic zeal. He wished to contribute to the Catholic restoration by transcending the apparent antagonism between modern philosophy and the teachings of the Church. Although he recognized the great danger which Kant's criticism and Fichte's idealism posed for the Christian faith, he was too fascinated by these philosophical systems to discard them completely.

[5] He continued to develop it in his *Philosophie der Geschichte* (1829).

[6] See above, pp. 221f.

[7] Sailer shows a similar development in his attitude toward the catechism. His constant concern for concrete and Bible-oriented thought is manifested by the emphasis with which he repeatedly refers to the moral example of biblical personalities; but subsequently he demanded above all that religious instruction emphasize the Passion and Salvation of Christ.

[8] Considering Schlegel, Vienna should be added to a certain degree. But Schlegel's strong influence was effective chiefly in the areas related to ecclesiastical knowledge. After the departure of Jam in 1806, the theological department, being under strict secular control, no longer exercised significant influence. See A. Wappler, op. cit., 254–62.

Instead, he wanted to fight Kant with his own weapons. Hermes carried the criticism of human knowledge a step further than Kant by regarding agreement with the truths of faith as a necessary conclusion of proof. He then proceeded to give an a priori description of all—including supernatural—reality on a rational basis, consonant with the demands of idealism.[9] Because of his remarkable teaching ability and his priestly charisma, together with the support of Archbishop Spiegel of Cologne, who was desirous of providing his diocese with educated and open-minded priests, Hermes was able to gain the enthusiasm of a portion of the young intellectuals. Upon his death, he left convinced followers in more than thirty philosophical and theological teaching posts and, in some cases, also in important positions in ecclesiastical life. But in reality, his work, which seemed so modern at the time, lacked a sense of history. Hermes' limited interest in ecclesiastical tradition, coupled with his concept of religion as a doctrine which could be understood rationally rather than spiritually, caused him to regard the development of dogmas and the history of dogmas as genuine latecomers of the Enlightenment. Therefore, he had to suffer not only the well-founded criticism of a few far-seeing minds who chided him for his Pelagian and semirationalistic position, but also of those, particularly those outside of the universities, who, influenced by romanticism, placed feeling and heartfelt belief before cold reason or were under the influence of French traditionalism.[10]

Among Hermes' opponents, many of whom adhered to fideism, which relativized their position, his Bonn colleague Karl Joseph Windischmann (1775–1839) requires special treatment. This physician and philosopher, after having wavered between pantheism and deism, finally returned to the Catholic faith in 1813. Windischmann wanted to establish a Hegelian-oriented Christian philosophy based on revelation. Through his teaching, correspondence, and numerous personal contacts, much more than through his esoteric writings, he exerted a great influence and led many people back to their Christian faith. At the same time, he directed attention to the great teachers of the Middle Ages, whose essence he sought more in their mystical writings than in their doctrinal systems.

[9] The essence of his principles is presented in his *Philosophische Einleitung in die Christkatholische Theologie* (1819) and its supplement *Positive Einleitung* (1829). His *Christkatholische Dogmatik* was published posthumously by his student Achterfeld.

[10] On the remarkable influence of Lamennais's traditionalism in Germany and especially in the Rhineland, see H. Schrörs, *Ein vergessener Führer aus der rheinischen Geistesgeschichte des 19. Jahrhunderts, J. W. J. Braun* (Bonn 1925), 289–95, and St. Lösch, *Döllinger und Frankreich* (München 1955). The chief publication of the movement was the *Aschaffenburger Kirchenzeitung; Der Katholik* (Mainz) also evinced some sympathies.

While in the Rhineland Hermes was working on an apologia with which to confront the problems caused by Kantianism and rationalism, a group of theologians at Tübingen,[11] fascinated by the philosophy of idealism but determined not to deviate from Catholic orthodoxy, sought a happy medium between the unhealthy mysticism of many romantics and the narrow-minded rationalism of many late students of the Enlightenment. They were courageous researchers, open to contemporary movements, who took advantage of the fact that certain terms of the new philosophy were already theologically adapted by contemporary Protestant thinkers. On this basis they presented a new theological synthesis which, although critical of the basic positions of Protestantism, was both modern and traditional and presented a bold program for the reform of liturgy and Church discipline.

In some areas the Tübingen theologians followed those precursors who have received attention through most recent historiography.[12] Among these men were Sailer, whose profound influence on the theology of romanticism has become increasingly clear; Geiger and Gügler, Sailer's students at Lucerne, who may be regarded as the link between the beginning of traditionalism and Hegel's philosophy; Brener, a professor at the Bamberg seminary, who, in an outline which was at the same time theology, philosophy, and history,[13] sketched dogma from the vantage point of the idea of the Empire of God; Seber, a professor at Bonn and later at Louvain, who saw the Church under the guidelines of a developing spiritual organism; and Ziegler at Vienna, who already employed the concept of a "living tradition." But only the Tübingen School managed to articulate the intellectual currents and to combine the great topics of romanticism in a comprehensive synthesis.

For Godet it was "primarily a school of speculative theology," but for Bihlmeyer it was "chiefly historically and critically" oriented. In reality, the Tübingen School stands out precisely because of its close blend of positive and speculative methods. It attempted to understand dogmatism not in the narrow sense of classical theology, for which it was merely a kind of catalogue of orthodox doctrines, but speculatively as revealed realities which demonstrate their inner harmony. The Tübingen theologians desired a more suitable instrument for the expansion of Schelling's philosophy or Hegel's dialectic, then very much in

[11] The Catholic Theological department created in 1812 was moved from Ellwangen to Tübingen in 1817. See *ThQ* 108 (1927), 77–158. A number of professors in 1819 founded the *Theologische Quartalschrift,* the hallmark of the new school.

[12] See the document collection of J. R. Geiselmann, *Geist des Christentums und des Katholizismus. Ausgewählte Schriften katholischer Theologie im Zeitalter des deutschen Idealismus und der Romantik* (Mainz 1938).

[13] See F. Dressler, *Lebensläufe aus Franken* VI, (München 1960), 32–53.

vogue, than was the case with regard to scholastic philosophy. From Schelling's philosophy, which closely related to the romantic movement, they took the idea of life and the organism as well as the strong emphasis on mystical knowledge. From Hegel they adopted, among others, the concept of a living spirit giving life to the continuing unfolding of the "Christian idea." In fact, as a result of its encounter with the writings of the Church Fathers, the history of dogma, together with the concept of a living tradition, constituted a kind of collective conscience of the Church acting under the effect of God's spirit. As such it became significant for theological renewal. In Germany, earlier than in Romance countries, the turn to the genetic method became compelling as the significance of the researches of Protestant scholars in the history of the development of Christianity became accepted. The development of a historical perspective became the characteristic method with which the nineteenth century approached all questions.

Three names dominated the Tübingen School. Its founder, Johann Sebastian Drey (1777–1851), was still tentative in his progress and tied to the ideas of Schelling and Schleiermacher. Yet his services were twofold; he incorporated the contributions of Protestant historians in his theology without falling victim to archeologism, and he developed a theology from the perspective of transcendental idealism in order to lead Catholicism back to a fundamental and comprehensive idea. He emphasized that this idea was not based a priori upon reason, but was grounded in revealed realities; and that it was not a pure idea, but God's eternal plan manifesting itself in time: a gift from supernatural life to man. These considerations led him to a treatment of the organic unity of the Church, its continuing development, and the life of the community inspired by the Holy Spirit; topics which were to concern German theology for a long time and later all of European theology.

Johann Baptist Hirscher (1788–1865) was a reformer of the pastoral and catechetical areas and developed daring and useful thoughts, some of which were rather far from reality. He was also a rejuvenator of moral theology[14] and introduced, as Drey had, a social dimension into this discipline. Hirscher presented moral theology in a less abstract manner, which was reminiscent of Pauline kerygma, and strove for a close connection between dogma and spirituality in order to counteract the naturalistic moralism of the eighteenth century and the casuistry of the preceding centuries.

Johann Adam Möhler (1776–38) towered above both Drey and

[14] There were forerunners in the first years of the nineteenth century. See, for example, C. Schmeing, *Studien zur "Ethica christiana" M. v. Schenkls und zu ihren Quellen* (Regensburg 1959).

Hirscher just as "genius surpasses talent" (de Grandmaison). In the course of his brief professorship he reformulated all topics which he treated: the basic dogmas of Christianity as much as the knowledge of faith, the supernatural, grace, and the Church. Not only did his thought grow in precision between his impressive early *The Unity of the Church* (1825) and his later *Symbolism* (1832), but also in the four later editions of this latter work,[15] which came to be the most important treatment of controversial theology since the end of the sixteenth century. Möhler was an autodidact to a much smaller degree than assumed by Goyau. Instead we see in him the unfolding of a theological renewal influenced in its beginnings by rich, deep, and tradition-molded insights but also including a nonreflective enthusiasm vulnerable in its philosophical assumptions. If Möhler was inferior to Drey in speculative thought, he was yet the greater of the two in that he succeeded in freeing his synthesis from the system-immanent pantheistic tendencies of idealistic philosophy. Thus his well-considered and balanced work, in a style which conveys an enthusiastic conviction, can be regarded as the most significant example of the intellectually awakened and fundamentally very Catholic theology of romanticism.[16]

The University of Munich, transferred from Landshut in 1825, did not contribute to the theological rejuvenation of the first third of the century to the same degree as Tübingen. However, through the activity of King Ludwig I and his intimate friend Ringseis, the first president of the university, it grew within a few years into the most important intellectual center of Catholicism in central Europe in the areas of philosophy, history, literature, and the arts. Among its professors were Schelling, a Protestant who was very open-minded toward Catholicism and whose brilliant philosophical-religious synthesis of Christianity was universally acclaimed; the historian Döllinger; the able exegete Allioli; and the poet Brentano, who popularized the *Revelations* of Katharina Emmerick. In addition to these, two others, both laymen, drew attention. The philosopher Franz von Baader (1765–1841), enthusiastically acclaimed by some contemporaries as the rejuvenator of speculative theology, was closer in his work to theosophy than theology. Inspired by Thomas Aquinas and Meister Eckhart as well as by the Protestant mystic Jakob Böhme, his was a very religious, daring, and original mind.

[15] Of these two works, J. R. Geiselmann issued critical editions (Cologne-Olten 1957 and 1958/61), preceded by important introductions which reconstruct the history of their development.

[16] A. Minon in *EThL* 16 (1939), 375. Counter to the currently rejected view of Vermeil, who saw in Möhler the founding father of modernism, see L. de Grandmaison in *RSR* 9 (1919), 400–09 and especially S. Lösch in ThQ 99 (1917/18), 28–59, 129–52.

He was interested in bringing about a union of the Churches outside of the domination of the Pope. Although very difficult to understand as a writer, he was incomparable as a conversationalist and "as shrewd as Plato and as witty as Voltaire" (C. Sainte-Foi). Baader drew attention once again to medieval scholasticism, while simultaneously working toward the destruction of rationalism.

The second influential layman was Johann Joseph Görres (1776–1848), a typical representative of the development which returned a number of young intellectuals to their faith. These young intellectuals, without losing the positive values of their intellectual positions, moved from a lack of faith, so popular in the eighteenth century, to a rediscovery of the spiritual demands within the atmosphere of romanticism, to the Christian faith, and finally to a vital and profound understanding of the Catholic Church. In 1826 Görres became a professor of history and literature at Munich and for about twenty years was the leader of an intellectually and artistically very active group. He also provided the stimulus for a German Catholic movement against an established Church.[17] His lectures, conducted with a high degree of scholarship, were more concerned with the philosophy of history than with history as a science. He developed a universal view of history in the romantic style, and his "eagle's perspective" (Diepenbrock) was impressive to his contemporaries. These views became the foundation for Görres's work on *Christian Mysticism* (1836/42), a work which displayed very little critical spirit, but which for half a century was a point of departure for many scholarly works on speculative mysticism.

The Munich School, in which the spirit of the Illuminati occupied a wide berth, exerted an unusual force. The significance of the Munich School for all of Europe was demonstrated by its contacts with Lamennais, Rio, and Montalembert in France, and Wiseman in England.

France: On the Way to a New Apologia

The revival of theological studies proceeded much slower in France than in Germany, as a result of the lack of an institutional framework. The suppression of the religious orders and the destruction of monastic libraries had occurred at roughly the same time as the disappearance of the theological schools of the Old Regime and most of the French centers of learning. The few schools which were reestablished by Napoleon after an interval of fifteen years remained insignificant and were not able to replace what had been lost, as they were not canonically constituted. The plan devised in 1824 by Monsignor Frayssinous, minis-

[17] See above, p. 222, and below, p. 333.

ter for ecclesiastical concerns and education, to found an institute in Paris for the university training of the clergy foundered on the lack of understanding on the part of the episcopate. For several generations, therefore, the entire intellectual training of the clergy was concentrated in the seminaries of the dioceses. There the curriculum left much to be desired for two reasons. Competent professors were not available, as a consequence of the interruption occasioned by the Revolution, and the shortage of priests compelled the bishops to be more concerned with rapid ordinations than with the quality of their education. Training of priests was of a purely practical nature. In seventy-five out of eighty seminaries, Church history was not taught at all, exegesis was generally limited to a devotional commentary without any critical content, moral theology was limited to the usual casuistry, and the study of dogma consisted of the memorization of simple and antiquated texts.[18] Only two seminaries stood a little above this general mediocrity. The first of these was the seminary of Saint Sulpice, in which a few competent people taught the Old Testament, but where tradition was hostile to all innovations, including attempts to adapt theology to modern thought. Above average training was also provided after 1827 by the seminary of Strasbourg in conjunction with the École des Hautes-Études at Molsheim. The École des Hautes-Études had been entrusted to Abbé Bautain, a convert who kept in touch with German academic developments and succeeded in gathering around him such excellent professors as Gratry. However, the hostile influence of Lamennais's followers, who saw it as competition, and that of the conservative clergy, who were alarmed about the new doctrines of Bautain and his students, soon dispersed the small school.[19]

Louis Bautain (1796–1867) is generally regarded only as a champion of fideism. But in reality, as Father Poupard has demonstrated, his orientation toward Plato and Augustine made him much more differentiated. Bautain possessed a profound if somewhat fanatical mind, and his university education made him a rarity in those days. He was very much concerned with a unity of thought and life, and he attempted to solve the intellectual problems of his age with a truly Catholic spirit. Unfortunately, Bautain was not familiar with scholastic tradition, a dangerous ignorance, but it allowed him a fresh and free approach to problems.[20] Beyond a sharp criticism of rationalism, his work was de-

[18] The gradual replacement of the *Institutiones Theologicae* (1818/33) by J.-B. Bouvier by L. Bailly's *Theologia dogmatica et moralis* or *Theologie de Toulouse* improved the situation only marginally.

[19] See P. Poupard, op. cit., 184–91, 255–56.

[20] See H. Walgrave in *RHE* 58 (1963), 641–42. A synthesis of Bautain's thought can be found in his *Philosophie du christianisme* (1835).

signed to offer a genuinely theological synthesis from the perspective of German idealism. Reflecting upon the wealth of ideas contained in revelation, he attempted to describe the complete agreement of dogmas and to demonstrate how they explained the riddles of nature and human life. His theological wisdom, presented to the faithless as the only true philosophy, acquired an apologetic significance. Throughout this time, apologetic intentions dominated Catholic thought in France, where destruction as a consequence of unbelief had been greater than in other countries. In many instances, however, the need for a rejuvenation in the area of methodology was not recognized. Until 1830, only the polemical writings of Duvoisin, Cardinal de la Luzerne, and Abbé Bergier against Voltaire and the encyclopedists were issued over and over. Most of the apologetic works published in the first quarter of the nineteenth century were written from this same perspective. Even the *Conférences de Monseigneur Frayssinous sur la Defénse du christianisme,*[21] which were so successful, were imbedded in classicism. The numerous editions of these works, many of which were merely mediocre efforts, point up how undemanding the ecclesiastical public was.

Occasionally an attempt was made to channel apologetics into new paths which would be better suited to the mentality of the period. These attempts contributed to a certain degree of revival in Catholic education, without, however, being able to achieve a solid and lasting synthesis.

Eckstein,[22] who had studied in Germany, followed the example of Görres in favoring a comprehensive study of the past of humanity with the aim of discovering within it the essence of the one divine history.[23] As a student of Schlegel, Eckstein opened up for the contemporaries of Champollion the significance of Near Eastern studies for the defense of Christianity. In this scientific area, Catholics occupied an honorable place until the middle of the century.

In a number of new books, two other laymen, Louis de Bonald and Joseph de Maistre, whose writings first appeared at the time of the Revolution, took up the topics raised since 1796.[24] Their intention was not that of the classical apologists to prove the truth of religion, but

[21] Held from 1803 to 1809 and 1814 to 1820; published in 1825, reprinted seventeen times; translated into English, German, Italian, and Spanish.

[22] See above, p. 231.

[23] It should be noted that even the Protestant Benjamin Constant with his multi-volume *De la religion*—rich in facts and ideas and also influenced by contemporary German scholarship—in his own way contributed to the success of traditional apologetics by showing that a documented work on prehistory confirms the unique nature of Christian revelation.

[24] See above, p. 70, and G. Constant in *RHE* 30 (1934), 54–60.

rather its necessity. This they did by applying the pragmatic perspective of Chateaubriand to the area of politics. Not only does revelation satisfy to the highest degree the demands of the heart and man's noblest motives, but it also confirms through experience that it is the necessary foundation of the activities of spiritual and social life, just as the destructive nature of the revolution had proved the error of the philosophy of the Enlightenment. For Bonald, individual reason, incapable of arriving at the truth, must be replaced by external authority, divine in origin and social in its realization, a revelation transmitted with the aid of tradition. This philosophically and theologically questionable concept became in France the impulse for the development of the study of the history of religion and of sociology and guided the attention of theologians to the social aspects of Christianity. De Maistre took an analogous but clearly differentiated direction. In a visionary fashion and without concern for early tradition, he examined the historical experience of the past few centuries in order to divine the laws of providence and the immutable principles of society. He also arrived at the conclusion that monarchy was the best form of government, but he insisted on the necessity of its association with Catholicism and warned that any attempt at independence with respect to the Holy See would necessarily lead to disruptions. In this way de Maistre became a champion of ultramontane revival as well as of that movement which favored the return of divided Christianity to Roman unity.[25]

This counterrevolutionary apologetic, abandoning individualistic rationalism for social salvation based upon a return to a religion of authority, had much to offer a world which saw society shaken to its foundations. But in order to be truly acceptable, especially to the young, it had to be less dogmatic and had to be able to express itself in a language fitted to the romantic mentality. In addition, it had to be shown as less directly political and no longer primarily as justification for a monarchical social order. It must stand as a strongly intellectual system of Catholic philosophy. This task was left for Lamennais, whom we encounter once more in this connection in his *Essai sur l'indifférence en matière de religion* (4 volumes, 1817–23). Lamennais continued to be inspired by themes of the apologists of the seventeenth century: Pascal, Bossuet, de Maistre, and especially Bonald. These themes were newly expressed by Lamennais even if not newly thought through. In a remarkable way Lamennais understood the mentality and the difficulties of his contemporaries and for that reason allowed himself momentarily to be fascinated by the ideology of the eighteenth century. He returned to the Church, however, not out of a reactionary reflex as so many

[25] See above, pp. 109f., and M. Jugie, *Joseph de Maistre et l'Église gréco-russe* (Paris 1922).

followers of de Maistre or Bonald had done, nor through a purely emotional attraction like Chateaubriand, but in the name of the demands of spiritual and intellectual freedom, which had been threatened by the despotism of the state and the domination of Napoleon.[26]

This brilliant apologia of Lamennais, which articulated many commonly held ideas with prophetic force and enriched them with fruitful if immature insights, was paired with a philosophical traditionalism which in Lamennais's eyes constituted its irreducible rational foundation. Out of the genuine desire to provide the doctrine of the Church with a valid philosophical justification, he started with a theory of knowledge which, inspired by Bonald, placed the criterion of certainty in the *sensus communis* instead of with the insight of the individual and that of general reason. Lamennais saw his justification in a dimension of social reality which had been a constant part of the faith of humankind since its beginnings. For him, Catholic Christianity was its only valid form of expression. His system contained positive aspects which had been neglected in preceding centuries. These were the emphasis on the social character of religious man and on the historical perspective of the intellectual development of mankind; a demonstration of the thesis confirming the moral necessity of revelation; the thought, in contrast to the Protestant view, that tradition preceding the writing of Holy Scripture is the chief organ of revelation; and the working out of a non-a priori religious theory based on fact. But the passionate criticism of individual reason which is the basis for Lamennais's apologia contains dual dangers. One is fideism, which in the act of accepting religious faith suspends the autonomy of the individual conscience; the other is naturalism, which confuses the truths of general reason with supernaturally revealed truth and the authority of humankind with the authority of the Church.

The new system therefore not only earned the scorn of the rationalists but also the partially justified criticism of the theologians from Saint Sulpice who had remained true to the classical concepts. In more than three hundred small pamphlets the critics attempted a refutation, but they found only a small echo outside of the group of expert theologians. Their criticism was formulated in the name of a traditional and no longer living philosophy and one whose Cartesian infiltration Lamennais demonstrated with temperament. The educated public was much more re-

[26] Lamennais principally fought against "political indifference," i.e., the attitude of a state whose institutions do not rest on the voluntary and exclusive acknowledgment of Catholic truth; he did not do so merely because Catholicism through legitimizing monarchical authority formed the only firm foundation for an enduring society, but equally as much because in obligating this authority to act only in agreement with a moral law respecting the individual as a human being could freedom of conscience be effectively protected.

ceptive to the striving of Lamennais for a Catholic doctrine which would integrate the tradition of the Church with the philosophies of classical antiquity and classical religions while keeping itself open to the future. Lamennais, a self-taught man, who was "ignorant of the classics" (Lambruschini) and who stood chronologically and ideologically at the turn from the eighteenth to the nineteenth century, became the originator of a new Christian humanism. For a decade he was the leading spiritual power of the most dynamic wing of the young clergy. These young clergymen were equally interested in an unmerciful criticism of Gallicanism and in the new and more modern political theology which Lamennais presented in *De la religion considerée dans ses rapports avec l'ordre politique et civil* (1826). Lamennais's influence reached far beyond the borders of France. He had admirers not only in Belgium,[27] which was traditionally tied to France, but there was also a numerically small but highly interested public in the northern part of the Kingdom of the Netherlands,[28] in Italy,[29] and even in Germany.[30]

The dynamic effect of Lamennais on the revival of speculative theology and philosophy in France resulted not only from his writings but also from his charisma. Convinced that one of the principal causes of the inferiority of Catholics in France for the past several centuries must be seen in the cultural and scientific backwardness of the clergy, together with his brother Jean-Marie[31] he developed in 1828 the idea of a new congregation which was to take the place of the old orders which were no longer capable of meeting the needs of the time. Aware that the task surpassed the strength of any individual, he hoped to enlist the assistance of the young intellectuals who had gathered around him. Under a simple rule which would permit membership to priests as well as to laymen, the new congregation would train scholars according to the example of the Benedictines, college and seminary professors according to the model of the Jesuits and Sulpicians, and preachers according to the way of the Dominicans.

[27] The philosophy of the *sensus communis,* enthusiastically presented in the *Spectateur belge,* edited by Abbé De Foere, quickly spread in the Belgian seminaries, especially through the efforts of Abbé De Ram, the future organizer of the University of Louvain. See E. de Moreau in *NRTh* 55 (1928), 560–601; Jürgensen, 107–13; Simon, *Rencontres,* 54–56, 107–12.

[28] The spread of Lamennais's apologetics was accomplished chiefly by the publicists Broere and Le Sage ten Broek as well as by van Bommel, the future archbishop of Liège. See Vrijmoed, op. cit.

[29] See below, p. 255.

[30] See above, p. 244, footnote 10.

[31] He was of decisive importance as organizer. See Le Guillou, op. cit., 76–78 and A. Dargis, op. cit.

In order to solve the great problems of the nineteenth century through a reconciliation of science and faith, the new congregation was to intensify learning through a development of Eckstein's ideas and a reliance on German philosophy and science.[32] The scope of study was to include philosophy, theology, exegesis, Church history, languages, and all of the profane sciences including mathematics and chemistry. Within this ambitious and rather unrealistic program, ideals frequently assumed the place of clear concepts and empty phrases replaced serious scientific work. A major cause was that Lamennais and his followers "like the whole clergy in France suffered from a lack of basic education in spite of their prophetic intuitions" (Leflon), and their activity proved it. Even though Lamennais's apostasy caused the circle at La Chênaie and the Congrégation de St. Pierre to last only briefly, they did impart a lasting impulse to the intellectual revival of the French clergy. In this area, as well as in many others, Lamennais was a great initiator even though the concepts he presented did not have lasting value.

Among Lamennais's associates at La Chênaie, his closest confidant, Philippe Gerbet (1798–1864), was the outstanding theologian. His sharp intelligence impressed all who met him. As the most active promoter of the *Mémorial catholique* after 1826, Gerbet, employing Lamennais's theory of proof, developed an analysis of the act of faith which attracted the justified attention of theologians. More important was the publication of his *Considérations sur le dogme générateur de la piété catholique* (1829), a treatise of the Eucharist which was both a dogmatic and a devotional tract.[33] It was the most perfect and typical result of Lamennais's method and, according to J. R. Derré, "perhaps the chief work of piety of the romantic period." It was also the start of a comparative examination of Catholicism and Protestantism which, had it been completed, might have become the French counterpart to Möhler's *Symbolism*.

Italy: Renaissance of the Christian Philosophy

Despite the upheavals of the revolution, the ecclesiastical centers of education in Italy survived in greater numbers than in France. The scholarly tradition of the eighteenth century was continued laudably in

[32] Lamennais himself was familiar with the publications on the other side of the Rhine only second-hand through Eckstein, B. Constant, Villers, etc., but he recommended his students urgently to learn German, "a language which appears to have taken the place of Latin" (C. Sainte-Foi, *Souvenirs de jeunesse,* 125).

[33] Introduction, p. v.

the areas of patrology, epigraphics, and Near Eastern studies, but stagnated in that of theology. No rejuvenation could be expected from the northern university departments, which were strongly supervised by government. The Roman schools, reorganized by Leo XII, and especially the Gregorian University, which had been entrusted again to the Jesuits in 1824, together with the Spanish schools were almost the only ones preserving the scholastic tradition in higher education. But it was an obdurate scholasticism, corrupted by the doctrines of Locke and Condillac, whose views were very much in fashion among the Italian clergy at the beginning of the nineteenth century. Even apologetics, which had reached a high point north of the Alps, did not achieve its potential in Italy. Caught up in long-outdated polemics against Protestantism, Jansenism, and Febronianism, Italian apologetics justified the harsh remarks of Lamennais: "If I had to judge the Romans according to the books coming out of their country, I would be forced to say that they have fallen behind their society. Reading them I gain the impression that for half a century nothing has changed in the world."[34]

These conditions in Italy make understandable the enthusiastic attitude which the public held toward the work of Lamennais, which had been translated by the Neapolitan Theatine G. Ventura. The first volume of the *Essai sur l'indifférence* was received with great acclaim, and the sympathies for the author increased on the occasion of his journey to Italy in 1824. This was the case above all in Piedmont, where Lamennais and the *Mémorial catholique* were frequently and positively mentioned in the *Amico d'Italia.* Yet the effect of Lamennais in Italy must not be overstated; it was less a case of influence than of a meeting of analogous thoughts. If Lamennais's views received acceptance it was because he expressed already existing ideas more fittingly and elegantly and because he was regarded as disseminating the ideas which de Maistre had already publicized for a number of years. Lamennais was admired as the defender of the Church against revolutionary rationalism, as the champion of theocracy, as the rejuvenator of the concept of authority, and as the apologist who voiced a general agreement with religious truth. The Italians evinced more reserve toward the philosophical system which he wanted to make the foundation of his intellectual revival. The doctrine of the *sensus communis* found a few adherents, in particular Ventura, who favored it in his *De methodo philosophandi* (1828). But most others were

[34] Letter of 2 January 1821, reproduced in *Lettres et opuscules inédits du comte Joseph de Maistre* I (Paris 1873), 120–221; this judgment is confirmed by the *Memoriale* of Cardinal Pacca of 11 April 1829 (edited by P. Perali [Rome 1928]). See Gemelli-Vismara, op. cit., 20ff., 83ff. and Colapietra, 111–12.

disturbed by the unclear relationship between the authorities of Church and humankind and by the consequences of a radical rejection of the possibilities of individual reason.

Thus at the very moment when the German Catholics were fascinated by post-Kantian systems and the French for a generation were involved with traditionalism, there grew in Italy, within a scholasticism corrupted by Cartesianism and empiricism, tender shoots of a renascence of original Thomism. The center of this movement was Piacenza. There, after 1806, Canon Vincenzo Buzzetti[35] (1777–1824) taught and succeeded in winning to his ideas two young Jesuits, the brothers Sordi, and Father Taparelli d'Azeglio. The latter, rector of the *Collegium Romanum* from 1824 to 1829, attempted in vain to introduce Thomism into this citadel of Suarezianism.[36] After his "promotion" to provincial of Naples in 1831, d'Azeglio entrusted Serafino Sordi with the teaching of philosophy at the school in Naples, which henceforth became a second center of this movement.

Other Catholic thinkers in Italy did not believe, however, that a simple return to the Middle Ages would effect the liberation of the educated from the sensualism of Locke or Condillac or from the moderate rationalism of the encyclopedists. They were convinced that traditional philosophy was in need of rejuvenation. This was the path taken by Pasquale Galuppi (1770–1846), who introduced Kant to Italy. His effort was continued in comprehensive fashion by Antonio Rosmini (1797–1855), one of the best Italian metaphysicians of the nineteenth century. Rosmini also began with the suggestion of a return to Thomism, but he gradually developed a more personal system in which Thomistic elements were combined with inspirations by Plato, Augustine, Anselm of Canterbury, Leibniz, and Hegel. He was a pious and ardent priest, a champion of the Catholic cause in the north of the Italian peninsula,[37] a personal friend of Manzoni, and a skilled educator, whose *Dell'unita dell'educazione* (1826) is still regarded well today. Pius VIII encouraged Rosmini in his philosophical and theological work,

[35] There has not yet been an end to the discussion of whether Buzzetti rediscovered Thomism by himself (the view adopted in 1923 by Masnovo and Fermi and repeated by Dezza) or through his Lazarist professors at the Collegio Alberoni (the view taken by Fabro, adopted by numerous scholars, and recently defended by Rossi on the basis of hitherto important unpublished documents). Even though it must be admitted that Buzzetti in fact, albeit only to a limited degree, fell under the influence of the eclectic scholasticism taught at his time at the Collegio Alberoni and under that of the brothers Masdeu, two Spanish ex-Jesuits, the direct sources of his philosophical development seem to stem from the continuing tradition of Thomism of the Dominicans in Italy. See M. Battlori in *AHSI* 29 (1960), 180–85.

[36] He was able at least to win the brothers Pecci to his views.

[37] See above, p. 236.

and, in 1830, there appeared the first fruit of these labors, his *Nuove saggio sull'origine delle idee,* which has become his fundamental work. The first reaction to his attacks upon contemporary idols was negative on the part of shocked laymen. There soon followed attacks by Gioberti, another defender of spiritualism in Italy, who even at that time could not be regarded as a Catholic thinker, and by scholastic circles who thought they detected in Rosmini's system traces of ontologism. Yet gradually Rosmini's philosophy, modern and religious in equal measure, was accepted. This acceptance was due in large part to the ease with which Rosmini's philosophy adapted itself to many characteristics of the national temperament. Between 1830 and 1850, large numbers of Rosminic groups of priests and laymen were formed. Their members admired in him the thinker as much as the priest. In the course of time, Rosmini's ideas were taught at the universities and in numerous seminaries of Northern Italy, where they remained strongly influential until the time of Leo XIII.

PART THREE

Between the Revolutions of 1830 and 1848

Introduction

Gregory XVI

Pius VIII died on 30 November 1830, at a critical point in European history. Even if the year 1830 was not as important a turning point as 1789, 1815, and 1848, it was nevertheless a significant caesura. The July revolution in France marked the victory of the middle class and of the parliamentary system over the vain attempts to restore the Old Regime, and caused a chain reaction in Europe: from Belgium, where the Vienna settlement was first breached, to Poland, Ireland, Piedmont, the Duchies of Parma and Modena, and the Papal States. This political fermentation, which soon involved the Iberian Peninsula with its dynastic and ideological conflicts, was only the symptom of a much deeper discontent. Intelligence and fantasy had advanced faster than the general development of a world whose economic and social structures were only just beginning to change and in which large landed estates continued to play a predominant role. New ideas of freedom and justice were born and raised expectations for the future. These new ideas were expressed in liberal newspapers and pamphlets, in the systems of utopian socialism, and in romanticism, which was, as Victor Hugo explained in his foreword to *Hernani* (March 1830), only "liberalism in literature." The desire for change was an overwhelming concern of the young intellectuals, whose dreams of transformations were impossible because they did not correspond to actual power realities. These suppressed desires came to the fore at the slightest opportunities and finally exploded in 1848.

The members of the Sacred College were as little able as any other statesmen of the period to analyze the situation in ways possible to the historian of a hundred years later. But all of them sensed that the Pope whom they had to choose would have to confront a particularly difficult situation. They sought a solution in traditional approaches, especially as the two parties opposing one another at the conclave of 1829 were present in virtually unchanged strength. There were the "politicals" who were still interested in a defense of the Papal States through close cooperation with Metternich's Austria, and the "zealots," who were more interested in the independence of the Church from governments than in diplomatic combinations. Of fifty-five cardinals, thirty-four were present at the opening of the conclave on 14 December 1830. Contrary to all expectations, the conclave lasted for fifty days. Pacca's candidacy was supported by the pro-Austrian party led by the old Cardinal Albani.

Victory for Pacca seemed likely, especially as the hesitant reply given by the candidate of the "zealots," Cardinal de Gregorio, to the speech of the French ambassador, was received with disappointment and reduced his initially strong chances. On 28 December the "zealots" voted for Giustiniani, who received twenty-one votes. But on 9 January the Spanish ambassador rejected this candidate, because during his nunciature at Madrid he had defended the rights of the clergy so energetically as to arouse the hostility of the government. Now the "zealots" cast their votes for the Camaldolese Cardinal Cappellari, prefect of the Congregation for the Propagation of the Faith, who earlier had been considered one of the *papabili* but who so far had never received more than seven votes. Finally, the pro-Austrian party gave up the hope of winning a two-thirds majority for Pacca and presented Macchi as their new candidate. But his candidacy also lacked a good chance of success, as he was suspected by the French government because of his relationship with ex-King Charles X. The duel between Pacca and Cappellari continued for three weeks, in spite of the growing dissatisfaction of the Roman population and the worsening political situation in Italy. It required all of the skills of Cardinal Bernetti and the announcement of a rebellion in the Romagna to persuade Albani to give up. Thus Cappellari was elected Pope on 2 February 1831. He chose the name Gregory XVI.[1]

Bartolomeo Alberto Cappellari, known in his order as Fra Mauro, was born on 18 September 1765 at Belluno in Venetia. In 1783 he had joined the Camaldolese, the strictest offshoot of the Benedictines, and for more than a quarter of a century devoted himself to theological studies. In 1799, at the nadir of the papacy, he published *Il trionfo della Santa Sede e della Chiesa contro gli assalti dei Novatori (The Triumph of the Holy See and the Church over the Attacks by the Innovators).* Directed against Febronians and Jansenists, it was to have great influence on the development of the ultramontane movement.[2] Gradually this monk, theologian, and scholar became acquainted with the complexities of ecclesiastical affairs. After he had been sent to Rome in 1795, he became abbot of San Gregorio al Celio in 1805 and shortly afterwards procurator superior of his order. This position enabled him to show his administrative talents at a particularly difficult time. Shortly after his return to Rome in 1814, Pius VII followed the advice of Cardinal Fontana and appointed Cappellari as consultant to several congrega-

[1] The last Pope of the same name had founded the *Sacra Congregatio de Propaganda Fide* at the beginning of the seventeenth century. But the newly elected Pope surely also was thinking of Gregory the Great as well as possibly of Gregory VII, the medieval champion of freedom of the Church against the intervention of secular power.

[2] Concerning this work and its influence, see vol. VIII in this series, chap. 1, n. 1.

tions, including the Congregation for Extraordinary Ecclesiastical Affairs, and as examiner of candidates for the episcopate. After he had become vicar general of his order in 1823, Leo XII, who regarded his knowledge of doctrinal matters highly, made Cappellari a cardinal in 1826 and appointed him prefect of the Congregation for the Propagation of the Faith. As such he was concerned not only with missions in general, but also with the Churches in America, the Uniate Churches of the Near East and Russia, and Catholic affairs in England and the Netherlands. The secretary of state consulted Cappellari regularly, and frequently his opinion was decisive.

Although he had spent the greatest part of his life in a monk's cell, as Pope Cappellari was surprisingly well versed not only in the affairs of the Curia, but also with the concrete difficulties facing the Church almost everywhere. Historians, frequently more politically oriented, tended to lose sight of this aspect. Capellari was intelligent and quite capable of grasping the ramifications of problems, as long as their aspects were within the framework of his thinking, which was linked to the eighteenth century. He was also an educated man according to the standards of this century and encouraged scholarly work, especially archeological research.[3] On the other hand, this monk had difficulties in his contacts with people and hardly any sensitivity for the interests of the laity of the Papal States. This was a handicap for a Pope who also must function as a secular ruler. A further obstacle was that Cappellari knew no foreign languages, had never met any of the statesmen of his time, and did not know much about politics. This left him at the mercy of advisers who were not always either enlightened or nonpartisan. This strict theologian, who had gleaned all of his knowledge from books, was incapable of grasping the problems of the new currents swirling around him. As a man of tradition, who had lived in the climate of counterrevolution for forty years, Cappellari harbored nothing but mistrust toward the liberal aspirations of the coming new society and resolutely took the part of the defenders of the established order.[4]

One can better understand the general directions of Gregory XVI's pontificate if one keeps in mind his basic orientation. This obstinate and

[3] On this aspect of his papal activity, see in *Gregorio XVI, Miscellanea commemorativa* I, the articles by A. Bartoli, "Gregorio XVI, le antichità e belle arti" (1–98), R. Fausti, "Gregorio XVI e l'archeologia cristiana" (405–56), and by P. Perali (365–403), R. Lefèvre (223–87), and E. Josi (201–21) on the organization of the papal museum for Etruscan art in 1837, the museum for Egyptian art in 1839, and the Greco-Roman Lateran museum in 1841.

[4] The statement "One must never revolt" (*Ris* 5 [1962], 82–83), made to the Belgian envoy in 1833, is typical for him. It explains especially his conduct during the Polish rising (cf. above, pp. 156f.), for which he was criticized.

authoritarian doctrinarian, ascending the chair of Saint Peter in far better health than his predecessors, was determined to face the dangers against which the "zealots" had warned for half a century. Interested wholly in religious concerns, the Pope opposed vague romantic religiosity and, in particular, rationalistic naturalism. For the purpose of combatting them, he preferred to employ the religious orders, whose difficult rebirth he promoted with all of his strength. He saw the root of the evil from which the Church suffered in the secret societies. Therefore he charged the French writer Crétineau-Joly to prepare an exposé of their activities. Tenaciously the Pope used his magisterial office to remind people of the great traditional principles and to characterize as error whatever attempted to evade submission to the supernatural.

He also made himself the unbending defender of ecclesiastical principles and of the independence of the Church from all notions of an established Church. Energetically he opposed all governmental systems which asserted the right to subjugate the pastoral office to secular domination,[5] especially in the area of nomination of bishops. Equally energetically the Pope rejected compromises in questions involving dogmatic principles, especially in the case of mixed marriages,[6] which had been treated rather laxly by Rome for many years. With equal determination he defended the supreme authority of the Pope within the Church against all remnants of Febronianism and Gallicanism. Without realizing the anachronism of such pretensions, he systematically employed the nunciatures to obtain the acknowledgment by the Catholic governments of papal monarchy, as whose savior he saw himself ever since the publication of his *Trionfo della Santa Sede.*[7] Sharing the shortsightedness of the "zealots" concerning the changes modern society was undergoing; incapable of recognizing the weakness of the political and social system of the Old Regime, which he regarded as an expression of divine will; and haunted by the thought that the Papal States, in which he saw the guarantee for the spiritual independence of the Pope, could be destroyed by liberal aspirations, Gregory XVI was determined to mobilize all means at the disposal of the reviving papacy in order to stop all

[5] Encyclical *Commissum divinitus* of 17 May 1835 (Roskovany IV, 134).

[6] In addition to the affairs at Cologne and Gnesen (see below, pp. 331–34), the most spectacular events, Gregory XVI repeatedly referred to this question: Encyclical of 27 May 1832 (A. Bernasconi, op. cit. I, 140ff.); letter of 8 February 1836 (id. II, 97f.); brief of 9 February 1839 (id. II, 292ff.); letter of 30 November 1839 (id. II, 385f.); instructions of 30 April and 22 May 1841 (id. III, 122ff., 132ff.); and letter of 23 May 1846 (id. III, 357f.).

[7] Concerning this new policy, see the comments by A. Simon, "Signification politique de la nonciature de Bruxelles" in *BIHBR* 33 (1961), 617–48.

further advances of the "revolution." For the same reasons the Pope obstinately refused to cooperate with any "subversive forces," even in Poland and Ireland, where they seemed to work toward the liberation of Catholics.

The pontificate of Gregory XVI appears as a "pontificate of struggle" (Pouthas), in the service of a conservative, even a reactionary, ideal. Thus it is not astonishing that in contrast to the events half a century later under Leo XIII, laity and clergy engaged in initiatives aimed at a reconciliation of the Church with modern society without the participation of the papacy. They provided Catholicism with a face totally different from that of 1815. Among many people the impression grew that a new and more progressive attitude prevailed, and it is this impression which explains the many illusions during the first months of Pius IX's pontificate.

During the fifteen years in which Gregory XVI guided the fortunes of the Church, such a development was possible not only because the Holy See—in contrast to the subsequent pontificate—was not yet able effectively to restrain the tendencies of which it disapproved. It was also possible because the work of Gregory XVI had many positive aspects which were directed toward the future; so much so that in more than one case Pius IX only needed to pluck the fruits of the patient preparations undertaken by his predecessor. For example, the former prefect of the Congregation for the Propagation of the Faith gave new impulses to missionary work, even if these impulses are overrated by most historians. In addition to this frequently mentioned aspect there were others which many liberal historians tended to overlook. Gregory XVI's battle against the excesses of rationalism, indifferentism, and Kantian subjectivism helped to achieve a balance between the sense of the supernatural and the value of human reason, and thus laid the firm foundations for the future development of the Catholic spirit and Catholic spirituality. By insisting inflexibly on the prerogatives of the Holy See and the independence of the Church, however, the Pope also prepared the way for those future successes of ultramontanism which ultimately stifled pluralism and endangered the collegial nature of ecclesiastical authority.

The immediate effect of Gregory's position, however, was the overcoming of that ecclesiastical nationalism in which the autonomy won by the regional Churches with respect to Rome had to be paid for with the submission of the Church to secular power. On the other hand, it must not be forgotten that in spite of the unyielding nature of the Camaldolese Pope, Gregory could be flexible in the practical applications of his principles. He proved this, for example, in the events at Cologne when he agreed to the dismissal of Archbishop Clemens August von Droste zu Vischering after the archbishop had gained his objectives;[8] by supporting Louis-Philippe in the Guillon affair in 1831; and by the temporary expulsion of the Jesuits in 1845.[9] In addition, many "zealots" had accused Cardinal Cappellari before the papal election of being too soft with respect to the Protestants in the negotiations for a concordat with King William I of the Netherlands. In addition to these special cases, Gregory XVI demonstrated his suppleness in his Bull *Sollicitudo Ecclesiarum* of 7 August 1831. Although personally holding the legitimist view, he declared that in case of changes of political regimes the Holy See would negotiate with the governments in de facto possession of power.[10] He employed this principle in the delicate case of the new South American republics, which had been a continuing problem for his three predecessors. Here, as well as with respect to the problem caused by the passing of a liberal constitution[11] in Catholic Belgium, the Pope understood how to apply in practical terms the famous difference between "thesis" and "hypothesis," even before it was coined. Monsignor Simon even wrote that occasionally Gregory XVI showed himself "not as a Pope of the past, but as a Pontiff introducing the future." Such characterization is misleading, for it must not be forgotten that Gregory XVI agreed to such political accommodations only with extreme reluctance and attempted to limit them as far as possible.

The Pope showed the same ambivalence with respect to past and future in the selection of his assistants and advisers. Cappellari, counted among the "zealots," chose as his first secretary of state a former associate and friend of Consalvi. Cardinal Bernetti[12] was a man of the world, little concerned with the religious aspect of problems, a pure technician of politics and diplomacy, who clearly recognized the deficiencies in the administration of the Papal States. Metternich valued his "knowledge of the needs of the time," while Lamennais accused him of giving in too much to the demands of governments.[13] But, formed in the atmosphere

[8] Below, p. 335.

[9] See J. P. Martin, *La nonciature de Paris* (Paris 1949), 127, 130, 354.

[10] Text in A. Bernasconi I, 38ff.; commentary in Leflon, 453–54.

[11] See below, pp. 279ff.

[12] Tommaso Bernetti (1779–1852) was an energetic, selfless, and intelligent man, albeit with a rather limited horizon, and occasionally very impulsive. As governor of Rome and director of police he had demonstrated that he could be forceful without brutality. After he had been secretary of state for a few months under the pontificate of Leo XII, he acted during the conclave as the head of the group opposing Albani's pro-Austrian policy. See *ECatt*, 1443–44 and *DBI* IX, 338–43 (Lit.). A good study is E. Morelli, *La politica estera di Tommaso Bernetti* (Rome 1953). Nothing, however, is available on his entire Church policy.

[13] J. R. Derré, *Metternich et Lamennais* (Paris 1963), 27.

of the first Roman restoration following the Jacobin interlude, Bernetti shared with the "zealots" the resolute hostility to liberal political regimes and the conviction that the only hope for a continuation of the Papal States rested in a conservative policy.

The growing opposition of the College of Cardinals, which accused Bernetti of attempting—like Consalvi—to centralize all power in his hands,[14] caused Gregory XVI to dismiss him in 1836.[15] His next choice, Cardinal Lambruschini,[16] was a man of totally different character, a strictly pious son of the Church. Like the Pope himself, he sympathized with the pastoral aspect of problems and was closely allied with the Jesuits. But he belonged to those members of the Curia who most resolutely closed their minds to modern ideas. Yet if he was a reactionary as a result of his innate personality and his development, and very much intent on fighting unmercifully any legacies of the revolution, his diplomatic experience had taught him that in practice he must moderate the rigidity of his principles. This showed itself in the administration of the Papal States, whose harsh police regime has been exaggerated, as well as in his general ecclesiastical policy which, when necessary, he adapted to constitutional conditions.

One must also take into account that Gregory XVI, to a far higher degree than his predecessors, personally participated in the conduct of papal affairs. He worked hard and in addition to his secretaries also relied on other advisers. Lützow noted in 1833 that Bernetti complained that the decisions of the Pope did not always agree with his suggestions and that the Pope allowed himself to be influenced by more rigorous prelates.[17] On the other hand, Monsignor Simon has reported

[14] An accusation which was not quite justified. See L. Pásztor in *AHPont* 6 (1968), 269–70. It must be added that the mediocrity of the higher Roman prelates noted by several observers (for example, Lützow in H. Bastgen, op. cit., 240, or Bautain in P. Poupard, *Journal romain de l'abbé L. Bautain 1838* [Rome 1964], 31) in part explains the decline of the influence of the college of cardinals.

[15] Concerning Bernetti's fall, in which Austrian intrigues apparently played a lesser role than has hitherto been assumed, see E. Morelli, op. cit., 156–68; E. Morelli in *ChStato* II, 559–60; N. Nada, *Metternich e le riforme nello Stato Pontificio* (Turin 1957), 170–87; and H. Bastgen, op. cit., 2.

[16] Concerning Luigi Lambruschini (1776–1854)—Barnabite, theologian, archbishop of Genoa (1819–27), nuncio in France (1827–31), where he was intimately involved in the Lamennais affair, prefect of the SC Stud. (1831–36), where he demonstrated that he opposed new currents of thought—see L. Manzini, *Il Cardinale Lambruschini* (together with *RStRis* 48 [1961], 319–24); *ECatt* VII, 844–45; *DThC* VIII, 2471–73; M. A. Giampaolo, "La preparazione politica del cardinale Lambruschini" in *RStRis* 18 (1931), 81–163; E. Piscitelli in *RStRis* 40 (1953), 158–82; F. Andreu, "Il cardinale Lambruschini e il P. Ventura" in *Regnum Dei* 10 (1954), 219–49; G. Bofitto, *Scrittori barnabiti* II, (Florence 1933), 312–36.

[17] H. Bastgen, op. cit., 237–38.

that the influence of Monsignor Capaccini, the deputy secretary of state and a man more open to modern currents, occasionally outweighed Lambruschini's.[18] This does not alter the fact that Lambruschini was chiefly responsible for the immobility characterizing the last years of the pontificate of Gregory XVI in many areas. It contrasted glaringly with the vitality which the Catholic Church outside of Rome displayed at this same time.

[18] *Documents relatifs à la nonciature de Bruxelles* (Brussels-Rome 1958) 12.—Concerning Franceso Capaccini (1784–1845), former secretary of Consalvi, deputy of the state secretariat from 1831–37, then secretary of the *Sacra Congregatio pro Negotiis Ecclesiasticis extraordinariis* from 1839–44—see *Biographie Nationale* XXX (Brussels 1958), 262–64.

SECTION ONE

The First Phase of Catholic Liberalism

In the eyes of the Catholics of the restoration period, liberal concepts were identified with the revolution and needed to be rooted out. In France, the last remaining sympathies disappeared which a number of the Constituent clergy held for the liberal ideas of the eighteenth century. But around 1830, when in all of Europe the majority of the priests and of the faithful continued to see salvation for the Church exclusively in a restoration of the political conditions of the Old Regime and in the reconquest of the privileged position of the Church in society, a growing number of young clergymen and laymen began to question this course. Fascinated by the mysticism of freedom which jointly inspired the writers and artists of romanticism, liberal conspirators, and people opposed to the Holy Alliance, they began to wonder about the possibility of reconciling Catholicism with liberalism to a certain extent and, without betraying their own faith, of accepting a social order based on the principles of 1789. These principles were: personal freedom in place of despotism; political freedoms which were no longer conceded privileges but legally anchored; the right of peoples to self-determination; primacy of the principle of nationality over the principle of legitimacy; and, in the area directly concerning religious life, freedom of the press and freedom of religion together with a limitation of ecclesiastical privileges, possibly even separation of Church and state.

Some promoted the reconciliation of Church and liberalism for practical reasons. For them it was either a means of winning the young intellectuals back to the Church or an unavoidable necessity in light of irreversible developments which should be adapted in the best possible way to the interests of the Church. Some voiced the thought that in countries with a Protestant or Orthodox majority and in which Catholics were the victims of a system of established religions, the introduction of a more liberal government would result in noticeable advantages for the Catholics. Others pointed out that the same advantages would accrue in Catholic countries in which regalistic governments posed serious obstacles to the work of the Church. Thinking that from the apostolic point of view liberal institutions were to be preferred to the protectionism to which the union of throne and altar frequently degenerated, they believed it to be necessary not merely to tolerate the contemporary movement but to encourage it. In fact, where it had not yet started, they thought it ought to be provoked. Others favored closer relations between Church and liberalism for reasons of principle. They shared the optimistic confidence of the philosophes of the eighteenth century in man's potential and regarded the development of society in a liberal direction as progress. Put differently, they regarded the democratic ideal which inspired the liberals as a realization of the message of the Gospel which invites the replacement of the inequality of conditions with the equality of nature and the domination of a few with the freedom for all. Others would soon go even further and want to introduce liberal ideas in the Church itself: less authoritarian relations between bishops and flock; greater autonomy of Catholic thinkers with respect to the official theological systems; greater leeway for the clergy in relation to traditional pastoral methods. No matter of what type the concrete applications might be, they were fundamentally an outgrowth of the same freedom which inspired the reform efforts of Hirscher in Tübingen, of Raffaele Lambruschini and Rosmini in Italy, and of Lamennais in France.

This general movement, comprising some very different tendencies, was called "Catholic liberalism" or "liberal Catholicism." It was to develop into one of the main problems, especially in the Latin countries, which agitated Catholics throughout the nineteenth century. The solution was the more difficult as the liberals, when the ecclesiastical authorities refused to follow the path suggested by them, now became emphatic in their anticlericalism. In their eyes, the Church was the main obstacle to political freedom, intellectual liberation, and progress in general. This attitude in turn stiffened the backs of the leaders of the Church, who saw themselves confirmed in their view of the incompatibility of the Church with those forces which, in collaboration with Freemasons and the heirs of the philosophes of the eighteenth century, wished to overturn the established religious and political order.

For a long time, Lamennais was considered to be the founder of Catholic liberalism. He was seen as the first person who with prophetic vision had enunciated the advantages which would accrue to the Church once it entered the arena of modern liberties. More recent examinations have brought forth a more differentiated picture. It was recognized that for several years prior to Lamennais others in France had begun to develop analogous ideas. This is true especially for Eckstein, who produced some of the first followers of Lamennais. The examinations undertaken by A. Simon and H. Haag and confirmed by K. Jürgensen have also definitively proven that the connection between Catholicism and modern liberties was systematically established in Belgium between 1825 and 1828. It did not, as had been assumed, receive its impulses from Lamennais's theories. On the contrary, the practical union between Belgian Catholics and liberals influenced the intellectual development of Lamennais. Yet Lamennais's ingenious intuition immediately grasped that the new procedure used by the Belgians to solve specific problems could be applied generally. He developed it into a theoretical system which included a new social philosophy, and he did not hesitate to urge the Church to follow the movement which was pushing nations toward democracy. By placing his considerable reputation in the service of this idea, he obtained for it the widespread attention which it had hitherto lacked. In this respect he continues to deserve to occupy a leading position in the beginnings of Catholic liberalism.

CHAPTER 16

From Belgian Unionism to the Campaign of L'Avenir

The Decision of Belgian Catholics in Favor of Liberty

Belgian Catholics in general and the clergy in particular had shown themselves very reactionary in 1815. The episcopate had gone so far as to forbid the oath of the constitution because it proclaimed freedom of the press and freedom of religion. This attitude had only served to increase the hostility of the liberals toward the clergy, which appeared to them as the defender of an anachronistic theocracy.

The remarkable aspect of the campaign ten years later against the seminary decrees of June 1825[1] was that, while it rested on an appeal to the right of the Church to train its priests, it soon took on broader outlines. At the end of 1825, Catholic parliamentarians and journalists liked to refer to constitutional freedoms. They demanded freedom of education as a natural extension of the freedom of conscience, and called for the independence of the Church from any governmental interference in the appointment of ecclesiastical dignitaries in the name of religious freedom. Publicists eventually discovered in freedom of the press the best protection against arbitrary governmental actions to which the Catholics were exposed. Even in entering this arena, though, the Catholics did not renounce their principles, which were very different from the ideals of the liberals who desired an increasing laicization of society. But in order to safeguard the permanent goal of instilling Christian values in public life, the Catholics considered it more realistic to resort to means other than those of the Old Regime. The Catholic view could be summarized as follows: In a parliamentary state, guaran-

[1] See above, pp. 144f.

teeing freedom of education and the press, Catholics would have the unrestricted right to influence consciences and to gain predominance legally. Laws passed by a majority would then enable them to construct a Christian society which heretofore had always depended exclusively on the good will of a Catholic sovereign.

In the course of 1826 the two most important Catholic newspapers began to emphasize the advantages of liberty; cautiously in the case of the *Courrier de la Meuse,* animated by Pierre Kersten of Liège, and with greater emphasis by the *Catholique des Pays-Bas* of Ghent. Adolphe Bartels used it to say that truth could prevail without official protection, and that the political desire of the liberals to have a government which expressed the will of the citizens and was no longer the governing instrument of a monarch was compatible with Catholic orthodoxy.

With the Catholics embarking on this course, some young liberals became convinced that the tactic of the old freethinkers of supporting the government in its chicanery of the Church was nothing more than a fool's paradise, as it enabled the government to pursue a policy of enlightened despotism. They considered it more important to oppose the absolutist tendencies of the monarchical government than to stifle the Church at any price. They thought of offering the Catholics a broad-based alliance on the following quid pro quo basis: We renounce any exclusion of the Church from education or any control over its activity aimed at limiting its influence on society; you, in turn, will no longer attempt to reach a privileged position in the state by way of a concordat or any other method, and will join us in demanding the exercise of modern freedoms.

When Devaux made this liberal appeal in the spring of 1827, many Catholics hesitated. At that very time they thought that they could reach a separate agreement with the King. They believed that they could achieve the most important of their demands on the basis of the concordat of 18 June 1827 without having to make common cause with the liberals. But when it became clear four months later that the government was delaying an agreement,[2] they began to have second thoughts. On 1 November the *Courrier de la Meuse* agreed to Devaux's offer and during 1828 the idea of a union of Catholics and liberals on the basis of the mutual demand for constitutional freedoms became widely accepted in the country, especially in Flanders. It did so without arousing the opposition of the clergy, which hated the government more than it disliked the liberals. Publicly the ecclesiastical authorities were reserved, but basically they viewed the development approvingly in spite

[2] See above, p. 146.

of the warnings of internuncio Capaccini, who was horrified by the "monstrous alliance" between Catholics and liberals.

Hence by the end of 1828 Catholics had been won for "unionism," i.e., for the tactic of uniting with the liberals in order to demand the independence of the Church on the basis of modern liberty and its right to establish an educational system directed exclusively by itself. Can one say that from this moment on they became the "liberal Catholics" who favored those theories which Lamennais presented two years later in *L'Avenir?* That would simplify matters too much. The unionists of 1828 in reality regarded their alliance with the liberals and the acceptance of the liberal viewpoint only as a provisional arrangement and not as a system representing a permanent ideal. They had no intention, as Lamennais was to do soon, to speak of a "natural alliance between Catholicism and democracy," nor to raise their demands for freedom to the point of a complete separation of Church and state. Matters were very clear for the ecclesiastical authorities as well as for the young noblemen of the Robiana-Merode group, whose real intentions were revealed in their private papers. In no way did they favor the principles of 1789; on the contrary, they wished to have the Church once again assume the spiritual control of civil society. De Gerlache and Kersten also insisted on avoiding an overemphasis of human rights. They were unwilling to accept the principle of popular sovereignty, just as much as they viewed the union with the liberals merely as the smaller of two evils, dictated by the circumstances. To be sure, Bartels—with the approval of a number of Flemish clerics—continued to be progressive and in 1828 developed several theses which appeared in the writings of Lamennais in the following year. One of them was that the people had primacy over the King, but he qualified this by saying that he desired general liberty not as an inherent good but as the smaller evil. This was still quite different from the demand for liberty for its own sake, as *L'Avenir* was to champion it later. But the positions assumed by the Belgian Catholics in their opposition to William I were by themselves and in spite of their limited character a revelation for Lamennais.

Lamennais's Development as a Liberal

Lamennais, the reactionary editor of the *Conservateur* and the *Drapeau blanc,* appeared hardly destined to become the leader of Catholic liberalism. During the first decade of the restoration[3] he was one of the most ardent advocates of a return to the Old Regime. His ideal of a

[3] Concerning Lamennais and his activity during these years, see above, pp. 232–35, 251–54.

protected Church in a divine-right monarchy was opposed to a free Church in a free state. When in 1826 in his book *De la Religion considerée dans ses rapports avec l'ordre politique* he advised the Church to cast itself free from the Bourbon regime, he did so because he thought that its compromises with liberalism would destroy it. His ideal was still a Christian, nay, a theocratic state.

Christian Maréchal[4] believed to have discovered several indications proving that Lamennais's turn to liberalism had started as early as 1820. True, the seed of change can be seen in his Bretonic temperament with its inherent desire for independence, his disgust with any type of absolutism, and his great concern for the spiritual freedom of Christians and the independence of the Church in the wake of anti-Gallican struggles. But Maréchal attached a meaning to these elements which they did not have in their contemporary context. Although in his articles Lamennais often wrote of freedom, and although his ultramontanism was based, as A. Simon and G. Verucci have shown, on the idea of freedom, he meant the freedom of the Christian against the powers of evil and the freedom of the Church with respect to the government. It was not, as Jürgensen states, a freedom for all, "but a freedom without toleration." In his writings before 1828 there is no sympathy for political liberalism or democracy. But Maréchal was quite correct in pointing out that during this period Lamennais thought more theocratically than monarchically. From this vantage point it becomes understandable that—once he grew disillusioned with monarchy—he found it easy to turn away from it. He associated the Church with the growing cause of the people and strove to achieve what Verucci has called a "democratic theocracy." In this perspective, illustrated by a few examples from the Middle Ages to Pius VII, the Pope appears as the protector of the weak and as the arbiter guaranteeing right over might. This development must have come about the more easily as Lamennais had already demonstrated in his apologetics the extent to which he understood the mentality of his time and the necessity to adapt to it.[5]

The struggles for the independence of the Church, especially in the field of education, brought Lamennais to a tentative acceptance of the idea of separation of Church and state. He openly defended it in his

[4] Especially in *La dispute de "l'Essai sur l'indifférence"* (Paris 1925) VIII, 443 and *passim* and in *Lamennais au "Drapeau blanc"* (Paris 1946), where he "discovers the ultra behind the democrat" (Moreau).

[5] He provides proof for this adaptability in his *Mémoire confidentiel à Léon XII,* written at the beginning of 1827, in which he points to the danger in allowing the Church to appear "as the natural ally of all kinds of despotism" (Text of the first chapters in A. Blaise, *Œuvres inédites de Lamennais* II, 311–40, and of the last two chapters in *RSR* 1 [1910], 476–85).

book *De la Religion* (1825/26), at the same time as he began to develop the thesis that truth was more powerful than institutions. Strengthened in this idea by the writings of Eckstein and Benjamin Constant and especially by the example of foreign countries (the United States, Ireland, and especially Belgium, where for their defense the Catholics did not appeal to protection by the state but to the principle of freedom), Lamennais frequently mentioned his idea in his correspondence during the following months. At the same time he discovered in Paris in the newspaper *Le Globe* a less antireligious liberalism, which demanded not additional supervision of the Church but "all freedoms for all."

Under the impact of these diverse influences, Lamennais in February 1829 published his book *Des progrès de la Révolution et de la guerre contre l'Église.* He still regarded an ultramontane Catholicism as the only solution for society, and rejected liberalism, statism, and secularism. But he also touched upon a number of new ideas. Liberalism, he wrote, could be different from the way it presented itself in France at the time, and there was an essential inner connection between Catholicism and a healthy liberalism which aimed at the liberation of people from any suppression by other people. He stated that freedom of the press was a small evil and could be advantageous for the Church, and that revolutions could be instruments of providence for the purpose of discarding a number of antiquated institutions under which the Church had suffered for a long time.

The book was a great success, and even if it encountered the violent opposition of royalists, jurists, and the episcopate, it confirmed his position in the eyes of his young followers, who to an increasing degree were disgruntled with the compromises the bishops made with the royal government. With rather romantic optimism they concluded that only a few gestures by the Church were required to give liberalism a different turn and to place this growing force in the service of the Catholic apostolate. They expressed these sentiments with increasing vehemence in their journals *Mémorial catholique* and *Revue catholique.* The evolution of the events in Belgium only confirmed them in these beliefs and soon they no longer hesitated to go even further than the Belgians and to assert that the alliance between Catholicism and liberalism was the only way of salvation for the Church.

These ideas fell on prepared soil.[6] Baron Eckstein in his journal *Le Catholique* emphasized the "admirable alliance" between Catholicism and a regime of political liberty.[7] Historians have not properly gauged the influence which he thereby exercised on a part of Parisian Catholic

[6] M. Prélot, op. cit., 53–72.

[7] See J. R. Derré, op. cit., 156–66, 199–206.

youth. Young noblemen, who had worked with him and hardly ever had had contact with Lamennais, founded the *Correspondant*[8] in March 1829. In it they declared themselves in favor of religious freedom for Protestants, which Lamennais had rejected, demanded the right for members of orders to join together, emphasized freedom of education independent from a state monopoly, and pointed to the dangers of too close a relationship between throne and altar. They did not go as far as Lamennais's followers later in demanding a complete separation of state and Church and a complete cessation of Church support in the state budget. It was these young people from the *Correspondant* who first received the appellation "liberal Catholics" from the editors of the *Globe* with whom they had opened a dialogue.

The July Revolution of 1830 and the outbreak of anticlericalism associated with it confirmed Lamennais and his followers in their conviction. The Church should welcome those political forms of government which replaced arbitrary action with control by the people, in order both to avoid accusations against it and to provide these new forms of government "with a soul." In the face of the hostile attitude of the government, separation of Church and state was more imperative than ever.

Harel de Tancrel, a young convert, suggested to Abbé Gerbet, Lamennais's most important assistant, the creation of a newspaper for the purpose of publicizing these views. Lamennais liked the idea greatly; even though he did not accept the position of editor, he settled near Paris at the Collège Juilly in order to be able to keep a close eye on it. On 20 August Gerbet announced the impending publication, an announcement which was received enthusiastically.[9] Among the supporters were most notably the young Charles Montalembert,[10] Abbé Lacordaire, and the economist Charles de Coux. On 16 October 1830,

[8] This group has been examined much less than the followers of Lamennais. See L. de Carné, *Souvenirs de ma jeunesse* (Paris 1873); E. Trogan in *Le Correspondant* 315 (1929), 5–13; L. C. Gimpfl, *The "Correspondant"* (Washington 1959), 2–8; see also the unpublished dissertation by Mother Flavia-Augustina, "*Le Correspondant,* liberal Catholic Review, 1829–55" (Catholic University of America 1958) and the unpublished work by J. Darmon, "Le groupe du premier *Correspondant* 1829–31" (Sorbonne 1959).

[9] Text in *Articles de "L'Avenir"* I, i–viii.

[10] Concerning Charles de Montalembert (1810–70), the well-documented but one-sided biography by Lecanuet (3 vol., Paris 1895/1902) is to be complemented by A. Trannoy, *Le romantisme politique de Montalembert avant 1843* (Paris 1942); P. de Lallemand, *Montalembert et ses amis dans le romantisme* (Paris 1927); A. Schnütgen in *AHVNrh* 148 (1949), 62–144; Lösch, 138–75. See also C. Trannoy, *Montalembert, Dieu et la liberté* (Paris 1970). Works: *Œuvres de Montalembert,* 9 vol. (Paris 1860/68; see *DThC* X, 2344–55) and *Les Moines d'Occident,* 7 vol. (Paris 1860/77). Letters: *LThK* VII, 294.

the first issue of *L'Avenir* saw the light of day with a lead article from the pen of Lamennais.[11]

The name of the paper said much, but even more its motto: "God and Liberty." The paper intended to fight a two-front war. On the one hand it gave the liberals the assurance to support impartially and enthusiastically the freedoms announced by the revolution of 1789. This was to be valid for all freedoms, however, including that of education, which many liberals were reluctant to concede for fear of aiding and abetting ultramontane propaganda. On the other hand, *L'Avenir* tried to make Catholics and clergy understand that it was time to dissociate themselves from the Old Regime and to turn to the future for the creation of a new humanism. The comprehensive attempt to rejuvenate Catholic thought and action, incorporating the new artistic, scientific, and democratic trends of the time, explains the attraction of this paper and its founder for many young people. A decided turn to modernity became indeed evident in all areas. *L'Avenir* proved itself open to the new romantic literature;[12] it demanded general disarmament and the unification of Europe;[13] and it supported the national revolts of the Belgians, the Irish, and the Poles in the name of the right of peoples to self-determination.[14] Increasingly it accepted universal franchise and republican government,[15] and emphasized the providential character of the revolutions then shaking Europe. It also displayed an open mind with respect to social democracy[16] and underscored the connection between the independence of the Church and its voluntary poverty, as only through it could it feel solidarity with all of humankind and become meaningful to common and oppressed people.

On the political and religious level, *L'Avenir* at first limited itself to praising the regime of liberty and the separation—or better, the differentiation—of Church and state as the most suitable springboard for winning back the faithless. The paper presented this relationship

[11] On the campaign of *L'Avenir* see especially Lecanuet, *Montalembert* I, 152–218, *DThC* IX, 527–45, and M. Prélot, op. cit., 84–109; and for the facts, in addition to the biographies of Lamennais, C. de Ladoue, *Mgr. Gerbet* (Paris 1872), I, 176–207, Lecanuet, op. cit., 132–51, 219–68, and A. Trannoy, *Le romantisme,* 143–62. Also *Procès de "L'Avenir"* (Paris 1831).

[12] J. R. Derré, op. cit., 529–614.

[13] M. Prélot, op. cit., 102–09.

[14] But he was much more reserved with respect to the revolts in Spain and Italy, plotted by secret societies of Jacobin tendencies, which appeared to him to go counter to the true spirit of liberalism as it developed in America. See G. Verucci in *RSIt* 67 (1955), 31–51.

[15] See the introduction by G. Verucci, *L'Avenir,* XIII–LXIV.

[16] See Duroselle, 36–59.

between Church and state as a necessity, without, however, accepting it as the ideal. It demanded the renunciation of the concordat, because in a society "which God had forgotten" it actually hindered the freedom of the Pope and bishops. If the clergy were rid of this unholy tie, Catholicism would experience a new awakening, as Ireland had shown. By the spring and summer of 1831, the paper progressed to an acceptance of the liberal system as the ideal form of government for a mature society.

While the paper, whose circulation never exceeded three thousand, day by day spread its ideas with a zeal which cared little for concrete conditions, Lacordaire, Montalembert, and de Coux, not satisfied with a mere campaign of ideas, established a "general agency for the defense of religious freedom."[17] It organized in the provinces a systematic campaign of influencing public opinion, attacking administrative chicanery about which Catholics had reason to complain, especially in the field of education. By doing so legally with small groups of people in the name of constitutional liberties, they succeeded in gaining the sympathies of the young clergy and in shaking a relatively large number of laity out of its lethargy.

Following a suggestion by the Dutch journalist Le Sage ten Broek, the campaign was quickly expanded to foreign countries, where it appealed for support of Catholics in Ireland, Poland, Germany, and the Netherlands. With the intention of creating genuine international solidarity in obtaining religious and political freedoms, and of opposing the Holy Alliance of Kings with a "Holy Alliance of Peoples," *L'Avenir* on 15 November 1831 published the draft of an "Act of Union, to be submitted to all who, despite the murder of Poland, still hope for freedom in the world and want to bring it about."[18] It was a manifesto which governments interpreted as an instrument of international revolution.

To what extent were the religious-political ideas propagated by *L'Avenir* accepted in the neighboring countries? In Germany, Lamennais's philosophy was received with interest by the Munich group, but the leaders of the Catholic movement regarded the attempt to come to an accommodation with liberalism with suspicion.[19] In Italy, the conservative Catholics who once had acclaimed the defender of throne and altar rejected his ideas. Liberal Catholics were disappointed by the ultramon-

[17] Statutes in *Articles de "L'Avenir"* I, 456–58. Lamennais's role in this campaign, planned and executed by his assistants, was a secondary one, as he was not a man of action.

[18] *Articles de "L'Avenir"* VII, 176–85.

[19] The influence of Lamennais in Germany has hardly been touched (the work by L. Ahrens, *La Mennais und Deutschland* examines only the German influence on Lamennais). See some references in J. R. Derré, op. cit., 461–92, Schnabel, *G* IV, 181–202, and Lösch, 88–137.

tane doctrines of *L'Avenir* and its defense of the secular power of the Pope; some members of orders, though, especially in Tuscany (with the exception of Father Ventura), greeted them with approval.[20] In Holland, on the other hand, the campaign of *L'Avenir* was observed with wide acclaim. It was a justification for those who, in a country with a Catholic minority, had discovered the advantages of religious freedom while they lived under the French regime. In addition to Le Sage ten Broek, the publicist Broere and the Redemptorist Bernard Haskenscheid supported Lamennais.[21] But nowhere was the influence of *L'Avenir* greater and more effective than in Belgium.

The Belgian Constitution of 1831

Until the beginning of 1831, unionism was for Belgian Catholics nothing more than a tactic, a temporary coalition, from which they expected to derive the greatest possible advantages; as a purely empirical innovation it owed nothing to Lamennais. After the publication of *Progrès de la Révolution,* which in Belgium generated an unbelievable echo because a man as famous as Lamennais used Belgium as an example, a goodly number of Catholics began to hold a different view.[22] Inspired by the recent publications by Lamennais and his associates, many people came to the conclusion that a regime of modern freedoms was inherently the best form of government. It corresponded to the wishes of the people in accordance with the principle of *vox populi vox Dei* and the views of philosophical traditionalism, and provided the essential connection between Christianity and freedom. Hence, on the eve of the September revolution of 1830, several currents of thought were in evidence among Belgian Catholics. There was the group around Lamennais, numerically clearly in the minority, which with its enthusiasm soon infected the majority of Catholics and was instrumental in renewing the somewhat loosened bonds between Catholicism and liberalism. In the group, swelling from month to month, especially in Flanders and around Tournai, were laymen as well as priests. The latter had more confidence in their faith, which had survived recent persecutions, than in the protection

[20] See A. Gambaro, "La fortuna di Lamennais in Italia" in *Studi francesi* 2 (1958), 198–219.

[21] See F. Vrijmoed, *Lamennais avant sa défection et la Néerlande catholique* (Paris 1930), to be complemented by G. Gorris, *J. Le Sage ten Broek* II, (Amsterdam 1949).

[22] H. Haag, A. Simon, and K. Jürgensen agree in a number of important points, but their opinions differ about the extent of the ties between the Belgian Catholics and liberalism: Is there an ideological growth or did they stop, as Haag thinks, with the simple tactic introduced in 1828? See especially H. Haag in *RHE* 54 (1959), 593–98 and A. Simon in *Revue belge de philosophie et d'histoire* 37 (1959), 408–18.

offered by the civil powers. Without completely identifying with the liberals, they shared their admiration for the opportunities offered by liberty in apostolic and political respects. Some of them openly acknowledged themselves as democrats or republicans. In opposition to episcopal directives they emphasized their personal freedom of interpretation in matters of theological tradition as long as defined dogmas were not involved. The followers of Lamennais were joined by many other liberal Catholics who actually admired English institutions more than Lamennais's thought.

There were also numerous conservatives who were unionists only from necessity. Unwilling to concede the natural character of an alliance between Catholicism and liberalism, they instead, as loyal monarchists, hoped for a quick return to the old unity of throne and altar.

Between these two extremes stood the Mechelen group.[23] Numerically it was very small, but it became very influential through the support of the archbishop of the Belgian Church, the strong personality of his vicar general Sterckx, and the new bishop of Liège, Van Bommel. Their thought also spread to other dioceses. Although showing sympathies for Lamennais's theories, the adherents of this third group, relatively strongly represented in the clergy, were not persuaded by them. Quite realistically they concluded that a return to the Old Regime was no longer possible in view of the revolution which thinking had undergone. In fact, such a return was no longer even desirable, as a close connection between Church and state invariably produced secular interference in ecclesiastical matters which, as the experience of the past fifty years had demonstrated, quickly became intolerable. Mutual independence of the two forces seemed preferable, and all religious communities should be afforded religious freedom. The decision for freedom was not taken in the name of Lamennais's demand for a total separation of Church and state. The Mechelen group attempted to combine the advantages of the liberal system and the Old Regime in keeping with Van Bommel's view, who was thinking chiefly of financial subsidies, that "freedom should not exclude protection, and protection should not stifle freedom."

The Dutch-Belgian union came to an end in September 1830, after a revolution which had been made by people who generally were not

[23] See *Collectanea Mechliniensia* 22 (1952), 349–64. The conceptions of this group find expression in the voluminous correspondence held in the archives of the archbishopric of Mechelen and in the Rijksarchief at The Hague, as well as in a brochure by C. Van Bommel published in October 1829: *Système de liberté illimitée des cultes et des opinions religieuses.*

strong in their faith[24] and whose outbreak the majority of the clergy had observed with concern. Now a constitution for the new state had to be drafted. The bishops did everything in their power to assure that the constituent assembly had a Catholic majority.[25] But many of the elected Catholics, open to the ideas of Lamennais, were more than ready to trust completely in liberty. The Mechelen group, however, which desired a certain protection of the Church within the framework of religious freedom, attempted to amend the first draft of the constitution with this objective. In November it published the brochure *Considérations sur la liberté religieuse, par une unioniste.* It received widespread attention and was supported a month later in a letter from Archbishop de Méan to the president of the national congress.

The letter was well received, as it proved in a semi-official manner that the Belgian Church abjured the system of an established Church and unequivocally accepted the notion of freedom. But the atmosphere of the national congress, and the Catholics represented in it, was too strongly influenced by Lamennais as to be able to realize fully the program enumerated in the brochure and the letter. But even if the Church was not successful in obtaining all desired concessions, especially with reference to religious congregations, the constitution adopted on 7 February 1831 granted it a rather advantageous position. Freedom of education was guaranteed (Art. 17), as well as the right to free association (Art. 20), i.e., freedom for orders. The state continued to be responsible for ecclesiastical salaries (Article 117).[26] Article 16 guaranteed the Church a degree of independence unknown at this time in any other Catholic country. The state was permitted neither to impose any conditions for the appointment of bishops and the publication of papal announcements nor to attempt to achieve this control through a concordat.

The lifting of all ecclesiastical privileges, and especially the liberal atmosphere in which the constitution had been worked out, worried the Holy See, which thought it detected the influence of Lamennais. Warned by Capaccini, Sterckx, who meanwhile had become chapter vicar of Mechelen, wrote a skillful defense in which he pointed out that while the traditional union between the two powers no longer existed,

[24] Concerning the religious policy of the Provisional Government, which was very liberal and yet considerate of the Church, see A. Simon, *L'Église catholique et les débuts de la Belgique indépendante* (Wetteren 1949), 14–24.

[25] Concerning their debates, see L. de Lichtervelde, *Le Congrès national* (Brussels 1945). Suggestions, amendments, and speeches in E. Huyttens, *Discussions du Congrès national de Belgique,* 5 vols. (Brussels 1844/45).

[26] See R. Georges in *Revue diocèse de Namur* 17 (1963), 1–46.

the separation actually was only apparent and was not complete.[27] His explanations were crafty, but from his position in the midst of the Belgian religious and political reality he comprehended that this *modus vivendi* was the only possible one. He hoped that the Church in Belgium possessed enough respect to regain in practice what it had lost in theory. At least his intervention, supported by several Jesuits, succeeded in warding off a formal disapproval by the Holy See. Henceforth the Belgian constitution gained European significance for the future development of Catholic liberalism. For many years it was the ideal of many Catholics who likewise demanded freedom as it was practiced in Belgium.

Briefly summarized, the unionism of the Belgian Catholics in its beginnings intended to be only a temporary and tactical association with modern liberty. But a genuine Catholic liberalism developed in dual fashion in the years 1829–31. One resulted from the theoretical writings of Lamennais and his associates, especially in *L'Avenir,* and the other from the embodiment in the Belgian constitution of conditions which would prove the fruitfulness of these ideas.

[27] Printed in *Mélanges d'histoire offerts à L. van der Essen* II, (Brussels-Louvain 1947), 983–90.

CHAPTER 17

The Roman Reaction

The Appeal to Rome

Lamennais's polemics against Gallicanism and scholastic philosophy earned him the animosity of bishops and theologians, especially the Sulpicians and the Jesuits.[1] His liberalism and the campaign waged by *L'Avenir* for a reconciliation of Church and democracy increased the number of his opponents.They were additionally embittered by the provocative tone and the personal attacks of *L'Avenir,* which for longer than a generation were to be the hallmark of Lamennais's followers. The government of Louis-Philippe accused him of political radicalism and resented his attacks on the religious policy of the July Monarchy. The legitimists, who had not forgiven him his turnabout, were incensed about his unjustified criticism of them and attacked him stridently in their press. Dupanloup hardly exaggerated when he described Lamen-

[1] See L. Le Guillou, *L'évolution et la pensée religieuse de Félicité Lamennais,* 199–216.

nais as "the idol of the young priests . . . but a vexation to all old clergymen and pious believers."[2] They resented his bold political ideas and suspected him of wanting to reform the Catholic religion itself. The bishops were irritated because, being legitimists and Gallicans, they were unable to distinguish between what was false and exaggerated in this movement and what was reasonable. They accused *L'Avenir* of asking for the cancellation of the concordat, whose advantages in their eyes made up for its disadvantages, and of undermining episcopal authority by its constant sarcasm and by permitting laymen to discuss questions which were subject to ecclesiastical authority. They did not wish to see such difficult questions debated on a journalistic level and were justifiably worried by the divisions which it generated among their clergy.[3] Most of them hesitated, however, to attack the well-known apologist and defender of the Roman cause with pastoral letters. But many of them purged their seminaries and pressured their priests to stop reading the paper. A number of older followers, actually in favor of a more open attitude toward liberal tendencies, were worried by the increasingly radical posture of *L'Avenir* in political matters. They thought like Father Ventura, who, in an article published in February 1831, approved of the liberal Catholic view of the paper but accused it of "preaching revolution in the name of religion." This reaction of a Roman friend was the more telling as the nunciature was increasingly reserved.

The editors of *L'Avenir* attempted to clarify the situation with the aid of a declaration[4] addressed to the new Pope, in which they extensively explained their philosophical, theological, religious, and political positions. But when Rome did not respond positively, cancellations of subscriptions increased and the financial condition of the paper became untenable. At the end of October it was decided to cease publication of *L'Avenir* and the activities of the agency.

[2] Letter to Cardinal de Rohan, quoted in F. Lagrange, *Vie de Mgr. Dupanloup* I, 132. To be compared with the letter by the internuncio in P. Dudon, op. cit., 123.

[3] For in this lay the whole problem of the apostolate beyond the relationship between Church and state in a fundamentally new world. Even graver was that of the relationship between faith and reason and between Church and world based on man's position outside of a hierarchical and authoritarian concept of society. Numerous unpublished letters, which L. Le Guillou is preparing for publication, show to what extent the problems posed by Lamennais, being pressing and essential for the conscience of many priests, split even the religious orders. Followers and opponents struggled so violently that occasionally they ignored the most elementary commandments of love. (*L'Information littéraire* 18 [1966], 141).

[4] Text in G. Verucci, *L'Avenir* (Rome 1967), 288–307. The Pope probably never saw this declaration written by Gerbet and published on 6 February.

An unexpected turn of events occurred when Lacordaire suggested that Lamennais present his case to the Pope personally. Then, equipped with a certification of his orthodoxy, he could return and begin anew with strengthened authority.[5] On 15 November *L'Avenir* appeared for the last time, with the announcement that for the time being it would cease publication. One week later, Lamennais, Lacordaire, and Montalembert started on their journey to Rome. They did so in the face of the warnings of the archbishop of Paris, who pointed out to them the danger of forcing the Holy See to adopt a position. Lamennais, deeply engaged in the battle for what he considered to be the only way of salvation for the Church, believed that the only reason the Pope did not support his cause was that the Curia had failed to inform the Pope of the actual situation. The Holy See, he believed, could not afford to remain neutral between good and evil, between the true and the false. Preoccupied with matters in France, Lamennais failed to realize that aside from ecclesiastical aspects and from the worries which the Pope had about the developments in Belgium,[6] the campaign of *L'Avenir* for democracy had to be particularly threatening to Rome. After all, it was the capital of a state whose existence most recently had been endangered by a liberal revolution.

Arriving in Rome on 30 December, the "Pilgrims of God and Freedom" visited a few well-disposed influential persons. They wanted to see Lamennais well received in spite of the "real errors" of his political writings, because they acknowledged his achievements as apologist, as champion of ultramontanism, and as defender of the freedom of the Church. They were also impressed by the evangelistic echo which *L'Avenir*'s appeals to a poorer Church, less compromised by Metternich's system, evoked. This view was shared by the Capuchin Cardinal Micara, a few other members of the Sacred College, a few theologians like Father Olivieri, *Magister Sacri Palatii,* and Father Ventura, who was once again totally reconciled with Lamennais and eager to help him.[7]

The opponents were many and powerful. There were the secretary of state, whom the judgment of *L'Avenir* concerning his suppression of the revolts in the Papal States had offended, and Cardinal Lambruschini, who as former nuncio in Paris was regarded as the expert on matters affecting France. He was a decided reactionary, who found it easy to gather adherents for his indignation about this "arrogant spirit" who

[5] See his autobiographical comments in P. Foisset, *Vie du R. P. Lacordaire* I (Paris 1870), 180–81.

[6] Concerning the importance of the Belgian situation in Lamennais's condemnation, see A. Simon in *Ris* 6 (1963), 15–16; id., *Reccontres*, 129–38.

[7] See his vote in P. Dudon, op. cit., 126–32.

thought he could give lessons in diplomacy to experienced nuncios and lessons in religion to the Pope. There were several theologians and canonists, especially Jesuits under the leadership of Father Rozaven, always a bitter enemy of Lamennais's philosophical ideas, who were outraged by the condescension with which Lamennais treated respected theologians. Finally there were French legitimists—supported by the Austrian and Russian embassies—assembled around the auditor of the *Rota* and Cardinal de Rohan, who articulated the concerns of the bishops.

The role of the foreign diplomats was discussed heatedly, and Lamennais himself in his *Affaires de Rome* ascribed to them a predominant influence. Access to the archives has made possible a more balanced view. The French government did not intervene directly, but its hostility to *L'Avenir* was known, and Gregory XVI under no circumstances wanted to increase the tensions between the Church and the new government. The influence of Russia, extremely irritated by *L'Avenir*'s support of the Polish revolt, seems to have been much more important than historians have generally admitted.[8] They have been more concerned with Metternich's role, which Father Dudon was at pains to minimize.[9] But the archives of Vienna, which Dudon did not consult, demand, as L. Ahrens and J. R. Derré have shown, a correction of some of his assertions. It is true that Gregory XVI even before the complaints of Austria's ambassador in December 1831[10] was not kindly disposed toward Lamennais and regarded as unbecoming his presumption to demand from the Holy See a declaration concerning his case. But the intervention of the ambassador strengthened the unfavorable impression of the Pope and militated against those who suggested that the pilgrims should be given a friendly reception. Metternich intervened several times during Lamennais's stay in Rome. Later, after the publication of *Mirari vos,* Metternich sent the Holy See numerous compromising letters which had been intercepted by his censor. Metternich had annotated them with comments and advice which corresponded to the personal opinion of the Pope and contributed to his hardening attitude. The vivid interest of the representatives of the Holy Alliance

[8] See especially Montalembert's letter to Guéranger in P. Dudon, op. cit., 151–52 and the passage of his diary quoted by A. Trannoy, op. cit., 181. See also A. Vidler, op. cit., 210–12, as well as more generally A. Boudou, *Le Saint-Siège et la Russie* I, chap. 5. The Tsar did not ascribe to *L'Avenir* the revolt in Poland, but its prolongation and the religious character which the battle had assumed.

[9] His article in *BLE* 33 (1932), 16–34, an answer to the book by L. Ahrens, presents no new aspects.

[10] See the telegrams by Lützow of 18 December and 25 December 1831, in L. Ahrens, op. cit., 237–40.

in Lamennais's case definitely convinced the Pope that he had to take a stand and publicly condemn the new school of thought.

Whatever the case may be, Lamennais and his associates met a wall of polite silence during their first weeks in Rome. At the beginning of February they delivered to the Pope a lengthy memorandum, written by Lacordaire,[11] in which they presented their views. Cardinal Pacca, the deacon of the Sacred College, brought a reply. It was a polite plea to let the matter rest. Lacordaire understood immediately and decided to return to France without delay.[12] But Lamennais, convinced that the opposition against him was exclusively of a political nature and that he was blameless with respect to doctrine, was determined to force Rome to reply. He extended his stay until July. When by that time he still had not heard anything, he decided, encouraged by some Roman friends, to resume publication of *L'Avenir.* He left Rome, bitter that he had been denied the opportunity to present his case personally. The fact that the authorities had systematically avoided any serious discussion convinced him that Rome, overly busy with problems of the day and purely secular problems, had no interest in the general welfare of the Church.

The Encyclical *Mirari vos*

Contrary to Lamennais's assumption, his case had been under serious investigation by the Congregation of Extraordinary Ecclesiastical Affairs since March. The report edited by Cardinal Lambruschini emphasized the international aftereffects of *L'Avenir*'s campaign: discontent among the bishops of France and Belgium[13] and concern in the cabinets of the Catholic powers. The advisers were unanimous in their view that the Pope could be silent no longer, as he otherwise might create the impression that he approved the subversive doctrine published by Lamennais during the past two years. Instead of compiling a list of the theses to be condemned, a process which would have taken too much time, the advisers suggested to the Pope that, without mentioning *L'Avenir* expressly, he condemn the theses about the legitimacy of revolution, the separation of Church and state, and freedom of religion and the press. A draft of the encyclical, presented by Monsignor Frezza, the secretary of the congregation, was ratified on August 9. The arguments set forth were primarily of a theological nature. The incriminated theories were accused of being derived from a "certain religious indifferentism, which

[11] Text in *Les Affaires de Rome,* 45–104.

[12] Concerning this decision, see P. Foisset, *Vie du R. P. Lacordaire* I, 197–99.

[13] See the letter of 29 January 1832 by Van Bommel to Gregory XVI in A. Simon, *Rencontres,* 136–37.

faith must reject," and countered notions of popular sovereignty with texts like *"omnis potestas a Deo."* But it is likely that the cardinals and the Pope himself were also persuaded to intervene by extratheological factors, such as renewed remarks by the diplomats, renewed outbreaks of liberal agitation in the Papal States, and the Belgian problem.

The Encyclical *Mirari vos* of 15 August 1832[14] painted a pessimistic picture of the conditions which Gregory XVI encountered upon his accession to the throne. After a condemnation of rationalism and Gallicanism, which Lamennais also had opposed for fifteen years, the encyclical railed against liberalism in its various manifestations, "this false and absurd maxim, or better this madness, that everyone should have and practice freedom of conscience." It spoke against freedom of the press, "this loathsome freedom which one cannot despise too strongly" and from which to expect anything good would be an illusion, attacked the invitation to revolt against sovereigns (this point was developed with special pathos), and opposed the separation of Church and state. Yielding on any of these points was condemned "with a biblical tone which seemed to stem from another age" (Droulers). Neither Lamennais nor *L'Avenir* were mentioned directly, but all of their theses were rejected by connecting them erroneously with naturalistic indifferentism. The fact that Rome did not regard this encyclical as a condemnation of the Belgian constitution indicated a willingness to remain on the ground of principles and to accept a regime which tolerated modern freedoms, under the condition that the essential rights of the Church remained untouched. What was condemned was the assertion of the legal equality of all religions and that the freedom to dispense any doctrine was an ideal and progress.[15] Equally, the doctrine of popular sovereignty was condemned, inspired more by the theoreticians of the divine right of Kings than by the Aristotelian positions of Thomas of Aquinas about the origin of power. It motivated a few Dominicans to react, even in Rome where they were not the only ones to question the opportunism of the encyclical or its authority.

Lamennais was sent a copy of the encyclical, accompanied by a letter from Cardinal Pacca, who explained that Lamennais was alluded to because of his tactics which he seemed to believe necessary for the defense of the Church, and because of his doctrines on religious policies. Lamennais received the message in Munich, where he wanted to make contact with some of his German followers.[16] In agreement with

[14] Text in *Acta Gregorii PP XVI,* ed. by A. Bernasconi (Rome 1901), I, 169–74.

[15] See R. Aubert, "L'enseignement du magistère ecclésiastique au XIXe siècle sur le libéralisme" in *Tolérance et communauté humaine* (Tournai 1952), 75–82.

[16] Concerning the stay in Munich, see L. Ahrens, op. cit., 86ff.

his collaborators he published a declaration which recanted nothing but announced that, "devoted to the supreme authority of the Vicar of Christ, the battleground would be vacated on which for two years a loyal fight had taken place." Furthermore, *L'Avenir* would not appear again and the agency would remain closed. The declaration satisfied Rome, which had feared a storm of indignation.

From *Mirari vos* to *Singulari nos*

The encyclical convinced a number of Lamennais's followers that they had been on the wrong path and they renounced the theories which heretofore they had defended. But Lamennais and many of his students—convinced that the encyclical was "more an act of government than of magisterial office" (Le Guillou)—believed that they were merely enjoined to silence and could continue to hold their earlier ideas without change.

The Belgian Catholics faced a special conflict of conscience,[17] as for them Catholic liberalism was not only a theoretical system but was also embodied in a constitution whose concrete advantages were appreciated more every day. The conservatives, who had criticized this constitution, which was too liberal in their eyes, were jubilant; the unionists were at first dismayed, and some of them asked themselves whether the antirevolutionary statements of the encyclical did not also condemn their active opposition to the regalism of William I and the revolution of 1830. But the bishops were not worried at all. They rightly assumed that the declarations of principle concerning an ideal regime did not refer to the constitution, an agreement of civil and not theological nature. Soon the Catholic papers began to interpret the encyclical in the same sense, and some of them added that an encyclical was not binding for the faith. Some early unionists like Gerlache, out of loyalty to the Roman doctrine, felt obliged to give up their parliamentary activity; but most of them after a few weeks of contemplation decided that for them nothing had changed. Metternich was extremely incensed and did not hesitate to pass his alarm on to Rome, insisting that a new, clearer declaration was mandatory.

Numerous French voices also called for another papal intervention, one which would obligate the followers of Lamennais to a genuine recantation. They desired above all that the Pope condemn the list of fifty-six theses by Lamennais which Monsignor d'Astros had submitted to the Holy See in 1832 and which for this reason was known by the

[17] See H. Haag, op. cit., 180–96, Jürgensen, op. cit., 254–69, and A. Simon, *Rencontres,* 149–53.

name of "Censure of Toulouse."[18] But while some secretly hoped to compel Lamennais to throw off his mask and believed they could triumph over the rebellious apostle of ultramontanism, Gregory XVI, disregarding the advice which he received from Metternich, the Jesuits, and many others, preferred to wait. He agreed with the opinion of the Congregation of Extraordinary Ecclesiastical Affairs not to follow the "Censure of Toulouse"; instead, a brief was composed in which the Pope confined himself to an expression of unmitigated joy over the way in which his encyclical had been received.

At the same time two other events occupied the center of attention. A Belgian paper published an excerpt from a letter by Lamennais in which he expressed his intention of resuming publication of *L'Avenir.* In spite of appearances, the letter actually was written prior to the encyclical,[19] but in Rome the news was received as proof of his duplicity. The effect of this tragic misunderstanding was heightened by the shattering foreword of Mickiewicz's *Book of the Polish Pilgrims.* The papal brief to Monsignor d'Astros (8 May 1833) was immediately amended by the insertion of a statement directed at Lamennais. Lamennais's letter of explanation failed to satisfy the Pope, who addressed an even stricter brief to the bishop of Rennes. An exchange of letters between Lamennais and Rome followed. The Breton abbé, no longer concerned with religious freedom or the separation of Church and state, but now interested in the cause of exploited peoples and oppressed nations, was prepared to announce his submission to the Holy See in questions of faith, morals, and Church discipline. But, relying on the radical difference between spiritual and secular matters, he wanted to retain his full freedom of thought and action in the political sphere, even after the encyclical. Gregory XVI was unwilling to concede this, as he was of the opinion that the call to revolt against established authorities questioned moral and religious principles. Lamennais was therefore asked to agree expressly to the totality of the statements made in *Mirari vos,* including those concerned with political activity.

Physically exhausted by the weeks of tiring discussions, embittered by the intensified attacks of the Catholic press doubting his loyalty, and desirous of "peace at any price," Lamennais finally surrendered on 11 December. His private letters, though, reveal his true attitude: he was ready to sign everything, "even if it had been an acknowledgement that

[18] On its origin and history, see P. Droulers, op. cit., 132–44, complemented by P. Dudon, op. cit., 243–63. Two thirds of the sentences concerned the philosophical theory of certainty and about one third the church-political theses of *L'Avenir.*

[19] This fact was discovered by G. Charlier. See *Revue d'histoire littéraire de la France* 11 (1933), 109–14.

the Pope were God."[20] It was the end of the process which had begun with his stay in Rome. He now harbored "very strong reservations about several points of Catholicism," convinced that "the Church could not remain as it is, because no attempt had ever been made to distinguish in it between the divine and the human."

It is probable that the papal brief of June 1832 to the Polish bishops made a deeper impression on Lamennais than the condemnation of *L'Avenir.* The brief condemned the national insurgency and justified its brutal suppression by the Tsar in the name of the obedience owed to a legitimate rule.[21] The Polish revolt was for Lamennais not only an attempt to liberate a people, but also a religious rising for the defense of the rights of Catholics violated by the Russian schismatics. The more he now reflected on these events during the following months, the more he began to wonder to what extent a Pope could be believed who so clearly betrayed his spiritual mission for political reasons. To Lamennais it appeared as though the Pope was looking for support from Russia, the better to resist the rebellious Romagna. Logically this led him to the question: "What is the Church?" Is it the hierarchy and the papacy, opposing the strivings of a people for its liberty, or is it all of humankind?" With his apocalyptic view, he saw the beginning of a development analogous to that which replaced the Jewish synagogue with a hierarchical Church. Henceforth the time had passed for him in which the papacy acted in the divinely sanctioned role of interpreter of the truth entrusted by God and humankind. Now it was necessary to await the coming of a new religious society, emerging from the Catholic Church like a butterfly from its chrysalis. More than a rebel incapable of obeying a reprimand, Lamennais thus appeared as a disappointed man who had placed precipitous hope in the Catholic Church for the liberation of man; when he realized that it did not act accordingly, he concluded that its hierarchy could not possibly be God's instrument on earth.

His outward submission gained him a few weeks of respite, but soon he began to accuse himself for his lukewarm attitude. From Ventura and other Roman friends he learned that even at the center of Catholicism the views of Gregory XVI were not accepted without reservations and that French and European policy was becoming increasingly reactionary. He decided to take an unequivocal stand. In April 1834, against the advice of his friends, he published a series of poems under the title

[20] Letter to Montalembert of 1 January 1834 (op. cit., 231). See also the letter to Marion of 4 January 1834 in A. du Bois de la Villerabel, *Confidences de Lamennais, lettres inédites* (Paris 1886), 94–95.
[21] See above, pp. 156f.

Paroles d'un croyant. He had written them in order to proclaim in the style of the prophets of the Old Testament the arrival of a new age in which the renewed intervention of Christ would free the peoples from the tyranny of despots and rulers. This hymn to everything the Pope had condemned in *Mirari vos* made a great stir.[22] Catholics saw in the work, which was very religious but whose concept of Christianity was vaguely drawn, a proof of Lamennais's definite apostasy. This was actually a premature conclusion,[23] but Rome reacted without delay. Lambruschini was ordered to prepare a report, and although he came to the conclusion that a papal brief would suffice, and although the archbishop of Paris recommended total silence, the Pope on 21 June 1834 published the Encyclical *Singulari nos.*[24] It recounted the events, extensively condemned the revolutionary doctrines of Lamennais's work, especially as these purported to be based on the doctrines of the Bible, and concluded with a short and rather generally worded condemnation of philosophical traditionalism.

Lamennais did not react immediately and his break with the Pope became evident only with the publication of *Affaires de Rome*[25] in November 1836. All of his former followers quickly announced their submission to the papal decision. Yet the influence of the movement started by Lamennais was a deep and lasting one in the Catholic Church. As the following chapters will show, the impetus generated by the Breton prophet retained its influence on thought and action, notwithstanding the severe strain to which the impatience of its founder exposed it. Lamennais was unable to respect God's patience and incapable of surrendering his excessive individualism, an individualism which did not

[22] See in Forgues, *Correspondance* II, 368–69 the collection of ingenious expressions, collected by Vitrolles in Paris: *"un bonnet rouge planté sur une croix," "Babeuf débité par le prophète Ezéchiel," "Robespierre en surplis"* . . .

[23] Lamennais stopped believing in the fundamental truths of Christianity only in 1835–36. See the last two chapters of L. Le Guillou, *L'évolution de la pensée religieuse de Félicité Lamennais.*

[24] Texts in *Acta Gregorii PP XVI* I, 433–34. Concerning the preparation of the encyclical, see P. Dudon, op. cit., 323–29, to be supplemented by the letter of E. d'Alzon of 5 July 1834 (*Lettres inédites de Lamennais à Montalembert,* 307–09). The archives at Vienna indicate Metternich's extraordinary activity in the weeks before the issuance of the encyclical, but in contrast to Harispe, L. Ahrens believes that the stunning parallels between the encyclical and the letters of the Austrian chancellor are more the expression of an already existing agreement than the result of an express influence.

[25] He announced in it that he gave up the "Christianity of the Pontificate" in favor of a "Christianity of Humanity," analogous to deism. He took up residence in Paris, devoted himself to journalism, but henceforth remained isolated even among the groups of the left, for whom he was too religious. After a vain attempt in 1848 to enter politics, he died on 17 February 1854.

permit his prolific intuitions to be cleansed and purged by the contact with the experience of ecclesiastical collectivity. He also suffered from a superficial understanding of religion, a lack which was to be a burden for the various forms of "political Catholicism" generated in the nineteenth century in the wake of Lammenais.

SECTION TWO

Church and State in Europe from 1830 to 1848

More than once it was assumed that the condemnation of *L'Avenir* in the Encyclical *Mirari vos* dealt a deathblow to Catholic liberalism. But this was not the case. Those followers of Lamennais who continued to be convinced of the viability of his ideas gave up developing theories about the ideal relationship between Church and state and ceased pursuing a systematic apologetics of the separation of the two powers. They turned to a translation of theory into practice by employing modern institutions in favor of religion and by demanding the application of common law instead of privileges wherever the freedom of Catholics was constrained as a consequence of governmental actions. At the same time, they tried to adapt Catholic culture to the movements and tendencies of modern society. The militant wing of Catholicism was resolutely engaged in this development, especially in France. It was also the policy of Belgian and Dutch Catholics, noticeably supported by their bishops. In Italy some attempted to take the same path. In the German states, only little influenced by Lamennais, there were parallel tendencies in the attempts of Görres and the Munich group to make Catholic thought palatable to Protestant intellectuals and to free the Church from the yoke of the regionalism of the Old Regime. It was not happenstance that the followers of Lamennais in France and Belgium observed the resistance of Prussian Catholics during the events at Cologne with enthusiasm. The second spring (Newman) which English Catholicism experienced during these years was due above all to the Emancipation Act of 1829, a Catholic and liberal success. It had its origin in O'Connell's activity; his example convinced the followers of Lamennais, and Montalembert emphasized its significance. In spite of the prevailing reactionary atmosphere in Rome and Vienna the most important Catholic developments in western and central Europe during the fifteen years of Gregory's pontificate thus occurred under the banner of liberty.

Chapter 18

The Continuation of Catholic Liberalism in Western Europe

France

The July Revolution of 1830, replacing the alliance of throne and altar so beneficial for the French clergy with a regime in which the influence of the anticlerical and liberal middle class was predominant, caused great consternation among the clergy. Upon the advice of Austria and against the counsel of his Curia and the nuncio in Paris, Pius VIII quickly recognized the new regime, which promised to honor the concordat. But a few anticlerical institutional measures[1] generated in the already suspicious clergy the fear that persecutions would begin anew. These measures were often of a local nature,[2] but they were augmented by attacks of the Paris press and theaters on the clergy. Additionally, there was the tendency of some community councils, especially in the cities, to reduce clerical influence on public life, and finally there were some unfortunate appointments of bishops during the first months following the revolution. Several priests and three bishops, among them Cardinals de Latil and de Rohan, left France and regarded themselves as the first in a wave of emigration similar to that of 1789. Actually, ecclesiastical reconstruction was consolidated during the eighteen years of the July Monarchy. In some areas—thanks to the sensible application of the tactic recommended by *L'Avenir*—there was even a continuation of the Catholic renewal which had begun during the restoration period.

Although they were indifferent in religious matters, neither the King nor his ministers were hostile to the Church. Not wanting anarchy to spread among the people, they made their peace with the clergy, whose influence in the countryside and the small towns remained considerable. In order to prevent the clergy from placing its influence at the disposal

[1] Abrogation of the article of the constitution which named Catholicism as the established religion, abolition of military chaplains and hospital chaplains, reduction of the salaries of bishops and canons and suspension of the subsidies for boys' seminaries, removal of crucifixes from court houses, and designation of the church of Saint Geneviève as a mausoleum of great men (Pantheon).

[2] The majority of the cases concerned Paris: destruction of the residence of the archbishop and of the church Saint Germain l'Auxerrois (see R. Limouzin-Lamothe in *Éfranc* 13 [1963], 184–208, 14 [1964], 58–76), destruction of the Jesuit novitiate and demonstrations against habit-wearing priests. The atmosphere in the provinces was hardly disturbed, except for the looting of the seminaries of Metz, Lille, and Nîmes, and the destruction of mission crosses displaying the Bourbon coat of arms.

of the legitimist opposition it was necessary to prove that there was no intention of restricting its apostolic work. To be sure, at the beginning the government was not able to commit itself to a certain policy, as it had to be mindful of public opinion, but thanks to the skills of the internuncio Garibaldi, who in August 1831 became the successor of the extremely reactionary Lambruschini, it was possible to overcome the initial difficulties. To the degree that the government felt more secure, the authorities became more sympathetic.

This development was enhanced by the death in 1839 of the archbishop of Paris, Monsignor de Quélen, who was one of the few bishops who resolutely refused to become reconciled to the "usurper." Increasingly the clergy was valued as the most important preserver of public order in the face of the threat of socialism. The ministries of religion also from the very beginning showed their good intentions. When the Chambers in 1832 demanded the dissolution of the thirty dioceses which during the restoration period had been added to the concordat dioceses, the demand was ignored. In fact, an additional one was created in 1838 in Algiers.[3] After 1837, the religious budget was increased regularly, and the number of parishes grew by 10 percent. Although the Council of State put more obstacles in the way of ecclesiastical purchase requisitions than during the restoration period, the Church invested 25,220,548 francs during the eighteen years of the July Monarchy, in contrast to the 13,664,760 francs during the fifteen years of the preceding government. The biographies of bishops of this period demonstrate throughout that after the first few years, notwithstanding local opposition and the reserve of nobles loyal to the Bourbons, the government and the local authorities did not hinder the creation of pious foundations and Catholic welfare organizations; occasionally they even assisted them.[4]

The handling of episcopal appointments was characteristic of the improvement of relations. After the unfortunate selections of the first few months, the government agreed to make appointments with the advice of the bishops. The correspondence between Monsignor Garibaldi and Mathieu, archbishop of Besançon, reveals the important role played by the latter. He was effective in bringing about a genuine separation of the prerogatives of episcopal appointments between the secular and

[3] Concerning the difficulties in establishing the Catholic Church in Algeria after the conquest, see M. Emerit in *Revue africaine* 97 (1953), 66–97; J. Leflon, *E. de Mazenod* III, 26–29; P. Poupard, op. cit., 166–70.

[4] The support given to the Church by the traditional forces of society in spite of the change in government is emphasized by A. J. Tudesq, *Les grands notables,* 124–26, 199, 213–15, 227–28, 439–40. Too many historians have erroneously judged the French attitude toward Catholicism exclusively on the basis of the Paris press.

spiritual forces, a separation far exceeding the provisions of the condordat. Government and nunciature jointly tried to exclude the most intimate followers of the deposed King as well as those of Lamennais, the progressivists of the time. The majority of the seventy-seven bishops appointed by Louis-Philippe came from the middle class and were relatively young (between forty and fifty), gradually displacing the pre-1789 generation. Many of them were former vicars general who with great prudence took care of the business of their dioceses. The result was a solid and pious episcopate more concerned with administration than with problems of intellectual and pastoral accommodation caused by the new society.[5] These bishops strove to keep the Church free from any political exposure and to maintain their independence from the government. Yet their conduct toward their clergy was often very authoritarian, as the concordat permitted them to act as they pleased. Their capriciousness was aggravated by a general ignorance of canon law: In 1837 alone, thirty-five hundred irremovable priests, more than 10 percent of the total, were transferred; in some dioceses, all priests were forced to change locations between 1836 and 1842. This led to a protest movement, meetings, and publications, started by the brothers Allignol from the diocese of Viviers. Their book *De l'état actuel du clergé de France* (1839) was moving proof of the precarious situation of the country clergy, the victims of dual dependence on lay notables and ecclesiastical superiors.

The numbers of active clergy changed dramatically. At first, the fear caused by the new government's hostility to the Church and the cancellation of stipends for the seminaries resulted in a clear reduction of ordinations, from 2357 in 1830 to 1095 in 1845. The time span between entrance into minor seminary and ordination normally was ten years. But owing to a low mortality rate, the total number of active priests increased from 38,388 to 45,456; thus in spite of a population increase of 21 percent, there was one priest for every 752 inhabitants in contrast to one for every 777 in 1830.[6] This was the result of the rejuvenation of the clergy during the preceding twenty years, a process which continued. The proportion of sixty-year-olds sank from 29 percent in 1830 to 10 percent in 1840 and in 1847 reached its lowest point

[5] With a few brilliant exceptions: Doney, Parisis, and principally the new archbishop of Paris, Affre (1839–48), appointed under the influence of Montalembert, who most astutely of all prelates seems to have recognized the problems, but whose tendency to exercise a certain primacy over the Church of France met the resistance of his colleagues.

[6] With great differences among the dioceses: one priest for 1450 people in 1841 in the dioceses of Bourges, but one for 348 people in the diocese of Rodez.

with 5.6 percent. Unfortunately, the young clergy, while more dynamic than the clergy of the restoration period and free from a longing for the Old Regime, which it had not experienced, was hardly better educated than the older clergy. Trained in seminaries whose standards continued to remain mediocre, the clergy did not adapt its pastoral efforts to new problems and its effectiveness remained limited.

The mediocrity of the diocesan clergy opened a wide field of activity for the orders which suffered from the July Revolution. There were riots against the Jesuits, and Casimir Périer, minister of religion, banished the Trappists, Carthusians, and Capuchins from Marseille. But by 1835 tolerance gained ground. New male and female congregations devoted to elementary education and welfare were permitted, together with the old orders which had been absent since the great revolution. In 1833 Dom Guéranger again introduced the Benedictines in France, and when Lacordaire in 1841 did the same with the Dominicans, the government did not dare oppose the move, in spite of the warnings of anticlerical deputies and newspapers which pointed to the orders' illegality.[7] The Jesuits, who in 1828 had only twelve houses, by 1840 had seventy-four of them. When in 1845 the dissolution of the order was demanded as revenge for the Jesuits' fight for freedom of education, the matter ended with a compromise, arranged by Pellegrino Rossi, Louis-Philippe's envoy, and Secretary of State Lambruschini. Officially, the Jesuits remained dispersed across the country as simple priests, but in actuality they were hardly restricted in their work.[8] In 1845, Emmanuel d'Alzon formed a new congregation, the Assumptionists. The growing influence assumed by the orders in the French Church was not to the liking of all bishops. Some of them did not care at all for these "guerillas," who were not subject to episcopal jurisdiction and whose untimely initiatives could endanger the détente between Church and state. Moreover, the new congregations, frequently favored by the upper classes, siphoned off contributions by the faithful.

Even more than on the structural level, the vitality of the Church proved itself in the field of Catholic action. Of course, not only successes could be recorded. After the apostasy of Lamennais, the romanticists, representing the active wing of the literary movement, became alienated from the Church. Many people of the middle class respected the Church, but in their religious practices confined themselves to an uncommitted conformism and directed all of their attention to material pursuits. In several rural areas like Bauce, there was a noticeable shrinking in the number of communicants and a diminution of religious feel-

[7] See vol. VIII in this series, chap. 1.

[8] For details see Burnichon II, 611–73, III, 1–113.

ing.[9] Protestantism competitively intensified its efforts and thanks to the dynamic of its revival movement was able to register some successes.[10] On the other hand, the urban youth was frequently more open to religious impulses than it had been during the restoration period. In a few dioceses, able prelates contributed to the growth which had started even before 1830. But above all there was a growth of small but very dynamic elite groups led by noted personalities, such as Bautain at Strasbourg, Blanc de Saint-Bonnet at Lyon, Guerrier de Dumast at Nancy, Salinis at the Collège de Juilly, and Madame Swetchine and Count de Montalembert at Paris.

Additionally, there were the young student Frédéric Ozanam,[11] who in 1833 together with E. Bailly organized the first Vincent Conference, L. Rendu, the creative force behind the *Cercle catholique scientifique et littéraire* (1840), and Abbé Ledreuille, the "workers' priest" and founder of the Society of Saint Francis Xavier (1840), which comprised thousands of workers and even had branches across the country. The groups were numerous and their most active members were legitimists with ties to the notables.[12] Their militant wing was formed by the disciples of Lamennais, who unmercifully made life difficult for a clergy trained in the old ways. Without having given up their old ideal of a reconciliation between the Church and the modern movements, they recognized that *L'Avenir*'s mistake had been to propagate ideas for which the time was not yet ripe, and that it would be more productive to act in a practical way in order to prove the validity of the recommended methods. They advocated cooperation between laity and clergy in a joint struggle for

[9] Inasmuch as systematic studies have not yet been undertaken, we have to rely on rather vague impressions with respect to the religious condition of the working class in 1848. It must be taken into consideration that it was still far from homogeneous, and one has to differentiate between Paris, where the areligiosity of the workers stretches back to the Jacobin clubs of 1793, and the provinces; between the few industrial centers and the handcraft industries; between the elite with a certain education, which preserved a weak Christian feeling but could hardly bear ecclesiastical paternalism, and the masses of the proletariat who were positively affected by the considerable measures of support made by the Church after 1830, differing from the egotism of the primarily anticlerical employers.

[10] Concerning the situation of the Protestants in France under the constitutional monarchy, see E. Léonard, *Histoire générale du protestantisme* III (Paris 1964), 217–48.

[11] No reliable study is available on Frédéric Ozanam (1813–53). See *LThK* VII, 1325–26 and also L. Baunard, *Frédéric Ozanam d'après sa correspondance* (Paris 1913); Duroselle, 154–83 (social action); C. Moeller in *RHE* 14 (1913), 304–30 (historical achievement); *Lettres de Frédéric Ozanam,* ed. by L. Celier and J. Caron, 2 vol. (Paris 1960/71).

[12] J. B. Duroselle on the national level and P. Droulers within the framework of Toulouse have clearly shown the extremely active participation of the legitimists in the Catholic efforts of this period.

the faith, realizing that effective work in the Church was possible only in agreement with the hierarchy and not in opposition to it. Between 1832 and 1848 their activity developed in two-fold fashion.

A number of young Catholics, inspired by the ambitious program of Lamennais at La Chênaie, continued to develop an academic basis for Catholicism to make it acceptable to future generations and to regain for the Church the respect of the intellectual world. After 1830, A. Bonnetty published the *Annals of Christian Philosophy* for the purpose of finding in ancient history and ethnology the proof for primitive revelation, thereby responding to the historicist and positivist needs of the nineteenth century. Ozanam, professor at the Sorbonne after 1841, revived the study of the Christian Middle Ages. In the Notre Dame Conferences, started in 1835 by Ozanam, Lacordaire continued the efforts to establish a revived apologetics by removing Catholicism from antiquated forms of thought. E. d'Alzon assigned tasks to his Assumptionists quite similar to those earlier developed by Lamennais for his Congregation of Saint Peter. In November 1833, Abbé Migne began to publish a new newspaper, *L'Univers,* which looked at events from the Catholic point of view; its beginnings were difficult, but soon it received the support of an extraordinary convert, Louis Veuillot.[13] In 1843, Lenormant resumed the publication of the *Correspondant* and campaigned for freedom of education.[14]

Montalembert, who had held back after *Mirari vos,* during the last ten years of the July Monarchy fought for freedom of education on the parliamentary level. He also was active on behalf of the right to existence for religious congregations, a right which was continually questioned by the authorities. In view of the lacking willingness of the authorities to make compromises, he sought the backing of the people instead of waiting for a solution through diplomatic negotiations between the Holy See and the King, a course of action favored by the Pope and most of the bishops.

The question of freedom of education, embodied in the constitution but in need of statutory regulation, had been discussed by *L'Avenir.* When at the beginning of 1831 the administration of Casimir Périer closed the music schools of Lyon, in which choirboys had been trained free of charge, the editors of *L'Avenir* decided to establish an elemen-

[13] An impartial biography of Louis Veuillot (1813–83) is not yet written. See E. and F. Veuillot, *Louis Veuillot,* 4 vol. (Paris 1899/1913); *DThC* XV, 2799–2835; E. Gauthier, *Le vrai Louis Veuillot* (Paris, no date); E. Gauthier, *Le génie satirique de Louis Veuillot* (Paris 1953); J. Gadille in *Cahiers d'histoire* 14 (1969), 275–88. Works: *Œuvres complètes,* 40 vol. (Paris 1924/40), of them 12 volumes are correspondence.

[14] Details concerning the founding of Catholic newspapers and journals in C. de Ladoue, *Monseigneur Gerbet* II, 71–146.

tary school without official permission in order to bring the question into the open.[15] Two years later the Guizot Law of 28 June 1833 granted freedom of education for elementary schools and recognized members of orders as public teachers, thereby breaching the monopoly of the universities. The rapid growth of the congregations of teaching brothers and sisters enabled the Church to make comprehensive use of the law, even though it was regretted that the state's teachers were not sufficiently subordinated to the parish priests.[16]

Montalembert's enthusiasm and oratorical gift succeeded in imbuing the French with a crusade mentality with respect to secondary schools, a mentality which was at work during the next several generations. In practice, however, this attitude—contrary to the idealizing reports by Lecanuet and many other Catholic historians—frequently degenerated into a "war without discipline" (Dupanloup), marked by excesses and polemics in which laymen and clerics competed with one another in stridency and spitefulness. For many years, Catholic newspapers and pamphlets accused the public high schools of being "breeding grounds of pestilence," offering "atheistic and materialistic" instruction, and changing children into "dirty and wild animals." In fact, the majority of the teachers were freethinkers, and in philosophy classes the eclecticism of Victor Cousin predominated, regarded as infamous by clerics.

At the same time, though, 5 percent of public teachers were priests, among them many principals, and more than 20 percent of the teachers were practicing Catholics. For this reason, the bishops, basically satisfied with freedom of education for minor seminaries, would have preferred a discreet agreement with the government to a public debate. But Montalembert, who in the Chamber of Peers had developed into a courageous representative of Catholic interests, decided to act on the basis of common law. He demanded for the Church neither the privilege nor the right—which many bishops still called for[17]—to control public education, but only the constitutionally guaranteed freedom of education. Properly applied, it would permit the Church to organize its own school system, in addition to the public one, not only for future priests, but for all children. Many Catholics actually did not see the public schools in sinister colors, and public opinion initially was only hesitantly on Montalembert's side, especially after it was recognized that the episcopate

[15] Lecanuet, *Montalembert* I, 229–51.

[16] The discontent of many parish priests about the "kind of equality" (Parisis) assigned to the teachers in relation to the priests led to many disputes on the local level. A few examples in L. A. Meunier, *Défense des instituteurs laïcs contre les attaques du clergé* (Évreux 1847).

[17] The *Mémoire adressé au roi par les évêques de la province de Paris* of 1841 (Paris 1844) is characteristic.

itself held back because it saw in his demands a revival of Lamennais's ideas. But the draft presented by Secretary of Education François Villemain in 1841 disappointed many and persuaded a few prelates to become more vocal. This new attitude was also supported by the growing number of militant Catholics who demanded for Catholic education the same degree of unrestricted freedom which prevailed in Belgium after the adoption of the constitution of 1831. The struggle raged until 1847. While many bishops like Monsignor Affre preferred to send secret petitions to the government, others joined the fray openly. Among them were Monsignor Clausel de Montals, the choleric bishop of Chartres, fighting in the name of the rights of the Church, and Monsignor Parisis, the young bishop of Langres, who in close contact with the bishop of Liège, Van Bommel, followed the path outlined by Montalembert. In 1843 he published a pamphlet, *Du devoir des catholiques dans la question de la liberté d'enseignement,* and created a great stir. Parisis followed this with the pamphlet *Liberté de l'enseignement, examen de la question au point de vue constitutionnel et social,* whose theses were approved by fifty-six bishops, including the cautious Monsignor Affre, as a direct consequence of their agitation over the recent publication of a pamphlet by Michelet against the Jesuits. At the same time, Abbé Dupanloup[18] became reconciled with Montalembert. He was well known in Paris society and the clergy as the only one among the leaders of the Catholic movement in the July Monarchy who from the beginning had opposed Lamennais. He adopted Montalembert's tactic of regarding the question of education as part of the constitutionally guaranteed freedoms. Inasmuch as the new draft presented by Villemain conceded only limited freedom to Catholic education (it was denied to the religious congregations, specifically the Jesuits), Monsignor Parisis came out with further aggressive pamphlets and a petition campaign was organized in 1844 and 1845. Dupanloup issued a moderately worded brochure in June 1845, *De la pacification religieuse.* In it he developed in large outlines a kind of concordat for schools, resting on mutual concessions by Church and state.

But the lack of cooperation of chambers and government, which attempted to divert attention by a direct attack on the Jesuits, led Montalembert, in spite of his youth the leader of the Catholic movement of

[18] Concerning Félix Dupanloup (1802–78), see in view of the lack of a reliable biography, F. Lagrange, *Vie de Monseigneur Dupanloup,* 3 vols. (Paris 1883/84; also E. de Pressensé in *Revue bleue* 34 [1884], 582–87 and U. Maynard, *Monseigneur Dupanloup et M. Lagrange son historien* [Paris 1884]); E. Faguet, *Monseigneur Dupanloup* (Paris 1914); R. Aubert in *DHGE* XIV, 1070–1122. Works: *De l'Éducation,* 6 vols. (Paris 1850/66); *Œuvres choisies,* 6 vols. (Paris 1862); *Nouvelles œuvres choisies,* 7 vols. (Paris 1874); *Dupanloup. Les meilleurs textes,* ed. by H. Duthoit (Paris 1933).

this time, to a change of tactics. Following the Belgian example, he tried to organize all Catholics in a large political party. He did so against the will of many bishops who, like the archbishop of Rouen, were of the opinion that laymen did not have any business in ecclesiastical matters, and the Holy See, which accused the leaders of the Catholic movement of jeopardizing with their loud methods Rome's attempts to reconstitute the former alliance between Church and state.[19] Encouraged by his friend Lacordaire, Montalembert together with de Vatimesnil and de Riancey founded the Committee for the Defense of Religious Freedom. It became very active outside of Paris, in spite of the resistance of many clerics who were enraged by this direct intervention in parliamentary politics. With the support of the newspaper *L'Univers* Montalembert in 1846 achieved the election of 144 representatives who favored freedom of education. It also happened to be the time of the election of Pius IX, which dispelled the fears of Rome. But this success, badly exploited by a leader "of more belligerent than political temperament" (Trannoy), was not translated into victory; for the Salvandy Law of April 1847 was hardly more satisfactory than preceding legislation, and the fall of the July Monarchy took place before the question was settled. The long conflict, in many respects regrettable because it deepened the rift between clergy and public teachers, yet produced two tangible advantages. It reawakened the energies of laymen who became aware of their responsibility to defend Catholic interests in the parliament (although these interests were pursued in rather narrow clerical fashion), and it broke the ties of the French Church to a government which shortly was to be brought down by the revolution of 1848.

Belgium

With every reason, the leaders of the Catholic movement in France enviously looked to Belgium in 1840. There, in the years after achieving independence, a truly remarkable upswing took place. It was the result of a Catholic, even clerical offensive on the basis of the constitutionally guaranteed freedoms of religion and education. The systematic intervention of the clergy, especially in Flanders,[20] gave the Catholics strong positions in parliament and government. Although a Protestant himself, Leopold I favored the Catholic Church, as he saw in it the best protection against the revolutionary spirit. His support assured the Church of an important position in the life of the nation, in spite of the

[19] Concerning this reaction by Gregory XVI and especially by Secretary of State Lambruschini, see J. Martin, op. cit., 315–27.

[20] In addition to the publications by A. Simon (especially *Lettres de Pecci,* 39–41), see E. Witte in *Revue belge d'histoire contemporaine* I (1969), 216–53.

constitutional regime which had an affinity for those who favored separation.[21] Laws and agreements, concluded in a spirit of friendship between Church and state for the protection of morals among the people, Catholicized liberal institutions. The outstanding success of this policy was the law of 23 September 1842, concerning elementary schools.[22] It established complete freedom of the Church in education and made religious instruction in public schools mandatory. The implementation of the law, thanks to the efforts of the Catholic minister de Theux, virtually gave the Catholic clergy control over education in elementary schools. In the area of secondary education, fifteen years after independence two-thirds of the seventy-four high schools of the country were directed by clerics or members of orders.

These positive results finally led to the recognition of the liberal constitution by all those who, through the Encyclicals *Mirari vos* and *Singulari nos,* had been strengthened in their opposition to everything which, rightly or wrongly, seemed to be inspired by Lamennais. The opposition was further strengthened by the unyielding attitude of large numbers of the Flanders clergy, which was very receptive to the democratic ideas of the lower middle class from which most of them came. By 1835, tension between the two camps was strong, but it soon was relieved. With the exception of the people around the *Journal des Flandres,* the majority of the former followers of Lamennais adopted a more conservative attitude as a consequence of the break between him and the Church. From a Catholic liberalism, retaining from the liberal ideal everything that appeared compatible with the Catholic faith, they changed to a liberal Catholicism which used liberty as a means for Christian activity. Many of the so-called "encyclicalists," even though they continued to yearn for the officially privileged position of the Church under the Old Regime, acknowledged the great apostolic advantages of a system which offered the clergy the support of the state without forcing it under its yoke. Consequently they took the position that, in spite of their concern over strict Roman orthodoxy, they had the freedom to support a system which was no longer a theoretical ideal but a small evil actually useful to the Church.

This was also the opinion of the bishops, who clearly distanced themselves from the encyclicalists, to the great dismay of the nunciature, many Jesuits, and Metternich. Without a doubt, the efforts of some of them to safeguard clerical influence within the framework of legality

[21] Although the government constitutionally played no role in the election of bishops, Rome quickly got accustomed to inquire by way of the nunciature about possible objections against the planned candidates.

[22] See M. Leveugle, "L' 'Exposé des vrais principes' de Monseigneur Van Bommel: son influence en Belgique et en France" (unpublished dissertation, Louvain 1956).

were motivated by the old theocratic desire to dominate civil society. But their supreme goal was pure: in spite of the mixture of politics and religion, characteristic of Belgian Catholicism for a century, they were above all pastors desirous of enabling the Church to perform its primary mission, the saving of souls. Nonetheless they were pastors who retained from the time of the Napoleonic regime and the enlightened despotism of William I the tendency to exercise their offices in strongly administrative and centralistic terms. They were also the heirs of a long tradition which knew how to combine an unconditional loyalty to the Pope with a remarkable independence from the Roman influence on the life of the local Churches. In this spirit they approached the planning of a reconstitution of diocesan administrations, taking account of the new situation but not always of canonical regulations.[23]

The unity of action of the six bishops—in 1834 the diocese of Bruges was added to the five dioceses of the concordat of 1801—was guaranteed by an annual conference. It was the first of this type in Europe and in the eyes of the bishops replaced the provincial councils. But the unity of action of the bishops was guaranteed even more by the pressure exerted by the archbishop of Mechelen, Cardinal E. Sterckx (1831–67), on his suffragans. A pious and industrious prince of the Church without special theological training, he appeared with his prudent behavior as a "remarkable precursor of the bishops of our own time, the time of a free Church in a free state" (Simon). He respected the autonomy of the state and was conciliatory to the new currents of thought, but remained loyal to the Holy See.

The long vacancies in most of the episcopal sees during the era of the Dutch government retarded the Catholic restoration, which was so necessary in view of the indifference toward religion among the population. Immediately after the achievement of independence restoration was renewed with emphasis. The foundation for the effort was the parish missions[24] which in the course of about 20 years were conducted in two-thirds of all parishes. They had an undeniable success in the countryside, where the number of people participating in Easter Communion increased noticeably.

In their reconstruction efforts the bishops could count on a numeri-

[23] See A. Simon, *Documents relatifs á la nonciature de Bruxelles,* 19–21, 39–42.

[24] See A. Simon, *Sterckx* II, 253–58; J. Vieujean in *Revue ecclésiastique de Liège* 25 (1934), 14–24; F. Holemans, *Le saint curé de Tildonck* (Brussels 1926); A. Marlier, *Missionaris in eigen land. I. van de Kerkhove* (Brussels 1960); E. de Moreau in *AHSI* 10 (1941), 259–82; S. d'Ydewalle in *Sources hist. rel. Belg.,* 64–69; and the Master's Theses by L. Grégoire, "Les missions paroissiales prêchées par les rédemptoristes dans le diocese de Liège de 1833 à 1852" (Louvain 1966) and M. Bodranghien, "Les missions paroissiales à Bruxelles et dans les environs 1833–1914" (Louvain 1970).

cally adequate clergy, whose quality improved in the course of the years. While the clergy after 1830 behaved rather independently, the bishops gradually assumed the leadership. After the turn of the century the Belgian priests accepted the increasing centralization of diocesan life with a greater degree of submission than their French brothers. Trained in seminaries whose programs were revised and unified in the years 1842–48, but taught by professors who were largely autodidacts and strongly under the influence of Lamennais, the Belgian clergy for a long time remained on a low qualitative level. But supported by annual exercises and monthly retreats which were reinstituted toward the end of the 1830s, the clergy was characterized by a strictness of morals, a simple and open attitude, the realism of its apostolic methods, and a piety which was regulated very methodically but contained few elements of mysticism. Even so, the main work of the parish clergy for a long time was confined to confessions, administration of the sacraments, and visits to the sick.

Owing to the constitutional freedom of association, religious congregations developed quickly. The bishops favored the small congregations, which were a valuable aid to them in education and welfare work, but they were much more reserved toward the older orders. The bishops wished to see their privileges restricted in order better to control their apostolic efforts, the more so as after a 40-year-long anomalous situation their discipline left much to be desired. The Holy See proved very understanding in this respect and allowed the direction of the orders temporarily to be withdrawn from the superiors and entrusted to an apostolic visitor whom the archbishop wished to see selected from the Belgian clergy.[25]

Orders and secular clergy could count on the cooperation of many influential laymen, serving the Catholic cause not only in parliament and communal councils, but also through their active participation in often subordinate positions and in those undertakings which were designed to keep the masses under the influence of the Church. In 1834 the bishops reopened the University of Louvain in order to assure themselves of a Catholic elite among the secular professions on which society rested in the nineteenth century. The reopening of the university was a consequence of freedom of education in Belgium, and quite consciously the bishops ignored the Roman desire to make it a papal institution.

But the successes which accrued to the Belgian Church from the skillful manipulation of constitutional freedoms could not conceal some weak points. One was the failure to understand the problem of the

[25] Concerning the achievements of the latter, Monseigneur F.-T. Corselis, see P. Frederix in *Sources hist. rel. Belg.,* 113–23.

workers, especially regrettable in a country which was in the midst of industrialization. While a few agencies were created for the purpose of raising morals among the lower classes or of ameliorating misery, priests as well as laymen, absorbed by the problem of adapting the Church to the new middle-class society, closed their eyes to the problems of social reform which the capitalist system made urgent. The few beginnings of a Christian socialism made by a few Flemish followers of Lamennais were quickly stifled by the conservative reaction introduced by Leopold I with the aid of the nunciature. Pastoral problems generated by the rapid development of workmen's districts in the industrial areas were ignored; the numerous new parishes in this period were generally created in the rural areas. It was not surprising, therefore, that the workers gradually lost touch with the official Church. In 1834 it was noted that a large proportion of the population in the Walloon area no longer bothered to receive the Sacraments. The liberal middle class, around 1830 still religious and practicing, also began to distance itself from the Church. The unfortunate circular of the bishops in 1837, which with the attitude of Catholic purism repeated the papal condemnation of the Freemasons,[26] contributed a great deal to the rift between Catholics and liberals and strengthened the anti-Christian orientation of the Freemasons. But the reconciliation in 1840 of the ultramontanes with the constitutional freedoms was the primary impulse for a transformation of the liberal Catholic spirit. The goal of most clerics and militants was no longer freedom for all in everything in the sense of mutual toleration, but the greatest possible freedom for the Church so that it could exercise its influence on society under the best possible conditions. This attitude, appearing to many as a planned clerical offensive, unavoidably resulted in a reawakening of anti-clericalism, which after the middle of the century was ever more aggressive.

The Netherlands

After the end of the Dutch-Belgian union, the Dutch Catholics were again in a minority.[27] While it took almost a quarter of a century to replace the mission administration with a diocesan organization, a con-

[26] About this circular, see Somon, *Sterckx* I, 320–28, and J. Bartier in *Revue de l'Université de Bruxelles,* n. ser. 16 (1963/64), 162–71, 203–11.

[27] A little bit less than 40 percent of the total population. Contrary to the general assumption, they were relatively numerous in the north: while Catholics constituted 87.64 percent in Brabant and 97.80 percent in Limburg, and only 9.05 percent in Friesland and 3.83 percent in Drenthe, they constituted 39.43 percent in the province of Utrecht, 38.03 percent in Geldern, and 27.15 percent and 24.46 percent in the provinces of South and North Holland.

tinual development to a less anomalous situation occurred. In 1833, a former professor at the seminary of Warmond, Baron van Wijckerslooth, was ordained as bishop *in partibus;* his elevation made the Netherlands independent from foreign clerics with respect to confirmations and ordinations of priests. In 1840, a royal decree granted the Catholic Church certain subsidies, but under conditions regarded as controversial by the clergy.[28] New vistas were opened by the accession of William II (1840–49). He was an intimate friend of the pastor of Tilburg, J. Zwijsen, and saw Catholicism as an antirevolutionary force; there was talk of a new concordat. The Agreement of 1827 had been badly received by most of the Dutch clergy, who thought it conceded too much influence in ecclesiastical affairs to the monarchy. Thereafter the influence of Lamennais and his followers, who had emphasized the great advantages of freedom, had strengthened the revulsion against a concordatic solution. But Rome was always in favor of such an approach, and in the fall of 1840 negotiations were begun by the internuncio Capaccini. After a few months the talks produced a partial success: the Dutch government accepted the principle of a concordat which was to bring about the establishment of a diocesan hierarchy in the southern provinces. But in view of the vehement opposition of the Protestants it was decided to postpone an agreement. In the meantime, the number of vicariates apostolic in these provinces was to be raised[29] and their titulars were to receive episcopal rank, but without involving the King in their nomination in any way.

The good will of William II for the future development of Dutch Catholicism was significant. The lifting of the restrictions against the orders permitted their rapid recovery even to the north of Moerdijk, and especially the congregations of women active in education and charity flourished.

This blossoming was proof of the vitality of Dutch Catholicism and also became visible in the spiritual and intellectual growth of the clergy. It came about under the influence of the new director of the seminary at Warmond, F. J. Van Vree, and one of his professors, C. Broere. The latter was an able writer, deeply influenced by Lamennais, and placed

[28] See J. Gasman in *Archief voor de Geschiedenis von de Aartsb. Utrecht* 72 (1952), 47–84.

[29] In 1840 an apostolic vicariate was established for the Grand Duchy of Luxemburg, which in 1839 was separated from Belgium and subordinated to the King of the Netherlands. Its first titular was J. T. Laurent, who in 1848 was forced to leave the country because of a conflict with the liberals (see J. Goedert in *Biographie nationale du pays de Luxembourg,* VIII [1957]). Frequently interrupted negotiations with Rome finally led to the establishment of a bishopric in 1870. See N. Majerus, *L'érection de l'évêché de Luxembourg* (Luxemburg 1951).

his energies into the service of the Church. He followed the example of Le Sage ten Broek, but on a less popular level.

In order to promote the growth of a necessary Catholic intellectual class, Van Vree and Broere in 1842 founded the newspaper *De Katholiek* which, while it did not succeed in breaking out of the isolation which characterized Dutch Catholicism for a long time to come, yet made a remarkable contribution to the Catholic revival for half a century. Three years later, Abbé J. Smits founded the daily *De Tijd* and gained the cooperation of two talented laymen: J. W. Cramer, an admirer of Veuillot, whose cutting intransigence he shared, and J. Alberdingk Thijm, an enthusiastic follower of the romantic movement, who contributed materially to supplying the paper with that cultural prestige and genuine national spirit which at the middle of the century was still very rare among the Catholics of the Netherlands.

The improvement of the condition of Catholicism in the Netherlands during the second third of the nineteenth century was without a doubt the fruit of the dynamic activity of such enterprising personalities as Le Sage and Broere, as well as of the zeal of numerous clerics like Zwijsens[30] who were not particularly intelligent but conscientiously carried out their pastoral duties. Catholicism profited also from two broader currents which contributed to a change of minds in its favor, namely romanticism and liberalism.

Under the influence of the novels of Walter Scott and studies by German philologists of Dutch literature during the Middle Ages, many Protestants became interested in their national traditions preceding the Reformation. Simultaneously, they gained an understanding of some Catholic values, as for example liturgy, which previously had been treated with nothing more than proud contempt. Prejudices dissolved, the more easily as the romantic rediscovery of the Middle Ages was not the work of Catholics who actually for a long time were tied to a limited classicism, but of pastors and scholars without any connection to the Church. It freed them of any tinge of suspect apologetics.

Liberalism pilloried as anachronistic the Calvinistic attempts to preserve a privileged established religion, and at the same time actively supported the entrance of the Catholics into public life. It has been shown earlier[31] with what enthusiasm the writings of Lamennais had been greeted by some of the most important spiritual leaders of Dutch Catholicism. Especially Le Sage ten Broek was very liberal in his pro-

[30] Concerning Johannes Zwijsen (1794–1877), who in 1853 became the first bishop of Utrecht, see J. Witlox, *Mgr. Johannes Zwijsen* ('s-Hertogenbosch 1927, 1941), to be read with Rogier, *Kath. Herleving,* passim, especially 192–95.
[31] See above, p. 279.

nouncements before the publication of *Mirari vos.* Not satisfied with calling concordats useless and even dangerous, he did not hesitate to declare that "truth owed its victory to itself and therefore error must be permitted to be free." The condemnation by Gregory XVI effected a change. Le Sage conceded that "liberty has its dangers and excesses" and that wisdom must "set limits" for it. Ten years later he no longer even encouraged a détente between Catholics and liberals on the parliamentary level, although earlier he had seen Belgian unionism as a victory over prejudices.

If this reserved attitude predominated until 1848 in the traditionally more conservative southern provinces, such was not the case in the area north of Moerdijk, where many Catholics, without wishing to bring about a doctrinary reconciliation between Church and liberalism, felt that there were reasons to support the liberal opposition. The opposition's program corresponded to the interests of Catholics in trade and economics, strongly represented in the large cities (25 percent in Amsterdam, 35 percent in Rotterdam, and 40 percent in Utrecht and Haarlem), and the religious indifference of many liberals fostered hopes for a more tolerant attitude toward the Church than that of the conservative Protestants in power. The work by Witlox on the early history of the Catholic Party[32] traces this slow shift of the Catholics to the left which took place in spite of Le Sage's reservations. A significant role in this context was played by a man long overlooked: the intelligent F. J. Van Vree, the future bishop of Haarlem. Together with the journalist Smits he encouraged and carefully and tenaciously guided the development of the new Catholic populations of the northern provinces.They gathered in the movement "Young Holland" and contributed a great deal to the electoral victory of the liberals, which in turn produced the change in the laws in 1848. This change produced a double advantage for the Catholics. The introduction of ministerial responsibility provided protection from royal arbitrariness, and it gave the Church a hitherto unknown independence. Its first result was the restoration of the hierarchy in 1853, achieved independently from any concordat by the more or less conscious application of Lamennais's principle of a free Church in a free state.

[32] To be supplemented by G. Beekelaar, *Rond grondwetherziening en herstel der hierarchie. De Hollandse Katholieke jongeren 1847–52* (Hilversum 1964).

Chapter 19

The Beginning of the Risorgimento in Italy

Ferment in the Papal States

The secretly growing discontent of the middle class and the young intellectuals after 1815 with the "priest government" continued to grow with Consalvi's resignation. The July Revolution in France and the revolution in Belgium brought it to a head. This double failure of the principle of legitimacy and the blow given to some important clauses of the Vienna Settlement encouraged renewed doubts about the maintenance of the traditional system of government in the Papal States as well as in the rest of Italy. A few French politicians declared their willingness to help the Italians against the intervention of Metternich's Austria. On 4 February 1831, two days after the election of Gregory XVI, Bologna, following the example of Parma and Modena, rose in revolt and under pressure from the *Carbonari* proclaimed the end of the Pope's secular rule in the province. During the subsequent days the revolt extended to the entire Romagna, the Marches, and Umbria, i.e., to four-fifths of the Papal States. Cardinal Benvenuti, bishop of Osimo, who because of his popularity in the area had been appointed special legate in charge of organizing counterrevolutionary resistance, was taken prisoner. On 25 February a "Provisional Government of the United Italian Provinces" was formed and expected French support in warding off Austrian intervention. It immediately undertook the drafting of a constitution and attempted to march on Rome, where the bulk of the people remained faithful to the Papal government. The revolution had been improvised by lawyers intoxicated by romantic notions, but it was not supported by the majority of the people. Thus it was quelled within a few weeks by an Austrian army for the intervention of which the papal government asked on 17 February after it had failed to put the revolution down with its own forces.[1] The revolt had weighty consequences. It proved the uselessness of local plots prepared by secret societies, brought about the decline of the *Carbonari,* and led to the rise of a new national movement. This was Giuseppe Mazzini's "Young Italy," with the much further-reaching aim of establishing a united republic with Rome as its capital. The consequences on the international level were even more important, as public opinion saw the Roman question in a new light,

[1] Bologna was occupied on 31 March, and Ancona, the last remaining holdout, surrendered on 26 March.

which predominated until 1870. It was no longer as in the eighteenth century a matter of incompatibility of religious values with the problems of politics, but a concern for the interests of the subjects of the Papal States as part of the interplay of the two great Catholic powers of Austria and France, with the latter once again resuming a central role on the stage of European politics after a fifteen-year hiatus.

Occasioned by the Austrian intervention in the Romagna, the rivalry between the two states concerning supremacy in Italy surfaced again. An international conference was convened in Rome by the great powers of England, Russia, Prussia, Austria, and France, and in spite of differences of opinion, skillfully exploited by Bernetti, they drafted a memorandum and handed it to the secretary of state on 21 May.[2] The document suggested a number of reforms regarded as absolutely necessary if the Roman government was to have the foundation required by the European interest. It demanded especially the restitution of the *motu proprio* of 1816, partially ignored by Leo XII, allowing general admission of laymen to offices of justice and administration, and the introduction of elections in the municipalities and provinces. The Pope was irritated by the intervention of the European powers in the internal affairs of the Roman state and together with his advisers regarded the suggested program as too liberal. Consequently the edict of 5 July confined itself to a few unimportant changes in the administration of the municipalities and provinces[3] and caused deep disappointment. Shortly after the Austrian troops left the Papal States on 15 July, fresh disturbances occurred in the Romagna. Four other edicts made slight concessions to the Romagna in the fall.[4] When they failed to bring about an improvement, the papal Curia resorted to the use of force and in December appointed Cardinal Albani to supervise the action.[5] The brutal behavior of his troops in Forli caused a general uprising. In order to quell it and without consulting with the Pope, he asked the Austrians for help, and once again they marched into the Romagna in January 1832. But this time France, interested in preventing the Papal States from becoming an Austrian satellite, reacted immediately and occupied Ancona. In spite of his indignation, shared by the other European governments, the Pope was forced to reconcile himself to the situation and agreed to the French occupation until the departure of Austria's army.

[2] Text in F. A. Gualterio, op. cit. I, 277–79 (better than Bastgen I, 91–92).

[3] A. M. Bernasconi, *Acta Gregorii Papae XVI* IV (Rome 1904), 25–31.

[4] Edicts of 5 and 31 October and 5 and 15 November 1831 (ibid. IV, 42, 53, 74, 117).

[5] L. Pásztor has clearly shown that for a long time historians overemphasized the antagonism which is supposed to have existed between Albani and Bernetti. The latter tried to use the prestige enjoyed by Albani at Vienna in order to save the independence of the Roman government.

This took place only at the end of 1838, however. While Bernetti wanted to retain Austria's conservative influence, he did not wish the Papal States to fall under Austria's tutelage.[6]

Propped up by foreign bayonets, the papal government ruthlessly punished the ringleaders, but afterwards was still confronted with the problem of reforms. These were demanded not only by the liberal governments of England and France, but from a different perspective also by Metternich, who was an enlightened and realistic conservative. He shared the hostility of Gregory XVI and his advisers to anything that smacked of constitutional government and regarded the maintenance of an absolutist government in the Italian states as mandatory for the preservation of Austria's interests. But in contrast to reactionary elements in Vienna and Rome he considered changes necessary if an end was to be put to the endemic discontent in central Italy. In his opinion, the discontent was largely caused by the incompetence of the Roman administration. He considered it absolutely necessary to make improvements designed to take into account the justified complaints of the population and to organize the powers of the state in such a way that in case of danger it could react effectively. In February 1832 he sent Court Councillor G. Sebregondi to Bologna as adviser to Cardinal Albani, who was entrusted with restoring order in the Romagna. But the Austrian envoy was powerless with the old cardinal, who was unwilling to make any changes. Gregory XVI then spontaneously invited Sebregondi to Rome, where for the next three years he was the moving power behind attempts to reorganize the Papal States.

Gregory XVI and Bernetti were radical opponents of political reforms which would permit the population to share in the governing of the state and refused to entrust laymen with important positions, but they genuinely desired administrative and economic improvements. Thus they took some useful steps even though these were esteemed too highly by the defenders of the Holy See. Sebregondi was not able completely to cure the catastrophic financial condition, but he succeeded in reducing the budget deficits. Some members of the Curia passively resisted his efforts, and he was able to realize only a portion of his original reform program. During the first years of the pontificate, he was also supported by others. Monsignor Brignole and Cardinal Ber-

[6] Hoping no longer to be dependent on foreign aid in the defense of public order, Bernetti, after vain attempts to reorganize the regular army, hit upon the idea of forming local militias consisting of volunteers, the "Centurions." Their capricious behavior in the service of the counterrevolution occasioned many justified complaints (see E. Morelli, *La politica estera di T. Bernetti,* 148–54).

netti in February 1833 reorganized the secretariat of state by dividing it into two branches, one for internal and one for external affairs, each one headed by a cardinal. It was without a doubt the first step in the direction of significant reforms.[7]

For various reasons, the reform plans devised by Metternich produced only very limited results. It was insufficient to pass edicts which then were not implemented as a consequence of the lethargy of the bureaucracy and the lack of support by high government officials. Reforms were moreover difficult in a state whose economy rested on a backward agriculture, crafts ill suited to modern means of production, a primitive industry, and a totally inadequate network of transportation. Above all, it was anachronistic to exclude laymen from the government of a state with three million inhabitants. Bernetti, like Consalvi before him, agreed only to reforms which did not go beyond the paternalistic despotism of the eighteenth century, even though almost everywhere else in Europe after 1830 attempts at a complete restoration were running afoul of liberal attitudes.

But even this timid and long overdue reformism was too progressive for the majority of the "zealots." In 1836 they welcomed with satisfaction the replacement of Bernetti by Lambruschini. As has already been shown, he was no blind reactionary and attempted to moderate police repression as well as to improve elementary education[8] and the road system. Neither was he a total slave to the Austrians.[9] But rot dominated the entire system. The policy of the secretary of state was limited to reserving the important positions and privileges for the followers of the government. This naturally embittered the liberals, who had no difficulty in presenting to the enlightened public opinion of Europe the backwardness of the government, in particular the refusal of Gregory XVI to permit railroads in his state.[10] It was typical that most of the members of the committees of revolutionary Italian refugees came from the Papal States. There the situation grew worse in the course of the years. After 1843 local revolts multiplied and the Dutch envoy in

[7] L. Pásztor, "La riforma della Segreteria di Stato di Gregorio XVI," *La Bibliofilia* 60 (Florence 1958), 285–305.

[8] Formiggini-Santamaria, *L'istruzzione popolare nello Stato pontificio 1824*–70 (Rome 1909). He was much less open-minded concerning secondary schools and universities. See M. A. Giampaolo in *RStRis* 18 (1931), 124–30.

[9] See, for example, M. A. Giampaolo, ibid., 137–39.

[10] As P. Negri has shown in "Gregorio XVI e le ferrovie," *Rassegna degli Archivi di Stato* 28 (1968), 103–26, the rejection was occasioned chiefly by political reasons, although this was denied with apologetic intentions. See also C. de Biase, *Il problema delle ferrovie nel Risorgimento* (Modena 1940).

Rome wrote that "all elements of the population are struggling against the yoke and are eager to throw it off."[11] Special military courts were in session permanently, and thousands of people were persecuted, banished, and punished for their political opinions. But repression was not able to maintain internal peace. In the fall of 1845, the Bolognese lawyer Galetti distributed broadsheets in which he exhorted the "brothers" of the Romagna to kill officials and loot churches under the banner of "Liberty, Order, Unity!" A group of revolutionaries from San Marino occupied Rimini and distributed a "Manifesto of the Population of the Roman State to the Princes and Peoples of Europe."[12] The suggested reforms were very moderate and less demanding than the memorandum of 1831. But in his reply[13] Lambruschini spoke of the "criminal declarations of a mad mob," revealing the depth of incomprehension which separated the papal government from the aspirations of a considerable portion of the people of the Papal States outside of the city of Rome.

The expressions of joy which greeted the news of the death of the Pope on 1 June 1846 provided a picture of the hatred of the Pope and the system of government embodied by him that had grown in the population. Discontent had been further fueled by the completely negative attitude of Gregory XVI and his secretary of state toward the attempts of Italian patriots to free the peninsula from Austrian intervention and toward the manifestations of national feeling which for a decade had grown mightily in the population, including the clergy.

The Catholics and the Problem of Italian Unity

A national consciousness, awake in Italy since the middle of the eighteenth century, gradually spread among a Jacobin minority when the French invasion toppled the dynasties. This national consciousness was fostered both by the revolutionary principle of the right of people to self-determination and the concrete experiences in the Kingdom of Italy. After 1815, the often rather vague concepts of unification of a peninsula liberated from the antiliberal Austrian yoke survived chiefly among the young from middle class backgrounds who longed for the Italy of Napoleon, but also among a part of the educated public living on the memories of the grandeur of Rome and the resistance of the Lombard cities to the German Emperors. The broad masses also were

[11] Quoted by A. M. Ghisalberti, *Cospirazioni del Risorgimento* (Palermo 1938), 8–11.
[12] Text in F. A. Gualterio, op. cit. II, 359–69. See also P. Zama in *Studi romagnoli* 2 (1951), 373–87.
[13] Reproduced by G. Margotti, *Le vittorie della Chiesa* (Milan 1857), 490ff.

infected by the movement of the *Risorgimento,* fed by the atmosphere of romanticism which promoted historical awareness. It was further promoted by such literary bestsellers as Silvio Pellico's *Le mie prigione* which related the terrible experiences of the author during his imprisonment in Austrian jails, constituting a terrible indictment of the methods of the Austrian police. The unrest of 1830/31 enlarged the number of Italian patriots; renewed Austrian intervention made it clear to all that constitutional and liberal aspirations could only be satisfied by a common front of all Italians. In subsequent years, the periodic congresses of scientists held in Italian capitals contributed to the breakdown of parochialism by pushing national questions[14] into the foreground. The economic development, illustrated by the growth of railroads, tended in the same direction. Initially there were among the *Carbonari* convinced Catholics, even priests and members of orders, often with a tradition of Jansenism.[15] But between 1830 and 1840 the wish for the unification of all of Italy was represented chiefly by men who were hostile to the Church, either because they saw in the Pope, the secular ruler obedient to the Austrians, the primary obstacle, or because under the influence of Freemasonry they regarded liberty incompatible with religion and viewed the priests as the main defenders of an authoritarian society opposed to their striving for popular sovereignty. There was also Mazzini, who in 1831 founded the organization "Young Italy." His program called for liberation from all dogmas and Churches, so that under the motto "God and People" a new religion of humanity could be created and with universal brotherhood a democracy of the future could be realized. The systematic use of violence by the secret societies and the radical character of Mazzini's program, aimed at replacing the legitimate rulers with a democratic republic, tended to increase the distrust of many Catholics and explained the almost totally negative reaction of the hierarchy toward the national movement. Around 1840 a new development occurred under the influence of intellectuals who favored a somewhat vague but genuinely religious Christianity and realized that in Italy loyalty to Catholicism represented the foremost national tradition. Consequently they tried to bring about the unification of their country not against the will of the Church, but with its support. This movement of neo-Guelphism replaced with convergence, cooperation,

[14] Lambruschini was well aware of the political significance of these congresses and refused to permit them in Rome. On the importance of the congresses, see F. Bartocini-S. Verdini, *Sui congressi degli scienzati* (Rome 1952).

[15] See M. Vaussard, *Jansénisme et gallicanisme aux origines religieuses du Risorgimento* (Paris 1959), 101–36.—On the Carbonari-priests in the kingdom of Naples, see A. de Santis in *Archivi,* 2nd ser. 25 (1958), 13–28.

and occasionally even uniformity the antithesis of the revolutionary left, which saw *Risorgimento* and Catholicism and Italy and Papacy as mutually exclusive hostile forces.

The starting point of neo-Guelphism was the conviction that the combination of religious and patriotic sentiments could form a powerful national lever, as had been shown by the examples of Spanish resistance to Napoleon, the liberation of Greece from the Ottoman yoke, and the emancipation of Belgium from Protestant Dutch domination. A few years earlier, Manzoni had attempted to awaken national feeling through an appeal to religious sentiment and by drawing attention to the role of protector played by the Pope at the time of the Lombards, when he had become the focal point for Italy after the collapse of the Roman Empire. At the same time, historians were attempting to bring back into prominence the tradition of national Guelphism through dubious reconstructions of the resistance to the Hohenstaufen Emperors. Among others there was the Neapolitan G. Troya (1782–1858), who wrote a monumental work in order to prove that the Pope, representing in medieval Italy the opposition to the "barbarians" from north of the Alps, once again had to wrest it from them.

Only Tommaseo,[16] banished to France since 1833, suggested in his work *Dell'Italia* (1835) that the Pope should take the lead in Italy's rebirth. He demanded the expulsion of the Austrians from the Italian peninsula, called for a united Italy, and proclaimed his belief in the unity of liberty and Christianity. The true initiator and spiritual leader of neo-Guelphism, however, was Vincenzo Gioberti,[17] a Piedmontese priest who because of his publicly announced sympathies for Mazzini had been banished to Brussels. Later he had broken with Mazzini's followers. The reason for the break was the fruitlessness of their agitation and their ideological inconsistency, which prevented them from

[16] Concerning Niccolò Tommaseo (1802–74), poet, philologist, and essayist, see R. Ciampini, *Vita di Niccolò Tommaseo* (Florence 1945); M. L. Astaldi, *Tommaseo come era* (Florence 1966); R. Ciampini, *Studi e ricerche su Niccolò Tommaseo* (Rome 1944), especially 107–210.

[17] Vincenzo Gioberti (1801–52) was a professor in the Department of Theology at Turin and almoner of the court from 1825 to 1833, even though he maintained intimate contact with the liberal and revolutionary movements; 1848–49 he was president of the Piedmontese government. See A. Bruers, *Gioberti* (Rome 1924); A. Anzilotti, *Gioberti* (Milan 1922; fundamental); U. Padovani, *Vincenzo Gioberti ed il cattolicismo* (Milan 1927); R. Rinaldi, *Gioberti e il problema religioso del Risorgimento* (Florence 1929); T. Vecchietti, *Il pensiero politico di Vincenzo Gioberti* (Milan 1941); A. Omodeo, *Vincenzo Gioberti e la sua evoluzione politica* (Turin 1941); G. Bonafede, *Gioberti e la critica* (Palermo 1950). Works: *Opere complete,* 35 vols. (Naples 1877/1937); new critical edition (Rome-Milan 1938ff.); *Epistolario,* 11 vols. (Florence 1927/37).

supplying the Italians with a constructive concept. After wavering between skepticism and pantheism, Gioberti retraced his way to a position close to his original Catholicism, and in January 1843 published a huge, almost indigestible tome, *Del primato morale e civile degli Italiani.* The response to it was compared to that which Fichte had evoked with his *Addresses to the German Nation.* After praising in his book the genius of Italy and reminding the readers of its contributions to the cultural legacy of humanity, he announced that the rebirth of the country, which encompassed liberty, national unity, and independence, in cooperation with a moderate liberalism, should utilize the alliance between modern currents and existing institutions, i.e., between monarchy and Catholicism. From this vantage point he called for the unification of Italy in a federation of states, with the Pope as president. As in almost all such cases, his thoughts were not quite new; some of them had been expressed by Rosmini some time before.[18] But never before had these thoughts been offered with such eloquence, and never before had the secular, political, and practical value of Catholicism and its main support, the papacy, been glorified as the spiritual source of national rebirth with such force. Of course, the book was not welcomed by anticlerical liberal circles; they had no difficulty in contrasting Gioberti's ideal Pope with the reality of Rome under Gregory XVI. Traditional Catholics also criticized the study because they were disturbed by its innovative views and its call for reform. For this reason Lambruschini quickly forbade the distribution of the book in the Papal States. But it was welcomed by very many Catholics and clergy, including some cardinals,[19] and immediately after its publication it was said that the idea of Italian unification was no longer identified with Mazzini but with Gioberti. The book's surprising success was especially astonishing in view of its difficult style. It proved that its content corresponded to a widespread attitude. People longed to reconcile what previously appeared irreconcilable: attachment to the ancestral religion and the desire for political rejuvenation, national sentiment and the revulsion against revolutionary violence. Marxist historiography has explained the success of the neo-Guelph program with an equivocal class reaction, with the antiquated nobility seeing in the Pope the protector of the feudal hierarchy, and with the propertied middle class tying its interests to a limited monar-

[18] See C. Callovini, "Il primato del neoguelfismo rosminiano," *Atti del Congresso internazionale di filosofia A. Rosmini* I (Florence 1957), 481–95. A. Anzilotti, *Gioberti,* 242, had already said: "Rosmini appare più neoguelfo del Gioberti stesso." Concerning Rosmini and the Risorgimento, see also below, pp. 323ff. and footnote 42.

[19] It is known that the work made a deep impression on the future Pope Pius IX, then bishop of Imola in the Romagna.

chy which in the name of Christian personal rights was to guarantee the essential principles of 1789, i.e., liberty and property.[20] In any case, for whatever reasons, neo-Guelphism for several years was considerably successful, even after Gioberti in his *Prolegomeni al Primato* (1845) admitted reduced confidence in a reform pope and directed attention to the reactionary forces within the Church, especially the Society of Jesus.

Gioberti's thoughts were seized upon by several Catholic writers. They regarded the continuation of the secular power of the Pope as the guarantee for the free exercise of his spiritual office, but they also thought that this principle could be reconciled with a federative Italy by a few changes in the statute of the Papal States. In his book *Speranze d'Italia,* published in 1844 and dedicated to Gioberti, the Piedmontese nobleman Cesare Balbo[21] concerned himself less with the future situation of the Pope than with Europe's diplomatic perspectives which justified the expectation of an evacuation of the Italian peninsula by the Austrians in the near future. Four other books, appearing in the first months of 1846, three of them outside of Italy and one in the Italian underground, dealt with the problem of adjusting the secular powers of the Pope to the political realities of the nineteenth century. In his *Pensieri sull'Italia,* the Lombard Luigi Torelli[22] suggested the division of an Italy liberated from the Austrians into three kingdoms, Savoy, Central Italy, and Naples, with Rome, as the seat of the Pope, a free city. In his *Della nazionalità italiana,* Giacomo Durando[23] developed the plan of withdrawing the Pope from the influence of the various European powers, so damaging to his freedom as head of the Church, leaving him only Rome and Civitavecchia, with the remainder of his states being turned over to the kings of Piedmont and Naples; they were expected to replace the absolutist system by parliamentary institutions. The Tuscan Leopoldo Galeotti,[24] one of the best liberal Catholic publicists of his time, concluded a sharp criticism of the leadership of the Papal States in

[20] See L. Bulferetti, "Il Neoguelfismo," *Quaderni di Rinascita* I (Rome 1948).

[21] Cesare Balbo (1789–1853) came from a liberal family and wrote several art-historical and art-philosophical works before becoming actively involved in politics after 1848. See *DBI* V, 395–405 (Lit.) and N. Valerie, *Cesare Balbo. Pagine scelte precedute da un saggio* (Milan 1960).

[22] Concerning Luigi Torelli (1810–67), aristocrat and scientist, see A. Monti, *Il conte Luigi Torelli* (Milan 1931) and E. Morelli in *RStRis* 36 (1949), 3–25.

[23] Concerning Giacomo Durando (1807–94), banished after 1831, soldier and after 1848 a very active politician, see N. Nada in *BStBis* 60 (1962), 147–60 and P. M. Toesca, "Italia e cattolicesimo nel pensiero di Giacomo Durando," *Il Saggiatore* 3 (1953).

[24] On Leopoldo Galeotti (1813–84), see G. Calamari, *Leopoldo Galeotti e il moderatismo toscano* (Modena 1935).

his *Della sovranità e del governo temporale dei Papi* with the suggestion that the solution consisted of a return to the conditions of the Middle Ages: nominal sovereignty of the Pope over the communes, which would retain their full local liberties. Massimo d'Azeglio,[25] one of the few Piedmontese aristocrats passionately in favor of Italy's unity, in his *Degli ultimi casi de Romagna* concluded his attacks on the persecutions after the Rimini matter with an enthusiastic portrait of a liberal reform pope whom he desired to see as successor to Gregory XVI.

It must be noted that in the case of all of these neo-Guelphs, national and unitary striving went hand in hand with the desire to create liberal institutions. These two aspects were intimately tied together since the beginnings of the *Risorgimento.* It explains to a large degree the mistrust and the often unconcealed hostility with which the movement was regarded by many members of orders, especially the Jesuits,[26] and by the majority of the hierarchy. They could not permit this attempt, reminiscent of Lamennais, to "Catholicize the revolution." Yet the success achieved by the neo-Guelphs among a considerable portion of Italy's Catholic population on the eve of the pontificate of Pius IX proved that in Italy also, even though in forms substantially different from the various West European countries and in spite of the much less favorable political and social conditions, a liberal Catholic movement was in the making.

The Varieties of Catholic Liberalism in Italy

Even though it is common usage in Italian historiography to speak of "liberal Catholics" and "intransigents," some people have doubted for a number of years that there ever existed before 1848 a Catholic liberalism comparable to that developing at the same time in France or Belgium. In contrast to French Catholics under the July Monarchy or Belgian Catholics after 1830, Italian Catholics in fact did not have to confront the question of what advantages and disadvantages a regime of constitutional liberties or the possible separation of Church and state

[25] Massimo Taparelli d'Azeglio (1798–1866) was the son of one of the strongest representatives of Piedmontese Catholicism during the restoration period, in his youth a painter and novelist, later active in politics as a very moderate constitutionalist. See N. Vaccaluzzo, *Massimo d'Azeglio* (Rome 1930); A. M. Ghisalberti, *Massimo d'Azeglio, un moderato realizzatore* (Rome 1953); *DBI* IV, 746–52.

[26] In fairness it must be added that the resistance of some Jesuits to the neo-Guelph program had other reasons than fear of liberal reforms. P. Curci in his *Fatti ed argomenti in risposta alle molte parole di Vincenzo Gioberti* (1845) declared that men of the Church should not be concerned with political problems but should confine themselves to be apostles of the gospels. Concerning the criticism by Father Taparelli d'Azeglio of the "braggarts of patriotism," see Jemolo, 34, footnotes 1 and 2.

would entail for the Catholic apostolate. In spite of the agitation of a dynamic but numerically small portion of the middle class and intellectuals, liberal institutions were nowhere in Italy introduced before the big crisis of the middle of the century, and relations between Church and state continued to function within the framework of the Old Regime. There existed a privileged established Church, strictly supervised by the government, a situation confirmed by the various concordats and agreements from the time of the pontificate of Gregory XVI.

On 16 April 1834 a concordat was concluded between the Holy See and the State of Naples, supplemented by the convention of 29 August 1839,[27] concerning the prerogatives of ecclesiastical courts and the continuation of the personal immunity of clerics. On 30 April 1841, the duke of Modena signed a similar concordat, guaranteeing the juridical privileges of the clergy and the statute of the ecclesiastical estates.[28] Piedmont, the first Italian state to travel a liberal path after 1848, until this date also followed a traditional course. In 1836 an agreement was concluded by Rome and Turin concerning the keeping of personal registries by the clergy.[29] In 1839 the nunciature in Turin, which had been closed in 1753, was reopened, largely as a result of the personal efforts of Count Solaro della Margarita, who wished to strengthen the alliance between Church and state.[30] In 1841 a concordat was signed concerning the privileged juridical status of the clergy.[31] This agreement, required by the political opposition and the plots in which clerics participated, was without a doubt a genuine concession of the Holy See to the legal needs of a state which under pressure from an anti-Curial administration was increasingly becoming secularized. Yet it still rested on a recognition of the principle of a privileged clergy and therefore, similar to all of the other cited examples, was not liberally motivated.

With exceptions, the majority of militant Catholics in France and Belgium went along with the liberal tendencies. The situation was fundamentally different in Italy, however. There, even in the northern provinces which were more receptive to modern currents of thought, militant Catholics joined the ranks of the counterrevolutionaries and traditionalists of the preceding period. It can be said that the failure of

[27] Mercati I, 724–25. See W. Maturi in *Archivio storico per le Prov. Napoletane* 73 (1955), 319–69.

[28] Mercati I, 739–42. It was supplemented on 13 April 1846 and 24 February 1851 by additional documents (ibid., 742–47). See P. Forni in *RSTI* 8 (1954), 356–82.

[29] Mercati I, 727–36; see 725–26. See J. A. Albo, *Relationes inter Santa Sedem et Gubernium Sardiniae 1831–46* (Rome 1940).

[30] See C. Ricciardi in *RSTI* 10 (1956), 396–436. Also L. Madaro in *Il Risorgimento italiano* 23 (1930), 515–26 and N. Nada in *BstBiS* 48 (1950), 119–38.

[31] Mercati I, 736–38. See V. Naymiller in *Il Risorgimento italiano* 24 (1931), 424–41.

the revolutionary movements of 1831 actually strengthened the reactionary character of the "intransigents" and their alliance with legitimism. Weekly or monthly periodicals such as *La Voce della verita*[32] in Modena (1831/41), *La Voce della ragione*[33] in Pesaro (1832/35), and *La Pragmalogia*[34] in Lucca (1828), were indicative of this attitude. Among its most marked defenders was Count Monaldo Leopardi,[35] a foe of any revolution, even if the ruler was clearly violating the principle of justice, as in his opinion nothing could justify a rebellion against constituted authority. Unceasingly he castigated liberty, the "dearest and most faithful friend of the devil," and especially freedom of the press, for it made possible "obscenities and scandalous stupidities of all kinds, rebellious writings, and blasphemous expressions against God and saints." These intransigent Catholics promoted a stiffer attitude toward the Protestants, especially in Tuscany and Piedmont,[36] and were emphatically suspicious of all initiatives not hewing to the denominational line. They were opposed to the religious indifferentism of the Bible societies as well as to activities concerning education and charities, because they threatened the monopoly of the Church in these areas. They commended the essentially religious and essentially monarchial kind of education of the Jesuit colleges and attacked the custom of the schools to leave groups of students in charge of student monitors, as they did not keep the children under the "precious yoke" of authority. The bitter campaign for years against the kindergartens of Ferrante Aporti,[37] which were accused of preparing the ground for a seculariza-

[32] See E. Clerici in *La Nuova Antologia* 221 (1908), 646–55.

[33] See N. Quilici in *Otto Saggi* (Ferrara 1934), 256ff.

[34] See M. Stanghellini in *RSTI* 9 (1955), 58–69. After 1838, when Monsignor Bertolozzi, a follower of Rosmini, became director, the weekly embarked on a more open-minded course.

[35] Concerning M. Leopardi (1776–1847), the father of the poet, and editor of *Voce della ragione,* see M. Angelastri, *Monaldo Leopardi* (Milan 1948) and L. Salvatorelli, op. cit., 191–96. His *Dialoghetti sulle materie correnti* (1831) were reissued by A. Moravia under the title *Viaggio di Pulcinella* (Rome 1945).

[36] At the beginning of the thirties, several factors contributed to making Protestant propaganda appear in a special and worrisome light, especially the effect generated in Florence by Vieusseux and his *Antologia* and the temporary turn of the young duke of Lucca to the Reformation. See G. Spini, 153–210, especially 188, 202–06, 210 and N. Nada in *Atti della Accademia delle Scienze di Torino* 89 (1954/55), 39–115.

[37] Ferrante Aporti (1791–1858), director of elementary schools at Cremona, one of the most important Italian pedagogues of the first half of the nineteenth century, after 1829 founded kindergartens for the broad masses (*"Asili infantili"*), which from Lombardy spread to Tuscany and then gradually to all Italian states. The Protestant origin of this method and the fact that laymen were used caused a violent reaction among the "intransigents." See A. Gambaro, *Ferrante Aporti e gli asili infantili nel Risorgimento,* 2 vols. (Turin 1937) and *Ferrante Aporti nel primo centenario della morte* (Brescia 1962).

tion of education, were partly the result of the recognition that liberals used such institutions for their own purposes, but even more so revealed the reactionary and fearful attitude toward any innovation which characterized a large part of Italy's Catholics at the time.

Although these attitudes prevailed among the majority of people, there were also some Catholics in Italy during the two decades before 1848 who were seriously concerned with the problem of confronting religious beliefs with the liberal tendencies of the time. But they did not band together, even though it would have been quite easy for like-minded men to acquaint one another with the doctrines of *L'Avenir* of how to use constitutional liberties for the benefit of the Church. On the contrary, they remained split in many small groups, with hardly any contact among them, attacked problems from totally different perspectives, and differed in many important respects.

There were indeed free spirits who raised the question of reform of Catholicism in its institutions and occasionally even in its dogmas, in order to adapt it to modern currents of thought. This was especially the case in Tuscany, where under the joint influence of the Enlightenment under Grand Duke Leopold, Jansenism, and Swiss Protestanism,[38] a number of people joined Marquis Gino Capponi[39] and Raffaele Lambruschini.[40] They strove for tolerance, human progress, and a reduction

[38] G. Capponi (1792–1876) developed his thoughts in the course of travels to Germany, Switzerland, Belgium, and Holland. He wrote several books on the Italian Middle Ages from a romantic perspective, but was known primarily through his educational writings. See G. Capponi, *Scritti inediti preceduti da una bibliografia ragionata,* ed. by G. Macchia (Florence 1957) and *Lettere di Gino Capponi e di altri a lui,* ed. by A. Carraresi, 6 vols. (Florence 1884/90). Also A. Gambaro, *La critica pedagogica di Gino Capponi* (Bari 1956); G. Gentile, op. cit.; E. Sestan, "Gino Capponi storico," *Nuova Rivista storica* 27 (1943), 270–306.

[39] Raffaele Lambruschini (1788–1873) came from Genoa. After having held ecclesiastical positions until 1817, he retired to his estates in Tuscany in order to concern himself with pedagogy and religious problems. See A. Gambaro, op. cit. (basic); R. Gentili, *Lambruschini. Un liberale cattolico dell'800* (Florence 1967); M. Casotti, *Raffaele Lambruschini e la pedagogia italiana dell'Ottocento* (Brescia 1964); G. Sofri, "Ricerche sulla formazione religiosa e culturale di Raffaele Lambruschini," *Annali della Scuola Normale di Pisa,* 2nd Series, 29 (1960), 149–89. Lambruschini's very dispersed works were collected and critically edited by A. Gambaro, *Primi scritti religiosi* (Florence 1918); *Dell'autorità e della libertà* (id. 1932; critical edition with many hitherto unpublished documents); *Scritti politici e di istruzione pubblica* (id. 1937); *Scritti di varia filosofia e di religione* (id. 1939).

[40] Either directly through the Genevan Sismondi (as his *Epistolario,* ed. by C. Pellegrini, 4 vols. [Florence 1933/54], shows) or indirectly with Vieusseux as intermediary (see R. Ciampini, *G. P. Vieusseux. I suoi viaggi, i suoi giornali, i suoi amici* [Turin 1953]; also G. Spini in *RStRis* 45 [1954], 30ff.); the significant influence of Vieusseux was confirmed by the *Carteggio inedito Niccolò Tommaseo-G. P. Vieusseux,* ed. by R. Ciampini-P. Ciureanu, I (Rome 1956).

of ecclesiastical power and its increasing spiritualization. But above all they desired a reform of Catholicism and papacy analogous to the principles of the Protestant revival movement. Lambruschini developed plans for a reform of the Church which were as far-reaching as those of Ricci and Degola. Parishes were to be governed jointly by an elected parish priest and an elected lay consistory, both of them forming a counterweight to ecclesiastical power. Beyond such organizational reform plans, these men were opposed to a religion of authority and in favor of an intensification of Christianity, which they looked upon more as a force for individual ethical perfection than as a communal religion of salvation.

In addition to this liberal Catholicism, touching the limits of ecclesiastical doctrine and occasionally overstepping them and demonstrating certain similarities with contemporary liberal Protestantism, there were also reformers who not in the least wished to question Catholic dogma in its Tridentine formulation, but who were interested in a limited democratization of ecclesiastical institutions. They were primarily the spiritual heirs of the Jansenists of the preceding generation, whose aims in this respect coincided with certain liberal tendencies: priests or members of orders who demanded the election of bishops by the faithful and a greater degree of independence from their superiors, and laymen such as the Tuscan Bettino Ricasoli,[41] who considered it unseemly to endanger the message of the gospels by concordatal negotiations with the secular power. For this reason they demanded the separation of Church and state, not in the name of the laicism of the state, but in the name of the transcendentalism of religion.

Special mention must be made of the philosopher, theologian, and political theorist Antonio Rosmini.[42] He was probably the strongest

[41] Bettino Ricasoli (1809–80) was more a man of action than a thinker, one of the leaders of the moderate liberal movement in Tuscany. During the first years of the kingdom of Italy he held an important position (see *ECatt* X, 853–54); see especially his *Carteggio,* ed. by S. Camerani (Rome 1939ff.) and the articles by P. Gismondi, "Dottrina e politica ecclesiastica in Ricasoli," *RStRis* 24 (1937), 1071–1113, 1256–1301 and by G. Gentile, "Bettino Ricasoli e il problema dei rapporti tra Stato e Chiesa," *Gino Capponi e la cultura toscana* (Florence 1942).

[42] On Antonio Rosmini-Serbati (1797–1855) there exists extraordinarily rich bibliographical material; see p. 396. Biography by G. B. Pagani, newly issued by G. Rossi, 2 vols. (Rovereto 1959); *Epistolario,* 13 vols. (Casale Monferrato 1889/94). From the point of view of interest here, there are especially L. Bulferetti, *Antonio Rosmini nella Restaurazione* (Florence 1942); P. Piovani, *La teodicea sociale di Rosmini* (Padua 1957); above all, F. Traniello, *Società civile e società religiosa in Rosmini* (Bologna 1966; also *Rivista di storia e lettera religiosa* 4 [1968], 397–401 and *CivCatt* III, [1967] 402–05). Also, "Il pensiero di Antonio Rosmini e il Risorgimento," (Convegno of Turin 1961) *RRosm* 56 (1962), 81–339 (especially E. Passerin, *La fortuna del pensiero di Rosmini nella*

personality of Italian Catholicism in the nineteenth century, in part because of the originality of some of his propositions, and in part because of the reception given his ideas, especially in northern Italy. The young aristocrat in his early years was a follower of religious and political restoration along theocratic and legitimist lines as represented by de Maistre and Haller. Thanks to a deeper connection with patristic and scholastic tradition he grew beyond them, and became increasingly aware of the difference between bourgeois society and the Church as an essentially spiritual community, without subscribing to their separation. Yet in many important points he differed from the purely liberal point of view. Until the end he remained an opponent of the Enlightenment and the principles of the French Revolution, but attempted to revive their deepest aspirations in another context, as he was convinced of the necessity to differentiate between destructive innovations and those which enrich the values inherited from the past. Thus he placed more and more emphasis on freedom of the person, the right of nationalities to develop freely, and the necessity of reconciling Catholicism with modern civilization.

In this fashion he appeared as early as 1830 as a forerunner of the neo-Guelphs of the 1840s. In contrast to Gioberti, who attempted to draw the Church into the service of his political and national ideals by assigning it a mission in the secular area, Rosmini was chiefly interested in the freedom of the Church to exercise its apostolic mission and to pursue its supernatural goal. Equating the independence of the Pope from regalistic governments with Italy's independence from Austria, he demanded national freedom as a prerequisite for the freedom of the Church. On the other hand, his radical rejection of regalistic governments, which he shared with the "intransigents" of the restoration period, caused him—unlike them—to turn against absolutism of any kind. In the name of the cultural traditions of medieval Italy discovered by the romanticists, he developed a Christian concept of politics and law which opposed equally Metternich's despotism in the style of the eighteenth century and the Jacobin predominance of the state preached by some so-called liberals of the time. In contrast to Lamennais and Gioberti, Rosmini underscored the essentially supernatural character of the Church, but assigned it the task within bourgeois society of defend-

---

cultura del Risorgimento, 97–109); C. Callovini, *Antonio Rosmini come uomo del Risorgimento italiano* (Rome 1953); S. Colonna, *L'educazione religiosa nella pedagogia di Antonio Rosmini* (Lecce 1963); G. Ferrarese, *Ricerche sulle riflessioni teologiche di Antonio Rosmini negli anni 1819–28* (Milan 1967). A good anthology is M. F. Sciacca, *Il pensiero giuridico e politico di Antonio Rosmini* (Florence 1962).

ing and promoting true freedom (a freedom not totally identical with that expounded by democratic liberals).

But Rosmini was also deeply convinced, thereby approaching the reform movement of Tuscany's liberal Catholics from another direction, that the independence of the Church from the governments, which alone would enable the Church to become the "Mother of Liberty," was tied essentially to an inner renewal of eccleciastical society. The Church, he said, which is primarily a spiritual entity, must gain its influence through truth and an appeal to conscience, not through force, and in the process it must renounce many an expensive support which it frequently seeks from the secular power. It must also come closer to the people by making a place for the Christian laity parallel to the hierarchy and show the utmost respect for the traditional rights of the particular Churches threatened by post-Tridentine centralization. This was also one of Lamennais's themes, but Rosmini approached it from a totally different perspective.

For a long time, this ecclesiological aspect of Rosmini's thought—at the time a bold innovation, but in its nucleus of a traditional nature—was not given the attention it deserved. It is the great accomplishment of F. Traniello to have brought it to light and to have demonstrated that it is the key which makes it possible correctly to understand *Le cinque piaghe della Santa Chiesa.*[43] Rosmini dared only in 1848 to publish this critical diagnosis of the Italian and Austrian Catholicism of his time, even though he wrote the work between November 1832 and March 1833 after an exchange of views with N. Tommaseo. He also frequently expressed his thoughts during this time in discussions and letters.[44] But before 1848 these expressions were limited to a number of his students and did not develop into a large movement, as was the case with Lamennais in France and with Gioberti in Italy.

The desire for greater freedom, focusing on reforms within the Church, which one encounters with variations in Rosmini, Capponi, Raffaele Lambruschini, and the men who more or less were under their influence, lent Italian Catholicism between 1830 and 1850 a façade

[43] The "five wounds of the Holy Church" indicated were: the rift between clergy and the faithful, caused by the use of Latin in liturgy; the inadequate education of the clergy; the excessive dependence of the episcopate on the princes; the exclusion of the lower clergy and the faithful from the nomination of bishops; and the control of the estates of the Church by the state. A critical edition of the work with an introduction placing it in its historical context was published by C. Riva (Brescia 1966). See also G. Martina in *RRosm* 62 (1968), 384–409, 63 (1969), 24–49.

[44] See, for example, G. Radice, *Antonio Rosmini e il clero ambrosiano. Epistolario,* 3 vols. (Milan 1962/64).

differing fundamentally from the Catholic liberalism of Montalembert's friends and the constitutionalism of the Belgian Catholics. To be sure, there were also in Italy Catholics who were primarily interested in the question of bourgeois and liberal freedoms. But they approached them from a perspective quite different from that of their fellow believers north of the Alps. There it was chiefly a case of militant Catholics, for whom the reconciliation with the modern and liberal governmental systems come to power in the course of the revolutions of 1830 posed a problem of conscience, inasmuch as liberal thought since the end of the eighteenth century tended to be anticlerical and occasionally anti-Christian. Still, the Catholics north of the Alps were of the opinion that by making peace with the new regime the Church had more to gain than to lose. After all, reconciliation would allow it to defend its rights more effectively and provide it with the opportunity to perform its apostolic work in a sector of leading public opinion which was threatening to slip away.

In Italy, however, Catholics engaged in reform politics faced the task of replacing the still prevailing absolutist governments with liberal institutions. They were primarily concerned not with the defense and the rights of the Church, but with the victory of liberalism. They were more comparable to the still believing and practicing liberals of France and Belgium than to the disciples of Lamennais. Several historians have therefore suggested designating them as "liberals and Catholics" rather than "Catholic liberals," as they had no difficulty reconciling their liberal views with their religious convictions. After all, the Italian liberalism of 1825 was not Voltairean and certainly not atheistic, not even in the secret societies in which the oath was often taken on a crucifix. As for foreign influence, that of the Cortes of Cádiz was more a guiding factor than that of the revolutionary French assemblies. Besides, in Italy, where the demand for liberal institutions was concretely tried to the awakening of a national consciousness and a rejection of foreign influences, the support was appreciated which the clergy in Spain, in Tyrol, and even in Italy itself had provided for the resistance to the Napoleonic policy of conquest. Even the almost total counterrevolutionary attitude of the ecclesiastical hierarchy hardly posed a problem for these men. Many of them had learned from Jansenism how to separate their religious convictions from submission to the ecclesiastical authorities in nondogmatic areas; condemnations of liberalism by the Pope diverted them from Catholicism as little as their teachers were diverted earlier by the papal condemnation at the Synod of Pistoia.

But the fact that a Jansenist mentality possibly facilitated the concurrence of some Catholics with liberalism does not mean at all that one has to seek in the Jansenism of the eighteenth century the source of

Catholic liberalism in Italy. A. Jemolo has clearly put forth the radical difference which, in spite of many parallels, separated the Jansenists from those who placed their confidence in progress and liberty. The decisive influence is to be sought in the ideas of the philosophes of the eighteenth century and in the innovations effected during the period of the Directory. Again in contrast to France, there was no such deep gap in Italy between the democratic Catholics of the last years of the eighteenth century and the liberal Catholics after 1830. Because Italy had not experienced the excesses of the Reign of Terror, there also did not exist, as north of the Alps, the radical reaction against everything reminiscent of the revolutionary epoch. These ideas came down from one generation to the next in diverse fashion: through clerics, who initially had harbored genuine sympathies for the new thought at the time of the French invasion and who had not completely forgotten them in the restoration period, and through former Jacobins who initially had been decidedly anticlerical, but later returned to the traditional loyalty toward the Catholic Church without renouncing their youthful enthusiasm for liberty. After giving up the revolutionary formula "Liberty without Religion" without adopting that of "Religion without Liberty" within the meaning of the Holy Alliance, they now were the heralds of the liberal Catholic "Religion with Liberty."

The "liberals and Catholics" of this movement, standing between the followers of Mazzini who clearly had divorced themselves from Church and Christianity and the reactionary militant Catholics, had many followers among the intellectuals. Two persons among them stand out: Niccolo Tommaseo and Allessandro Manzoni. Tommaseo combined the influences of the Tuscan group, of Rosmini, and of Lamennais. His passionate work *Dell'Italia* (1935) was an echo to the motto of *L'Avenir:* "Christianity separated from liberty will always remain a slave; the combination of the two will be an indication of the nearness of world peace. Only the banner having both names on it will rise victoriously. . . ." It is difficult to define Manzoni's precise attitude toward Catholic liberalism.[45] After his conversion under Jansenist auspices he discovered in religion the source of true spiritual liberty, the principle of autonomy of conscience with respect to those forces which exert pressure on it from the outside, and the leader of liberty who will keep it within reasonable boundaries and will prevent its descent into anarchy and tyranny as was the case during the French Revolution. This view is reminiscent of Lamennais's position in 1826–27. But Manzoni developed it completely independently from the French theoretician and

[45] See A. Jemolo in *RStT* 4 (1958), 242–43. On Alessandro Manzoni (1785–1873), see above, p. 239.

fitted it into the framework of a national tradition reminiscent of Savonarola's aphorism: *"Unus ex potissimis vitae christianae effectibus est animi libertas."* There is also no trace in him and others of Lamennais's earlier theocratic tendencies. In the case of Manzoni it was not a matter of a renascence of society through a free Church, but of the development of the person owing to a free conscience;[46] this explains his statement that the Lamennaic temptation of a "political Catholicism" was incompatible with the purity of religion.

Does this mean that there was in Italy no equivalent to the liberal Catholicism as it existed in France under the July Monarchy? That would go too far. The Lamennais of *L'Avenir* found no great response[47] in Italy, and the liberals generally regarded with skepticism his hope to effect an agreement between liberalism and an excessive papal sovereignty. But he had the satisfaction of approval by several recognized Italian ecclesiastics, among them the Servite Superior General Battini, the Capuchin Cardinal Micara, a few Roman theologians, and Father Ventura, the general of the Theatines.[48] There were even a few genuine disciples, especially among the young regular and secular clergy of Tuscany[49] and Lombardy.

Mirari vos put a quick end to the enthusiasm for Lamennais's doctrines among many clerics and laymen who were excited by the concept of a liberal ultramontanism. Possibly, though, the hopes awakened by Lamennais explain to a certain extent the success which the neo-Guelphs had ten years later among broad masses of the ecclesiastical world. Many people saw in neo-Guelphism an opportunity to reconcile their loyalty to Roman Catholicism with their patriotic and liberal tendencies, in spite of the skepticism of many liberals who immediately diagnosed the illusionary nature of the movement, which was a late product of romantic enthusiasm.

Finally, there were in Italy on the eve of 1848 also many Catholics

[46] This aspect was underscored by P. Scoppola, *Dal neoguelfismo alla democrazia cristiana* (Rome 1957), 13–14.

[47] Concerning the influence of Lamennais in Italy during his liberal Catholic phase, see A. Gambaro in *Studi francesi* I (1958), 204–06, 211–15. According to A. Simon in *RHE* 54 (1959), 213, Lamennais is supposed to have exerted a greater influence on Gioberti than is commonly assumed.

[48] Gioacchino Ventura (1792–1861) was a Sicilian. Gregory XVI did not permit him to continue as general of his order after 1833. See L. Tomeucci, "'Libertà e religione' nel pensiero di Gioacchino Ventura," *Archivio storico messinese* 55 (1954/55), 21–62. About his relationship to Lamennais, see F. Salinitti in *Salesianum* 2 (1940), 318–48. Concerning his support of the Sicilian revolution in 1848, see E. Di Carlo in *Regnum Dei* 5 (1949), 134–47 and *RstRis* 37 (1950), 119–24.

[49] See, for example, C. Cannarozzi, "I Frati Minori di Toscana e il Risorgimento," *StudFr* 52 (1955), 406–12.

whose principles were much like those of Montalembert. This was the case, for example, with the Jesuit Taparelli d'Azeglio. He not only unequivocally opposed despotism, thereby departing from the accepted political theology of the Society of Jesus and approaching that of Thomism, but also declared his confidence that a governmental system of constitutional liberties would bring advantages for the Church. He called upon Catholic laymen to organize themselves on the basis of common law for the defense of their religious interests.[50] This proves that the ideas matured elsewhere slowly made their way and penetrated even to the Jesuits, of whom it was too quickly thought that in Italy they were always identified with the defense of reactionary absolutism.

At the end of this survey it is understandable that A. Jemolo could ask whether with respect to Italy the phrase "Catholic liberalism" was more than a mere label, as the realities which the term subsumed were fundamentally different from case to case. Yet all these diverse attempts, regardless of the differences of viewpoints and suggested solutions, were based on a common reality. Jemolo himself spoke of the encounter of the Catholic sentiment and the liberal sentiment. Passerin d'Entrèves declared that numerous Catholics were beginning to realize that in order to do justice to the new problems posed by modern society and modern civilization, it was no longer possible to be satisfied with a return to traditional solutions, but that a somewhat radical adaptation was unavoidably necessary. But while this conviction was widely accepted by many Catholics north of the Alps, it was present in Italy before the middle of the century only in a small circle of intellectuals, none of whom was able to find acceptance by the public. The only exception was neo-Guelphism at the end of this period, and even it was more concerned with national than with liberal considerations.

[50] This fact was brought to light by G. De Rosa, *I gesuiti in Sicilia e la rivoluzione del 48* (Rome 1963). On the religious policy of the Sicilian Republic of 1848, see M. Condorelli, *Stato e Chiesa nella rivoluzione siciliana del 1848* (Catania 1965).

CHAPTER 20

The States of the German Confederation and Switzerland, 1830–1848

The July Revolution demonstrated to all who believed that revolutionary ideas had been overcome the continuing vitality of such ideas, put in question the political system of 1815, and raised fears of a new age of crisis. Its general impact was more significant than its concrete effects, which differed from country to country. Of the states treated in this chapter, Switzerland experienced the most profound changes, while the structure of the German Confederation and its member states generally survived the crisis. It had far-reaching consequences, however, which touched upon the ecclesiastical realm. Everywhere conservative forces found themselves on the defensive, and in Austria especially the tendency toward an alliance between throne and altar was strengthened. More important, liberal movements, the efforts to acquire modern constitutions, and protests against the authoritarian use of power by the states were buoyed. Changed views also impinged upon the renewed Catholic movement.[1] Resistance to the system of established Churches and demands for the realization at last of the religious parity promised in most constitutions were articulated more emphatically. Occasionally there was limited cooperation between liberals and Catholics against the common foe,[2] and in the Catholic camp more than in the liberal one there were the beginnings of popular movements.

The Roman Curia held back until the 1840s, when it seized the leadership. Gregory XVI, in any case a full-blown reactionary, became Pope during the July Revolution which created the first crisis endangering the existence of the internally weak Papal States. For this reason the new Pope sought the backing of the authoritarian states even more than before. Gregory XVI shortly after his election influenced the development in Germany by the first German publication of his *Triumph of the Holy See.*[3] It became one of the programmatic tracts of the movement of renewal and contributed substantially to its ultramontane orientation.

Clinging to the system of absolutist established Churches, most of the governments exacerbated the existing tensions. Denominational minorities resided mostly in areas acquired by the states between 1803 and 1815. Church policy, therefore, was part of the larger context of integrating these territories, and the opposition to the new authorities often combined ecclesiastical, regional, and historical desires for autonomy. This was most pronounced in the Rhineland, acquired by Prussia in 1815, where in the decade after 1830 the first great dispute between state and Church took place at Cologne. The occasion for it was the Roman condemnation of the Bonn philosopher Hermes[4] and the prob-

[1] See chapter 13.

[2] In the Rhineland, for example, where middle-class liberalism comprised many active Catholics and where the Belgian example was remembered. On the latter, see L. Schwahn, *Die Beziehungen der katholischen Rheinlande und Belgiens in den Jahren 1830–40* (Strasbourg 1914); H. Schrörs in *AHVNrh* 107–08 (1923/26).

[3] Capellari's work *Il trionfo della Santa Sede e della Chiesa contro gli assalti dei novatori,* which championed the universal episcopate and the infallibility of the Pope, first appeared in 1799 in Venice. The first German edition was published in 1833 in Augsburg.

[4] See above, pp. 243f.

lem of mixed marriages. For the population, the latter issue was a very weighty problem, as it affected ecclesiastical policy in no longer denominationally uniform states.

Count Ferdinand August von Spiegel,[5] archbishop of Cologne, had invited Hermes to the University of Bonn and found in him as well as in many of his students suitable supporters for the spiritual and organizational reconstruction of ecclesiastical life. Strict opponents denounced Hermes' doctrine, Rome subjected it to lengthy examinations, and Gregory XVI condemned it in his summary Brief *Dum acerbissimas* of 26 September 1835.[6] The Curia did not notify the state authorities of the brief, it was not published officially, and its implementation caused difficulties. For the Hermesians, the papal decision came as a great surprise. The nuncios at Munich and Brussels assigned the task of distributing the brief to the opponents of Hermes, who were most eager to do so and who used the brief as a weapon in their fight against an established Church. The Catholic press supported them, and the involvement of the nuncios was a clear indication of the expanding ultramontanism.

The strictly Tridentine law concerning mixed marriages proved impossible to maintain everywhere in the eighteenth century. Mitigation of the law was conceded to Prussia, whose government refused to apply the law in its original form; with respect to Silesia, Pius VI in 1777 had left the implementation to the bishop of Breslau. The clergy was generally content with the provisions of the Common Law Code of Prussia, according to which sons were brought up in the religion of the father, daughters in that of the mother. Even the declaration of 1803, according to which legitimate children were to be raised in the religion of the father, raised no objections. The government hesitated to take further steps before the ecclesiastical reorganization was finished; but in 1825 a cabinet order extended the declaration of 1803 to the western provinces where canon law applied and where an established Church of the Prussian type had no tradition. The order violated the guarantees which had been given to the Church when Prussia assumed possession of the Rhenish provinces and was a determined effort to Protestantize the western provinces, as almost only Protestant officials and officers were stationed there. Bishops and Curia did not dare resist, but many clerics, especially those close to the movement of revival, refused to carry out the order. Their appeal to freedom of conscience was also supported by many liberals. Because the government was unwilling to give up its

[5] See above, p. 225. The biography by Lipgens and Schrörs, *Kölner Wirren,* chapters II and III, as well as Bastgen in *RQ* 39 (1931) provide the most thorough information on Spiegel's multifaceted work and eminent personality.

[6] Bernasconi, *Acta Gregorii XVI* I, 85f.; D 1618–20.

claims and insisted on the clerical blessing of mixed marriages, it began new negotiations with the Curia, conducted by Christian Karl Josias von Bunsen (1791–1860), Niebuhr's active successor as envoy to Rome.[7] With his Brief *Litteris altero abhinc* of 25 March 1830, Pius VIII tried to be conciliatory. He permitted priests to provide "passive help" in all cases in which a mixed marriage was not preventable in spite of attempts at dissuasion and in which agreement was not obtained to raise children as Roman Catholics. But the government refused the official acceptance of the papal brief, insisting on formal wedding ceremonies and renunciation of the priestly attempts at dissuasion.

Inasmuch as Rome now stuck to its position, the government attempted to persuade the Rhenish-Westphalian bishops to interpret the papal decision most liberally, using massive pressure in the process as well as promises which later were not kept. The bishops of Münster, Paderborn, and Trier gave in quickly; not so Archbishop Spiegel of Cologne, on whom everything depended and who was always interested in asserting the Church's independence. Eventually he also agreed, only because the Prussian emissaries were able to convince him that the Pope desired the most liberal interpretation of the brief possible. When the Prussian government then accepted the brief for transmission to the bishops, the Curia was convinced that it had won a victory. But on 19 June 1834 Spiegel and Bunsen signed a secret convention in Berlin which required for formal marriage vows no more than the "religious intention on the part of the Catholic partner to adhere to the faith and fulfill the duties involved in raising children" and limited passive assistance to cases of evident frivolity. Spiegel's suffragan bishops concurred.

But the expected calming of the waters failed to occur. In fact, the protest against Prussia's religious policy, now combined with criticism of the archbishop's yielding and Rome's silence, only grew more vehement. In Prussia, police and censorship were able to suppress many expressions of opposition, but outside of its borders leading publicists of the Catholic movement such as Räss and Weis[8] took up the cudgels.

Clemens August Baron von Droste-Vischering (1773–1845)[9] be-

[7] After the failure of the Prussian mixed marriage policy, Bunsen was forced to resign his position. In addition to the literature about the Cologne disturbances, there is a three-volume biography about him by F. Nippold (Leipzig 1868/69), and concerning his ecclesiastical concepts there is L. v.Ranke, *Aus dem Briefwechsel Friedrich Wilhelms IV. mit Bunsen* (Leipzig 1874); F. H. Reusch, *Briefe an Bunsen . . .* (Leipzig 1897); W. Bussmann, *NDB* 3, 17f.

[8] See above, p. 223.

[9] An adequate biography is lacking. So far the most thorough but occasionally too critical treatment is Schrörs, *Kölner Wirren,* chapters IV–IX. See also Schnabel, *G* IV, 133–38.

came Spiegel's successor in 1836. As a member of the Gallitzin circle he had acquired a fideistic hostility to science, lived an ascetic life, and because of his authoritarian regimen in Cologne failed to win the sympathies of either subordinates or associates. The few advisers whom he trusted all came from the militant wing of the Catholic movement. Droste's first aim was the destruction of Hermesianism, which he had always distrusted; he also wanted to hurt the University of Bonn's department of theology. His distant goal was a type of Tridentine seminary for all theological instruction. To achieve his objectives, Droste used means which were illegal in the eyes of state and Church and maneuvered himself into a corner. He and his advisers were aching for a test of strength with the state and the time seemed right for it. In the spring of 1837 the archbishop seized upon the problem of mixed marriages, which appeared to him as a wonderful battle instrument. He was determined to apply the Berlin convention, which by now as a result of better information was also contested by the Curia,[10] only to the extent to which it corresponded to the brief of Pius VIII. He refused to be intimidated by the ultimatum of the Prussian government either to give in or to resign. Employing the means of an authoritarian police state, the government on 20 November 1837 had Droste arrested and incarcerated in the fortress of Minden. An official explanation accused him of having broken his word and of revolutionary intentions.

Gregory XVI on 10 December 1837 protested against this act of violence in the solemn form of an allocution to the cardinals. At the same time he placed in question Prussia's entire conduct in the question of mixed marriages and rejected the convention of Berlin. But Görres with his polemic *Athanasius* (January 1838) was much more effective. The talented publicist succeeded in painting Droste as the great champion of freedom of the Church and to make his cause that of all German Catholics. Numerous brochures followed, and Church newsletters experienced a tremendous rise in circulation. In 1838 Görres and his friends founded the *Historisch-politische Blätter,*[11] which under the lead-

[10] Broad revelations in the Liège *Journal historique et littéraire* (October 1835) caused the Curia to protest. It took an even harder line after Bishop von Hommer of Trier immediately before his death had withdrawn from the Convention and informed the Pope of its creation and content. In the face of the Roman protests, Bunsen employed a shortsighted tactic of stonewalling.

[11] F. Rhein, *10 Jahre Hist.-Pol. Blätter 1838–48* (Diss., Bonn 1916); K.-H. Lucas, *Joseph Edmund Jörg. Konservative Publizistik zwischen Revolution und Reichsgründung 1852 bis 1871* (Diss., Cologne 1969); Pesch, *Kirchlich-politische Presse,* 166f. The rise of the other Catholic presses is treated by Pesch, op. cit., 167–84, 209–19.

ership of George Phillips,[12] Görres's son Guido, and Carl Ernst Jarcke[13] laid the foundations for the Catholic-conservative doctrine of state and society. To an increasing degree the polemic was also directed to Protestants, the great majority of whom sided with the Prussian government; the events at Cologne contributed to a lasting hardening of the denominational fronts.

Out of the dispute over mixed marriages grew the first mass movement for freedom of the Church, finding support in the Pope, and forcing the Prussian state to the limits of its power in a way previously unknown. Within a few months after Droste's arrest the government had to endure "modest inquiries" about the Catholic education of children from mixed marriages. Immediately after the papal allocution, canon law with respect to mixed marriages was applied in the western provinces and soon it was also employed in the eastern provinces, where for the time being only Leopold Count Sedlnitzky,[14] prince-bishop of Breslau and a defender of the concept of an established Church, continued the old practice. A further attempt by the government to stabilize the situation with the arrest of Archbishop Martin von Dunin of Gnesen-Posen (1774–1842)[15] also was a failure. Almost completely united, the Poles took the side of their archbishop, whose cause was also supported by all of Catholic Germany.

[12] George Phillips (1804–72), historian of law, canonist, publicist, Catholic since 1828, became a professor in Munich in 1834, in Innsbruck in 1850, and in Vienna in 1851. His work on Church law (7 vols., Regensburg 1845/72) did much to promote the papalistic concept of the Church. G. von Pölnitz in *HZ* 155 (1937); Vigener, op. cit., 99ff.

[13] Carl Ernst Jarcke, lawyer (see chapter 13, footnote 14), was professor in Vienna after 1832 and became one of Metternich's associates with respect to religious policy. F. Peters, *Jarckes Staatsauffassung* (Berlin 1926); O. Weinberger in *HF* 46 (1926); A. Wegener in *Festschrift für Ernst Heinrich Rosenfeld* (Berlin 1949); O. Köhler in *StL* IV, 621f.

[14] Leopold Count Sedlnitzky von Choltitz (1787–1871), prince-bishop after 1835, believed that conciliation served peace with the state as well as among the denominations; he was severely attacked by the Catholic press in connection with the dispute over mixed marriages. Although Frederick William IV approved of his policy, he followed a request by the Pope and resigned in 1840 without struggle, evidently realizing that his enlightened views were being overtaken by events. Sedlnitzky continued to live in Berlin and became a Protestant in 1863. Sedlnitzky's autobiography (Berlin 1872); *Schlesische Lebensbilder* IV (Breslau 1931); J. Gottschalk in *ArSKG* 2 (1936), 5 (1940); W. Urban (Warsaw 1955, chauvinistic distortion); Lill, *Beilegung der Kölner Wirren* 64–67, 102–06; H. Jedin, "Von Sedlnitzky zu Diepenbrock," *ArSKG* 29 (1971), 173–204 (letters of chapter vicar Ritter, 1841–47).

[15] In Dunin's case at least due process was applied. The archbishop was removed from his office by the Posen district court and sentenced to confinement in a fortress. B. Stasiewski in *LThK* III, 601 (Lit.).

The ascension of the throne of Prussia by Frederick William IV in June 1840 brought about a fundamental turn of events. The new King was imbued with the thought of political romanticism and despised established Churches and bureaucracies. Believing in one Church with different denominations, he wanted to create a Christian state. He desired the independence of the Churches and their coordination with the state, and in Berlin he displayed an unusual degree of sympathy for specifically Catholic forms of worship and traditions.[16] In negotiations with the Curia, in which Ludwig I of Bavaria and Metternich acted as mediators, the King quickly made far-reaching concessions. Gregory XVI's diplomacy thus succeeded in reaching the compromise in the summer of 1841 which granted the Catholic Church in Prussia a larger degree of freedom than it enjoyed in any other German state and which considerably enhanced the reputation of the Holy See in Germany. The Munich nuncio Viale-Prela acted as the prudent interpreter of Roman intentions and generally extended the influence of the nunciature to non-Bavarian dioceses.[17] Prussia gave up the demand to approve and interfere in the practice of mixed marriages, the bishops were allowed to correspond freely with Rome, the freedom of episcopal elections was guaranteed according to the agreement of 1821, and a separate branch for Catholic affairs was created in the ministry of religion.[18] Dunin was permitted to return to his office; Droste, whom the Curia was not loath to see pushed into the background because of his rudeness, had to be content with an apology.

The administration of the archbishopric of Cologne was assumed by the bishop of Speyer, Johannes von Geissel (1796–1864).[19] Geissel energetically used the freedoms granted to the Church and integrated the impulses generated by the Catholic movement into his hierarchical concept. By way of Viale-Prela he maintained close contact with Rome,

[16] E. Schaper, *Die geistespolitischen Voraussetzungen der Kirchenpolitik Friedrich Wilhelms IV.* (Stuttgart 1938); W. Bussmann, "Spiegel der Geschichte," *Festschrift für Max Braubach* (Münster 1964); K. Borries in *NDB* 5, 563–66. On the church policy of the King, see also his correspondence with Bunsen; E. Friedberg, *Die Grundlagen der preussischen Kirchenpolitik unter König Friedrich Wilhelm IV.* (Leipzig 1882); Lill, op. cit.

[17] Michele Viale-Prelà (1798–1860), nuncio in Munich (1838–45) and Vienna (1845–55, after 1852 cardinal and pronuncio), after 1855 archbishop of Bologna. Engel-Janosi, *Österreich und der Vatikan* I, 39, 71, 117; Hacker, *Bayern und der Heilige Stuhl,* 109–13, 115–29.

[18] V. Conzemius, *Die Briefe Aulikes an Döllinger. Ein Beitrag zur Geschichte der "Katholischen Abteilung" im preussischen Kultusministerium* (Rome–Freiburg–Vienna 1968).

[19] *Schriften und Reden Geissels,* 4 vols., ed. by K. Th. Dumont (Cologne 1869/76); biographies by J. A. F. Baudri (Cologne 1881) and O. Pfülf (2 vols., Freiburg 1895/96); Schnabel *G* IV, 75–80, 153ff., 197f.; R. Haas in *NDB* 6, 157f.; R. Lill, *Rheinische Lebensbilder* 3 (Düsseldorf 1968).

but always safeguarded his own autonomy. The unnecessarily harsh exclusion of the last remaining Hermesians was Geissel's first measure to achieve internal uniformity; he regarded it as necessary for the struggle with opposing forces, for the organizational expansion of the Church, and for the activation of its remaining reserves. Soon he began the creation of Catholic clubs which reached beyond the borders of his diocese; the founding of the Borromäus Association in 1844 was a promising beginning.[20] Geissel also established contact with many other German bishops, preparing the ground for common action by the episcopate, first tested in 1848. Even before the revolution he achieved concerted action on the part of his bishops in a way which the government had not permitted before 1840. He was supported by Wilhelm Arnoldi (1798–1864), whose appointment as bishop of Trier in 1842 was also possible only as a result of the change in Prussia's religious policy.[21] In 1844 he organized a pilgrimage to the Holy Coat; with more than a million pilgrims it was a powerful proof of the revival of Catholicism, even though it was attacked by many Protestants and liberals as a challenge to the spirit of the century. It was the overt reason for the splitting-off of German Catholicism,[22] which as a national and superficially rationalistic countermovement against the ecclesiastical rejuvenation in eastern and central Germany achieved initial successes. The short-lived movement, supported by liberal and democratic publicists, used essentially nonecclesiastical arguments incapable of supporting a separate Church; it was eventually absorbed partially by Protestantism, partially by folkish groups. The sensible defense against German Catholic attacks was guided by Melchior von Diepenbrock (1789–1853), a student of Sailer, who became prince-bishop of Breslau in 1845 after having overcome strong reservations on the part of conservative clerics.[23] In contrast to the belligerent and defensive activism of

[20] The aim of the association was to deepen Catholic sentiments through the distribution of good books and to provide an alternative to the liberal works widely available in the Rhineland. The founders, Franz X. Dieringer (professor of dogma at Bonn and adviser to Geissel), Baron Max von Loë, and August Reichensperger came from the social class which continued to provide the leaders of the association movement (clergy, nobility, middle class intellectuals). W. Spael, *Das Buch im Geisteskampf. 100 Jahre Borromäus-Verein* (Bonn 1950).

[21] Biography by J. Kraft (Trier 1862, 1865); A. Thomas in *NDB* 1, 390f.

[22] The leaders of the movement were Johannes Ronge (1813–87) and Johann Czerski (1813–93). K. Algermissen, *Konfessionskunde* (Hanover 1930), 181–221; K. Algermissen in *LThK* III, 279; H. J. Christiani, *J. Ronges Werdegang bis zu seiner Exkommunikation* (Breslau 1924).

[23] Biographies by H. Förster (Breslau 1878) and J. H. Reinkens (Leipzig 1881); H. Finke in *Westfälische Zeitschrift* 55 (1897); J. Jungnitz, *Die Beziehungen des Kardinals M. von Diepenbrock zu König Friedrich Wilhelm IV.* (Breslau 1903); F. Vigener, *Drei Gestalten*

Geissel, Diepenbrock adhered to the conciliatory principles and broad ecclesiastical concept of his mentor and thereby gained the full confidence of Frederick William IV. In a period of ultramontane hardening, he preserved a decided awareness of episcopal autonomy.

The development in Bavaria at first proceeded totally within the course mapped out by Ludwig I.[24] The revolution was followed by a more conservative policy. The King knew how to combine adherence to an established Church with strictly conservative ecclesiastical rejuvenation. As he strongly supported the Church, the Curia was willing to make concessions to his regalism, for example in the dispute over mixed marriages in which Gregory XVI initially attempted to have canon norms accepted.[25] Pressured by the King and his government, the Holy See gave in with respect to this problem which was of such great importance to Catholic rejuvenation. An instruction to the Bavarian bishops[26] of 12 September 1834 contained the same concessions which Pius VIII had granted the Prussians. Ludwig, in contrast to the government in Berlin familiar with the limits of Roman willingness to compromise, was satisfied.

The men led by Ringseis, Görres, and Döllinger reached their greatest effectiveness during the thirties; among the younger associates there were George Phillips, the lawyer Karl Ernst von Moy de Sons (1799–1867), and the theologian Friedrich Windischmann (1811–61). Phillips influenced Carl August von Abel (1788–1859), secretary of the interior after 1837. Abel continued the Catholic state traditions of Bavaria and followed an extremely conservative, and at the same time militantly Catholic policy; conversions were favored, and new creations of Protestant communities were hindered.

Abel's appointment was symptomatic for the reaction of Ludwig I to the religious events in Prussia. Especially during the Cologne disturbances, the King believed that he had to act as *defensor ecclesiae*[27]; it was due to him and Abel that Bavaria presented the Catholic point of view.

---

aus dem modernen Katholizismus (Munich 1926); J. H. Beckmann, *Westfälische Lebensbilder* 1 (Münster 1930); J. H. Beckmann in *HJ* 55 (1935); A. Nowack, *Ungedruckte Briefe von und an Kardinal M. von Diepenbrock* (Breslau 1931); *M. Kardinal von Diepenbrock, Gedenkschrift,* ed. by E. Bröker (Bocholt 1953); J. Glossner-Gitschner in *NDB* 3, 651f.

[24] See above, p. 222.

[25] Brief *Summo iugiter studio* (27 May 1832). Text in Bernasconi I, 140ff.

[26] Text in Bernasconi I, 459ff.

[27] With the historical concept of his office, the King liked to refer to the Catholic Counter-Reformation traditions of the House of Wittelsbach. Hacker, op. cit., 106. On the reaction of the King to the Cologne events, see also J. Grisar, "Bayern und Preussen zur Zeit der Kölner Wirren" (typed dissertation, Munich 1923).

The Cologne events and Ludwig's partisanship had the effect in Bavaria of aiding the growth of the Catholic movement and especially of strengthening its intransigent wing. In the heat of the dispute, Sailer's conciliatory legacy receded into the background. A short period of particularly close ties between Rome and Munich began; Ludwig's mediation role in the Cologne dispute has already been mentioned; following the Prussian example, he also in 1841 permitted the bishops of his state and the Curia to correspond freely.

In the appointment of bishops, Ludwig generally steered a middle course, but the nomination of the young Count of Reisach[28] as bishop of Eichstätt in 1836 meant a strengthening of the militant forces. Reisach, personally close to Gregory XVI, was the first real curialist among the German bishops of the nineteenth century. While most of his fellow bishops wanted to retain a modest degree of autonomy even during the height of ultramontanism, Reisach was eager to adjust all ecclesiastical structures and forms to the Roman standards and examples.

While the King tried to follow a moderate course once the situation had become calm again, the Catholic leaders retained their militancy. Their intransigence, often protected by Abel, increased,[29] they turned against Ludwig's established Church, endangered the internal peace of the state, and provided the strong liberal attacks on the ministry with nourishment. Reisach, archbishop of Munich after 1846, and Windischmann, whom he appointed to be his vicar general, were mainly responsible for the hardening of the fronts. The consequence was a gradual alientation between the Catholic movement and the King, who remembered his earlier dislike of ecclesiastical excesses and once again exercised his prerogatives over the Church. Abel's influence decreased,

[28] Karl August Count von Reisach (1800–69), after studies at the Germanicum appointed as teacher in 1830 at the Roman College of the Propaganda Congreation, bishop of Eichstätt in 1836, coadjutor in 1841, archbishop of Munich-Freising in 1846, and Curia cardinal in 1855 after disputes with King Maximilian II (see chapter 29). He negotiated the Convention between the Holy See and Württemberg and Baden and became a member of all important congregations. After 1865 he was also a member of the executive committee in charge of preparations for Vatican I, after 1867 also president of the council commission concerned with Church policy. H. Rall in *LThK* VIII, 1151f.

[29] The objections by Baader and Diepenbrock against this intransigence caused by the continuing violent anti-Catholicism of many Protestants and the Southwest German system of an established church signal the internal Catholic disagreements of the 1850s and 1860s. Although Döllinger warned against unnecessary excesses in the crisis of 1847, he nevertheless was a militant. In many articles in the *Historisch-Politische Blätter* and especially through his *History of the Reformation* (3 vols, Regensburg 1846/48), directed against Ranke, he participated in the battle against Protestantism.

and in 1846 he was forced to resign from the ministry. A few months later the crisis erupted openly in conjunction with the Lola Montez scandal. After Abel's critical memorandum concerning the attempt to give the King's lover citizenship became public, he and his colleagues were replaced by a liberal cabinet and leading Catholic civil servants and professors lost their positions.

In southwest Germany, the rigorously applied laws imposed on the Church in 1830[30] precluded any free development of ecclesiastical life. The bishops essentially were confined to the ordination of priests, diocesan coordination was impossible, and the bishop became alientated from his clergy because of his dependence on the state's authority. As in neighboring Switzerland, internal tensions complicated the situation. The rejuvenation of the Church gained ground only slowly; many clerics saw in Josephinist ties to the state a better guarantee for effective religious work than in closer ties to Rome; a considerable portion of the clergy derived radical consequences from Wessenberg's reforms and demanded far-reaching democratization; and frequently there was solidarity with parallel political movements.

The first two archbishops of Freiburg, Bernhard Boll (1756–1836)[31] and Ignaz Anton Demeter (1773–1842),[32] attempted to obtain concessions from the state through conciliation and continuation of Wessenberg's liturgical reforms. Demeter opposed the synodal movement; he obtained the establishment of a state school of theology and the appointment of two eminent theologians, the catechist Hirscher and the dogmatist Staudenmaier, at the University of Freiburg. Archbishop Hermann von Vicari, after the revolution an outspoken champion of freedom of the Church,[33] during the first years of his long episcopate (1842–68) also had to make many concessions, but under the impact of the Cologne disturbances he was at least able to have the canon law on

[30] See above, p. 139.

[31] P. P. Albert in *FreibDiözArch* 56 (1928); J. Klein in *FreibDiözArch* 61 (1933); W. Müller in *LThK* II, 570.

[32] W. Reinhard-H. Bastgen in *FreibDiözArch* 56 (1928); H. Schiel in *FreibDiözArch* 57 (1929); H. Baier in *FreibDiözArch* 61 (1933); W. Müller in *NDB* 3, 591; *LThK* III, 214f.

[33] Vicari (1773–1868) was named spiritual councillor in 1802, official in Constance in 1816, and as the only member of that curia was called as cathedral canon to Freiburg, where he became suffragan bishop in 1832. Inadequate biographies exist by L. von Kübel (Freiburg 1869), H. Hansjakob (Würzburg 1873), and R. Aichele (Stuttgart 1932). A. Rösch in *FreibDiözArch* 55 (1927); H. Bastgen in *FreibDiözArch* 56 (1928), 57 (1930); W. Müller in *LThK* X, 764f.

mixed marriages recognized. Josph Vitus Burg (1786–1833)[34] and Johann Baptist von Keller (1774–1845),[35] the first bishops of Mainz and Rottenburg, were convinced Josephinists and partisans of the government. Keller's weak efforts at a reconciliation among the different factions of his bishopric were in vain, and the movement of revival, with its spiritual center in the Tübingen School, he never understood. Only under pressure from Rome and the Catholic public did he become active in the cause of greater ecclesiastical autonomy; but an appeal which he directed to the provincial diet for this purpose was rejected in 1841.

The more important attempts to free the Church from supervision by the police state in southwest Germany were made by laymen. The process was accompanied by the first stirrings of a Catholic party. In Baden, Heinrich Bernhard von Andlaw-Birseck (1802–71)[36] and Franz Josef Buss (1803–78, after 1836 professor of law in Freiburg)[37] were active. Andlaw was in favor of a strictly conservative course, Buss attempted a synthesis of conservative and liberal forces. Buss independently continued to develop the doctrine of a corporative state, and more strongly than the Viennese political romanticists he emphasized individual responsibility. He was the first to designate the solution of social problems, in addition to achieving freedom for the Church, as the chief task of German Catholics. In Württemberg, the Catholic nobility of Upper Swabia, with the Hereditary Count Konstantin von Waldburg-Zeil and Baron von Hornstein in the forefront, led the mostly conservatively motivated opposition to the established Church.[38]

After 1830, Metternich championed an alliance with the Church more strongly than before. He was doubtless motivated more by political sentiments than by religious conviction.[39] He had become completely convinced that the universal authoritarian power of the Catholic Church and the supra-national monarchy of the Habsburgs had to take a common stand against revolutionary forces. He was also interested in a recovery of Austrian prestige in the Catholic world, obscured by Josephinism and its repercussions on Austria's international and Ger-

[34] L. Lenhart in *Jahrbuch für das Bistum Mainz* 2 (1947); L. Lenhart in *LThK* X, 786; A. Ph. Brück in *NDB* 3, 43.

[35] Hagen *R* I.

[36] Biography by F. Dor (Freiburg 1910); M. Wellner in *NDB* 1, 272.

[37] Biography by F. Dor (Freiburg 1910); J. Dorneich, *Der badische Politiker F. J. Buss* (Dissertation, Freiburg 1921); R. Lange, *F. J. Ritter von Buss und die soziale Frage seiner Zeit* (Freiburg 1955); J. Dorneich in *NDB* 3, 72f.

[38] Waldburg-Zeil to an increasing degree used liberal arguments and became a liberal in 1848.

[39] See above, pp. 141 and 219f.

man positions.[40] It was easy for the chancellor to confirm Gregory XVI in his reactionary principles. The military aid given the Papal States in 1830–31 enhanced the solidarity. It was more difficult to make the concessions desired by the Pope and recognized as necessary by Metternich. The concessions were opposed by the liberal civil service, which continued to see in Josephinism the best guarantee for the monarchy. But the chancellor gained considerable ground domestically under the reign of the incompetent Emperor Ferdinand (1835–48).[41] Besides, the ecclesiastical policy testament of Francis II, in whose formulation Metternich had had a hand, formally empowered him to revise Josephinist legislation.[42] Metternich therefore strove for a cautious coordination of the two powers; the contradictions between the laws of the state and the Church were to be removed through joint agreement, and the demands of both sides were to be carefully separated.[43] Carl Ernst Jarcke[44] and the titular Abbot Joseph Otmar von Rauscher (1797–1875) aided him; Rauscher[45] came from a family of civil servants with strong ties to the state and had received his intellectual impulses from Hofbauer. Viale-Prela, nuncio in Vienna after 1845, also was in close agreement with Metternich. The efforts of Metternich and his associates helped prepare the concordat of 1855, but prior to 1848 success was denied to them; their proposals died in committees.

But partial results were achieved, as for instance in the problem of mixed marriages. Under the impact of the Cologne disturbances, the problem grew into a serious one for Austria. As the most important prerequisite for a normalization of relations, the Curia demanded the

[40] Presentation by Metternich at the State Conference on 13 June 1841 in Hussarek, op. cit., 688ff.; Weinzierl-Fischer, op. cit., 24.

[41] Metternich's violent opposition to Minister Count Kolowrat, who together with him was a member of the State Conference governing for Emperor Ferdinand, also extended to Church policy. Kolowrat was a convinced Josephinist. Srbik, op. cit., 8f., 42ff. Liberal resistance against Vienna's reactionary Church policy was fueled by the brutal and unwise expulsion of the "inclinants" of the Zillertal, ordered by the government in 1837 in the interest of the religious conformity of Tyrol. The expulsion was compatible with the Federal Act, Article 16, because the "inclinants" belonged to none of the recognized religions.

[42] Text in Weinzierl-Fischer, op. cit., 18.

[43] Among other things, Metternich was interested in easing the restrictions on the correspondence between bishops and Pope, permitted only by way of the State Conference, the restoration of the connection between Austrian superiors of orders and their Roman generals, and the renewed permission of theological studies at the Collegium Germanicum.

[44] See above, p. 334.

[45] On Rauscher, in addition to the biography by Wolfsgruber, see M. Hussarek in *AÖG* 109 (1922), 112 (1933); E. Weinzierl-Fischer, *Grosse Österreicher* XI (1957).

removal of the Josephinist marriage laws which contravened the Tridentine marriage laws. In opposition to Kolowrat, Metternich insisted on bilateral talks as suggested by Rome in 1839. The result of the negotiations[46] in 1841 corresponded to the principles of the chancellor, who insisted on retaining religious toleration and freedom of conscience as long as they coincided with his concepts of the state. For Hungary, the validity of a mixed marriage performed by a non-Catholic pastor was expressly recognized. For the other parts of the monarchy, the validity of mixed marriages without a commitment to raise children as Catholics was made dependent on the passive assistance of the Catholic priest, but could not be denied by the clergy.

In Switzerland, the July Revolution put an end to the predominance of conservative principles of state, and in twelve cantons liberal democratic constitutions were introduced. In the process of change, many Catholics also expressed desires for reform along Josephinist-Wessenberg lines and found support among the liberals. The seven cantons which in 1832 had united for a liberal change of the federal constitution, in 1834 at the Baden conferences also formulated a joint program of religious policy. They demanded the sovereignty of the state over the Church to the same degree as achieved in southwest Germany,[47] including permission for all ecclesiastical decrees; state supervision of synods, positions, and legal and educational systems of the Church; and the oath of clerics. They also wanted a nationally influenced uniformity and autonomy of the Church, in particular the creation of a Swiss Church province with Basel as archbishopric, and the expansion of episcopal prerogatives vis-à-vis Pope and nunciature. Monasteries were to lose their exemption and were to pay taxes for social purposes.

The Articles of Baden lastingly aggravated the differences among Catholics as well as between Catholics and liberals. They were condemned by Pope and episcopate alike,[48] and a large majority of the Catholic population voted against them. In consequence, the radical-liberal forces grew more hostile to Catholicism, and the initially political opposition between liberal and conservative estates shifted to the religious area. Liberal Catholics, who in the cantons of Aargau, Saint Gallen, and Solothurn had won great political influence, attempted to im-

[46] Brief of Gregory XVI of 30 April 1841; Instructions of the cardinal secretary of state, 30 April, and 22 May 1841. Texts in Bernasconi III 122ff., 125f., 132ff. See also O. Weinberger in *Zeitschrift für öffentliches Recht* 5 (1925).

[47] See above, pp. 339 and 137ff.

[48] Encyclical of Gregory XVI, 17 May 1835. Text in Bernasconi II, 32–36.

pose their program on the majority, The most excessive action was taken by the canton of Aargau, which in 1841 in violation of the constitution dissolved all monasteries.[49] The general anger of the Catholics, not pacified by the restoration of a few convents, brought about the fall of the liberals in the neighboring canton of Lucerne. The new Catholic administration recalled the Jesuits, thereby arousing the ire not only of the radicals but of all Swiss Protestants.[50] Both sides were increasingly dominated by militants. When in 1844 the radicals organized irregular troops for the purpose of toppling the Lucerne government and favored a far-reaching revision of the federal constitution in order to make it centralistic and liberal, the Catholic cantons[51] formed a defensive alliance, seeing in the undiminished maintenance of their sovereignty the irreducible prerequisite for freedom of the Church. They refused the demand of the Diet to disband their league (1846/47). The Diet consequently resolved to use military force. In the short war of the Separatist League, the last religious war in central Europe, the Catholics were defeated.[52]

The liberal majority of the Diet was now in a position to pursue its program. The Protestant victory was cheered lustily by the liberals in all of Europe and stimulated the development of events in 1848. In several cantons monasteries were dissolved, several of the defeated cantons received liberal governments in favor of established Churches, and the federal constitution of 1848 contained the discriminating prohibition of the Jesuits. The Swiss Catholics were forced into a ghetto to which they adjusted spiritually and socially. The connection with Rome was intensified, the greatest possible internal cohesion was attempted, and all areas of life were dominated by the Church. Encounters with new ideas were avoided, and participation in public life was reduced to the absolutely essential. Catholic principles and interests were equated with those of the ultramontane and conservative movements.

[49] Among them the famous abbeys of Muri (OSB) and Wettingen (OCist), which found new homes in Austria (Bozen/Gries and Bregenz/Mehrerau).

[50] The old anti-Catholic resentments of Reformed Switzerland had increased with the renewed strength of Catholicism and especially with the spectacular conversions of the Bern political scientist von Haller (see above, pp. 220 and 226) and of Friedrich Hurter (1787–1863) from Schaffhausen.

[51] Freiburg, Lucerne, Schwyz, Unterwalden, Uri, Wallis, and Zug.

[52] In vain Metternich tried to obtain the intervention of the European powers in favor of the Catholic cantons and thus in favor of the system of 1815. See E. Streiff, *Die Einflussnahme der europäischen Mächte auf die Entwicklungskämpfe in der Schweiz 1839–45* (Zurich 1931), and Näf, op. cit., passim and Srbik, op. cit., 160–74.

CHAPTER 21

Great Britain and Ireland, 1830–1848

English Catholicism survived punitive legislation as a small community, dominated by a lay aristocracy. Even before the Emancipation Act of 1829, however, forces were at work which were to change its nature. Influenced by romanticism, there were a number of famous conversions, among them those of Kenelm Digby (1823), Ambrose Philips de Lisle (1825), George Spencer (1829), and Augustus Welby Pugin (1834), the neo-Gothic architect. Actually, these converts fit badly into traditional Catholicism, which continued to be suspicious of religious enthusiasm and only slowly emerged from its tradition of isolation from public life.

The converts, finding their way to the Catholic Church via romanticism, raised hopes of mass conversions, but their influence was much smaller than that of the Oxford Movement. The Oxford Movement arose from a dissatisfaction within the Church of England, a dissatisfaction which turned more toward contemporary Rome than to the Church of the Middle Ages. There was general agreement on the need for reform of the Anglican Church, but it was not quite so clear from where the spiritual strength for reform was to come, considering that the Church in many of its aspects was controlled by Parliament. After 1829, Parliament was open to men of all Christian denominations. A crisis erupted in 1833, when Parliament dissolved a number of Protestant bishoprics in Ireland. While it could not be denied that these sees were not needed by Irish Protestants, the action of Parliament raised the general question of parliamentary control, and the possibility of disestablishmentarianism was discussed. A number of prominent people at Oxford concluded that the danger of submitting the Church to the state according to the theory of Erastus could be avoided effectively only if the Church reformed itself.

The leaders of this group were clerics belonging to the established Church. Some of them, like Keble and Pusey, remained loyal to it, but others, especially the representatives of the younger generation like Ward and Faber, converted to Catholicism. The most famous of these converts was John Henry Newman (1801–90). Although in no way an official leader of the movement, he became its spiritual and intellectual focus because of his character and his intellectual capacity.

Newman's all-encompassing sense of religion and responsibility for human beings, as well as his life-long concern with Scripture and Church Fathers, can be traced back to a spiritual crisis during his early years in 1826. In 1817 he entered Trinity College at Oxford and became a Fellow of Oriel in 1822, even though he did not achieve honors. He was ordained in 1825 and in 1828 was appointed vicar of the university church of Saint Mary's. It was during these years that he began to develop his ideas of the Church: the Church as connecting link between man and Christ, based on the teachings resting on its tradition, its Sacraments, and the apostolic succession of its hierarchy. When the crisis came in 1833, he already had gained considerable influence in the religious circles of Oxford.

The protest began in July with Keble's sermon, "The National Apostasy." It was continued in the writings known as *Tracts for the Times,* as a result of which the Anglo-Catholics gained a powerful position within the established Church.[1] The group met resistance, even though Newman in the tracts written by him interpreted the Anglican Church as the *via media* between the errors of Protestantism on the one hand and those of Rome on the other. The *via media* opposed both, and instead relied on antiquity, Scripture, and the Fathers. He opposed what constituted in his eyes a constant threat for Anglicanism, namely the "liberalism" which wanted to submit revealed truth to human judgment.[2]

Gradually he was forced to admit that age alone could not be regarded as a source of ecclesiastical authority in modern times. Catholicity, not age, was the sole measuring stick; but Catholicity, he asserted, was only incompletely realized in the Anglican, Roman, and Eastern branches of the Church, and Rome had deformed its Catholicity through accretions to the symbols of the early Church. Tract 90 appeared on 27 February 1841. It asserted that the Anglican 39 Articles were not incompatible with the nature of Catholicism. The tract created a storm of indignation[3] and was condemned by the university and twenty-four bishops. In consequence, Newman retired to Littlemore near Oxford. Later he said that with respect to the Anglican Church he was at that time already on his death bed, even though he was becoming aware of this only gradually.[4] Rome's accretions to the original symbols continued to be for him a real obstacle. There is only one faith, the Anglican in him argued, and Rome failed to preserve it; his reading of the Fathers always made him reject the Roman reply that "there is only one Church, and the Anglicans are not part of it."[5] But by 1843 he was "much more certain that England was schismatic than that the Roman

[1] John Henry Newman, *Apologia pro Vita sua,* 76.

[2] See *Tracts* 38, 40, 71; *The Prophetical Office of the Church* (1847); *Lectures on the Doctrine of Justification* (1838).

[3] Newman, *Apologia,* 88.

[4] Ibid., 147.

[5] Ibid., 106.

accretions to the confession of faith were not developments springing from a bold and vital articulation of the *depositum fidei*."[6] After his sermon in September on "The Parting of Friends," he quietly retired to the lay community in order to devote himself to what eventually emerged as his *Essay on the Development of Christian Doctrine.* Even before it was published, he was received into the Catholic Church on 9 October 1845, by the Italian Passionist Dominicus Barberi.

Influenced by Newman, a number of his friends took the same step; but hopes for a mass conversion, harbored by many, especially by Nicholas Wiseman, who in 1840 had become coadjutor to Bishop Walsh in the Midland District, were not realized. Wiseman, born in Spain as the son of an Irish father and a Spanish mother, received his education at Ushaw and the English College in Rome, whose dean he became in 1828. His London lectures, held on the occasion of a stay in England in 1835, received great attention not only because of their scholarship, but also because he presented in them something which went beyond the traditional and insular nature of Catholic England. In 1836, financially supported and encouraged by Daniel O'Connell, he founded the *Dublin Review* as the organ for Catholic scholarship.[7] When he returned to England for good in 1840, it was only natural that he placed great hopes in the Oxford Movement. But at this time the most pressing problem for the bishops in England consisted of the growing number of Catholic immigrants from Ireland.

Irishmen had migrated to England in small numbers during the eighteenth century and had settled chiefly in London. The immigration quota rose with British industrialization, especially after the Act of Union in 1800. By 1840, there were four hundred fifty thousand Catholics in England and Wales. About half of them were native Irishmen, and about 80 percent were Irish by birth and extraction. In Scotland, there were about one hundred fifty thousand Catholics, 80 percent of them also of Irish extraction. Many Irish Catholics served in the army and the navy, but most of them worked in heavy industry, in railway construction, in ports and mines, and in steel and textile mills. Most of them were very poor and lived under confined and terrifying conditions in London and the industrial areas of the Midlands, Lancashire, South Wales, and Scotland. They were ill adjusted to English life, which began to develop into a democracy under the impact of the Reform Bill of 1832. The Irish proletariat was viewed with suspicion and fear as the germ cell of political and radical unrest. Catholic England

[6] Ibid., 208–09.

[7] The title was in recognition of O'Connell's generous financial support, but in reality the journal always remained an English publication.

was badly prepared for the spiritual care which they required, but it was precisely the needs of this Irish Catholic proletariat which broke the traditional mold far more than the conversions of Englishmen, no matter how important those might be. Although wealthy English Catholics proved themselves very generous, churches and schools in the industrial centers had to rely largely on the contributions of the poor.[8] As long as England continued to regard education primarily as a task of the Churches, the schools could rely on a certain amount of state subsidies for whose optimal utilization organizations were founded. The rapid numerical increase of the Catholics and the pastoral problems connected with it led in 1840 to an increase in the number of vicars apostolic from four to eight. But the establishment of a diocesan hierarchy was only possible in 1850, given the suspicions by English Catholics of such an organization.

In Ireland, the emigration to England had contributed only little to the easing of the job situation. Ireland's population had grown from about 5 million people in 1780 to more than 8 million in 1840. But industry was present only in Protestant Ulster. In all other areas, cities and centers were in decay, as English manufactured goods drove out local industrial production. Two-thirds of the population were directly dependent on agriculture and, especially in the west, constituted a large rural proletariat subjected to very uncertain conditions of life.

The Catholic Emancipation Act of 1829 was of little significance for the poor. Political power was closely tied to property and that was largely in Protestant hands. The Protestant established Church continued tithing, even though its members everywhere constituted only a minority and in some areas only a very small minority. Daniel O'Connell decided to use his political organization, which he had built for obtaining Catholic emancipation, to achieve the repeal of the Act of Union. He argued convincingly that the clergy should support his new movement as it had supported the old one, because repeal was also a religious problem. His reason was that in return for supporting the union the Catholics had been promised full emancipation but had not been granted it.

Emancipation had been granted in 1829, because political opinion in the United Kingdom was generally convinced of its reasonableness and necessity. There was no such unity with respect to repealing the union, but O'Connell succeeded in building a mighty organization in Ireland. Although some bishops hesitated to support it, most clerics had no difficulty in doing so. It was most strongly supported by the influential

[8] For an exact description of the problems in a key area of London, see B. Bogan, *The Great Link: A History of St. George's Cathedral, Southwark, 1786–1958* (London 1958).

bishop of Kildare and Leighlin, James Doyle. When he died in 1834 at the age of forty-eight, his place was taken by John MacHale, who in the same year had been appointed archbishop of Tuam despite the opposition of the government.

The government attempted to deal with the Irish discontent through such laws as the Tithe Composition Act and the new Poor Law, both passed in 1838. Neither of these laws was radical enough to be effective. The government also tried to keep the Irish clergy within bounds through pressure on Rome. But here it was in a difficult position; formal diplomatic relations were unacceptable, and the loyalty oath imposed on the Catholics in connection with the Emancipation Act forced them to swear that the Pope had no political authority in the United Kingdom. But the Curia of Gregory XVI feared the risks of revolution and in general was so badly informed about conditions in Ireland that it sharply remonstrated with MacHale.

When the Tories came to power in 1841 with Robert Peel as Prime Minister, they were determined to suppress the repeal movement. By this time, Archbishop Murray of Dublin (1768–1852) was almost the only bishop opposed to the movement. Additional laws were passed: the Charitable Bequests Act of 1844, the Queen's Colleges Act of 1845, and the Maynooth Act of 1845 for the increase of the state's subsidy to this college. Pressure on Rome continued and finally on 15 October 1844 led to a decree[9] in which the priests were requested to keep away from politics. But the phrasing of the decree was cautious and vague and devoid of any judgment concerning the repeal movement and the right of Catholic laymen to support it.

Neither Rome's warnings nor the palliative laws were able to stop the support of the clergy for the repeal movement. In 1846 the organization Young Ireland was created as a challenge to O'Connell's unqualified rejection of physical force. By this time O'Connell's health was debilitated and his death in 1847, together with the great famine of that year, put an end to the problem of repeal.

Despite their poverty, the Irish Catholics built churches, hospitals, and schools. The modest repentance chapels were replaced. For the schools and hospitals, the new orders were of great help: the Presentation Sisters (1782), the Irish Christian Brothers (1802), the Sisters of Charity (1815), the Loreto Sisters (1821), and the Sisters of Mercy (1831). In 1834 the Sisters of Charity opened Saint Vincent Hospital, the first Catholic hospital in Dublin.

[9] Cardinal Fransoni to Archbishop Crolly of Armagh, 15 October 1844, printed in Broderick, *The Holy See and the Irish Movement for the Repeal of the Union with England,* 232f.

Finances, especially in the field of education, were always inadequate. The first census in 1841 revealed an illiteracy rate of 53 percent, and whatever interpretation one wishes to give this figure, it can not have been far from the truth. The Stanley Act of 1831 created a governmental system of elementary schools by creating a national office for the administration of nondenominational schools and offering guarantees for the faith of the pupils. The Irish Catholics already had enough experience with state subsidies for education, designed to win the children for Protestantism, but the system of 1831 appeared to offer enough guarantees and was generally accepted. With its approval of state supervision it was far ahead of contemporary developments in England. A Roman rescript of 1841 left the regulation of education to each bishop and his diocese. Only the archbishop of Tuam, MacHale, refused to recognize these publicly administered schools. The bishops were in much less agreement on the Queen's Colleges Act of 1845, concerning nondenominational higher education. The problem was eventually solved in 1850 at the Synod of Thurles.

BIBLIOGRAPHY

GENERAL BIBLIOGRAPHY

I. GENERAL HISTORY

WORLD HISTORY: O. Westphal, *Weltgeschichte der Neuzeit, 1750–1950* (Stuttgart 1953); F. Valjaveč, ed., *Historia Mundi* IX and X (Bern 1961); G. Mann, ed., *Propyläen-Weltgeschichte* VII and VIII (Berlin 1960); D. K. Fieldhouse, *Die Kolonialreiche seit dem 18. Jahrhundert (Fischer-Weltgeschichte 29)*, (Frankfurt am Main 1965); G. N. Clark, ed., *The New Cambridge Modern European History* VIII, IX, and X (Cambridge 1960, 1960, 1965).

EUROPE: B. Croce, *History of Europe in the 19th Century* (New York 1963); W. Mommsen, *Geschichte des Abendlandes von der Französischen Revolution bis zur Gegenwart, 1789–1945* (Munich 1951); H. Herzfeld, *Die moderne Welt, 1789–1945,* 2 vols. (Brunswick 1966); L. Salvatorelli, *Storia del novecento* (Florence 1957); C. Zaghi, *Napoleone e Europa* (Naples 1969); R. R. Palmer, *The Age of Democratic Revolution,* 2 vols. (Princeton 1959–64); M. Beloff, ed., *L'Europe du XIXe et du XXe siècle* I (Paris 1959); J. B. Duroselle, *L'Europe de 1815 à nos jours. Vie politique et relations internationales* (*Nouvelle Clio* 38), (Paris 1964); G. A. Craig, *Europe since 1815* (Englewood 1966); G. Lefebvre, *La Révolution Française* (*Peuples et Civilisations* 13), (Paris 1968); G. Lefebvre, *Napoléon* (*Peuples et Civilisations* 14), (Paris 1953); F. Ponteil *L'Éveil des Nationalités et le Mouvement Libéral, 1815–1848* (*Peuples et Civilisations* 15), (Paris 1968); C. H. Pouthas, *Démocraties et Capitalisme, 1848–1860* (*Peuples et Civilisations* 16), (Paris 1948); H. Hauser et al., *Du Libéralisme à L'Impérialisme* (*Peuples et Civilisations* 17), (Paris 1952); E. Weis, *Der Durchbruch des Bürgertums, 1776–1847* (*Propyläengeschichte Europas* 4), (Frankfurt am Main 1978); T. Schieder, *Staatensystem als Vormacht der Welt, 1848–1918 (Propyläengeschichte Europas 5)*, (Frankfurt am Main 1977); A. Sorel, *L'Europe et la Révolution française,* 8 vols; (Paris 1885–1911). J. L. Godechot, *La grande nation. L'expansion révolutionnaire de la France dans le monde de 1789 à 1799,* 2 vols. (Paris 1956); E. Naujoks, *Die Französische Revolution und Europa* (Stuttgart 1969); L. Bergeron, F. Furet, and R. Koselleck, *Das Zeitalter der europäischen Revolution 1780–1848* (*Fischer-Weltgeschichte* 26), (Frankfurt am Main 1969); L. Salvatorelli, *La rivoluzione europea. 1848–1849* (Milan 1949); P. Robertson, *Revolutions of 1848* (New York 1960); A. J. P. Taylor, *The Struggle for Mastery in Europe, 1848–1918* (Oxford 1954); C. Brinton, *A Decade of Revolution, 1789–1799* (New York 1934); G. Bruun, *Europe and the French Imperium, 1799–1814* (New York 1938); F. B. Artz, *Reaction and Revolution, 1814–1832* (New York 1934); W. F. Langer, *Political and Social Upheaval, 1832–1852* (New York 1969); R. C. Binkley, *Realism and Nationalism, 1852–1871* (New York 1935).

FRANCE: *Nouvelle histoire de la France,* 1–10. Editions du Seuil (Paris 1972); P. Gaxotte, *La Révolution française.* Nouvelle edition avec Jean Tulard (Paris 1977); M. Vovelle, *Religion et Révolution: La dechristianisation de l'An II* (Paris 1976); P. H. Beik, *The French Revolution Seen from the Right* (New York 1970); J. N. Moody, *French Education since Napoleon* (Syracuse 1978); F. Furet and D. Richet, *The French Revolution* (London 1970);

J. Godechot, *The Counter-Revolution* (New York 1971); G. de Bertier de Sauvigny, *The Restoration* (New York 1967); R. Rémond, *La vie politique en France depuis 1789,* 2 vols. (Paris 1965/69); R. Rémond, *La Droite en France de 1815 à nos jours* (Paris 1963); J. L. Godechot, *Les révolutions, 1770–1799* (Paris 1965); J. L. Godechot, *L'Europe et l'Amérique à l'époque napoléonienne, 1800–1815* (Paris 1967); B. Groethuysen, *Philosophie de la Révolution française* (Paris 1956); I. Kaplow, ed., *New Perspectives on the French Revolution* (New York 1965); A. Gérard, *La Révolution française, mythes et interprétations, 1799–1970* (Paris 1970); J. Chastenet, *Histoire de la Troisième République,* 7 vols. (Paris 1952/63); G. Dupeux, *La Société française, 1789–1960* (Paris 1964); J. L. Godechot, *Les institutions de la France sous la Révolution et l'Empire* (Paris 1968); F. Ponteil, *Les institutions de la France de 1814 à 1870* (Paris 1966); A. Prost, *L'enseignement en France 1800–1967* (Paris 1968); L. Duguit, H. Monnier, R. Bonnard, *Les constitutions et les principales lois politiques de la France depuis 1789* (Paris 1952); *Le Moniteur Universel* (1799/1868) and *Journal officiel* (Paris 1869seqq.) for legislation and parliamentary debates.

BELGIUM, NETHERLANDS, LUXEMBURG: S. Schama, *Patriots and Liberators: Revolution in the Netherlands, 1780–1813* (New York 1977); C. H. E. De Wit, *De Strijd tussen Aristocratie en Democratie in Nederland, 1780–1848* (Heerlen 1965); P. Gerin, S. Vervaeck, J. De Belder, J. Hannes, *Bibliographie de l'histoire de Belgique, 1789–1914,* 3 vols. (Louvain 1960/66); H. Pirenne, *Histoire de Belgique* VI/VII (Brussels 1926/32); J. Van Houtte, ed., *Algemene Geschiedenis der Nederlanden* VIII/XII (Antwerp-Zeist 1955/58); J. Deharveng, ed., *Histoire de la Belgique contemporaine, 1830–1914,* 3 vols. (Brussels 1928/30); T. Luykx, *Politieke geschiedenis van Belgie van 1789 tot heden* (Brussels 1969); A. Simon, *Le parti catholique belge* (Brussels 1958).

SPAIN AND PORTUGAL: M. Artola, *Los origines de la España contemporanea,* 2 vols. (Barcelona 1958); F. G. Bruguera, *Histoire contemporaine d'Espagne. 1789–1950* (Paris 1953); R. Carr, *Spain, 1808–1939* (Oxford 1966); M. Fernández Almagro, *Historia politica de la España contemporánea,* 2 vols. (Madrid 1956/59); H. V. Livermore, *A New History of Portugal* (Cambridge, 1966).

ITALY: C. Spellanzon, *Storia del Risorgimento e dell' unità d'Italia,* 5 vols. (Milan 1932/40); W. Maturi, *Interpretazioni del Risorgimento* (Turin 1962); L. Salvatorelli, *Spiriti e figure del Risorgimento* (Florence 1962); D. Mack Smith, *Italy. A Modern History* (Ann Arbor 1959).

GERMAN STATES AND SWITZERLAND: B. Gebhardt, H. Grundmann, *Handbuch der deutschen Geschichte* I and II (Stuttgart 1960); L. Just, ed., *Handbuch der deutschen Geschichte* III (Constance 1956); H. Holborn, *A History of Modern Germany* II and III (New York 1959); E. Marcks, *Der Aufstieg des Reiches, 1807–78,* 2 vols. (Stuttgart 1936); A. H. Springer, *Geschichte Österreichs seit dem Wiener Frieden 1809,* 2 vols. (Leipzig 1863/65); G. Mann, *Deutsche Geschichte im 19. und 20. Jahrhundert* (Frankfurt am Main 1966); A. Ramm, *Germany, 1789–1919* (London 1967); T. S. Hamerow, *Restoration, Revolution, Reaction. Economics and Politics in Germany, 1815–71* (Princeton 1958); H. Hantsch, *Die Geschichte Österreichs* II (Graz 1962); G. A. Craig, *Germany, 1866–1945* (New York 1978); F. Schnabel, *Deutsche Geschichte im 19. Jahrhundert,* 4 vols. (Freiburg 1929/37); V. Valentin, *Geschichte der deutschen Revolution von 1848–49,* 2 vols., (Berlin 1930/31); R. Charmatz, *Österreichs innere Geschichte von 1848 bis 1895,* 2 vols. (Leipzig 1918); V. Bibl, *Der Zerfall Österreichs,* 2 vols. (Vienna 1922/24); H. v. Srbik, *Deutsche Einheit,* 4 vols. (Munich 1935/42); E. Fueter, *Die Schweiz seit 1848* (Zurich 1928).

GREAT BRITAIN: G. M. Trevelyan, *British History in the Nineteenth Century and after* (London 1937); E. Halévy, *History of the English People in the Nineteenth Century,* 6 vols. (London 1949/52); L. Woodward, *The Age of Reform, 1815–70 (Oxford History of England),* (Oxford 1962).

UNITED STATES OF AMERICA: H. G. Dahms, *Geschichte der Vereinigten Staaten von Amerika* (Munich 1953); E. Samhaber, *Geschichte der Vereinigten Staaten von Nordamerika* (Munich 1954); E. Angermann, "Die Vereinigten Staaten von Amerika," *Historia Mundi* X (1961), 253–331; R. Hofstadter, W. Miller, D. Aaron, W. Jordan, and L. Litwack, *The United States* (Englewood Cliffs 1976); J. A. Garraty, *The American Nation* (New York 1979); J. M. Blum, E. S. Morgan, W. L. Rose, A. M. Schlesinger, Jr., K. M. Stampp, C. Vann Woodward, *The National Experience: A History of the United States* (New York 1973); R. N. Current, T. H. Williams, F. Freidel, *American History: A Survey* (New York 1979); B. Bailyn, D. B. Davis, D. H. Donald, J. L. Thomas, R. H. Wiebe, G. S. Wood, *The Great Republic: A History of the American People* (Lexington, Mass. 1977).

LATIN AMERICA: S. de Madariaga, *The Fall of the Spanish American Empire* (London 1947); H. V. Livermore, ed., *Portugal and Brazil* (Oxford 1953); A. P. Whitaker, "Die iberoamerikanische Welt von 1825–1920," *Historia Mundi* X (1961), 332–57.

II. CHURCH HISTORY

1. GENERAL CHURCH HISTORY

L. A. Veit, *Die Kirche im Zeitalter des Individualismus* II: *1800 bis zur Gegenwart* (Freiburg i. Br. 1933); L. Rogier, R. Aubert, D. Knowles, *Geschichte der Kirche* IV (Einsiedeln 1966); E. E. Y. Hales, *The Catholic Church in the Modern World. A Survey from the French Revolution to the present* (London 1958); K. S. Latourette, *Christianity in a Revolutionary Age. A History of Christianity in the 19th and 20th Centuries,* 5 vols. (New York 1958/62); J. Lortz, *Geschichte der Kirche in ideengeschichtlicher Betrachtung* II (Münster 1964); L. Girard, *Le catholicisme en Europe de 1814 à 1878* (Les Cours de Sorbonne), (Paris 1962); Daniel-Rops, *L'Église des Révolutions,* 2 vols. (Paris 1960/63); H. Hermelink, *Das Christentum in der Menschheitsgeschichte von der Französischen Revolution bis zur Gegenwart,* 3 vols. (Stuttgart 1951/55); K. D. Schmitt, *Grundriss der Kirchengeschichte* IV: *Geschichte der Kirche im Zeitalter des Individualismus und des Säkularismus* (Göttingen 1960); K. D. Schmitt, E. Wolf, *Die Kirche in ihrer Geschichte. Ein Handbuch* IV, Lieferung Nl; F. Heyer, *Die katholische Kirche vom Westfälischen Frieden bis zum ersten Vatikanischen Konzil* (Göttingen 1963); A. Fliche-V. Martin, *Histoire de l'Église* XX, XXI (Paris 1949, 1964); K. Bihlmeyer-H. Tüchle, *Church History,* 3 vols., (New York 1979).

2. PAPACY

J. Schmidlin, *Papstgeschichte der neuesten Zeit,* 4 vols. (Munich 1933/39); F. X. Seppelt, G. Schwaiger, *Geschichte der Päpste* (Munich 1964); P. Paschini, P. Brezzi, *I papi nella storia* II (Rome 1961); C. Ledré, *Un siècle sous la tiare. De Pie IX à Pie XII* (Paris 1955); G. Mollat, *La Question romaine de Pie VI à Pie XI* (Paris 1932); V. Del Giudice, *La Questione romana* (Rome 1948); C. Berthelet, *Conclavi pontifici e cardinali nel secolo XIX* (Rome 1903); E. De Marchi, *Le Nunziature apostoliche dal 1800 al 1956* (Rome 1957);

Notizie dell'anno (until 1860); *Annuario pontificio* (1861/70, 1912seqq.); *La Gerarchia cattolica* (1872/1911).

3. The Catholic Church in Individual Countries

Germany: H. Brück, *Geschichte der katholischen Kirche in Deutschland im 19. Jahrhundert* (Mainz 1902/03); G. Goyau, *L'Allemagne religieuse. Le Catholicisme,* 4 vols. (Paris 1905/09); F. Schnabel, *Deutsche Geschichte im 19, Jahrhundert* IV: *Die religiösen Kräfte* (Freiburg i. Br. 1937); P. Funk, *Von der Aufklärung zur Romantik* (Munich 1925); F. Heyer, *Die katholische Kirche von 1648 bis 1870* (Göttingen 1963); H. Schrörs, *Die Kölner Wirren. Studien zu ihrer Geschichte* (Berlin–Bonn 1927); H. Bastgen, *Die Verhandlungen zwischen dem Berliner Hof und dem Heiligen Stuhl über die konfessionell gemischten Ehen* (Paderborn 1936); H. Bastgen, *Die Besetzung der Bischofssitze in Preussen in der ersten Hälfte des 19. Jahrhunderts,* 2 parts (Paderborn 1941); R. Lill, *Die Beilegung der Kölner Wirren* (Düsseldorf 1962); J.-B. Kissling, *Geschichte der deutschen Katholikentage,* 3 vols. (Münster 1920/21); R. Lill, *Die ersten deutschen Bischofskonferenzen* (Freiburg i. Br. 1964); A. K. Huber, *Kirche und deutsche Einheit im 19. Jahrhundert* (Königstein 1966); K. Buchheim, *Ultramontanismus und Demokratie. Der Weg der deutschen Katholiken im 19. Jahrhundert* (Munich 1963); K. Bachem, *Vorgeschichte, Geschichte und Politik der deutschen Zentrumspartei* I (Cologne 1927, reprint Aalen 1967); F. Hanus, *Die preussische Vatikangesandtschaft, 1747–1920* (Munich 1954); G. Franz-Willing, *Die bayerische Vatikangesandtschaft, 1803–1934* (Munich 1965); F. Engel-Janosi, *Österreich und der Vatikan 1846–1918* I (Graz- Vienna- Cologne 1958); R. Hacker, *Die Beziehungen zwischen Bayern und dem Heiligen Stuhl in der Regierungszeit Ludwigs I.* (Tübingen 1967); H. Schiel, *Johann Michael Sailer,* 2 vols. (Regensburg 1948/52); W. Schellberg, *Johann Görres* (Cologne 1926); J. Janssen, *Friedrich Leopold Graf zu Stolberg* (Freiburg i. Br. 1877); E. Hosp, *Hofbauer* (Vienna 1951); R. Till, *Hofbauer und sein Kreis* (Vienna 1951); O. Pfülf, *Kardinal Johannes von Geissel,* 2 vols. (Freiburg i. Br. 1895/96); L. Lenhart, *Bischof Ketteler,* 3 vols. (Mainz 1966/68); L. v. Pastor, *August Reichensperger,* 2 vols. (Freiburg i. Br. 1899); F. Schmidt, *Peter Reichensperger* (Mönchengladbach 1913); S. J. Schäffer, J. Dahl, *Adolf Kolping* (Cologne 1961); J. Friedrich, *Ignaz von Döllinger,* 3 vols. (Munich 1899/1901).

Austria: F. Engel-Janosi, *Österreich und der Vatikan,* 2 vols. (Graz 1958/60); F. Engel-Janosi, *Die politische Korrespondenz der Päpste mit den österreichischen Kaisern 1804–1918* (Vienna 1964); J. Grisar, *De historia Ecclesiae catholicae austriacae saeculi XIX* (Rome 1936); A. Hudal, *Die österreichische Vatikanbotschaft 1806–1918* (Munich 1952); C. Wolfsgruber, *Joseph Otmar von Rauscher* (Vienna 1888); C. Wolfsgruber, *Kardinal Schwarzenberg,* 3 vols. (Vienna 1905/17).

France: A. Latreille, *L'Église catholique et la révolution française,* 2 vols. (Paris 1950); G. Bourgin, "Les sources manuscrites de l'histoire religieuse de la France moderne," *RHEF* 10 (1924), 27–66, 172–206, 333–58, 466–92; J. Gadille, "Les sources privées de l'histoire contemporaine du catholicisme en France," *RH* 238 (1967), 333–46; G. Weill, "Le catholicisme français au XIXe siècle," *Revue de synthèse historique* 15 (1907), 319–56; A. Latreille, J.-R. Palanque, É. Delaruelle, R. Rémond, *Histoire du catholicisme en France* III (Paris 1962); W. Gurian, *Die politischen und sozialen Ideen des französischen Katholizismus, 1789–1914* (Freiburg im Breisgau 1929); A. Dansette, *Histoire religieuse de la France contemporaine,* 2 vols. (Paris 1948/51); A. Debidour, *Histoire des rapports de l'Église et de l'État en France de 1789 à 1870,* 2 vols. (Paris 1891); A. Debidour, *L'Église* *catholique et l'État sous la IIIe Republique, 1870–1906,* 2 vols. (Paris 1906); A. Rivet, *Traité du culte catholique et des lois civiles d'ordre religieux* (Paris 1947); J. Brugerette, *Le prêtre français et la société contemporaine,* 3 vols. (Paris 1933/38); F. Boulard, *Essor ou déclin du clergé français* (Paris 1950); L. Baunard, *L'Épiscopat français depuis le Concordat jusqu'à la Séparation* (Paris 1907); L. Baunard, *Un siècle de l'Église de France, 1800–1900* (Paris 1901); L. Grimaud, *Histoire de la liberté d'enseignement en France,* 6 vols. (Grenoble–Paris 1944/54); P. Nourisson, *Histoire légale des congrégations religieuses en France depuis 1789,* 2 vols. (Paris 1928); G. Le Bras. *Études de sociologie religieuse,* 2 vols. (Paris 1955/56); G Weill, *Histoire de l'idée laïque en France au XIXe siècle* (Paris 1929); A. Mellor, *Histoire de l'anticléricalisme français* (Paris 1966); P. Droulers, *Action pastorale et problèmes sociaux sous la Monarchie de Juillet chez Monseigneur d'Astros* (Paris 1954); E. Sevrin, *Un évêque militant et gallican au XIXe siècle, Monseigneur Clausel de Montals,* 2 vols. (Paris 1955); F. Lagrange, *Vie de Monseigneur Dupanloup,* 3 vols. (Paris 1883/84); also *DHGE* XIV, 1070–1122; A. de Falloux, *Mémoires d'un royaliste,* 2 vols. (Paris 1888); E. Veuillot, *Le comte de Falloux et ses Mémoires* (Paris 1888); C. de Ladoue, *Monseigneur Gerbet, sa vie, ses œuvres,* 3 vols. (Paris 1870); F. Gousset, *Le cardinal Gousset* (Besançon 1903); P. Delatte, *Dom Guéranger, abbé de Solesmes,* 2 vols. (Paris 1909/10); J. Paguelle de Follenay, *Vie du cardinal Guibert,* 2 vols. (Paris 1896); T. Foisset, *Vie du R. P. Lacordaire,* 2 vols. (Paris 1870); L. Baunard, *Le cardinal Lavigerie,* 2 vols. (Paris 1896); X. de Montclos, *Lavigerie, le Saint-Siège et l'Église, 1846–78* (Paris 1965); G. Bazin, *Vie de Monseigneur Maret,* 3 vols. (Paris 1891/92); F. Besson, *Vie de S. É. le cardinal Mathieu,* 2 vols. (Paris 1882); J. Leflon, *Eugène de Mazenod,* 3 vols. (Paris 1896/1902); A. d'Andigné, *Un apôtre de la charité, Armand de Melun* (Paris 1962); E. Lecanuet, *Montalembert,* 3 vols. (Paris 1896/1902); C. Guillemant, *P.-L. Parisis,* 3 vols. (Paris 1916/25); L. Baunard, *Histoire du cardinal Pie,* 2 vols. (Paris 1893); C.-J. Destombes, *Vie de S.É. le cardinal Régnier,* 2 vols. (Paris 1885); M. de Hédouville, *Monseigneur de Ségur, sa vie, son action* (Paris 1957); F. Poujoulat, *Vie de Monseigneur Sibour* (Paris 1857); M. J. Rouet de Journel, *Une russe catholique. La vie de Madame Swetchine* (Paris 1953); E. and F. Veuillot, *Louis Veuillot,* 4 vols. (Paris 1902/13).

ITALY: *Archiva Ecclesiae* 3/4 (1960/61), 87–179, 223–87; Silvino da Nadro OFMCap, *Sinodi diocesani italiani. Catalogo bibliografico degli atti a stampa, 1574–1878* (Vatican City 1960); A.-C. Jemolo, *Chiesa e Stato in Italia negli ultimi cento anni* (Turin 1963); P. Scoppola, *Chiesa e Stato nella storia d'Italia. Storia documentaria dall'Unità alla Repubblica* (Bari 1967); P. Scoppola, *Dal Neoguelfismo alla Democrazia cristiana* (Rome 1957); A. Della Torre, *Il cristianesimo in Italia dai filosofisti ai modernisti* (Milan 1912); G. De Rosa, *Storia del movimento cattolico in Italia,* 2 vols. (Bari 1966); *I cattolici italiani dall'800 ad oggi* (Brescia 1964); T. Chiuso, *La Chiesa in Piemonte dal 1797 ai giorni nostri,* 4 vols. (Turin 1888); T. Salvemini, *La statistica ecclesiastica con speciale riguardo al clero in Italia* (Ferrara 1941); G. Spini, *Risorgimento e protestanti* (Naples 1956); C. Castiglioni, *Gaysruck e Romilli, arcivescovi di Milano* (Milan 1938); C. Castiglioni, *Monsignor Nazari di Calabiana* (Milan 1952); E. Federici, *Sisto Riario Sforza* (Rome 1945); G. Russo, *Il cardinale Sisto Riario Sforza e l'unità d'Italia* (Naples 1962); J. E. Borrel, *Vie de Monseigneur Charvaz* (Chambéry 1909); P. Stella, *Don Bosco nella storia della religiosità cattolica,* 2 vols. (Zurich 1968/69); A. Castellani, *Il b. Leonardo Murialdo,* 2 vols. (Rome 1966/68).

SPAIN: J. del Burgo, *Fuentes de la Historia de España. Bibliografia de las guerras carlistas y de las luchas politicas del siglo XIX,* 4 vols. (Pamplona 1954/60); V. de la Fuente, *Historia ecclesiástica de España* VI (Barcelona 1875); P. Gams, *Die Kirchengeschichte von Spanien* III/2 (Regensburg 1872, reprint Graz 1956); E. A. Peers, *The Church in Spain, 1737–*

1937 (London 1938); E. A. Peers, *Spain, the Church, and the Orders* (London 1939); J. M. Cuenca, *La Iglesia española ante la Revolución liberal* (Madrid 1971); J. Becker, *Relaciones diplomáticas entre España y la Santa Sede durante el siglo XIX* (Madrid 1909); M. Menéndez y Pelayo, *Historia de los heterodojos españoles* VII (Madrid 1932).

BELGIUM: *Sources de l'histoire religieuse de la Belgique. Époque contemporaine. Colloque de Bruxelles 1967* (Louvain 1968); A. Simon, *Réunions des évêques de Belgique. Procès-verbaux, 1830–83,* 2 vols. (Louvain 1960/61); A. Simon, *Instructions aux nonces de Bruxelles, 1835–89* (Brussels 1961); R. Aubert, "Kirche und Staat in Belgien im 19. Jahrhundert," W. Conze, ed., *Beiträge zur deutschen und belgischen Verfassungsgeschichte im 19. Jahrhundert* (Stuttgart 1967); V. Mallinson, *Power and Politics in Belgian Education, 1815–1961* (London 1963); A. Tihon, *Le clergé et l'enseignement moyen pour garçons dans le diocèse de Malines, 1802–1914* (diss., Louvain 1970); "Prêtres de Belgique, 1838–1930," *NRTh* 57 (1930), 617–744; S. Scholl, ed., *150 jaar katholieke arbeidersbeweging in België, 1789–1939,* 3 vols. (Brussels 1963/66); N. Piepers, *La "Revue générale" de 1865 à 1940* (Louvain 1968).

PORTUGAL: F. de Almeida, *Historia da Igreja em Portugal* IV, 1/4 (Coimbra 1917/23); M. de Oliveira, *Historia eclesiástica de Portugal* (Lisbon 1940).

GREAT BRITAIN AND IRELAND: J. H. Whyte, "Historians of XIXth-century English Catholicism," *Clergy Review* 52 (1967), 791–801; G. A. Beck, ed., *The English Catholics, 1850–1950* (London 1950); D. Mathew, *Catholicism in England* (London 1936); P. J. Corish, ed., *A History of Irish Catholicism* IV/V (Dublin 1968seqq.) A. Bellesheim, *Geschichte der katholischen Kirche in Schottland* (Mainz 1883); P. Thureau-Dangin, *La renaissance catholique en Angleterre au XIXe siècle,* 3 vols. (Paris 1899/1906); O. Chadwick, *The Victorian Church,* 2 vols. (London 1966/70); C. Butler, *The Life and Times of Bishop Ullathorne,* 2 vols. (London 1926); W. Ward, *The Life and Times of Cardinal Wiseman,* 2 vols. (London 1897); W. Ward, *The Life of John Henry Cardinal Newman,* 2 vols. (London 1912); E. Purcell, *Life of Cardinal Manning,* 2 vols. (London 1895).

THE NETHERLANDS: L. J. Rogier, N. De Rooy, *In vrijheid herboren. Katholiek Nederland, 1853–1953* (The Hague 1957); P. Albers, *Geschiedenis van het herstel der hiërarchie in de Nederlanden,* 2 vols. (Nijmegen–The Hague 1903/04); A. Commissaris, *Van toen wij vrij werden, 1795–1903,* 2 vols. (Groningen 1929); J. Witlox, *De Katholieke Staatspartij,* 2 vols. ('s-Hertogenbosch 1919/27); J. A. De Kok, *Nederland op de breuklijn Rome-Reformatie. Numerieke aspecten van protestantisering en katholieke herleving in de Noordelijke Nederlanden, 1580–1880* (Assen 1964).

SWITZERLAND: A. Büchi, *Die katholische Kirche in der Schweiz* (Munich 1902); T. Schwegler, *Geschichte der katholischen Kirche in der Schweiz* (Stans 1945); K. Müller, *Die katholische Kirche in der Schweiz seit dem Ausgang des 18. Jahrhunderts* (Einsiedeln 1928); F. Strobel, *Die Jesuiten und die Schweiz im 19. Jahrhundert* (Olten 1954).

SCANDINAVIA: A. Palmqvist, *Die römisch-katholische Kirche in Schweden nach 1781,* 2 vols. (Uppsala 1954/58); K. Kjelstrup, *Norvegia catholica, 1843–1943* (Rome 1947); J. Metzler, *Die apostolischen Vikariate des Nordens* (Paderborn 1919).

RUSSIA AND POLAND: A. M. Ammann, *Abriss der Ostslawischen Kirchengeschichte* (Vienna 1950); A. Boudou, *Le Saint-Siège et la Russie,* 2 vols. (Paris 1922/25); E. Winter, *Russland und das Papsttum* II (Berlin 1961); W. Urban, *Ostatni etap dziejów Kościola w Polsce przed nowym tysiącleciem, 1815–1965* (Rome 1966); O. Beiersdorf, *Papietswo wobec sprawy polskiej w latach 1772–1864 wybor źródel* (Wroclaw 1960); J. Wasilewski,

Arcybiskupi i administratorowie archidiecezji Mohylowskiej (Pinsk 1930); J. A. Malinowski, *Die deutschen katholischen Kolonien am Schwarzen Meere* (Stuttgart 1927); S. Załęski, *Jezuici w Polsce*, V (Cracow 1907); J. Bjelogolovov, *Akten und Dokumente in Bezug auf die Organisation und Verwaltung der römisch-katholischen Kirche in Russland* (St. Petersburg 1905); A. Welykyj, *Documenta Pontificum Romanorum historiam Ukrainiae illustrantia* II (Rome 1954); S. Olszamowska-Skowronska, *La correspondance des papes et des empereurs de Russie (1814–78) selon les documents authentiques* (Rome 1970).

SOUTHEASTERN EUROPE AND THE NEAR EAST: G. G. Golubovich, *Biblioteca bio-bibliografica della Terra Santa e dell'Oriente cristiano*, 8 vols. (Karachi 1906/30); E. von Mülinen, *Die lateinische Kirche im Türkischen Reiche* (Berlin 1903); F. W. Hasluck, *Christianity and Islam under the Sultans*, 2 vols. (Oxford 1929); A. Schopoff, *Les Réformes et la protection des chrétiens en Turquie, 1673–1904* (Paris 1904); G. Goyau, *Le protectorat de la France sur les chrétiens de l'Empire ottoman* (Paris 1895); J. Friedrich, *Die christlichen Balkanstaaten in Vergangenheit und Gegenwart* (Munich 1916); B. Rupčič, *Entstehung der Franziskanerpfarreien in Bosnien und Herzegowina und ihre Entwicklung bis zum Jahre 1878* (Breslau 1937); I. Simrak, *Graeco-catholica Ecclesia in Jugoslavia* (Zagreb 1931); P. Tocanel, *Storia della Chiesa cattolica in Romania* III: *Il Vicariato apostolico e le missioni dei Frati Minori Conventuali in Moldavia*, 2 vols. (Padua 1960/65); K. Lübeck, *Die katholische Orientmission in ihrer Entwicklung dargestellt* (Cologne 1917); Hilaire de Barenton OFMCap, *La France catholique en Orient durant les trois derniers siècles* (Paris 1912); *Les jésuites en Syrie, 1831–1931* (Paris 1931); A. Posseto, *Il patriarcato latino di Gerusalemme* (Milan 1938); F. de Portu, *Notice sur le diocèse de Smyrne et le vicariat apostolique de l'Asie Mineure* (Smyrna 1908).

UNITED STATES: J. T. Ellis, *A Guide to American Catholic History* (Milwaukee 1959); C. R. Fish, *Guide to the Materials for American History in Roman and other Italian Archives* (Washington 1911); T. McAvoy, "Catholic Archives and Manuscript Collections," *The American Archivist* 24 (1961), 409–14; P. Cadden, *The Historiography of the American Catholic Church, 1785–1943* (Washington 1944); H. J. Browne, "American Catholic History, A Progress Report, Research and Study," *CH* 26 (1957), 372–80; J. G. Shea, *History of the Catholic Church in the United States*, 4 vols. (New York 1886/92); T. McAvoy, *A History of the Catholic Church in the United States* (Notre Dame 1969); J. T. Ellis, *American Catholicism* (Chicago 1956); L. Hertling, *Geschichte der katholischen Kirche in den Vereinigten Staaten* (Berlin 1954); R. F. McNamara, "Etats-Unis," *DHGE* XV, 1109–47; A. Greeley, *The Catholic Experience. An Interpretation of the History of American Catholicism* (Garden City 1968); F. Kenneally, *United States Documents in the Propaganda Fide Archives*, 2 vols. (Washington 1966/68); J. T. Ellis, *Documents of American Catholic History* (Milwaukee 1956); D. Shearer, *Pontificia Americana. A Documentary History of the Catholic Church in the United States, 1784–1884* (Washington 1933); P. Guilday, *The National Pastorals of the American Hierarchy, 1792–1910* (Washington 1923); P. Guilday, *A History of the Councils of Baltimore* (New York 1932); E. Shaughnessy, *Has the Immigrant kept the Faith? A Study of Immigration and Catholic Growth in the United States* (New York 1925); J. A. Burns, *The Growth and Development of the Catholic School System in the United States* (New York 1912); J. A. Burns, J. Kohlbrenner, *A History of Catholic Education in the United States* (New York 1937); D. T. McColgan, *A Century of Charity: the first one hundred Years of the Society of St. Vincent de Paul in the United States*, 2 vols. (Milwaukee 1951); P. J. Dignan, *A History of the Legal Incorporation of Catholic Property in the United States, 1784–1932* (Washington 1933); F. McDonald, *The Catholic Church and the Secret Societies in the United States* (New York 1946); R. Corrigan, *Die Propaganda-Kongregation und ihre Tätigkeit in Nord-Amerika*

(Munich 1928); T. Roemer, *The Ludwig-Missionsverein and the Catholic Church in the United States, 1838–1918* (Washington 1933); R. Clarke, *Lives of Deceased Bishops of the Catholic Church in the United States,* 3 vols. (New York 1888); J. B. Code, *Dictionary of the American Hierarchy* (New York 1940); R. Baudier, *The Catholic Church in Louisiana* (New Orleans 1939); W. Casper, *History of the Catholic Church in Nebraska,* 3 vols. (Milwaukee 1960/66); R. Trisco, *The Holy See and the Nascent Church in the Middle Western United States* (Rome 1962); W. Schoenberg, *A Chronicle of the Catholic Historiography of the Pacific Northwest, 1743–1960* (Spokane 1962); E. V. O'Hara, *Pioneer Catholic History of Oregon* (Portland 1907); C. Blanchard, *History of the Catholic Church in Indiana,* 2 vols. (Logansport 1898); H. H. Heming, *The Catholic Church in Wisconsin* (Milwaukee 1895/98); J. F. Kempker, *History of the Catholic Church in Iowa* (Iowa City 1887); J. H. Lamott, *History of the Archdiocese of Cincinnati* (New York 1921); M. J. Hynes, *History of the Diocese of Cleveland* (Cleveland 1953); G. Garraghan, *The Catholic Church in Chicago* (Chicago 1921); G. Paré, *The Catholic Church in Detroit* (Detroit 1951); J. Smith, *The Catholic Church in New York,* 2 vols. (New York 1905); L. J. Kirlin, *Catholicity in Philadelphia* (Philadelphia 1909); F. J. Magri, *The Catholic Church in the City and Diocese of Richmond* (Richmond 1906); J. H. Bailey, *A History of the Diocese of Richmond, the Formative Years* (Richmond 1956); J. E. Rothensteiner, *History of the Archdiocese of St. Louis,* 2 vols. (St. Louis 1928); J. M. Reardon, *The Catholic Church in the Diocese of St. Paul* (St. Paul 1952); F. Parkman, *The Jesuits in North America* (Boston 1963); V. O'Daniel, *The Dominican Province of St. Joseph* (New York 1942); G. Herbermann, *The Sulpicians in the United States* (New York 1916); A. Gabriel, *The Christian Brothers in the United States* (New York 1948); M. de L. Walsh, *The Sisters of Charity of New York, 1809–1959,* 3 vols. (New York 1960); T. P. McCarty, *Guide to the Catholic Sisterhoods in the United States* (Washington 1964); W. Sweet, *The Story of Religion in America* (New York 1950); C. Olmstead, *History of Religion in the United States* (New Jersey 1960); S. Ahlstrom, *A Religious History of the American People* (New Haven 1972); S. Ahlstrom, *Theology in America: The Major Protestant Voices from Puritanism to Neo-Orthodoxy* (Indianapolis 1976); N. Burr, *A Critical Bibliography of Religion in America* (New Jersey 1961); N. Burr, *Religion in American Life* (New York 1971); L. Loetscher, *American Christianity: An Historical Interpretation with Representative Documents,* 2 vols. (New York 1960–63); J. Brauer, *Reinterpretation in American Church History* (Chicago 1968); E. Gaustad, *Historical Atlas of Religion in America* (New York 1962); R. Handy, *A History of the Churches in the United States and Canada* (Oxford 1976); M. Marty, *Righteous Empire: The Protestant Experience in America* (New York 1970); A. Stokes, *Church and State in the United States,* 3 vols. (New York 1950); S. Mead, *The Lively Experiment: The Shaping of Christianity in America* (New York 1963); E. Humphrey, *Nationalism and Religion in America* (New York 1965); W. McLoughlin, *Modern Revivalism: Charles Grandison Finney to Billy Graham* (New York 1959); W. Kennedy, *The Shaping of Protestant Education: An Interpretation of the Sunday School and the Development of Protestant Educational Strategy in the United States, 1789–1860* (New York 1966); R. Billington, *The Protestant Crusade, 1800–1860: A Study of the Origins of American Nativism* (New York 1938); C. Griffin, *Their Brother's Keepers: Moral Stewardship in the United States, 1800–1865* (New Brunswick 1960); D. Riemers, *White Protestantism and the Negro* (New York 1975); R. Michaelson, *Piety in the Public Schools: Trends and Issues in the Relationship Between Religion and the Public School in the United States* (New York 1970); R. Handy, *A Christian America: Protestant Hopes and Historical Realities* (New York 1971); K. Bailey, *Southern White Protestantism in the Twentieth Century* (New York 1964); P. Gaston, *The New South Creed, A Study in Southern Mythology* (New York 1970); G. Lenski, *The Religious Factor: A Sociological Study of Religion's Impact on Politics,*

Economics, and Family Life (New York 1961); M. Ewens, *The Role of the Nun in Nineteenth-Century America* (University of Minnesota 1971); B. J. Meiring, *Educational Aspects of the Legislation of the Councils of Baltimore, 1829–1884* (diss., University of California 1963); P. Gleason, ed., *Documentary Reports on Early American Catholicism* (New York 1978); A. H. Dorsey, *The Flemmings* (New York 1869); J. England, *The Works of the Right Rev. John England, First Bishop of Charleston,* 5 vols. (New York 1849); A. M. Greeley, "Catholicism in America: 200 Years and Counting," *The Critic* XXXIV (1976), 14–47, 54–70; H. J. Nolan, ed., *Pastoral Letters of the American Hierarchy, 1792–1970* (Huntington 1971); R. F. Hueston, *The Catholic Press and Nativism, 1840–1860* (New York 1976); W. B. Faherty, *Dream by the River. Two Centuries of Saint Louis Catholicism, 1766–1967* (St. Louis 1973); J. P. Gallagher, *A Century of History: the Diocese of Scranton, 1869–1968* (Scranton 1968); R. H. Lord, J. E. Sexton, E. T. Harrington, *History of the Archdiocese of Boston in the various Stages of its Development 1604 to 1943,* 3 vols. (New York 1944); G. J. Garraghan, *The Jesuits of the Middle United States,* 3 vols. (New York 1938); J. Rippinger, "Some Historical Determinants of American Benedictine Monasticism, 1846–1900," *American Benedictine Review* XXVII (1976), 63–84; T. Radzialowski, "Reflections on the History of the Felicians in America," *Polish-American Studies* XXXII (1975), 19–28; J. M. Daley, *Georgetown University: Origin and Early Years* (Washington 1957); J. T. Ellis, *The Formative Years of the Catholic University of America* (Washington 1946); M. H. Sanfilippo, "Personal Religious Expressions of Roman Catholicism: A Transcendental Critique," *Catholic Historical Review* LXII (1976), 366–87; J. Dolan, *Catholic Revivalism in the United States, 1830–1900* (Notre Dame 1977); J. P. Gaffey, "Patterns of Ecclesiastical Authority: The Problem of the Chicago Succession," *Church History* XLII (1973), 257–70; D. Spalding, "Martin John Spalding's 'Dissertation on the American Civil War,'" *Catholic Historical Review* LII (1966), 66–85; J. R. G. Hassard, *Life of the Most Reverend John Hughes, D.D., First Archbishop of New York* (New York 1969); T. W. Spalding, *Martin John Spalding: American Churchman* (Washington 1973); T. R. Ryan, *Orestes A. Brownson* (Huntington 1976); R. M. Leliaert, "The Religious Significance of Democracy in the Thought of Orestes A. Brownson," *Review of Politics* XXXVIII (1976), 3–26; P. H. Lemcke, *Life and Work of Prince Demetrius Augustine Gallitzin* (London–New York 1940); J. Oetgen, *An American Abbott: Boniface Wimmer, O.S.B., 1809–1887* (Latrobe, Pa. 1976); P. L. Johnson, *Crosier on the Frontier: A Life of John Martin Henni, Archbishop of Milwaukee* (Madison 1959); P. L. Johnson, *Stuffed Saddlebags: The Life of Martin Kundig, Priest, 1805–1879* (Milwaukee 1942); P. Horgan, *Lamy of Santa Fe; His Life and Times* (New York 1975); V. R. Greene, *For God and Country: The Rise of Polish and Lithuanian Ethnic Consciousness in America, 1860–1910* (Madison 1975); W. Galush, "The Polish National Catholic Church: A Survey of its Origins, Development and Missions," *Records of the American Catholic Historical Society of Philadelphia* LXXXIII (1972), 131–49; A. Kuzniewski, "The Polish National Catholic Church—The View From People's Poland," *Polish-American Studies* XXXI (1974) 30–34; H. B. Leonard, "Ethnic Conflict and Episcopal Power: The Diocese of Cleveland, 1847–1870," *Catholic Historical Review* LXII (1976), 388–407; D. P. Killen, "Americanism Revisited: John Spalding and *Testem Benevolentiae,*" *Harvard Theological Review* LXVI (1973), 413–54; A. I. Abell, *American Catholicism and Social Action; A Search for Social Justice* (Garden City 1960); T. O. Hanley, ed., *The John Carroll Papers,* 3 vols. (Notre Dame 1976); P. Gleason, "The Main Sheet Anchor: John Carroll and Catholic Higher Education," *Review of Politics* XXXVIII (1976), 576–613; J. W. Sanders, *The Education of an Urban Minority: Catholicism in Chicago, 1833–1965* (New York 1977); V. P. Lannie, "The Emergence of Catholic Education in America," *Notre Dame Journal of Education* III (1973), 297–309.

CANADA: M. Sheehan, *A Current Bibliography of Canadian Church History: Canadian Historical Association Report;* D. de St-Denis OFMCap, *L'Église catholique au Canada. Précis historique et statistique* (Montreal 1956); H. H. Walsh, *The Christian Church in Canada* (Toronto 1956); J. S. Moir, *Church and State in Canada, 1627–1867. Basic documents* (Toronto 1967); L. Pouliot, "Canada," *DHGE* XI, 675–98; A. de Barbézieux OFMCap, *Histoire de la province ecclésiastique d'Ottawa,* 2 vols. (Paris 1925); W. P. Bull, *From MacDonnell to McGuignan. The History of the Growth of the Roman Catholic Church in Upper Canada* (Toronto 1939); A. Morice, *Histoire de l'Église catholique dans l'Ouest canadien* III/IV (Winnipeg 1928); A. A. Johnston, *A History of the Catholic Church in Eastern Nova Scotia* (Antigonish 1963); H. Têtu, *Les évêques de Québec. Notices biographiques* (Québec 1889); Mgr. Tangay, *Répertoire général du clergé canadien* (Montréal 1893); L. E. Hamelin, "Évolution numérique du clergé catholique dans le Québec," *Recherches sociographiques* 2 (1961), 189–243; *Mandements, lettres pastorales et circulaires des évêques de Québec,* 9 vols. (Québec 1887/98); *Mandements, lettres pastorales et circulaires des évêques publiés dans le diocèse de Montréal,* 13 vols. (Montréal 1887/1926); J. Grant, *A History of the Christian Church in Canada,* 3 vols. (Toronto 1966/72); J. Moir, *Church and State in Canada, 1627–1867: Basic Documents* (Toronto 1967); P. Carrington, *The Anglican Church in Canada: A History* (Toronto 1963); W. Reid, *The Church of Scotland in Lower Canada: Its Struggle for Establishment* (Toronto 1936); M. Armstrong, *The Great Awakening in Nova Scotia, 1776–1809* (Hartford 1948); E. Norman, *The Conscience of the State in North America* (Cambridge 1968); S. Crysdale, *The Industrial Struggle and Protestant Ethic in Canada* (Toronto 1961); J. Grant, *The Canadian Experience of Church Union* (London 1967); C. Silcox, *Church Union in Canada: Its Causes and Consequences* (New York 1933); C. Sissons, *Church and State in Canadian Education* (Toronto 1959).

AUSTRALIA: P. F. Moran, *History of the Catholic Church in Australasia,* 2 vols. (Sydney 1896); P. O'Farrell, *The Catholic Church in Australia, 1788–1967* (London 1968); P. O'Farrell, ed., *Documents in Australian Catholic History,* 2 vols. (London 1969).

LATIN AMERICA: R. Streit, J. Dindinger, *Bibliotheca Missionum* III (Freiburg i. Br. 1927); J. L. Mecham, *Church and State in Latin America* (Chapel Hill 1966); E. Ryan, *The Church in the South American Republics* (New York 1932); F. B. Pike, ed., *The Conflict between Church and State in Latin America* (New York 1964); J. J. Kennedy, *Catholicism, Nationalism and Democracy in Argentina* (Notre Dame 1958); J. S. Campobassi, *Laicismo y catolicismo en la educación pública argentina* (Buenos Aires 1961); F. López Menéndez, *Compendio de la historia eclesiástica de Bolivia* (La Paz 1965); P. F. da Silveria Camargo, *Historia eclesiástica do Brasil* (Petrópolis 1955); J. Dornas Filho, *O padroado e la Igreja brasileira* (São Paulo 1939); Julio Maria, *A Religiâo: Livro do Centenario* I (Rio de Janeiro 1900); C. Silva Cotapos, *Historia eclesiástica de Chile* (Santiago de Chile 1925); M. Cruchaga Montt, *De las relaciones entre la Iglesia y el Estado en Chile* (Madrid 1929); J. M. Groot, *Historia eclesiástica y civil de Nueva Granada,* 4 vols. (Bogotá 1889/93); J. P. Restrepo, *La Iglesia y el Estado en Colombia* (London 1885); B. E. Haddox, *Sociedad y religion en Colombia* (Bogotá 1965); J. Maramillo, *El pensiamento colombiano en el siglo XIX* (Bogotá 1964); J. T. Donoso, *La Iglesia ecuatoriana en el siglo XIX,* 2 vols. (Quito 1934/36); M. Cuevas, *Historia de la Iglesia en México,* V (Mexico 1928); J. Bravo Ugarte, *Diocesis y obispos de la Iglesia mexicana, 1519–1939* (Mexico 1941); J. Ramirez Cabañas, *Las relaciones entre México y el Vaticano* (Mexico 1928); G. Decorme, *Historia de la Campañia de Jesús en la República Mexicana durante el siglo XIX,* 2 vols. (Guadalajara 1914/21); R. Vargas Ugarte, *Historia de la Iglesia en el Perú* V (Burgos 1962); A. Watters, *A History of the Church in Vnezuela, 1819–1930* (Chapel

Hill 1933); F. B. Pike, "The Catholic Church in Central America," *RPol* 21 (1959), 83–113.

4. Catholic Churches with Eastern Rites

J. Hajjar, *Les chrétiens uniates du Proche-Orient* (Paris 1962); J. Hajjar, *L'apostolat des missionnaires latins dans le Proche-Orient selon les directives romaines* (Jerusalem 1956); S. Sidarous, *Les patriarcats dans l'Empire ottoman et spécialement en Égypte* (Paris 1907); *Statistica con cenni storici della gerarchia e dei fedeli di rito orientale* (Vatican City 1932); C. de Clercq, *Conciles des Orientaux catholiques,* 2 vols. (Paris 1949/52); *S. Congregazione per la Chiesa Orientale. Codificazione canonica orientale. Fonti,* 3rd series, (Rome 1931seqq.); C. Charon (= C. Korolewski), *Histoire des patriarcats melkites* II/III (Rome–Paris 1910/11); A. D'Avril: *ROC* 3 (1898), 1–30, 265–81; T. Anaissi, *Bullarium Maronitarum* (Rome 1911); G. Beltrami, *La Chiesa caldea nel secolo dell'unione* (Rome 1933); M. Cramer, *Das christlich-koptische Ägypten einst und heute. Eine Orientierung* (Wiesbaden 1959); V. Inglisian, *Hundertfünfzig Jahre Mechitaristen in Wien, 1811–1961* (Vienna 1961); The articles "Maronites," "Nestorienne (Église)," "Roumanie," "Syrienne (Église)," *DThC;* The articles "Alep," "Antioche," "Antonins," "Arménie," "Audo," "Beyrouth," "Constantinople," "Égypte," *DHGE;* E. Likowski, *Dzieje Kosciola unickiego na Litwie i Rusi w XVIII i XIX wieku,* 2 vols. (Warsaw 1906); A. Korczok, *Die griechisch-katholische Kirche in Galizien* (Leipzig 1921); N. Nilles, *Symbolae ad illustrandam historiam Ecclesiae in terris Coronae S. Stephani,* 2 vols. (Innsbruck 1885); I. Radu, *Istoria diocezei romane-unite a Orazü-Mari* (Oradea Mare 1930).

5. Mission History

Bibliotheca Missionum, R. Streit, J. Dindinger, eds. (Freiburg im Breisgau 1916seqq.), VIII, XII–XIV, XVII–XXI, XXVII; *Collectanea S. Congregationis de Propaganda Fide* I (1622–1866), II (1867–1906), (Rome 1907); S. Delacroix, *Histoire Universelle des Missions Catholiques* III: *Les Missions Contemporaines* (1800–1957), (Paris 1958); K. S. Latourette, *A History of the Expansion of Christianity* IV/VI: *The Great Century* (New York 1941); A. Launay, *Histoire Générale de la Société des Missions Étrangères,* 3 vols. (Paris 1894); F. Schwager, *Die katholische Heidenmission der Gegenwart* I–IV (Steyl 1907).

6. Orders and Congregations

M. Heimbucher, *Die Orden und Kongregationen der katholischen Kirche,* 2 vols. (Paderborn 1932/34); M. Escobar, ed., *Ordini e Congregazioni religiose,* 2 vols. (Turin 1951/53); C. Tyck, *Notices historiques sur les congrégations et communautés religieuses et les instituts missionnaires du XIXe siècle* (Louvain 1892); H. C. Wendlandt, *Die weiblichen Orden und Kongregationen der katholischen Kirche und ihre Wirksamkeit in Preussen von 1818 bis 1918* (Paderborn 1924); S. Hilpisch, *Geschichte des benediktinischen Mönchtums* (Freiburg im Breisgau 1929); P. Schmitz, *Histoire de l'Ordre de S. Benoît* VI/VII (Maredsous 1948/56); P. Weissenberger, *Das benediktinische Mönchtum im 19./20. Jahrhundert* (Beuron 1958); L. F. Lekai, *Geschichte und Wirken der Weissen Mönche. Der Orden der Cisterzienser* (Cologne 1958); N. Backmund, *Monasticon Praemonstratense,* 3 vols. (Straubing 1949/56); A. Walz, *Compendium historiae Ordinis Praedicatorum* (Rome 1948); A. Mortier, *Histoire des Maîtres généraux de l'ordre des Frères Prêcheurs* VII (Paris 1915); H. Holzapfel, *Manuale historiae Ordinis FF. Minorum* (Freiburg i. Br. 1909); M. de Pobladura, *Historia generalis Ordinis Fratrum Minorum capucinorum* III (Rome 1951); R. Villoslada, *Manual de historia de la Compañia de Jesús* (Madrid 1954); P. Albers, *Liber saecularis historiae Societatis Iesu ab anno 1814 ad annum 1914* (Rome 1914); H. Azzolini in *AHSI* 2 (1933), 88–92; J. Burnichon, *La Compagnie de Jésus en France. Histoire d'un siècle. 1814–1914,* 4 vols. (Paris 1914/22); L. Frias, *Historia de la Compañia de Jesús en su Asistencia moderna de España,* 2 vols. (Madrid 1923/44); B. Basset, *The English Jesuits* (New York 1968); P. Galletti, *Memorie storiche intorno alla Provincia Romana della Compagnia di Gesù, 1814–1914* (Prato 1914); A. Monti, *La Compagnia di Gesù nel territorio della Provincia torinese* V (Chieri 1920); A. Aldegheri, *Breve storia della Provincia veneta della Compagnia di Gesù, 1814–1914* (Venice 1914); Volpe, *I Gesuiti nel Napoletano, 1804–1914,* 3 vols. (Naples 1914/15); F. Strobel, *Die Jesuiten und die Schweiz* (Olten 1955); G. Decorme, *Historia de la Compañiá de Jesús en la República mejicana durante del siglo XIX* (Guadalajara 1914); T. Hugues, *History of the Society of Jesus in North America* II/IV (New York 1908/14); A. Brou, *Cent ans de missions, 1815–1934. Les jésuites missionnaires au XIXe et XXe siècle* (Paris 1935); E. Hosp, *Die Kongregation des Allerheiligsten Erlösers* (Graz 1924); M. de Meulemeester, *Histoire sommaire de la Congrégation du T. S. Rédempteur* (Louvain 1958); G. Rigault, *Histoire générale de l'Institut des Frères des Écoles chrétiennes,* 9 vols. (Paris 1936/53); K. Zähringer, *Die Schulbrüder* (Freiburg im Breisgau 1962); H. Neufeld, *Die Gesellschaft Mariens* (Munich 1962); P. Coste, G. Goyau, *Les Filles de la Charité* (Paris 1933); J. F. Devaux, *Les Filles de la Sagesse* II (Cholet 1955); L. Ziegler, *Die Armen Schulschwestern von Unserer Lieben Frau* (Munich 1935); A. Hillengass, *Die Gesellschaft vom heiligen Herz Jesu* (Stuttgart 1917).

7. History of Theology

E. Hocedez, *Histoire de la théologie au XIXe siècle,* 3 vols. (Brussels 1947/52); M. Grabmann, *Die Geschichte der katholischen Theologie seit dem Ausgang der Väterzeit* (Freiburg i. Br. 1933); L. Scheffczyk, *Theologie in Aufbruch und Widerstreit. Die deutsche katholische Theologie im 19. Jahrhundert* (Bremen 1965).

BIBLIOGRAPHY TO INDIVIDUAL CHAPTERS

Part One

The Catholic Church and the Revolution

Introduction: *The Catholic Church at the End of the Eighteenth Century*

PIUS VI: Pastor XVI/3 (Lit.); V. Gendry, *Pie VI,* 2 vols. (Paris 1907); J. Flory, *Pie VI* (Paris 1942); *DThC* XII, 1653–69; Seppelt-Schwaiger V (Munich 1959), 484–90, 547 (Lit.); I. Rinieri, *Relazioni storiche tra Pio VI e la corte di Napoli negli anni 1776–1799* (Turin 1910); G. Soranzo, *Peregrinus Apostolicus. Lo spirito pubblico e il viaggio di Pio VI a Vienna* (Milan 1937).

ON THE CONCLAVE: E. Pacheco y de Leyva, *El conclave de 1774–1775* (Madrid 1915); J. Gendry: *Revue des questions historiques* 51 (1892), 424–85; F. Masson, *Le cardinal de Bernis* (Paris 1903), 300–18; E. Harder, *Der Einfluss Portugals bei der Wahl Pius' VI.* (Königsberg 1882).

ON THE ADMINISTRATION OF THE PAPAL STATES: C. De Cupis, *Le vicende dell'agricoltura e della pastorizia nell'agro romano* (Rome 1911), 330–47, 367; E. Piscitelli, *La riforma di Pio VI e gli scrittori economici italiani* (Milan 1958); F. Venturi in *RSIt* 71 (1959), 135–42; L. Del Pane, *Lo Stato pontificio e il movimento riformatore del Settecento* (Milan 1959).

1. *The French Revolution and Pius VI*

SOURCES

Overviews, especially with respect to still unpublished sources, are to be found in P. Caron, *Manuel pratique pour l'étude de la Révolution française* (Paris 1947); L. Le Grand, *Les sources de l'histoire religieuse de la Révolution aux Archives Nationales* (Paris 1914); G. Bourgin, *Les sources manuscrites de l'histoire religieuse de la France moderne* (Paris 1929), 97–115; E. Audard, "Histoire religieuse de la Révolution française aux Archives Vaticanes," *RHEF* 4 (1913), 516–45; E. Sevestre, *Étude critique des sources de l'histoire religieuse de la Révolution en Normandie* (Paris 1916).

A. Theiner, *Documents inédits relatifs aux affaires religieuses de la France 1790–1800,* 2 vols. (Paris 1857); J. Guillon, ed., *Collection générale des brefs et instructions du Pape Pie VI relatifs à la Révolution française* (Paris 1798); G. Bourgin, *La France et Rome de 1788 à 1797. Regeste des dépêches du cardinal secretaire d'État* (Paris 1909); de Richemont, ed., *Correspondance secrète de l'abbé de Salamon, chargé d'affaire du Saint-Siège pendant la Révolution* (Paris 1898), complemented in *MAH* 18 (1898), 419–50; A. Barruel, *Collection ecclésiastique,* 14 vols. (Paris 1791–92); S. Viviani, *Témoignage de l'Église de France sur la Constitution civile du clergé,* 16 vols. (Rome 1791–94); J. Maury, *Correspondance dip-*

lomatique et mémoirs inédits, ed. by A. Ricard, 2 vols. (Lille 1891); *Archives parlementaires,* 1st series: 1787–99, 87 vols. (Paris 1867–1968); A. Debidour, ed., *Actes du Directoire exécutif,* 4 vols. (Paris 1910–17); A. Aulard, *La Révolution française et les congrégations* (Paris 1903).

ON THE ATTITUDE OF THE CLERGY IN THE ESTATES-GENERAL AND THE CONSTITUENT ASSEMBLY: The diaries of *Jallet,* ed. by J. J. Brethé (Fontenay-le-Comte 1871), *Thibault* and *Coster,* ed. by A. Houtin (Paris 1916); Durand de Maillane, *Histoire apologétique du Comité ecclésiastique de l'Assemblée nationale* (Paris 1791).

ON THE CONSTITUENT CHURCH: H. Carnot, ed., *Mémoires de Grégoire,* 2 vols. (Paris 1840); The correspondence of *Grégoire* with *Ricci* and *Defraisse,* ed. by M. Vaussard (Florence 1963, Paris 1962), with *Le Coz,* ed. by L. Pingaud (Besançon 1906), and with *Dom Grappin,* ed. by B. Plongeron (Paris 1969); The correspondence of *Le Coz,* ed. by A. Roussel (Paris 1900); *Annales de la Religion* (1795–1803).

LITERATURE

A. Martin and G. Walter, *Catalogue de l'histoire de la Révolution française,* 5 vols. (Paris 1936–43).

GENERAL WORKS: A. Latreille, *L'Église catholique et la Révolution française* I (Paris 1946); K. D. Erdmann, *Volkssouveränität und Kirche* (Cologne 1949); C. Ledré, *L'Église de France sous la Révolution* (Paris 1949); Leflon, 7–158; Hermelink I, 1–95; Daniel-Rops I, 7–116; H. Maier, *Revolution und Kirche* (Freiburg i. Br. 1965); J. Godechot, *Les institutions de la France sous la Révolution et l'Empire* (Paris 1968), 250–70, 421–32, 526–35; A. Gazier, *Étude sur l'histoire religieuse de la Révolution* (Paris 1887); A. Sicard, *Les évêques pendant la Révolution* (Paris 1894); id., *Le clergé de France pendant la Révolution,* 2 vols. (Paris 1912–27); Giobbio, *La Chiesa e lo Stato in Francia durante la Rivoluzione* (Rome 1905); P. de la Gorce, *Histoire religieuse de la Révolution,* 5 vols. (Paris 1909–23); A. Mathiez, *La Révolution et l'Église* (Paris 1910); J. Lacouture, *La politique religieuse de la Révolution* (Paris 1924); B. Plongeron, *Conscience religieuse en Révolution. Regards sur l'historiographie religieuse de la Révolution française* (Paris 1969).

THE CONDITION OF THE FRENCH CHURCH ON THE EVE OF THE REVOLUTION: A. Sicard, *L'ancien clergé de France* I (Paris 1912); E. Sevestre, *Les idées gallicanes et royalistes du haut-clergé à la fin de l'Ancien Régime* (Paris 1917); id., *L'organisation du clergé paroissial à la veille de la Révolution* (Paris 1911); P. de Vaissière, *Curés de campagne de l'ancienne France* (Paris 1933); C. Gérin in *RQH* 19 (1876), 449–91, 21 (1877), 35–99 (Benedictines, Augustinians, and Dominicans); P. Lecarpentier, *La propriété foncière du clergé sous l'Ancien Régime* (Paris 1902); H. Marion, *La dîme ecclésiastique en France au XVIIIe siècle et sa suppression* (Paris 1912); E. Préclin, *Les jansénistes du XVIIIe siècle et la Constitution civile du clergé* (Paris 1929); J. Delumeau, *Le catholicisme entre Luther et Voltaire* (Paris 1971).

THE CIVIL CONSTITUTION OF THE CLERGY AND THE CONSTITUENT CHURCH: L. Sciout, *Histoire de la constitution civile du clergé 1790–1801,* 4 vols. (1872–81); A. Mathiez, *Rome et le clergé français sous la Constituante* (Paris 1910); H. Leclercq, *L'Église constitutionnelle 1790–1791* (Paris 1934); J. Haak, *De discussie over de Constitution civile du clergé, 1790* (Groningen 1964); *DThC* III, 1537–1604. There is as yet no comprehensive work on the Constituent Church, but see P. Pisani, *Répertoire biographique de l'épiscopat constitutionnel* (Paris 1907). The most notable monographs are: J. Leflon, *N.*

Philibert, évêque constitutionnel des Ardennes (Mézières 1954); H. Lacape, *P. Pontard, évêque constitutionnel de la Dordogne* (Bordeaux 1962); C. Grelier, *Bulletin de la Société archéologique et historique de Nantes* 99 (1960), 177–88 (for the Vendée); A. Sabathès in *BLE* 62 (1961), 245–74 (election of priests in Aude); E. Sevestre, *L'acceptation de la Constitution civile du clergé en Normandie* (Laval 1922); C. Constantin, *L'évêché du département de la Meurthe* (Nancy 1935); R. Reuss, *La constitution civile du clergé et la crise religieuse en Alsace,* 2 vols. (Strasbourg 1922–23); P. Mesple in *Mémoire de l'Académie de Toulouse* 128 (1966), 73–83; M. Chartier: *Revue du Nord* 45 (1963), 307–16; P. Tartat in *AHRF* 22 (1950), 221–46; W. Edington in *Bulletin de la Société des antiquaires de Normandie* 54 (1957–58), 492–501; J. Camelin, *Les Prêtres de la Révolution* (Lyon 1944; for the diocese of Rhône-et-Loire).

REVOLUTIONARY RELIGIONS: A. Aulard, *Le culte de la Raison et de l'Etre suprême* (Paris 1901); A. Mathiez, *Les origines des cultes révolutionnaires* (Paris 1904); id., *La Théophilanthropie et le culte décadaire* (Paris 1904); A. Soboul in *AHRF* 29 (1957), 193–213; M. Dommanget, *Le symbolisme et le prosélytisme révolutionnaire à Beauvais et dans l'Oise* (Beauvais 1932).

THE RELIGIOUS POLICY OF THE DIRECTORY: L. Séché, *Les origines du concordat* I (Paris 1894); E. Sol, *Sous le régime de la séparation* (Paris 1931); V. Pierre, *La déportation ecclésiastique sous le Directoire* (Paris 1896); A. C. Sabatié, *La déportation révolutionnaire du clergé français* (Paris 1916).

RELIGIOUS ORDERS DURING THE REVOLUTION: P. Nourisson, *Histoire légale des congrégations religieuses en France depuis 1789* I (Paris 1928); B. Plongeron, *Les réguliers de Paris devant le serment constitutionnel* (Paris 1964); J. Boussoulade, *Moniales et hospitalières dans la tourmente révolutionnaire* (Paris 1962; for the bishopric of Paris); A. Lestra, *Le P. Coudrin, fondateur de Picpus* I (Lyon 1952); J. Letort in *Cahiers L. Delisle* 15 (1966), 107–31 (for the bishopric of Évreux); C. Schmitt in *Mémoires de l'Académie de Metz,* 5th ser. 10 (1964–65), 21–61; Armel d'Etel, "Les historiens et la question des réguliers," *Éfranc* (1925), 355–79, 601–16, (1926), 57–77.

REGIONAL MONOGRAPHS: Many of them limit themselves to what actually happened and to anecdotes and are written from an outdated point of view. Most noteworthy are: J. Gallerand, *Les cultes sous la Terreur en Loir-et-Cher* (Blois 1929); P. Clémendot, *Le département de la Meurthe à l'époque du Directoire* (Nancy 1966); C. Aimond, *Histoire religieuse de la Révolution dans le département de la Meuse* (Paris 1949); J. Annat, *Le clergé du diocèse de Lescar pendant la Révolution* (Paris 1954); P. Bois, *Paysans de l'Ouest* (Paris 1959); E. Bouchez, *Le clergé du pays rémois pendant la Révolution* (Reims 1913); C. Brelot, "Besançon révolutionnaire" in *Cahiers d'Études comtoises* 9 (1966), 33–212; F. Bridoux, *Histoire religieuse du département de Seine-et-Marne pendant la Révolution,* 2 vols. (Paris 1953–55); J. Eich, *Histoire religieuse du département de la Moselle pendant la Révolution* (Metz 1964); id., *Les prêtres mosellans pendant la Révolution,* 2 vols. (Metz 1959–64); M. Giraud, *Essai sur l'histoire religieuse de la Sarthe de 1789 à l'an IV* (La Flêche 1920); J. Hérissay, *La vie catholique à Paris sous la Terreur* (Paris 1952); J. Boussoulade, *L'Église de Paris du 9 thermidor au Concordat* (Paris 1950); C. Ledré, *Le diocèse de Rouen et la législation révolutionnaire de 1793 à 1800* (Paris 1939); J. Nicolas, "Annecy sous la Révolution," *Annesci* 13 (1966), 11–148; J. Peter and C. Poulet, *Histoire religieuse du département du Nord pendant la Révolution,* 2 vols. (Lille 1930); A. Prevost, *Histoire du diocèse de Troyes pendant la Révolution,* 3 vols. (Troyes 1908–09); id., *Répertoire biographique* (Troyes 1914); M. Reinhard, *Le département de la Sarthe sous le régime directorial* (St-Brieuc 1935); de Roux, *Histoire religieuse de la Révolution dans la Vienne* (Paris 1952); E. Sevestre, *La vie religieuse dans les principales villes normandes pendant la Révolution,* 2 vols. (Paris 1945); C. Tilly, *The Vendée* (London 1964), 100–12, 227–62; E. Lavaquery, "L'histoire religieuse de la Révolution dans le cadre diocésain," *RHEF* 20 (1934), 216–30.

BIOGRAPHIES: J. Leflon, *M. Émery* I (Paris 1944; according to Godechot one of the keys to the history of the Church during the revolution); id., *É. A. Bernier* I (Paris 1938); F. Masson, *Le cardinal de Bernis* (Paris 1903), 449–560; J. Sudreau, *Un cardinal diplomate F. J. de Pierre de Bernis* (Paris 1969); C. Ledré, *L'abbé de Salamon* (Paris 1966); E. Lavaquery, *Le cardinal de Boisgelin* II (Paris 1920); L. Mahieu, *Mgr L. Belmas* I (Paris 1934).

NON-CATHOLIC RELIGIONS: B. C. Poland, *French Protestantism and the French Revolution* (Princeton 1957); D. Ligou: *Bulletin de la Société d'histoire du protestantisme français* 103 (1957), 25–52; M. A. Wemyss in *Annales du Midi* 69 (1957), 307–22; Z. Szakowsky, "The Attitude of the French Jacobines toward the Jewish Religion," *Historia judaica* 18 (1956), 107–20.

EFFECTS IN NEIGHBORING COUNTRIES: J. Godechot, *La grande nation* II (Paris 1956), 501–35. The only comprehensive work on the religious problems in Belgium is that by P. Verhaegen, *La Belgique sous la domination française,* 5 vols. (Brussels–Paris 1922–29) especially II, 268–349, III, 203–82. It has the advantage of resting on the sources, but requires revision in view of its systematic hostility toward the revolutionary regime. See also *DHGE* VII, 711–16. Monographs are available in large numbers, but frequently they lack the required scientific discipline. Of note are: J. Plumet, *L'évêché de Tournai pendant la révolution française* (Louvain 1963); and F. Claeys-Bounaert, *Les déclarations et serments imposés par la loi civile aux membres du clergé belge sous le Directoire* (Gembloux 1960), whose questions are obsolete but which exploit a comprehensive and still unpublished documentation. With respect to the oath see also the correspondence of *S. P. Ernst,* published by C. de Clercq (Reference in *DHGE* XV, 812); id., *SE* 8 (1956), 349–78; id., *Taxandria* 27 (Turnhout 1955), 3–35; W. Munier, *Bulletin de la Société d'art et d'histoire du diocèse de Liège* 44 (1964), 51–124. On the sale of church lands: J. Delatte, *La vente de biens nationaux dans le département de Jemappes* (Brussels 1938); id., *La vente des biens du clergé dans le département de l'Ourthe* (Liège 1951); id., *Annales de la Société archéologique de Namur* 40 (1934), 189–339; J. Paquay, *Bulletin de la Société scientifique et littéraire du Limbourg* 42 (1928), 25–52. Also A. Thys, *La persécution religieuse en Belgique sous le Directoire* (Antwerp 1898); F. Prims, "De Kerk van Antwerpen onder het Directoire," *Antwerpiensia* VIII (Antwerp 1935), 231–87; L. Lefebvre, "La crise religieuse dans la region de Bastogne 1794–1814," *Mémorial A. Bertrang* (Arlon 1964), 127–58; A. Verhaegen, *Le cardinal de Franckenberg* (Bruges–Lille 1889), 299–426. C. De Clercq, *SE* 10 (1958), 298–328, 15 (1964), 341–411; id., *SE* 9 (1957), 286–375, 10 (1958), 238–97 (on Bishop Nelis of Antwerp).

RHINELAND: P. Sagnac, *Le Rhin français pendant la Révolution et l'Empire* (Paris 1918); F. C. Dreyfus, *Sociétés et mentalités à Mayence dans la 2e moitié du XVIIIe siècle* (Paris 1968).

UNITED NETHERLANDS: M. van der Heyden, *De dageraad van de emancipatie der Katholieken* (Nijmegen 1947; basic). Also *Romeinse bescheiden voor de geschiedenis der Rooms-Katholieke Kerk in Nederland,* II: *1754–1795,* edited by P. Polman (The Hague 1963), 467–877; id., *Katholieke Nederland in de 18^e^ eeuw* (Hilversum 1968), II, 246–86 III, 291–305; P. Noordeloos, *De restitutie der Kerken in de Fransche tijd* (Utrecht 1937); M Spiertz, *Maastricht in het vierde kwart van de 18e eeuw* (Assen 1964); H. van den Eerenbeemt, *'s-Hertogenbosch in de Bataafse en Franse tijd 1794–1814* (Nijmegen 1955).

SWITZERLAND: E. Chapusat, *La Suisse et la Révolution française* (Geneva 1945); G. Gautherot, *La Révolution française et l'évêché de Bâle,* 2 vols. (Paris 1907); J. R. Suratteau, *Le département du Mont-Terrible sous le régime du Directoire* (Paris 1965) 227–79.

ITALY: A. de Stefano, *Rivoluzione e religione nelle prime esperienze constituzionali italiane* (Milan 1954); M. Vaussard, *Jansénisme et gallicanisme aux origines religieuses du Risorgimento* (Paris 1959); id., "Les jansénistes italiens et la constitution civile du clergé," *RH* 205 (1951), 243–59; id., *Correspondance Sc. de'Ricci H. Grégoire 1796–1807* (Florence 1963); V. Giuntella, *Nuove questioni di storia di Risorgimento* I (Milan 1961), 320–25; id., *RStRis* 42 (1955), 289–96 (inspiring research program); M. Finocchiaro in *Archivio giuridico F. Serafini* 171 (1966), 136–54; A. Aquarone, "Giansenismo italiano e rivoluzione francese prima del triennio giacobino," *RStRis* 49 (1962), 559–624; P. Stella, *Il Giansenismo in Italia. Piemonte* (Zürich 1970); B. Plongeron, "Questions pour l'Aufklärung catholique en Italie," *Il pensiero politico* 3 (1970), 30–58; R. De Felice, *Italia giacobina* (Naples 1965); id., *Giacobini italiani, a cura di D. Cantimori,* 2 vols. (Bari 1956–64).

CISALPINE REPUBLIC: J. Leflon, *Pie VII* (Paris 1958), 360–529; U. Marcelli, *La vendita dei beni nazionali nella Repubblica cisalpina* (Bologna 1967); id., "Polemiche religiose a Bologna nel sec. XVIII," *Atti e Memorie della Dep. di storia patria per la Romagna* n. s. 6 (1954–55), 103–177.

LIGURIAN REPUBLIC: C. Caristia, "La Repubblica ligure e il giansenismo democratico," *Atti dell'Accademia di Torino* 94 (1960), 427–505; Cassiano di Langasco, *Nuove ricerche storiche sul Giansenismo* (Rome 1954), 211–29; A. Coletti, *La chiesa durante la Repubblica ligure* (Genoa 1950).

ON DEMOCRATIC PRIESTS: R. De Felice, "L'evangelismo giacobino e l'abate Cl. Della Valle," *RSIt* 60 (1957), 196–249, 378–410; A. Bersano, *L'abate F. Bonardi e i suoi tempi* (Turin 1957).

THE DIRECTORY AND THE HOLY SEE: P. Gaffarel, *Bonaparte et la République italienne* (Paris 1895); A. Sorel, *Hoche et Bonaparte en 1797* (Paris 1896); A. Dufourcq, *Le régime jacobin en Italie* (Paris 1900); J. du Teil, *Rome, Naples et le Directoire* (Paris 1902); R. Guyot, *Le Directoire et la paix de l'Europe* (Paris 1911); de Richemont: *Correspondant* 188 (1897) 801–49; F. Bouvier, "Bonaparte, Cacault et la papauté," *Revue d'histoire diplomatique* 21 (1907), 340–56.

THE TREATY OF TOLENTINO: G. Filippone, *Le relazioni tra lo Stato pontificio et la Francia rivoluzionaria,* 2 vols. (Milan 1961–67); also *RSTI* 16 (1962), 145–49; R. Olaecha in *MCom* 43 (1965), 95–292; L. Pásztor in *AHPont* 1 (1963), 295–383.

ROMAN REPUBLIC: V. Giuntella, *Bibliografia della Repubblica romana* (Rome 1957); id., *ASRomana* 73 (1950), 1–213; id., *La crisi del potere temporara alle fine del Settecento e la parentesi constituzionale del 1798–99* (Bologna 1954); R. De Felice, *La vendita dei beni nazionali nella Repubblica Romana* (Rome 1960); M. Battaglini, "La soppressione dei conventi nella Repubblica Romana giacobina," *Palatino* 9 (1965), 13–23.

THE LAST MONTHS OF PIUS VI: G. Merck, *La captivité et la mort de Pie VI* (London 1814); P. Baldassari, *Histoire de l'enlèvement et de la captivité du pape Pie VI* (Paris–Lyon 1839); T. de la Rive, *L'esilo e la morte di Pio VI* (Rome 1899); C. Poncet, *Pie VI à Valence* (Paris 1868).

2. *Napoleon and Pius VII*

SOURCES

BullRomCont XI–XIII (Rome 1846–47); G. Sala, ed., *Documenti relativi alle contestazioni insorte fra la S. Sede ed il Governo Francese,* 6 vols. (Rome 1833–34); *Correspondance de Napoléon Ier,* 32 vols. (Paris 1958–70); P. Feret, *La France et le St-Siège sous le Ier Empire* (Paris 1911; diplomatic correspondence); Bastgen I, 42–72; E. Consalvi, *Memorie,* ed. by M. Nasalli Rocca, 2 vols. (Rome 1950; also *DHGE* XIII, 521–22; the French translation by J. Crétineau-Joly which appeared in Paris in 1864 is not reliable); B. Pacca, *Memorie,* 3 vols. (Rome 1830; also J. Leflon and C. Perrat in *ChStato* II, 355–81); E. de Lévis-Mirepoix, ed., *Mémoires et papiers de Lebzeltern* (Paris 1949; Austrian ambassador to the Pope); J. Jauffret, *Mémoires pour servir à l'histoire de la religion au XIXe siècle,* 3 vols. (Paris, n.d.; very useful for reorganization of the Church in France); E. A. Bernier, *Lettres, Notes diplomatiques, Mémoires inédits,* ed. by J. Leflon (Reims 1938); A. Roussel, ed., *Correspondance de Le Coz, archevêque de Besançon,* 2 vols. (Paris 1900–03); L. Pingaud, ed., *Correspondance de Le Coz et Grégoire 1801–15* (Besançon 1906); J. Puraye, ed., *La correspondance de Mgr Zaepfel* (Bruges-Paris 1951; bishop of Liège); Mgr. de Barral, *Fragments relatifs à l'histoire ecclésiastique du XIXe siècle* (Paris 1814); F. de Lamennais, *Réflexions sur l'état de l'Église de France et sur sa situation actuelle* (Paris 1821; written in 1808); *Annales littéraires et morales,* 4 vols. (Paris 1803–06; viewpoint of former refractory priests); *Journal des curés,* 6 vols. (Paris 1806–11; viewpoint of former Constituent Church members); Lemière d'Argy, *Précis historique du voyage et de la captivité de Pie VII* (Paris 1804); A. de Beauchamp, *Histoire des malheurs et de la captivité de Pie VII* (Paris 1815).

LITERATURE

THE PONTIFICATE OF PIUS VII UNTIL 1815: Schmidlin, *PG* I, 39–130; Leflon, 159–273; Pouthas, 60–172; Hermelink, I, 95–171; Belvederi, 820–67; *DThC* XII, 1670–83; *ECatt* IX, 1504–08; Rogier, *KG* IV, 183–203; Daniel-Rops I, 117–234; C. Wunderlich, *Der Pontifikat Pius' VII. in der Beurteilung der deutschen Umwelt* (Leipzig 1913); Mollat, 69–99; Salvatorelli, 16–26; A. Latreille, *Napoléon et le Saint-Siège 1801–08. L'ambassade du cardinal Fesch à Rome* (Paris 1935).

CONSALVI: G. A. Angelucci, *Il grande segretario della S. Sede, E. Consalvi* (Rome 1924); M. R. Wichterich, *Sein Schicksal war Napoleon. Leben und Zeit des Kardinals Consalvi* (Heidelberg 1951); L. von Ranke, *Cardinal Consalvi und seine Staatsverwaltung unter dem Pontifikat Pius' VII.* in *Sämtliche Werke* XLI/XLII (Leipzig 1877–78), 3–180; *Nel primo centenario della morte del cardinale Consalvi* (Rome 1925); I. Rinieri in *CivCatt* I (1925), 289–300, 395–402; *DHGE* XIII, 509–23; Colapietra, 18–36, 139.

REORGANIZATION OF THE CHURCH IN FRANCE: J. Leflon in *RHEF* 34 (1948), 103–17, a good introduction; The best comprehensive work is A. Latreille, *L'Église catholique et la Révolution* II: *L'Ère napoléonienne* (Paris 1950); *HistCathFr,* 155–218; S. Delacroix, *La réorganisation de l'Église de France* (Paris 1962; the first part of a typed doctoral dissertation, Sorbonne, 1957, together with a volume of documents. A basic work); J. d'Haussonville, *L'Église romaine et le Premier Empire,* 5 vols. (Paris 1866–68; still useful, although neither the state archives nor the Vatican archives could be consulted and the work was written from an anti-Bonapartist viewpoint); I. Rinieri, *La diplomazia pontificia nel sec. XIX* II (Rome 1904); id., *Napoleone e Pio VII, 1804–13,* 2 vols. (Rome

1906); Debidour, *Histoire* II (Paris 1891), 5–324; V. Bindel, *Histoire religieuse de Napoléon,* 2 vols. (Paris 1940); Dansette I, 159–231; E. Walder, *Staat und Kirche in Frankreich* II (Bern 1953).

NAPOLEON'S CORONATION: E. Celani, *Il viaggio di Pio VII a Parigi* (Rome 1893); F. Masson, *Le sacre et le couronnement de Napoléon* (Paris 1908); J. Leflon, *Bernier* II, 197–222.

CLERGY AND ORDERS: J. Leflon, "Le clergé de second ordre sous le Consulat et L'Empire," *RHEF* 31 (1945), 97–119; L. Preneel in *De Leiegouw* 4 (Kortrijk 1962), 73–101, 205–30, 5 (1963), 5–29 (on the clergy of the diocese of Ghent); id. in *Bijdragen* 23 (Nijmegen 1962), 63–74 (on clerical garb); L. Deries, *Les congrégrations religieuses au temps de Napoléon* (Paris 1928); P. Imbert, *Le droit hospitalier de la Révolution et de l'Empire* (Paris 1954); C. Rigault, *Histoire de l'Institut des Frères des Écoles chrétiennes* IV (Paris 1942), 1–413; P. Zind, *Les nouvelles congrégations de Frères enseignants en France de 1800 à 1830* I (Le Montet 1969), 47–71; *DSAM* II, 974–79 (on the foundings of P. de Clorivière).

REGIONAL MONOGRAPHS: C. Ledré, *La réorganisation d'un diocèse au lendemain de la Révolution. Le cardinal Cambacerès* (Paris 1943); P. Mouly, *Le concordat en Lozère et en Ardèche* (Mende 1943); F. Le Douarec, *Le concordat dans un diocèse de l'Ouest, Mgr Cafarelli et le préfet Boullé* (Paris 1958); R. Pinet, *Le diocèse de Valence 1802–15* (Valence 1963); G. Lacroix, *Ch. de la Tour d'Auvergne* (Arras 1965); J. Godel, *La reconstruction concordataire dans le diocèse Grenoble* (Grenoble 1968); F. Uzureau, *Les premières applications du concordat dans le diocèse d'Angers* (Paris 1901); J. Contrasty, *Le mouvement religieux en Haute-Garonne sous le consulat* (Paris 1907); P. Pisani, *Histoire de l'Église de Paris sous la Révolution* V (Paris 1911); L. Lévy-Schneider, *L'application du consulat par une évêque d'Ancien régime, Champion de Cicé* (Paris 1921; for the diocese of Aix); P. Genevray, *L'administration et la vie ecclésiastique dans le diocèse de Toulouse* (Paris 1921); A. Poirier, *Mgr Paillou et les débuts du concordat en Vendée* (Paris 1924); C. Le Sueur, *Le clergé picard et le Concordat,* 2 vols. (Paris 1929–30); On the Belgian dioceses: L. Preneel in *RHE* 57 (1962), 871–900 (concerning the determination of diocesan boundaries); C. de Clercq, "L'opposition à Mgr de Roquelaure dans le département de la Dyle," *SE* 13 (1962), 194–265; F. Jacques, *Le rètablissement du culte catholique à Namur* (Gembloux 1962); W. Munier, "Het concordaat van Napoleon en de opheffing van het oude bisdom Roermond," *Publications de la Société historique et archéologique dans le Limbourg* 98/99 (1962–63), 147–214.

THE REBIRTH OF RELIGIOUS FEELING: G. Constant, "Le réveil religieux en France au début du XIXe siècle," *RHE* 29 (1933), 905–50, 30 (1934), 54–84; J. Goretti, *Bonald. La Révolution française et le réveil religieux* (Paris 1962); C. Sainte-Beuve, *Chateaubriand et son groupe littéraire* 2 vols. (Paris 1960); C. Pouthas, *La jeunesse de Guizot* (Paris 1936).

BIOGRAPHIES: J. Leflon, *E. A. Bernier,* 2 vols. (Paris 1938) id., *M. Émery* II (Paris 1946); L. Mahieu, *Belmas,* 2 vols. (Paris 1934); A. Delacroix, *Boulogne* (Paris 1880); J. Lenfant, "Broglie," *RHEF* 17 (1931), 312–47; E. Gabory, *Duvoisin* (Nantes 1947); J. P. Lyonnet, *Fesch,* 2 vols. (Paris-Lyon 1841, to be augmented by *DHGE* XVI, 1315–19); A. Roussel, *Le Coz* (Paris 1898); A. G. Bonet-Maury, *Maury* (Paris 1892, inadequate); A. Durand, *Périer* (Paris 1902); F. L'Huillier, *Recherches sur l'Alsace napoléonienne* (Paris 1947).

THE CONFLICT BETWEEN PIUS VII AND NAPOLEON: H. Welschinger, *Le pape et l'empereur* (Paris 1905); L. Madelin, *La Rome de Napoléon* (Paris 1906); B. Melchior-

Bonet, *Napoléon et le pape* (Paris 1958); E. Hales, *The Emperor and the Pope* (New York 1961); H. de Mayol de Luppé, *La captivité de Pie VII* (Paris 1912); M. Crépon, "Nomination et institution canonique des évêques," *Le Correspondant* 210 (1903), 843–78; L. Maddi in *RStRis* 22 (1935), 685–745; A. LeGlay, *Mgr d'Arezzo, une victime de Napoléon* (Cambrai 1908); J. Destrem, "Documents sur les déportations de prêtres sous le Premier Empire," *RH* 11 (1879), 331–88; Borrey, *L'esprit public chez les prêtres franc-comtois pendant la crise de 1813 à 1815* (Paris 1912); F. Claeys-Bouvaert, *Le diocèse et le séminaire de Gand pendant les dernières années de la domination française* (Ghent 1913); A. Milet, *L'opposition à la politique religieuse de Napoléon dans le département de Jemappes* (Tournai 1970).

Biographies of Pius VII: E. Pistolesi, *Vita del S. Pontefice Pio VII,* 2 vols. (Rome 1824/30); A. F. Artaud de Montor, *Histoire de la vie et du pontificat du Pie VII* (Paris 1836); G. Giucci, *Storia della vita e del pontificato di Pio VII* (Rome 1857); M. Allies, *The Life of Pope Pius the Seventh* (London 1875); D. Bertolotti, *Vita di Pio VII* (Turin 1881); J. Leflon, *Pie VII* (Paris 1958; basic, but only to 1800).

The Conclave: J. Leflon, *Pie VII* I, 532–606, to be supplemented by L. Pásztor, *ASRomana* 83 (1960), 99–187 (newly discovered diary of Consalvi); see also id., *AHPont* 3 (1965), 239–308; G. Incisa della Rocchetta: *Boll. dell'Istituto di storia della societa e dello Stato veneziano* (1962), 268–323 (diary of Prince Chigi); E. Celani, "I preliminari del conclave di Venezia," *ASRomana* 26 (1913), 475–518; C. Van Duerm, *Un peu plus de lumière sur le conclave de Venise et sur les commencements du pontificat de Pie VII* (Louvain 1896); A. Ricard, *Correspondances et Mémoires du cardinal Maury* I (Lille 1891), 200–374; R. Cessi, "L'Austria al conclave di Venezia," *Il Risorgimento italiano* 15 (1922), 356–413; A. Mater, *La République au conclave* (Paris 1923); G. Damerini, *L'Isola e il cenobio di S. Giorgio Maggiore* (Venice 1956), 201–36 (following the diary of cardinal L. Flangini); B. Bastgen in *HJ* 79 (1960), 146–74 (Letters of Consalvi).

The First Restoration of the Papal States: Schmidlin, *PG* I, 28–39; Mollat, 73–86; J. Leflon in *Revue des travaux de l'Académie des sciences morales et politiques* 114/II (1961), 173–182 (following the diary of Despuig); L. Dal Pane, "Le riforme economiche di Pio VII," *Studi romagnoli* 16 (1965), 257–76; F. Grosse-Wietfeld, *Justizreformen im Kirchenstaat* (Paderborn 1932), 1–27; Ardent, *Pape et paysans* (Paris 1891); L. Madelin, *La Rome de Napoléon* (Paris 1906).

The Concordat of 1801: A. Boulay de la Meurthe, *Documents sur la négociation du concordat,* 6 vols. (Paris 1901–05); J. Portalis, *Discours, rapports et travaux inédits sur le concordat de 1801* (Paris 1845); F. D. Mathieu, *Le concordat de 1801* (Paris 1902); I. Rinieri, *Il concordato tra Pio VII e il Primo Console* (Rome 1902); E. Sevestre, *L'histoire, le texte et la destinée du concordat de 1801* (Paris 1905); A. Boulay de la Meurthe, *Histoire de la négociation du concordat* (Tours 1920); A. Rayez in *RHE* 46 (1951), 624–80, 47 (1952), 142–62.

Southern Europe, Italy: I. Rinieri, *La diplomazia pontificia nel sec. XIX* II (Rome 1902); F. Melzi d'Eril, *Memorie,* 2 vols. (Milan 1865); A. Fugier, *Napoléon et l'Italie* (Paris 1947); M. Roberti, "La legislazione ecclesiastica nel periodo napoleonico," *Chiesa e Stato, Studi storici* I (Milan 1939), 253–332; A. Theiner, *Histoire des deux concordats de la République française et de la République Cisalpine* II (Bar-le-Duc 1869), 1–53; id., *Pièces justificatives,* 249–85; A. Latreille, *L'ambassade du cardinal Fesch* (Paris 1935); G. Manganella, "L'applicazione del Concordato italiano," *Miscellanea di studi storici ad A. Luzio II* (Florence 1933), 143–68; Stanislao da Campagnola in *Laurentianum* 5 (1964), 245–

82, 11 (1970), 129–53; id. in *Collectanea franciscana* 39 (1969), 304–61; J. Rambaud, "L'Église de Naples sous la domination française," *RHE* 9 (1908), 294–312; C. Tori, "Lo schema di concordato del 1804 fra la Repubblica democratica di Lucca e la Santa Sede," *RSTI* 20 (1966), 328–52; P. Barbaini, *Problemi religiosi del Risorgimento in Toscana* (Turin 1961), 56–58.

SOUTHERN EUROPE, SPAIN: F. Marti Gilabert, *La Iglesia en España durante la Revolución francesa* (Pamplona 1971); M. Artola, *Los orígenes de la España contemporanea,* 2 vols. (Madrid 1959), especially I, 34–44, 506–36, II, 115–245; L. Sierra, *La reacción del episcopado español ante los decretos de matrimonios del ministro Urquijo de 1799 a 1803* (Bilbao 1964); M. Menéndez y Pelayo, *Historia de los heterodoxos españoles* II (BAC Madrid 1956), 770–841; G. de Grandmaison, *L'Espagne et Napoléon,* 3 vols. (Paris 1908/31); J. M. Cuenca Toribio, "La actitud de la jerarquía barcelonesa ante la Revolucíon francesa 1790–95," *Analecta sacra Tarraconensia* 40 (1967), 355–69; A. Pérez Goyena, "El espíritu religioso de la guerra de la Independencia," *RF* 21 (1908), 5–18; id., "La masonería en España durante la guerra de la Independencia," *RF* 22 (1908), 413–28; Isidoro de la Villapadierna, "Conflicto entre el Cardenal Primado y el Nuncio Mons. Gravina en 1809–14," *Anthologica annua* 5 (1957), 261–311; id. in *Nuove ricerche storiche sul giansenismo* (Rome 1954), 275–303; on the Cortes of Cádiz; id. in *HS* 8 (1955), 275–335; L. M. de Mendijur, *Scriptorium Victoriense* 12 (1965), 300–41; J. M. Cuenca Toribio, *HS* 15 (1962), 149–62.

Part Two

The Catholic Church and the Restoration

SECTION ONE

The Reorganization of the Churches

3. *The Catholic Church after the Congress of Vienna*

On the world and Europe after the Napoleonic wars see in addition to the general works "Bilan du monde en 1815" in *XII*[e]*Congrès international des sciences historiques* I: *Grands Thèmes* (Vienna 1965), 451–573, especially L. Trénard, "Bilan idéologique," 547–73.

RELIGIOUS REVIVAL AND INFLUENCE OF ROMANTICISM: P. Funk, *Von der Aufklärung zur Romantik* (Munich 1925); A. Béguin, *L'âme romantique et le rêve* (Paris 1947); H. F. Hedderich, *Die Gedanken der Romantik über Kirche und Staat* (Gütersloh 1941); B. Magnino, *Romanticismo e cristianesimo,* 3 vols. (Brescia 1962/63); L. Cellier, *Fabre d'Olivet. Contribution à l'étude des aspects religieux du romantisme* (Paris 1953); L. Guinet, *De la franc-maçonnerie mystique au sacerdoce ou la vie romantique de F. L. Z. Werner* (Caen 1964); A. von Martin, *Logos* 17 (1928), 141–64; L. Trénard, Y. M. Hilaire, "Idées, croyances et sensibilité religieuse du XVIIIe siècle," *Comité des travaux historiques. Bulletin de la section d'histoire moderne et contemporaine* 5 (1964), 7–27.

THE PONTIFICATE OF PIUS VII AFTER 1814: Schmidlin, *PG* I, 131–366; Belvederi, 832–87; Pouthas, 173–261; Rogier, *KG,* 204–09; L. von Ranke, *Cardinal Consalvi und siene Staatsverwaltung: Sämtliche Werke* XLI/XLII (Leipzig 1877/78), 3–180 and *Historische Meisterwerke. Geschichte der Päpste* III/IV (Hamburg, no date), 301–439.

LEO XII: R. Colapietra, *La Chiesa tra Lamennais et Metternich. Il pontificato di Leone XII* (Brescia 1963; basic); Schmidlin, *PG* I, 367–474; also A. F. Artaud de Montor, *Histoire du pape Léon XII,* 2 vols. (Paris 1843); Belvederi, 887–98; Pouthas, 262–73; Leflon, 379–408.

THE CONCLAVE OF 1823: M. Rossi, *Il conclave di Leone XII* (Perugia 1935); R. Colapietra: *AstIt* 120 (1962), 76–146; also C. Terlinden in *RHE* 14 (1913), 272–343.

PIUS VIII: Schmidlin, *PG* I, 474–510 and O. Fusi-Pecci, *La vita di Papa Pio VIII* (Rome 1965); A. F. Artaud de Montor, *Histoire du pape Pie VIII* (Paris 1844); G. Malazanza, *Cenni storico-biografici su Pio VIII* (Cingoli 1931); Belvederi, 898–903; Leflon, 409–25; C. Vidal, "La Santa Sede e la spedizione francese in Algeria," *ASRomana* 77 (1954),

77–89; id., "La Monarchie de Juillet et le St-Siège au lendemain de la Révolution de 1830," *Revue d'histoire diplomatique* 46 (1932), 497–517.

THE CONCLAVE OF 1829: P. Dardano, *Diario dei conclavi del 1829 e del 1830–31* (Florence 1879); *Chateaubriand, Journal d'un conclave,* ed. by Thomas (Paris 1913); M. Y. Durry, *L'ambassade romaine de Chateaubriand* (Paris 1927); R. Jacquin in *RevSR* 31 (1957), 299–308; R. Moscati in *RstRis* 20 (1933), 257–74; J. Marche in *RHEF* 48 (1962), 49–53; R. Colapietra in *Critica storica* 1 (1962), 517–41, 636–61.

RESTORATION IN THE PAPAL STATES: M. Petrocchi, *La restaurazione, il cardinale Consalvi e la Riforma del 1816* (Florence 1941); id., *La restaurazione romana, 1815–23* (Florence 1943); details by A. Aquarone, "La restaurazione nello Stato pontificio ed i suoi indirizzi legislativi," *ASRomana* 78 (1955), 119–88. Also R. Colapietra, *La dottrina economica della Restaurazione romana* (Naples 1966); also Card. B. Pacca, *Il mio secondo ministero,* ed. by A. Quacquarelli, *La ricostituzione dello Stato Pontificio* (Città di Castello 1969), 160ff.; Mollat, 128–50; A. Ventrone, *L'amministrazione dello Stato Pontificio dal 1814 al 1850* (Rome 1942); G. Cassi, *Il cardinale Consalvi ed i primi anni della Restaurazione pontificia 1815–1819* (Milan 1931); M. Moscarini, *La Restaurazione pontificia nelle provincie di prima recupera* (Rome 1933); F. Grosse-Wietfeld, *Justizreformen im Kirchenstaat in den ersten Jahren der Restauration, 1814–16* (Paderborn 1932); E. Lodolini, "L'ordinamento giudiziario nello Stato pontificio," *Ferrara viva* (1959), 43–73; id., "L'amministrazione periferica e locale nello Stato pontificio dopo la Restaurazione," *Ferrara viva* (1959), 5–32; G. Forchellini, "Un progetto di codice civile del 1818 nello Stato Pontificio," *Scritti in onore di U. Borsi* (Bologna 1955), 89–164.

SECRET SOCIETIES: D. Spadoni, *Sette, cospirazioni e cospiratori nello Stato Pontificio all'indomani della Restaurazione* (Macerata 1904); G. Bandini, *Giornali e scritti politici clandestini della Carboneria Romagnola, 1819–21* (Rome 1908); G. Leti, *Carboneria e Massoneria nel Risorgimento* (Genoa 1925), 98ff.; A. Berselli: *L'apporto delle Marche al Risorgimento* (Florence 1961), 67–106; A. Bersano, *L'abate Fr. Bonardi e i suoi tempi* (Turin 1957); G. De Caesaris in *RstRis* 19/II (1932), 335–56.

4. *The Rejuvenated Position of the Holy See within the Church*

ARCHITECTURAL AND ARTISTIC IMPROVEMENTS IN ROME: Schmidlin, *PG* I, 163–78.

CONCORDAT POLICIES: See chapters 5–7 below and works on Consalvi (bibliography for chapter 2); Also Ranke, *Consalvi und seine Staatsverwaltung,* chap. 5; I. Rinieri, *La diplomazia pontificia nel sec. XIX,* 2 vols. (Rome 1902); Hermelink I, 356–62; Colapietra, 71–90; L. Pásztor in *AHPont* 6 (1968), 220–34.

THE ROMAN CURIA: L. Pásztor in *RHE* 65 (1970), 474–85.

PROGRESS OF ULTRAMONTANISM: Y. Congar, "L'ecclésiologie . . . sous le signe de l'affirmation de l'autorité," *L'ecclésiology au XIXe siècle* (Paris 1960), 77–114; R. Aubert, "La géographie ecclésiologique au XIXe siècle," id., 11–32; Colapietra, 56–69, 429–47; Maass V, 244–59; Friedrich I, 1–95, 173–202; G. Alberigo, *Lo sviluppo della dottrina sui poteri nella Chiesa universale* (Bologna 1964), 349–89. In France: C. Latreille, *J. de Maistre et la papauté* (Paris 1906); C. Maréchal, *La jeunesse de La Mennais* (Paris 1913), 299–357, 386–434, 468–92; id., *La Mennais. La dispute de l' "Essai sur l'indifférence"* (Paris 1925), 147–64; A. Bardoux, *Le comte de Montlosier et le gallicanisme*

(Paris 1881); E. Sevrin, *Mgr Clausel de Montals* I (Paris 1955), 94–100; R. Limouzin-Lamothe, *Mgr de Quélen* I (Paris 1955), 230ff. See also the biographies of Frayssinous, Gerbet, Rohrbacher, and Combalot.

In Germany and Austria: F. Vigener, "Gallikanismus und episkopalistische Strömungen im deutschen Katholizismus," *HZ* 111 (1913), 495–581; H. Becher, *Der deutsche Primas* (Colmar 1943); G. Krüger, "Der Mainzer Kreis und die katholische Bewegung," *PrJ* 148 (1912), 395–414; Schulte III; Maass V, especially 51–73, 173–95, 275ff.

CHURCH UNITY: O. Rousseau, "Les attitudes de pensée concernant l'unité chrétienne au XIXe siècle," *L'ecclésiologie au XIXe siècle* (Paris 1960), 351–65; M. Jugie, *J. de Maistre et l'Église gréco-russe* (Paris 1922); F. Kantzenbach, *J.M. Sailer und der ökumenische Gedanke* (Munich 1955); J. M. Congar, "La signification œcuménique de l'œuvre de Moehler," *Irénikon* 15 (1938), 113–30; J. Doyle, *Letters on the Reunion of the Churches of England and Rome* (Dublin 1824); D. Robert, *Les Églises réformées en France* (Paris 1961), 177–85, 193–203, 446–57.

5. *The Alliance of Throne and Altar in France*

SOURCES

For laws and parliamentary debates, see the General Bibliography. Numerous memoirs and correspondences for this period are available (see G. de Bertier, *La Restauration,* 462) and especially Card. Lambruschini, *La mia nunziature di Francia* (Bologna 1934) and L. de Carné, *Souvenirs de ma jeunesse* (Paris 1872) as well as the correspondence of Lamennais, which unfortunately is rather dispersed (see literature to chapter 14). The most important newspapers and journals are: *L'Ami de la Religion et du Roi, Le Drapeau blanc, Le Journal des débats, La Quotidienne, and Le Mémorial Catholique.* Additionally, there is a large number of pamphlets (see *Catalogue de l'Histoire de France* III, 280–554, and XI, 230–92 at the Bibliothèque Nationale, Paris). These soures can be augmented by the numerous unpublished documents in the Archives Nationales, Paris (especially Series F), the archives of departments and dioceses, and the Roman archives. See G. de Bertier, "L'histoire religieuse de la Restauration aux Archives du Vatican," *RHEF* 38 (1952), 77–89.

LITERATURE

GENERAL: In addition to the works of Schmidlin, *PG* (I, 178–86, 394–405), Leflon (328–36, 393–401), Debidour, *Histoire* (II, 325–412), Brugerette (I, 1–62), Dansette (I, 233–84), Gurian, (76–101), Dupeux (103–29), Rémond (25–59), see especially *HistCathFr* (III, 219–93), C. Pouthas, *L'Église de France sous la Monarchie constitutionelle* (Cours de Sorbonne [Paris 1942]), and G. de Bertier de Sauvigny, *La Restauration* (Paris 1963), especially 299–326. Also E. de Guichen, *La France morale et religieuse sous la Restauration,* 2 vols. (Paris 1911); S. Charléty, *La Restauration* (Paris 1921); F. Artz, *France under the Bourbon Restoration* (Cambridge 1931); P. Dudon in *RHEF* 20 (1934), 79–114.

SPECIAL ASPECTS: P. Pouthas, "Le clergé sous la Monarchie constitutionelle," *RHEF* 29 (1943), 19–53; P. Broutin, "La piété sacerdotale au début du XIXe siècle," *RAM* 20

(1939), 158–80; R. Limouzin-Lamothe in *BLE* 55 (1954), 144–63; H. Forestier in *Annales de Bourgogne* 28 (1956), 195–203; Burnichon I; E. Piscitelli, "Lambruschini e alcune fasi della sua attività diplomatica," *RStRis* 40 (1953), 158–82; Colapietra, 73–74, 371–79, 387–98, 413–17, 431–43; D. Robert, *Les Églises réformées en France, 1800–1830* (Paris 1861), Park II, especially 446–61. On the anticlerical movement in Weill, *Histoire,* 11–55; Mellor, 262–79; R. Casanova, *Montlosier et le Parti prêtre* (Paris 1970).

EDUCATION: R. Severin, *L'enseignement primaire en France sous la Restauration* (Paris 1933); Grimaud; A. Garnier, *Frayssinous, son rôle dans l'Université sous la Restauration* (Paris 1925); id., *Les ordonnances du 16 juin 1828* (Paris 1919); R. Limouzin-Lamothe in *Annales du Midi* 65 (1953), 457–74, 69 (1957), 259–65; G. de Bertier in *RHEF* 46 (1960), 70–78.

MISSIONS: E. Sevrin, *Les missions religieuses en France sous la Restauration* 2 vols. (Paris 1948/59); A. Omodeo, *Aspetti del cattolicesimo della Restaurazione* (Turin 1946), 11–78; G. Richard in *Annales de l'Est,* 5th ser. 10 (1959), 39–71.

BIOGRAPHIES: There are numerous biographies of bishops and of founders of religious societies, many of which are too uncritical; most useful are: C. Baillé, *Le cardinal de Rohan-Chabot* (Paris 1904); A. Garnier, *Frayssinous;* J. Dissard, *Mgr Ch.-Fr. d'Aviau* (Bordeaux 1953); E. Sevrin, *Mgr Clausel de Montals, évêque de Chartres* I (Paris 1955); R. Limouzin-Lamothe, *Mgr de Quélen, archevêque de Paris* I (Paris 1955); J. Leflon, *É. de Mazenod* II (Paris 1960); A. P. Laveille, *Jean-Marie de Lamennais,* 2 vols. (Paris 1903).

MONOGRAPHS: There are few that concern themselves with local matters. P. Genevray, *L'administration et la vie ecclésiastique dans le grand diocèse de Toulouse* (Toulouse 1943); P. Guillaume, *Essai sur la vie religieuse dans l'Orléanais de 1801 à 1878* (Orléans 1959); P. Leuillot, *L'Alsace au début du XIXe siècle* III (Paris 1960), especially 1–154; J. Vidalenc, *Le département de l'Eure sous la Monarchie constitutionelle* (Paris 1952), especially 546–602; P. Huot-Pleuroux, *Le recrutement sacerdotal dans le diocèse de Besançon de 1801 à 1960* (Besançon 1966); M. Faugeras, *Le diocèse de Nantes sous la Monarchie censitaire,* 2 vols. (Fontenay 1964).

6. *The Continuation of the Old Regime in Southern Europe*

ITALY

Schmidlin, *PG* I, 186–96, 425–26, 500–01; Leflon, 322–25, 402; S. Fontana, *La controrivoluzione cattolica in Italia, 1820–30* (Brescia 1968), especially 211–344; L. Bulferetti, "La Restaurazione 1815–30," *Storia d'Italia* III (Turin 1959), 361–504; Spini, 70–152.

KINGDOM OF THE TWO SICILIES: W. Maturi, *Il concordato del 1818* (Florence 1929); L. Pásztor: *AHPont* 6 (1968), 226–31; R. Romeo in *RSIt* 67 (1955), 402–08; G. Catalano, "I Borboni e la manomorta ecclesiastica di Sicilia," *Il diritto ecclesiastico* 59 (1948), 198–213; G. M. Monti, *Chiesa e Stato* I (Milan 1939), 355–405 (concerning the revolution of 1820–21).

TUSCANY: P. Pieri, *La Restaurazione in Toscana, 1814–21* (Pisa 1922), especially 79ff.; A. Aquarone in *RStRis* 43 (1956), 18–21; P. Barbaini, *Problemi religiosi del Risorgimento in Toscana* (Turin 1961), 58–69.

DUCHIES: D. Corsi in *RSTI* 7 (1953), 256–66.

KINGDOM OF LOMBARDY-VENETIA: Maass IV and V (Vienna 1957 and 1961); C. Castiglione, *Gaysruck e Romilli* (Milan 1938); G. Mantese in *AHPont* 4 (1966), 259–80.

PIEDMONT: G. Pellicia, "Il concordato del 17 luglio 1817" *Palestra del clero* 32 (1953), 1173–83, 1243–54, 33 (1954), 36–54 (new documents); R. Colapietra, "Le relazioni tra Roma e Torino sotto Leone XII," *Rassegna di politica e di storia* 12 (1966), 23–32; P. Stella, *Crisi religiose nel primo Ottocento piemontese* (Turin 1959); L. Berra in *Bolletino della Società per gli studi storici nella provincia di Cuneo* 36 (1955), 18–59.

SPAIN

In addition to the works cited in the General Bibliography, see Schmidlin, *PG* I, 200–03, 427–28; J. A. Diaz Merino, *Colección ecclesiástica española,* 14 vols. (Madrid 1823/24; documents concerning the religious policy of the liberal government from 1820 to 1823); P. Leturia in *HJ* 46 (1926), 233–332; M. Pinto-Vieites, *La politica de Fernando VII entre 1814 y 1820* (Pamplona 1958); M. Artola Gallego, *La España de Fernando VII* (Madrid 1968); J. S. Laboa, *Doctrina canónica del Dr. Villanueva. Su actuación en el conflicto entre la Sancta Sede y el gobierno de España, 1820–23* (Vitoria 1957); see also *Revista española de derecho canónico* 12 (1957), 747–61; J. M. Cuenca Toribio, *D. Pedro de Inguanzo y Rivero (1764–1836), último primado del antiguo régimen* (Pamplona 1965); id., "La Iglesia española en el trienio constitucional," *HS* 18 (1965), 333–64; id. in *Ius Canonicum* 10 (Pamplona 1970), 412–25; A. Rodriguez Eiras, "La Junta apostólica y la restauración realista en Galicia," *Cuadernos de estudios galegos* 22 (1967), 198–220; A. C. Jemolo, "Il conte Solaro della Margarita ed il nunzio Tiberi," *Atti della Reale Accademia di Torino* 77 (1941/42), 119–43; Colapietra, 379–87, 399, 402; F. Suárez, ed., *Informes sobre el Estado de España, 1825* (Pamplona 1966).

CONCERNING THE END OF THE SPANISH INQUISITION: L. Alonso Tejada, *Ocaso de la Inquisición* (Madrid 1969); M. Defourneaux in *Annales histoires de la Révolution française* 35 (1963), 160–84; A. C. Jemolo in *Atti della Reale Accademia di Torino* 76 (1940/41), 433–58.

PORTUGAL: In addition to F. de Almeida (General Bibliography), especially IV/2, 205–89, see Schmidlin, *PG* I, 205–06, 428–29.

7. *Ecclesiastical Reorganization and Established Church in the German Confederation and Switzerland*

SOURCES

F. Walter, *Fontes iuris ecclesiastici antiqui et hodierni* (Bonn 1862); P. Schneider, *Die partikulären Kirchenrechtsquellen in Deutschland und in Österreich* (Regensburg 1898); A. Mercati, *Raccolta di Concordati su materie ecclesiastiche tra la Santa Sede e le Autorità Civili* I (Vatican City 1954); L. Schöppe, *Konkordate seit 1800. Originaltext und deutsche Übersetzung der geltenden Kondordate* (Frankfurt-Berlin 1954; limited to continuing valid provisions!), E. R. Huber, *Dokumente zur deutschen Verfassungsgeschichte* I (Stuttgart 1961); F. Maass, *Der Jospehinismus* IV (Vienna-Munich 1957); I. H. von Wessenberg, *Autobiog-*

raphische Aufzeichnungen (Unpublished manuscripts and letters I/1), ed. by K. Aland (Freiburg–Basel–Vienna 1968).

LITERATURE

GENERAL: H. Brück, *Geschichte der katholischen Kirche in Deutschland im 19. Jahrhundert* I (Mainz 1902), 254–62, II (Mainz 1903), 1–273; Schmidlin, *PG* I, 206–65, 270–87, 492ff.; Leflon (Fliche-Martin 20) 232ff., 336f., 340–49; Schnabel, *G* IV: *Die religiösen Kräfte* (Freiburg 1955), 21–43; E. R. Huber, *Deutsche Verfassungsgeschichte seit 1789* I (Stuttgart 1957, reprint 1961), 387–450; Bihlmeyer-Tüchle III, 312–21; Feine, *RG, Die katholische Kirche* (Cologne–Graz 1964), 613–27; F. Vigener, *Gallikanismus und episkopalistische Strömungen im deutschen Katholizismus zwischen Tridentinum und Vatikanum* (first published 1913; now under the title: *Bischofsamt und Papstgewalt . . ., ed. by G. Maron* [Göttingen 1964]); H. Becher, *Der deutsche Primas* (Colmar 1943); E. Plassmann, *Staatskirchenrechtliche Grundgedanken der deutschen Kanonisten an der Wende vom 18. zum 19. Jahrhundert* (Freiburg-Basel-Vienna 1968).

NATIONAL CONCORDAT AND CHURCH AT THE CONGRESS OF VIENNA: H. Bastgen, *Dalbergs und Napoleons Kirchenpolitik in Deutschland* (Paderborn 1917); E. Ruck, *Die römische Kurie und die deutsche Kirchenfrage auf dem Wiener Kongress* (Basel 1917); Becher, op. cit., 31–130; A. K. Huber, *Kirche und deutsche Einheit im 19. Jahrhundert* (Königstein 1966), 18–24; H. Raab, "Karl Theodor von Dalberg. Das Ende der Reichskirche und das Ringen um den Wiederaufbau des kirchlichen Lebens 1803–15," *AMrhKG* 18 (1966), 27–39.

REORGANIZATION ON THE LEVEL OF INDIVIDUAL STATES: E. Friedberg, "Der Staat und die Bischofswahlen in Deutschland . . . Mit Aktenstücken," *Das 19. Jahrhundert* (Leipzig 1874; reprint Aalen 1965); U. Stutz, *Der neueste Stand des deutschen Bischofswahlrechtes. Mit Exkursen in das Recht des 18. und 19. Jahrhunderts* (Stuttgart 1909); H. E. Feine, "Persona grata, minus grata," *Festschrift A. Schultze* (Weimar 1934); W. Weber, *Die politische Klausel in den Konkordaten. Staat und Bischofsamt* (Hamburg 1939); L. Link, *Die Besetzung der kirchlichen Ämter in den Konkordaten Pius' XI.* (Bonn 1942, reprint Amsterdam 1964; with an extensive description of the legal situation in the nineteenth century); J. H. Kaiser, *Die politische Klausel der Konkordate* (Berlin-Munich 1949).

BAVARIA: H. von Sicherer, *Staat und Kirche in Bayern . . . 1799*–1821 (Munich 1873); M. Freiherr von Lerchenfeld, *Zur Geschichte des bayerischen Konkordates* (Nördlingen 1883); K. A. Geiger, *Das bayerische Konkordat vom 5. Juni 1817* (Regensburg 1917); M. Doeberl, *Entwicklungsgeschichte Bayerns* II (Munich 1928), 480ff., 576ff.; A. Scharnagle, "Das königliche Nominationsrecht für die Bistümer in Bayern 1817–1918," *ZSavRGkan* 17 (1928); B. Bastgen, *Bayern und der Heilige Stuhl in der l. Hälfte des 19. Jahrhunderts*, 2 vols. (Munich 1940); Link, *Besetzung der kirchlichen Ämter*, 112ff., 231ff., 345ff.; G. Schwaiger, *Die altbayerischen Bistümer Freising, Passau und Regensburg zwischen Säkularisation und Konkordat 1803–17* (Munich 1959); G. Franz-Willing, *Die bayerische Vatikangesandtschaft 1803–1934* (Munich 1965), 13–32.

PRUSSIA: W. Rudolphi, *Zur Kirchenpolitik Preussens* (Paderborn 1897); C. Mirbt, *Die preussische Gesandtschaft am Hofe des Papstes* (Leipzig 1899); W. Wendland, *Die Religiösität und die kirchenpolitischen Grundsätze König Friedrich Wilhelms III.* (Giessen 1909); J. B. Kissling, *Geschichte des Kulturkampfes im Deutschen Reiche I: Vorgeschichte* (Freiburg 1911); L. Kaas, *Die geistliche Gerichtsbarkeit der katholischen Kirche in Preussen,*

2 vols. (Stuttgart 1915/16); J. Löhr, *Das Preussische Allgemeine Landrecht und die katholischen Kirchengesellschaften* (Paderborn 1917); J. Hansen, ed., J. Hansen and U. Stutz, *Die Rheinprovinz 1815–1915,* 2 vols. (Bonn 1917); H. Müssener, *Die finanziellen Ansprüche der katholischen Kirche an den preussischen Staat auf Grund der Bulle De salute animarum* (Mönchengladbach 1926); M. Bierbaum, *Vorverhandlungen zur Bulle De salute animarum* (Paderborn 1927); Link, *Besetzung der kirchlichen Ämter,* 119ff., 239ff., 356ff.; F. Hanus, *Die preussische Vatikangesandtschaft 1747–1920* (Munich 1954), 78–195; W. Lipgens, *Ferdinand August Graf Spiegel und das Verhältnis von Kirche und Staat 1789–1835,* 2 vols. (Münster 1965).

HANOVER AND CENTRAL AND NORTH GERMAN STATES: L. Dreves, *Geschichte der katholischen Gemeinden zu Hamburg und Altona* (Schaffhausen 1866); H. Meurer, "Die Säkularisation und Wiederherstellung des Stifts Osnabrück," *AkathKR* 33 (1875); J. Freisen, *Staat und katholische Kirche in den deutschen Bundesstaaten Lippe, Waldeck, Anhalt . . .,* 2 vols. (Stuttgart 1906); J. Metzler, *Die Apostolischen Vikariate des Nordens* (Paderborn 1919); A. Bertram, *Geschichte des Bistums Hildesheim* III (Hildesheim–Leipzig 1925); G. Langer, *Landesherrliches Patronatsrecht und staatliches Oberaufsichtsrecht gegenüber der katholischen Kirche Sachsens* (Leipzig 1929); E. Hegel, *Die kirchenpolitischen Beziehungen Hannovers, Sachsens und der norddeutschen Kleinstaaten zur römischen Kurie 1800–46* (Paderborn 1934); Link, *Besetzung der kirchlichen Ämter,* 244f., note 81, 356, note 78, 367f., note 109, 422, note 42.

UPPER RHENISH CHURCH PROVINCES: I. von Longner, *Beiträge zur Geschichte der oberrheinischen Kirchenprovinz* (Tübingen 1863); H. Brück, *Die oberrheinische Kirchenprovinz* (Mainz 1868); E. Göller, "Zur Vorgeschichte der Bulle *Provida sollersque,*" *FreibDiözArch* 55 (1927), 56 (1928); M. Miller, "Die Errichtung der oberrheinischen Kirchenprovinz, im besonderen des Bistums Rottenburg," *HJ* 54 (1934); Link, *Besetzung der kirchlichen Ämter,* 125ff., 255ff., 375ff.; Frankfurter Konferenzen: A. Williard, *FreibDiözArch* 61 (1933), 63 (1935); H. Maas, *Geschichte der katholischen Kirche im Grossherzogtum Baden* (Freiburg 1891); H. Lauer, id. (Freiburg 1908); R. Gönner, J. Sester, *Das Kirchenpatronatsrecht im Grossherzogtum Baden* (Stuttgart 1904).—A. Hagen, *Geschichte der Diözese Rottenburg* I (Stuttgart 1957).—C. J. Reidel, *Die katholische Kirche im Grossherzogtum Hessen* (Paderborn 1904); K. Walther, *Hessen-Darmstadt und die katholische Kirche 1803–1830* (Darmstadt 1933). T. Apel, "Die Versuche zur Errichtung eines katholischen Bistums für Kurhessen . . .," *ZSavRGkan* 41 (1920); St. Hilpisch, *Die Bischöfe von Fulda von der Gründung des Bistums (1752) bis zur Gegenwart (1957).*—M. Höhler, *Geschichte des Bistums Limburg* (Limburg 1908); W. Nicolay, *Die Beteiligung der Freien Stadt Frankfurt an der Stiftung des Bistums Limburg* (Frankfurt 1921); id., "Zur Vorgeschichte des Bistums Limburg," *FreibDiözArch* 55 (1927); H. Natale, "Zur Vorgeschichte des Bistums Limburg," *AMrhKG* 21 (1969); J. Weier, "Das bischöfliche Kommissariat Frankfurt am Main," *AMrhKG* 7 (1955).

AUSTRIA: A. Beer, "Kirchliche Angelegenheiten in Österreich 1816–1842," *MIÖG* 18 (1897); H. Bastgen, *Die Neueinrichtung der Bistümer in Österreich nach der Säkularisation* (Vienna 1914); Maass, *Josephinismus* IV; E. Tomek, *Kirchengeschichte Österreichs* III (Innsbruck–Vienna–Munich 1959), 507–677; E. Weinzierl-Fischer, *Die österreichischen Konkordate von 1855 und 1933* (Vienna–Munich 1960), 10–25; E. Winter, *Der Josefinismus* (Berlin 1962), 204ff.; P. Pototschnig, "Die Entwicklung des österreichischen Patronatsrechtes im 19. Jahrhundert," *ÖAKR* 18 (1967).

SWITZERLAND: In addition to the works of K. Müller, T. Schwegler, W. Martin (General Bibliography) and of Schmidlin, *PG* I, 279–88, 413–16, 492–98, see *Urkunden zur*

Geschichte der kirchlichen Veränderungen in der Schweiz 1803–30 (Mannheim 1851); C. Gareis und P. Zorn, *Staat und Kirche in der Schweiz,* 2 vols. (Zürich 1877/78); A. Büchi, *Die katholische Kirche in der Schweiz* (Munich 1902); H. Seeholzer, *Staat und römisch-katholische Kirche in den paritätischen Kantonen der Schweiz* (Zürich–Leipzig 1912); E. His, *Geschichte des neueren Schweizer Staatsrechts,* 3 vols. (Basel 1920/38), I, 360ff., II, 539ff., III, 2, 828ff.; U. Lampert, *Kirche und Staat in der Schweiz,* 3 vols. (Basel 1929/39).—C. Attenhofer, "Die Besetzung des bischöflichen Stuhls und der Domkapitularstellen in . . . Basel," *AKKR* 19 (1868), 20 (1869); F. Fleiner, *Staat und Bischofswahl im Bistum Basel* (Leipzig 1897); J. Kälin et al., *Das Bistum Basel 1828–1928* (Solothurn 1928); G. Boner, "Das Bistum Basel . . . bis zur Neuordnung 1828," *FreibDiözArch* 88 (1968), 5–101; A. Bölle, *Die Seminarfrage im Bistum Basel* (Rome 1964); J. Danuser, *Die staatlichen Hoheitsrechte des Kantons Graubünden gegenüber dem Bistum Chur* (Diss., Zürich 1897); H. Fehr, *Staat und Kirche im Kanton St. Gallen* (Diss., Bern 1899); F. Gschwend, *Die Errichtung des Bistums St. Gallen* (Stans 1909); J. Meile, ed., *Hundert Jahre Diözese St. Gallen* (Uznach 1947); C. Trezzini, *Le diocèse de Lugano . . .* (Fribourg 1948); G. Staffelbach, "Der Plan eines von Konstanz gelösten schweizerischen Nationalbistums der Waldstätte," *HJ* 72 (1953); O. Karmin, *Le transfert de Chambéry à Fribourg de l'évêché de Genève* (Annecy 1890); Martin-Fleury, *Histoire de M. Vuarin et du rétablissement du catholicisme à Genève* (Geneva 1861); J. Widmer, *Chorherr F. Geiger* (Lucerne 1843); J. L. Schiffmann, *Lebensgeschichte A. Güglers,* 2 vols. (Augsburg 1833); A. Renner, *Görres und die Schweiz* (Freiburg i. Br. 1930); E. Reinhard, *Schweizer Rundschau* 25 (1925/26), 557ff., 669ff., 768ff.; id., *C. L. von Haller. Ein Lebensbild aus der Zeit der Restauration* (Cologne 1915); id., *Zeitschrift für die gesamte Staatswissenschaft* 111 (1955), 115–30.

8. *The Other European Churches*

THE NETHERLANDS: In addition to Rogier, *KathHerleving,* and Albers, *Herstel,* see C. Terlinden, *Guilleaume Ier, roi de Pays-Bas, et l'Église catholique en Belgique, 1814–30,* 2 vols. (Brussels 1906); J. Witlox, *De Noord-Nederlandsche Katholieken in de politiek onder Koning Willem I* ('s-Hertogenbosch 1919); S. Stokman, *De religieuzen en de onderwijspolitiek der Regering in het Ver. Kon. der Nederlanden 1814–30* (The Hague 1935); A. F. Manning, *De betekenis van C.R.A. van Bommel voor de Noordelijke Nederlanden* (Utrecht 1946); G. Gorris, *J. G. Le Sage ten Broek en de eerste faze van de emancipatie der katholieken* I (Amsterdam 1947); Simon, *Sterckx* I, 31–123; Jürgensen, 62–158. also H. J. Allard, *A. van Gils* ('s-Hertogenbosch 1875); J. Demarteau, *F.A. de Méan* Brussels 1944); J. Kleyntjens, "Les instructions données par le St Siège à Mgr Capaccini en 1827," *Bulletin de la Commission royale d'histoire* 114 (1949), 227–55; A. van Peer in *Bossche Bijdragen* 19 (1948), 113–37; A. M. Frenken in ibid. 20 (1950/51), 118–226; id. in ibid. 22 (1954), 69–96; W. Munier in ibid. 29 (1969), 1–61, 30 (1970), 1–59; J. Muyldermans, "Vereeniging ter verspreiding van goede boeken 1826–30," *Ons Geloof* 15 (Antwerp 1929), 49–64, 111–27; A. Marlier, *L. V. Donche* (Louvain 1948); A. Alkemade, *Geschiedenis van 19 religieuze congregaties 1800–1850* ('s-Hertogenbosch 1966); M. De Vroede, "Het openbaar lager onderwijs in België onder Willem I," *Bijdragen en mededelingen van het Hist. Gennootschap* 78 (1964), 10–44; A. Ribberink in *AGKKN* 8 (1966), 98–110; J. Bornewasser, "Duitse bemoeienissen met de strijd om het collegium philosophicum," *Bijdragen tot geschiedenis der Nederlanden* 14 (1960), 273–301; L. Rogier, *Het tijdschrift "Katholikon" 1827–30* (Amsterdam 1957); J. C. Van der Loos, *Geschiedenis van het Seminarie Warmond tot 1853* (Haarlem 1932); J. Meyhoffer, "Le protestantisme belge de 1815 à 1830," *Annales de la Société d'histoire du protestantisme belge* 16 (1955), 152–74.

GREAT BRITAIN: In addition to Matthew, 150–86, Bellesheim, *Irland* III, 273–377, Schmidlin, *PG* I, 298–307, 429–32, 501–02, and Leflon, 349–51, 405–06, 461–62, see B. Ward, *The Eve of the Catholic Emancipation,* 3 vols. (London 1911/13); J. T. Ellis, *Cardinal Consalvi and Anglo-papal Relations 1814–24* (Washington 1942); G. I. Machin, *The Catholic Question in English Politics 1820 to 1830* (Oxford 1964); J. W. Osborne in *CHR* 49 (1963/64), 382–89; D. Gwynn, *The Struggle for Catholic Emancipation 1750–1829* (London 1928); J. Reynolds, *The Catholic Emancipation's Crisis in Ireland 1823–29* (New Haven 1954); R. B. McDowell, *Public Opinion and Government Policy in Ireland 1801–46* (London 1952); T. Wyse, *Historical Sketch of the Late Catholic Association of Ireland,* 2 vols. (London 1829); J. A. Murphy, "The Support of the Catholic Clergy in Ireland 1750–1850," *Historical Studies* 5 (1965), 103–21; J. B. Bockery, *Collingridge* (Newport 1959; Apostolic vicar of the Western District from 1809 to 1829).

Biographies of *D. O'Connell* by A. Zimmermann (Paderborn 1909), D. Gwynn (London 1929), and M. Thierney (Dublin 1949; also J. Hennig in *Modern Language Review* 54 [1959], 573–78); *Correspondence* ed. by W. J. Fitzpatrick, 2 vols. (London 1888).—F. Husenbeth, *J. Milner* (Dublin 1862); *DictEnglCath* V, 15–53.—F. P. Carey, *J. Murray* (Dublin 1951); *Pastoral Letters and Religious Discourses,* 2 vols. (Dublin 1859); W. J. Fitzpatrick, *J. Doyle,* 2 vols. (Dublin 1861); *DHGE* XIV, 771–73.

RUSSIA: In addition to the general works by Lescœur, Boudou I, Ammann, Winter, Wasilewski, Malinowski, Schmidlin, *PG* I, 325–32, 433–36, 505, 627–32, the two collections of documents by J. Bieloholowy, *Akty i dokumenty otnosjaśćiesja k nstrojstvu i upravlenju rimsko-katoliskoj cerkvi v Rossii I 1762–1825* (Petrograd 1915) and *Allocuzione della Santità di . . . Gregorio P. P. XVI . . . seguita da una Esposizione corredata di documenti sulle incessanti cure della stessa S.S. a riparo dei gravi mali da cui è afflitta la Religione Cattolica negli imperiali e reali dominii di Russia e Pologna* (Rome 1842; 90 documents), see E. Theiner, *Die neuesten Zustände der katholischen Kirche beider Ritus in Polen und Russland seit Katharina II. bis auf ünsere Tage,* 2 vols. (Augsburg 1841); M. Loret, *Watykan a Polska 1815–32* (Warsaw 1913); K. Piwarski, *Kuria rzymska a polski ruch naradowo-wyzwolenczy 1794–1863* (Warsaw 1955); B. Pawloski, *Grzegorz XVI a Polska po powstaniu listopadowem* (Warsaw 1911); M. Żywczyński, *Geneza i nasępstwa encykliki "Cum primum"* (Warsaw 1935); G. Bozzolato, *RStRis* 51 (1964), 319–44, 455–80. Also H. Lutteroth, *Russland und die Jesuiten von 1772 bis 1820* (Stuttgart 1846); P. Bliard, "L'empereur Alexandre Ier, les jésuites et J. de Maistre," *Études* 130 (1912), 234–44; A. Brumanis, *Mgr St Siestrzencewicz* (Louvain 1968); L. Chodzko, *Un évêque polonais, K.G. Colonna Cieciszewski et son temps 1745–1831* (Paris 1866); M. Czapska, "Stosunek Michiewicza do religii i Kościola w świetle jego listów i przemowień," *SPM* 2 (1955), 73–128 (concerning the religious views of A. Mickiewicz); F. A. Symon, "De seminario principali Vilnensi," *Academia Rom. Cath. Ecclesiastica Petropolitana 1887/88* (see also M. Godlewski, *Documenta ad historiam seminarii principalis Vilnensis pertinentia 1805–22,* (St. Petersburg 1911).

OTTOMAN EMPIRE: In addition to works listed in the General Bibliography such as Schmidlin, *PG* I, 333–36, 462–64, 505–06, 664–67, see P. Gams, *Geschichte der Kirche Christi im XIX. Jahrhundert* I (Innsbruck 1854), 175ff.; Article "Türkei," *Kirchenlexikon,* ed. by H. Wetzer and B. Welte, 2nd ed., XII, 126–34; J. Hajjar, *L'Europe et les destinées du Proche-Orient, 1819–1848* (Paris 1970).

BULGARIA: *DHGE* X, 1188–89.

RUMANIA: Tocanel III/1; N. Jorga, *Studii si documente cu privire la istoria Românilor* I, (Bucharest 1901), 340–405, 443–44; R. Cândea, *Der Katholizismus in den Donaufürstentümern. Sein Verhältnis zum Staat und zur Gesellschaft* (Leipzig 1916); F. Pall, "Les consuls des Puissances étrangères et le clergé catholique en Valachie au début du XIXe siècle," *Mélanges de l'École rou maine en France* 15 (1939/40), 145–264.

GREECE: G. Hoffmann in *OrCHrP* 2 (1936), 164–90, 395–436; id., "Papa Gregorio XVI e la Grecia," *Gregorio XVI. Miscellanea commemorativa* II (Rome 1948), 135–57.

9. *The Churches of America*

SPANISH AMERICA

P. de Leturia, *Relaciones entre la Santa Sede e Hispano-américa* II, III (Rome-Caracas 1959/60; basic). Also Schmidlin, *PG* I, 313–21, 437–45, 504; L. Tormo, *Historia de la Iglesia en América latina II: La Iglesia en la crisis de independencia* (Bogotá 1962); D. Olmedo, "La crisis máxima de la Iglesia católica en la América española," *Memorias de la Academia mexicana de la historia* 9 (1950), 274–324; R. Vargas Ugarte, *El episcopado en los tiempos de la emancipación sudamericana* (Buenos Aires 1945); G. Furlong, *La Santa Sede y la emancipación hispano-americana* (Buenos Aires 1957); R. F. Schwaller, "The Episcopal Succession in Spanish America 1800–50," *The Americas* 24 (1968), 207–71; P. de Leturia, M. Batllori, *La primera misión pontificia a Hispanoamérica 1823–25* (Vatican City 1963); A. de la Peña y Reyes, *León XII y los países hispanoamericanos* (Mexico 1924); J. Pérez de Guzmán, "El ambajador de España en Roma, don Antonio de Vargas Laguna," *La ilustración española y americana* 29 (Madrid 1906), 18–79; C. Sáenz de Santa María, "Bolívar y Pio VIII," *Rev. de Hist. de América* 49 (Mexico 1960), 147–71, L. Frias, *Historia de la Compañia de Jesús en su asistencia moderna de España* I (Madrid 1923), 94–97, 274–83, 349ff.; F. Blanco and R. Azpurúa, *Documentos para la historia de la vida pública del Libertador de Colombia, Perú y Bolivia,* 14 vols. (Caracas 1875/78).

Concerning individual countries, the reader should consult the following works in addition to those mentioned in the General Bibliography:

CHILE: S. Cotapos, *Don J.S. Rodríguez Zorrilla, obispo de Santiago de Chile 1752–1832* (Santiago 1915); W. J. Coleman, *La restauración del episcopado chileno en 1828 según fuentes Vaticanos* (Santiago 1954); A. Undurraga Huidobro, *Don Manuel Vicuña Larrain* (Santiago 1887).

ECUADOR: J. J. Donoso, op. cit. (General Bibliography).

MEXICO: M. Cuevas, op. cit. (General Bibliography) V, 73–209; L. Medina Ascensio, *La Santa Sede y la emancipación mexicana* (Guadalajara 1946, 1965) A. Gómez Robledo, *Historia Mexicana* 13 (1963/64), 18–58; E. Shiels in *CHR* 28 (1942), 206–28; M. P. Costeloe, *Church Wealth in Mexico. A Study of the "Juzgado de capellanias," 1800–56* (Cambridge 1967); L. Frias, op. cit., 349–88, 668–700.

PERU: J. P. de Rada y Gamio, *El arzobispo Goyeneche y apuntes para la historia del Perú* (Rome 1917).

RIO DE LA PLATA: R. Carbia, *La revolución de mayo y la Iglesia* (Buenos Aires 1945); J. F. Sallaberry, *La Iglesia en la independencia del Uruguay* (Montevideo 1930); A. A. Tonda,

Rivadavia y Medrano, sus actuaciones en la reforma eclesiástica (Sante Fe 1952); id., *Las facultades de los vicarios capitulares porteños, 1812–53* (Buenos Aires 1953); id., *El deán Funes y la reforma de Rivadavia* (Sante Fe 1961; concerning the support of a portion of the secular clergy for the steps against the religious Orders); A. P. Carranza, *El clero argentino de 1810 a 1820* (Buenos Aires 1917); G. Furlong, "Clero patriótico y clero apatriótico entre 1810–16," *Archivum* 4 (Buenos Aires 1960), 569–612; G. Gallardo in ibid., 106–56; R. C. González, "Las órdenes religiosas y la revolución de mayo," ibid., 42–86; E. Ruiz Guiñazu, *El deán de Buenos Aires, D.E. de Zavaleta* (Buenos Aires 1952); G. Nowack, *La personalidad de monsignor M. Escalada* (Zamora 1958).

SAN SALVADOR: S. Malaina, *Historia de la erección de la diócesis de San Salvador* (San Salvador 1944); S. R. Vilanova, *Apuntamientos de historia patria eclesiástica* (San Salvador 1911), 92–141.

BRAZIL: In addition to the works listed in the General Bibliography, see M. de Oliveira Lima, *O movimento da Independencia 1821–22* (São Paulo 1922); C. Magalhaes de Azevedo, *O reconhecimento da Independencia e do Imperio do Brasil pela Santa Sè* (Rome 1932); L. Silva, *O clero nacional e a independencia do Brasil* (Rio de Janeiro 1922); M. C. Thornton, *The Church and Freemasonry in Brazil. A Study in Regalism* (Washington 1958), 27–68; W. J. Coleman, *The First Apostolic Delegation in Rio de Janeiro and its Influence in Spanish America, 1830–40* (Washington 1950); H. Accioly, *Os primeros nuncios do Brasil* (São Paulo 1948); I. Silveira, "Tentativas de concordato no Brasil Imperio," *Revista eclesiastica brasileira* 21 (1961), 361–79 (covering 1824 to 1837); Metodio da Nambro, "Le missioni cappuccine nel Brasile 1822–40," *CollFr* 27 (1957), 385–415; R. B. Lopes, *Monte Alverno, pregador imperial* (Petropolis 1958).

THE UNITED STATES

In addition to Shea III, Ellis, *AmCath,* 40–81, and *Documents,* 167–259; McAvoy, 61–162, and *DHGE* XV, 1121–26, see Schmidlin, *PG* I, 321–24, 445–46, 645–48, Latourette, *Christianity* III, 4–241 and Rogier, *KG,* 272–84. Also F. Kenneally, *United States Documents in the Propaganda Fide Archives* I (Washington 1966); C. Metzger, *Catholics and the American Revolution* (Chicago 1962); J. Baisnée, *The Catholic in the United States, 1784–1829; RACHS* 56 (1945), 133–62, 245–92; T. McAvoy, "The Catholic Minority in the United States 1789–1821," *HRSt,* 39–40 (1952), 33–50; P. J. Foik, *Pioneer Catholic Journalism* (New York 1930); M. C. Sullivan, "Some Non-Permanent Foundations of Religious Orders and Congregations of Women in the United States 1793–1850," *HRSt* 31 (1940), 7–118; V. J. Fecher, *A Study of the Movement for German National Parishes in Philadelphia and Baltimore, 1784–1832* (Rome 1955).

REGIONAL MONOGRAPHS: P. Guilday, *The Catholic Church in Virginia 1815–22* (New York 1924); R. F. Trisco, *The Holy See and the Nascent Church in the Middle Western United States, 1826–50* (Rome 1962); R. Mattingly, *The Catholic Church on the Kentucky Frontier 1785–1812* (Washington 1936); T. McAvoy, *The Catholic Church in Indiana 1780–1834* (New York 1940); W. McNamara, *The Catholic Church in the Northern Indiana Frontier 1789–1844* (Washington 1931). See also the reports addressed to Rome by Monsignor Flaget, 1815 (*CHR* 1 [1915/16], 305–09), by Monsignor Maréchal, 1818 (ibid., 439–53), and by Monsignor Bruté, 1836 (ibid. 29 [1943], 177–233) as well as the correspondence of Monsignor Dubourg with the Congregation Propaganda Fide

(*St. Louis Catholic Historical Review* 1–3 [1918/21], *passim*) and M. J. Spalding, *Sketches of the Early Catholic Missions of Kentucky 1787–1826* (Louisville 1844).

THE PROVINCIAL COUNCILS OF BALTIMORE: *Concilia provincialia Baltimori habita ab anno 1829 ad anno 1849* (Baltimore 1851). See T. Casey, *The Sacred Congegation de propaganda fide and the Revision of the First Provincial Council of Baltimore* (Rome 1957).

CATHOLIC EDUCATION AND TRAINING OF THE CLERGY: E. J. Goebel, *A Study of Catholic Secondary Education during the Colonial Period up to 1852* (New York 1957); F. P. Cassidy, *Catholic College Foundations in the United States 1667 to 1850* (Washington 1924); H. J. Browne, "Public Support of Catholic Education in New York 1825–42," *CHR* 39 (1953), 1–27; J. M. Daley, *Georgetown University, Origin and Early Years* (Washington 1957); P. P. McDonald, *The Seminary Movement in the United States 1784–1833* (Washington 1927); J. W. Ruane, *The Beginnings of the Society of St. Sulpice in the United States 1791–1829* (Washington 1935).

FOREIGN SUPPORT THROUGH SENDING OF PRIESTS AND FINANCIAL AID: J. A. Baisnée, *France and the Establishment of the American Catholic Hierarchy* (Baltimore 1934); J. Griffin, *The Contribution of Belgium to the Catholic Church in America* (Washington 1932), 63–189; J. Thauren, *Ein Gnadenstrom zur Neuen Welt: Die Leopoldinen–Stiftung* (Vienna 1940); G. Kummer, *Die Leopoldinen–Stiftung 1829 bis 1914* (Vienna 1966); L. Laurent, *Québec et l'Église aux États-Unis sous Monsignor Briand et Monsignor Plessis* (Washington–Montreal 1945).

TRUSTEEISM: P. J. Dignan, *A History of the Legal Incorporation of Catholic Church Property in the United States* (New York 1935); R. F. McNamara, "Trusteeism in the Atlantic States," *CHR* 30 (1944), 136–54; A. G. Stritch, "Trusteeism in the North-West," ibid., 155–64.

NATIVISM: R. A. Billington, *The Protestant Crusade 1800–50* (New York 1938). For a study of this phenomenon on the local level see L. D. Scisco, *Political Nativism in New York State* (New York 1901) and W. D. Overdyke, *The Know-Nothing Party in the South* (Baton Rouge 1950) as well as "A Selection of Sources dealing with the Nativist Riots of 1844," *RACHS* 80 (1969), 68ff. and a number of dissertations written for the Catholic University of America.

BIOGRAPHIES: American historiography is especially rich in biographies. See P. Guilday, *The Life and Times of John Carroll* (New York 1922); id., *The Life and Times of John England*, 2 vols. (New York 1927); H. J. Nolan, *The Most Rev. Father P. Kenrick* (Washington 1948); also the biographies of the bishops *Rosati* (by F. J. Easterly, Washington 1942), *David* (by M. C. Fox, New York 1925), *Bruté* (by T. Maynard, New York 1943), *de Cheverus* (by A. M. Melville, Milwaukee 1958), *Flaget* (J. H. Schauinger, *Cathedrals in the Wilderness*, Milwaukee 1952) and *E. D. Fenwick* (by V. F. O'Daniel, Washington 1921); those of *Saint Elizabeth Seton*, founder of the Sisters of Charity (by A. M. Melville, New York 1951, and by J. I. Dirvin, id., 1962) and those of two laymen, *W. Gaston*, one of the first Catholic politicians (by J. H. Schauinger, Milwaukee 1939) and *R. B. Taney*, the first Catholic chief justice (by C. B. Swisher, New York 1935).

CANADA

L. Lemieux, *L'établissement de la première province ecclésiastique au Canada 1783–1844* (Montreal 1968); J.-P. Wallot, "Jewell et son projet d'asservir le clergé canadien, 1801,"

Revue d'histoire de l'Amérique française 16 (1963), 549–66; Ferland, *J. O. Plessis* (Quebec 1864); H. J. Somers, *The Life and Times of A. McDonnell, First Bishop of Upper Canada* (Washington 1931); L. Pouliot, "Lord Gosford and Monsignor Lartigue," *Canadian Historical Review* 46 (1965), 238–46; id., *Monsignor Bourget et son temps I: Les années de préparation 1799–1840* (Montreal 1955); A. A. Johnston, *A History of the Catholic Church in Eastern Nova Scotia* I (Antigonish 1960; until 1827); M. Trudel, *L'influence de Voltaire au Canada,* 2 vols. (Montreal 1945); F. Quellet, "L'enseignement primaire, responsabilité des Églises ou de l'État 1801–36," *Recherches sociographiques* 2 (Quebec 1961), 171–87 (also L. Lemieux, op. cit., 27–28, note 22). See also H. Têtu, ed., *Journal d'un voyage en Europe de Monsignor J. O. Plessis 1819–20* (Quebec 1903), and the *Report on the Affairs of British North America from the Earl of Durham* (London 1839).

10. *The Churches of the Eastern Rite*

Uniates of the Near East

Maronites: P. Curzon, *Visits to the Monasteries in the Levant* (London 1849); A. Laurent, *Relation historique des affaires de Syrie 1840–42.* 2 vols. (Paris 1846).

Melkites: J. Hajjar, *Un lutteur infatigable, le patriarch Maximos III Mazloum* (Harissa 1957), which replaces the work of K. Lübeck (Aachen 1919).

Chaldeans: S. Bello, *La congrégation de S. Hormisdas et l'Église chaldéenne dans la première moitié du XIXe siècle* (Rome 1939); I. X. Morand, *Voyage en Turquie et en Perse 1846–48,* 4 vols. (Paris 1854/60).

Copts: J. Metzlar in *ED* 14 (1961), 36–62, 15 (1962), 70–105.

Armenians: Berberian, *History of the Armenians 1772–1860* (Constantinople 1871; in Armenian; from the Gregorian point of view; many documents); A. Alexandrian, *Historical Sketch of the 12 Catholicos of Cilicia* (Venice 1906; in Armenian).

Rumania: Article "Roumanie," *DThC* XIV; de Clercq I, 211–14; A. de Gerando, *La Transylvanie et ses habitants,* 2 vols. (Paris 1845); C. Sucin, *Missionari greco-cattolici in Valachia 1718–1829* (Blaj 1934).

Ruthenians: Ammann, 637–58; Boudou I, 153–69, 213–40; Winter, *Byzanz,* 138–64; de Clercq I, 184–90; A. Theiner, *Die neuesten Zustände der Katholischen Kirche beider Riten in Polen und Russland* (Augsburg 1841); J. Zelechowski, *Joann Sniegurski, ego zizn i djejatelnost v Galitskoj Rusi* (Lemberg 1894); W. Lencyk, *The Eastern Catholic Church and Czar Nicholas I* (Rome 1966); disagrees with N. Riazanowsky, *Nicholas I and Official Nationality in Russia 1825–1855,* Berkeley 1950).

11. *The Resumption of Missionary Work*

Streit, VIII, XII–XIV, XVII–XXI, XXVII. *Collectanea Santa Congregationis de Propaganda Fide* I (1622–1866) (Rome 1907) (=*CPF*); *Juris Pontificii de Propaganda Fide,* Pars V (Rome 1898) (=*JP*); S. Delacroix, "Histoire Universelle des Missions Catholiques III," *Les Missions Contemporaines (1800–1957)* (Paris 1958); K. S.

Latourette, "A History of the Expansion of Christianity IV/V," *The Great Century* (New York 1941); A. Launay, *Histoire Générale de la Société des Missions Étrangères,* 3 vols. (Paris 1894); J. Leflon, *La crise révolutionnaire 1789–1846* (*Histoire de l'Église* XX) (Paris 1951); A. Mulders, *Missionsgeschichte* (Regensburg 1960); J. A. Otto SJ, *Gründung der neuen Jesuitenmission durch General Johann Philipp Roothaan* (Freiburg 1939); F. Schwager, *Die katholische Heidenmission der Gegenwart* I–IV (Steyl 1907); J. Schmidlin, *Papstgeschichte der neuesten Zeit* I (Munich 1933).

SECTION TWO

The Awakening of Catholic Vitality

12. *The Rebirth of the Old Orders and the Blossoming of New Congregations*

READMISSION OF THE SOCIETY OF JESUS: *Synopsis historiae SJ* (Louvain 1950), 368–426; Albers, *Lib. saec.*, 5–74; P. Dudon, "La résurrection de la Compagnie de Jésus 1773–1814," *Revue des questions historiques* 133 (1939), 21–59; M. J. Rouët de Journel, *La Compagnie de Jésus en Russie* (Paris 1922); P. Galletti, *Brevie notizie intorno alla Compagnia di Gesù in Italia dall'1773 all'1814,* 2 volumes, (Rome 1926); P. Chadwick, "Paccanarists in England," *AHSI* 20 (1951), 142–66; E. I. Dewitt, "The Suppression and Restauration of the Society in Maryland," *Woodstock Letters* 34 (1905), 113–30, 203–35; O. Pfülf, *Die Anfänge der deutschen Provinz der Gesellschaft Jesu und ihr Wirken in der Schweiz 1805–47* (Freiburg i. Br. 1922); J. Joachim, *Le P.A. Kohlmann* (Paris 1938: on Germany and the Dutch); A. Rayez, "Clorivière et les Pères de la Foi," *AHSI* 21 (1952), 300–28; A. Guidée, *Vie du Père Varin* (Paris 1860); J. Burnichon, *La Compagnie de Jésus en France* I (Paris 1914); L. Frías, *Historia de la Compañia de Jesús en su Asistencia moderna de España,* 2 volumes (Madrid 1923/44) I, 69–187, 274–83, 349–88, 668–700; I. Beretti, *De vita Al. Fortis* (Verona 1833); *DHGE* XVII, 1160–63.

OLD ORDERS: In addition to M. Heimbucher, *Die Orden und Kongregationen der katholischen Kirche,* 2 volumes (Paderborn 1932/34) and M. Escobar, ed., *Ordini e Congregazioni religiose,* 2 volumes (Turino 1951/53), see the great works of A. Walz, *Compendium historiae Ordinis Praedicatorum* (Rome 1948) and A. Mortier, *Histoire des Maîtres généraux de l'ordre des Frères Prêcheurs* VII (Paris 1914) and S. M. Villaro, *Del ristabilimento della Provincia domenicana nel Piemonte dopo la soppressione francese* (Chieri 1929; V. F. O'Daniel *Dominican Province of St. Joseph* (New York 1942) on the Dominicans. On the Franciscans, see H. Holzapfel, *Manuale historiae Ordinis FF. Minorum* (Freiburg i. Br. 1909); A. Barrado Manzano in *AIA* 24 (1964), 353–87. Concerning the Capuchins there is Melchior de Pobladura, *Historia generalis Ordinis Fratrum Minorum capucinorum* III (Rome 1951). The Benedictines are treated by P. Schmitz, *Histoire de l'Ordre de S. Benoît* VI and VII (Maredsous 1948 and 1956); S. Hilpisch, *Geschichte des benediktinischen Mönchtums* (Freiburg i. Br. 1929); P. Weissenberger, *Das benediktinische Mönchtum im 19./20. Jahrhundert* (Beuron 1958); P. Sattler, *Die Wiederherstellung des Benediktinerordens durch Ludwig I. von Bayern* (Munich 1931), and the Cistercians by L. F. Lekai, *Geschichte und Wirken der Weissen Mönche. Der Orden der Cisterzienser* (Cologne 1958); J. du Halgoüet in *Cîtaux* 17 (1966), 89–118, 18 (1967), 51–74, 240–62, 20 (1969), 36–68. For the Premonstratensians see N. Backmund, *Monasticon Praemonstratense,* 3 vols. (Straubing 1949/56), and for the Redemptorists see E. Hosp, *Die Kongregation des Allerheiligsten Erlösers* (Graz 1924); M. De Meulemeester, *Histoire sommaire de la Congrégation du T.S. Rédempteur* (Louvain 1958); J. Hofer, *Der hl. Klemens Maria Hofbauer* (Freiburg i. Br. 1923); *Monumenta Hofbaueriana,* 8 vols., (Cracow 1915/39); H. Girouille, *Vie du vén. P.J. Passerat* (Paris 1924); A. Sampers in *Spicilegium hist. Congr. SS Redempt.* 9 (1961), 129–202. On the Christian Schoolbrothers, see G.

Rigault, *Histoire générale de l'Institut des Frères des Écoles chrétiennes,* 9 vols. (Paris 1936/53); M. de Vroede in *Paedagogica historica* 10 (Ghent 1970), 49–79; The Daughters of Charity are treated by P. Coste, G. Goyau, *Les Filles de la Charité* (Paris 1933); Marboutin in *Revue de l'Agenais 1916,* 267–87, and the Daughters of Wisdom by J. F. Devaux, *Les Filles de la Sagesse* II (Cholet 1955); A. P. Laveille, C. Collin, *G. Deshayes et ses familles religieuses* (Brussels 1924).

NEW CONGREGATIONS: See Heimbucher II, Escobar II, and K. Zähringer, *Die Schulbrüder* (Freiburg i. Br. 1962); also P. Zind, *Les nouvelles congrégations de frères enseignants en France de 1800 à 1830* (St. Genis–Laval 1969); P. Broutin in *NRTh* 82 (1960), 607–32; J.-B. Furet, *Marcellin Champagnat* (Landshut 1958); A. P. Laveille, *Jean-Marie de Lamennais,* 2 vols. (Paris 1903); F. Symphorien-Auguste, *A travers la correspondance de l'abbé J.-M. de Lamennais,* 7 vols. (Vannes 1937/60); L. Cnockaert, "Le chanoine Triest et ses fondations" (unpublished dissertation, Louvain 1971); K. G. Reichgelt, *De Broeders van Liefde* I (Ghent 1957); S. Perron, *Vie du T. R. P. Coudrin* (Paris 1900); A. Delaporte, *Vie du T. R. P. J.-B. Rauzan* (Paris 1857); J. Leflon, *Eug. de Mazenod* (Paris 1957/65) II, 38–198, 260–97, 604–14, III, 129–84; P. Mayet, *Le T. R. P. J. C. Colin* (Lyon 1895); H. Neufeld, *Die Gesellschaft Mariens* (Munich 1962); G. Goyau, *Chaminade, fondateur des marianistes* (Paris 1914); P. Broutin in *NRTh* 65 (1938), 413–36; F. S. Zanon, *I servi di Dio P.A.A. e P.M. Cavanis,* 2 vols. (Venice 1925); T. Piatti, *Un precursore dell'Azione cattolica, Br. Lanteri* (Turin 1934); A. P. Frutaz, *Positio super introductione causae . . .* (Vatican City 1945); G. Pusineri, *Rosmini, fondatore dell'Istuto della carità* (Domodossola 1929); T. Réjalot, *La bienheureuse Julie Billiart* (Namur 1922); D. Voss, *Die hl. M.M. Postel* (Werl 1959); G. Bernoville, *Ste Émilie de Rodat* (Paris 1959); I. Giordani, *Maddalena di Canossa* (Rome 1963); L. Baunard, *Histoire de Madame Barat,* 2 vols. (Paris 1925); A. Hillengass, *Die Gesellschaft vom heiligen Herz Jesu* (Stuttgart 1917); G. Goyau, *Un grand homme, Mère Javouhey* (Paris 1929); E. C. Scherer, *Schwester J. Jorth und die Einführung der Barmherzigen Schwestern in Bayern* (Cologne 1932); L. Ziegler, *Mutter Theresia v. J. Gerhardinger* (Munich 1950); L. Ziegler, *Die Armen Schulschwestern von Unserer Lieben Frau* (Munich 1935); M. B. Degnan, *Mercy unto thousands: Life of Mother Mary Catherine McAuley* (Westminster, Md. 1957); A. J. Alkemade, *Vrouwen XIX. Geschiedenis van 19 religieuze congregaties 1800–50* ('s-Hertogenbosch 1966).

13. *The Beginnings of the Catholic Movement in Germany and Switzerland*

GENERAL

V. Cramer, *Bücherkunde zur Geschichte der katholischen Bewegungen in Deutschland im 19. Jahrhundert* (Mönchengladbach 1914); P. Funk, *Von der Aufklärung zur Romantik* (Munich 1925); K. Bachem, *Vorgeschichte, Geschichte und Politik der deutschen Zentrumspartei* I (Cologne 1927, reprint Aalen 1967); Leflon (Fliche-Martin 20), 359ff., 474ff.; Schnabel IV, 44–97; E. Ritter, *Die katholisch-soziale Bewegung Deutschlands im 19. Jahrhundert und der Volksverein* (Cologne 1954), chaps. 1–2; Bihlmeyer-Tüchle III, 326–30, 336f.; K. Buchheim, *Ultramontanismus und Demokratie. Der Weg der deutschen Katholiken im 19. Jahrhundert* (Munich 1963); F. Heyer, *Die katholische Kirche von 1648 bis 1870 (Die Kirche in ihrer Geschichte. Ein Handbuch,* ed. by K. D. Schmidt and E. Wolf, vol. 4, Section N, Part I, Göttingen 1963), 94–100, 102–05, 108f.; Vigener, 57–77. K. Löffler, *Geschichte der katholischen Presse Deutschlands* (Mönchengladbach 1924); R. Pesch, *Die kirchlich-politische Presse der Katholiken in der Rheinprovinz vor 1848*

(Mainz 1966). A. von Martin, "Das Wesen der romantischen Religiosität," *DVfLG* 2 (1924); id., "Romantische Konversionen," *Logos* 17 (1928); A. L. Mayer, "Liturgie, Romantik und Restauration," *JLW* 10 (1930); H. F. Hedderich, *Die Gedanken der Romantik über Kirche und Staat* (Gütersloh 1941); R. Benz, *Die deutsche Romantik* (Leipzig 1956); J. Droz, *Le Romantisme allemand et l'État* (Paris 1966).

Individual Centers

MÜNSTER: J. Galland, *Die Fürstin Gallitzin und ihre Freunde* (Cologne 1880); P. Brachin, *Le cercle de Münster et la pensée religieuse de F. L. Stolberg* (Lyon-Paris 1952); E. Reinhard, *Die Münsterische familia sacra* (Münster 1953); E. Trunz, *Fürstenberg, Fürstin Gallitzin und ihr Kreis* (Münster 1955); S. Sudhof, *Hochland* 52 (1960); E. Hegel, *Geschichte der katholisch-theologischen Fakultät Münster 1773–1964,* I (Münster 1966), 21–79; H. Heuveldop, *Bernard Overberg* (Münster 1933); W. Sahner, *Overberg als Pädagoge* (Gelsenkirchen 1949; K. Kruchen, *Die Bibel Overbergs* (Diss. Münster 1956); T. Rensing, *Franz von Fürstenberg* (Münster 1961); A. Hanschmidt, *Franz von Fürstenberg als Staatsmann . . .* (Münster 1969); J. Janssen, *Friedrich Leopold Graf zu Stolberg* (Freiburg 1877, 1910 ed. by L.v.Pastor); P. Brachin, "Friedrich Leopold zu Stolberg und die deutsche Romantik," *LJ,* new ed. 1 (1960); H. Raab, "Friedrich Leopold zu Stolberg und Karl L. von Haller," *ZSKG* 62 (1968); F. Beelert, *Bernard Georg Kellermann* (Münster 1935); K. Gründer, "Hamann in Münster," *Westfalen* 33 (1955); W. H. Bruford, *Fürstin Gallitzin und Goethe* (Cologne–Opladen 1957).

VIENNA: *Monumenta Hofbaueriana,* 15 vols. (Thorun–Cracow–Rome 1915/51); M. B. Schweitzer in *HJ* 48 (1928); E. Winter, "Die Differenzierungen der katholischen Restauration in Österreich," *HJ* 52 (1932); E. Hosp, *Hofbauer* (Vienna 1951); R. Till, *Hofbauer und sein Kreis* (Vienna 1951); E. Winter, *Romantismus, Restauration und Frühliberalismus im österreichischen Vormärz* (Vienna 1968); F. Schlegel, *Kritische Ausgabe der Werke,* ed. by E. Behler (Paderborn 1958seqq.); B. v. Wiese, *F. Schlegel* (Berlin 1927); L. Wirz, *F. Schlegels philosophische Entwicklung* (Bonn 1939); J. J. Anstett, *La pensée religieuse de F. Schlegel* (Paris 1941); E. Behler, "Neue Ergebnisse der F. -Schlegel-Forschung," *GRM,* new ed. 8 (1958); G. P. Hendrix, *Das politische Weltbild F. Schlegels* (Diss., Cologne 1962); A. von Martin, "Die politische Ideenwelt Adam Müllers," *Festschrift für Walter Goetz* (Leipzig 1927); J. Baxa, *Adam Müller* (Jena 1930); A. von Klinckowström, *Friedrich August von Klinckowström* (Vienna 1877); P. Hankamer, *Zacharias Werner* (Bonn 1920).

LANDSHUT: J. M. Sailer, *Werke,* 41 vols. (Sulzbach 1830/45); B. Lang, *Bischof Sailer und seine Zeitgenossen* (Regensburg 1932); H. Schiel, *J.M. Sailer,* 2 vols. (Regensburg 1948/52); J. R. Geiselmann, *Von lebendiger Religiosität zum Leben der Kirche* (Stuttgart 1952); G. Fischer, *Sailer und Kant* (Freiburg i. Br. 1953); *idem, Sailer und Pestalozzi* (Freiburg i. Br. 1954); id., *Sailer und Jacobi* (Freiburg i. Br. 1955); F. W. Kantzenbach, *J.M. Sailer und der ökumenische Gedanke* (Nuremberg 1955); H. J. Müller, *Die ganze Bekehrung* (Salzburg 1956); J. Vonderach, "Sailer und die Aufklärung," *FZThPh* 5 (1958); R. Adamski in *ThJ* (Leipzig 1960).

MUNICH: M. Spindler, "Die kirchlichen Erneuerungsbestrebungen in Bayern im 19. Jahrhundert," *HJ* 71 (1952), now also in M. Spindler, *Erbe und Verpflichtung. Aufsätze und Vorträge zur bayerischen Geschichte* (Munich 1966); J. Görres, *Historischkritische Neuausgabe der Werke,* ed. by W. Schellenberg, A. Dryoff, L. Just (Cologne 1926seqq., so far 16 vols.); J. N. Sepp, *J. Görres und seine Zeitgenossen* (Nördlingen 1877);

H. Kapfinger, *Der Eos-Kreis 1828–32* (Munich 1928); W. Schellberg, *J. Görres* (Cologne 1926); *Görres-Festschrift,* ed. by K. Hoeber (Cologne 1926); J. Grisar, "Görres' religiöse Entwicklung," *StdZ* 112 (1927); A. Schorn, *Görres' religiöse Entwicklung* (Diss., Cologne 1927); R. Saitschick, *J. Görres und die abendländische Kultur* (Olten-Freiburg 1953); G. Bürke, *Vom Mythos zur Mystik* (Einsiedeln 1958); E. R. Huber, "J. Görres und die Anfänge des katholischen Integralismus in Deutschland," E.R. Huber, *Nationalstaat und Verfassungsstaat* (Stuttgart 1965); B. Lang, *J. N. Ringseis* (Fribourg 1931); D. Baumgardt, *F. Baader und die philosophische Romantik* (Halle 1927); E. Susini, *F. Baader et le romantisme mystique,* 2 vols. (Paris 1942); J. Friedrich, *I.v. Döllinger* I and II, (Munich 1899); G. Schwaiger, *I.v. Döllinger* (Munich 1963); J. Finsterhölzl, *I.v. Döllinger* (Graz–Vienna–Cologne 1969); A. Doeberl, "Ludwig I. und die katholische, Kirche," *HPBl* (1916/17), 158–60; M. Spindler, *Der Briefwechsel zwischen König Ludwig I. und Ed. v. Schenk 1824–41* (Munich 1930); R. Hacker, *Die Beziehungen zwischen Bayern und dem Heiligen Stuhl in der Regierungszeit Ludwigs I.* (Tübingen 1967); G. Schwaiger, "Ludwig I. von Bayern," *ZKG* 79 (1968).

MAINZ: J. Guerber, *F. L. Liebermann* (Freiburg 1880); J. Wirth, *Monsign. Colmar* (Paris 1906); A. Schnütgen, *Das Elsass und die Erneuerung des katholischen Lebens in Deutschland von 1814 bis 1848* (Strassburg 1913); S. Merkle, "Zu Görres' theologischer Arbeit am *Katholik,*" *(Görres-Festschrift 1926);* L. Lenhart, *Das Mainzer Priesterseminar als Brücke von der alten zur neuen Mainzer Universität* (Mainz 1947); id., *Die erste Mainzer Theologenschule des 19. Jahrhunderts* (Mainz 1956); H. Schwalbach, *Der Mainzer "Katholik" . . . 1821–1850* (Diss. Mainz 1966).

Other Personalities and Circles

A. F. Ludwig, *Weihbischof Zirkel von Würzburg . . ., 22* vols. (Paderborn 1904/06); A. Dyroff, *Karl Josef Windischmann und sein Kreis* (Cologne 1916); W. Schellberg, *Klemens Brentano* (Mönchengladbach 1916); H. Rupprich, *Brentano, Luise Hensel und Ludwig v. Gerlach* (Vienna–Leipzig 1927); G. Schönig, *Anton Jos. Binterim (1779–1855) als Kirchenpolitiker und Gelehrter* (Düsseldorf 1933); O. Dammann, "Johann Friedrich Schlosser auf Stift Neuburg und sein Kreis," *Neue Heidelberger Jahrbücher* (1934); E. Ritter, *Radowitz* (Cologne 1948); A. Klein, "Werner v. Haxthausen und sein Freundeskreis am Rhein," *AHVNrh* 155/156 (1954); K. G. Faber, "Rheinisches Geistesleben zwischen Restauration und Romantik," *RhVJBll* 21 (1956); E. Kleinstück, *Johann Friedrich Böhmer* (Frankfurt 1959); A. Brecher, "L. A. Nellessen (1783–1859) und der Aachener Priesterkreis," *ZAGV* 76 (1964); H. Witetschek, *Studien zur kirchlichen Erneuerung im Bistum Augsburg in der l. Hälfte des 19. Jahrhunderts* (Augsburg 1965); W. Hoffmann, *Clemens Brentano* (Berlin–Munich 1966); C. Weber, *Orthodoxie und Aufklärung am Mittelrhein 1820–50* (in preparation).

Eminent Bishops

A. Schnütgen, "Das religiös-kirchliche Leben im Rheinland unter den Bischöfen Graf Spiegel und Hommer," *AHVNrh* 119 (1931); W. Lipgens, *Ferdinand August v. Spiegel* (see ch. 7); P. Sieweck, *L. A. Freiherr v. Gebsattel* (Diss., Munich 1955); On Hommer, see A. Thomas in *TThZ* 58 (1949), *AMrhKG* 1 (1949), 15 (1963); J. Schiffhauer in *Festschrift für Alois Thomas* (Trier 1967).

14. *The Catholic Movement in France and Italy*

France

CATHOLIC CLUBS: G. de Grandmaison, *La Congrégation* (Paris 1889); J. B. Duroselle, "Les "filiales" de la Congrégation," *RHE* 50 (1955), 867–91; G. de Bertier de Sauvigny, *Ferdinand de Bertier et l'énigme de la Congrégation* (Paris 1948), especially 353–407; A. Lestra, *Histoire secrète de la Congrégation de Lyon. De la clandestinité à la fondation de la Propagation de la Foi, 1801–31* (Paris 1967).

CATHOLIC PUBLICATIONS: On Bonald and Maistre see *LThK* II, 581–82 and VI, 1305–06; also R. A. Lebrun, *Throne and Altar. The Political and Religious Thought of J. de Maistre* (Ottawa 1965).—E. Reinhard, *Haller, Ein Lebensbild aus der Zeit der Restauration* (Cologne 1915); H. Weilenmann, *Untersuchungen zur Staatstheorie C.L. von Hallers* (Aarau 1955).—P. M. Burtin, *Un semeur d'idées au temps de la Restauration, le baron d'Eckstein* (Paris 1931); *DHGE* XIV, 1405–06.—A. Viatte, *Le catholicisme chez les romantiques* (Paris 1922); V. Giraud, *De Chateaubriand à Brunetière* (Paris 1939), 113–19; J. R. Derré, *Lamennais, ses amis et le mouvement des idées à l'époque romantique, 1824–34* (Paris 1962).

LAMENNAIS: *Œuvres complètes,* 12 vols. (Paris 1836/37) and 10 vols. (Paris 1844), also contain the three volumes of *Mélanges* (Paris 1819, 1826, 1835) in which Lamennais published collections of his smaller writings and newspaper articles; *Œuvres posthume,* ed. by E. Forgues, 6 vols. (Paris 1855/59).—Lamennais's correspondence, which constitutes a main source, unfortunately is widely dispersed and in part still has not yet been published (L. Le Guillou is preparing the publication of general correspondence: Volume I, 1805–20 (Paris 1971); the chief collections are listed in *Catholicisme* V, 1723; see also the chronological listing of the printed letters (which, however, needs complementing) in A. Feugère, *Lamennais avant l' "Essai sur l'Indifférence"* (Paris 1906), 249–437 (Index 445–50). F. Duine, *Essai de bibliographie de Lamennais* (Paris 1923). On life and thought there are A. Roussel, *Lamennais d'après des documents inédits,* 2 vols. (Rennes 1893); C. Boutard, *Lamennais, sa vie et ses doctrines,* 3 vols. (Paris 1905/13); F. Duine, *Lamennais* (Paris 1922); A. Vidler, *Prophecy and Papacy. A Study of Lamennais, the Church and the Revolution* (London 1954); L. Foucher, *La philosophie catholique en France au XIXe siècle* (Paris 1955), 31–71; G. Verucci, *F. Lamennais dal cattolicesimo autoritario al radicalismo democratico* (Naples 1963); L. Le Guillou, *L'évolution de la pensée religieuse de F. Lamennais* (Paris 1966); volume I of the *Bulletin Lamennais,* ed. by L. Le Guillou (Paris 1971).—For the epoch of the restoration there are also C. Maréchal, *La jeunesse de Lamennais* (Paris 1913), *La Dispute de l' "Essai sur l'Indifférence"* (Paris 1925), and *Lamennais au "Drapeau blanc"* (Paris 1946); E. Sevrin, *Dom Guéranger et Lamennais* (Paris 1933); Y. Le Hir, *Lamennais écrivain* (Paris 1948). On Lamennais's influence outside of France, there are A. Gambaro in *Studi francesi* 2 (1958), 198–219; A. Simon, *Rencontres mennaisiennes en Belgique* (Brussels 1963); F. Vrijmoed, *Lamennais avant sa défection et la Néerlande catholique* (Paris 1930); S. Lösch, *Döllinger und Frankreich* (Münster 1955), 88ff.; W. G. Roe, *Lamennais and England* (London 1966); C. de Carilla, "Lamennais y el Río de la Plata," *Rev. de hist. de las ideas . . . (1950), 63–68.*

Italy

A broad overview and literature are provided by G. Verucci, "Per una storia del cattolicesimo intransigente in Italia dal 1815 al 1848," *Rassegna storia toscana* 4 (1958),

251–85. Basic are the works of S. Fontana, *La controrivoluzione cattolica in Italia 1820–30* (Brescia 1968) and C. Bona, *Le "Amicizie". Società segrete e rinascita religiosa, 1770–1830* (Turin 1962). Also G. De Rosa, *L'Azione cattolica I* (Bari 1953), 28–45; P. Pirri, "C. d'Azeglio e gli albori della stampa cattolica in Italia," *CivCatt* III (1930), 193–212; G. Verucci in *Rassegna di politica e di storia* 5 (1959), 12–16; L. Bulferetti, *A. Rosmini nella Restaurazione* (Florence 1942); G. Pusineri, "La 'Società degli amici.' Rosmini precursore dell'Azione cattolica," *Charitas* 5 (1931), 7 (1933), *passim;* U. Biglia in *Novarien,* 3 (1969), 207–46 (concerning the fraternities for young intellectuals carried on by P. Scavini).

ON THE INFLUENCE OF LAMENNAIS: A. Gambaro, *Sulle orme del Lamennais in Italia* I (Turin 1958; basic). Also P. Pirri in *CivCatt* IV (1930), 3–19, III (1932), 313–27, 567–83; P. Dudon in *Gr* 18 (1937), 88–106; G. Verucci, op. cit., 264–67; C. Bona, op. cit., 396–406.

ON LANTERI: A. P. Frutaz, *Positio . . . Servi Dei P. B. Lanteri* (Vatican City 1945); T. Piatti, *Un precursore dell'Azione cattolica, P. B. Lanteri* (Turin 1954).

ON VENTURA: A. Rastoul, *Le Père Ventura* (Paris 1906); A. Cristofoli, *Il pensiero religioso del P. Ventura* (Milan 1927); R. Rizzo, *Teocrazia e neocatolicismo nel Risorgimento. Genesi e sviluppo del pensiero politico del P. Ventura* (Palermo 1938); F. Salinitri in *Salesianum* 2 (1940), 318–48 (Ventura and Lamennais); works and literature in *Regnum Dei* 20 (1969), 148–210.

ON ROSMINI AND GIOBERTI: Survey and literature in *ECatt* X, 1359–71, VI, 414–22.

ON MANZONI: M. Parenti, *Bibliografia manzoniana* (Florence 1936) to be supplemented by F. Ghisalberti, *Critica manzoniana di un decennio 1939–48* (Milan 1949); A. Galletti, *Le origini del romanticismo italiano e l'opera di A. Manzoni* (Milan 1942); id., *Manzoni* (Milan 1958); R. Amerio, *A. Manzoni filosofo e teologo* (Turin 1958); M. Bendiscioli, *Scritti stor. e giurid, in memoria di A. Visconti* (Milan 1955), 145–55.

15. *The Complex Revival of Religious Studies*

GENERAL DESCRIPTIONS

Hocedez I (with literature); Grabmann, 218ff. (Literature 337ff.); B. Magnino, *Romanticismo e cristianesimo,* 3 vols. (Brescia 1962/63). Also Hurter, *Nomenclator* V/l (Innsbruck 1912).

GERMANY

K. Werner, *Geschichte der katholischen Theologie* (Munich 1889); D. Gla, *Repertorium der katholisch-theologischen Literatur in Deutschland, Österreich und der Schweiz* I (Paderborn 1895/1904); Goyau I, 161–391, II, 2–111; Schnabel IV, 62–97, 164f.f.; Scheffczyk, 1–233; P. Funk, *Von der Aufklärung zur Romantik. Studien zur Vorgeschichte der Münchener Romantik* (Munich 1925); A. Reatz, *Reformversuche in der katholischen Dogmatik Deutschlands zu Beginn des 19. Jahrhunderts* (Mainz 1917); J. Diebolt, *La théologie morale catholique en Allemagne 1750–1850* (Strasbourg 1926); A. Anwander, *Die allgemeine Religionsgeschichte im katholischen Deutschland während der Aufklärung und Romantik* (Salzburg 1932).

THEOLOGICAL FACULTIES: M. Braubach, "Die katholischen Universitäten Deutschlands und die französische Revolution," *HJ* 49 (1929), 263–303; H. Schrörs, *Geschichte der katholisch-theologischen Fakultät zu Bonn 1818–31* (Cologne 1922); M. Huber, *Ludwig I. von Bayern und die Universität in München* (Würzburg 1939); H. Witetschek in *HJ* 86 (1966), 107–137 (for Munich); S. Merkle, A. Bigelmair et al., *Aus der Vergangenheit der Universität Würzburg* (Berlin 1932); F. Haase, *Die schriftstellerische Tätigkeit der Breslauer theologischen Fakultäten 1811–1911* (Breslau 1911); A. Wappler, *Geschichte der theologischen Fakultät zu Wien* (Vienna 1884).—L. Lenhart, *Die erste Mainzer Theologenschule 1805–30* (Maize 1956); A. F. Ludwig, *Weihbischof Zirkel von Würzburg in seiner Stellung zur theologischen Aufklärung und zur kirchlichen Restauration,* 2 vols. (Paderborn 1904/06); L. Scheffczyk, *L.F. zu Stolbergs Geschichte der Religion Jesu Christi. Die Abwendung der katholischen Kirchengeschichtsschreibung von der Aufklärung und ihre Neuorientierung im Zeitalter der Romantik* (Munich 1952); P. Brachin, *Le Cercle de Munster et la pensée religieuse de F.L. Stolberg* (Paris 1952); L. Wirz, *Fr. Schlegels philosophische Entwicklung* (Bonn 1939); J. Anstett, *La pensée religieuse de Fr. Schlegel* (Paris 1941); J. R. Geiselmann, *Von lebendiger Religiosität zum Leben der Kirche. J.M. Sailers Verständnis der Kirche geistesgeschichtlich gedeutet* (Stuttgart 1952); A. Dyroff, *C.J. Windischmann und sein Kreis* (Cologne 1916); A. Sonnenschein, *Görres, Windischmann und Deutinger als christliche Philosophen* (Bonn 1937); E. Susini, *F. Baader et le romantisme mystique,* 2 vols. (Paris 1942); T. Steinbüchel: *WiWei* 10 (1943), 41–60, 103–26; S. Lösch, *Professor A. Gengler. Die Beziehungen des Bamberger Theologen zu I. Döllinger und J.A. Möhler* (Würzburg 1963).

HERMES: K. Eschweiler, *Die zwei Wege der neueren Theologie. G. Hermes - M.J. Scheeben* (Augsburg 1926); K. Thimm, *Die Autonomie der praktischen Vernunft in der Philosophie und Theologie des Hermesianismus* (Munich 1939); other literature in R. Schlund in *LThK* V, 258–60. On the beginning of the dispute, see H. Schrörs, op. cit., 69–91, 166–90, 371–79.

TÜBINGEN SCHOOL: J. Zeller, "Die Errichtung der katholisch-theologischen Fakultät in Tübingen 1817," *ThQ* 108 (1927), 77–158; S. Lösch, *Die Anfänge der Tübinger Theologischen Schule, 1819–31* (Rottenburg 1938); P. Schanz in *ThQ* 80 (1898), 1–49; E. Vermeil, *J. A. Möhler et l'école catholique de Tubingue, 1815–40* (Paris 1913); P. Chaillet in *RSPhTh* 26 (1937), 483–98, 713–26; J. R. Geiselmann, *Lebendiger Glaube aus geheiligter Überlieferung. Der Grundgedanke der Theologie J.A. Möhlers und der katholischen Tübinger Schule* (Mainz 1942); id., *Die katholische Tübinger Schule* (Freiburg 1964; also B. Dupuy in *RSPhTh* 50 (1966), 311; H. J. Brosch, *Das Übernatürliche in der katholischen Tübinger Schule* (Essen 1962); F. W. Kantzenbuch in *ZRGG* 15 (1963), 55–86; A. Hagen, *Gestalten aus dem schwäbischen Katholizismus I und II* (Stuttgart 1948/50). Survey and literature concerning Drey, see J. R. Geiselmann in *LThK* III, 574.—Concerning Hirscher, see works and literature in F.X. Arnold in *LThK* V, 383–84; also J. Rief, *Reich Gottes und Gesellschaft nach J.S. Drey und J.B. Hirscher* (Paderborn 1965); E. Keller, *J. B. Hirscher* (Graz 1969). Concerning Möhler, see older literature in S. Lösch, *J.A. Möhler* I (Munich 1928), XXIIff.; recent literature in J. R. Geiselmann in *LThK* VII, 521–22.

FRANCE

A. Baudrillart, *Le renouvellement intellectuel du clergé en France au XIXe siècle. Les hommes, les institutions* (Paris 1903); *DThC* VI, 695–712; L. Foucher, *La philosophie catholique en France au XIXe siècle* (Paris 1955), 11–98; J. A. At, *Les apologists français au XIXe siècle*

(Paris 1909); N. Hötzel, *Die Uroffenbarung im französischen Traditionalismus* (Munich 1962).

MONOGRAPHS: P. Poupard, *L'abbé L. Bautain* (Paris 1961); S. Merkle, "Die Anfänge französischer Laientheologie im 19. Jahrhundert," *Festschrift K. Muth* (Munich 1927), 325–27.

SCHOOL OF LA CHÊNAIE: C. Sainte-Foi (=É. Jourdain), *Souvenirs de jeunesse,* ed. by C. Latreille (Paris 1911), 37–134; A. Roussel, *Lamennais à la Chênaie* (Paris 1909); J. R. Derré, *Lamennais, ses amis et le mouvement des idées à l'époque romantique* (Paris 1962), 278–305; A. Dargis, "La Congrégation de Saint-Pierre" (unpubl. Diss., Louvain 1971), 248–66, 346–83; *LThK* IV, 711.

ITALY

A. Gemelli, S. Vismara, *La riforma degli studi universitari negli Stati pontifici* (Milan 1933); *L'Università Gregoriana nel 1° secolo della restituzione* (Rome 1924).

BEGINNINGS OF NEOTHOMISM: A. Masnovo, *Il neotomismo in Italia, origine e prime vicende* (Milan 1923); P. Dezza, *Alle origini del neotomismo* (Milan 1940); C. Fabro in *ECatt* XI, 135–40; G. F. Rossi, *La filosofia nel Collegio Alberoni e il neotomismo* (Piacenza 1959); A. Fermi, *Origine del tomismo piacentino* (Piacenza 1959).

ROSMINI: *Works, Edizione nazionale,* ed. by E. Castelli (Rome 1934ff.); older literature in Volume I, recent literature in *LThK* IX, 55. See also C. Bergamaschi, *Bibliografia rosminiana,* 2 vols. (Milan 1967); G. Pagani, *Vita di A. Rosmini,* revised by G. Rossi, 2 vols. (Rovereto 1959); *A. Rosmini nel I° centenario della morte,* ed. by C. Riva (Florence 1958); *Atti del Congresso internazionale di filosofia A. Rosmini* (Florence 1957); A. Gambaro, "A. Rosmini nella cultura del suo tempo," *Rivista Rosminiana* 49 (1955), 162–96; F. Traniello, *Società religiosa e società civile in Rosmini* (Bologna 1966); G. Ferrarese, *Ricerche sulle riflessione teologiche di A. Rosmini negli anni 1819–1928* (Milan 1967); D. Mancini, *Il giovane Rosmini* I (Urbino 1963).

Part Three

Between the Revolutions of 1830 and 1848

Introduction: *Gregory XVI*

Sources

BullRomCont XIX (Rome 1835); *Acta Gregorii Papae,* ed. by A. M. Bernasconi, 4 vols. (Rome 1901/04); *Raccolta delle leggi e disposizioni di pubblica amministrazione dello Stato Pontificio* (Rome 1834/71); H. Bastgen, *Forschungen und Quellen zur Kirchenpolitik Gregors XVI.* (Paderborn 1929); Moroni XXXII, 312–28; N. Wiseman, *Recollections of the Last Four Popes* (London 1858).

Literature

There exists as yet no scholarly study of Gregory's life and his whole pontificate. Numerous valuable elements concerning various aspects of his personality and his activities as Pope and secular ruler can be found in *Gregorio XVI, Miscellanea commemorativa,* 2 vols. (Rome 1948). D. Federici, *Gregorio XVI tra favola e realtà* (Rovigo 1948; literature pp. 17–25; too glorifying, but in reaction to the prevailing tendency to view Gregory XVI more as sovereign than as Pope). F. Fabi-Montanari, *Notizie istoriche di Gregori XVI* (Rome 1846); B. Wagner, *Papst Gregor XVI., sein Leben und sein Pontifikat* (Sulzbach 1846); G. Audisio, *Storia religiosa e civile dei Papi* V (Rome 1868), 356–94; C. Sylvain, *Grégoire XVI et son pontificat* (Lille 1889); F. Hayward, *Le dernier siècle de la Rome pontificale* II (Paris 1928), 174–215; E. Vercesi, *Tre pontificati. Leone XII, Pio VIII, Gregorio XVI* (Turin 1936); M. Vincenti, *Gregorio XVI* (Rome 1941).

Treatments of the Pontificate: Schmidlin, *PG* I, 511–687; Leflon, 426–516; Pouthas, 275–315; Belvederi, 903–22; Daniel-Rops I, 341–427; *DThC* VI, 1822–36; *ECatt* VI, 1148–56; A. Simon, "Vues nouvelles sur Grégoire XVI," *RGB* 63 (1951), 395–408.

Concerning the Conclave: L. Alpago-Novello, "Il conclave di Gregorio XVI," *Archivio veneto-tridentino* 6 (1924), 68–114; G. Cacciamani, *Storia del conclave di Papa Gregorio XVI* (Camaldoli 1960); D. Silvagni, *Diarii dei conclavi di Mons. Dardano* (Rome 1879), 73ff.; L. Wahrmund, *Das Ausschliessungsrecht bei den Papstwahlen* (Vienna 1888), 233f. (based on Vienna archives); A. Eisler, *Das Veto der katholischen Staaten bei den Papstwahlen* (Vienna 1907), 238ff.; T. M. March, "La exclusiva dada por España contra el cardinale Giustiniani en el conclave de 1830–31," *RF* 98 (1932), 50–64, 337–48, 99 (1932), 43–61.

SECTION ONE

The First Phase of Catholic Liberalism

STATUS OF RESEARCH

R. Aubert, J.-B. Duroselle, A. Jemolo, "Le libéralisme religieux au XIXe siècle" in *X Congresso internazionale di Scienze storiche. Relazioni* V (Florence 1955), 305–83.

LITERATURE

Beyond the more general description in handbooks of the church history of the nineteenth century and the historiography of the pontificate of Gregory XVI, see the general surveys by Weill, *Cath. lib.* and by P. Constantin in *DThC* IX, 506–65 (outdated, but still useful for facts), by Gurian, 101–47, and Salvatorelli, 21–49; the anthology by M. Prélot, *Le libéralisme catholique* (Paris 1969), 9–141; H. Maier, *Revolution und Kirche. Studien zur Frühgeschichte der christlichen Demokratie* (Freiburg i. Br. 1959); the works on Lamennais listed on p. 393, especially those by G. Verucci and L. Le Guillou, to which should be added: K. Jürgensen, *Lamennais und die Gestaltung des belgischen Staates. Der liberale Katholizismus in der Verfassungsbewegung des 19. Jahrhunderts* (Wiesbaden 1963); E. Sevrin, *Dom Guéranger et Lamennais* (Paris 1933); and the biographies (listed in General Bibliography) of Lacordaire, Montalembert, Gerbet, d'Astros, and Mazenod.

16. *From Belgian Unionism to the Campaign of* L'Avenir

BELGIUM: C. Terlinden, *Guillaume Ier roi des Pays-Bas, et l'Église catholique en Belgique* II (Paris–Louvain 1906; antiquated, but still useful); H. Haag, *Les origines du catholicisme libéral en Belgique* (Louvain 1950); A. Simon, *Rencontres;* A. Simon, *Aspects de l'unionisme* (Wetteren 1958), 9–81; A. Simon, *Sterckx* I, 65–155, II, 461; K. Jürgensen, op. cit., 62–228 (in addition, A. Simon, *Revue belge de philosophie et d'histoire* 37 [1959], 408–18); S. Stockman, *De religieuzen en de onderwijspolitiek der regering in het Vereenigd Koninkrijk der Nederlanden* (The Hague 1935); A. Manning, *De betekenis van C.R.A. Van Bommel voor de Noordelijke Nederlanden* (Utrecht 1956), 42–161; E. Perniola, "De internuntius Cappaccini en de belgische Omwenteling," *Mededelingen van het Nederl. hist. Instituut te Rome,* 3rd s. 4 (1947), 53–169; H. Wagnon, "Le Congrès national belge de 1830–31 a-t-il établi la séparation de l'Église et de l'État?," *Études d'histoire du droit canonique dédiées à G. Le Bras* II (Paris 1965), 753–81. A. Boland, *Adolphe Bartels, révolutionnaire et démocrate* (Louvain 1960).

FRANCE: In addition to the newspaper articles and books by Lamennais, his correspondence is the most important source. See especially E. Forgues, *Lamennais, Correspondance,* 2 vols. (Paris 1863); E. Forgues, *Correspondance inédite entre Lamennais et le baron de Vitrolles* (Paris 1886); A. Blaize, *Œuvres inédites de Félicité Lamennais,* 2 vols.

(Paris 1866); G. Goyau, *Le portefeuille de Lamennais 1818–36* (Paris 1930). The most important articles of *L'Avenir,* systematically arranged, were at that time published again with a few cuts in the *Mélanges catholiques. Extraits de "l'Avenir",* 2 vols. (Paris 1831) and chronologically in *Articles de "l'Avenir",* 7 vols. (Louvain 1830/31); and recently, with an introduction and comments, by G. Verucci, *"L'Avenir." Antologia degli articoli* (Rome 1967).—To the works on Lamennais listed above on p. 398 are to be added J. R. Derré, *Lamennais, ses amis et le mouvement des idées à l'époque romantique* (Paris 1962), especially 156–63, 199–206, 385–459, and Weill, *Histoire,* 28–50.

17. *The Roman Reaction*

Sources

Lamennais stated his views in *Les affaires de Rome* (Paris 1836); see also his correspondence listed on p. 393 and *Lettres inédites de Lamennais à Montalembert,* ed. by E. Forgues (Paris 1898). P. Dudon, *Lamennais et le Saint-Siège* (Paris 1911) is valuable because of its numerous extracts and documents from the Vatican Archives, but must be supplemented and differentiated by L. Ahrens, *Lamennais und Deutschland* (Münster 1930) and J. L. Derré, *Metternich und Lamennais* (Paris 1963), both of whom have also used the archives at Vienna. In addition there should be consulted the diaries of Montalembert (at the castle of La-Roche-en-Breny); selections from his biography by Lecanuet and by A. Trannoy, *Le romantisme politique de Montalembert avant 1843* (Paris 1942) and his correspondence (especially *Lettres de Montalembert à Lamennais,* ed. by G. Goyau [Paris 1932]), the memoirs of Lacordaire (*Le testament du Père Lacordaire* [Paris 1865]), and the memoirs of the period as well as G. Procacci, *Le relazioni diplomatiche fra lo Stato pontificio e la Francia,* 2nd ser., I–II (Rome 1962/63).

Literature

Consult the works listed in the bibliography to chapter 16. The two most recent treatments, differentiated and familiar with sources and monographs, are A. Vidler, *Prophecy and Papacy* (London 1954), 184–284 and P. Droulers, *Action pastorale et problèmes sociaux chez Mgr d'Astros* (Paris 1954), 125–62. Concerning the development of Lamennais after *Mirari vos* see primarily L. Le Guillou, *L'évolution de la pensée religieuse de Félicité Lamennais* (Paris 1966), 170–402; L. Le Guillou, *Les "Discussions critiques," journal de la crise mennaisienne* (Paris 1967); L. Le Guillou, "L'information romaine de Lamennais," *Annales de Bretagne* 71 (1964), 373–421; G. Verucci, *Félicité Lamennais dal cattolicesimo autoritario al radicalismo democratico* (Naples 1963), 228–339, and the introduction by Y. LeHir of the critical edition of *Paroles d'un croyant* (Paris 1949).

SECTION TWO

Church and State in Europe from 1830 to 1848

18. *The Continuation of Catholic Liberalism in Western Europe*

FRANCE

SOURCES: For legal codes and parliamentary debates, see the General Bibliography. The episcopal pastoral letters are one of the most important sources (incomplete collection in the National Archives of Paris, F 5473–88, and in the *Bibliothèque Nationale,* ser. E). Numerous memoirs, especially those of Guizot, 8 vols. (Paris 1857/58), and correspondence, especially of Lamennais, Lacordaire (consult *LThK* VI, 726), and Veuillot (*Œuvres complètes* XV–XVI, [Paris 1931]). The most important newspapers are *L'Avenir* (1830/31), *L'Ami de la Religion* (since 1830), *L'Univers religieux* (since 1833), and *Le Journal des villes et des campagnes.* For brochures, consult the *Catalogue de l'histoire de France* of the Bibliothèque Nationale in Paris, III, 555–804 and XI, 292–319. Also G. Procacci, *Le relazioni diplomatiche fra lo Stato pontificio e la Francia, 2nd Series, 1830–48,* 3 vols. (Rome 1962/69, to 1838); P. Poupard, *Correspondance inédite entre Mgr. Garibaldi, internonce à Paris, et Mgr Mathieu, archevêque de Besançon* (Paris 1961). For unpublished sources, consult G. Bourgin, *Les sources manuscrites de l'histoire religieuse de la France moderne* (Paris 1925). Especially important are the Series F in the National Archives of Paris and the archival collections of the *Nunziatura di Francia* in the Vatican Archives.

LITERATURE: In addition to the works of Schmidlin, *PG* (I, 556–67), Leflon (440–52, 478–84, 489–509), Brugerette (I, 63–122), Gurian (124–84), Dansette (I, 285–337), and *HistCathFr* (274–365), see C. Pouthas, *L'Église de France sous la Monarchie constitutionnelle* (Cours de Sorbonne 1942).

Among the numerous biographies of bishops, clerics, and other important men of the period, note especially P. Droulers, *Action pastorale et problèmes sociaux sous la Monarchie de Juillet chez Mgr d'Astros* (Paris 1954; the concern of the work exceeds considerably the character of a biography); J. Leflon, *E. de Mazenod* II–III (Paris 1960/65; the same as above applies here); E. Sevrin, *Mgr Clausel de Montals,* 2 vols. (Paris 1957); R. Limouzin-Lamothe, *Mgr de Quélen, archevêque de Paris* II (Paris 1957); R. Limouzin-Lamothe and J. Leflon, *Mgr D.-A. Affre* (Paris 1971); C. Guillemant, *P.L. Parisis* I–II (Paris 1916/17); S. Vailhé, *Le P.E. d'Alzon,* 2 vols. (Paris 1927); Lecanuet, *Montalembert* I–II (Paris 1895/99); M. J. Rouë de Journel, *Mme Swetchine* (Paris 1929).—Equally useful, though less critical, are the biographies of Dupanloup (by F. Lagrange I [Paris 1883]), Mathieu (by Besson I [Paris 1882]), Gerbet (by C. de Ladoue I–II [Paris 1882]), Sibour (by Poujoulat [Paris 1857]), Gousset (by F. Gousset [Besançon 1903]), Guibert (by J. Paguelle de Follenay, 2 vols. [Paris 1896]), Lacordaire (by T. Foisset, 2 vols. [Paris 1870]), and Veuillot (by E. and F. Veuillot I–II [Paris 1899/1901]).

RELATIONS BETWEEN CHURCH AND STATE: P. Thureau-Dangin, *L'Église et l'État sous la Monarchie de Juillet* (Paris 1895); Debidour, *Histoire* II, 413–90; Rémond, 75–94; E. Piscitelli, *Stato e Chiesa sotto la Monarchia di Luglio attraverso i documenti vaticani* (Rome

1950); J. P. Martin, *La nonciature de Paris et les affaires ecclésiastiques en France sous le règne de Louis-Philippe* (Paris 1949); L. Manzini, *Il cardinale Lambruschini* (Vatican City 1960), 160–238.—Concerning the recognition of the July Monarchy by the Holy See, see C. Vidal in *Revue d'histoire diplomatique* 46 (1932), 497–517; S. Celli in *ChStato* I, 67–104.
Dioceses.
C. Pouthas, "Le clergé sous la Monarchie constitutionnelle," *RHEF* 29 (1943), 19–74; P. Poupard, "L'épiscopat angevin sous la Monarchie de Juillet," *Mémoires de l'Académie d'Angers,* 8th ser. 5 (1961), 15–29 and especially the introduction to the correspondence Garibaldi-Mathieu by the same author with the subtitle *Contribution à l'histoire de l'administration ecclésiastique sous la Monarchie de Juillet;* J.-B. Duroselle, "L'abbé Clavel et les revendications du bas-clergé sous Louis-Philippe," *Études d'histoire moderne et contemporaine* 1 (1947), 99–126.

Freedom of Education: In addition to the biographies of Montalembert, Parisis, Dupanloup, Clausel and Veuillot, see Grimaud VI; L. Follioley, *Montalembert et Mgr Parisis* (Paris 1901); L. Trénard, *Salvandy et son temps* (Paris 1968); P. Gerbod, *La condition universitaire en France au XIXᵉ siècle* (Paris 1965), 141–56, 176–81; A. J. Tudesq, *Les grands notables en France 1840–49* (Paris 1964), 695–730; A. Rivet in *Actes du 88ᵉ congrès national des sociétés savantes* (Paris 1964), 181–200 (elementary schools).

Catholic Movement: F. Mourret, *Le mouvement catholique en France de 1830 à 1850* (Paris 1917); Weill, *Cath. lib.,* 51–90; M. Prélot, *Le libéralisme catholique* (Paris 1969), 148–78; P. Fernessole, *Les conférenciers de Notre-Dame* I (Paris 1935); E. Martin, *La Mère de Gondrecourt* (Nancy 1895), 1–54 (for Nancy).

Religious Life: Y. M. Hilaire in *L'information historique* 25 (1963), 57–69, 29 (1967), 31–35; C. Marcilhacy, *Le diocèse d'Orléans au milieu du XIXᵉ siècle* (Paris 1964); C. Marcilhacy in *ArchSR* 6 (1958), 91–103; the works (listed in chap. 5) by M. Faugeras, P. Huot-Pleuroux, and J. Vidalenc; G. de Bertier in *RHEF* 55 (1969), 273–78; L. Trénard, "Aux origines de la déchristianisation, le diocèse de Cambrai de 1830 à 1848," *Revue du Nord* 47 (1965), 399–459; H. Pomme, "La pratique religieuse dans les campagnes de la Meurthe vers 1840," *Annales de l'Est,* 5th ser. 21 (1968), 137–157; H. Forestier in *Bulletin de la société des sciences histoires et naturelles de l'Yonne* 97 (1957/58), 33–54; M. Vincienne-H. Courtois in *ArchSR* 6 (1958), 104–18; F. Isambert in *ArchSR* 6 (1958), 7–35; M.-H. Vicaire, "Les ouvriers parisiens en face du catholicisme de 1830 à 1870," *Schweizerische Zeitschrift für Geschichte* 1 (1951), 226–45; R. Voog, "Le problème religieux à Lyon pendant la Monarchie de Juillet d'après les journaux ouvriers," *Cahiers d'histoire* 8 (1963), 405–21. Concerning anticlericalism, see Weill, *Idée laïque,* 56–104; Mellor, 271–85.

Catholics and the Social Question: Duroselle, 80–287, to be complemented by the cited work of P. Droulers about Mgr. d'Astros and by the articles of the same author in *Revue d'histoire moderne et contemporaine* 4 (1957), 281–301; *Cahiers d'histoire* 6 (1961), 265–85; *Revue de l'Action populaire* 47 (1961), 442–60; *Saggi storici intorno al Papato* (Rome 1959), 401–63. Also, A. d'Andigné, *Un apôtre de la charité, A. de Melun* (Paris 1962); F.-A. Isambert, *Politique, religion et science de l'homme chez Ph. Buchez* (Paris 1967).

Belgium

Sources: In addition to pastoral letters and the *Journal historique et littéraire* (1834seqq.), the publications of documents by A. Simon, with their valuable introductions, are of fundamental importance: *Réunions des évêques de Belgique 1830–1867. Procès-verbaux* (Louvain 1960); *Documents relatifs à la nonciature de Bruxelles 1834–38* (Brussels 1958); *Correspondance du nonce Fornari 1838–43* (Brussels 1956; also *BIHBR* 29 [1955], 33–68 and *RHE* 49 [1954], 462–506, 808–34); *Lettres de Pecci 1843–46* (Brussels 1959); *La politique religieuse de Léopold Ier* (Brussels 1953); *Aspects de l'Unionisme 1830–57* (Wetteren 1958). Also L. Jadin in *BIHBR* 11 (1931), 421–62 (concerning the bishops).

LITERATURE: In addition to the titles listed in the General Bibliography, see especially Simon, *Sterckx;* Simon, *Rencontres,* 147–265; H. Haag, *Les origines du catholicisme libéral en Belgique* (Louvain 1950), 199–292; C. Lebas, *L'union des catholiques et des libéraux de 1839 à 1847* (Louvain 1960); H. Wagnon, "Le Saint-Siège et la nomination des évêques belges," *Miscellanea hist. A. De Meyer* (Louvain 1946), 1248–67; G. Simenon, "Mgr Van Bommel," *Revue ecclésiastique de Liège* 32 (1945), 313–27, 33 (1946), 341–51 (also A. Simon, *Catholicisme et politique* [Wetteren 1959], 41–61); E. de Moreau, *A. Deschamps* (Brussels 1911), 43–199; C. Pieraerts, A. Desmet, *Vie du chan. C. Van Crombrugghe* (Brussels 1937); J. Willequet, *La vie tumultueuse de l'abbé Helsen* (Brussels 1956); A. Milet in *Revue diocésaine de Tournai* 9 (1954), 209–28, 10 (1955), 355–61 (about the seminary of Tournai); P. Janssens in *Spicilegium hist. Congregationis SS. Redemptoris* 12 (1964), 185–202, 13 (1965), 380–403; P. Gérin, *150 Jaar katholieke Arbeidersbeweging in België*, ed. by S. Scholl, I (Brussels 1963), 223–45. On the Catholic press, E. Lamberts in *BIHBR* 40 (1969), 389–467; A. Cordewiener, *Revue belge d'histoire contemporaine* 2 (1970), 27–44; R. Van Eenoo in *Revue belge d'histoire contemporaine* 2 (1970), 55–100. There are also the unpublished dissertation of E. Lamberts, "Kerk en liberalisme in het bisdom Gent 1821–57" (Louvain 1970) and the theses (Louvain) by A. Arnould, "Le clergé paroissial dans le diocèse de Namur 1836–65" (1964), St. van Outryve d'Ydewalle, "Structuren van het bisdom Brugge 1834–48" (1966), and L. Billiouw, "De sekuliere roepingen in het arrondissement Roeselare, 1833–63" (1964).

Netherlands

In addition to the cited works in the General Bibliography and in chap. 8, there are chiefly Albers, *Herstel* I, 432–67, II, 1–92; J. Witlox, *De katholieke Staatspartij,* 2 vols. ('s-Hertogenbosch 1919/27); G. Brom, *Romantiek en Katholicisme in Nederland,* 2 vols. (Groningen 1926); G. Brom, *Corn. Broere* (Utrecht 1955); G. Gorris, *J. Le Sage ten Broek* II (Amsterdam 1949); A. Manning, *C. van Bommel* (op. cit. in chap. 16), 162–83; R. Reinsma in *AGKKN* 3 (1961), 50–72; W. Munier in *AGKKN* 9 (1967), 259–321; A. J. Alkemade, *Vrouwen XIX. Geschiedenis van 19 religieuze congregaties, 1800–1850* ('s-Hertogenbosch 1966).

19. *The Beginning of the Risorgimento in Italy*

The Ferment in the Papal States

Schmidlin, *PG* I, 520–56; Leflon, 432–40; Mollat, 150–90; E. Morelli, *La politica estera di T. Bernetti* (Rome 1953); L. Manzini, *Il cardinale Lambruschini* (Vatican City 1960), 188–208, 280–306, 539–43 (panegyrical; see also M. G. Giampaolo in *RStRis* 18 [1931], 103–36); F. A. Gualterio, *Gli ultimi rivolgimenti italiani. Memorie storiche con documenti inediti* I (Naples 1861); F. Engel-Janosi, *Die politische Korrespondenz der Päpste mit den österreichischen Kaisern* (Vienna 1964), 21–25, 199–222; *Le relazioni diplomatiche fra lo Stato pontificio e la Francia,* 2nd ser. 1830–48, 3 vols. (Rome 1962/69); see also E. Calvi, *Bibliografia di Roma nel Risorgimento* (Rome 1912), nos. 2083–2281.

THE DISTURBANCES OF 1831–32: E. Morelli, *Lo Stato pontificio e l'Europa nel 1831–32* (Rome 1966); E. Morelli, *Studi storici in onore di G. Volpi* II (Florence 1958), 665–77; E. Morelli in *ChStato* II, 549–62; N. Nada, *L'Austria e la Questione Romana, agosto 1830–luglio 1831* (Turin 1953); N. Nada, *La polemica fra Palmerston e Metternich sulla Questione romana nel 1832* (Turin 1955); L. Pásztor, P. Pirri, *L'archivio dei Governi provvisori di Bologna e delle Provincie Unite del 1831* (Vatican City 1956); P. Pirri, "Il Memorandum del 1831 nei dispacci del cardinale Bernetti al Nunzio di Vienna," *GregMC* II, 353–72; L. Pásztor in *RSTI* 8 (1954), 95–128; L. Pásztor, *Boll. del Museo del Risorgimento di Bologna* 3 (1958), 167–202; L. Pásztor in *Studi romagnoli* 8 (1957), 529–95; S. Celli, "Il cardinale Benvenuti nella rivoluzione del 1831," *RSTI* 14 (1960), 48–93. Also *Nel primo centenario della Rivoluzione del 1831* (Bologna 1931); *Contributi alla storia della rivoluzione italiana del 1831* (Bologna 1931); B. Gamberale in *RStRis* 14 (1927), 657–715; R. Dal Piano, *Roma e la rivoluzione del 1831* (Imola 1931); P. Zama, *La marcia su Roma del 1831* (Milan 1931); F. Falaschi in *RStRis* 19 suppl. (1932), 117–27; E. Docci, *Deputati romagnoli a Roma nel maggio 1831* (Faenza 1957).

THE PAPAL STATES AND REFORM ATTEMPTS: D. Demarco, *Il tramonto dello Stato pontificio. Il papato di Gregorio XVI* (Turin 1949; see also *RStRis* 44 [1957], 191–258); G. Quazza, *La lotta sociale nel Risorgimento* (Turin 1951), 113–42; N. Nada, *Metternich e la Riforma nello Stato pontificio. La missione Sebregondi a Roma 1832–1836* (Turin 1957; important, but to be qualified according to E. Morelli in *ChStato* II, 554–60 and L. Pásztor in *La Bibliofilia* 60 [1958], 285–97); P. Dalla Torre, "L'opera riformatrice e amministrativa di Gregorio XVI," *GregMC,* 29–121; P. Ciprotti in *GregMC* I, 113–121. See also A. Boyer d'Agen, *La prélature de Léon XIII. De Bénévent à Pérouse, 1838–45* (Paris 1907).

RECENT DISTURBANCES: In addition to Schmidlin, *PG* I, 549–56, see A. M. Ghisalberti in *GregMC* II, 123–34; A. M. Ghisalberti in *RStRis* 19 (1932), 70–88; O. Montenovesi, "I casi di Romagna, sett. 1845," *RStRis* 8 (1921), 307–426; J. A. v. Helfert, *Gregor XVI. und Pius IX. vom Oktober 1845 bis November 1846* (Prague 1895). See also M. d'Azeglio, *Degli ultimi casi di Romagna* (Florence 1846).

CATHOLICS AND THE PROBLEM OF ITALIAN UNITY

A. M. Ghisalberti, *Il movimento nazionale del 1831 alla vigilia della prima guerra d'indipendenza d'Italia* III, ed. by N. Valeri (Turin 1965), 533–712; Jemolo, 19–36; W. Maturi in *EnI* XXIX, 437–39; A. Anzilotti, *La funzione storica del giobertismo* (Florence 1923); S. A. Kähler, "Über zwei italienische Programmschriften zur Neuordnung Italiens und Europas von 1843," *NAG,* Phil.-Hist. Kl. (1944), 33–62; A. M. Ghisalberti, "Reazioni cattoliche alle 'Speranze d'Italia'" AstIt 112 (1954), 195–216; A. Luzio, *La massoneria e il Risorgimento* I (Bologna 1925); G. Ambrosetti, "Illuminismo e tradizione cattolica nei concetti del Risorgimento," *I cattolici e il Risorgimento* (Rome 1963), 35–49; L. Bulferetti, "Albori del Risorgimento fra illuminismo e diritto naturale cristiano," *BStBiS* 19 (1947), 55–75; D. Massè, *Il caso di coscienza del Risorgimento italiano* (Alba 1946); D. Massè, *Cattolici e Risorgimento* (Rome 1961); M. Apollonio, "La letteratura d'ispirazione cattolica e il Risorgimento," *Vita e Pensiero* 42 (1959), 918–32; A. Manno, *L'opinione religiosa e conservatrice in Italia del 1830 al 1850* (Turin 1912); P. Treves, *L'idea di Roma e la cultura italiana del secolo XIX* (Milan–Naples 1962).

The Varieties of Catholic Liberalism in Italy

This topic is treated in the publications on the origins of the Risorgimento and in the numerous studies devoted to its leaders: Manzoni (see p. 394), G. Capponi (see p. 322, footnote 38), R. Lambruschini (see p. 322, footnote 39), A. Rosmini (see p. 323, footnote 42), V. Gioberti (see p. 316, footnote 17), G. Ventura (see p. 394 and 328 footnote 48) etc. For a general view, see A. C. Jemolo in *Relazioni del X Congresso internazionale di scienze storichi* V (Florence 1955), 325–31, 365–71; A. C. Jemolo, "Il cattolicesimo liberale dal 1815 al 1848," *RStT* 4 (1958), 239–50; E. Artom, "Il problema politico dei cattolici italiani nel XIX secolo," *RStT* 4(1958), 215–37; E. Passerin d'Entrèves, "Il cattolicesimo liberale ed il movimento neoguelfo in Italia," *Nuove Questioni di storia del Risorgimento* I (Milan 1961), 565–88; L. Salvatorelli, "Il problema religioso nel Risorgimento," *RStRis* 43 (1956), 193–216; L. Salvatorelli, *Il pensiero politico italiano del 1700 al 1870* (Bari 1943), 187–221, 259–90. Also, F. De Sanctis: *Opere,* ed. by C. Muscetta, G. Candeloro, XI (Turin 1953); A. Anzilotti, "Dal neoguelfismo all'idea liberale," *Nuova Rivista storica* 1 (1917), 227–56, 385–422; F. Landogna, *Saggio sul cattolicesimo liberale in Italia* (Livorno 1925); P. Fossi, *Italiani dell'Ottocento, Rosmini, Capponi, Lambruschini, Tommaseo, Manzoni* (Florence 1941); A. Pietra, *Storia del movimento cattolico liberale* (Milan 1947). The anthology by R. Tisato, *I liberali cattolici. Testi scelti e commentati* (Treviso 1959) is very disputable (see *Nuova Rivista storica* 44 [1960], 156–61).

Concerning the Tuscan group, see A. Gambara, *Riforma religiosa nel carteggio inedito di R. Lambruschini,* 2 vols. (Turin 1926); P. Barbaini, *Problemi religiosi nella vita politica-culturale del Risorgimento in Toscana* (Turin 1961), 157–215; R. Mori in *I cattolici italiani dall'800 ad oggi* (Brescia 1964), 29–47; G. Gentile, *G. Capponi e la cultura toscana nel secolo XIX* (Florence 1942); S. Jacini, *Un reformatore toscano dell'epoca del Risorgimento, il conte P. Guicciardini* (Florence 1940); M. L. Trebiliani in *Studium* 53 (1957), 527–40.

20. *The States of the German Confederation and Switzerland, 1830–1848*

General: Brück, *Geschichte* II, 274–592; L. Bergsträsser, *Studien zur Vorgeschichte der Zentrumspartei* (Tübingen 1910); Bachem, *Zentrumspartei* I; Schmidlin, *PG* I, 488–92, 567–95, II, 190 ff.; Leflon (Fliche-Martin 20), 415f., 464f., 465–70; Schnabel, *G* IV, 97–220; Ritter, *Die Katholisch-soziale Bewegung,* chap. 3; S. Huber, *Verfassungsgeschichte* II (Stuttgart 1960), 185–265, 345–70; Bihlmeyer-Tüchle III, 321, 328–35, 336f.; Buchheim, *Ultramontanismus und Demokratie,* 25ff., 48–55; Heyer, *Die katholische Kirche 1648–1870,* 93f., 99f., 117–22, 129; Pesch, *Die kirchlich-politische Presse,* 154–94, 203–26.

Prussia: J. Bachem, *Preussen und die katholische Kirche* (Cologne 1887), 56–71; J. Hansen: *Geschichte des Rheinlandes* I (Bonn 1922), 270–98; W. Schulte, *Volk und Staat. Westfalen im Vormärz und in der Revolution 1848/49* (Münster 1954); F. H. Fonk, *Das staatliche Mischehenrecht in Preussen vom Allgemeinen Landrecht an* (Bielefeld 1961); B. Poll, "Preussen und die Rheinlande," *ZAGV* 76 (1964); R. Vierhaus, "Preussen und die Rheinlande," *RhVJBll* 30 (1965); Lipgens, *Spiegel;* K.-G. Faber, *Die Rheinlande zwischen Restauration und Revolution. Probleme der rheinischen Geschichte 1814–1848 im Spiegel der zeitgenössischen Publizistik* (Wiesbaden 1966); A. Klein, *Die Personalpolitik der Hohenzollernmonarchie bei der Kölner Regierung* (Düsseldorf 1967).

Cologne Disturbances: H. Schrörs, *Die Kölner Wirren. Studien zu ihrer Geschichte* (Berlin–Bonn 1927); H. Bastgen, *Forschungen und Quellen zur Kirchenpolitik Gregors*

XVI. (Paderborn 1929); H. Bastgen, *Die Verhandlungen zwischen dem Berliner Hof und dem Heiligen Stuhl über die konfessionell gemischten Ehen* (Paderborn 1936); Schönig, *Binterim;* J. Grisar, "Die Allokution Gregors XVI. vom 10. Dezember 1837," *Misc. Hist. Pont.* XIV (Rome 1948); R. Lill, *Die Beilegung der Kölner Wirren* (Düsseldorf 1962).

BAVARIA: M. Doeberl, *Entwicklungsgeschichte Bayerns* III, ed. by M. Spindler (Munich 1931), 15–31, 123f., 125–47; B. (H.) Bastgen, *Bayern und der Heilige Stuhl* and articles by Bastgen in *HJ* 49 (1929), *AkathKR* 109 (1929), *Mitteilungen des Historischen Vereins der Pfalz* 50 (1930/32); W. Mathäser, *Der Ludwigs-Missionsverein in der Zeit Ludwigs I.* (Munich 1939); H. Gollwitzer, "Carl v. Abel und seine Politik 1837–47" (unpubl. diss., Munich 1944); M. Spindler, "Die politische Wendung von 1847/48 in Bayern," *Bayern. Staat und Kirche, Land und Reich, Gedenkschrift für Wilhelm Winkler* (Munich 1961), now also in Spindler, *Erbe und Verpflichtung* (Munich 1966); Franz-Willing, *Bayerische Vatikangesandtschaft,* 36–45; W. M. Hahn, *Romantik und katholische Restauration. Das Wirken des Sailerschülers und Bischofs von Regensburg Franz X. von Schwäbl* (*Misc. Bavarica Monacensis,* 24, Munich 1970).

SOUTHWEST GERMANY: Literature on the Upper Rhenish Church Province in chapter 7, especially the works by Brück, Maas, Lauer, Gönner-Sester, Hagen, Reidel, and Höhler. Also O. Bechtold, *Der "Ruf nach Synoden" als kirchenpolitische Erscheinung im jungen Erzbistum Freiburg 1827–60* (diss., Freiburg 1958); E. Keller, "Das erste Freiburger Rituale von 1835," *FreibDiözArch* 80 (1960).—C. Bauer, *Politischer Katholizismus in Württemberg bis 1848* (Freiburg 1929); A. Hagen, *Der Mischehenstreit in Württemberg 1837–55* (Paderborn 1931); A. Hagen, *Gestalten aus dem schwäbischen Katholizismus,* 3 vols. (Stuttgart 1948/54); A. Hagen, *Die kirchliche Aufklärung in der Diözese Rottenburg* (Stuttgart 1953); P. Blickle, "Katholizismus, Aristokratie und Bürokratie im Württemberg des Vormärz," *HJ,* 88 (1968).—H. Becker, "Der nassauische Geheime Kirchenrat Johann Ludwig Koch, ein Exponent der episkopalistischen . . . Bewegung," *AMrhKG* 15 (1963).

AUSTRIA: Literature in chapter 7, especially the works of Beer, Maass, Tomek, Weinzierl-Fischer, and Pototschnig, also C. Wolfsgruber, *Joseph Othmar Cardinal Rauscher* (Freiburg 1888); M. Hussarek, "Die Verhandlung des Konkordates vom 18. August 1855," *AÖG* 109 (1921); H. v. Srbik, *Metternich. Der Staatsmann und der Mensch* II (Munich 1925, reprint 1957), 1–45; F. Engel-Janosi, *Österreich und der Vatikan 1846–1918* I (Graz–Vienna–Cologne 1958), chaps. 1 and 2; Winter, *Romantismus, Restauration und Frühliberalismus im österreichischen Vormärz* (Vienna 1968).

SWITZERLAND: Literature in chapter 7, especially the works by Gareis, Zorn, Büchi, Seeholzer, Lampert, and Schwengler, as well as W. Näf, *Der schweizerische Sonderbundskrieg als Vorspiel der deutschen Revolution* (diss., Munich 1920); H. Dommann, "Die Kirchenpolitik im ersten Jahrzehnt des neuen Bistums Basel," *ZSKG* 22/23 (1928/29); E. J. J. Müller, "Religion und Politik. Vom Sinn des 'Sonderbund'-Geschehens," *Schweizer Rundschau* 47 (1947); E. F. J. Müller-Büchi, "Die Anfänge der katholisch-konservativen Tagespresse in der Schweiz," *ZSKG* 54 (1960); F. Glauser, "Der Kanton Solothurn und die Badener Artikel 1834–35," *Jahrbücher für solothurnische Geschichte* 33/34 (1960/61); F. Glauser, "Ludwig von Roll und die solothurnische Ausgleichsbewegung von 1830–31," *SZG* 12 (1962); F. Glauser, "Luzern und der Zürcher Putsch von 1839," *ZSKG* 57 (1963); R. Flury, *Johann Matthias Hungerbühler . . . Werdegang und Wirken bis 1848* (St. Gallen 1962); E. Bucher, *Die Geschichte des Sonderbundkrieges* (Zürich 1966); K. Büchi, *Die Krise der Luzerner Regeneration 1839–41*

(Zürich 1967); H. Raab, "Friedrich Leopold zu Stolberg und Karl Ludwig von Haller," *ZSKG* 62 (1968); K. Büchi, "Joseph von Görres und die Schweiz," *HJ* 89 (1969).

21. *Great Britain and Ireland 1830–1848*

The Letters of the Most Reverend John MacHale (Dublin 1847); W. J. Fitzpatrick, *The Life, Times, and Correspondence of Right Reverend Dr. Doyle,* 2 vols. (Dublin 1880); B. O'Reilly, *John MacHale, Archbishop of Tuam,* 2 vols. (New York 1890); J. Healy, *Maynooth College 1795–1895* (Dublin 1895); W. Ward, *The Life and Times of Cardinal Wiseman,* 2 vols. (London 1897); B. Ward, *The Sequel to Catholic Emancipation 1830–1850,* 2 vols. (London 1915); J. E. Handley, *The Irish in Scotland 1798–1845* (Cork 1943); J. D. Fitzpatrick, *Edmund Ignatius Rice* (Dublin 1945); D. Gwynn, *O'Connell, Davis, and the Colleges Bill* (Cork 1948); M. Tierney, ed., *Daniel O'Connell* (Dublin 1949); J. F. Broderick, *The Holy See and the Irish Movement for the Repeal of the Union with England* (Rome 1951); R. B. MacDowell, ed., *Social Life in Ireland 1800–1845* (Dublin 1957); T. J. Walsh, *Nano Nagle and the Presentation Sisters* (Dublin 1959); R. Chapman, *Father Faber* (London 1961); J. A. Jackson, *The Irish in Britain* (London 1963); B. Fothergill, *Nicholas Wiseman* (London 1963); K. B. Nowlan, *The Politics of Repeal* (London 1965); O. Chadwick, *The Victorian Church* I (London 1966); J. Hickey, *Urban Catholicism in England and Wales from 1829 to the Present Day* (London 1967); D. H. Akenson, *The Irish Education Experiment* (London 1970).

The following parts of P. J. Corish, ed., *A History of Irish Catholicism* have been published: D. Gwynn, J. E. Handley, *Great Britain* (Dublin 1968); T. P. Cunningham, *Church Reorganization;* T. P. Kennedy, *Church Building;* J. Corkery, *Ecclesiastical Learning* (Dublin 1970); I. Murphy, S. V. Ó. Súilleabháin, F. McGrath, *Catholic Education* (Dublin 1970).

The Oxford Movement and John Henry Newman

SOURCES: *Newman's Works* (London 1868/81); A. Mozley, ed., *Letters and Correspondence of John Henry Newman during his Life in the English Church,* 2 vols. (London 1891); *Correspondence of John Henry Newman with John Keble and Others 1839–45* (Birmingham 1917); H. Tristram, ed., *John Henry Newman, Autobiographical Writings* (London 1956); C. S. Dessain, V. Blehl, *The Letters and Diaries of John Henry Newman* XI–XX (1845–63), (London 1961/70; to be continued).

LITERATURE: H. Tristram, J. Bacchus, "Newman," *DThC* XI, 327–98; R.W. Church, *The Oxford Movement* (London 1891); P. Thureau-Dangin, *La renaissance catholique en Angleterre au XIXe siècle,* 3 vols. (Paris 1899/1906); W. Ward, *The Life of John Henry Newman,* 2 vols. (London 1912); M. Laros, *Newman* (Mainz 1921); H. Tristram, *Newman and His Friends* (London 1933); J. Guitton, *La philosophie de Newman* (Paris 1933); M. Nédoncelle, *La philosophie religieuse de J. H. Newman* (Strasbourg 1946); G. Söhngen, *Newman, sein Gottesgedanke und seine Denkergestalt* (Bonn 1946); H. Fries, *Die Religionsphilosophie Newmans* (Stuttgart 1948); H. Fries,W. Becker, eds., *Newman-Studien* (Nuremberg 1948seqq.); F. McGrath, *Newman's University: Idea and Reality* (London 1951); J. Seynaeve, *Cardinal Newman's Doctrine on Holy Scripture* (Louvain 1953); J. H. Walgrave, *Newman, le développement du dogme* (Paris–Tournai 1957); H. Fries, "Newmans Beitrag zum Verständnis der Tradition," M. Schmaus, ed., *Die mündliche Überlieferung* (Munich 1957), 281–308; G. Biemer, *Überlieferung und Offen-*

barung: Die Lehre von der Tradition nach J. H. Newman (Freiburg 1960); J. Artz, "Der Ansatz der Newmanschen Glaubensbegründung," *Newman-Studien* IV (1960), 249–68; A. T. Bochraad, H. Tristram, *The Argument from Conscience to the Existence of God according to John Henry Newman* (Louvain 1961); F. McGrath, *The Consecration of Learning* (Dublin 1962); J. Altholz, *The Liberal Catholic Movement in England* (London 1962); H. A. MacDougall, *The Acton-Newman Relations* (New York 1962); M. Trevor, *Newman,* 2 vols. (London 1962); C. S. Dessain, *John Henry Newman* (London 1966).

INDEX